Advance Praise for H

"There are books you buy, books you keep, books you keep on your desk, and thanks to O'Reilly and the Head First crew, there is the penultimate category, Head First books. They're the ones that are dog-eared, mangled, and carried everywhere. Head First SQL is at the top of my stack. Heck, even the PDF I have for review is tattered and torn."

— Bill Sawyer, ATG Curriculum Manager, Oracle

"This is not SQL made easy; this is SQL made challenging, SQL made interesting, SQL made fun. It even answers that age-old question 'How to teach non-correlated subqueries without losing the will to live?' This is the right way to learn—it's fast, it's flippant, and it looks fabulous."

— Andrew Cumming, Author of *SQL Hacks*, Zoo Keeper at *sqlzoo.net*

"Outrageous! I mean, SQL is a *computer* language, right? So books about SQL should be written for *computers*, shouldn't they? *Head First SQL* is *obviously* written for *human beings*! What's up with *that*?!

— Dan Tow, Author of *SQL Tuning*

Praise for other *Head First* books

"This book's admirable clarity, humor and substantial doses of clever make it the sort of book that helps even non-programmers think well about problem-solving."

— Cory Doctorow, co-editor of Boing Boing
Author, *Down and Out in the Magic Kingdom*
and *Someone Comes to Town, Someone Leaves Town*

"If you thought Ajax was rocket science, this book is for you. Head Rush Ajax puts dynamic, compelling experiences within reach for every web developer."

— Jesse James Garrett, Adaptive Path

"I received the book yesterday and started to read it...and I couldn't stop. This is definitely très 'cool.' It is fun, but they cover a lot of ground and they are right to the point. I'm really impressed."

— Erich Gamma, IBM Distinguished Engineer, and co-author of Design Patterns

"*Head First Design Patterns* managed to mix fun, belly-laughs, insight, technical depth and great practical advice in one entertaining and thought provoking read. Whether you are new to design patterns, or have been using them for years, you are sure to get something from visiting Objectville."

— Richard Helm, co-author of *Design Patterns*

"One of the funniest and smartest books on software design I've ever read."

— Aaron LaBerge, VP Technology, ESPN.com

"I just finished reading HF OOA&D and I loved it! The thing I liked most about this book was its focus on why we do OOA&D—to write great software!"

— Kyle Brown, Distinguished Engineer, IBM

I *heart* *Head First HTML with CSS & XHTML*—it teaches you everything you need to learn in a 'fun coated' format!"

— Sally Applin, UI Designer and Fine Artist, *http://sally.com*

Praise for the *Head First* Approach

"It's fast, irreverant, fun, and engaging. Be careful—you might actually learn something!"

— Ken Arnold, former Senior Engineer at Sun Microsystems
Co-author (with James Gosling of Java),
The Java Programming Language

"I feel like a thousand pounds of books have just been lifted off of my head."

— Ward Cunningham, inventor of the Wiki
and founder of the Hillside Group

"This book is close to perfect, because of the way it combines expertise and readability. It speaks with authority and it reads beautifully."

— David Gelernter, Professor of Computer Science, Yale University

"Just the right tone for the geeked-out, casual-cool guru coder in all of us. The right reference for practical development strategies--gets my brain going without having to slog through a bunch of tired, stale professor-speak."

— Travis Kalanick, Founder of Scour and Red Swoosh Member of the MIT TR100

"The combination of humour, pictures, asides, sidebars, and redundancy with a logical approach to introducing the basic tags and substantial examples of how to use them will hopefully have the readers hooked in such a way that they don't even realize they are learning because they are having so much fun."

— Stephen Chapman, Fellgall.com

Other related books from O'Reilly

The Art of SQL

Learning SQL

SQL in a Nutshell

SQL Cookbook

SQL Hacks

SQL Pocket Guide

The Relational Database Dictionary

Database in Depth

Other books in O'Reilly's *Head First* series

Head First PMP

Head First Object-Oriented Analysis and Design

Head Rush Ajax

Head First HTML with CSS and XHTML

Head First Design Patterns

Head First Servlets & JSP™

Head First Java™

Head First EJB™

Head First JavaScript (2007)

Head First C# (2007)

Head First SQL

Wouldn't it be dreamy if there was a book that could teach me SQL without making me want to relocate to a remote island in the Pacific where there are no databases? It's probably nothing but a fantasy...

Lynn Beighley

O'REILLY®

Beijing • Cambridge • Köln • Paris • Sebastopol • Taipei • Tokyo

Head First SQL

by Lynn Beighley

Printed in the United States of America.

Published by O'Reilly Media, Inc., 1005 Gravenstein Highway North, Sebastopol, CA 95472.

O'Reilly Media books may be purchased for educational, business, or sales promotional use. Online editions are also available for most titles (*safari.oreilly.com*). For more information, contact our corporate/institutional sales department: (800) 998-9938 or *corporate@oreilly.com*.

Series Creators: Kathy Sierra, Bert Bates

Series Editor: Brett D. McLaughlin

Editor: Catherine Nolan

Design Editor: Louise Barr

Cover Designers: Louise Barr, Karen Montgomery

Production Editor: Sanders Kleinfeld

Indexer: Julie Hawks

Page Viewer: Andrew Fader

Printing History:

August 2007: First Edition.

He's incredibly patient.

No clowns, doughnuts, or Girl Sprouts were harmed in the making of this book. Just my car, but it's been fixed.

RepKover. This book uses RepKover™, a durable and flexible lay-flat binding.

ISBN-10: 0-596-52684-9

ISBN-13: 978-0-596-52684-9

[M]

To our world, awash in data.
And to you, who want to master it.

Author of Head First SQL

Lynn Beighley

SQL? Shouldn't it be called Head First SQRL?

The view from Lynn's window.

Lynn is a fiction writer stuck in a technical book writer's body. Upon discovering that technical book writing actually paid real money, she learned to accept and enjoy it.

After going back to school to get a Masters in computer science, she worked for the acronyms NRL and LANL. Then she discovered Flash, and wrote her first bestseller.

A victim of bad timing, she moved to Silicon Valley just before the great crash. She spent several years working for Yahoo! and writing other books and training courses. Finally giving in to her creative writing bent, she moved to the New York area to get an MFA in creative writing.

Her Head First–style thesis was delivered to a packed room of professors and fellow students. It was extremely well received, and she finished her degree, finished *Head First SQL*, and can't wait to begin her next book.

Lynn loves traveling, cooking, and making up elaborate background stories about complete strangers. She's a little scared of clowns.

Table of Contents (Summary)

Table of Contents (the real thing)

Intro

Your brain on SQL. Here *you* are trying to *learn* something, while here your *brain* is doing you a favor by making sure the learning doesn't *stick*. Your brain's thinking, "Better leave room for more important things, like which wild animals to avoid and whether naked snowboarding is a bad idea." So how *do* you trick your brain into thinking that your life depends on knowing SQL?

data and tables

1 A place for everything

Don't you just hate losing things? Whether it's your car keys, that 25% off coupon for Urban Outfitters, or your application's data, there's nothing worse than not being able to **keep up with what you need**... when you need it. And when it comes to your applications, there's no better place to store your important information than in a **table**. So turn the page, come on in, and take a walk through the world of **relational databases**.

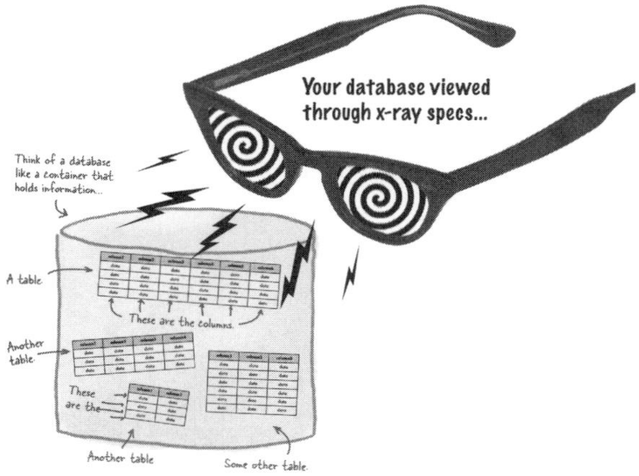

Your database viewed through x-ray specs...
Think of a database like a container that holds information...
A table
These are the columns.
Another table.
These are the
Another table
Some other table.

2 the SELECT statement

Gifted data retrieval

Is it really better to give than retrieve? When it comes to databases, chances are you'll need to **retrieve your data** as often than you'll need to insert it. That's where this chapter comes in: you'll meet the powerful **SELECT** statement and learn how to **gain access to that important information** you've been putting in your tables. You'll even learn how to use **WHERE**, **AND**, and **OR** to selectively get to your data and even avoid displaying the data that you *don't* need.

3 DELETE and UPDATE

A change will do you good

Keep changing your mind? Now it's OK! With the commands you're about to learn—**DELETE** and **UPDATE**—you're no longer stuck with a decision you made six months ago, when you first inserted that data about mullets coming back into style soon. With UPDATE, you **can change data**, and DELETE lets you **get rid of data** that you don't need anymore. But we're not just giving you the tools; in this chapter, you'll learn how to be selective with your new powers and avoid dumping data that you really do need.

4

smart table design

Why be normal?

You've been creating tables without giving much thought to them. And that's fine, they work. You can `SELECT`, `INSERT`, `DELETE`, and `UPDATE` with them. But as you **get more data**, you start seeing **things you wish you'd done** to make your `WHERE` clauses simpler. What you need is to make your tables more *normal*.

Wait a second. I already have a table full of data. You can't seriously expect me to use the DROP TABLE command like I did in chapter 1 and type in all that data again, just to create a primary key for each record...

5 ALTER

Rewriting the Past

ver wished you could correct the mistakes of your past? Well, now is your chance. By using the **ALTER command**, you can apply all the lessons you've been learning to tables you designed days, months, even years ago. Even better, you can do it without affecting your data. By the time you're through here, you'll know what **normal** really means, and you'll be able to apply it to all your tables, past and present.

It's time to turn your tired old hooptie table into a date magnet and take it to a level of table pimpification you never knew existed.

6 advanced SELECT

Seeing your data with new eyes

It's time to add a little finesse to your toolbox. You already know how to SELECT data and use WHERE clauses. But sometimes you need more **precision** than SELECT and WHERE provide. In this chapter, you'll learn about how to **order and group** your data, as well as how to **perform math operations** on your results.

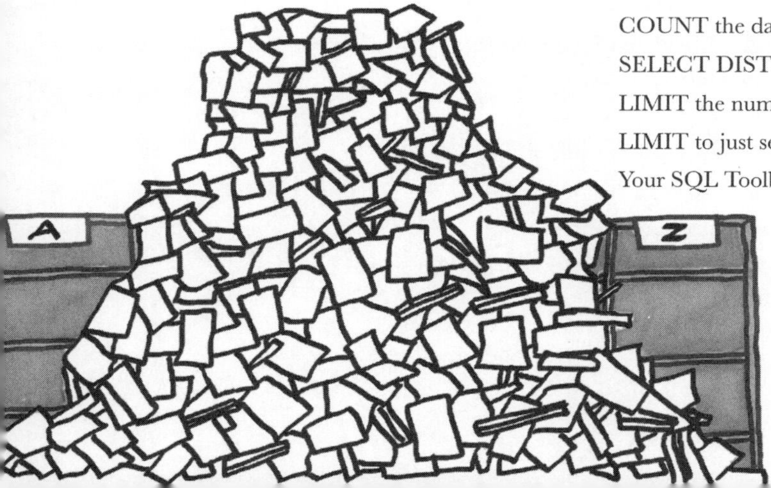

7 multi-table database design

Outgrowing your table

Sometimes your single table isn't big enough anymore. Your data has become more complex, and that **one table** you've been using just **isn't cutting it**. Your single table is full of redundant data, wasting space and slowing down your queries. You've gone as far as you can go with a single table. It's a big world out there, and sometimes you need **more than one table** to contain your data, control it, and ultimately, be the master of your own database.

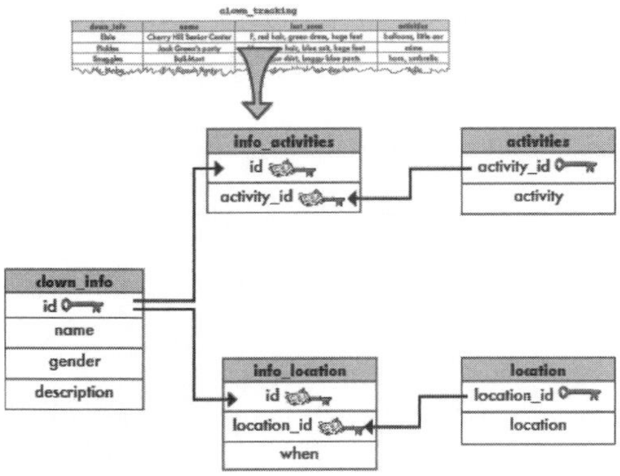

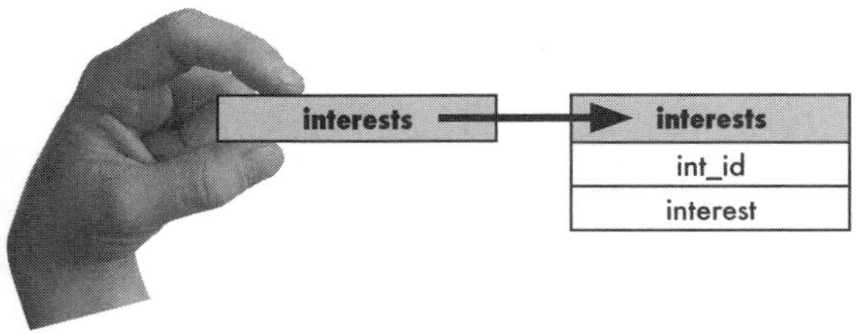

8 joins and multi-table operations

Can't we all just get along?

Welcome to a multi-table world. It's great to have **more than one table** in your database, but you'll need to learn some ***new tools and techniques*** to work with them. With multiple tables comes confusion, so you'll need **aliases** to keep your tables straight. And **joins** help you connect your tables, so that you can get at all the data you've spread out. Get ready, it's time to **take control of your database** again.

...and that's where little result tables really come from.

subqueries

9 Queries within queries

Yes, Jack, I'd like a two-part question, please. Joins are great, but sometimes you need to ***ask your database more than one question***. Or ***take the result of one query and use it as the input to another query***. That's where **subqueries** come in. They'll help you **avoid duplicate data**, **make your queries more dynamic**, and even get you in to all those high-end concert afterparties. (Well, not really, but two out of three ain't bad!)

Outer query

Inner query

```
SELECT some_column, another_column
FROM table
WHERE column = (SELECT column FROM table);
```

10 outer joins, self-joins, and unions

New maneuvers

You only know half of the story about joins. You've seen cross joins that return every possible row, and inner joins that return rows from both tables where there is a match. But what you haven't seen are **outer joins** that give you back rows that *don't have matching counterparts in the other table*, **self-joins** which (strangely enough) *join a single table to itself*, and **unions** that *combine the results of queries*. Once you learn these tricks, you'll be able to get at all your data exactly the way you need to. (And we haven't forgotten about exposing the truth about subqueries, either!)

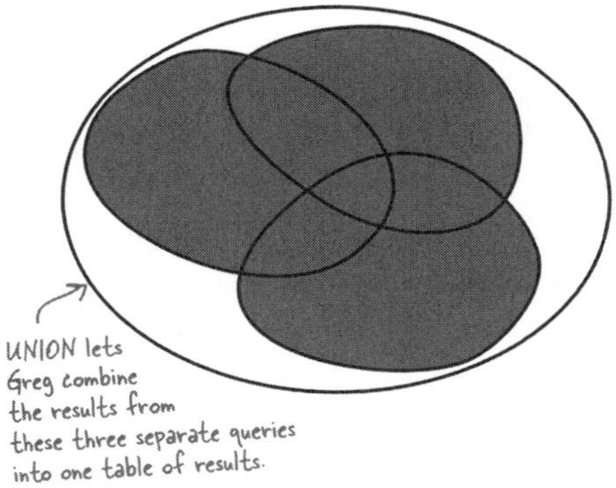
UNION lets Greg combine the results from these three separate queries into one table of results.

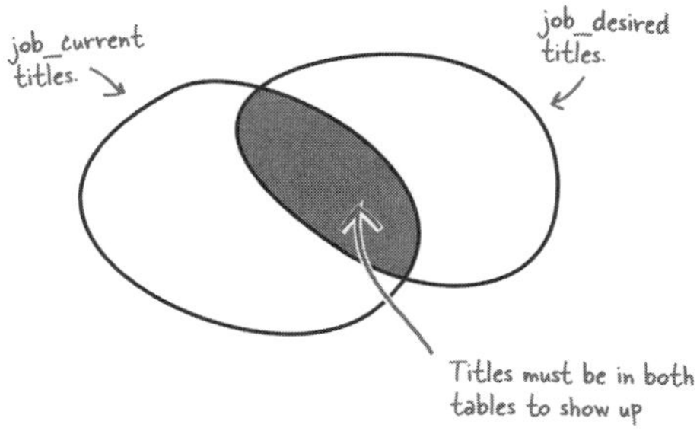
job_current titles.
job_desired titles.
Titles must be in both tables to show up

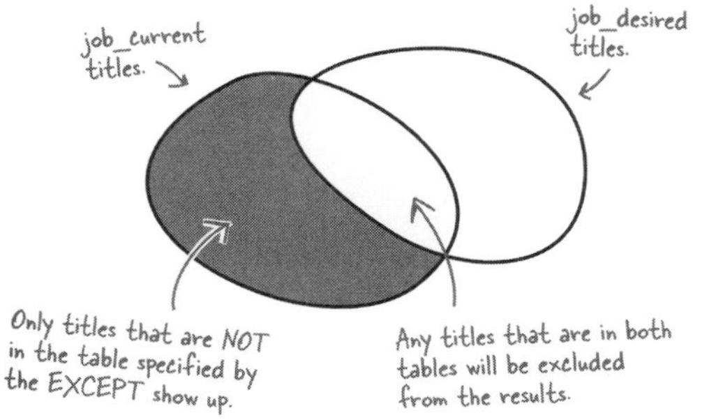
job_current titles.
job_desired titles.
Only titles that are NOT in the table specified by the EXCEPT show up.
Any titles that are in both tables will be excluded from the results.

11 constraints, views, and transactions

Too many cooks spoil the database

Your database has grown and other people need to use it. The problem is that some of them won't be as skilled at SQL as you are. You need ways to **keep them from entering the wrong data**, techniques for allowing them to **only see part of the data**, and ways to **stop them from stepping on each other when they try entering data at the same time**. In this chapter we begin protecting our data from the mistakes of others. Welcome to Defensive Databases, Part 1.

12 security

Protecting your assets

You've put an enormous amount of time and energy into creating your database. And you'd be devastated if anything happened to it. You've also had to give other people **access to your data**, and you're worried that they might insert or update something incorrectly, or even worse, **delete the wrong data**. You're about to learn how databases and the objects in them can be made more **secure**, and how you can have complete control over ***who can do what with your data.***

leftovers

The Top Ten Topics (we didn't cover)

Even after all that, there's a bit more. There are just a few more things we think you need to know. We wouldn't feel right about ignoring them, even though they only need a brief mention. So before you put the book down, take a read through these **short but important SQL tidbits**. Besides, once you're done here, all that's left is another appendix... and the index... and maybe some ads... and then you're really done. We promise!

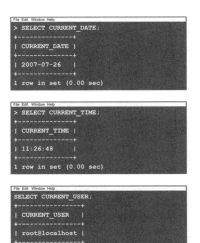

ii

mySQL installation

Try it out for yourself

All your new SQL skills won't do you much good without a place to apply them. This appendix contains instructions for getting your very own MySQL RDBMS for you to work with.

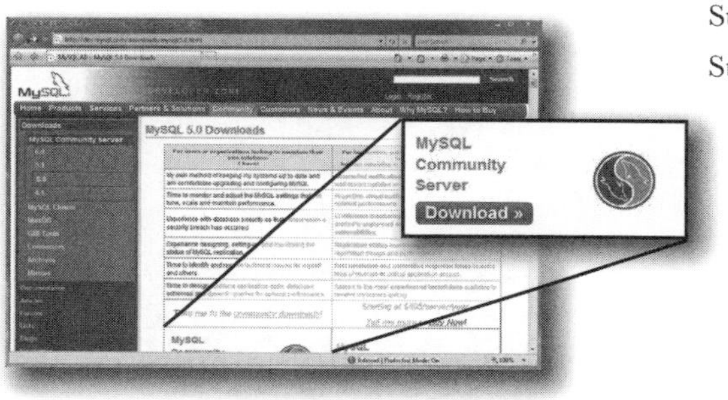

iii

tools roundup

All your new SQL tools

Here are all your SQL tools in one place for the first time, for one night only (kidding)! This is a roundup of all the SQL tools we've covered. Take a moment to *survey the list and feel **great**—***you learned them all**!

Intro

In this section, we answer the burning question:
"So why DID they put that in an SQL book?"

Who is this book for?

If you can answer "yes" to all of these:

1. Do you have access to a computer with an RDBMS installed on it, like Oracle, MS SQL, or MySQL? Or one that you can install MySQL, or other RDBMS on?
2. Do you want to **learn**, **understand**, **and remember how to create tables, databases, and write queries using the best and most recent standards?**
3. Do you prefer **stimulating dinner party conversation** to **dry**, **dull**, **academic lectures**?

We'll help you learn SQL concepts and syntax in a way that will definitely make it easier for you to understand and actually use SQL precisely the way you need to use it.

this book is for you.

Who should probably back away from this book?

If you can answer "yes" to any of these:

1. Are you **completely comfortable** with beginning SQL syntax and seeking something that will help you with advanced database design?
2. Are you already an experienced SQL programmer and looking for a ***reference* book** on SQL?
3. Are you **afraid to try something different**? Would you rather have a root canal than mix stripes with plaid? Do you believe that a technical book can't be serious if SQL concepts are anthropomorphized?

But if you would like a refresher, and never quite understood normal form and one-to-many and left outer joins, this book can help you.

this book is not for you.

[Note from marketing: this book is for anyone with a credit card.]

We know what you're thinking.

"How can *this* be a serious SQL book?"

"What's with all the graphics?"

"Can I actually *learn* it this way?"

And we know what your *brain* is thinking.

Your brain thinks THIS is important.

Your brain craves novelty. It's always searching, scanning, *waiting* for something unusual. It was built that way, and it helps you stay alive.

So what does your brain do with all the routine, ordinary, normal things you encounter? Everything it *can* to stop them from interfering with the brain's *real* job—recording things that *matter*. It doesn't bother saving the boring things; they never make it past the "this is obviously not important" filter.

How does your brain *know* what's important? Suppose you're out for a day hike and a tiger jumps in front of you, what happens inside your head and body?

Neurons fire. Emotions crank up. *Chemicals surge.*

And that's how your brain knows...

This must be important! Don't forget it!

But imagine you're at home, or in a library. It's a safe, warm, tiger-free zone. You're studying. Getting ready for an exam. Or trying to learn some tough technical topic your boss thinks will take a week, ten days at the most.

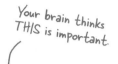

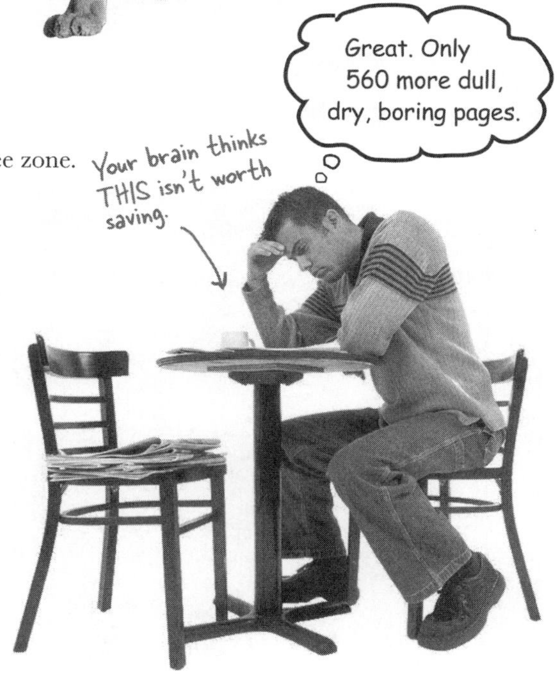
Great. Only 560 more dull, dry, boring pages.
Your brain thinks THIS isn't worth saving.

Just one problem. Your brain's trying to do you a big favor. It's trying to make sure that this *obviously* non-important content doesn't clutter up scarce resources. Resources that are better spent storing the really *big* things. Like tigers. Like the danger of fire. Like how you should never again snowboard in shorts.

And there's no simple way to tell your brain, "Hey brain, thank you very much, but no matter how dull this book is, and how little I'm registering on the emotional Richter scale right now, I really *do* want you to keep this stuff around."

We think of a "Head First" reader as a learner.

So what does it take to *learn* something? First, you have to *get* it, then make sure you don't *forget* it. It's not about pushing facts into your head. Based on the latest research in cognitive science, neurobiology, and educational psychology, *learning* takes a lot more than text on a page. We know what turns your brain on.

Some of the Head First learning principles:

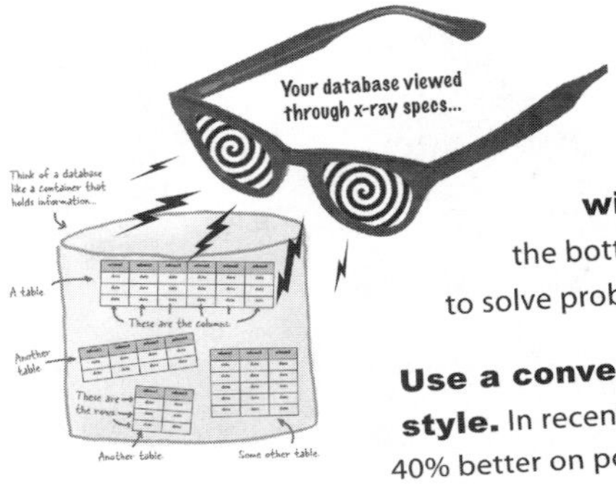
Your database viewed through x-ray specs...
Think of a database like a container that holds information...
A table
These are the columns
Another table
These are the rows
Another table
Some other table.

Make it visual. Images are far more memorable than words alone, and make learning much more effective (up to 89% improvement in recall and transfer studies). It also makes things more understandable. **Put the words within or near the graphics** they relate to, rather than on the bottom or on another page, and learners will be up to *twice* as likely to solve problems related to the content.

But I'm funny how? I mean, funny like I'm a clown, I amuse you?

Use a conversational and personalized style. In recent studies, students performed up to 40% better on post-learning tests if the content spoke directly to the reader, using a first-person, conversational style rather than taking a formal tone. Tell stories instead of lecturing. Use casual language. Don't take yourself too seriously. Which would *you* pay more attention to: a stimulating dinner party companion, or a lecture?

Get the learner to think more deeply. In other words, unless you actively flex your neurons, nothing much happens in your head. A reader has to be motivated, engaged, curious, and inspired to solve problems, draw conclusions, and generate new knowledge. And for that, you need challenges, exercises, and thought-provoking questions, and activities that involve both sides of the brain and multiple senses.

Get—and keep—the reader's attention. We've all had the "I really want to learn this but I can't stay awake past page one" experience. Your brain pays attention to things that are out of the ordinary, interesting, strange, eye-catching, unexpected. Learning a new, tough, technical topic doesn't have to be boring. Your brain will learn much more quickly if it's not.

Wait a second... 'Try out these queries,' you said. You implied that they would all work. And I trusted you! But one of them doesn't work. And some of them don't look like they should work.

Touch their emotions. We now know that your ability to remember something is largely dependent on its emotional content. You remember what you care about. You remember when you *feel* something. No, we're not talking heart-wrenching stories about a boy and his dog. We're talking emotions like surprise, curiosity, fun, "what the...?", and the feeling of "I Rule!" that comes when you solve a puzzle, learn something everybody else thinks is hard, or realize you know something that "I'm more technical than thou" Bob from engineering *doesn't*.

Metacognition: thinking about thinking

If you really want to learn, and you want to learn more quickly and more deeply, pay attention to how you pay attention. Think about how you think. Learn how you learn.

Most of us did not take courses on metacognition or learning theory when we were growing up. We were *expected* to learn, but rarely *taught* to learn.

But we assume that if you're holding this book, you really want to learn about project management. And you probably don't want to spend a lot of time. And since you're going to take an exam on it, you need to *remember* what you read. And for that, you've got to *understand* it. To get the most from this book, or *any* book or learning experience, take responsibility for your brain. Your brain on *this* content.

I wonder how I can trick my brain into remembering this stuff...

The trick is to get your brain to see the new material you're learning as Really Important. Crucial to your well-being. As important as a tiger. Otherwise, you're in for a constant battle, with your brain doing its best to keep the new content from sticking.

So just how *DO* you get your brain to think that SQL is a hungry tiger?

There's the slow, tedious way, or the faster, more effective way. The slow way is about sheer repetition. You obviously know that you *are* able to learn and remember even the dullest of topics if you keep pounding the same thing into your brain. With enough repetition, your brain says, "This doesn't *feel* important to him, but he keeps looking at the same thing *over* and *over* and *over*, so I suppose it must be."

The faster way is to do ***anything that increases brain activity,*** especially different *types* of brain activity. The things on the previous page are a big part of the solution, and they're all things that have been proven to help your brain work in your favor. For example, studies show that putting words *within* the pictures they describe (as opposed to somewhere else in the page, like a caption or in the body text) causes your brain to try to makes sense of how the words and picture relate, and this causes more neurons to fire. More neurons firing = more chances for your brain to *get* that this is something worth paying attention to, and possibly recording.

A conversational style helps because people tend to pay more attention when they perceive that they're in a conversation, since they're expected to follow along and hold up their end. The amazing thing is, your brain doesn't necessarily *care* that the "conversation" is between you and a book! On the other hand, if the writing style is formal and dry, your brain perceives it the same way you experience being lectured to while sitting in a roomful of passive attendees. No need to stay awake.

But pictures and conversational style are just the beginning.

Here's what WE did:

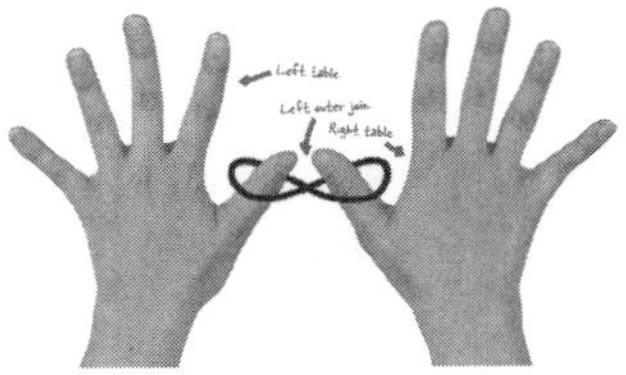

We used ***pictures***, because your brain is tuned for visuals, not text. As far as your brain's concerned, a picture really *is* worth a thousand words. And when text and pictures work together, we embedded the text *in* the pictures because your brain works more effectively when the text is *within* the thing the text refers to, as opposed to in a caption or buried in the text somewhere.

We used ***redundancy***, saying the same thing in *different* ways and with different media types, and *multiple senses*, to increase the chance that the content gets coded into more than one area of your brain.

We used concepts and pictures in ***unexpected*** ways because your brain is tuned for novelty, and we used pictures and ideas with at least *some* ***emotional*** *content*, because your brain is tuned to pay attention to the biochemistry of emotions. That which causes you to *feel* something is more likely to be remembered, even if that feeling is nothing more than a little ***humor***, ***surprise***, or ***interest.***

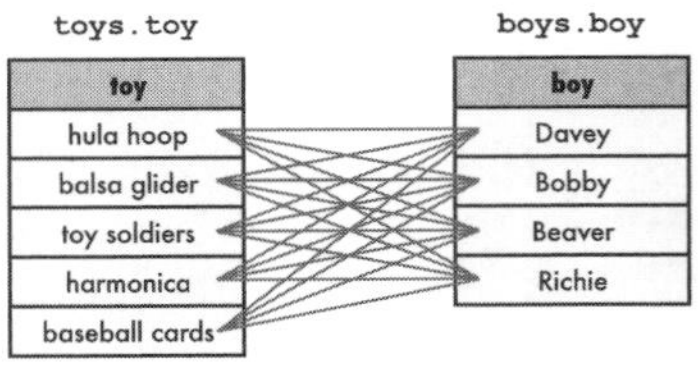

We used a personalized, ***conversational style***, because your brain is tuned to pay more attention when it believes you're in a conversation than if it thinks you're passively listening to a presentation. Your brain does this even when you're *reading*.

We included more than 80 ***activities***, because your brain is tuned to learn and remember more when you ***do*** things than when you *read* about things. And we made the exercises challenging-yet-do-able, because that's what most people prefer.

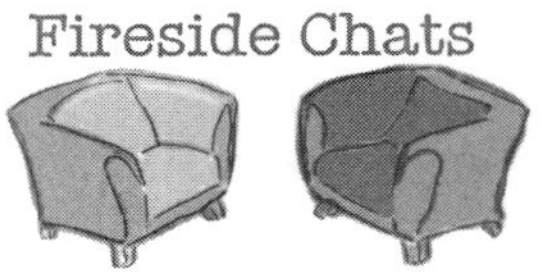

We used ***multiple learning styles***, because *you* might prefer step-by-step procedures, while someone else wants to understand the big picture first, and someone else just wants to see an example. But regardless of your own learning preference, *everyone* benefits from seeing the same content represented in multiple ways.

We include content for ***both sides of your brain***, because the more of your brain you engage, the more likely you are to learn and remember, and the longer you can stay focused. Since working one side of the brain often means giving the other side a chance to rest, you can be more productive at learning for a longer period of time.

And we included ***stories*** and exercises that present ***more than one point of view,*** because your brain is tuned to learn more deeply when it's forced to make evaluations and judgments.

We included ***challenges***, with exercises, and by asking ***questions*** that don't always have a straight answer, because your brain is tuned to learn and remember when it has to *work* at something. Think about it—you can't get your *body* in shape just by *watching* people at the gym. But we did our best to make sure that when you're working hard, it's on the *right* things. That ***you're not spending one extra dendrite*** processing a hard-to-understand example, or parsing difficult, jargon-laden, or overly terse text.

We used ***people***. In stories, examples, pictures, etc., because, well, because *you're* a person. And your brain pays more attention to *people* than it does to *things*.

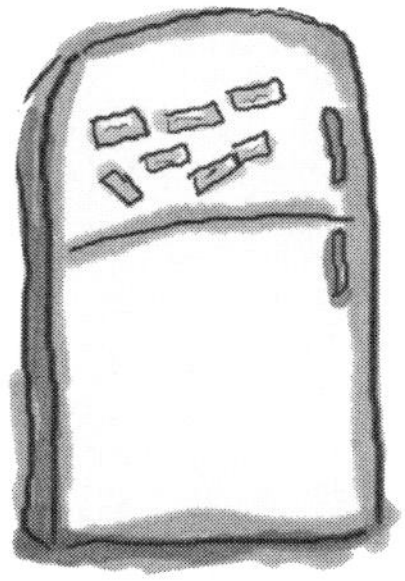

Here's what YOU can do to bend your brain into submission

So, we did our part. The rest is up to you. These tips are a starting point; listen to your brain and figure out what works for you and what doesn't. Try new things.

cut this out and stick it on your refrigerator.

1. **Slow down. The more you understand, the less you have to memorize.**

   Don't just *read*. Stop and think. When the book asks you a question, don't just skip to the answer. Imagine that someone really *is* asking the question. The more deeply you force your brain to think, the better chance you have of learning and remembering.

2. **Do the exercises. Write your own notes.**

   We put them in, but if we did them for you, that would be like having someone else do your workouts for you. And don't just *look* at the exercises. **Use a pencil.** There's plenty of evidence that physical activity *while* learning can increase the learning.

3. **Read the "There are No Dumb Questions"**

   That means all of them. They're not optional sidebars—***they're part of the core content!*** Don't skip them.

4. **Make this the last thing you read before bed. Or at least the last challenging thing.**

   Part of the learning (especially the transfer to long-term memory) happens *after* you put the book down. Your brain needs time on its own, to do more processing. If you put in something new during that processing time, some of what you just learned will be lost.

5. **Drink water. Lots of it.**

   Your brain works best in a nice bath of fluid. Dehydration (which can happen before you ever feel thirsty) decreases cognitive function.

6. **Talk about it. Out loud.**

   Speaking activates a different part of the brain. If you're trying to understand something, or increase your chance of remembering it later, say it out loud. Better still, try to explain it out loud to someone else. You'll learn more quickly, and you might uncover ideas you hadn't known were there when you were reading about it.

7. **Listen to your brain.**

   Pay attention to whether your brain is getting overloaded. If you find yourself starting to skim the surface or forget what you just read, it's time for a break. Once you go past a certain point, you won't learn faster by trying to shove more in, and you might even hurt the process.

8. **Feel something!**

   Your brain needs to know that this *matters*. Get involved with the stories. Make up your own captions for the photos. Groaning over a bad joke is *still* better than feeling nothing at all.

9. **Create something!**

   Apply this to your daily work; use what you are learning to make decisions on your projects. Just do something to get some experience beyond the exercises and activities in this book. All you need is a pencil and a problem to solve…a problem that might benefit from using the tools and techniques you're studying for the exam.

Read me

This is a learning experience, not a reference book. We deliberately stripped out everything that might get in the way of learning whatever it is we're working on at that point in the book. And the first time through, you need to begin at the beginning, because the book makes assumptions about what you've already seen and learned.

We begin by teaching basic SQL syntax, then SQL database design concepts, and then advanced querying.

While it's important to create well-designed tables and databases, before you can, you need to understand the syntax of SQL. So we begin by giving you SQL statements that you can actually try yourself. That way you can immediately do something with SQL, and you will begin to get excited about it. Then, a bit later in the book, we show you good table design practices. By then you'll have a solid grasp of the syntax you need, and can focus on *learning the concepts*.

We don't cover every SQL statement, function, or keyword.

While we could have put every single SQL statement, function, and keyword in this book, we thought you'd prefer to have a reasonably liftable book that would teach you the most important statements, functions, and keywords. We give you the ones you need to know, the ones you'll use 95 percent of the time. And when you're done with this book, you'll have the confidence to go look up that function you need to finish off that kick-ass query you just wrote.

We don't address every flavor of RDBMS.

There's Standard SQL, MySQL, Oracle, MS SQL Server, PostgreSQL, DB2, and quite a few more RDBMSs out there. If we covered every variation in syntax for every command in the book, this book would have many more pages. We like trees, so we're focusing on Standard SQL with a nod toward MySQL. All the examples in the book will work with MySQL. And most will work with any of the RDBMSs listed above. Remember that reference book we just suggested you buy? Buy one for the particular RDBMS that you use.

The activities are NOT optional.

The exercises and activities are not add-ons; they're part of the core content of the book. Some of them are to help with memory, some are for understanding, and some will help you apply what you've learned. ***Don't skip the exercises.*** The crossword puzzles are the only thing you don't *have* to do, but they're good for giving your brain a chance to think about the words and terms you've been learning in a different context.

The redundancy is intentional and important.

One distinct difference in a Head First book is that we want you to *really* get it. And we want you to finish the book remembering what you've learned. Most reference books don't have retention and recall as a goal, but this book is about *learning*, so you'll see some of the same concepts come up more than once.

The examples are as lean as possible.

Our readers tell us that it's frustrating to wade through 200 lines of an example looking for the two lines they need to understand. Most examples in this book are shown within the smallest possible context, so that the part you're trying to learn is clear and simple. Don't expect all of the examples to be robust, or even complete—they are written specifically for learning, and aren't always fully-functional.

We've placed many of the commands on the Web so you can copy and paste them into your terminal or database software. You'll find them at
http://www.headfirstlabs.com/books/hfsql/

The Brain Power exercises don't have answers.

For some of them, there is no right answer, and for others, part of the learning experience of the Brain Power activities is for you to decide if and when your answers are right. In some of the Brain Power exercises, you will find hints to point you in the right direction.

The technical review team

Cary Collett

Chaucer helped too.

Steve Milano

Shelley Rheams

LuAnn Mazza

Jamie Henderson

Our amazing reviewers:

Huge thanks go to our tech review team. They caught innumerable blatant mistakes, subtle errors, and pathtetic typos. Without them, this book wouldn't be anywhere near as clean and correct as it is. They did a thorough job of getting the errors out of this book.

Cary Collett put his 15 years of experience working at startups, government labs, and currently in the financial sector to use while reviewing the book, and is looking forward to getting back to enjoying his non-work things like cooking, hiking, reading and terrorizing his dogs.

LuAnn Mazza found time in her busy Illinois professional life as a Software Developer and Analyst, to do some incredibly timely and detailed reviews, we're happy that she can now spend her spare time enjoying her hobbies including biking, photography, computers, music, and tennis

When **Steve Milano** isn't coding in half a dozen different languages at his day job, doing a top-notch review of Head First SQL, or playing punk rock with his band Onion Flavored Rings in unventilated basements throughout the land, he can be found at home with his cats Ralph and Squeak.

"Shelley" Moira Michelle Rheams, MEd, MCP, MCSE teaches and runs the Early Childhood Education Program at Delgado Community College in New Orleans: West Bank Campus. Currently she enjoys putting education courses online to meet the needs of the changing New Orleans community post-Katrina, and we thank her for being able to fit us into her overbooked schedule.

Jamie Henderson is a senior systems architect sporting purple hair and dividing what spare time she has between cello, reading, video games, and watching movies on DVD.

This fantastic team is the reason that the code and exercises in this book will actually do what they are supposed to, and why, when you are finished with this book, you'll be a confident SQL programmer. Their attention to detail also kept us from being too cute or too patronizing, or even, sometimes, too weird.

Acknowledgments

My editors:

First of all, I want to thank my editor, **Brett McLaughlin**, for not one, but two Head First boot camps. Brett was more than an editor—he was a combination sounding board and sherpa. There's absolutely no way this book would have been written without his guidance, support, and interest. Not only did he "get me" from the very first audition, his appreciation of my sometimes over-the-top humor made this the best book writing experience I've ever had. He gave me a whole lot of advice, hints, and more than a little coaching throughout this whole process. Thanks, Brett!

Brett McLaughlin

Catherine Nolan

Editor **Catherine Nolan** has a huge ulcer now, thanks to some incredibly bad luck I had near the end of the editorial process. She's the reason this book didn't come out in 2008, and perhaps the reason it exists at all. It was a bit like kitten juggling at the end, and she didn't drop a single one. I badly needed a schedule, and Catherine is the best scheduler I've ever met. And I think I've been her biggest challenge so far. Let's hope her next project goes more smoothly, she's more than earned it.

The O'Reilly team:

Design Editor **Louise Barr** has been both a great friend and an amazing graphic designer. Somehow she was able to channel my crazy ideas into impressive art that make the difficult concepts very clear. All the great design is hers, and I have no doubt that at many points in this book you'll want to thank her too.

Lou Barr

But we would have gone to press with a whole lot of errors had it not been for the technical review process, and **Sanders Kleinfeld** did a great job as production editor, getting this book ready for press. He also went far, far beyond the call of duty, pointing out some conceptual chasms that really needed to be bridged. Thanks, Sanders!

Finally, I want to thank **Kathy Sierra** and **Bert Bates** for creating this wonderful series and for the best and most mentally challenging training I've ever had at the first Head First boot camp. Without those three days, well, I don't even want to think about how much harder it would have been to be Head First-y. And Bert's final editorial comments were painfully accurate, and vastly improved this book.

1 data and tables

A place for everything

I used to keep track of all my patients on paper, but I kept losing them! I finally learned SQL and now I never lose a soul. Learning about tables won't hurt a bit!

Don't you just hate losing things? Whether it's your car keys, that 25% off coupon for Urban Outfitters, or your application's data, there's nothing worse than not being able to **keep up with what you need**... when you need it. And when it comes to your applications, there's no better place to store your important information than in a **table**. So turn the page, come on in, and take a walk through the world of **relational databases**.

Defining your data

Greg knows many lonely single people. He likes keeping track of what his friends are up to, and enjoys introducing them to each other. He has lots of information about them scrawled on sticky notes like this:

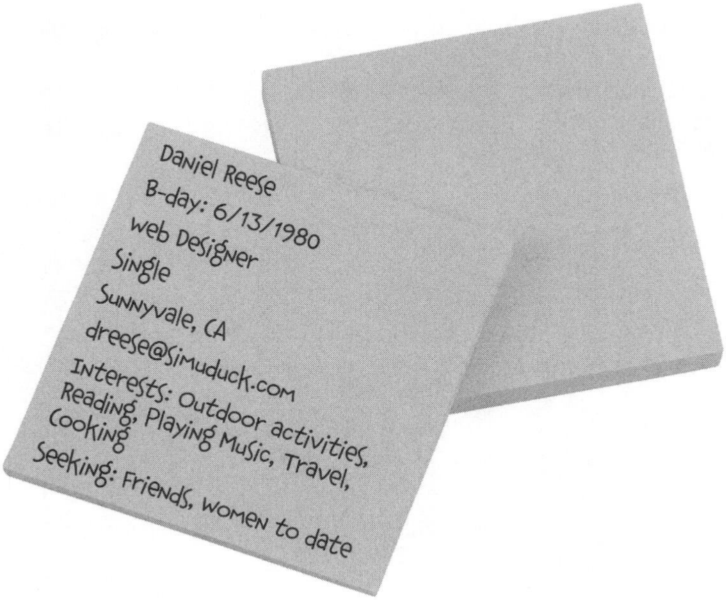
Daniel Reese
B-day: 6/13/1980
web Designer
Single
Sunnyvale, CA
dreese@simuduck.com
Interests: Outdoor activities, Reading, Playing Music, Travel, Cooking
Seeking: Friends, women to date

Greg's been using his system for a very long time. Last week he expanded his connections to include people who are seeking new jobs, so his listings are growing quickly. Very quickly…

Just a few of Greg's notes

BRAIN POWER

Is there a better way to organize this information?
What would you do?

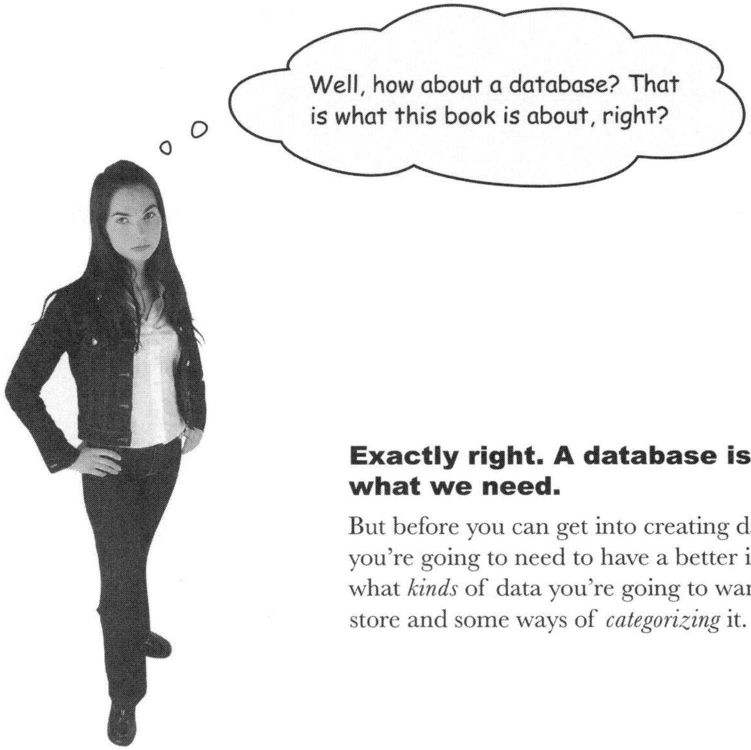

Well, how about a database? That is what this book is about, right?

Exactly right. A database is just what we need.

But before you can get into creating databases, you're going to need to have a better idea of what *kinds* of data you're going to want to store and some ways of *categorizing* it.

Sharpen your pencil

Here are some of Greg's notes. Look for similar information that Greg's collected about each person. Give each common bit of data a label that describes the category of information it is, then write those labels in the space below.

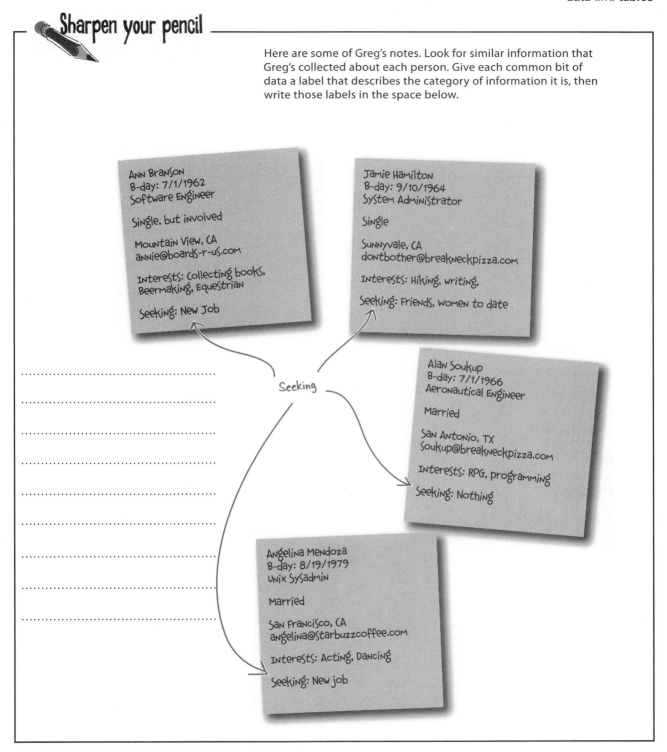

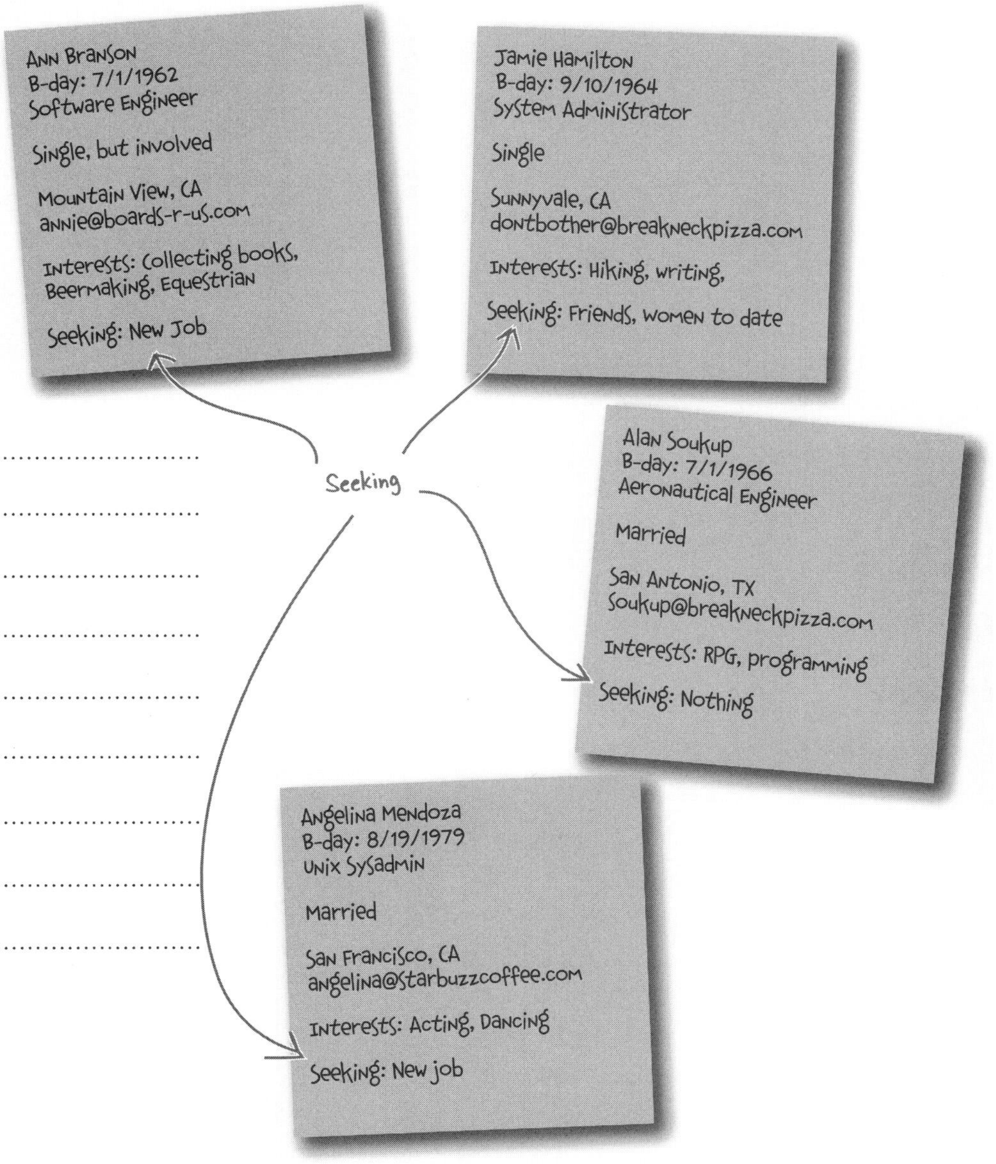

Sharpen your pencil
Solution

Here are some of Greg's notes. Look for similar information that Greg's collected about each person. Give each common bit of data a label that describes the category of information it is, then write those labels in the space below.

Now that we've created these categories, we can use them to organize our data.

First Name

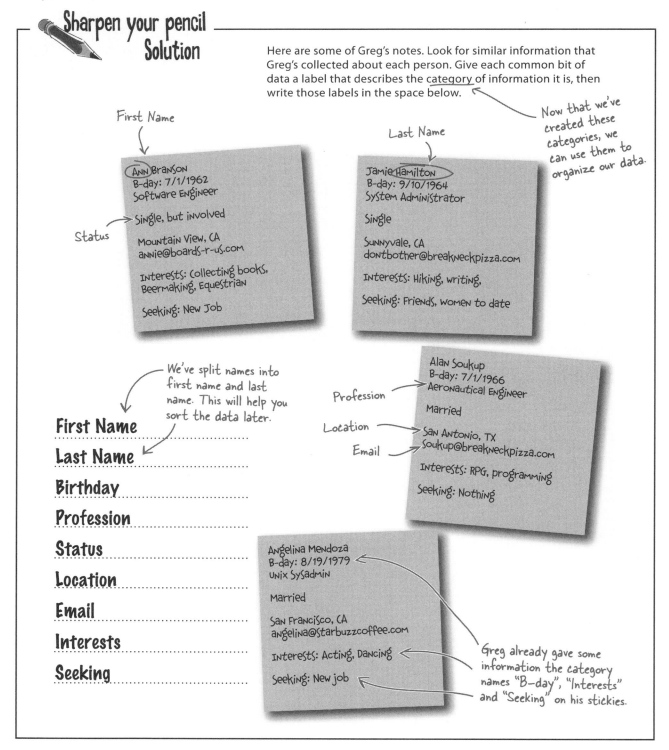

(Ann) Branson
B-day: 7/1/1962
Software Engineer

Single, but involved ← Status

Mountain View, CA
annie@boards-r-us.com

INTERESTS: Collecting books,
Beermaking, Equestrian

Seeking: New Job

Last Name

(Jamie Hamilton)
B-day: 9/10/1964
System Administrator

Single

Sunnyvale, CA
dontbother@breakneckpizza.com

INTERESTS: Hiking, writing,

Seeking: Friends, women to date

We've split names into first name and last name. This will help you sort the data later.

First Name ....

Last Name ....

Birthday ....

Profession ....

Status ....

Location ....

Email ....

Interests ....

Seeking ....

Alan Soukup
B-day: 7/1/1966
Aeronautical Engineer ← Profession

Married

San Antonio, TX ← Location
Soukup@breakneckpizza.com ← Email

INTERESTS: RPG, programming

Seeking: Nothing

Angelina Mendoza
B-day: 8/19/1979
Unix Sysadmin

Married

San Francisco, CA
angelina@starbuzzcoffee.com

INTERESTS: Acting, Dancing

Seeking: New job

Greg already gave some information the category names "B-day", "Interests" and "Seeking" on his stickies.

Look at your data in categories

Let's look at your data in a different way. If you cut each note into pieces, then spread the pieces out horizontally you'd get something that looked like this:

Then if you cut up another sticky note with the categories you just noticed, and put the pieces above their corresponding information, you'd have something that looks a lot like this:

Here's that same information nicely displayed in a **TABLE** in **columns** and **rows.**

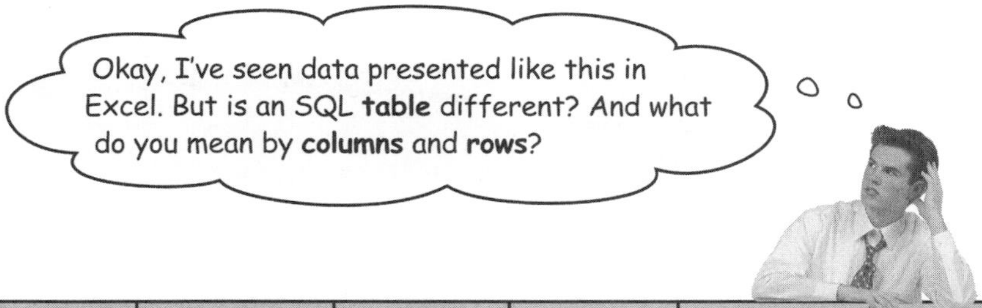

last_name	first_name	email	birthday	profession	location	status	interests	seeking
Branson	Ann	annie@boards-r-us.com	7-1-1962	Aeronautical Engineer	San Antonio, TX	Single, but involved	RPG, Programming	New Job
Hamilton	Jamie	dontbother@breakneckpizza.com	9-10-1966	System Administrator	Sunnyvale, CA	Single	Hiking, Writing	Friends, Women to date
Soukup	Alan	soukup@breakneckpizza.com	12-2-1975	Aeronautical Engineer	San Antonio, TX	Married	RPG, Programming	Nothing
Mendoza	Angelina	angelina@starbuzzcoffee.com	8-19-1979	Unix System Administrator	San Francisco, CA	Married	Acting, Dancing	New Job

What's in a database?

Before we get into the details of what tables, rows, and columns are, let's step back and look at the bigger picture. The first SQL structure you need to know about is the container that holds all your tables known as a ***database***.

> A **database** is a container that holds tables and other SQL structures related to those tables.

Every time you search online, go shopping, call information, use your TiVo, make a reservation, get a speeding ticket, or buy groceries, a database is being asked for information, otherwise known as being ***queried***.

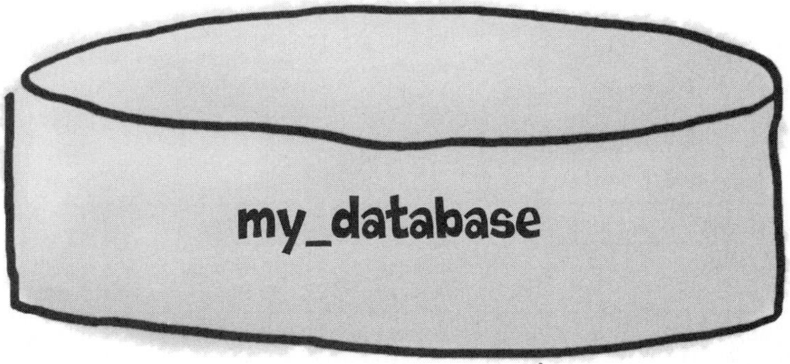

my_database
In diagrams and flow charts, databases are depicted as cylinders. So when you see this, think database.

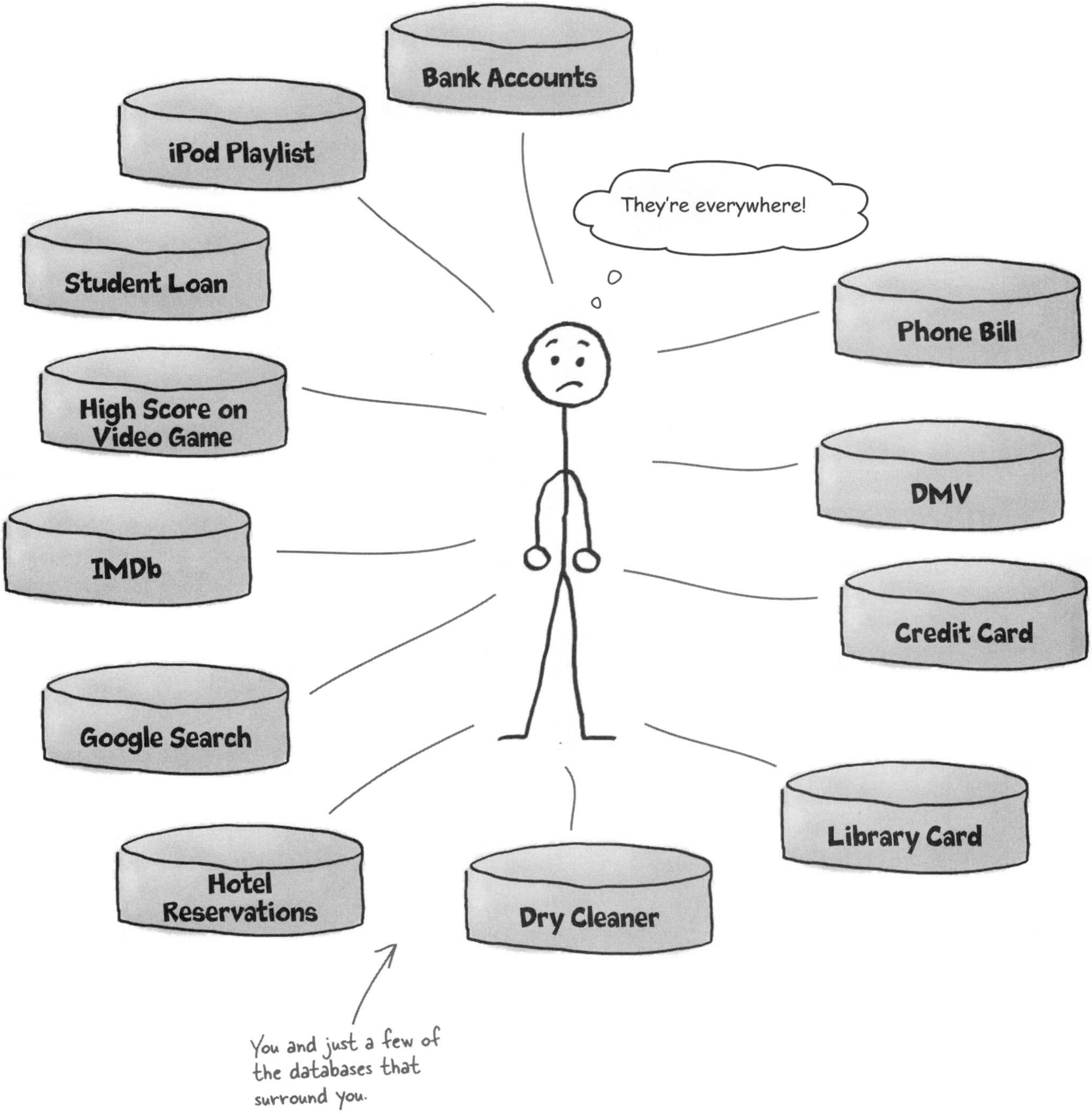
Bank Accounts
iPod Playlist
They're everywhere!
Student Loan
Phone Bill
High Score on Video Game
DMV
IMDb
Credit Card
Google Search
Library Card
Hotel Reservations
Dry Cleaner
You and just a few of the databases that surround you.

Anatomy of a Database

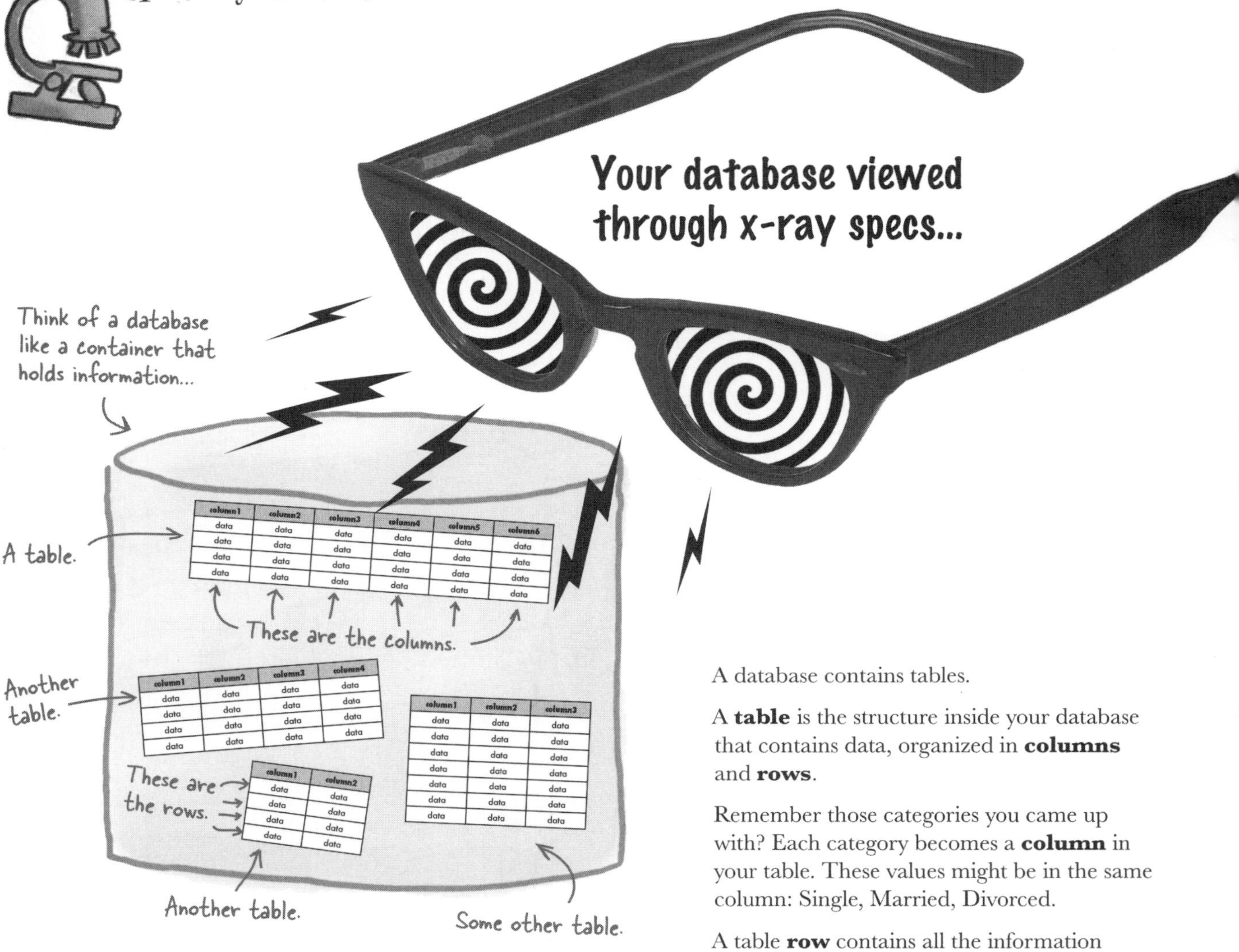
Your database viewed through x-ray specs...
Think of a database like a container that holds information...
A table.
These are the columns.
Another table.
These are the rows.
Another table.
Some other table.

A database contains tables.

A **table** is the structure inside your database that contains data, organized in **columns** and **rows**.

Remember those categories you came up with? Each category becomes a **column** in your table. These values might be in the same column: Single, Married, Divorced.

A table **row** contains all the information about one object in your table. In Greg's new table, a row would be all the data about one person. Here's an example of some of the data that might be in one row: John, Jackson, single, writer, jj@boards-r-us.com.

The information inside the database is organized into **tables**.

BE the table

Below, you'll find some sticky notes and a table. Your job is to be the partially formed table and fill in the empty bits to create inner peace. After you've done the exercise, turn the page to see if you've become one with the table.

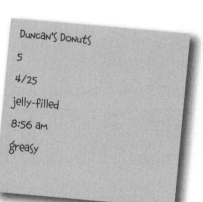

Duncan's Donuts
7
4/24
not enough jelly
10:35 pm
jelly-filled

Starbuzz Coffee
4/23
jelly filled
9
7:43 am
almost perfect

Duncan's Donuts
5
4/25
jelly-filled
8:56 am
greasy

jelly-filled
stale, but tasty
6
Krispy King
4/26
9:39 pm

Use one of the fields as a title that gives the table a meaningful name. →

shop				
			9	
		4/25	5	
				not enough jelly

BE the table Solution

Your job was to be the partially formed table and fill in the empty bits to increase inner peace.

You should have been able to work out what the table's title could be from the stickies.

jelly_doughnuts

shop	time	date	rating	comments
Starbuzz Coffee	7:43 am	4/23	9	almost perfect
Duncan's Donuts	8:56 am	4/25	5	greasy
Krispy King	9:39 pm	4/26	6	stale, but tasty
Duncan's Donuts	10:35 pm	4/24	7	not enough jelly

Don't worry if your answers for the column names don't match ours exactly.

Databases contain connected data

All of the tables in a database should be **connected** in some way. For example, here are the tables that might be in a database holding information about doughnuts:

Here's a database with three tables in it. The database is called 'my_snacks'.

Database and table names are not usually capitalized.

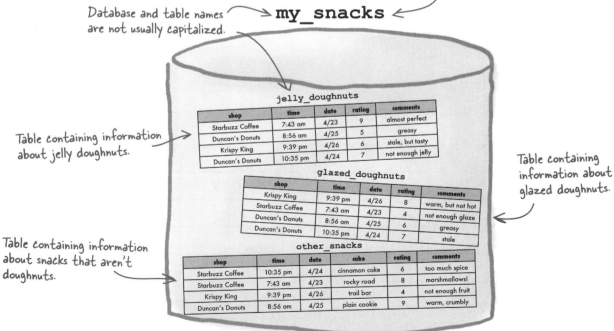

my_snacks

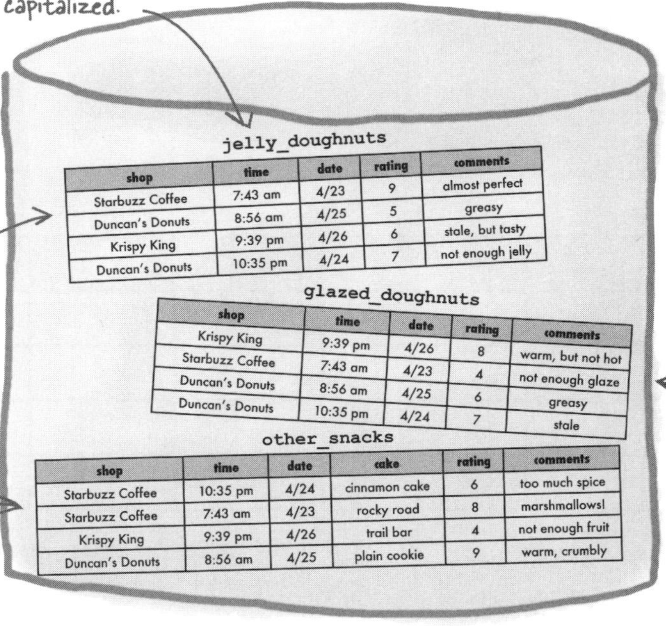

Table containing information about jelly doughnuts.

Table containing information about snacks that aren't doughnuts.

Table containing information about glazed doughnuts.

Tables Up Close

A column is a piece of data stored by your table. A row is a single set of columns that describe attributes of a single thing. Columns and rows together make up a table.

Here's an example of what an address book table containing your personal information might look like. You'll often see the word **field** used instead of **column**. They mean the same thing. Also, **row** and **record** are often used interchangeably.

These are the columns.

first_name	last_name	address	city	state	id_num

These are the rows.

Joe	Epps	data	data	data	data
Al	Jones	data	data	data	data
Mary	Morris	data	data	data	data
Lou	Green	data	data	data	data

Put the columns and rows together and you've got yourself a table.

first_name	last_name	address	city	state	id_num
Joe	Epps	data	data	data	data
Al	Jones	data	data	data	data
Mary	Morris	data	data	data	data
Lou	Green	data	data	data	data

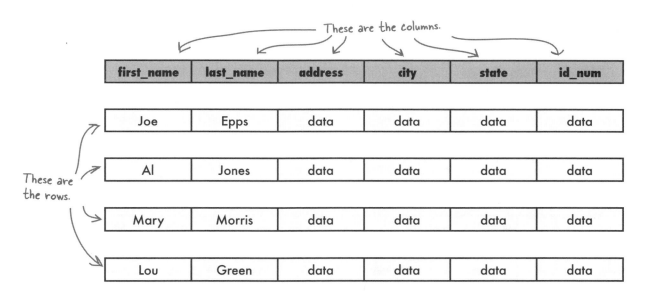

So we have enough data from my stickies to turn them into a table?

Exactly. You can identify categories for the type of data you're collecting for each person.

Your categories then become your columns. Each sticky note becomes a row. You can take all that information from your stickies and turn it into a table.

Categories from page 7.

First Name | Last Name | Birthday | Profession | Status | Location | Email | Interests | Seeking

Angelina | Mendoza | 8/19/1979 | Unix SysAdmin | Married | San Francisco, CA | angelina@starbuzzcoffee.com | Acting, Dancing | New job

Data from a single sticky laid out to form a row.

Now you know that the categories are called columns.

last_name	first_name	email	birthday	profession	location	status	interests	seeking
Branson	Ann	annie@boards-r-us.com	7-1-1962	Aeronautical Engineer	San Antonio, TX	Single, but involved	RPG, Programming	New Job
Hamilton	Jamie	dontbother@yahoo.com	9-10-1966	System Administrator	Sunnyvale, CA	Single	Hiking, Writing	Friends, Women to date
Soukup	Alan	fprose@yahoo.com	12-2-1975	Aeronautical Engineer	San Antonio, TX	Married	RPG, Programming	Nothing
Mendoza	Angelina	angel79@gmail.com	8-19-1979	Unix System Administrator	San Francisco, CA	Married	Acting, Dancing	New Job

...and that each sticky's data can be placed on a single row called a record.

Finally. Okay so how do I create my table?

Exercise

Consider the databases and tables below. Think about what categories of data you might find in each. Come up some likely columns for each table.

library_db

books: ....

library_patron: ....

bank_db

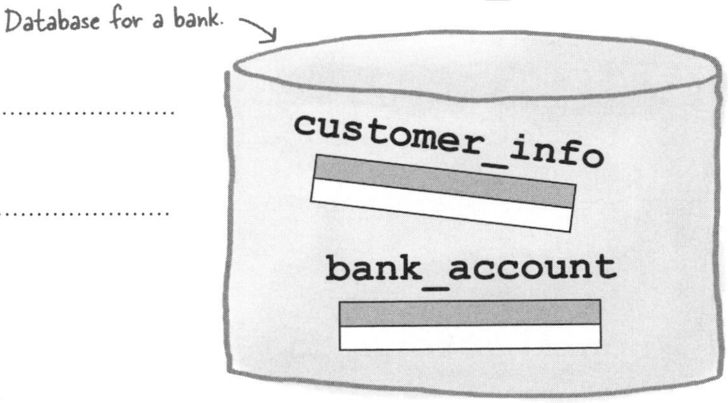

customer_info: ....

bank_account: ....

onlinestore_db

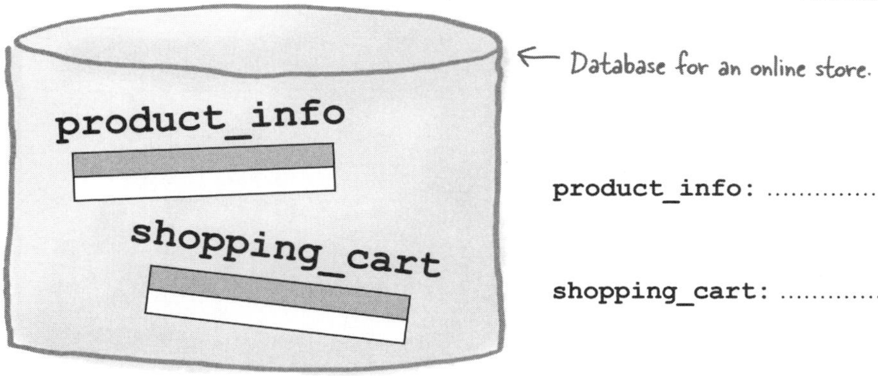

product_info: ....

shopping_cart: ....

Consider the databases and tables below. Think about what categories of data you might find in each. Come up some likely columns for each table.

library_db

Database for a library.

Don't worry if your answers for the column names don't match ours exactly.

books: title, author, cost, scan_code

library_patron: first_name, last_name, address

bank_db

Database for a bank.

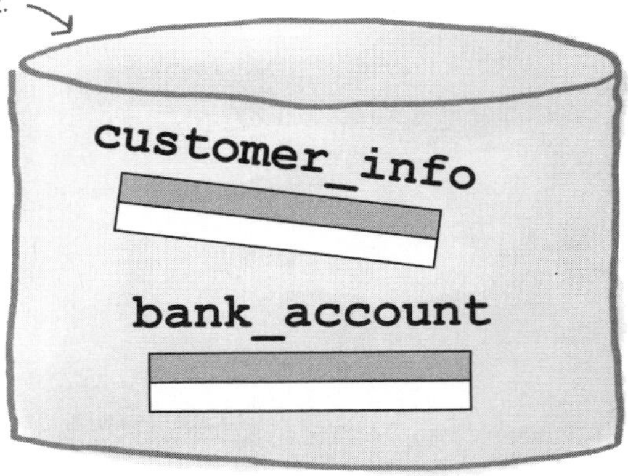

customer_info: first_name, last_name, address, account_number, ssn

bank_account: balance, deposits, withdrawals

onlinestore_db

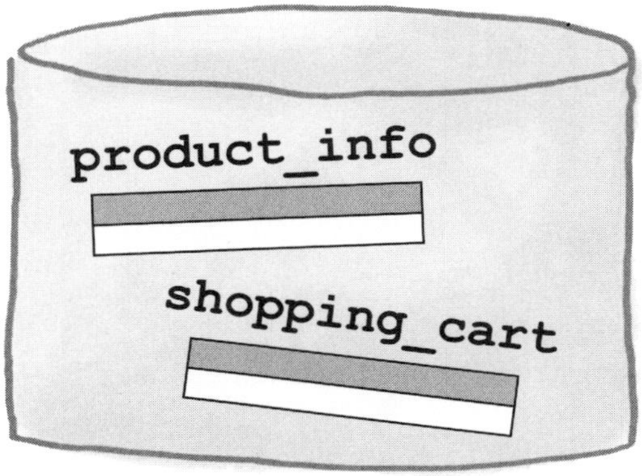

Database for an online store.

product_info: name, size, cost

shopping_cart: total_charge, customer_id

Take command!

Start up your SQL relational database management system (RDBMS) and open a command-line window or graphical environment that allows you to communicate with your RDBMS. Here's our terminal window after we start MySQL.

```
File Edit Window Help CommandMeBaby
Welcome to the SQL monitor. Commands end with ; or \g.

Type 'help;' or '\h' for help. Type '\c' to clear the buffer.

>
```

This angle bracket is the command prompt. You'll be typing your commands right after it.

First you're going to need to create a database to hold all your tables.

Spaces aren't allowed in the names of databases and tables in SQL, so an underscore can be used instead.

1 Type in the line of code below to create your database called **gregs_list**.

```
CREATE DATABASE gregs_list;
```

CREATE DATABASE is the command.

The name of the database is gregs_list

Your command must end with a semicolon.

```
File Edit Window Help CommandMeBaby
> CREATE DATABASE gregs_list;
Query OK, 1 row affected (0.01 sec)
```

This is feedback from the RDBMS, letting you know your query executed successfully.

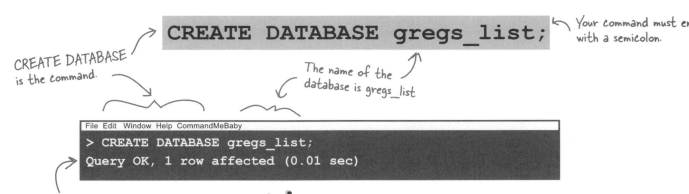

Did you read the intro?

We're using MySQL to command our databases, so commands in your Database Management System (DBMS) might look a little different. See Appendix II for instructions on installing MySQL on your server.

2. Now you need to tell your RDBMS to actually *use* the database you just created:

```
USE gregs_list;
```

Now everything we do will happen inside the gregs_list database!

```
File Edit Window Help USEful
> USE gregs_list;
Database changed
```

there are no Dumb Questions

Q: Why do I need to create a database if I only have one table?

A: The SQL language requires all tables to be inside of databases. There are sound reasons behind this. One of the features of SQL is the ability to control access to your tables by multiple users. Being able to grant or deny access to an entire database is sometimes simpler than having to control the permissions on each one of multiple tables.

Q: I noticed that we used all uppercase for the CREATE DATABASE command. Is that necessary?

A: Some systems do require certain keywords to be capitalized, but SQL is case insensitive. That means it's not necessary to capitalize commands, but it's considered a good programming practice in SQL. Look at the command we just typed,

```
CREATE DATABASE
gregs_list;
```

The capitalization makes it easy to tell the command (`CREATE DATABASE`) from the name of the database (`gregs_list`).

Q: Is there anything I should know about naming my databases, tables, and columns?

A: It's generally a good idea to create descriptive names. Sometimes this results in you needing to use more than one word in a name. You can't use spaces in your names, so the underscore lets you create more descriptive names. Here are variations you might see used:

```
gregs_list
gregslist
Gregslist
gregsList
```

Generally it's best to avoid capitalizing your names to avoid confusion since SQL is case insensitive..

Q: What if I prefer to use "gregsList" with no underscore?

A: Go right ahead. The important thing is to be consistent. If you use `gregsList` as the database name with no underscore and the second word capitalized, then you should stick to that naming convention throughout all your tables in this database, for example naming your table `myContacts`, to be consistent.

Q: Shouldn't the database be called greg's_list? Why leave out the apostrophe?

A: The apostrophe is reserved for a different use in SQL. There are ways you could include one, but it's far easier to omit it.

Q: I also noticed a semicolon at the end of the CREATE DATABASE command. Why did we need that?

A: The semicolon is there to indicate that the command has ended.

Capitalization and underscores help you program in SQL (even though SQL doesn't need them!)

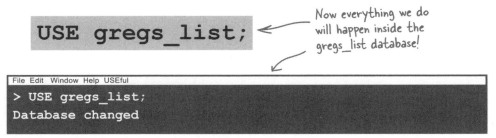

Setting the table: the CREATE TABLE statement

Let's see all this in action with the doughnut data. Say you were having trouble remembering what type of doughnuts a snack in your list was just from its name, you might ***create a table*** to save having to remember them instead. Below is a single command to type into your console window. When you've typed it, you can press RETURN to tell your SQL RDBMS to carry out the command.

doughnut_list

doughnut_name	doughnut_type
Blooberry	filled
Cinnamondo	ring
Rockstar	cruller
Carameller	cruller
Appleblush	filled

```
CREATE TABLE doughnut_list
(
    doughnut_name VARCHAR(10),
    doughnut_type VARCHAR(6)
);
```

Here's the SQL command to create the table—notice the caps.

Your table's name should be lowercase and have an underscore in place of any spaces.

Just hit return to start a new line in your command to make it easier to read what's what.

The opening parenthesis opens the list of columns to create.

The comma separates the colums being created.

The name of the first column in the table.

The name of the second column.

The closing parenthesis closes the list of columns.

The semicolon tells the SQL RDBMS that it's reached the end of the command.

This is a DATA TYPE. It stands for VARiable CHARacter and is used to hold information that's stored as text. The (6) means that the text it holds can be up to 6 characters long.

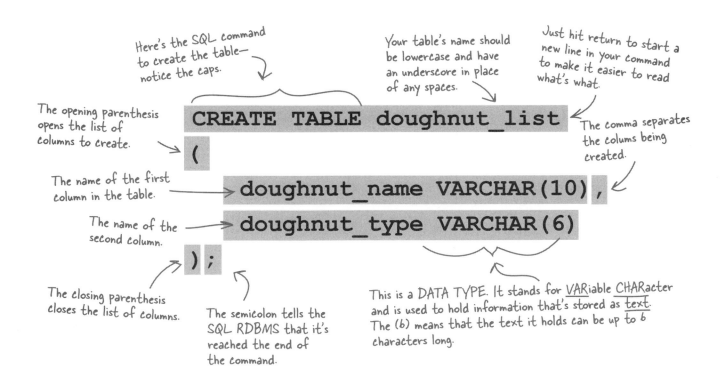

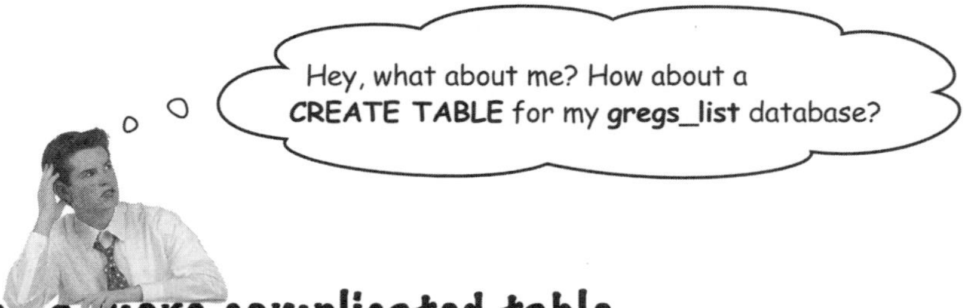
Hey, what about me? How about a
CREATE TABLE for my gregs_list database?

Creating a more complicated table

Remember the columns for Greg's table? We've jotted them down on a sticky note. You'll need those to write your **CREATE TABLE** command.

last name
first name
email
birthday
profession
location
status
interests
seeking

You'll be using the CREATE TABLE command to go from this...

...to this

last_name	first_name	email	birthday	profession	location	status	interests	seeking

BRAIN POWER

In which two ways do the column names on the sticky note differ from those in the table above? Why are they significant?

Look how easy it is to write SQL

You've seen that to create a table you categorize your data into columns. Then you come up with the right data type and length for each column. After you estimate how long each column needs to be, writing the code is straightforward.

Sharpen your pencil

The code to the left is our CREATE TABLE statement for Greg's new database. Try to guess what each line of the CREATE TABLE command is doing. Also include an example of the data that will go in each column.

```
CREATE TABLE my_contacts
(
   last_name VARCHAR(30),
   first_name VARCHAR(20),
   email VARCHAR(50),
   birthday DATE,
   profession VARCHAR(50),
   location VARCHAR(50),
   status VARCHAR(20),
   interests VARCHAR(100),
   seeking VARCHAR(100)
);
```

Sharpen your pencil Solution

Here's what each line of the CREATE TABLE command is doing, and some example data for each column type.

```
CREATE TABLE my_contacts
(
    last_name VARCHAR(30),
    first_name VARCHAR(20),
    email VARCHAR(50),
    birthday DATE,
    profession VARCHAR(50),
    location VARCHAR(50),
    status VARCHAR(20),
    interests VARCHAR(100),
    seeking VARCHAR(100)
);
```

Creates a table named 'my_contacts'	
Opens the list of columns to add	
Adds a column named 'last_name' that can hold up to 30 characters	'Anderson'
Adds a column named 'first_name' that can hold up to 20 characters	'Jillian'
Adds a column named 'email' that can hold up to 50 characters	'jill_anderson@breakneckpizza.com'
Adds a column named 'birthday' that can hold a date value	'1980-09-05'
Adds a column named 'profession' that can hold up to 50 characters	'Technical Writer'
Adds a column named 'location' that can hold up to 50 characters	'Palo Alto, CA'
Adds a column named 'status' that can hold up to 20 characters	'Single'
Adds a column named 'interests' that can hold up to 100 characters	'Kayaking, Reptiles'
Adds a column named 'seeking' that can hold up to 100 characters	'Relationship, Friends'
Closes the list of columns to add, and the semicolon ends the command	

Create the my_contacts table, finally

Now you know exactly what each line is doing, you can type in the **CREATE TABLE** command. You can enter it one line at a time, copying the code at the top of this page.

Or you can enter it all as one really long single line:

```
CREATE TABLE my_contacts(last_name VARCHAR(30), first_name VARCHAR(20), email VARCHAR(50), birthday DATE, profession VARCHAR(50), location VARCHAR(50), status VARCHAR(20), interests VARCHAR(100), seeking VARCHAR(100))
```

Trust us, this really is the command, it's just written out r-e-a-l-l-y small so it fits on the page!

Whichever way you choose to enter it, before you hit return after the semicolon, make sure you haven't missed any characters:
`last_name VARCHAR(3)` is a very different column than `lastname VARCHAR(30)`!

Your table is ready

```
File Edit Window Help AllDone
> CREATE TABLE my_contacts
    -> (
    ->     last_name VARCHAR(30),
    ->     first_name VARCHAR(20),
    ->     email VARCHAR(50),
    ->     birthday DATE,
    ->     profession VARCHAR(50),
    ->     location VARCHAR(50),
    ->     status VARCHAR(20),
    ->     interests VARCHAR(100),
    ->     seeking VARCHAR(100)
    -> );
Query OK, 0 rows affected (0.07 sec)
```

Did you notice how hitting return after the semicolon ended the command and told your SQL RDBMS to process it?

So I'll always store everything in either **VARCHAR** or **DATE** data types?

Actually, you'll need a few more data types for other kinds of data, like numbers.

Suppose we added a price column to our doughnut table. We wouldn't want to store that as a VARCHAR. Values stored as VARCHARs are interpreted as text, and you won't be able to perform mathematical operations on them But there are more data types you haven't met yet…

BRAIN POWER

Before going further, come up with other types of data that need a data type other than **VARCHAR** or **DATE**.

Take a meeting with some data types

These are a few of the most useful data types. It's their job to store your data for you without mucking it up. You've already met VARCHAR and DATE, but say hello to these.

CHAR or CHARACTER. He's rigid and prefers his data to be a set length.
INT or INTEGER thinks numbers should be whole, but he's not afraid of negative numbers.
DEC, short for DECIMAL. He'll give you all the decimal places you ask for, until he's full.
We don't know who he is, he just wandered in.
Call him BLOB. He likes large gobs of text data.
She goes by either DATETIME or TIMESTAMP depending on the SQL RDBMS. She keeps track of the date and time. She's also got a fraternal twin, TIME, who doesn't care what the date is.
DATE keeps track of your dates. She doesn't care about the time, though.
VARCHAR holds text data of up to 255 characters in length. She's flexible and can adapt to the length of your data.

Watch it!

These data type names may not work with your SQL RDBMS!

Unfortunately, there are no universally accepted names for various data types. Your particular SQL RDBMS might use different names for one or more of these types. Check your documentation to find the correct names for your RDBMS.

WHICH DATA TYPE?

Determine which data type makes the most sense for each column. While you're at it, fill in the other missing info.

These two numbers show how many digits the database should expect in front of the decimal, and how many after.

Column Name	Description	Example	Best Choice of Data Type
price	The cost of an item for sale	5678.39	DEC(5,2)
zip_code			
atomic_weight	Atomic weight of an element with up to 6 decimal places		
comments	Large block of text, more than 255 characters	Joe, I'm at the shareholder's meeting. They just gave a demo and there were rubber duckies flying around the screen. Was this your idea of a joke? You might want to spend some time on Monster.com.	
quantity	How many of this item in stock		
tax_rate		3.755	
book_title		Head First SQL	
gender	One character, either M or F		CHAR(1)
phone_number	Ten digits, no punctuation	2105552367	
state	Two-character abbreviation for a state	TX, CA	
anniversary		11/22/2006	DATE
games_won			INT
meeting_time		10:30 a.m. 4/12/2020	

there are no Dumb Questions

Q: Why not just use BLOB for all of my text values?

A: It's a waste of space. A VARCHAR or CHAR takes up a specific amount of space, no more than 256 characters. But a BLOB takes up much more storage space. As your database grows, you run the risk of running out of space on your hard drive. You also can't run certain important string operations on BLOBs that you can on VARCHARs and CHARs (you'll learn about these later).

Q: Why do I need these numeric types like INT and DEC?

A: It all comes down to database storage and efficiency. Choosing the best matching data type for each column in your table will reduce the size of table and make operations on your data faster.

Q: Is this it? Are these all the types?

A: No, but these are the most important ones. Data types also differ slightly by RDBMS, so you'll need to consult your particular documentation for more information. We recommend *SQL in a Nutshell* (O'Reilly) as a particularly good reference book that spells out the differences between RDBMSs.

Which Data Type?

Determine which data type makes the most sense for each column. While you're at it, fill in the other missing info.

A zip code may not always be 10 characters long, so we use VARCHAR to save space in the database. You might also have used CHAR here and assumed a specific length.

Column Name	Description	Example	Best Choice of Data Type
price	The cost of an item for sale	5678.39	DEC(5,2)
zip_code	Five to 10 characters	90210-0010	VARCHAR(10)
atomic_weight	Atomic weight of an element with up to 6 decimal places	4.002602	DEC(10, 6)
comments	Large block of text, more than 255 characters	Joe, I'm at the shareholder's meeting. They just gave a demo and there were rubber duckies flying around the screen. Was this your idea of a joke? You might want to spend some time on Monster.com.	BLOB
quantity	How many of this item in stock	239	INT
tax_rate	A percentage	3.755	DEC(4, 2)
book_title	A text string	Head First SQL	VARCHAR(50)
gender	One character, either M or F	M	CHAR(1)
phone_number	Ten digits, no punctuation	2105552367	CHAR(10)
state	Two character abbreviation for a state	TX, CA	CHAR(2)
anniversary	Month, day, year	11/22/2006	DATE
games_won	An integer representing number of games won	15	INT
meeting_time	A time and day	10:30 a.m. 4/12/2020	DATETIME

A phone number will always be exactly this length. And we treat it like a text string because we don't need to do any mathematical operations on it, even though it's a number.

TIMESTAMP is usually used to capture the current time. DATETIME is best used to store a future event.

BULLET POINTS

- Break your data up in categories before you create your table. Pay special attention to the type of data for each column.
- Use the **CREATE DATABASE** statement to create the database which will hold all of your tables.
- Use the **USE DATABASE** statement to get inside your database to create your table.
- All tables are created with a **CREATE TABLE** statement, containing column names and their corresponding data types.
- Some of the most common datatypes are **CHAR**, **VARCHAR**, **BLOB**, **INT**, **DEC**, **DATE**, and **DATETIME**. Each has different rules for what goes inside.

Wait a second. Where's the table I just created in the gregs_list database? I want to check that I got everything in there correctly.

Good call. Checking your work is important.

To see how the `my_contacts` table you created looks, you can use the **DESC** command to view it:

```
DESC my_contacts;
```

DESC is short for DESCRIBE

You try it.

```
File Edit Window Help DescTidy
> DESC my_contacts;
```

Your table, DESCribed

When you've entered the DESC command. You'll see something that looks similar to this:

Don't worry about these right now; we'll get to them shortly.

```
File  Edit  Window  Help  DescTidy
> DESC my_contacts;
+------------+-------------+------+-----+---------+-------+
| Column     | Type        | Null | Key | Default | Extra |
+------------+-------------+------+-----+---------+-------+
| last_name  | varchar(30) | YES  |     | NULL    |       |
| first_name | varchar(20) | YES  |     | NULL    |       |
| email      | varchar(50) | YES  |     | NULL    |       |
| birthday   | date        | YES  |     | NULL    |       |
| profession | varchar(50) | YES  |     | NULL    |       |
| location   | varchar(50) | YES  |     | NULL    |       |
| status     | varchar(20) | YES  |     | NULL    |       |
| interests  | varchar(100)| YES  |     | NULL    |       |
| seeking    | varchar(100)| YES  |     | NULL    |       |
+------------+-------------+------+-----+---------+-------+
9 rows in set (0.07 sec)
```

I wish I'd put a column in there for gender. Is it too late to add one?

BRAIN POWER

What do <u>you</u> think? What sorts of problems could adding a new column create?

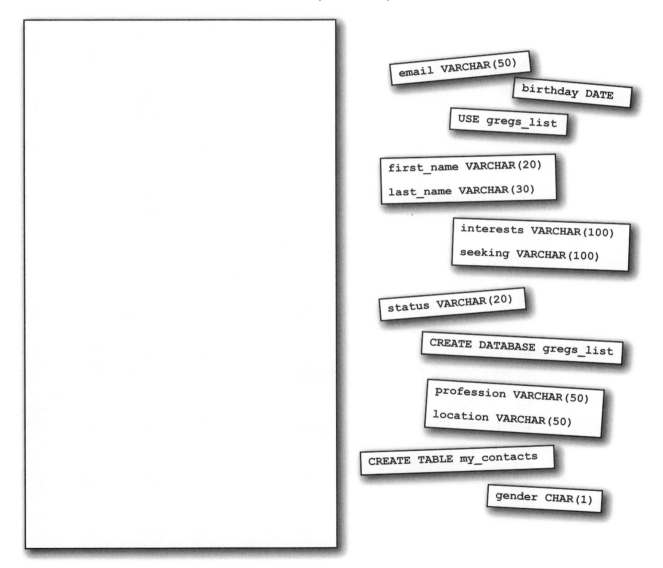

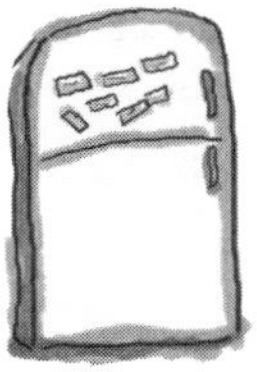

SQL Magnets

The code to create the database and table with the new gender column is all scrambled up on the fridge. Can you reconstruct the code snippets to make it work? Some of the parentheses and semicolons fell on the floor and they were too small to pick up, so feel free to add as many of those as you need!

```
email VARCHAR(50)
```

```
birthday DATE
```

```
USE gregs_list
```

```
first_name VARCHAR(20)
last_name VARCHAR(30)
```

```
interests VARCHAR(100)
seeking VARCHAR(100)
```

```
status VARCHAR(20)
```

```
CREATE DATABASE gregs_list
```

```
profession VARCHAR(50)
location VARCHAR(50)
```

```
CREATE TABLE my_contacts
```

```
gender CHAR(1)
```

When you finish, try typing the new CREATE TABLE code into your SQL console to add the new gender column!

SQL Magnets Solution

Your job was to reconstruct the code snippets to make the code that would create the database and table with the new gender column.

gregs_list already exists.

Here's the code reconstructed. Check your answer against it, then keep reading...

```
CREATE DATABASE gregs_list
USE gregs_list
CREATE TABLE my_contacts
(
last_name VARCHAR(20),
first_name VARCHAR(30),
email VARCHAR(50),
birthday DATE,
gender CHAR(1),
profession VARCHAR(50),
location VARCHAR(50),
status VARCHAR(20),
interests VARCHAR(100),
seeking VARCHAR(100)
);
```

You can't recreate an existing table or database!

Did you try entering the new CREATE TABLE statement? If you did, you'll already know that the solution to the exercise won't help you add the new column.

If you did enter it into your console, you probably saw something like this:

```
File Edit Window Help OhCrap!
> CREATE TABLE my_contacts
    -> (
    ->     last_name VARCHAR(30),
    ->     first_name VARCHAR(20),
    ->     email VARCHAR(50),
    ->     gender CHAR(1),
    ->     birthday DATE,
    ->     profession VARCHAR(50),
    ->     location VARCHAR(50),
    ->     status VARCHAR(20),
    ->     interests VARCHAR(100),
    ->     seeking VARCHAR(100)
    -> );
ERROR 1050 (42S01): Table 'my_contacts' already exists
```

The new column for gender.

Uh oh. That statement gives you an error message. Looks like the table wasn't created.

there are no Dumb Questions

Q: About that SQL Magnets exercise, why did I get an error?

A: You can't create a table that already exists. And once you create a database, you don't need to create it again. Other possible errors include you forgetting the semicolon. Also, check to see if you typoed any of the SQL keywords.

Q: Why isn't there a comma after "seeking VARCHAR(100)" like all the other columns have?

A: The column 'seeking" is the last of them before we reach the closing parenthesis. That tells the RDBMS that the end of the statement is here, so no comma is needed.

Q: So, is there a way to add the forgotten column or will I have to start over?

A: You're going to have to start over, but before you can create the table with the added gender column you have to get rid of the old one. Since there is no data in the table yet, we can simply get rid of the old one away and start over.

Q: But what if I've got a table with data in it, and I need to add a column? Is there a way to do it without deleting the whole table and starting over?

A: Great question! There is a way to change your table without damaging the data in it. We'll get to that a bit later, but for now, since our table is empty, we'll get rid of the table and create a new one.

If we're going to have to type over our CREATE TABLE command again, I bet we could save time and energy if we typed all our SQL statements in a text editor like NotePad or TextEdit.

That's a very good idea, and you'll want to use a text editor throughout this book.

That way, you can copy and paste the statements into your SQL console whenever you need to. This will keep you from having to retype everything. Also, you can copy and edit old SQL statements to make new ones.

Out with the old table, in with the new

1. Getting rid of a table is much easier than creating a table. Use this simple command:

The command to delete your table...

...and the name of the table to be deleted.

```
DROP TABLE my_contacts;
```

Don't forget the semicolon.

```
File Edit Window Help ByeByeTable
> DROP TABLE my_contacts;
Query OK, 0 rows affected (0.12 sec)
```

DROP TABLE will work whether or not there is data in your table, so *use the command with extreme caution*. Once your table is dropped, it's gone, along with any data that was in it.

DROP TABLE deletes your table and any data in it!

2. Now you can enter your new **CREATE TABLE** statement:

```
File Edit Window Help Success
> CREATE TABLE my_contacts
    -> (
    ->     last_name VARCHAR(30),
    ->     first_name VARCHAR(20),
    ->     email VARCHAR(50),
    ->     gender CHAR(1),
    ->     birthday DATE,
    ->     profession VARCHAR(50),
    ->     location VARCHAR(50),
    ->     status VARCHAR(20),
    ->     interests VARCHAR(100),
    ->     seeking VARCHAR(100)
    -> );
Query OK, 0 rows affected (0.05 sec)
```

This time it worked.

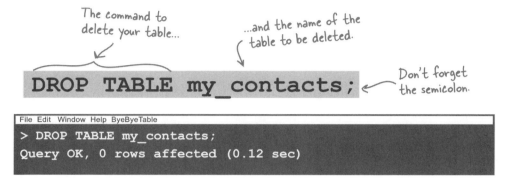

Who am I?

A bunch of SQL keywords and data types, in full costume, are playing the party game "Who am I?" They give you a clue, and you try to guess who they are, based on what they say. Assume they always tell the truth about themselves. If they happen to say something that could be true for more than one guy, then write down all for whom that sentence applies. Fill in the blanks next to the sentence with the names of one or more attendees.

Tonight's attendees:

CREATE DATABASE, USE DATABASE, CREATE TABLE, DESC, DROP TABLE, CHAR, VARCHAR, BLOB, DATE, DATETIME, DEC, INT

	Name
I've got your number.	....
I can dispose of your unwanted tables.	....
T or F questions are my favorite.	....
I keep track of your mom's birthday.	....
I got the whole table in my hands.	....
Numbers are cool, but I hate fractions.	....
I like long, wordy explanations.	....
This is the place to store everything.	....
The table wouldn't exist without me.	....
I know exactly when your dental appointment is next week.	....
Accountants like me.	....
I can give you a peek at your table format.	....
Without us, you couldn't even create a table.	....
	....

Answers on page 51.

Anatomy of a Statement

Okay, I've got my new table ready. Now, *how* do I get the data from the sticky notes into the table?

To add data to your table, you'll use the INSERT statement

This pretty much does what it says in the name. Take a look at the statement below to see how each part works. The values in the second set of parentheses have to be in the ***same order as the column names.***

The command below isn't a real command, it's a template of a statement to show you the format of an `INSERT` statement.

The keywords INSERT INTO begin the statement.

The name of your table. In Greg's case, it will be my_contacts.

This next part is a list of your column names, separated by commas. You already know that Greg's list will have columns like first_name, last_name, and email.

More column names follow, no comma after the last one.

```
INSERT INTO your_table (column_name1, column_name2,...)
    VALUES ('value1', 'value2',...);
```

Another keyword. This signals that the values for the columns follow.

This next part is a list of your values, separated by commas. In Greg's case, the list will contain the information from his sticky notes.

The single quotes are correct. Use them whenever you're inserting text, even if it's a single character like 'M', or 'F'.

More values follow, no comma after the last one.

The usual semicolon ending the statement.

IMPORTANT: the values need to be in the same order as the column names.

WHO DOES WHAT?

Before you can write your INSERT statement, you need to match up your column names and values.

Columns	Values
first_name	'Relationship, Friends'
status	'Anderson'
seeking	'1980-09-05'
gender	'Technical Writer'
birthday	'Jillian'
last_name	'Single'
location	'F'
interests	'Palo Alto, CA'
profession	'jill_anderson@breakneckpizza.com'
email	'Kayaking, Reptiles'

WHO DOES WHAT?

Before you can write your INSERT statement, you need to match up your column names and values.

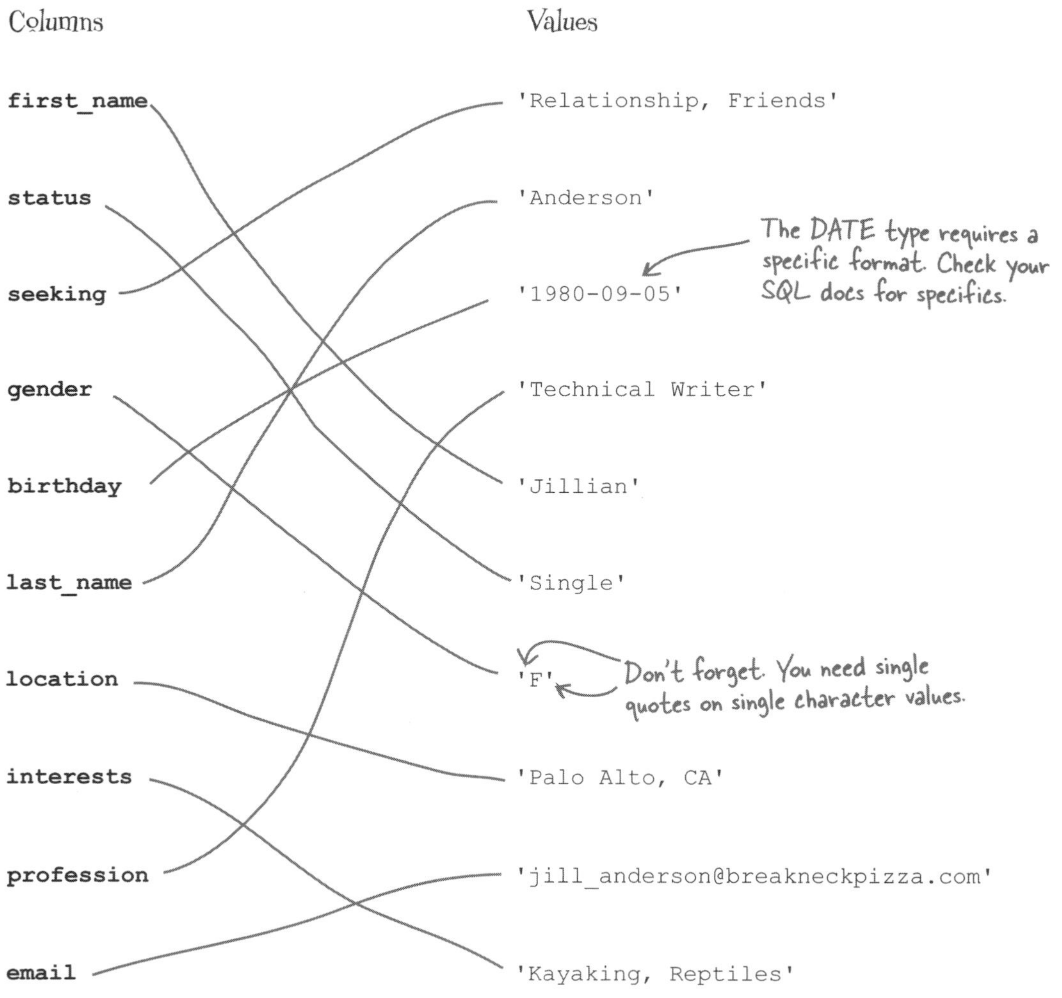
Columns
Values
first_name
status
seeking
gender
birthday
last_name
location
interests
profession
email
'Relationship, Friends'
'Anderson'
'1980-09-05'
'Technical Writer'
'Jillian'
'Single'
'F'
'Palo Alto, CA'
'jill_anderson@breakneckpizza.com'
'Kayaking, Reptiles'
The DATE type requires a specific format. Check your SQL docs for specifics.
Don't forget. You need single quotes on single character values.

Create the INSERT statement

Your column names are in the first set of parentheses and divided by commas.

You can hit return before the opening parenthesis to make the code easier to read in your console window.

```
INSERT INTO my_contacts
(last_name, first_name, email, gender, birthday,
profession, location, status, interests,
seeking)
VALUES
('Anderson', 'Jillian', 'jill_anderson@
breakneckpizza.com', 'F', '1980-09-05',
'Technical Writer', 'Palo Alto, CA', 'Single',
'Kayaking, Reptiles', 'Relationship, Friends');
```

Hit return after the closing columns parenthesis and another after VALUES to make the code easier to read.

The values for each column are in the second set of parentheses and are also separated by commas.

Any value that goes into a VARCHAR, CHAR, DATE, or BLOB column has single quotes around it.

Watch it!

Order matters!

*The **values** should be listed in **exactly** the **same order** as the **column names**.*

Exercise — **Try this at home**

This is one way to add a row to your table. Try typing it in yourself. Type it in a text editor first so if you make a mistake you won't have to retype the entire thing. Pay special attention to the single quotes and commas. Write the response you get here:

....

You just told me that **CHAR**, **VARCHAR**, **DATE**, and **BLOB** values have **single quotes** around them **in the INSERT** statement. So that means **numeric values** like **DEC** and **INT don't use quotes**?

Exactly right.

Here's an `INSERT` statement you might use if you had a table of doughnut purchases. Notice how, in the values, the numbers that match the dozens of donuts purchased and price columns have no quotes.

The dozens column is an INT, since you don't usually buy part of a dozen and don't need decimal places.

The price column is DEC(4,2) which means it's four digits long, with two decimal places.

```
INSERT INTO doughnut_purchases
(donut_type, dozens, topping, price)
VALUES
('jelly', 3, 'sprinkles', 3.50);
```

The values inserted into the dozens and price columns don't need quotes!

Sharpen your pencil

Your SQL RDBMS will tell you when something is wrong with your statement, but will sometimes be a bit vague. Take a look at each INSERT statement below. First try to guess what's wrong with the statement, and then try typing it in to see what your RDBMS reports.

```
INSERT INTO my_contacts

(last_name, first_name, email, gender, birthday, profession, location, status,
interests, seeking) VALUES ('Anderson', 'Jillian', 'jill_anderson@breakneckpizza.com',
'F', '1980-09-05', 'Technical Writer', 'Single', 'Kayaking, Reptiles', 'Relationship,
Friends');
```

What's wrong? ....

Your RDBMS says: ....

```
INSERT INTO my_contacts

(last_name, first_name, gender, birthday, profession, location, status, interests,
seeking) VALUES ('Anderson', 'Jillian', 'jill_anderson@breakneckpizza.com', 'F',
'1980-09-05', 'Technical Writer', 'Palo Alto, CA', 'Single', 'Kayaking, Reptiles',
'Relationship, Friends');
```

What's wrong? ....

Your RDBMS says: ....

```
INSERT INTO my_contacts

(last_name, first_name, email, gender, birthday, profession, location, status,
interests, seeking) VALUES ('Anderson', 'Jillian', 'jill_anderson@breakneckpizza.com',
'F', '1980-09-05', 'Technical Writer' 'Palo Alto, CA', 'Single', 'Kayaking, Reptiles',
'Relationship, Friends');
```

What's wrong? ....

Your RDBMS says: ....

```
INSERT INTO my_contacts

(last_name, first_name, email, gender, birthday, profession, location, status,
interests, seeking) VALUES ('Anderson', 'Jillian', 'jill_anderson@breakneckpizza.com',
'F', '1980-09-05', 'Technical Writer', 'Palo Alto, CA', 'Single', 'Kayaking, Reptiles',
'Relationship, Friends);
```

What's wrong? ....

Your RDBMS says: ....

If this one causes your RDBMS to "hang," try typing a single quote followed by a semicolon after you've entered the rest of the statement.

Sharpen your pencil Solution

Your SQL RDBMS will tell you when something is wrong with your statement, but will sometimes be a bit vague. Take a look at each INSERT statement below. First try to guess what's wrong with the statement, and then try typing it in to see what your RDBMS reports.

```
INSERT INTO my_contacts

(last_name, first_name, email, gender, birthday, profession, location, status,
interests, seeking) VALUES ('Anderson', 'Jillian', 'jill_anderson@breakneckpizza.com',
'F', '1980-09-05', 'Technical Writer', 'Single', 'Kayaking, Reptiles', 'Relationship,
Friends');
```

What's wrong? It's missing a location value ← We've got a location column in the column list, but no location in the values list, we're short one value.

Your RDBMS says: ERROR 1136 (21S01): Column count doesn't match value count at row 1

Notice that many different problems result in the same error. Watch out for typos; they can be tricky to track down.

```
INSERT INTO my_contacts

(last_name, first_name, gender, birthday, profession, location, status, interests,
seeking) VALUES ('Anderson', 'Jillian', 'jill_anderson@breakneckpizza.com', 'F',
'1980-09-05', 'Technical Writer', 'Palo Alto, CA', 'Single', 'Kayaking, Reptiles',
'Relationship, Friends');
```

What's wrong? Missing email in column list ← This time we have a value for all the columns, but we're missing our email column in the column list.

Your RDBMS says: ERROR 1136 (21S01): Column count doesn't match value count at row 1

```
INSERT INTO my_contacts

(last_name, first_name, email, gender, birthday, profession, location, status,
interests, seeking) VALUES ('Anderson', 'Jillian', 'jill_anderson@breakneckpizza.com',
'F', '1980-09-05', 'Technical Writer' 'Palo Alto, CA', 'Single', 'Kayaking, Reptiles',
'Relationship, Friends');
```

What's wrong? Missing comma between two values ← No comma in the values list between 'Technical Writer' and 'Palo Alto, CA'

Your RDBMS says: ERROR 1136 (21S01): Column count doesn't match value count at row 1

```
INSERT INTO my_contacts

(last_name, first_name, email, gender, birthday, profession, location, status,
interests, seeking) VALUES ('Anderson', 'Jillian', 'jill_anderson@breakneckpizza.com',
'F', '1980-09-05', 'Technical Writer', 'Palo Alto, CA', 'Single', 'Kayaking, Reptiles',
'Relationship, Friends);
```

What's wrong? It's missing a single quote after the last value

Your RDBMS says: ERROR 1064 (42000): You have an error in your SQL syntax; check the manual that corresponds to your MySQL server version for the right syntax to use near '' at line 4

Variations on an INSERT statement

There are three variations of **INSERT** statements you should know about.

1 Changing the order of columns

You can change the order of your column names, as long as the matching values for each column come in that same order!

```
INSERT INTO my_contacts

(interests, first_name, last_name, gender, email, birthday,
profession, location, status, seeking)

VALUES

('Kayaking, Reptiles', 'Jillian', 'Anderson', 'F',
'jill_anderson@breakneckpizza.com', '1980-09-05', 'Technical
Writer', 'Palo Alto, CA', 'Single', 'Relationship, Friends');
```

Notice the order of the column names? Now look at the values; they're in that same order. So long as the values match the column names, the order you INSERT them in doesn't matter to you, or your SQL RDBMS!

---

2 Omitting column names

You can leave out the list of column names, but the values must be **all** there, and all **in the same order** that **you added the columns in**. (Double-check the order on page 37 if you're unsure.)

```
INSERT INTO my_contacts

VALUES

('Anderson', 'Jillian', 'jill_anderson@breakneckpizza.com',
'F', '1980-09-05', 'Technical Writer', 'Palo Alto, CA',
'Single', 'Kayaking, Reptiles', 'Relationship, Friends');
```

We left the column names out altogether, but if you do that, you must include ALL the values, and in the EXACT ORDER that they are in the table!

---

3 Leaving some columns out

You can insert a few columns and leave some out.

```
INSERT INTO my_contacts

(last_name, first_name, email)

VALUES

('Anderson', 'Jillian', 'jill_anderson@
breakneckpizza.com');
```

This time, we're only inserting part of our data. Since your SQL RDBMS won't know which parts, you'll need to tell it by specifying the column names and values that you are entering.

BRAIN POWER

What do you think shows up in the table in columns that you don't assign a value to?

Columns without values

Let's insert a record into the my_contacts database from this incomplete sticky note:

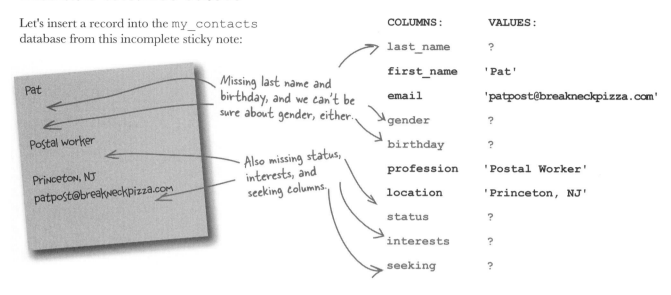

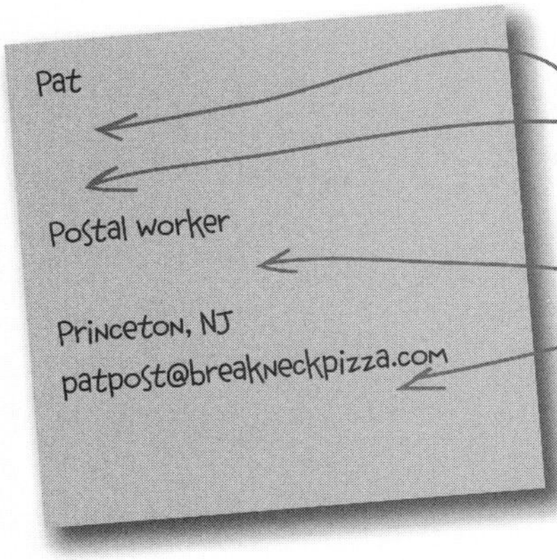

Missing last name and birthday, and we can't be sure about gender, either.

Also missing status, interests, and seeking columns.

COLUMNS:	VALUES:
last_name	?
first_name	'Pat'
email	'patpost@breakneckpizza.com'
gender	?
birthday	?
profession	'Postal Worker'
location	'Princeton, NJ'
status	?
interests	?
seeking	?

Because the sticky is missing some data, Greg will have to enter an incomplete record. But that's okay, he'll be able to add in the missing information later.

We're using the the version of INSERT where we don't have to provide data for all columns because it lets us include just the columns where we know the values.

```
INSERT INTO my_contacts
(first_name, email, profession, location)
VALUES
('Pat', 'patpost@breakneckpizza.com', 'Postal
Worker', 'Princeton, NJ');
```

```
File Edit Window Help MoreDataPlease
> INSERT INTO my_contacts (first_name, email, profession,
location) VALUES ('Pat', 'patpost@breakneckpizza.com',
'Postal Worker', 'Princeton, NJ');

Query OK, 1 row affected (0.02 sec)
```

Peek at your table with the SELECT statement

So you want to see what your table looks like? Well, DESC won't cut it anymore, because it only shows the *structure* of the table and not the information inside of it. Instead, you should use a simple SELECT statement so you can see what data is in your table.

We want to select all the data in our table...

... and the asterisk says to select EVERYTHING.

Our table name.

```
SELECT * FROM my_contacts;
```

Don't worry what the SELECT statement does for now.

We'll be looking at it in a lot more detail in chapter 2. For now, just sit back and marvel at the beauty of your table when you use the statement.

Now try it yourself. You'll have to stretch out your window to see all the results nicely laid out.

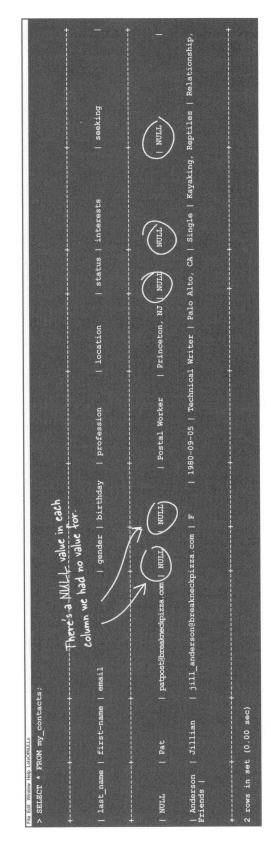

```
File Edit Window Help LotsOfNULLs
> SELECT * FROM my_contacts;
```

There's a NULL value in each column we had no value for.

last_name	first_name	email	gender	birthday	profession	location	status	interests	seeking
NULL	Pat	patpost@breakneckpizza.com	NULL	NULL	Postal Worker	Princeton, NJ	NULL	NULL	NULL
Anderson	Jillian	jill_anderson@breakneckpizza.com	F	1980-09-05	Technical Writer	Palo Alto, CA	Single	Kayaking, Reptiles	Relationship, Friends

2 rows in set (0.00 sec)

BRAIN POWER

Now you know that NULL appears in any columns with no assigned value. What do you think NULL actually *means*?

SQL Exposed

This week's interview: Confessions of a NULL

Head First: Welcome, NULL. I have to admit I didn't expect to see you. I didn't think you actually existed. Word on the street is that you're nothing more than a zero, or nothing at all.

NULL: I can't believe you'd listen to such lies. Yes, I'm here, and I'm quite real! So you think I'm nothing, just dirt under your feet?

Head First: Easy there, calm down. It's just that you show up whenever something has no value…

NULL: Sure, better me than, say, a zero, or an empty string.

Head First: What's an empty string?

NULL: That would be if you used two single quotes with nothing inside of them as a value. It's still a text string, but of length zero. Like setting a value for first_name in the my_contacts table to ''.

Head First: So you aren't just a fancy way of saying nothing?

NULL: I told you, I'm not nothing! I'm something… I'm just a bit… undefined, is all.

Head First: So you're saying that if I compared you to a zero, or to an empty string, you wouldn't equal that?

NULL: No! I'd never equal zero. And actually, I'd never even equal another NULL. You can't compare one NULL to another. A value can **be** NULL, but it never **equals** NULL because NULL is an undefined value! Get it?

Head First: Calm down and let me get this straight. You aren't equal to zero, you aren't an empty string variable. And you aren't even equal to yourself? That makes no sense!

NULL: I know it's confusing. Just think of me this way: I'm undefined. I'm like the inside of an unopened box. Anything could be in there, so you can't compare one unopened box to another because you don't know what's going to be inside of each one. I might even be empty. You just don't know.

Head First: I've been hearing rumors that sometimes you aren't wanted. That maybe there are times where you NULLs cause problems.

NULL: I'll admit that I've shown up where I wasn't wanted before. Some columns should always have values. Like last names, for example. No point to having a NULL last name in a table.

Head First: So you wouldn't go where you weren't wanted?

NULL: Right! Just tell me, man! When you're creating your table and setting up your columns, just let me know.

Head First: You don't really look like an unopened box.

NULL: I've had enough. I've got places to go, values to be.

Controlling your inner NULL

There are certain columns in your table that should always have values. Remember the incomplete sticky note for Pat, with no last name? She (or he) isn't going to be very easy to find when you have twenty more NULL last name entries in your table. You can easily set up your table to not accept NULL values for columns.

```
CREATE TABLE my_contacts
(
  last_name VARCHAR (30) NOT NULL,
  first_name VARCHAR (20) NOT NULL
);
```

Just add the words NOT NULL right after the data type.

If you use these, you *must* provide a value for the column in your INSERT statement. If you don't, you'll get an error.

Sharpen your pencil

```
CREATE TABLE my_contacts
(
  last_name VARCHAR(30) NOT NULL,
  first_name VARCHAR(20) NOT NULL,
  email VARCHAR(50),
  gender CHAR(1),
  birthday DATE,
  profession VARCHAR(50),
  location VARCHAR(50),
  status VARCHAR(20),
  interests VARCHAR(100),
  seeking VARCHAR(100)
);
```

Look at each of the columns in our my_contacts CREATE TABLE command. Which should be set to be NOT NULL? Think about columns that should never be NULL and circle them.

We've given you two to start, now finish up the rest. Primarily consider columns that you'll use later to search with or columns that are unique.

Sharpen your pencil Solution

```
CREATE TABLE my_contacts
(
   last_name VARCHAR(30) NOT NULL,
   first_name VARCHAR(20) NOT NULL,
   email VARCHAR(50),
   gender CHAR(1),
   birthday DATE,
   profession VARCHAR(50),
   location VARCHAR(50),
   status VARCHAR(20),
   interests VARCHAR(100),
   seeking VARCHAR(100)
);
```

Look at each of the columns in our my_contacts CREATE TABLE command. Which should be set to be NOT NULL? Think about columns that should never be NULL and circle them.

We've given you two to start, now finish up the rest. Primarily consider columns that you'll use later to search with or columns that are unique.

All of the columns should be NOT NULL.

You will use ALL your columns to search with. It's important to make sure your records are complete and your table has good data in it...

...but, if you have a column that you know will need to be filled in later, you may want to allow NULL values in it.

NOT NULL appears in DESC

Here's how the my_contacts table would look if you set all the columns to have NOT NULL values.

Here's where we create our table with NOT NULL in each column.

```
File Edit Window Help NoMoreNULLs
CREATE TABLE my_contacts
(
    last_name VARCHAR(30) NOT NULL,
    first_name VARCHAR(20) NOT NULL,
    email VARCHAR(50) NOT NULL,
    gender CHAR(1) NOT NULL,
    birthday DATE NOT NULL,
    profession VARCHAR(50) NOT NULL,
    location VARCHAR(50) NOT NULL,
    status VARCHAR(20) NOT NULL,
    interests VARCHAR(100) NOT NULL,
    seeking VARCHAR(100) NOT NULL
);
Query OK, 0 rows affected (0.01 sec)

> DESC my_contacts;
+------------+--------------+------+-----+---------+-------+
| Column     | Type         | Null | Key | Default | Extra |
+------------+--------------+------+-----+---------+-------+
| last_name  | varchar(30)  | NO   |     |         |       |
| first_name | varchar(20)  | NO   |     |         |       |
| email      | varchar(50)  | NO   |     |         |       |
| gender     | char(1)      | NO   |     |         |       |
| birthday   | date         | NO   |     |         |       |
| profession | varchar(50)  | NO   |     |         |       |
| location   | varchar(50)  | NO   |     |         |       |
| status     | varchar(20)  | NO   |     |         |       |
| interests  | varchar(100) | NO   |     |         |       |
| seeking    | varchar(100) | NO   |     |         |       |
+------------+--------------+------+-----+---------+-------+
10 rows in set (0.02 sec)
```

This is the table described. Notice the word NO under NULL.

Fill in the blanks with DEFAULT

If we have a column that we know is usually a specific value, we can assign it a **DEFAULT** value. The value that follows the DEFAULT keyword is automatically inserted into the table each time a row is added ***if no other value is specified***. The default value has to be of the same type of value as the column.

```
CREATE TABLE doughnut_list
(
  doughnut_name VARCHAR(10) NOT NULL,
  doughnut_type VARCHAR(6) NOT NULL,
  doughnut_cost DEC(3,2) NOT NULL DEFAULT 1.00
);
```

We want to make sure that we always have a value in this column. Not only can we make it NOT NULL, we can also assign it a DEFAULT value of $1.

This will be the value inserted in the table for the doughnut_cost column when no other value is designated.

doughnut_list

doughnut_name	doughnut_type	doughnut_cost
Blooberry	filled	2.00
Cinnamondo	ring	1.00
Rockstar	cruller	1.00
Carameller	cruller	1.00
Appleblush	filled	1.40

Here's how your table would look if you left the doughnut_cost values blank when you were inserted the records for the Cinnamondo, Rockstar, and Carameller doughnuts.

Using a DEFAULT value fills the empty columns with a specified value.

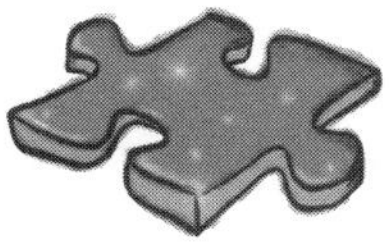

Tablecross

Take some time to sit back and give your left brain something to do. It's your standard crossword; all of the solution words are from this chapter.

Across

4. A _____ is a container that holds tables and other SQL structures related to those tables.
5. A _____ is a piece of data stored by your table.
6. This holds text data of up to 255 characters in length.
7. You can't compare one _____ to another.
10. End every SQL statement with one of these.
12. This is a single set of columns that describe attributes of a single thing.

Down

1. This is the structure inside your database that contains data, organized in columns and rows.
2. Use this in your CREATE TABLE to specify a value for a column if no other value is assigned in an INSERT.
3. Use this keyword to see the table you just created.
5. This word can be used in front of both TABLE or DATABASE.
8. To get rid of your table use _____ TABLE.
9. This datatype thinks numbers should be whole, but he's not afraid of negative numbers.
11. To add data to your table, you'll use the _____ statement.

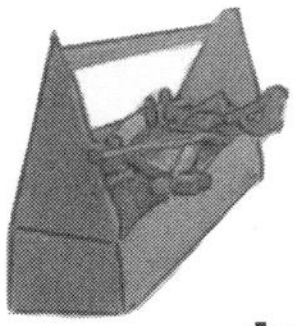

Your SQL Toolbox

You've got Chapter 1 under your belt, and you already know how to create databases and tables, as well as how to insert some of the most common data types into them while ensuring columns that need a value get a value.

BULLET POINTS

- If you want to see the structure of your table, use the **DESC** statement.

- The **DROP TABLE** statement can be used to throw away your table. Use it with care!

- To get your data inside your table, use one of the several varieties of **INSERT** statements.

- A **NULL** value is an undefined value. It does not equal zero or an empty value. A column with a **NULL** value **IS NULL**, but *does not* **EQUAL NULL**.

- Columns that are not assigned values in your **INSERT** statements are set to **NULL** by default.

- You can change a column to not accept a **NULL** value by using the keywords **NOT NULL** when you create your table.

- Using a **DEFAULT** value when you **CREATE** your table fills the column with that value if you insert a record with no value for that column.

CREATE DATABASE

Use this statement to set up the database that will hold all your tables.

USE DATABASE

Gets you inside the database to set up all your tables.

CREATE TABLE

Starts setting up your table, but you'll also need to know your COLUMN NAMES and DATA TYPES. You should have worked these out by analyzing the kind of data you'll be putting in your table.

NULL and NOT NULL

You'll also need to have an idea which columns should not accept NULL values to help you sort and search your data. You'll need to set the columns to NOT NULL when you create your table.

DEFAULT

Lets you specify a default value for a column, used if you don't supply a value for the column when you insert a record.

DROP TABLE

Lets you delete a table if you make a mistake, but you'll need to do this before you start using INSERT statements, which let you add the values for each column.

Who am I?

A bunch of SQL keywords and data types, in full costume, are playing the party game "Who am I?" They give you a clue and you try to guess who they are, based on what they say. Assume they always tell the truth about themselves. If they happen to say something that could be true for more than one guy, then write down all for whom that sentence applies. Fill in the blanks next to the sentence with the names of one or more attendees.

Tonight's attendees:

CREATE DATABASE, USE DATABASE, CREATE TABLE, DESC, DROP TABLE, CHAR, VARCHAR, BLOB, DATE, DATETIME, DEC, INT

	Name
I've got your number.	DEC, INT
I can dispose of your unwanted tables.	DROP TABLE
T or F questions are my favorite.	CHAR(1) ← Bonus points if you added the (1)!
I keep track of your mom's birthday.	DATE
I got the whole table in my hands.	CREATE DATABASE
Numbers are cool, but I hate fractions.	INT
I like long, wordy explanations.	BLOB
This is the place to store everything.	CREATE TABLE
The table wouldn't exist without me.	CREATE DATABASE
I know exactly when your dental appointment is next week.	DATETIME
Accountants like me.	DEC
I can give you a peek at your table format.	DESC
Without us, you couldn't even create a table.	CREATE DATABASE, USE DATABASE
	DROP TABLE

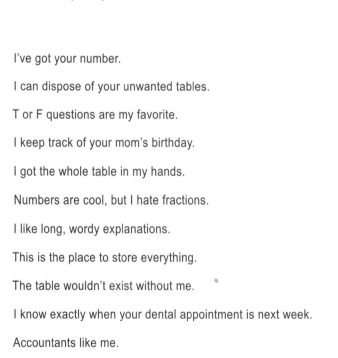

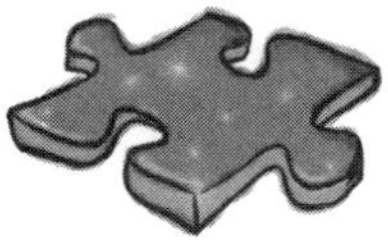

DataAndTablescross Solution

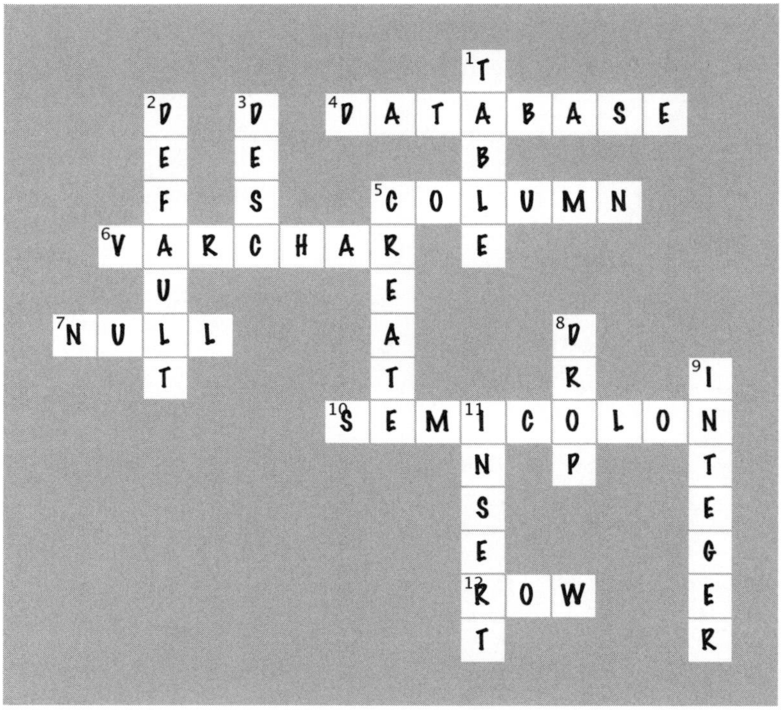

2 the SELECT statement

Gifted data retrieval

SELECT * FROM gifts
WHERE contents = "expensive";

Is it really better to give than retrieve? When it comes to databases, chances are you'll need to **retrieve your data** as often than you'll need to insert it. That's where this chapter comes in: you'll meet the powerful **SELECT** statement and learn how to **gain access to that important information** you've been putting in your tables. You'll even learn how to use **WHERE**, **AND**, and **OR** to selectively get to your data and even avoid displaying the data that you *don't* need.

Date or no date?

Greg's finished adding all the sticky notes into his `my_contacts` table. Now he's ready to relax. He's got two tickets to a concert, and he wants to ask one of his contacts, a girl from San Francisco, out on a date.

He needs to find her email address, so he uses the **SELECT** statement from Chapter 1 to view his table.

Her details are in Greg's table... somewhere.

```
SELECT * from my_contacts;
```

BE Greg

Your job is to play Greg. Search through the first part of the my_contacts table on the next page looking for Anne from San Fran.

The my_contacts table has quite a few columns. These are just the first few.

File Edit Window Help AnneWho

last_name	first_name	email	gender
Anderson	Jillian	jill_anderson@breakneckpizza.com	F
Joffe	Kevin	joffe@simuduck.com	M
Newsome	Amanda	aman2luv@breakneckpizza.com	F
Garcia	Ed	ed99@b0tt0msup.com	M
Roundtree	Jo-Ann	jojoround@breakneckpizza.com	F
Briggs	Chris	cbriggs@boards-r-us.com	M
Harte	Lloyd	hovercraft@breakneckpizza.com	M
Toth	Anne	Anne_Toth@leapinlimos.com	F
Wiley	Andrew	andrewwiley@objectville.net	M
Palumbo	Tom	palofmine@mightygumball.net	M
Ryan	Alanna	angrypirate@breakneckpizza.com	F
McKinney	Clay	clay@starbuzzcoffee.com	M
Meeker	Ann	ann_meeker@chocoholic-inc.com	F
Powers	Brian	bp@honey-doit.com	M
Manson	Anne	am86@objectville.net	M
Mandel	Debra	debmonster@breakneckpizza.com	F
Tedesco	Janis	janistedesco@starbuzzcoffee.com	F
Talwar	Vikram	vikt@starbuzzcoffee.com	M
Szwed	Joe	szwed_joe@objectville.net	M
Sheridan	Diana	sheridi@mightygumball.net	F
Snow	Edward	snowman@tikibeanlounge.com	M
Otto	Glenn	glenn0098@objectville.net	M
Hardy	Anne	anneh@b0tt0msup.com	F
Deal	Mary	nobigdeal@starbuzzcoffee.com	F
Jagel	Ann	dreamgirl@breakneckpizza.com	F
Melfi	James	drmelfi@b0tt0msup.com	M
Oliver	Lee	lee_oliver@weatherorama.com	M
Parker	Anne	annep@starbuzzcoffee.com	F
Ricci	Peter	ricciman@tikibeanlounge.com	M
Reno	Grace	grace23@objectville.net	F
Moss	Zelda	zelda@weatherorama.com	F
Day	Clifford	cliffnight@breakneckpizza.com	M
Bolger	Joyce	joyce@chocoholic-inc.com	F
Blunt	Anne	anneblunt@breakneckpizza.com	F
Bolling	Lindy	lindy@tikibeanlounge.com	F
Gares	Fred	fgares@objectville.net	M
Jacobs	Anne	anne99@objectville.net	F

location
Palo Alto, CA
San Jose, CA
San Fran, CA
San Mateo, CA
San Fran, CA
Austin, TX
San Jose, CA
San Fran, CA
NYC, NY
Princeton, NJ
San Fran, CA
NYC, NY
San Fran, CA
Napa, CA
Seattle, WA
Natchez, MS
Las Vegas, NV
Palo Alto, CA
NYC, NY
Phoenix, AZ
Fargo, ND
Boulder, CO
San Fran, CA
Boston, MA
San Fran, CA
Dallas, TX
St. Louis, MO
San Fran, CA
Reno, NV
Palo Alto, CA
Sunnyvale, CA
Chester, NJ
Austin, TX
San Fran, CA
San Diego, CA
San Jose, CA
San Jose, CA
Miami, FL

This isn't the end of the table! Greg had a LOT of sticky notes.

BE Greg Solutions

Your job was to play Greg, searching through the first part of the my_contacts table looking for Anne from San Fran.

You had to find all the San Fran Annes, and write down their first and last names, and their email addresses.

Toth, Anne: Anne_Toth@leapinlimos.com

Hardy, Anne: anneh@b0tt0msup.com

Parker, Anne: annep@starbuzzcoffee.com

Blunt, Anne: anneblunt@breakneckpizza.com

Here are all the Annes and their email addresses.

Greg's looking for Anne with an 'e'. If you found any Ann entries, you should ignore those.

Making contact

That took **far too much time** and was **extremely tedious**. There is also the very real possibility that Greg might miss some of the matching Annes, including the one he's looking for.

Now that Greg's got all their email addresses, he emails the Annes and discovers...

> To: Toth, Anne <Anne_Toth@leapinlimos.com>
> From: Greg <greg@gregslist.com>
> Subject: Did we meet at Starbuzz?
>
> I'm involved with a wonderful guy called Tim
> ___ at the moment. We met at a frat party.

> To: Blunt, Anne <anneblunt@breakneckpizza.com>
> From: Greg <greg@gregslist.com>
> Subject: Did we meet at Starbuzz?
>
> I've been looking for a cowpoke like you! Pick me up at five, and we'll rustle up some grub.

> To: Hardy, Anne <anneh@b0tt0msup.com>
> From: Greg <greg@gregslist.com>
> Subject: Did we meet at Starbuzz?
>
> I'm not the Anne you're looking for, but I'm sure she's a sweet girl. If things don't work out, drop me a line.

> To: Parker, Anne <annep@starbuzzcoffee.com>
> From: Greg <greg@gregslist.com>
> Subject: Did we meet at Starbuzz?
>
> Of course I remember you! I just wish you had contacted me sooner. I've made plans with my ex-boyfriend who wants to get back together.

BRAIN POWER

Can you think of a way we could write a SQL query to display only those records that have a first_name of "Anne"?

A better SELECT

Here's a `SELECT` statement that would have helped Greg find Anne a whole lot sooner than painstakingly reading through the entire huge table looking for Annes. In the statement, we use a **WHERE *clause that gives the RDBMS something specific to search for***. It narrows down the results for us and **only returns the rows that match the condition.**

The equal sign in the `WHERE` clause is used to test whether each value in the column `first_name` equals, or matches, the text `'Anne'`. If it does, everything in the row is returned. If not, the row is not returned.

This is the name of the table.

```
SELECT * FROM my_contacts
WHERE first_name = 'Anne';
```

Add the semicolon and hit Return to put it all together and ask "If the value of the first_name column is Anne, show me the record."

WHERE tells your software that you want to look at something specific.

Put this with your WHERE, and it says you want to look at just the values in the column called first_name.

= is SQL speak for 'is'.

The value for your first_name column. Don't forget to use single quotes for text strings.

The console below shows you the rows that have been returned by this query, where the first name equals Anne.

```
File Edit Window Help NoDate
> SELECT * FROM my_contacts WHERE first_name = 'Anne';
+-----------+------------+--------------------------+--------+-------------+--------------+
| last_name | first_name | email                    | gender | birthday    | location     |
+-----------+------------+--------------------------+--------+-------------+--------------+
| Toth      | Anne       | Anne_Toth@leapinlimos.com | F     | NULL        | San Fran, CA |
| Manson    | Anne       | am86@objectville.net     | F      | NULL        | Seattle, WA  |
| Hardy     | Anne       | anneh@b0tt0msup.com      | F      | NULL        | San Fran, CA |
| Parker    | Anne       | annep@starbuzzcoffee.com | F      | NULL        | San Fran, CA |
| Blunt     | Anne       | anneblunt@breakneckpizza.com | F  | NULL        | San Fran, CA |
| Jacobs    | Anne       | anne99@objectville.net   | F      | NULL        | San Jose, CA |
+-----------+------------+--------------------------+--------+-------------+--------------+
6 rows in set (3.67 sec)
```

These are the results from our SELECT statement.

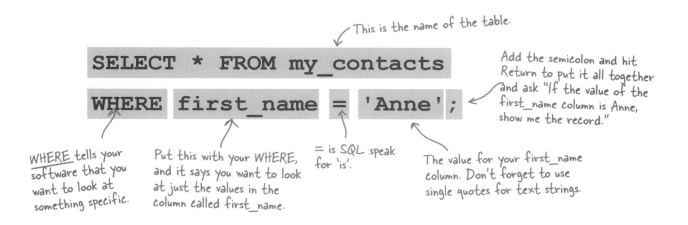

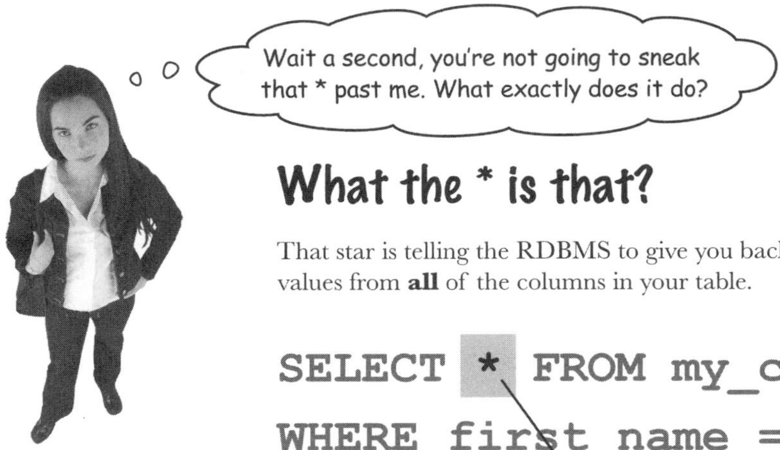
Wait a second, you're not going to sneak that * past me. What exactly does it do?

What the * is that?

That star is telling the RDBMS to give you back the values from **all** of the columns in your table.

```
SELECT * FROM my_contacts
WHERE first_name = 'Anne';
```

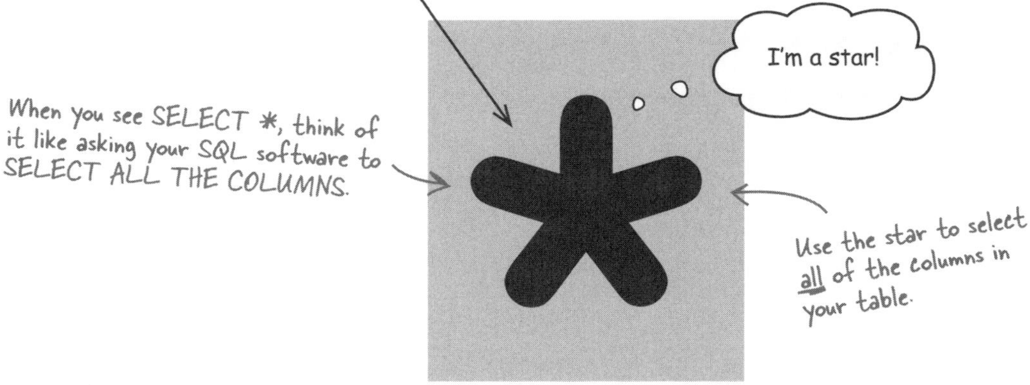
I'm a star!
When you see SELECT *, think of it like asking your SQL software to SELECT ALL THE COLUMNS.
Use the star to select all of the columns in your table.

there are no Dumb Questions

Q: What if I don't want to select all the columns? Can I use something else instead of the star?

A: Indeed you can. The star selects everything, but in a few pages you'll learn how to just select some of the columns, making your results easier to interpret.

Q: Is this star the same thing as an asterisk?

A: Yes, it's the same character on your keyboard, located above the 8 key. Hit SHIFT at the same time as the 8 to type one. This is the same for Mac and PC users.

But, although it's exactly the same character as asterisk, in SQL lingo, it's always referred to as *star*. This is a good thing, as saying "`SELECT asterisk from` ..." is not as easy as saying "`SELECT star from` ..."

Q: Are there other characters that have special meanings like the star does?

A: SQL does have other special, or reserved, characters. You'll see more of these later in the book. But the star is the only one you need to know about for right now. It's the only one used in the SELECT part of an SQL statement.

The Head First Lounge is adding mixed fruit drinks to its menu. Using what you learned in Chapter 1, create the table on this page and insert the data shown.

This table is part of a database called **drinks**. It contains the table **easy_drinks** with the recipes for a number of beverages that have only two ingredients.

`easy_drinks`

drink_name	main	amount1	second	amount2	directions
Blackthorn	tonic water	1.5	pineapple juice	1	stir with ice, strain into cocktail glass with lemon twist
Blue Moon	soda	1.5	blueberry juice	.75	stir with ice, strain into cocktail glass with lemon twist
Oh My Gosh	peach nectar	1	pineapple juice	1	stir with ice, strain into shot glass
Lime Fizz	Sprite	1.5	lime juice	.75	stir with ice, strain into cocktail glass
Kiss on the Lips	cherry juice	2	apricot nectar	7	serve over ice with straw
Hot Gold	peach nectar	3	orange juice	6	pour hot orange juice in mug and add peach nectar
Lone Tree	soda	1.5	cherry juice	.75	stir with ice, strain into cocktail glass
Greyhound	soda	1.5	grapefruit juice	5	serve over ice, stir well
Indian Summer	apple juice	2	hot tea	6	add juice to mug and top off with hot tea
Bull Frog	iced tea	1.5	lemonade	5	serve over ice with lime slice
Soda and It	soda	2	grape juice	1	shake in cocktail glass, no ice

amount1 and amount2 are in ounces.

Answer on page 117.

Watch it!

Before you start, do some planning.

Choose your data types carefully, and don't forget about NULL. Then ***check your code on page 117****.*

Sharpen your pencil

NAME THAT DRINK

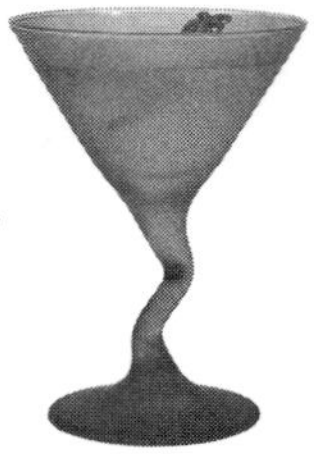

Don't worry about any characters in the queries you haven't seen yet. Just type them in as you see them for now, then see if they run.

Use the **easy_drinks** table you just created and try out these queries on your machine. Write down which drinks are returned as the result of each query.

```
SELECT * FROM easy_drinks WHERE main = 'Sprite';
```

Which drink(s)? ....

```
SELECT * FROM easy_drinks WHERE main = soda;
```

Which drink(s)? ....

```
SELECT * FROM easy_drinks WHERE amount2 = 6;
```

Which drink(s)? ....

```
SELECT * FROM easy_drinks WHERE second = "orange juice";
```

Which drink(s)? ....

```
SELECT * FROM easy_drinks WHERE amount1 < 1.5;
```

Which drink(s)? ....

```
SELECT * FROM easy_drinks WHERE amount2 < '1';
```

Which drink(s)? ....

```
SELECT * FROM easy_drinks WHERE main > 'soda';
```

Which drink(s)? ....

```
SELECT * FROM easy_drinks WHERE amount1 = '1.5';
```

Which drink(s)? ....

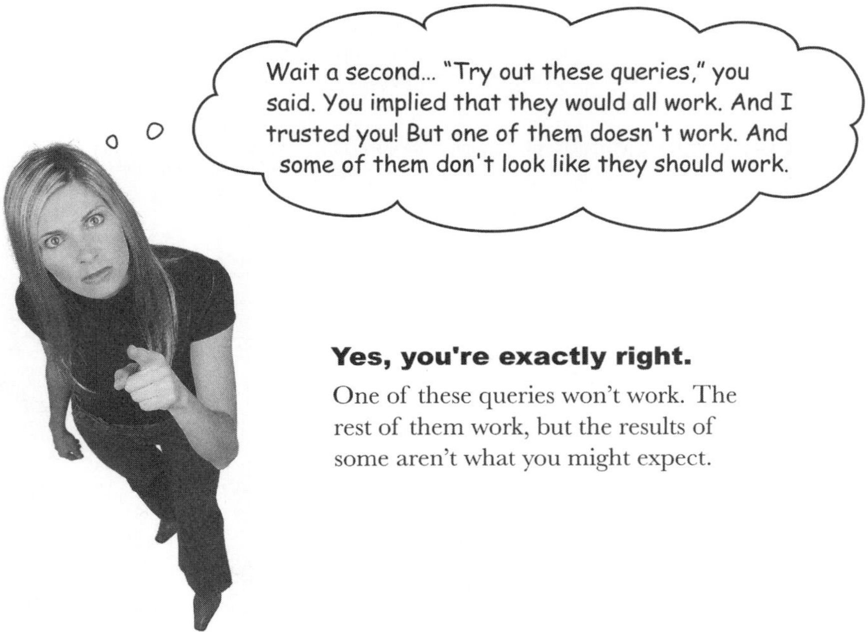
Wait a second... "Try out these queries," you said. You implied that they would all work. And I trusted you! But one of them doesn't work. And some of them don't look like they should work.

Yes, you're exactly right.

One of these queries won't work. The rest of them work, but the results of some aren't what you might expect.

For bonus points, write down here which query doesn't work...

....

... and which ones worked that you didn't expect to.

....

....

....

....

Sharpen your pencil Solution

NAME THAT DRINK

You tried out these queries on your **easy_drinks** table and wrote down which drinks are returned as the result of each query.

```
SELECT * FROM easy_drinks WHERE main = 'Sprite';
```

Which drink(s)? Lime Fizz

Notice the single quotes.

```
SELECT * FROM easy_drinks WHERE main = soda;
```

Which drink(s)? Error

Hmm. Looks like this is the query that wouldn't run.

```
SELECT * FROM easy_drinks WHERE amount2 = 6;
```

This one works. It's a DEC variable, so you don't use quotes at all.

Which drink(s)? Hot Gold, Indian Summer

```
SELECT * FROM easy_drinks WHERE second = "orange juice";
```

Which drink(s)? No results

```
SELECT * FROM easy_drinks WHERE amount1 < 1.5;
```

Which drink(s)? Oh My Gosh

```
SELECT * FROM easy_drinks WHERE amount2 < '1';
```

Which drink(s)? Blue Moon, Lime Fizz, Lone Tree

```
SELECT * FROM easy_drinks WHERE main > 'soda';
```

Another correctly formed WHERE clause.

Which drink(s)? Blackthorn, Lime Fizz

```
SELECT * FROM easy_drinks WHERE amount1 = '1.5';
```

Which drink(s)? Blackthorn, Blue Moon, Lime Fizz, Lone Tree, Greyhound, Bull Frog

For bonus points, write down here which query doesn't work…

```
WHERE main = soda;
```

This is the WHERE clause that won't work. You need quotes around that VARCHAR.

… and which ones worked that you didn't expect to?

```
WHERE second = "orange juice";
```

This query works and doesn't cause an error, but returns no results. SQL expects you to use single quotes, as you did when you inserted the value.

```
WHERE amount2 < '1';
```

But this one works, even though it shouldn't because DEC variables don't need quotes.

```
WHERE amount1 = '1.5';
```

And so does this one!

These last two queries will work because most SQL RDBMSes give you a little latitude. They will ignore the quotes and treat your DEC and INT values as numbers, even though the quotes indicate they are text values. The queries are NOT CORRECT, but your RDBMS is forgiving.

How to query your data types

To write valid WHERE clauses, you need to make sure each of the data types you include is formatted properly. Here are the conventions for each of the major data types:

CHAR or CHARACTER
Always use single quotes.
INT or INTEGER
Never use quotes.
DEC, short for DECIMAL.
Never use quotes.
He keeps asking for doughnuts.
BLOB
Always use single quotes.
DATETIME, TIME or TIMESTAMP Always use quotes.
DATE
Always use single quotes.
VARCHAR
Always use single quotes.

WE ♥ single quotes	No quotes for us
CHAR	DEC
VARCHAR	INT
DATE	
DATETIME, TIME, or TIMESTAMP	
BLOB	

The VARCHAR, CHAR, BLOB, DATE, and TIME data types need single quotes. The numeric types, DEC and INT, do not.

More punctuation problems

Greg picked up a few more contacts the other night. He's trying to add one to his table:

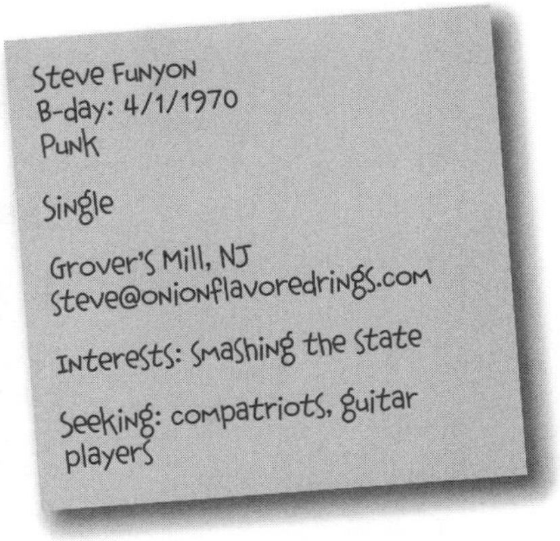
Steve Funyon
B-day: 4/1/1970
Punk
Single
Grover's Mill, NJ
steve@onionflavoredrings.com
Interests: Smashing the state
Seeking: compatriots, guitar players

```
INSERT INTO my_contacts
VALUES
('Funyon','Steve','steve@onionflavoredrings.com',
'M','1970-04-01','Punk','Grover's Mill, NJ',
'Single','smashing the state','compatriots,
guitar players');
```

But his program doesn't seem to be responding. He types a few semicolons, trying to get the query to end. No luck.

```
File Edit Window Help Aliens!
> INSERT INTO my_contacts VALUES ('Funyon', 'Steve', 'steve@
onionflavoredrings.com', 'M','1970-04-01', 'Punk', 'Grover's
Mill, NJ', 'Single', 'smashing the state', 'compatriots,
guitar players');
'>
'> ;
'> ;
'>
```

Every time he hits Return, he sees this prompt: '>

BRAIN POWER

What do you think is going on here?

Hmm, look at that single quote that keeps appearing before the prompt. I bet there's something wrong with the quotes in our INSERT statement...

Unmatched single quotes

Exactly! When Greg tried to add the record, the SQL program was expecting an even number of single quotes, one before and one after each VARCHAR, CHAR, and DATE value. The town name, **Grover's Mill**, confused matters because it added an extra apostrophe. The SQL RDBMS is still waiting for one more closing single quote.

Relax

You can get back control of your console.

End the statement by typing a single quote and a semicolon. This gives the RDBMS the extra single quote it's expecting.

You'll get an error when you type in the other quote and semicolon, and you'll have to enter your **INSERT** again from scratch.

You'll get an error after you do this, but at least you'll be able to try again.

File Edit Window Help TakeTwo

```
> INSERT INTO my_contacts VALUES ('Funyon', 'Steve', 'steve@
onionflavoredrings.com', 'M','1970-04-01', 'Punk', 'Grover's
Mill, NJ', 'Single', 'smashing the state', 'compatriots,
guitar players');

'>

'> ;

'> ;

'>

'> ';

ERROR 1064 (42000): You have an error in your SQL syntax;
check the manual that corresponds to your SQL server version
for the right syntax to use near 's Mill, NJ', 'Single',
'smashing the state', 'compatriots, guitar players');

' at line 1

>
```

Typing a single quote and semicolon ends the broken INSERT statement.

This error gives you a pretty clear idea of what's wrong. It quotes part of your query, beginning with the extra single quote.

Even though the record isn't inserted, that last > shows that at least the SQL program is responsive again.

Single quotes are special characters

When you're trying to insert a VARCHAR, CHAR, or BLOB containing an apostrophe, you must indicate to your RDBMS that it isn't meant to end the text, ***but is part of the text*** and needs to be included in the row. One way to do this is to **add a backslash** in front of the single quote.

```
INSERT INTO my_contacts
(location)
VALUES
('Grover\'s Mill');
```

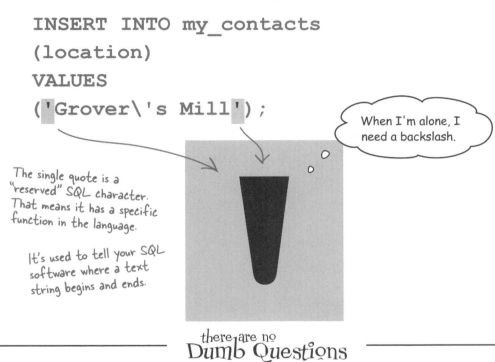

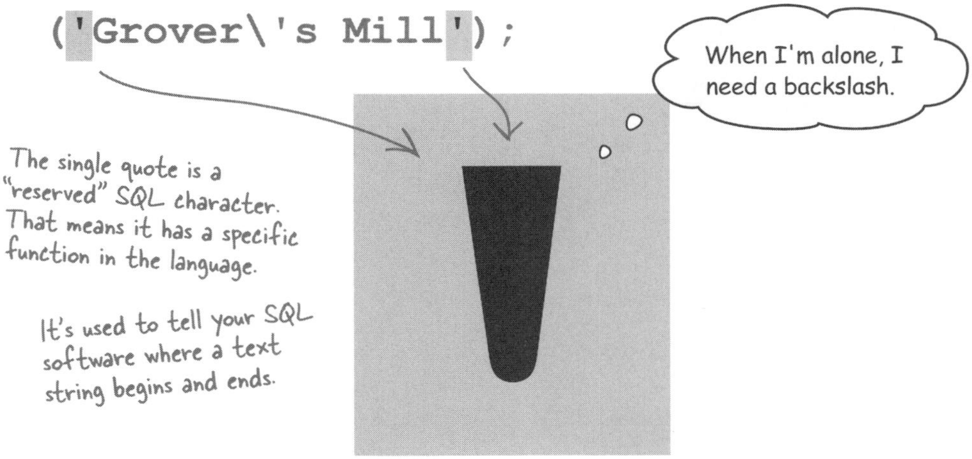
When I'm alone, I need a backslash.
The single quote is a "reserved" SQL character. That means it has a specific function in the language.
It's used to tell your SQL software where a text string begins and ends.

there are no Dumb Questions

Q: Isn't this the same thing as an apostrophe?

A: It's exactly the same thing as an apostrophe. SQL assigns it a very specific meaning, however. It's used to tell the SQL software that the data in between two of them is text data.

Q: What data types need them?

A: The text data types. Text data simply means that the data is a `VARCHAR`, `CHAR`, `BLOB`, or `TIMEDATE` column. Anything that isn't a number.

Q: Do `DEC` and `INT` columns need them?

A: No. Numeric columns have no spaces, so it's easy to tell when the number ends and the next word in the statement begins.

Q: So, it's only used for text columns?

A: Yes. Only trouble is, text columns have spaces. This causes problems when your data contains apostrophes. SQL doesn't know how to tell the difference between an apostrophe within the column, and one that tells it when the column begins or ends.

Q: Couldn't we make it easy to tell them apart by using a double quote instead of a single quote?

A: No. Don't use double quotes in case you use SQL statements with a programming language (like PHP) later. You use " in the programming language to say "this is where the SQL statement is"; that way, single quotes are recognized as being part of that statement and not part of the programming language.

INSERT data with single quotes in it

You need to tell your SQL software that your quote isn't there to begin or end a text string, but that it's *part of* the text string.

Handle quotes with a backslash

You can do this (and fix your `INSERT` statement at the same time) by adding a backslash character in front of the single quote in your text string:

```
INSERT INTO my_contacts
VALUES
('Funyon','Steve','steve@onionflavoredrings.
com', 'M', '1970-04-01', 'Punk','Grover\'s Mill,
NJ','Single','smashing the state','compatriots,
guitar players');
```

Telling SQL that a single quote is part of a text string by putting a backslash in front of it is called "escaping" it.

Handle quotes with an extra single quote

Another way to "escape" the quote is to put an extra single quote in front of it.

```
INSERT INTO my_contacts
VALUES
('Funyon','Steve','steve@onionflavoredrings.
com', 'M', '1970-04-01', 'Punk','Grover''s Mill,
NJ','Single','smashing the state','compatriots,
guitar players');
```

Or you can "escape" a single quote with an extra single quote in front of it.

BRAIN POWER

What other characters might cause similar problems?

Exercise

If you have data in your table with quotes, you might actually have to search for it with a WHERE clause at some point. To SELECT data containing single quotes in your WHERE clause, you need to escape your single quote, just like you did when you inserted it.

Rewrite the code below using the different methods of escaping the single quote.

```
SELECT * FROM my_contacts
WHERE
location = 'Grover's Mill, NJ';
```

1. ....

   ....

   ....

2. ....

   ....

   ....

Which method do you prefer?

Exercise Solution

If you have data in your table with quotes, you might actually have to search for it with a WHERE clause at some point. To SELECT data containing single quotes in your WHERE clause, you need to escape your single quote, just like you did when you inserted it.

Rewrite the code below using the different methods of escaping the single quote.

```
SELECT * FROM my_contacts
WHERE
location = 'Grover's Mill, NJ';
```

1.
```
SELECT * FROM my_contacts
WHERE
location = 'Grover\'s Mill, NJ';
```
Method 1, the backslash.

2.
```
SELECT * FROM my_contacts
WHERE
location = 'Grover''s Mill, NJ';
```
Method 2, the extra single quote.

SELECT specific data

Now you've mastered how to SELECT all the data types with quotes, and how to SELECT data where the data contains quotes.

Wait. Every time I do a SELECT * my data is a big mess because it wraps. Can I hide all those extra columns when maybe all I want is someone's email address.

You need to know how to only SELECT the columns you wish to see.

What we need here is more precision. Let's try narrowing our results some. Narrowing our results means getting fewer columns in our output. We select only the columns we want to see.

Try this at home

Exercise

Before you try this SELECT query, sketch how you think the table of results will look. (If you need to look at the easy_drinks table, you can find it on page 59.)

*We've replaced the * with these column names.*

```
SELECT drink_name, main, second
FROM easy_drinks
WHERE main = 'soda';
```

Exercise Solution

Try this at home

Before you try this SELECT query, sketch how you think the table of results will look.

drink_name	main	second
Blue Moon	soda	blueberry juice
Lone Tree	soda	cherry juice
Greyhound	soda	grapefruit juice
Soda and It	soda	grape juice

The old way

```
SELECT * FROM easy_drinks;
```

Here we get all the columns, and our results are too wide for our terminal window. They wrap to the next line and the display is a mess.

File Edit Window Help MessyDisplay

```
> SELECT * FROM easy_drinks;
+-----------------+--------------+----------+------------------+---------+----------------
-----------------------------------------+
| drink_name      | main         | amount1  | second           | amount2 | directions
|
+-----------------+--------------+----------+------------------+---------+----------------
-----------------------------------------+
| Kiss on the Lips | cherry juice |      2.0 | apricot nectar   |    7.00 | serve over ice
with straw                               |
| Hot Gold        | peach nectar |      3.0 | orange juice     |    6.00 | pour hot orange
juice in mug and add peach nectar        |
| Lone Tree       | soda         |      1.5 | cherry juice     |    0.75 | stir with ice,
strain into cocktail glass               |
| Greyhound       | soda         |      1.5 | grapefruit juice |    5.00 | serve over ice,
stir well                                |
| Indian Summer   | apple juice  |      2.0 | hot tea          |    6.00 | add juice to mug
and top off with hot tea                 |
| Bull Frog       | iced tea     |      1.5 | lemonade         |    5.00 | serve over ice
with lime slice                          |
| Soda and It     | soda         |      2.0 | grape juice      |    1.00 | shake in
cocktail glass, no ice                   |
| Blackthorn      | tonic water  |      1.5 | pineapple juice  |    1.00 | stir with ice,
strain into cocktail glass with lemon twist |
| Blue Moon       | soda         |      1.5 | blueberry juice  |    0.75 | stir with ice,
strain into cocktail glass with lemon twist |
| Oh My Gosh      | peach nectar |      1.0 | pineapple juice  |    1.00 | stir with ice,
strain into shot glass                   |
| Lime Fizz       | Sprite       |      1.5 | lime juice       |    0.75 | stir with ice,
strain into cocktail glass               |
+-----------------+--------------+----------+------------------+---------+----------------
-----------------------------------------+
11 rows in set (0.00 sec)
```

SELECT specific columns to limit results

By specifying which columns we want returned by our query, we can choose only the column values we need. Just as you use a `WHERE` clause to limit the number of rows, you can use column selection to limit the number of columns. It's about letting SQL do the heavy lifting for you.

```
SELECT drink_name, main, second
FROM easy_drinks;
```

...but we can narrow our results by selecting only the columns we want to see show up in the results.

File Edit Window Help JustEnough

```
> SELECT drink_name, main, second FROM easy_drinks;
+-----------------+--------------+-----------------+
| drink_name      | main         | second          |
+-----------------+--------------+-----------------+
| Kiss on the Lips | cherry juice | apricot nectar  |
| Hot Gold        | peach nectar | orange juice    |
| Lone Tree       | soda         | cherry juice    |
| Greyhound       | soda         | grapefruit juice |
| Indian Summer   | apple juice  | hot tea         |
| Bull Frog       | iced tea     | lemonade        |
| Soda and It     | soda         | grape juice     |
| Blackthorn      | tonic water  | pineapple juice |
| Blue Moon       | soda         | blueberry juice |
| Oh My Gosh      | peach nectar | pineapple juice |
| Lime Fizz       | Sprite       | lime juice      |
+-----------------+--------------+-----------------+
11 rows in set (0.00 sec)
```

SELECT specific columns for faster results

This is a good programming practice to follow, but it has other benefits. As your tables get larger, it speeds up retrieval of your results. You'll also see more speed when you eventually use SQL with another programming language, such as PHP.

Sharpen your pencil

Many ways to get a Kiss on the Lips

Remember our easy_drinks table? This SELECT statement will result in a Kiss on the Lips:

```
SELECT drink_name FROM easy_drinks
WHERE
main = 'cherry juice';
```

Finish the other four SELECT statements on the next page to get a Kiss also.

easy_drinks

drink_name	main	amount1	second	amount2	directions
Blackthorn	tonic water	1.5	pineapple juice	1	stir with ice, strain into cocktail glass with lemon twist
Blue Moon	soda	1.5	blueberry juice	.75	stir with ice, strain into cocktail glass with lemon twist
Oh My Gosh	peach nectar	1	pineapple juice	1	stir with ice, strain into shot glass
Lime Fizz	Sprite	1.5	lime juice	.75	stir with ice, strain into cocktail glass
Kiss on the Lips	cherry juice	2	apricot nectar	7	serve over ice with straw
Hot Gold	peach nectar	3	orange juice	6	pour hot orange juice in mug and add peach nectar
Lone Tree	soda	1.5	cherry juice	.75	stir with ice, strain into cocktail glass
Greyhound	soda	1.5	grapefruit juice	5	serve over ice, stir well
Indian Summer	apple juice	2	hot tea	6	add juice to mug and top off with hot tea
Bull Frog	iced tea	1.5	lemonade	5	serve over ice with lime slice
Soda and It	soda	2	grape juice	1	shake in cocktail glass, no ice

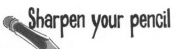

SELECT ....

WHERE ....

SELECT ....

WHERE ....

SELECT ....

WHERE ....

SELECT ....

WHERE ....

Now write three SELECT statements that will give you a Bull Frog.

1. ....

....

2. ....

....

3. ....

....

Sharpen your pencil Solution

Finish the other four SELECT statements to get a Kiss also.

SELECT drink_name FROM easy_drinks
WHERE second = 'apricot nectar';

SELECT drink_name FROM easy_drinks
WHERE amount2 = 7;

SELECT drink_name FROM easy_drinks
WHERE directions = 'serve over ice with straw';

SELECT drink_name FROM easy_drinks
WHERE drink_name = 'Kiss on the Lips';

This is one you'll seldom use, but it does give you the result you want. You might use something like this when you want to make sure your drink_name column doesn't have a typo.

Now write three SELECT statements that will give you a Bull Frog.

1. SELECT drink_name FROM easy_drinks
   WHERE main = 'iced tea';

2. SELECT drink_name FROM easy_drinks
   WHERE second = 'lemonade';

3. SELECT drink_name FROM easy_drinks
   WHERE directions = 'serve over ice with lime slice';

BULLET POINTS

- Use single quotes in your WHERE clause when when selecting from text fields.
- Don't use single quotes when selecting from numeric fields.
- Use the * in your SELECT when you want to select all of the columns.
- If you've entered your query and your RDBMS doesn't finish processing it, check for a missing single quote.
- When you can, select specific columns in your table, rather than using SELECT *.

there are no Dumb Questions

Q: What if I need all the columns from my table returned by a query? Should I actually be naming them in the SELECT rather than using the *?

A: If you need them all, then by all means use the *. It's only when you don't need them all that you should try not to use it.

Q: I tried to copy and paste a query from the Internet, and I kept getting errors when I tried to use it. Am I doing something wrong?

A: Queries pasted from web browsers sometimes contain invisible characters that look like spaces but mean something different to SQL Pasting them into a text editor is one way to see and remove these "gremlin" characters. Your best bet is to paste it into a text editor first and take a close look at it.

Q: So I should paste it into something like Microsoft Word?

A: No, Word isn't a good choice, since it does nothing to show you the invisible formatting that might be in the text. Try Notepad (PC) or TextEdit in plain-text mode (Mac).

Q: About escaping the apostrophe, is there any reason to use one method over the other?

A: Not really. We tend to use the backslash method only because we find that it's easier to spot where that extra apostrophe is when things go wrong in a query. For example, this is easier to process visually:

```
'Isn\'t that your sister\'s pencil?'
```

Than this:

```
'Isn''t that your sister''s pencil?'
```

Other than that, there's really no reason to favor one method over the other. Both methods allow you to enter apostrophes into your text columns.

Doughnut ask what your table can do for you...

To find the best glazed doughnut in the table, you need to do at least two `SELECT` statements. The first one will select rows with the correct doughnut type. The second will select rows with doughnuts with a rating of 10.

I want to find the best glazed doughnut without having to hunt through all those results.

doughnut_ratings

location	time	date	type	rating	comments
Starbuzz Coffee	7:43 am	4/23	cinnamon glazed	6	too much spice
Duncan's Donuts	8:56 am	8/25	plain glazed	5	greasy
Duncan's Donuts	7:58 pm	4/26	jelly	6	stale, but tasty
Starbuzz Coffee	10:35 pm	4/24	plain glazed	7	warm, but not hot
Krispy King	9:39 pm	9/26	jelly	6	not enough jelly
Starbuzz Coffee	7:48 am	4/23	rocky road	10	marshmallows!
Krispy King	8:56 am	11/25	plain glazed	8	maple syrup glaze

Imagine that this table contains 10,000 records.

1 One way is to search for the doughnut type:

You need to SELECT rating to search through the highest scores, and location because that gives you the name of the winner.

```
SELECT location, rating FROM doughnut_ratings
WHERE
type = 'plain glazed';
```

All of the results will be the correct type of doughnut.

First query results, but imagine hundreds more.

location	rating
Duncan's Donuts	5
Starbuzz Coffee	7
Krispy King	8
Starbuzz Coffee	10
Duncan's Donuts	8

Ask what you can do for your doughnut

2 Or you need to search for that high rating:

```
SELECT location, type FROM doughnut_ratings
WHERE
rating = 10;
```

You need to look through all the types, and then location will give you the name of your winner.

All of the results will be the highest rated.

location	type
Starbuzz Coffee	rocky road
Krispy King	plain glazed
Starbuzz Coffee	plain glazed
Duncan's Donuts	rocky road

Second query results, again, picture hundreds of these.

This doesn't really help. I could stop with either query and dig through the results, but that table has thousands of records... I'm hungry, and I want that doughnut ***now!***

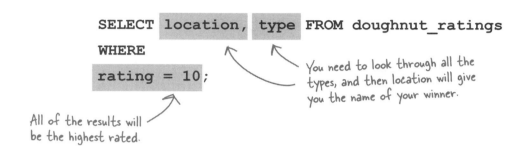

BRAIN POWER

In plain English, what is the question you're trying to answer with these queries?

Combining your queries

We can handle the two things we're searching for, 'plain glazed' for the type and 10 for the rating into a single query using the keyword AND. The results we get from the query must satisfy both conditions.

```
SELECT location
FROM doughnut_ratings
WHERE type = 'plain glazed'
AND
rating = 10;
```

Now all we need to SELECT is the location.

Use the word AND to combine your two WHERE clauses.

Here's the result of the AND query. Even if we received more than one row as a result of our query, you would know that all locations have glazed doughnuts with a rating of 10, so you could go to any of them. Or all of them.

location	rating
Duncan's Donuts	5
Starbuzz Coffee	7
Krispy King	8
Starbuzz Coffee	10
Duncan's Donuts	8

AND

location	type
Starbuzz Coffee	rocky road
Krispy King	plain glazed
Starbuzz Coffee	plain glazed
Duncan's Donuts	rocky road

This query combines the results for 'plain glazed' and rating= 10 to find any results that match both queries.

location
Starbuzz Coffee

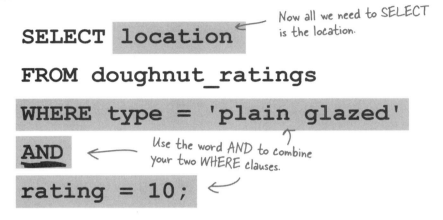

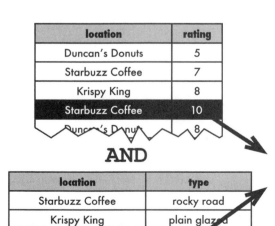

Mom? Can we go to Starbuzz? Pleeeeeease?!

Exercise

So I could have found Anne using AND?

Using the my_contacts table, write some queries for Greg. SELECT only the columns you really need to give you your answer. Pay attention to single quotes.

Write a query to find the email addresses of all computer programmers.

....

....

....

....

Write a query to find the name and location of anyone with your birthdate.

....

....

....

....

Write a query to find the name and email of any single people who live in your town. For extra points, only pick those of the gender you'd want to date.

....

....

....

....

Write the query Greg could have used to find all the Annes from San Francisco.

....

....

....

....

Exercise Solution

Using the my_contacts table, write some queries for Greg. SELECT only the columns you really need to give you your answer. Pay attention to single quotes.

Write a query to find the email addresses of all computer programmers.

```
SELECT email FROM my_contacts
WHERE profession = 'computer programmer';
```

We want the email column.

The profession we want is computer programmer.

Write a query to find the name and location of anyone with your birthdate.

```
SELECT last_name, first_name, location
FROM my_contacts
WHERE birthday = '1975-09-05';
```

This should be your birthdate in quotes.

Write a query to find the name and email of any single people who live in your town. For extra points, only pick those of the gender you'd want to date.

```
SELECT last_name, first_name, email
FROM my_contacts
WHERE location = 'San Antonio, TX'
AND gender = 'M';
```

Your town here.

The gender you wish to date here.

Write the query Greg could have used to find all the Annes from San Francisco.

```
SELECT last_name, first_name, email
FROM my_contacts
WHERE location = 'San Fran, CA'
AND first_name = 'Anne';
```

Looking back at the table, Greg seems to have shortened San Francisco to San Fran. Hope he was consistent.

Finding numeric values

Let's say you want to find all the drinks in the `easy_drinks` table that contain more than an ounce of soda in *a single query*. Here's the hard way to find the results. You can use two queries:

We just want the names of the drinks.

Soda drinks with 1.5 ounces of soda.

```
SELECT drink_name FROM easy_drinks
WHERE
main = 'soda'
AND
amount1 = 1.5;
```

```
File Edit Window Help MoreSoda
> SELECT drink_name FROM easy_drinks WHERE main = 'soda' AND
amount1 = 1.5;
+-----------+
| drink_name |
+-----------+
| Blue Moon  |
| Lone Tree  |
| Greyhound  |
+-----------+
3 rows in set (0.00 sec)
```

Soda drinks with 2 ounces of soda.

```
SELECT drink_name FROM easy_drinks
WHERE
main = 'soda'
AND
amount1 = 2;
```

```
File Edit Window Help EvenMoreSoda
> SELECT drink_name FROM easy_drinks WHERE main = 'soda' AND
amount1 = 2;
+-------------+
| drink_name  |
+-------------+
| Soda and It |
+-------------+
1 row in set (0.00 sec)
```

Wouldn't it be dreamy if I could find all the drinks in the easy_drinks table that contain **more than** an ounce of soda in a single query. But I know it's just a fantasy...

easy_drinks

drink_name	main	amount1	second	amount2	directions
Blackthorn	tonic water	1.5	pineapple juice	1	stir with ice, strain into cocktail glass with lemon twist
Blue Moon	soda	1.5	blueberry juice	.75	stir with ice, strain into cocktail glass with lemon twist
Oh My Gosh	peach nectar	1	pineapple juice	1	stir with ice, strain into shot glass
Lime Fizz	Sprite	1.5	lime juice	.75	stir with ice, strain into cocktail glass
Kiss on the Lips	cherry juice	2	apricot nectar	7	serve over ice with straw
Hot Gold	peach nectar	3	orange juice	6	pour hot orange juice in mug and add peach nectar
Lone Tree	soda	1.5	cherry juice	.75	stir with ice, strain into cocktail glass
Greyhound	soda	1.5	grapefruit juice	5	serve over ice, stir well
Indian Summer	apple juice	2	hot tea	6	add juice to mug and top off with hot tea
Bull Frog	iced tea	1.5	lemonade	5	serve over ice with lime slice
Soda and It	soda	2	grape juice	1	shake in cocktail glass, no ice

Once is enough

But it's a waste of time to use two queries, and you might miss drinks with amounts like 1.75 or 3 ounces. Instead, you can use a **greater than** sign:

```
SELECT drink_name FROM easy_drinks
WHERE
main = 'soda'
AND
amount1 > 1;
```

The GREATER THAN symbol will give you all the drinks that contain more than 1 ounce of soda.

```
File Edit Window Help DoItOnce
> SELECT drink_name FROM easy_drinks  WHERE main = 'soda' AND
amount1 > 1;
+------------+
| drink_name  |
+------------+
| Blue Moon   |
| Lone Tree   |
| Greyhound   |
| Soda and It |
+------------+
4 rows in set (0.00 sec)
```

BRAIN POWER

Why can't you combine the first two queries with an additional AND?

~~Smooth~~ Comparison Operators

So far, we've only used the **equal** sign in our `WHERE` clause. You just saw the **greater than** symbol, >. What that does is compare one value against another. Here are the rest of the comparison operators:

The equal sign looks for exact matches. This does us no good when we want to find out if something is less than or greater than something else.

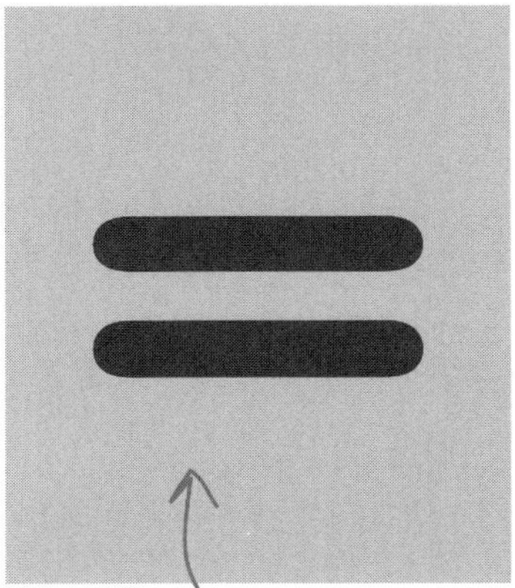

The EQUAL sign we all know and love.

This confusing sign is **not equal**. It returns precisely the opposite results of the equal sign. Two values are either equal, or they are not equal.

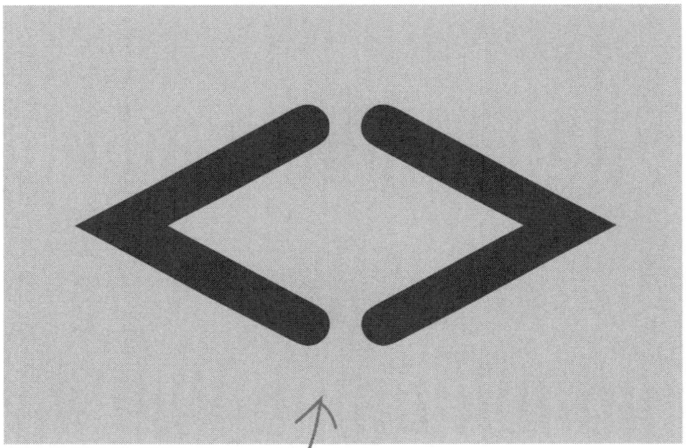

This one means NOT EQUAL. It returns all the records that don't match the condition.

BRAIN BARBELL

Have you noticed that every `WHERE` clause so far always has a column name on the left. Would it work if the column name was on the right?

The **less than** sign looks at the values in the column on the left and compares them to the value on the right. If the column value is less than the value on the right, that row is returned.

LESS THAN returns all values less than the condition.

The **greater than** sign is the reverse of the less than. It looks at the values in the column and compares them to the value on the right. If the column value is greater than the value on the right, that row is returned.

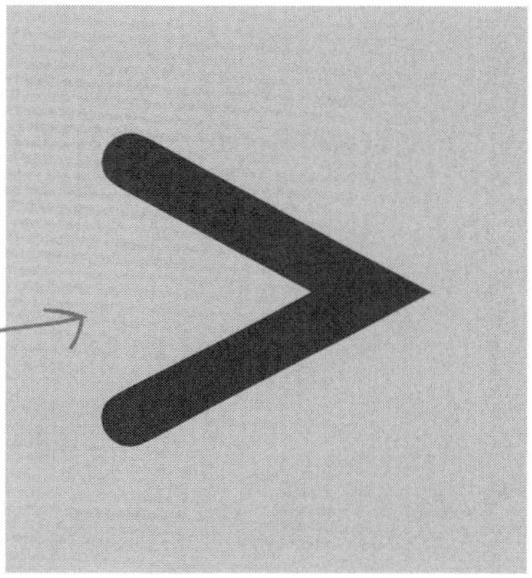

And of course there's a GREATER THAN.

The only difference with the **less than or equal to** sign is that column values equal to the condition value are also returned.

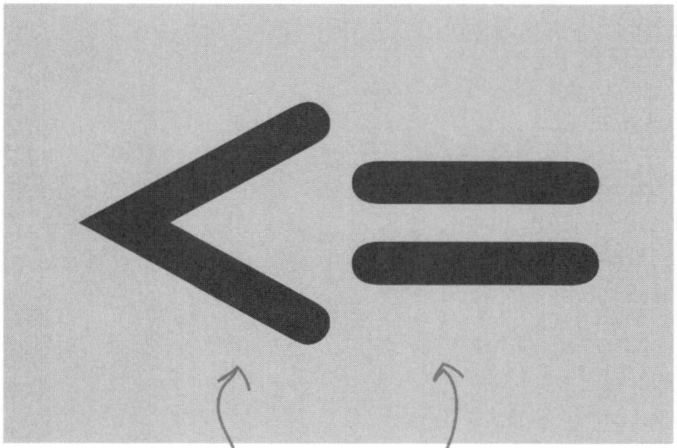

Any records that are LESS THAN OR EQUAL TO the condition are returned.

Same thing with this **greater than or equal to sign**. If the column value matches or is greater than the condition value, the row is returned.

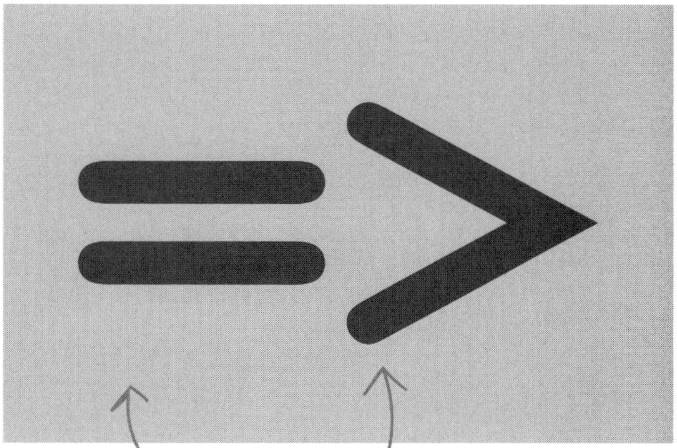

And there's a GREATER THAN OR EQUAL TO.

Finding numeric data with Comparison Operators

The Head First Lounge has a table with the cost and nutritional information about their drinks. They want to feature higher priced, lower calorie drinks to increase profits.

They're using comparison operators to find the drinks that are priced at least \$3.50 and have less than 50 calories in the `drink_info` table.

The total carbohydrate grams in each drink.

The calories in each drink.

drink_info

drink_name	cost	carbs	color	ice	calories
Blackthorn	3	8.4	yellow	Y	33
Blue Moon	2.5	3.2	blue	Y	12
Oh My Gosh	3.5	8.6	orange	Y	35
Lime Fizz	2.5	5.4	green	Y	24
Kiss on the Lips	5.5	42.5	purple	Y	171
Hot Gold	3.2	32.1	orange	N	135
Lone Tree	3.6	4.2	red	Y	17
Greyhound	4	14	yellow	Y	50
Indian Summer	2.8	7.2	brown	N	30
Bull Frog	2.6	21.5	tan	Y	80
Soda and It	3.8	4.7	red	N	19

```
SELECT drink_name FROM drink_info
WHERE
cost >= 3.5
AND
calories < 50;
```

This says: "find drinks that cost \$3.50 or more." This includes drinks that cost exactly \$3.50.

This says: "find drinks with calories less than 50".

This query only returns drinks where **both** of these conditions are met because of the AND combining the two results. The drinks that are returned are: Oh My Gosh, Lone Tree, and Soda and It.

Sharpen your pencil

Your turn to do some mixing. Write queries that will return the following information. Also write down what the result of each query is:

The cost of each drink with ice that is yellow and has more than 33 calories.

....

Result: ....

The name and color of each drink which does not contain more than 4 grams of carbs and uses ice.

....

Result: ....

The cost of each drink whose calorie count is 80 or more.

....

Result: ....

Drinks called Greyhound and Kiss on the Lips, along with each one's color and whether ice is used to mix the drink.

....

Result: ....

Sharpen your pencil Solution

Your turn to do some mixing. Write queries that will return the following information. Also write down what the result of each query is:

The cost of each drink with ice that is yellow and has more than 33 calories.

```
SELECT cost FROM drink_info
WHERE ice = 'Y'
AND
color = 'yellow'
AND
calories > 33;
```

Result: $4.00

The name and color of each drink which does not contain more than 4 grams of carbs and uses ice.

```
SELECT drink_name, color FROM drink_info
WHERE
carbs <= 4
AND
ice = 'Y';
```

Result: Blue Moon, blue

The cost of each drink whose calorie count is 80 or more.

```
SELECT cost FROM drink_info
WHERE
calories >= 80;
```

Result: $5.50, $3.20, $2.60

But this only works with numbers, right? If I want to find all the drinks with names beginning with a specific letter I'm out of luck?

Drinks called Greyhound and Kiss on the lips, along with each one's color and whether ice is used to mix the drink.

```
SELECT drink_name, color, ice FROM drink_info
WHERE
cost >= 3.8;
```

This one's tricky. You had to look through the table and find some column you could use to get those drinks and *just* those drinks.

Result: Kiss on the LIps, purple, Y
Greyhound, yellow, Y

Text data roping with Comparison Operators

Comparing text data works in a similar way with your text columns like `CHAR` and `VARCHAR`. The comparison operators evaluate everything **alphabetically**. So, say you want to select all the drinks that begin with an 'L', here's a query that will select all the drinks that match that criteria.

drink_info

drink_name	cost	carbs	color	ice	calories
Blackthorn	3	8.4	yellow	Y	33
Blue Moon	2.5	3.2	blue	Y	12
Oh My Gosh	3.5	8.6	orange	Y	35
Lime Fizz	2.5	5.4	green	Y	24
Kiss on the Lips	5.5	42.5	purple	Y	171
Hot Gold	3.2	32.1	orange	N	135
Lone Tree	3.6	4.2	red	Y	17
Greyhound	4	14	yellow	Y	50
Indian Summer	2.8	7.2	brown	N	30
Bull Frog	2.6	21.5	tan	Y	80
Soda and It	3.8	4.7	red	N	19

```
SELECT drink_name
FROM drink_info
WHERE
drink_name >= 'L'
AND
drink_name < 'M';
```

This query returns drinks whose first letter is L or later, but whose first letters come earlier in the alphabet than M.

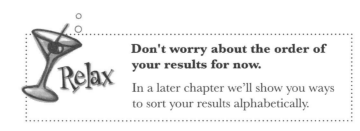

Don't worry about the order of your results for now.

In a later chapter we'll show you ways to sort your results alphabetically.

Selecting your ingredients

One of the bartenders has been asked to mix a cocktail that has cherry juice in it. The bartender could use two queries to find the cocktails:

Each query checks the two ingredients columns.

```
File Edit Window Help..
> SELECT drink_name FROM easy_drinks WHERE main = 'cherry juice';
+-------------------+
| drink_name        |
+-------------------+
| Kiss on the Lips  |
+-------------------+
1 row in set (0.02 sec)

> SELECT drink_name FROM easy_drinks WHERE second = 'cherry juice';
+------------+
| drink_name |
+------------+
| Lone Tree  |
+------------+
1 row in set (0.01 sec)
```

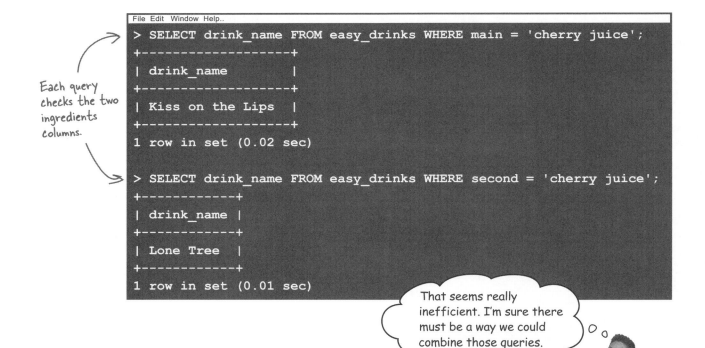

That seems really inefficient. I'm sure there must be a way we could combine those queries.

drink_info

drink_name	cost	carbs	color	ice	calories
Blackthorn	3	8.4	yellow	Y	33
Blue Moon	2.5	3.2	blue	Y	12
Oh My Gosh	3.5	8.6	orange	Y	35
Lime Fizz	2.5	5.4	green	Y	24
Kiss on the Lips	5.5	42.5	purple	Y	171
Hot Gold	3.2	32.1	orange	N	135
Lone Tree	3.6	4.2	red	Y	17
Greyhound	4	14	yellow	Y	50
Indian Summer	2.8	7.2	brown	N	30
Bull Frog	2.6	21.5	tan	Y	80
Soda and It	3.8	4.7	red	N	19

To be OR not to be

You can combine those two queries using OR. This condition returns records when ***any*** of the conditions are met. So, instead of two the two separate queries, you can combine them with OR like this:

```
File Edit Window Help.. SweetCherryPie
> SELECT drink_name from easy_drinks
WHERE main = 'cherry juice'
OR
second = 'cherry juice';
+-------------------+
| drink_name        |
+-------------------+
| Kiss on the Lips  |
| Lone Tree         |
+-------------------+
2 rows in set (0.02 sec)
```

Sharpen your pencil

Cross out the unnecessary parts of the two SELECTs below and add an OR to turn it into a single SELECT statement.

```
SELECT drink_name FROM easy_drinks WHERE
main = 'orange juice';

SELECT drink_name FROM easy_drinks WHERE
main = 'apple juice';
```

Use your new selection skills to rewrite your new SELECT.

....

....

Sharpen your pencil Solution

Cross out the unnecessary parts of the two SELECTs below and add an OR to turn it into a single SELECT statement.

```
SELECT drink_name FROM easy_drinks WHERE
main = 'orange juice';
  OR
SELECT drink_name FROM easy_drinks WHERE
main = 'apple juice';
```

We need to get rid of that semicolon so the statement doesn't end yet.

With this OR we get drink_names with main ingredients of orange juice OR apple juice.

We can simply cross out this line, we've already got this covered by the first part of the query (now joined by our OR.

Use your new selection skills to rewrite your new SELECT.

```
SELECT drink_name FROM easy_drinks
WHERE
main = 'orange juice'
OR
main = 'apple juice';
```

Here's the final query.

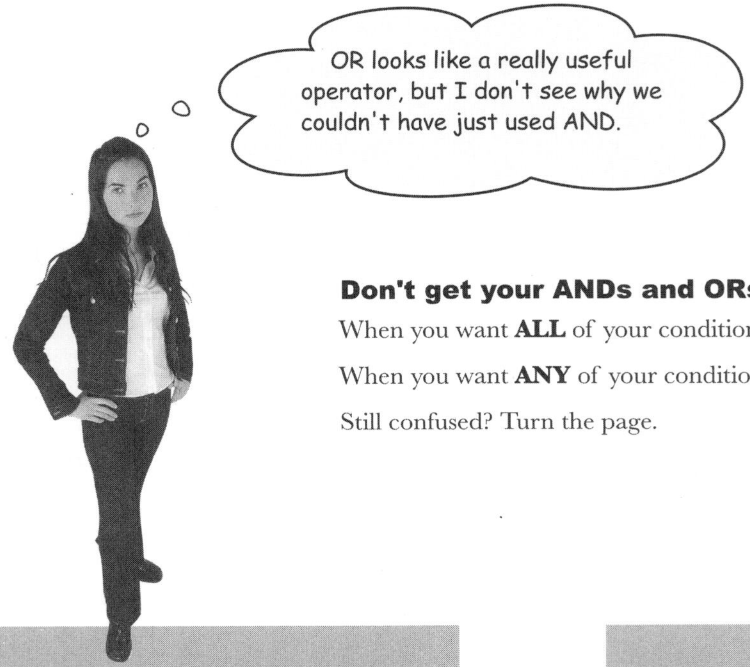
OR looks like a really useful operator, but I don't see why we couldn't have just used AND.

Don't get your ANDs and ORs confused!

When you want **ALL** of your conditions to be true, use **AND**.

When you want **ANY** of your conditions to be true, use **OR**.

Still confused? Turn the page.

AND
OR

there are no Dumb Questions

Q: Can you use more than one AND or OR in the same WHERE clause?

A: You certainly can. You can combine as many as you like. You can also use both AND and OR together in the same clause.

The difference between AND and OR

In the queries below you'll see examples of all the possible combinations of two conditions with AND and OR between them.

doughnut_ratings

location	time	date	type	rating	comments
Krispy King	8:50 am	9/27	plain glazed	10	almost perfect
Duncan's Donuts	8:59 am	8/25	NULL	6	greasy
Starbuzz Coffee	7:35 pm	5/24	cinnamon cake	5	stale, but tasty
Duncan's Donuts	7:03 pm	4/26	jelly	7	not enough jelly

```
SELECT type FROM doughnut_ratings                                    RESULTS

WHERE location = 'Krispy King' AND rating = 10;                      plain glazed

WHERE location = 'Krispy King' OR rating = 10;                       plain glazed

WHERE location = 'Krispy King' AND rating = 3;                       no results

WHERE location = 'Krispy King' OR rating = 3;                        plain glazed

WHERE location = 'Snappy Bagel' AND rating = 10;                     no results

WHERE location = 'Snappy Bagel' OR rating = 10;                      plain glazed

WHERE location = 'Snappy Bagel' AND rating = 3;                      no results

WHERE location = 'Snappy Bagel' OR  rating = 3;                      no results
```

Yes, there is a match (location = 'Krispy King')

Yes (rating = 10)

No matches (rating = 3)

No match (location = 'Snappy Bagel')

BE the Conditional

Below, you'll find a series of WHERE clauses with ANDs and ORs. Become one with these clauses and determine whether or not they will produce results.

```
SELECT type FROM doughnut_ratings
```

Did you get a result?

`WHERE location = 'Krispy King' AND rating <> 6;`	....
`WHERE location = 'Krispy King' AND rating = 3;`	....
`WHERE location = 'Snappy Bagel' AND rating >= 6;`	....
`WHERE location = 'Krispy King' OR rating > 5;`	....
`WHERE location = 'Krispy King' OR rating = 3;`	....
`WHERE location = 'Snappy Bagel' OR rating = 6;`	....

To improve your karma, note down why two of your results are a bit different than all the rest.

BE the Conditional Solution

Below, you'll find a series of WHERE clauses with ANDs and ORs. Become one with these clauses and determine whether or not they will produce results.

```
SELECT type FROM doughnut_ratings
```

Did you get a result?

`WHERE location = 'Krispy King' AND rating <> 6;`	plain glazed
`WHERE location = 'Krispy King' AND rating = 3;`	no result
`WHERE location = 'Snappy Bagel' AND rating >= 6;`	no result
`WHERE location = 'Krispy King' OR rating > 5;`	plain glazed, NULL, jelly
`WHERE location = 'Krispy King' OR rating = 3;`	plain glazed
`WHERE location = 'Snappy Bagel' OR rating = 6;`	NULL

To improve your karma, note down why two of your results are a bit different than all the rest.

Two queries return NULL.

Those NULL values may cause you problems in future queries. It's better to enter some sort of value than leave a NULL value in a column ***because NULLs can't be directly selected from a table.***

Use IS NULL to find NULLs

I tried selecting NULL values directly, but it didn't work. How do I find the NULLs in my tables?

drink_info

drink_name	cost	carbs	color	ice	calories
Holiday	NULL	14	NULL	Y	50
Dragon Breath	2.9	7.2	brown	N	NULL

You can't select a NULL value directly.

```
SELECT drink_name FROM drink_info
WHERE
calories = NULL ;
```

Won't work because nothing can be equal to NULL. It's an undefined value.

```
SELECT drink_name FROM drink_info
WHERE
calories = 0;
```

This won't work because NULL isn't the same thing as zero.

```
SELECT drink_name FROM drink_info
WHERE
calories = 'NULL';
```

And this won't work either, because NULL isn't a text string.

But you can select it using keywords.

```
SELECT drink_name
FROM drink_info
WHERE
calories IS NULL;
```

The only way to directly select a NULL value is to use the keywords IS NULL.

Keywords are not text strings, so they don't have quotes.

there are no Dumb Questions

Q: You say you can't "directly select" NULL without using IS NULL. Does that mean you can indirectly select it?

A: Right. If you wanted to get to the value in that column, you could use a `WHERE` clause on one of the other columns. For example, your result will be `NULL` if you use this query:

```
SELECT calories FROM drink_info
WHERE drink_name = 'Dragon Breath';
```

Q: What would my result from that query actually look like?

A: It would look exactly like this:

```
+-----------+
| calories  |
+-----------+
| NULL      |
+-----------+
```

Meanwhile, back at Greg's place...

Greg's been trying to find all the people in California cities in his `my_contacts` table. Here's part of the query he's been working on:

Typing all these OR clauses is exhausting!

```
SELECT * FROM my_contacts
WHERE
location = 'San Fran, CA'
OR
location = 'San Francisco, CA'
OR
location = 'San Jose, CA'
OR
location = 'San Mateo, CA'
OR
location = 'Sunnyvale, CA'
OR
location = 'Marin, CA'
OR
location = 'Oakland, CA'
OR
location = 'Palo Alto, CA'
OR
location = 'Sacramento, CA'
OR
location = 'Los Angeles, CA'
OR
And the list goes on and on...
```

He knows he's entered SF at least these two ways. And what about typos?

Saving time with a single keyword: LIKE

There are simply too many cities and variations, and possible typos. Using all those ORs is going to take Greg a very long time. Luckily, there's a timesaving keyword—LIKE—that, used with a wildcard, looks for part of a text string and returns any matches.

Greg can use LIKE like this:

```
SELECT * FROM my_contacts
WHERE location LIKE '%CA';
```

Place a percent sign inside the single quotes. This tells your software you're looking for all values in the location column that end with CA.

The call of the Wild(card)

LIKE teams up with two wildcard characters. Wildcards are stand-ins for the characters that are actually there. Rather like a joker in a card game, a wildcard is equal to any character in a string.

The call of the wild(card).

Wildcards are stand-in characters.

BRAIN BARBELL

Have you seen any other wildcards earlier in this chapter?

That's more LIKE it

LIKE likes to play with wildcards. The first is the percent sign, %, which can stand in for any number of unknown characters.

```
SELECT first_name FROM my_contacts
WHERE first_name LIKE '%im';
```

The percent is a stand-in for any number of unknown characters.

Results in names with any number of characters before the "im", like Ephraim, Slim, and Tim.

The second wildcard character that LIKE likes to hang out with is the underscore, _ which stands for just one unknown character.

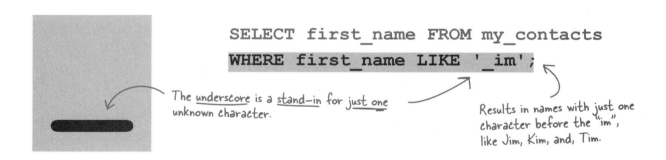

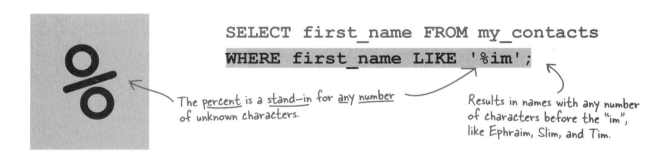

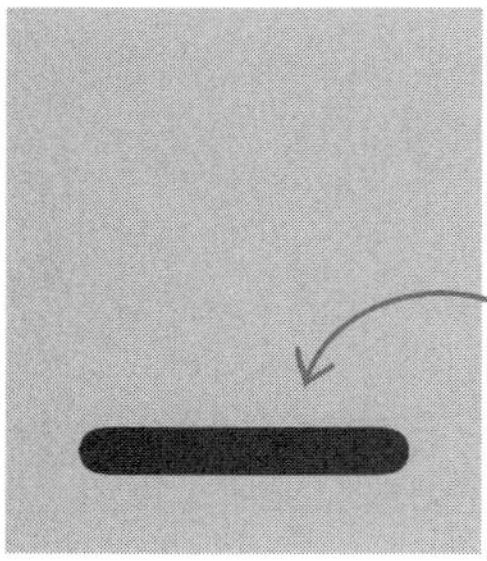

```
SELECT first_name FROM my_contacts
WHERE first_name LIKE '_im';
```

The underscore is a stand-in for just one unknown character.

Results in names with just one character before the "im", like Jim, Kim, and, Tim.

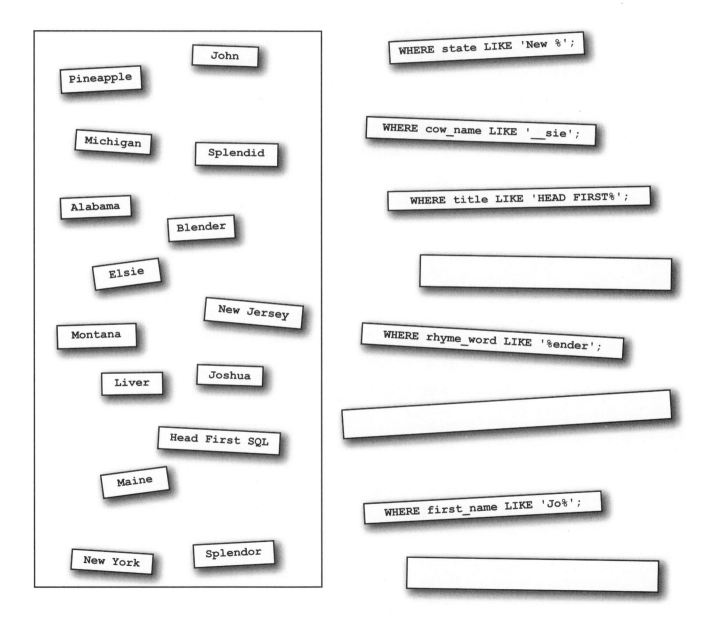

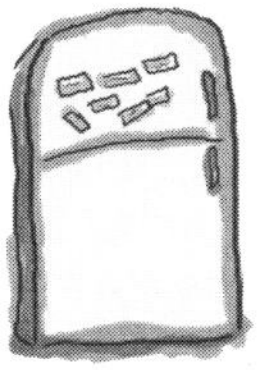

Magnet Matching

A bunch of WHERE clauses with LIKE are all scrambled up on the fridge. Can you match up the clauses with their appropriate results? Some may have multiple answers. Write your own LIKE statements with wild cards for any results that are left hanging around.

- John
- Pineapple
- Michigan
- Splendid
- Alabama
- Blender
- Elsie
- New Jersey
- Montana
- Liver
- Joshua
- Head First SQL
- Maine
- New York
- Splendor

```
WHERE state LIKE 'New %';
```

```
WHERE cow_name LIKE '__sie';
```

```
WHERE title LIKE 'HEAD FIRST%';
```

```
WHERE rhyme_word LIKE '%ender';
```

```
WHERE first_name LIKE 'Jo%';
```

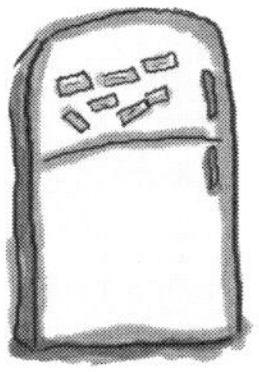

Magnet Matching Solutions

A bunch of WHERE clauses with LIKE are all scrambled up on the fridge. Can you match up the clauses with their appropriate results? Some may have multiple answers. Write your own LIKE statements with wild cards for any results that are left hanging around.

WHERE state LIKE 'New %';
New Jersey
New York
WHERE cow_name LIKE '__sie';
Elsie
WHERE title LIKE 'HEAD FIRST%';
Head First SQL
WHERE word LIKE 'Spl%';
Splendid
Splendor
WHERE rhyme_word LIKE '%ender';
Blender
WHERE state LIKE 'M%' OR state LIKE 'A%';
Michigan
Montana
Alabama
Maine
WHERE first_name LIKE 'Jo%';
John
Joshua
WHERE word LIKE '_i%';
Pineapple
Liver

Selecting ranges using AND and comparison operators

The people at the Head First Lounge are trying to pinpoint drinks with a certain range of calories. How will they query the data to find the names of drinks that fall into the range of calories between, and including, 30 and 60?

drink_info

drink_name	cost	carbs	color	ice	calories
Blackthorn	3	8.4	yellow	Y	33
Blue Moon	2.5	3.2	blue	Y	12
Oh My Gosh	3.5	8.6	orange	Y	35
Lime Fizz	2.5	5.4	green	Y	24
Kiss on the Lips	5.5	42.5	purple	Y	171
Hot Gold	3.2	32.1	orange	N	135
Lone Tree	3.6	4.2	red	Y	17
Greyhound	4	14	yellow	Y	50
Indian Summer	2.8	7.2	brown	N	30
Bull Frog	2.6	21.5	tan	Y	80
Soda and It	3.8	4.7	red	N	19

```
SELECT drink_name FROM drink_info
WHERE
calories >= 30
AND
calories <= 60;
```

The results will include drinks with calories equal to 30, if there are any, as well as the drinks with 60 calories, as well as drinks with calorie counts in between.

Just BETWEEN us... there's a better way

We can use the BETWEEN keyword instead. Not only is it shorter than the previous query, but it gives you the same results. Notice that the endpoint (30 and 60) are also included. BETWEEN is equivalent to using the <= and >= symbols, but not the < and > symbols.

```
SELECT drink_name FROM drink_info
WHERE
calories BETWEEN 30 AND 60;
```

This includes the drinks with 30 and 60 calories.

This will give you exactly the same results as the query on the previous page, but look how much quicker it is to type!

File Edit Window Help MediumCalories

```
> SELECT drink_name FROM drink_info
WHERE
calories BETWEEN 30 AND 60;
+-----------------+
| drink_name      |
+-----------------+
| Blackthorn      |
| Oh My Gosh      |
| Greyhound       |
| Indian Summer   |
| Soda and It     |
+-----------------+
```

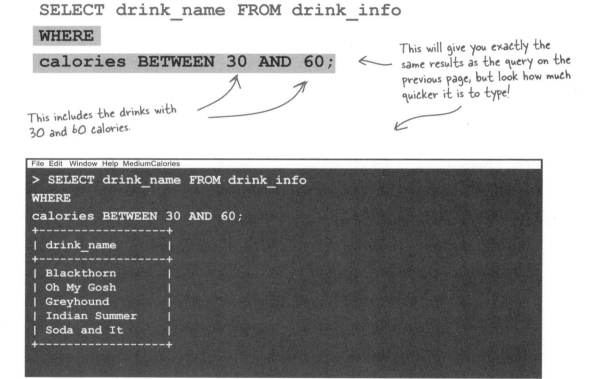

Sharpen your pencil

Rewrite the query on the previous page to SELECT all the names of drinks that have more than 60 calories and less than 30.

....

....

....

Try using BETWEEN on text columns. Write a query that will SELECT the names of drinks that begin with the letters G through O.

....

....

....

What do you think the results of this query will be?

```
SELECT drink_name FROM drink_info WHERE
calories BETWEEN 60 AND 30;
```

....

....

....

Sharpen your pencil Solution

Rewrite the query on the previous page to SELECT all the names of drinks that have more than 60 calories and less than 30.

```
SELECT drink_name FROM drink_info
WHERE
calories < 30 OR calories > 60;
```

This gives us drink names with calories greater than 60.

and these are the ones with calories less than 30.

Try using BETWEEN on text columns. Write a query that will SELECT the names of drinks that begin with the letters G through O.

```
SELECT drink_name FROM drink_info
WHERE
drink_name BETWEEN 'G' AND 'O';
```

We'll get drink names that begin with G and O, and all the letters in between.

What do you think the results of this query will be?

```
SELECT drink_name FROM drink_info WHERE
calories BETWEEN 60 AND 30;
```

Order matters, so you won't get any results from this query.

We're looking for values that are between 60 and 30. There are no values in between 60 and 30, because 60 comes after 30 numerically. The smaller number must always be first for the **BETWEEN** to be interpreted the way you expect.

After the dates, you are either IN...

Greg's friend Amanda has been using Greg's contacts to meet guys. She's gone on quite a few dates, and has started to keep a "little black book" table with her impressions of her dates.

She's named her table `black_book`. She wants to get a list of the good dates, so she uses her positive ratings.

black_book

date_name	rating
Alex	innovative
James	boring
Ian	fabulous
Boris	ho hum
Melvin	plebian
Eric	pathetic
Anthony	delightful
Sammy	pretty good
Ivan	dismal
Vic	ridiculous

These are the positive ratings.

```
SELECT date_name
FROM black_book
WHERE
rating = 'innovative'
OR
rating = 'fabulous'
OR
... ;
```

You need a line for each positive score.

Instead of using all those ORs, we can simplify it with the keyword `IN`. Use IN with a set of values in parentheses. When the value in the column matches one of the values in the set, the row or specified colums are returned.

```
SELECT date_name
FROM black_book
WHERE
rating IN ('innovative',
'fabulous', 'delightful',
'pretty good');
```

Using the keyword IN tells your RDBMS that a set of values is coming up.

This is the set of positive ratings.

```
File Edit Window Help GoodDates
> SELECT date_name FROM black_book
WHERE
rating IN ('innovative', 'fabulous',
'delightful', 'pretty good');

+------- ----+
| date_name  |
+------------+
| Alex       |
| Ian        |
| Anthony    |
| Sammy      |
+------------+
```

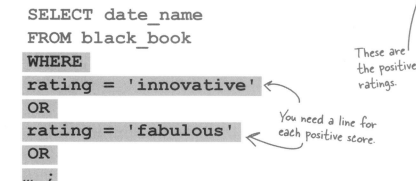

... or you are NOT IN

Of course, Amanda wants to know who got the bad ratings so that if they call she can be washing her hair or otherwise engaged.

To find the names of those she didn't rate highly, we're going to add the keyword `NOT` to our `IN` statement. `NOT` gives you the opposite results, anything that doesn't match the set.

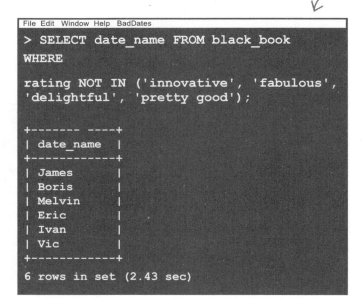

If you are NOT IN, you are out!

```
SELECT date_name
FROM black_book
WHERE
rating NOT IN ('innovative',
'fabulous', 'delightful',
'pretty good');
```

Using the keywords NOT IN tells your software that the results aren't in the set of terms.

The results of the NOT IN query are the people who didn't get positive ratings and won't get a second date, either.

```
File Edit Window Help BadDates
> SELECT date_name FROM black_book
WHERE
rating NOT IN ('innovative', 'fabulous',
'delightful', 'pretty good');

+------- ----+
| date_name  |
+------------+
| James      |
| Boris      |
| Melvin     |
| Eric       |
| Ivan       |
| Vic        |
+------------+
6 rows in set (2.43 sec)
```

BRAIN POWER

Why might you sometimes choose to use `NOT IN` rather than `IN`?

More NOT

You can use NOT with BETWEEN and LIKE just as you can with IN. The important thing to keep in mind is that **NOT goes right after WHERE** in your statement. Here are some examples.

```
SELECT drink_name FROM drink_info
WHERE NOT carbs BETWEEN 3 AND 5;
```

```
SELECT date_name from black_book
WHERE NOT date_name LIKE 'A%'
AND NOT date_name LIKE 'B%';
```

When you use NOT with AND or OR, it goes right after the AND or OR.

there are no Dumb Questions

Q: Wait, you just said that NOT goes after WHERE. What about when you use NOT IN?

A: That's an exception. And even moving the NOT after WHERE will work. These two statements will give you exactly the same results:

```
SELECT * FROM easy_drinks
WHERE NOT main IN ('soda', 'iced tea');

SELECT * FROM easy_drinks
WHERE main NOT IN ('soda', 'iced tea');
```

Q: Would it work with <> the "not equal to" comparison operator?

A: You could, but it's a double negative. It would make much more sense to just use an equal sign. These two queries return the same results:

```
SELECT * FROM easy_drinks
WHERE NOT drink_name <> 'Blackthorn';

SELECT * FROM easy_drinks
WHERE drink_name = 'Blackthorn';
```

Q: How would it work with NULL?

A: Just like you might guess it would. To get all the values that aren't NULL from a column, you could use this:

```
SELECT * FROM easy_drinks
WHERE NOT main IS NULL;
```

But this will also work:

```
SELECT * FROM easy_drinks
WHERE main IS NOT NULL;
```

Q: What about with AND and OR?

A: If you wanted to use it in and AND or OR clause, it would go right after that word, like this:

```
SELECT * FROM easy_drinks
WHERE NOT main = 'soda'
AND NOT main = 'iced tea';
```

Exercise

Rewrite each of the following WHERE clauses so they are as simple as possible. You can use AND, OR, NOT, BETWEEN, LIKE, IN, IS NULL, and the comparison operators to help you. Refer back to the tables used in this chapter.

```
SELECT drink_name from easy_drinks
WHERE NOT amount1 < 1.50;
```

```
SELECT drink_name FROM drink_info
WHERE NOT ice = 'Y';
```

```
SELECT drink_name FROM drink_info
WHERE NOT calories < 20;
```

```
SELECT drink_name FROM easy_drinks
WHERE main = 'peach nectar'
OR main = 'soda';
```

....

....

....

```
SELECT drink_name FROM drink_info
WHERE NOT calories = 0;
```

....

....

....

```
SELECT drink_name FROM drink_info
WHERE NOT carbs BETWEEN 3 AND 5;
```

....

....

....

```
SELECT date_name from black_book
WHERE NOT date_name LIKE 'A%'
AND NOT date_name LIKE 'B%';
```

....

....

....

Exercise Solution

Rewrite each of the following WHERE clauses so they are as simple as possible. You can use AND, OR, NOT, BETWEEN, LIKE, IN, IS NULL, and the comparison operators to help you. Refer back to the tables used in this chapter.

```
SELECT drink_name from easy_drinks
WHERE NOT amount1 < 1.50;
```

```
SELECT drink_name FROM easy_drinks
WHERE amount1 >= 1.50;
```

```
SELECT drink_name FROM drink_info
WHERE NOT ice = 'Y';
```

```
SELECT drink_name FROM drink_info
WHERE ice = 'N';
```

```
SELECT drink_name FROM drink_info
WHERE NOT calories < 20;
```

```
SELECT drink_name FROM drink_info
WHERE calories >= 20;
```

```
SELECT drink_name FROM easy_drinks
WHERE main = 'peach nectar'
OR main = 'soda';
```

SELECT drink_name FROM easy_drinks

WHERE main BETWEEN 'P' AND 'S';

This will only work because we don't have any other main ingredients that satisfy the condition. If our table had pomegranate juice, this wouldn't work.

```
SELECT drink_name FROM drink_info
WHERE NOT calories = 0;
```

SELECT drink_name FROM drink_info

WHERE calories > 0;

We never have negative calories, so we're safe with the greater than sign.

```
SELECT drink_name FROM drink_info
WHERE NOT carbs BETWEEN 3 AND 5;
```

SELECT drink_name FROM drink_info

WHERE carbs < 3

OR

carbs > 5;

```
SELECT date_name from black_book
WHERE NOT date_name LIKE 'A%'
AND NOT date_name LIKE 'B%';
```

SELECT date_name FROM black_book

WHERE date_name NOT BETWEEN 'A' AND 'B';

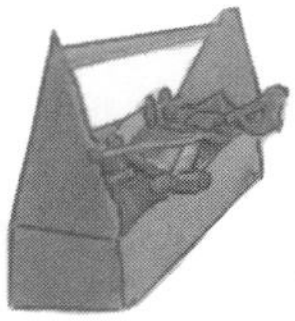

Your SQL Toolbox

You've got Chapter 2 under your belt and now you've added operators to your tool box. For a complete list of tooltips in the book, see Appendix iii.

`SELECT *`

Use this to select all the columns in a table.

`Escape with ' and \`

Escape out apostrophes in your text data with an extra apostrophe or backslash in front of it.

`= <> < > <= >=`

You've got a whole bunch of equality and inequality operators at your disposal. .

`IS NULL`

Use this to create a condition to test for that pesky NULL value.

`AND and OR`

With AND and OR, you can combine your conditional statements in your WHERE clauses for more precision.

`NOT`

NOT lets you negate your results and get the opposite values.

`BETWEEN`

Lets you select ranges of values.

`LIKE with % and _`

Use LIKE with the wildcards to search through parts of text strings.

Your new tools: operators!

Exercise Solution from page 59.

Greg wants to create a table of mixed drinks that bartenders can query for recipes for his speed-dating events. Using what you learned in Chapter 1, create the table on this page and insert the data shown.

This table is part of a database called **drinks**. It contains the table **easy_drinks** with the recipes for a number of beverages that have only two ingredients.

```
CREATE DATABASE drinks;

USE drinks;

CREATE TABLE easy_drinks

(drink_name VARCHAR(16), main VARCHAR(20), amount1 DEC(3,1),
second VARCHAR(20), amount2 DEC(4,2), directions VARCHAR(250));
```

It's a good idea to give yourself a few extra characters in case you ever need to enter a name that's longer than the existing ones.

Don't forget: numeric data types don't need quotes!

```
INSERT INTO easy_drinks

VALUES

('Blackthorn', 'tonic water', 1.5, 'pineapple juice', 1, 'stir with ice, strain
into cocktail glass with lemon twist'), ('Blue Moon', 'soda', 1.5, 'blueberry
juice', .75, 'stir with ice, strain into cocktail glass with lemon twist'),
('Oh My Gosh', 'peach nectar', 1, 'pineapple juice', 1, 'stir with ice, strain
into shot glass'),
('Lime Fizz', 'Sprite', 1.5, 'lime juice', .75, 'stir with ice, strain into
cocktail glass'),
('Kiss on the Lips', cherry juice', 2, 'apricot nectar', 7, 'serve over ice
with straw'),
('Hot Gold', 'peach nectar', 3,' orange juice', 6, 'pour hot orange juice in
mug and add peach nectar'),
('Lone Tree', 'soda', 1.5, 'cherry juice', .75, 'stir with ice, strain into
cocktail glass'),
('Greyhound', 'soda', 1.5, 'grapefruit juice', 5, 'serve over ice, stir well'),
('Indian Summer', 'apple juice', 2, 'hot tea', 6, 'add juice to mug and top off
with hot tea'),
('Bull Frog', 'iced tea', 1.5, 'lemonade', 5, 'serve over ice with lime slice'),
('Soda and It', 'soda', 2, 'grape juice', 1, 'shake in cocktail glass, no ice');
```

Each drink's set of values is in parentheses.

And between each drink is a comma.

3 DELETE and UPDATE

A change will do you good

Next time will you please try to take it easy with that DELETE statement? I can't afford to keep buying you get-well cigars.
My First SQL Commands

Keep changing your mind? Now it's OK! With the commands you're about to learn—**DELETE** and **UPDATE**—you're no longer stuck with a decision you made six months ago, when you first inserted that data about mullets coming back into style soon. With UPDATE, you **can change data**, and DELETE lets you **get rid of data** that you don't need anymore. But we're not just giving you the tools; in this chapter, you'll learn how to be selective with your new powers and avoid dumping data that you really do need.

Clowns are scary

Suppose we want to keep track of the clowns in Dataville. We could create a `clown_info` table to track them. And we could use a `last_seen` column to keep track of the clowns' whereabouts.

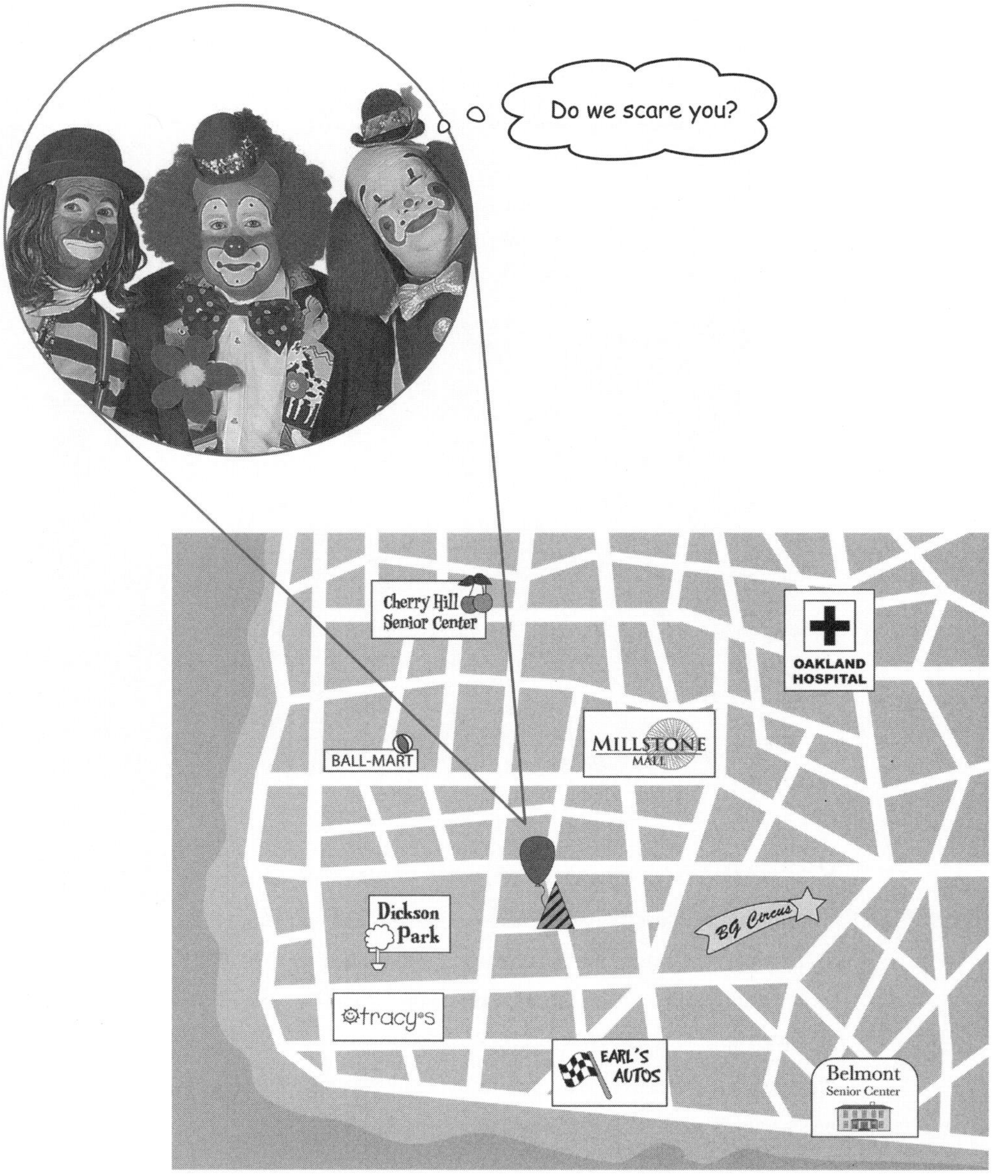

Clown tracking

Here's our table. We can leave out information we don't know and fill it in later. Every time we have a new clown sighting, we can add a new row. We'll have to change this table frequently to keep it up to date.

Where each clown was last spotted.

clown_info

name	last_seen	appearance	activities
Elsie	Cherry Hill Senior Center	F, red hair, green dress, huge feet	balloons, little car
Pickles	Jack Green's party	M, orange hair, blue suit, huge feet	mime
Snuggles	Ball-Mart	F, yellow shirt, baggy red pants	horn, umbrella
Mr. Hobo	BG Circus	M, cigar, black hair, tiny hat	violin
Clarabelle	Belmont Senior Center	F, pink hair, huge flower, blue dress	yelling, dancing
Scooter	Oakland Hospital	M, blue hair, red suit, huge nose	balloons
Zippo	Millstone Mall	F, orange suit, baggy pants	dancing
Babe	Earl's Autos	F, all pink and sparkly	balancing, little car
Bonzo		M, in drag, polka dotted dress	singing, dancing
Sniffles	Tracy's	M, green and purple suit, pointy nose	

We'll fill in the blank columns later.

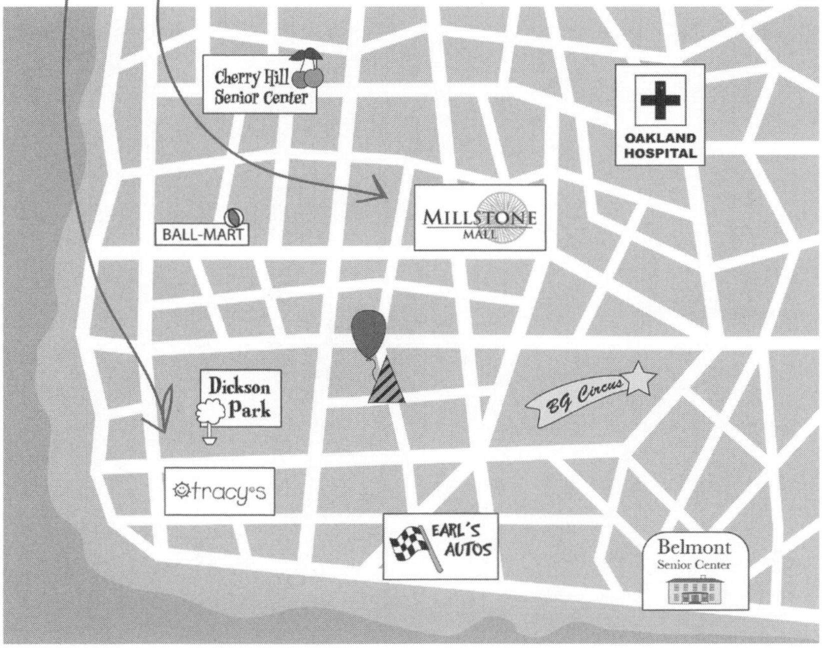

Sharpen your pencil

The clowns are on the move

Your job is to write the SQL commands to get each field report into the clown_info table. Notice that not all the information has changed for each clown, so you'll need to refer back to the table on page 121 to get the rest of the information to add.

Zippo spotted singing

```
INSERT INTO clown_info
VALUES
('Zippo', 'Millstone Mall', 'F, orange suit, baggy pants',
'dancing, singing');
```

Snuggles now wearing baggy blue pants

```
INSERT INTO clown_info
VALUES
('Snuggles', 'Ball-Mart', 'F, yellow shirt, baggy blue pants',
'horn, umbrella');
```

Bonzo sighted at Dickson Park

Sniffles seen climbing into tiny car

Mr. Hobo last seen at party for Eric Gray

Now fill in what that data in the clown_info table looks like once you've added the data using your INSERT commands.

name	last_seen	appearance	activities
Elsie	Cherry Hill Senior Center	F, red hair, green dress, huge feet	balloons, little car
Pickles	Jack Green's party	M, orange hair, blue suit, huge feet	mime
Snuggles	Ball-Mart	F, yellow shirt, baggy red pants	horn, umbrella
Mr. Hobo	BG Circus	M, cigar, black hair, tiny hat	violin
Clarabelle	Belmont Senior Center	F, pink hair, huge flower, blue dress	yelling, dancing
Scooter	Oakland Hospital	M, blue hair, red suit, huge nose	balloons
Zippo	Millstone Mall	F, orange suit, baggy pants	dancing
Babe	Earl's Autos	F, all pink and sparkly	balancing, little car
Bonzo		M, in drag, polka dotted dress	singing, dancing
Sniffles	Tracy's	M, green and purple suit, pointy nose	

Sharpen your pencil Solution

The clowns are on the move

Your job was to write the SQL commands to get each field report into the clown_info table, then fill in what that data in the table looks like after adding the data using your INSERT commands.

Zippo spotted singing

```
INSERT INTO clown_info
VALUES
('Zippo', 'Millstone Mall', 'F, orange suit, baggy pants',
'dancing, singing');
```

Snuggles now wearing baggy blue pants

```
INSERT INTO clown_info
VALUES
('Snuggles', 'Ball-Mart', 'F, yellow shirt, baggy blue pants',
'horn, umbrella');
```

Bonzo sighted at Dickson Park

```
INSERT INTO clown_info
VALUES
('Bonzo', 'Dickson Park', 'M, in drag, polka dotted dress',
'singing, dancing');
```

Sniffles seen climbing into tiny car

```
INSERT INTO clown_info
VALUES
('Sniffles', 'Tracy\'s', 'M, green and purple suit, pointy nose',
'climbing into tiny car');
```

Don't forget to escape quotes in your VARCHAR values.

Mr. Hobo last seen at party for Eric Gray

```
INSERT INTO clown_info
VALUES
('Mr. Hobo', 'Party for Eric Gray', 'M, cigar, black hair
tiny hat', 'violin');
```

name	last_seen	appearance	activities
Elsie	Cherry Hill Senior Center	F, red hair, green dress, huge feet	balloons, little car
Pickles	Jack Green's party	M, orange hair, blue suit, huge feet	mime
Snuggles	Ball-Mart	F, yellow shirt, baggy red pants	horn, umbrella
Mr. Hobo	BG Circus	M, cigar, black hair, tiny hat	violin
Clarabelle	Belmont Senior Center	F, pink hair, huge flower, blue dress	yelling, dancing
Scooter	Oakland Hospital	M, blue hair, red suit, huge nose	balloons
Zippo	Millstone Mall	F, orange suit, baggy pants	dancing
Babe	Earl's Autos	F, all pink and sparkly	balancing, little car
Bonzo		M, in drag, polka dotted dress	singing, dancing
Sniffles	Tracy's	M, green and purple suit, pointy nose	
Zippo	Millstone Mall	F, orange suit, baggy pants	dancing, singing
Snuggles	Ball-Mart	F, yellow shirt, baggy blue pants	horn, umbrella
Bonzo	Dickson Park	M, in drag, polka dotted dress	singing, dancing
Sniffles	Tracy's	M, green and purple suit, pointy nose	climbing into tiny car
Mr. Hobo	Party for Eric Gray	M, cigar, black hair, tiny hat	violin

BRAIN POWER

How can you find out the current location of a particular clown?

How our clown data gets entered

Our clown trackers work on a vounteer basis. Sometimes clown tracking reports sit in an inbox for a week or two before they get entered in. And sometimes two people **split the pile** of reports up and **enter data at the same time.**

Keeping that in mind, let's look at all the rows in our table for Zippo. We can do a SELECT statement to get them:

File Edit Window Help CatchTheClown

```
SELECT * FROM clown_info WHERE name = 'Zippo';
```

name	last_seen	appearance	activities
Zippo	Millstone Mall	F, orange suit, baggy pants	dancing
Zippo	Millstone Mall	F, orange suit, baggy pants	dancing, singing
Zippo	Oakland Hospital	F, orange suit, baggy pants	dancing, singing
Zippo	Tracy's	F, orange suit, baggy pants	dancing, singing
Zippo	Ball-Mart	F, orange suit, baggy pants	dancing, juggling
Zippo	Millstone Mall	F, orange suit, baggy pants	dancing, singing
Zippo	Oakland Hospital	F, orange suit, baggy pants	dancing, singing

These two records are exactly alike.

These are also exactly alike.

This info repeats again and again.

Is there a way to query our data and get only the most recent sighting of Zippo? Can you tell what her location was?

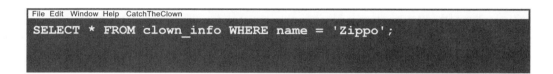

Sure, that's easy. You just look at the last record.

Unfortunately, you can't be certain that the last record is the newest.

We have more than one person entering data at the same time. And the reports might have gotten shuffled in the inbox. But even if that were the case, **you can't rely on the rows in the table being in chronological order**.

There are a number of internal database factors that can change the order in which rows in a table are stored. These include which RDBMS you use and indexes on your columns (which we'll get to later).

You can't guarantee that the last row in a table is the newest row added to that table.

Bonzo, we've got a problem

Since you can't count on the last record being the newest record, we've got a problem. Our clown table gives us a list of where clowns were at some point. **But the main reason the table exists is to tell us where the clown was last seen.**

And that's not all. Notice the duplicate records? We have two rows showing Zippo at the same place doing the same thing. They take up space and will slow down your RDBMS as your tables get bigger and bigger. Duplicate records **should never exist in a table**. In a few chapters, we'll be talking about why duplicates are bad and how to avoid them with ***good table design***. You'll see how to create tables that will never have duplicate records. But right now let's focus on what we can do to fix our existing table so that it will contain useful data.

there are no Dumb Questions

Q: Why can't we just assume the last record is the most recent?

A: The order of records in a table is not guaranteed, and soon you'll be modifying the order of the results you get. You can't have absolute confidence that the last entry is *really* the last inserted record. Also, simple human error could misorder a table. Suppose we enter two `INSERT` statements for the same clown. Unless we make a point of remembering which sighting came first, after that data is in your table, we won't know for sure which came first.

Q: Suppose we do remember the order. Again, why can't we just use the last record?

A: Let's extend the example. We've been tracking the same clowns for many years. Maybe we have assistants who track them as well and INSERT their own records. Some of the clowns have hundreds of records. When we SELECT, we get back those hundreds of records and have to wade through them to the last one, which we *hope* is the most recent.

Q: Aren't there times when we *do* want to keep data like this in a table? Does it ever make sense to `INSERT` new records and keep the old ones?

A: Absolutely. Take our current example. The table as it stands now not only gives us the last place a particular clown was spotted, but it also gives us a history of their movements. This is potentially useful information. The problem is that we don't have any clear information in each record that tells us when this took place. If we add in a column with the current time and date, suddenly we're able to track clowns with great accuracy.

But for now, we need to get those nearly duplicate records out of our table to simplify things.

Q: Okay, so at the end of this book I'll know how to design tables with no duplicate rows. But what if the guy who had the job before me left me with a badly designed table?

A: Badly designed tables are common in the real world, and most people who learn SQL find themselves having to fix other people's SQL messes.

There are a number of techniques for cleaning up duplicate rows. Some of the best ones involving joins, a topic covered later in this book. At this point you don't have all the tools you'll need to fix bad data, but you will when you're done.

Getting rid of a record with DELETE

It looks like we're going to have to get rid of some records. To make our table more useful to us, we should only have one row per clown. While we wait for a new Zippo sighting to come in, one that we know will be the most recent, we can get rid of some of the old Zippo records that don't help us.

The `DELETE` statement is your tool for deleting rows of data from your table. It uses the same type of `WHERE` clause that you've already seen. See if you can come up with the right syntax before we show it to you.

Here are the rows for Zippo again:

name	last_seen	appearance	activities
Zippo	Millstone Mall	F, orange suit, baggy pants	dancing
Zippo	Millstone Mall	F, orange suit, baggy pants	dancing, singing
Zippo	Oakland Hospital	F, orange suit, baggy pants	dancing, singing
Zippo	Tracy's	F, orange suit, baggy pants	dancing, singing
Zippo	Ball-Mart	F, orange suit, baggy pants	dancing, juggling
Zippo	Millstone Mall	F, orange suit, baggy pants	dancing, singing
Zippo	Oakland Hospital	F, orange suit, baggy pants	dancing, singing

DELETE Statement Magnets

We wrote a simple command that we could use to get rid of one of the Zippo records, but all the pieces fell off the refrigerator. Piece together the fragments, and annotate what you think each part of the new command does.

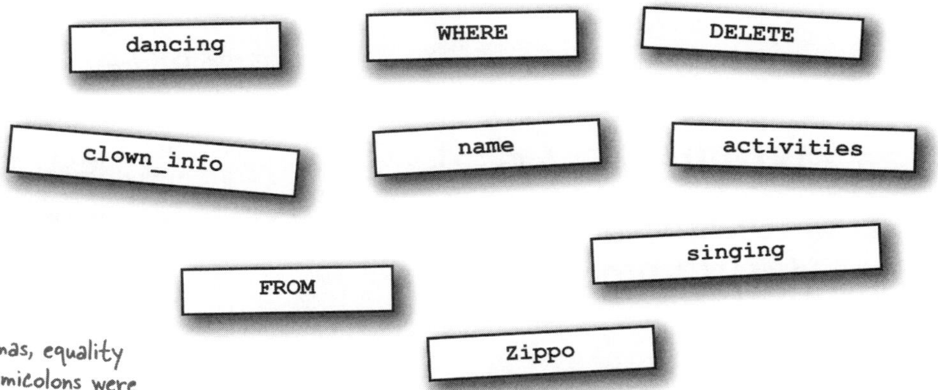

The quotes, commas, equality operators, and semicolons were too small to pick up. Feel free to add as many as you need.

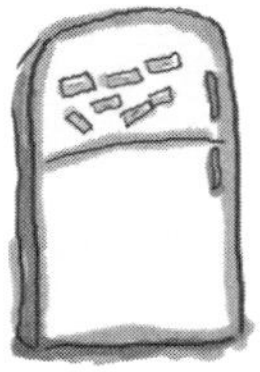

DELETE Statement Magnets Solution

We wrote a simple command that we could use to get rid of one of the Zippo records, but all the pieces fell off the refrigerator. Piece together the fragments, and annotate what you think each part of the new command does.

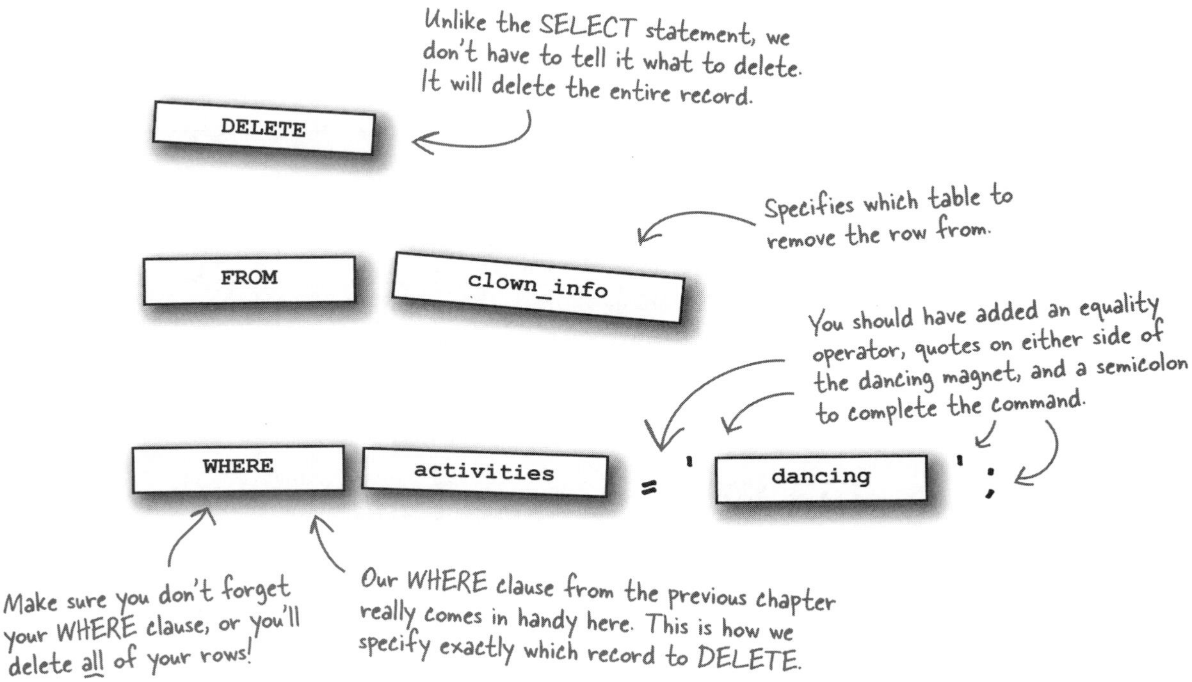
Unlike the SELECT statement, we don't have to tell it what to delete. It will delete the entire record.
DELETE
Specifies which table to remove the row from.
FROM
clown_info
You should have added an equality operator, quotes on either side of the dancing magnet, and a semicolon to complete the command.
WHERE
activities
=
'
dancing
'
;
Make sure you don't forget your WHERE clause, or you'll delete all of your rows!
Our WHERE clause from the previous chapter really comes in handy here. This is how we specify exactly which record to DELETE.

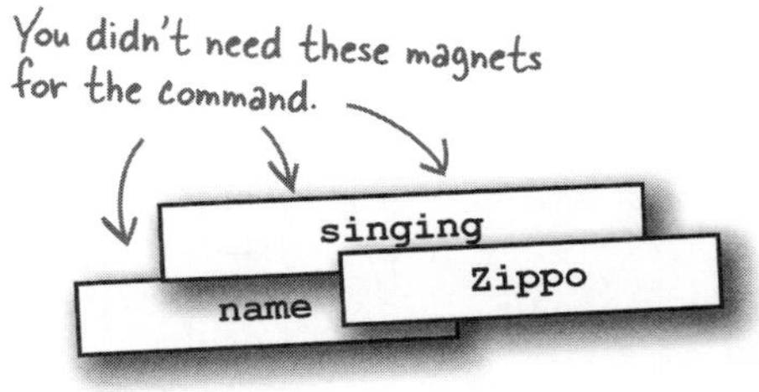
You didn't need these magnets for the command.
singing
name
Zippo

You can use WHERE clauses with DELETE statements the same way you use them with INSERT statements.

Using our new DELETE statement

Let's use the DELETE statement we just created. It does exactly what it sounds like it should. All records that match the WHERE condition will be deleted from our table.

```
DELETE FROM clown_info
WHERE
activities = 'dancing';
```

name	last_seen	appearance	activities
Elsie	Cherry Hill Senior Center	F, red hair, green dress, huge feet	balloons, little car
Pickles	Jack Green's party	M, orange hair, blue suit, huge feet	mime
Snuggles	Ball-Mart	F, yellow shirt, baggy red pants	horn, umbrella
Mr. Hobo	BG Circus	M, cigar, black hair, tiny hat	violin
Clarabelle	Belmont Senior Center	F, pink hair, huge flower, blue dress	yelling, dancing
Scooter	Oakland Hospital	M, blue hair, red suit, huge nose	balloons
Zippo	Millstone Mall	F, orange suit, baggy pants	dancing
Babe	Earl's Autos	F, all pink and sparkly	balancing, little car
Bonzo		M, in drag, polka dotted dress	singing, dancing
Sniffles	Tracy's	M, green and purple suit, pointy nose	
Zippo	Millstone Mall	F, orange suit, baggy pants	singing
Snuggles	Ball-Mart	F, yellow shirt, baggy blue pants	horn, umbrella
Bonzo	Dickson Park	M, in drag, polka dotted dress	singing, dancing
Sniffles	Tracy's	M, green and purple suit, pointy nose	climbing into tiny car
Mr. Hobo	Party for Eric Gray	M, cigar, black hair, tiny hat	violin

This is the record which will be deleted.

BRAIN POWER

Do you think you can delete a single column from a row using DELETE?

DELETE rules

- You can't use `DELETE` to delete the value from a single column or tableful of columns.
- You can use `DELETE` to delete a single row or multiple rows, depending on the WHERE clause.
- You've seen how to delete a single row from a table. We can also delete multiple rows from a table. For that, we use a `WHERE` clause to tell our `DELETE` which rows to choose. This `WHERE` clause is exactly the same as the one you used in Chapter 2 with your `SELECT` statements. It can use everything you used it with in Chapter 2, such as `LIKE`, `IN`, `BETWEEN`, and all the conditionals to tell your RDBMS precisely which rows to delete.
- And, watch out for this one, you can delete every row from a table with:

```
DELETE FROM your_table
```

there are no Dumb Questions

Q: Is there any difference in using a WHERE with a DELETE versus WHERE with SELECT?

A: No difference. The WHERE is the same, but what SELECT and DELETE do is significantly different. SELECT returns a copy of columns from rows that match the WHERE condition, but does not change your table. DELETE removes any rows that match the WHERE condition. It removes the entire row from the table.

BE the DELETE with WHERE Clauses

Become one with a series of DELETEs with WHERE clauses with ANDs and ORs to determine whether or not they would delete any rows.

Draw a line to the row or rows each query deleted:

```
DELETE FROM doughnut_ratings

WHERE location  = 'Krispy King' AND  rating <> 6;

WHERE location  = 'Krispy King' AND  rating = 3;

WHERE location  = 'Snappy Bagel' AND  rating >= 6;

WHERE location  = 'Krispy King' OR  rating > 5;

WHERE location  = 'Krispy King' OR  rating = 3;

WHERE location  = 'Snappy Bagel' OR  rating = 6;
```

doughnut_ratings

location	time	date	type	rating	comments
Krispy King	8:50 am	9/27	plain glazed	10	almost perfect
Duncan's Donuts	8:59 am	8/25	NULL	6	greasy
Starbuzz Coffee	7:35 pm	5/24	cinnamon cake	5	stale, but tasty
Duncan's Donuts	7:03 pm	4/26	jelly	7	not enough jelly

BE the DELETE with WHERE Clauses Solution

You became one with a series of DELETEs with WHERE clauses with ANDs and ORs to determine whether or not they would delete any rows.

Draw a line to the row or rows each query deleted:

```
DELETE FROM doughnut_ratings

WHERE location  = 'Krispy King' AND  rating <> 6;

WHERE location  = 'Krispy King' AND  rating = 3;

WHERE location  = 'Snappy Bagel' AND  rating >= 6;

WHERE location  = 'Krispy King' OR  rating > 5;

WHERE location  = 'Krispy King' OR  rating = 3;

WHERE location  = 'Snappy Bagel' OR  rating = 6;
```

No matches, did not DELETE

No matches, did not DELETE

No matches, did not DELETE

doughnut_ratings

location	time	date	type	rating	comments
Krispy King	8:50 am	9/27	plain glazed	10	almost perfect
Duncan's Donuts	8:59 am	8/25	NULL	6	greasy
Starbuzz Coffee	7:35 pm	5/24	cinnamon cake	5	stale, but tasty
Duncan's Donuts	7:03 pm	4/26	jelly	7	not enough jelly

Those NULL values may cause you problems in future queries. It's better to enter some sort of value than leave a NULL value in a column because NULLs can't be found with an equality condition.

The INSERT-DELETE two step

There's only one record for Clarabelle in the entire table. Since we only want one row per clown that holds their most recent information, we just need to create one new record and delete the old one.

Only her activity is different from the current row.

> Clarabelle spotted dancing at Belmont Senior Center.
> F, pink hair, huge flower, blue dress

Our job was to add this data to this table. We're just showing one line of the table on page 131 to save space.

name	last_seen	appearance	activities
Clarabelle	Belmont Senior Center	F, pink hair, huge flower, blue dress	yelling, dancing

1 First, use the INSERT to add the new information (and all the old information, too).

```
INSERT INTO clown_info
VALUES
('Clarabelle', 'Belmont Senior Center', 'F, pink hair,
huge flower, blue dress', 'dancing');
```

INSERT the record using all the original data and just altering the column you need to change.

name	last_seen	appearance	activities
Clarabelle	Belmont Senior Center	F, pink hair, huge flower, blue dress	yelling, dancing
Clarabelle	Belmont Senior Center	F, pink hair, huge flower, blue dress	dancing

INSERT →

2 Then, DELETE the old record using a WHERE clause.

```
DELETE FROM clown_info
WHERE
activities = 'yelling'
AND name = 'Clarabelle';
```

Use a WHERE clause to find and DELETE the old record.

Now we're left with just the new record.

name	last_seen	appearance	activities
Clarabelle	Belmont Senior Center	F, pink hair, huge flower, blue dress	dancing

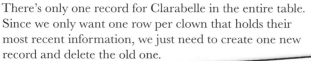

Sharpen your pencil

Use INSERT and DELETE to change the drink_info table as requested. Then draw the changed table on the right.

drink_info

drink_name	cost	carbs	color	ice	calories
Blackthorn	3	8.4	yellow	Y	33
Blue Moon	2.5	3.2	blue	Y	12
Oh My Gosh	3.5	8.6	orange	Y	35
Lime Fizz	2.5	5.4	green	Y	24
Kiss on the Lips	5.5	42.5	purple	Y	171
Hot Gold	3.2	32.1	orange	N	135
Lone Tree	3.6	4.2	red	Y	17
Greyhound	4	14	yellow	Y	50
Indian Summer	2.8	7.2	brown	N	30
Bull Frog	2.6	21.5	tan	Y	80
Soda and It	3.8	4.7	red	N	19

Change the calories of Kiss on the Lips to 170.

....

....

....

....

Change the yellow values to gold.

....

....

....

....

drink_info

drink_name	cost	carbs	color	ice	calories
Blackthorn					
Blue Moon					
Oh My Gosh					
Lime Fizz					
Kiss on the Lips					
Hot Gold					
Lone Tree					
Greyhound					
Indian Summer					
Bull Frog					
Soda and It					

Is this another of your trick exercises?

Make all the drinks that cost $2.50 cost $3.50, and make all drinks that currently cost $3.50 now cost $4.50.

....

....

....

....

....

Sharpen your pencil Solution

Use INSERT and DELETE to change the drink_info table as requested. Then draw the changed table on the right.

drink_info

drink_name	cost	carbs	color	ice	calories
Blackthorn	3	8.4	yellow	Y	33
Blue Moon	2.5	3.2	blue	Y	12
Oh My Gosh	3.5	8.6	orange	Y	35
Lime Fizz	2.5	5.4	green	Y	24
Kiss on the Lips	5.5	42.5	purple	Y	171
Hot Gold	3.2	32.1	orange	N	135
Lone Tree	3.6	4.2	red	Y	17
Greyhound	4	14	yellow	Y	50
Indian Summer	2.8	7.2	brown	N	30
Bull Frog	2.6	21.5	tan	Y	80
Soda and It	3.8	4.7	red	N	19

Change the calories of Kiss on the Lips to 170.

```
INSERT INTO drink_info VALUES ('Kiss on the Lips', 5.5, 42.5, 'purple', 'Y', 170);
DELETE FROM drink_info WHERE calories = 171;
```

Change the yellow values to gold.

```
INSERT INTO drink_info VALUES ('Blackthorn', 3, 8.4, 'gold', 'Y', 33),
('Greyhound', 4, 14, 'gold', 'Y', 50);
DELETE FROM drink_info WHERE color = 'yellow';
```

drink_info

drink_name	cost	carbs	color	ice	calories
Blackthorn	3	8.4	gold	Y	33
Blue Moon	3.5	3.2	blue	Y	12
Oh My Gosh	4.5	8.6	orange	Y	35
Lime Fizz	3.5	5.4	green	Y	24
Kiss on the Lips	5.5	42.5	purple	Y	170
Hot Gold	3.2	32.1	orange	N	135
Lone Tree	3.6	4.2	red	Y	17
Greyhound	4	14	gold	Y	50
Indian Summer	2.8	7.2	brown	N	30
Bull Frog	2.6	21.5	tan	Y	80
Soda and It	3.8	4.7	red	N	19

This is what your table should look like after you make the changes. Yours might be in a different order, but remember, the order doesn't really mean anything.

It's not a trick question, but it is one you need to think about. If you change the $2.50 drinks to $3.50, then the $3.50 to $4.50, you will have raised the price of the Blue Moon by two dollars. Instead, you need to change the larger values first ($3.50 to $4.50), and then the $2.50 Blue Moon to $3.50.

Is this another of your trick exercises?

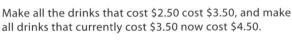

Make all the drinks that cost $2.50 cost $3.50, and make all drinks that currently cost $3.50 now cost $4.50.

```
INSERT INTO drink_info VALUES ('Oh My Gosh', 4.5, 8.6, 'orange', 'Y', 35);
DELETE FROM drink_info WHERE cost = 3.5;
INSERT INTO drink_info VALUES ('Blue Moon', 3.5, 3.2, 'blue', 'Y', 12),
('Lime Fizz', 3.5, 5.4, 'green', 'Y', 24);
DELETE FROM drink_info WHERE cost = 2.5;
```

Bonus points if you put both of your INSERT statements into a single INSERT!

Be careful with your DELETE

Each time you delete records, you run the risk of accidentally deleting records you didn't intend to remove. Take for example if we had to add a new record for Mr. Hobo:

Use DELETE carefully. Make sure you include a precise WHERE clause to target the exact rows you really want to delete.

Mr. Hobo sighted at Tracy's

Here's the information we need to add, and the INSERT to do it..

```
INSERT INTO clown_info
VALUES
('Mr. Hobo', 'Tracy\'s', 'M, cigar,
black hair, tiny hat', 'violin');
```

Don't forget about the backslash character in front of your apostrophe.

name	last_seen	appearance	activities
Elsie	Cherry Hill Senior Center	F, red hair, green dress, huge feet	balloons, little car
Pickles	Jack Green's party	M, orange hair, blue suit, huge feet	mime
Snuggles	Ball-Mart	F, yellow shirt, baggy red pants	horn, umbrella
Mr. Hobo	BG Circus	M, cigar, black hair, tiny hat	violin
Clarabelle	Belmont Senior Center	F, pink hair, huge flower, blue dress	yelling, dancing
Scooter	Oakland Hospital	M, blue hair, red suit, huge nose	balloons
Zippo	Millstone Mall	F, orange suit, baggy pants	dancing, singing
Babe	Earl's Autos	F, all pink and sparkly	balancing, little car
Bonzo		M, in drag, polka dotted dress	singing, dancing
Sniffles	Tracy's	M, green and purple suit, pointy nose	
Zippo	Millstone Mall	F, orange suit, baggy pants	singing
Snuggles	Ball-Mart	F, yellow shirt, baggy blue pants	horn, umbrella
Bonzo	Dickson Park	M, in drag, polka dotted dress	singing, dancing
Sniffles	Tracy's	M, green and purple suit, pointy nose	climbing into tiny car
Mr. Hobo	Party for Eric Gray	M, cigar, black hair, tiny hat	violin
Mr. Hobo	Tracy's	M, cigar, black hair, tiny hat	violin

DELETED

Now you be the DELETE

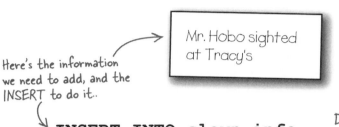

BE the DELETE

Below, you'll find a series of WHERE clauses for a DELETE statement designed to clean up the clown_info table on the facing page. Figure out which ones help us and which ones create new problems.

```
DELETE FROM clown_info
```

Does this help us? If not, state why not.

```
WHERE last_seen = 'Oakland Hospital';
```

....

....

```
WHERE activities = 'violin';
```

....

....

```
WHERE last_seen = 'Dickson Park'
AND name = 'Mr. Hobo';
```

....

....

```
WHERE last_seen = 'Oakland Hospital' AND
last_seen = 'Dickson Park';
```

....

....

```
WHERE last_seen = 'Oakland Hospital' OR
last_seen = 'Dickson Park';
```

....

....

```
WHERE name = 'Mr. Hobo'
OR last_seen = 'Oakland Hospital';
```

....

....

Now write a single DELETE statement that can clean up the extra Mr. Hobo records without touching any of the others.

....

....

....

....

BE the DELETE Solution

Below, you'll find a series of WHERE clauses for a DELETE statement designed to clean up the clown_info table on the facing page. Figure out which ones help us and which ones create new problems.

```
DELETE FROM clown_info
```
⌐ Scooter also has a row that matches this.
↓
```
WHERE last_seen = 'Oakland Hospital';
```

⌐ We don't want to delete the new record.
↓
```
WHERE activities = 'violin';
```

```
WHERE last_seen = 'Dickson Park'
AND name = 'Mr. Hobo';
```

⌐ The AND means both have to be true.
↓
```
WHERE last_seen = 'Oakland Hospital'
AND last_seen = 'Dickson Park';
```

```
WHERE last_seen = 'Oakland Hospital'
OR last_seen = 'Dickson Park';
```

```
WHERE name = 'Mr. Hobo'
OR last_seen = 'Oakland Hospital';
```

Now write a single DELETE statement that can clean up the extra Mr. Hobo records without touching any of the others.

Does this help us? If not, state why not.

Only deletes one of Mr. Hobo's records.
Also deletes Scooter's record.

Deletes all of Mr. Hobo's records,
including the new one.

Deletes only one of Mr. Hobo's
old records.

Doesn't delete anything.

Deletes Bonzo's and Scooter's records, along with
the old records for Mr. Hobo.

Deletes all of Mr. Hobo records including
the new one, and deletes Scooter's.

```
DELETE FROM clown_info
WHERE name = 'Mr. Hobo'
AND last_seen <> 'Tracy\'s';
```

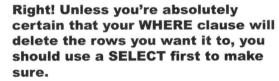

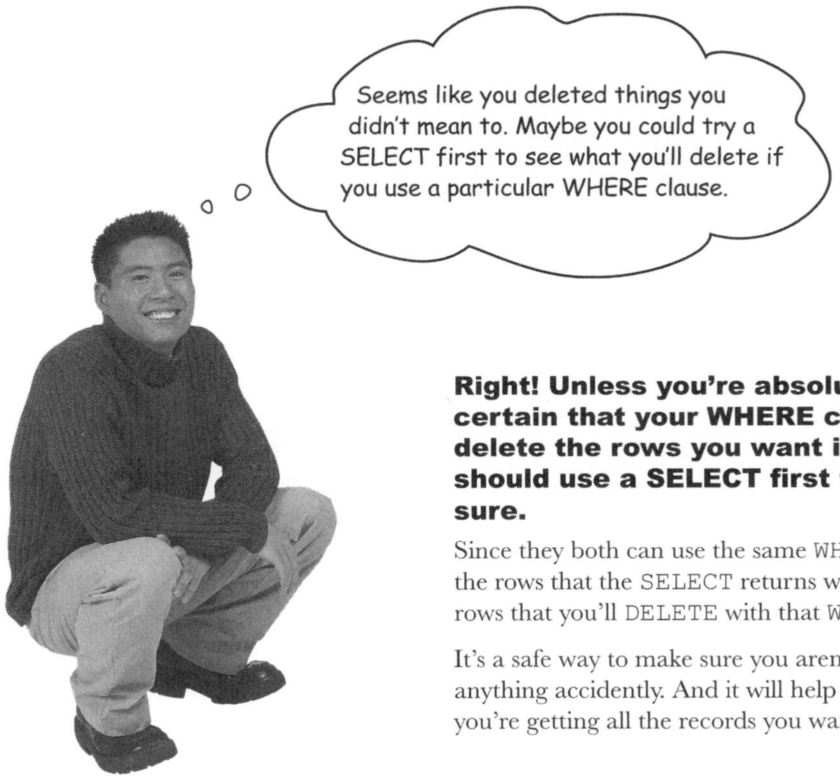

Seems like you deleted things you didn't mean to. Maybe you could try a SELECT first to see what you'll delete if you use a particular WHERE clause.

Right! Unless you're absolutely certain that your WHERE clause will delete the rows you want it to, you should use a SELECT first to make sure.

Since they both can use the same `WHERE` clause, the rows that the `SELECT` returns will echo the rows that you'll `DELETE` with that `WHERE` clause.

It's a safe way to make sure you aren't deleting anything accidently. And it will help you be sure you're getting all the records you want to delete.

The trouble with imprecise DELETE

`DELETE` is tricky. If we aren't careful, the wrong data will be targeted. We can avoid targeting the wrong data if we add another step to our `INSERT-DELETE` two-step.

Here's a THREE STEP plan we can follow:

Change only the records you mean to by using a SELECT statement first.

1. First, `SELECT` the record you know has to be removed to confirm you're going to delete the right record and none of the wrong ones.

```
SELECT FROM clown_info
WHERE
activities = 'dancing';
```

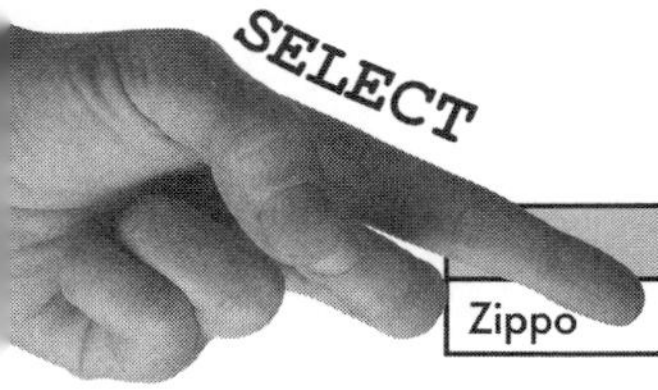

	last_seen	appearance	activities
Zippo	Millstone Mall	F, orange suit, baggy pants	dancing

2. Next, INSERT the new record.

```
INSERT INTO clown_info
VALUES
('Zippo', 'Millstone Mall', 'F, orange suit,
baggy pants', 'dancing, singing');
```

INSERT the record using all the original data and just altering the column you need to change.

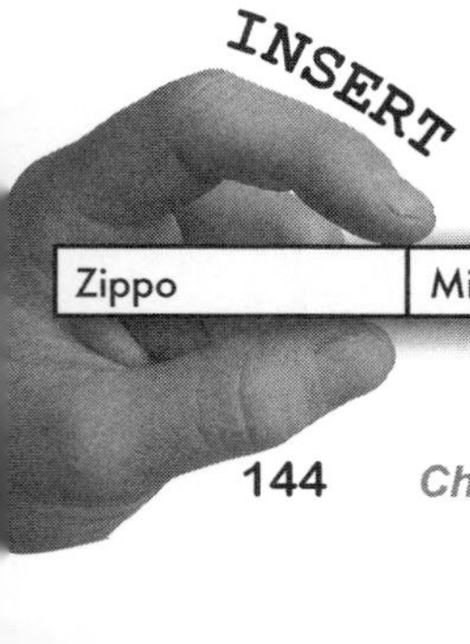

name	last_seen	appearance	activities
Zippo	Millstone Mall	F, orange suit, baggy pants	dancing
Zippo	Millstone Mall	F, orange suit, baggy pants	dancing, singing

3 Finally, `DELETE` the old records with the same `WHERE` clause you used with your `SELECT` back at the start of the ol' three-step.

```
DELETE FROM clown_info
WHERE
activities = 'dancing';
```

Use the WHERE clause you used to SELECT the record in the new step 1 to find and DELETE the old record.

name	last_seen	appearance	activities
Zippo	Millstone Mall	F, orange suit, baggy pants	dancing, singing

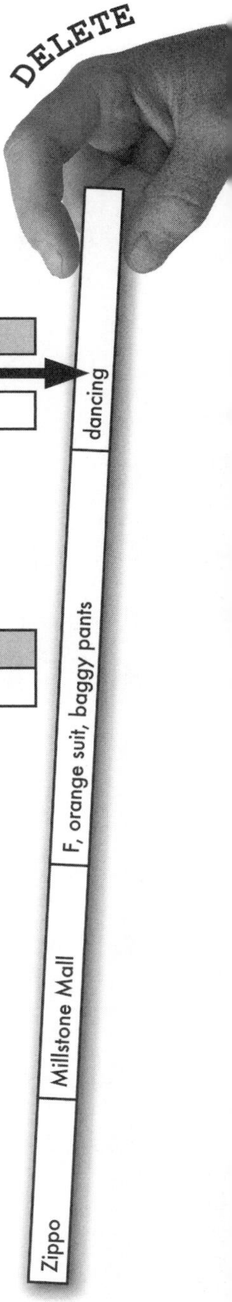

Now we're left with just the new record.

name	last_seen	appearance	activities
Zippo	Millstone Mall	F, orange suit, baggy pants	dancing, singing

Wouldn't it be dreamy if I could change a record in just one step without worrying if my new record gets deleted along with the old one. But I know it's just a fantasy...

Change your data with UPDATE

By now you should be comfortable using INSERT and DELETE to keep your tables up to date. And we've looked at some ways you can use them together to indirectly modify a particular row.

But instead of inserting a new row and deleting the old one, you can repurpose, or reuse, a row that's already in your table, changing only the column values you want to change.

The SQL statement is called UPDATE, and it does exactly what it sounds like it does. It updates a column, or columns, to a new value. And just like SELECT and DELETE, you can give it a WHERE clause to indicate which row you want to UPDATE.

Here's UPDATE in action:

```
UPDATE doughnut_ratings
SET
type = 'glazed'
WHERE type = 'plain glazed';
```

This is where we say what the new value should be.

Here's a standard WHERE clause, just like the ones you've seen with SELECT and DELETE.

The SET keyword tells the RDBMS that it needs to change the column before the equal sign to contain the value after the equal sign. In the case above, we're changing 'plain glazed' to just 'glazed' in our table. The WHERE says to only change rows where type is 'plain glazed'.

doughnut_ratings

location	time	date	type	rating	comments
Krispy King	8:50 am	9/27	plain glazed	10	almost perfect
Duncan's Donuts	8:59 am	8/25	NULL	6	greasy
Starbuzz Coffee	7:35 pm	5/24	cinnamon cake	5	stale, but tasty
Duncan's Donuts	7:03 pm	4/26	jelly	7	not enough jelly

doughnut_ratings

location	time	date	type	rating	comments
Krispy King	8:50 am	9/27	glazed	10	almost perfect
Duncan's Donuts	8:59 am	8/25	NULL	6	greasy
Starbuzz Coffee	7:35 pm	5/24	cinnamon cake	5	stale, but tasty
Duncan's Donuts	7:03 pm	4/26	jelly	7	not enough jelly

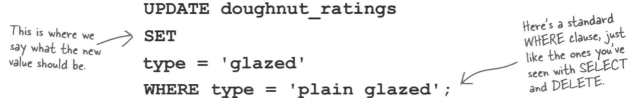

UPDATE rules

- You can use `UPDATE` to change the value of a single column or tableful of columns. Add more `column = value` pairs to the SET clause, and put a comma after each:

```
UPDATE your_table
SET first_column = 'newvalue',
second_column = 'another_value';
```

- You can use `UPDATE` to update a single row or multiple rows, depending on the `WHERE` clause.

there are no Dumb Questions

Q: What happens if I leave out the WHERE clause?

A: Then every column in the SET clause in your table will be updated with the new value.

Q: There are two equal signs over there in the SQL query on the left page that seem to be doing different things. Is that right?

A: Exactly. The equal sign in the SET clause says "set this column equal to this value," while the one in the WHERE clause is testing to see if the column value is equal to the value after the sign.

Q: Could I have used this statement to do the same thing over there?

```
UPDATE doughnut_ratings SET type =
'glazed' WHERE location = 'Krispy King';
```

A: Yes, you can. That would update the same row the same way. And it's fine for our four-row table. But if you had used that with a table with hundreds or thousands of records, you would have changed the type on every single Krispy King row.

Q: Ouch! How can I make sure I only update what I need to?

A: Just as you saw with DELETE, unless you know for certain you are targeting the correct rows with your WHERE clause, do a SELECT first!

Q: Can you have more than one SET clause?

A: No, but you shouldn't need to. You can put all your columns and the new values for them in the same SET clause, as shown above.

UPDATE is the new INSERT-DELETE

When you use **UPDATE**, you're ***not deleting anything***. Instead, you're **recycling the old record into the new one**.

Start with UPDATE...

...then the name of the table containing the record you want to use.

SET specifies the change you're going to make to the record.

```
UPDATE table_name
SET column_name = newvalue
WHERE column_name = somevalue;
```

Our trusty WHERE clause is here to help us precisely target which record to change.

UPDATE statements can replace DELETE/INSERT combinations.

Let's see this in action as a command that will work with the `clown_info` table.

UPDATE a record in the clown_info table.

Change the value in the last_seen column to Tracy's.

Don't forget the backslash to escape your quote.

```
UPDATE clown_info
SET last_seen = 'Tracy\'s'
WHERE name = 'Mr. Hobo'
AND last_seen = 'Dickson Park';
```

Here's the WHERE clause to precisely specify the record to change—in this case, the Mr. Hobo record with a last_seen value of Dickson Park.

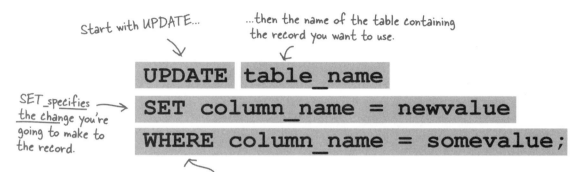

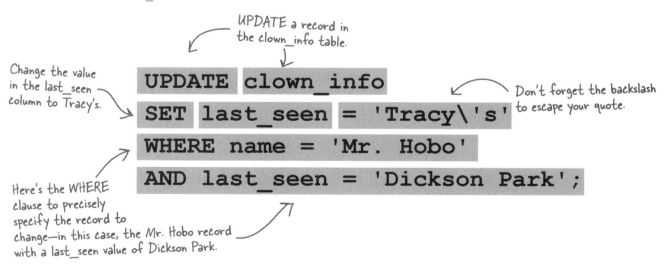

UPDATE in action

Using the UPDATE statement, the `last_seen` column of Mr. Hobo's record is changed from Dickson Park to Tracy's.

Mr. Hobo sighted at Tracy's

Here's the information we need to add, and the UPDATE we'll use to do it.

```
UPDATE clown_info
SET last_seen = 'Tracy\'s'
WHERE name = 'Mr. Hobo'
AND last_seen = 'Party for Eric Gray';
```

name	last_seen	appearance	activities
Elsie	Cherry Hill Senior Center	F, red hair, green dress, huge feet	balloons, little car
Pickles	Jack Green's party	M, orange hair, blue suit, huge feet	mime
nuggles	Ball-Mart	F, yellow shirt, baggy red pants	horn, umbrella
Hobo	BG Circus	M, cigar, black hair, tiny hat	violin
abelle	Belmont Senior Center	F, pink hair, huge flower, blue dress	yelling, dancing
[illegible]	Oakland Hospital	M, blue hair, red suit, huge nose	balloons
[illegible]	illstone Mall	F, orange suit, baggy pants	dancing, singing
[illegible]	rl's Autos	F, all pink and sparkly	balancing, little car
[illegible]	[illegible]	M, in drag, polka dotted dress	singing, dancing
[illegible]	acy's	M, gre nd purple suit, pointy	
[illegible]	Millstone Mall	F	singing
[illegible]	[illegible]	e pants	horn, umbrella
[illegible]	[illegible]	ess	singing, dancing
[illegible]	[illegible]	nty nose	climbing into tiny car
Mr. Hobo	Tracy's		violin

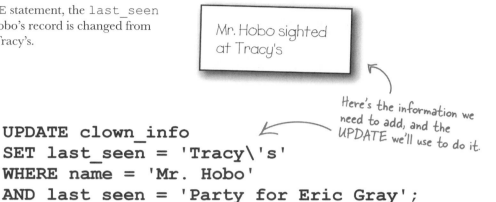

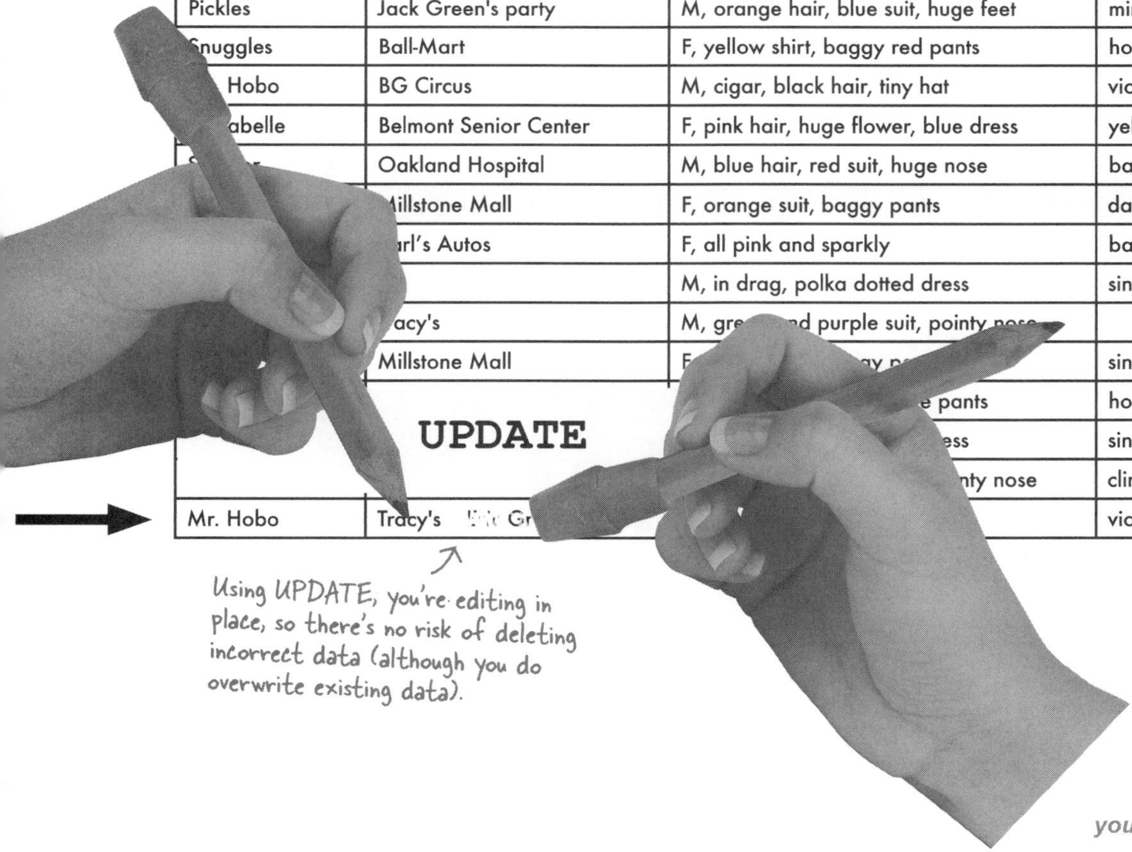

Using UPDATE, you're editing in place, so there's no risk of deleting incorrect data (although you do overwrite existing data).

Sharpen your pencil

Updating the clowns' movements

This time, let's do it right. Fill in an UPDATE statement for each sighting. We've done one to get you started. Then fill in the clown_info table as it will look after we execute all the UPDATE statements.

Zippo spotted singing

```
UPDATE clown_info
SET activities = 'singing'
WHERE name = 'Zippo';
```

Snuggles now wearing baggy blue pants

Bonzo sighted at Dickson Park

Sniffles seen climbing into tiny car

Mr. Hobo last seen at party for Eric Gray

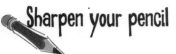

name	last_seen	appearance	activities
Elsie	Cherry Hill Senior Center	F, red hair, green dress, huge feet	balloons, little car
Pickles	Jack Green's party	M, orange hair, blue suit, huge feet	mime
Snuggles	Ball-Mart	F, yellow shirt, baggy red pants	horn, umbrella
Mr. Hobo	BG Circus	M, cigar, black hair, tiny hat	violin
Clarabelle	Belmont Senior Center	F, pink hair, huge flower, blue dress	yelling, dancing
Scooter	Oakland Hospital	M, blue hair, red suit, huge nose	balloons
Zippo	Millstone Mall	F, orange suit, baggy pants	dancing
Babe	Earl's Autos	F, all pink and sparkly	balancing, little car
Bonzo		M, in drag, polka dotted dress	singing, dancing
Sniffles	Tracy's	M, green and purple suit, pointy nose	

name	last_seen	appearance	activities
Elsie	Cherry Hill Senior Center	F, red hair, green dress, huge feet	balloons, little car
Pickles	Jack Green's party	M, orange hair, blue suit, huge feet	mime
Snuggles			
Mr. Hobo			
Clarabelle	Belmont Senior Center	F, pink hair, huge flower, blue dress	yelling, dancing
Scooter	Oakland Hospital	M, blue hair, red suit, huge nose	balloons
Zippo			
Babe	Earl's Autos	F, all pink and sparkly	balancing, little car
Bonzo			
Sniffles			

Sharpen your pencil Solution

Updating the clowns' movements

Your job was to fill in an UPDATE statement for each sighting, then fill in the clown_info table as it will look after we execute all the UPDATE statements.

Zippo spotted singing

```
UPDATE clown_info
SET activities = 'singing'
WHERE name = 'Zippo';
```

Snuggles now wearing baggy blue pants

```
UPDATE clown_info
SET appearance = 'F, yellow shirt, baggy blue pants'
WHERE name = 'Snuggles';
```

We don't want to throw away the other info that's already in the appearance column. Make sure it's included here.

Bonzo sighted at Dickson Park

```
UPDATE clown_info
SET last_seen = 'Dickson Park'
WHERE name = 'Bonzo';
```

Sniffles seen climbing into tiny car

```
UPDATE clown_info
SET activities = 'climbing into tiny car'
WHERE name = 'Sniffles';
```

Mr. Hobo last seen at party for Eric Gray

```
UPDATE clown_info
SET last_seen = 'Eric Gray\'s Party'
WHERE name = 'Mr. Hobo';
```

name	last_seen	appearance	activities
Elsie	Cherry Hill Senior Center	F, red hair, green dress, huge feet	balloons, little car
Pickles	Jack Green's party	M, orange hair, blue suit, huge feet	mime
Snuggles	Ball-Mart	F, yellow shirt, baggy red pants	horn, umbrella
Mr. Hobo	BG Circus	M, cigar, black hair, tiny hat	violin
Clarabelle	Belmont Senior Center	F, pink hair, huge flower, blue dress	yelling, dancing
Scooter	Oakland Hospital	M, blue hair, red suit, huge nose	balloons
Zippo	Millstone Mall	F, orange suit, baggy pants	dancing
Babe	Earl's Autos	F, all pink and sparkly	balancing, little car
Bonzo		M, in drag, polka dotted dress	singing, dancing
Sniffles	Tracy's	M, green and purple suit, pointy nose	

The gray records haven't changed because we didn't UPDATE those.

name	last_seen	appearance	activities
Elsie	Cherry Hill Senior Center	F, red hair, green dress, huge feet	balloons, little car
Pickles	Jack Green's party	M, orange hair, blue suit, huge feet	mime
Snuggles	Ball-Mart	F, yellow shirt, baggy blue pants	horn, umbrella
Mr. Hobo	Eric Gray's Party	M, cigar, black hair, tiny hat	violin
Clarabelle	Belmont Senior Center	F, pink hair, huge flower, blue dress	yelling, dancing
Scooter	Oakland Hospital	M, blue hair, red suit, huge nose	balloons
Zippo	Millstone Mall	F, orange suit, baggy pants	singing
Babe	Earl's Autos	F, all pink and sparkly	balancing, little car
Bonzo	Dickson Park	M, in drag, polka dotted dress	singing, dancing
Sniffles	Tracy's	M, green and purple suit, pointy nose	climbing into tiny car

Only the parts of each record that we SET on the UPDATE have changed. ~~We've finally filled in those gaps from~~ way back on page 121.

UPDATE your prices

Remember when we tried to change some of the prices in the `drink_info` table? We wanted to change the $2.50 drinks to $3.50, and the $3.50 drink to $4.50.

drink_info

drink_name	cost	carbs	color	ice	calories
Blackthorn	3	8.4	yellow	Y	33
Blue Moon	2.5	3.2	blue	Y	12
Oh My Gosh	3.5	8.6	orange	Y	35
Lime Fizz	2.5	5.4	green	Y	24
Kiss on the Lips	5.5	42.5	purple	Y	171
Hot Gold	3.2	32.1	orange	N	135
Lone Tree	3.6	4.2	red	Y	17
Greyhound	4	14	yellow	Y	50
Indian Summer	2.8	7.2	brown	N	30
Bull Frog	2.6	21.5	tan	Y	80
Soda and It	3.8	4.7	red	N	19

Let's look at how we can approach this problem using an `UPDATE` statement to go through each record individually and write a series of `UPDATE` statements like this one:

```
UPDATE drink_info
SET cost = 3.5
WHERE drink_name = 'Blue Moon';
```

Cost with $1 added.

We use a WHERE to choose a unique column so we know which record to update.

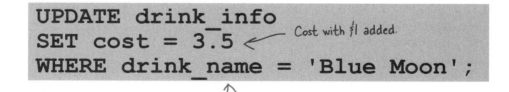

Sharpen your pencil

Write UPDATE statements for each record in the
`drinks_info` table to add another dollar to the cost of each.

drink_name	cost	carbs	color	ice	calories
Blackthorn	3	8.4	yellow	Y	33
Blue Moon	2.5	3.2	blue	Y	12
Oh My Gosh	3.5	8.6	orange	Y	35
Lime Fizz		4			24
Kiss of the					171
Hot G					

> Wait a minute. Why are you making us
> do all this work? Isn't there an operator we
> can use with UPDATE instead of changing
> **every single record by hand**?

You're right.

It looks like some clever operator
would be just the thing to help
out here. Let's update all those
drink prices without having to do
every single one by hand…and
risk overwriting data we already
changed once.

All we need is one UPDATE

Our age column is a number. In SQL, we can perform ***basic math*** operations on **number columns**. In the case of our cost column, we can just add 1 to it for each row in our table we need to change. Here's how:

```
UPDATE drink_info
SET cost = cost + 1;
WHERE
drink_name='Blue Moon'
OR
drink_name='Oh My Gosh'
OR
drink_name= 'Lime Fizz';
```

Add 1 to each of the three prices ($2.50 and $3.50 drinks) that we need to change.

there are no Dumb Questions

Q: Can I use subtraction with a numeric value? What else can I use?

A: Multiplication, division, subtraction—you can use any of them. And you can perform these operations using other numeric values, not just 1.

Q: Can you give me an example of when I might want to use multiplication?

A: Sure. Suppose you had a list of items in a table, each with a price. You could use an `UPDATE` statement and multiply the price of each with a fixed number to compute the price of the item with tax.

Q: So, are there other operations you can perform on data besides simple math?

A: There are quite a few. Later, we'll talk about things you can do with your text variables in addition to more with the numeric ones.

Q: Like what? Give us a hint.

A: Okay, for one thing, you can use the function `UPPER()` to change the entire text column in your table to uppercase. And as you might guess, `LOWER()` will make everything lowercase.

UPDATE statements can be used on multiple records in your table. Use them with basic math operators to manipulate your numeric values.

I guess it's good to know how to update my data, but I really wish I'd understood how to better design it in the first place.

Data does change, so knowing how to update your data is crucial.

But the better job you do designing your table, the less updating you'll have to do overall. Good table design frees you up to focus on the data in the table.

Interested? Next, we'll take a close, painless, look at table design made fishy...

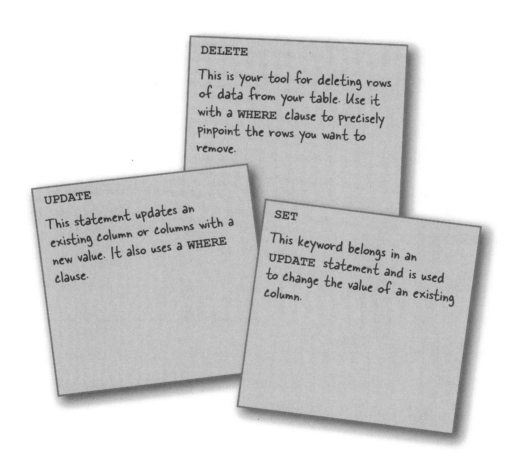

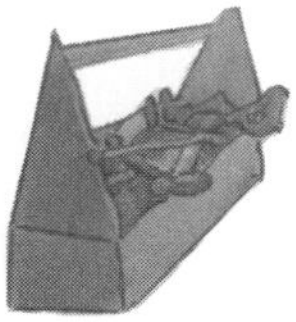

Your SQL Toolbox

Chapter 3 will soon be a memory. But here's a quick refresher of the new SQL statements you've learned. For a complete list of tooltips in the book, see Appendix iii.

DELETE

This is your tool for deleting rows of data from your table. Use it with a WHERE clause to precisely pinpoint the rows you want to remove.

UPDATE

This statement updates an existing column or columns with a new value. It also uses a WHERE clause.

SET

This keyword belongs in an UPDATE statement and is used to change the value of an existing column.

4 smart table design

Why be normal?

...and then Mummy called me her good little helper!
Okay, that's just not normal.

You've been creating tables without giving much thought to them. And that's fine, they work. You can SELECT, INSERT, DELETE, and UPDATE with them. But as you **get more data**, you start seeing **things you wish you'd done** to make your WHERE clauses simpler. What you need is to make your tables more *normal*.

Two fishy tables

Jack and Mark both created tables to store information about record-setting fish. Mark's table has columns for the species and common names of the fish, its weight, and where it was caught. It doesn't include the names of the people who caught the fish.

fish_info

common	species	location	weight
bass, largemouth	M. salmoides	Montgomery Lake, GA	22 lb 4 oz
walleye	S. vitreus	Old Hickory Lake, TN	25 lb 0 oz
trout, cutthroat	O. Clarki	Pyramid Lake, NV	41 lb 0 oz
perch, yellow	P. Flavescens	Bordentown, NJ	4 lb 3 oz
bluegill	L. Macrochirus	Ketona Lake, AL	4 lb 12 oz
gar, longnose	L. Osseus	Trinity River, TX	50 lb 5 oz
crappie, white	P. annularis	Enid Dam, MS	5 lb 3 oz
pickerel, grass	E. americanus	Dewart Lake, IN	1 lb 0 oz
goldfish	C. auratus	Lake Hodges, CA	6 lb 10 oz
salmon, chinook	O. Tshawytscha	Kenai River, AK	97 lb 4 oz

This table only has four columns. Compare it to the fish_records table over there.

I'm an ichthyologist. I only want to search my table for species name or common name to get the weight and location of record-setting fish.
Mark

Jack's table has the common name and weight of the fish, but it also contains the first and last names of the people who caught them, and it breaks down the location into a column containing the name of the body of water where the fish was caught, and a separate state column.

This table is also about record-breaking fish, but it has almost twice as many columns.

fish_records

first_name	last_name	common	location	state	weight	date
George	Perry	bass, largemouth	Montgomery Lake	GA	22 lb 4 oz	6/2/1932
Mabry	Harper	walleye	Old Hickory Lake	TN	25 lb 0 oz	8/2/1960
John	Skimmerhorn	trout, cutthroat	Pyramid Lake	NV	41 lb 0 oz	12/1/1925
C.C.	Abbot	perch, yellow	Bordentown	NJ	4 lb 3 oz	5/1/1865
T.S.	Hudson	bluegill	Ketona Lake	AL	4 lb 12 oz	4/9/1950
Townsend	Miller	gar, longnose	Trinity River	TX	50 lb 5 oz	7/30/1954
Fred	Bright	crappie, white	Enid Dam	MS	5 lb 3 oz	7/31/1957
Mike	Berg	pickerel, grass	Dewart Lake	IN	1 lb 0 oz	6/9/1990
Florentino	Abena	goldfish	Lake Hodges	CA	6 lb 10 oz	4/17/1996
Les	Anderson	salmon, chinook	Kenai River	AK	97 lb 4 oz	5/17/1985

Sharpen your pencil

Write a query for **each table** to find all records from New Jersey.

....

....

....

....

I'm a writer for *Reel and Creel* magazine. I need to know the names of the fishermen, dates, and locations of the big catches.

Sharpen your pencil Solution

Write a query for each table to find all records from New Jersey.

I almost never need to search by state. I inserted the data with states in the same column as the town.

We have to use a LIKE to get our results from the combined city and state.

```
SELECT * FROM fish_info
WHERE location LIKE '%NJ';
```

common	species	location	weight
perch, yellow	P. Flavescens	Bordentown, NJ	4 lb 3 oz

I often have to search by state, so I put in a separate state column when I created my table.

This query can look directly at the state column.

```
SELECT * FROM fish_records
WHERE state = 'NJ';
```

first_name	last_name	common	location	state	weight	date
C.C.	Abbot	perch, yellow	Bordentown	NJ	4 lb 3 oz	5/1/1865

there are no Dumb Questions

Q: So Jack's table is better than Mark's?

A: No. They're different tables with different purposes. Mark will rarely need to search directly for a state because he only really cares about the species and common names of the record-breaking fish and how much they weighed.

Jack, on the other hand, *will* need to search for states when he's querying his data. That's why his table has a separate column: to allow him to easily target states in his searches.

Q: Should we avoid LIKE when querying our tables? Is there something wrong with it?

A: There's nothing wrong with `LIKE`, but it can be difficult to use in your queries, and you risk getting results you don't want. If your columns contain complicated information, `LIKE` isn't specific enough to target precise data.

Q: Why are shorter queries better than longer ones?

A: The simpler the query, the better. As your database grows, and as you add in new tables, your queries will get more complicated. If you start with the simplest possible query now, you'll appreciate it later.

Q: So are you saying I should always have tiny bits of data in my columns?

A: Not necessarily. As you're starting to see with Mark's and Jack's tables, it depends on how you'll ***use*** the data.

For example, imagine a table listing cars for a mechanic and one for a car salesman. The mechanic might need precise information on each car, but the auto dealer might only need the car's make, model, and VIN number.

Q: Suppose we had a street address. Why couldn't we have one column with the entire address, then other columns that break it apart?

A: While duplicating your data might seem like a good idea to you now, consider how much room on your hard drive it will take up when your database grows to an enormous size. And each time you duplicate your data, that's one more clause in an UPDATE statement you'll have to remember to add when your data changes.

Let's take a closer look at how to design your tables the best possible way for your use.

How you're going to use your data will affect how you set up your table.

BRAIN POWER

SQL is the language used by relational databases. What do you think "relational" means in an SQL database?

A table is all about relationships

SQL is known as a Relational Database Management System, or RDBMS. Don't bother memorizing it. We only care about the word RELATIONAL*. All this means to you is that to design a killer table, you need to consider **how** the **columns *relate*** to each other **to describe a thing**.

The challenge is to describe the thing using columns in a way that makes getting the information out of it easy. This depends on what you need from the table, but there are some very broad steps you can follow when you're creating a table.

1. Pick your thing, **the one thing** you want your table to describe.

   What's the main thing you want your table to be about?

2. Make a **list of the information** you need to know about your one thing when you're **using the table**.

   How will you use this table?

3. Using the list, **break down the information** about your thing **into pieces** you can use for **organizing** your table.

   How can you most easily query this table?

* Some people think that RELATIONAL means multiple *tables* relating to each other. That's not correct.

Exercise

Can you spot the columns in this sentence Mark the ichthyologist used to describe how he wants to select from his table? Fill in the column names.

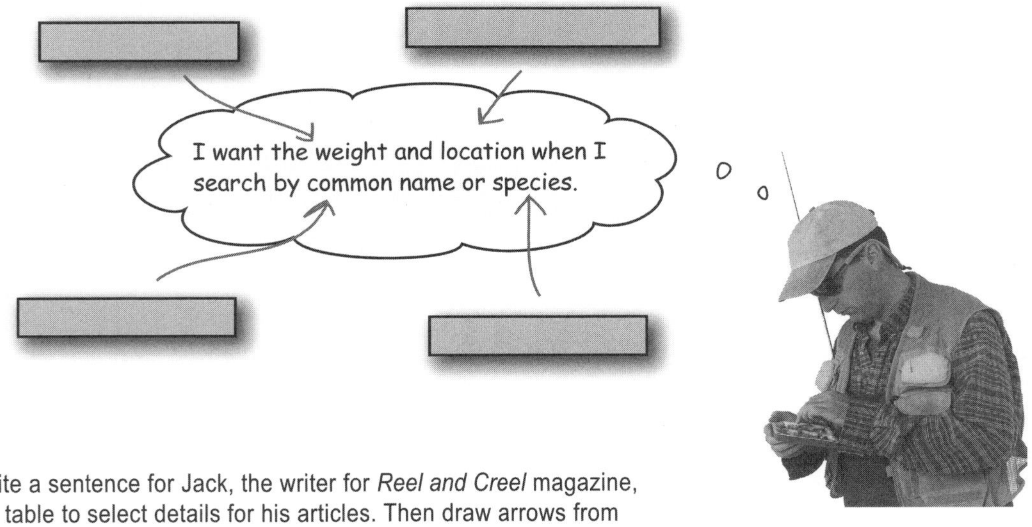

I want the weight and location when I search by common name or species.

Your turn. Write a sentence for Jack, the writer for *Reel and Creel* magazine, who uses his table to select details for his articles. Then draw arrows from each column to where it's mentioned in the sentence.

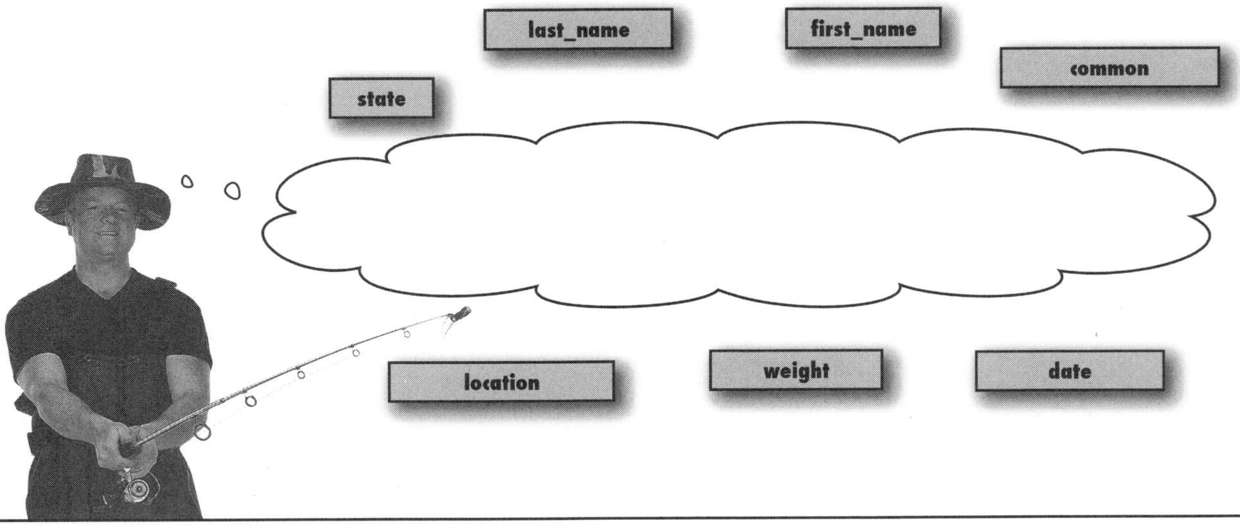

Exercise Solution

Can you spot the columns in this sentence Mark the ichthyologist used to describe how he wants to select from his table? Fill in the column names.

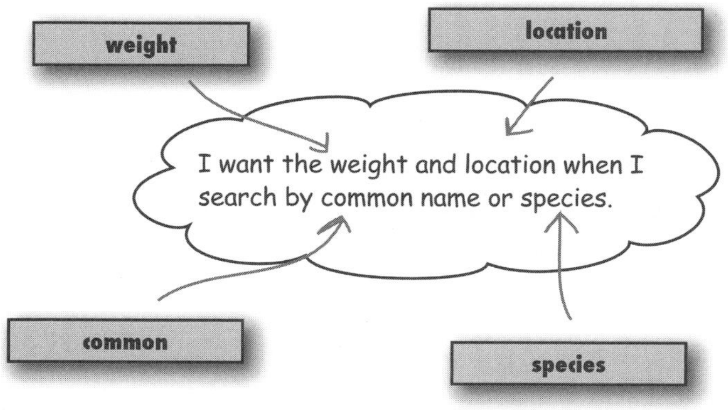
weight
location
I want the weight and location when I search by common name or species.
common
species

Your turn. Write a sentence for Jack, the writer for *Reel and Creel* magazine, who uses his table to select details for his articles. Then draw arrows from each column to where it's mentioned in the sentence.

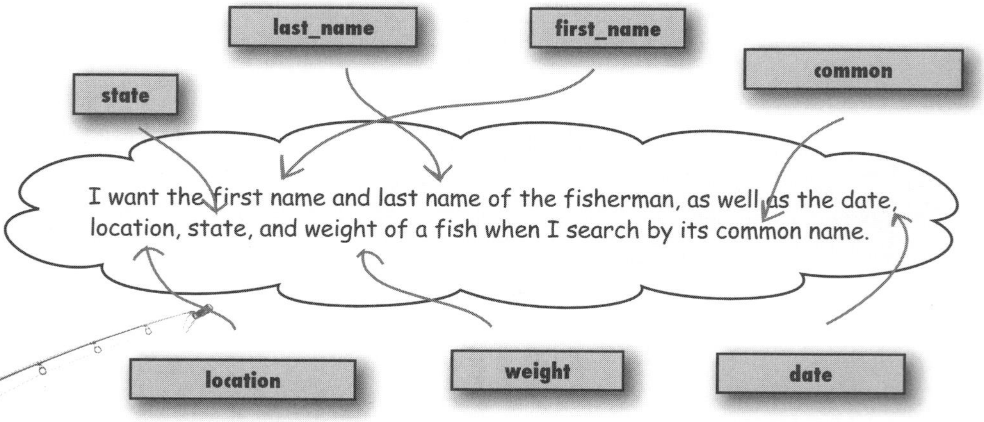
last_name
first_name
state
common
I want the first name and last name of the fisherman, as well as the date, location, state, and weight of a fish when I search by its common name.
location
weight
date

But why stop there with Jack's table? Couldn't you break up the date into month, day, and year? You could even break the location down into street number and street name.

We could, but we don't need the data broken down to that level.

At least, not in this case. If Jack had been writing an article about the best places to go on vacation and catch a big fish, *then* he might have wanted the street number and name so readers could find accommodations nearby.

But Jack only needed location and state, so he only added as many columns as he needed to save space in his database. At that point, he decided his data was broken down enough—it is ***atomic***.

BRAIN POWER

What do you think the word ***atomic*** means in terms of SQL data?

Atomic data

What's an atom? A little piece of information that can't or shouldn't be divided. It's the same for your data. When it's **ATOMIC**, that means that it's been broken down into the **smallest pieces of data *that can't or shouldn't be divided.***

30 minutes or it's free

Consider a pizza delivery guy. To get to where he's going, he just needs a street number and address in a single column. For his purposes, that's atomic. He never needs to look for a single street number on its own.

In fact, if his data were broken into street number and street name, his queries would have to be longer and more complicated, making it take him longer to get the pizza to your front door.

For the pizza guy, the entire street address in one column is atomic enough.

```
File Edit Window Help SimplePizzaFactory
+--------------+--------------------------+
| order_number | address                  |
+--------------+--------------------------+
| 246          | 59 N. Ajax Rapids        |
| 247          | 849 SQL Street           |
| 248          | 2348 E. PMP Plaza        |
| 249          | 1978 HTML Heights        |
| 250          | 24 S. Servlets Springs   |
| 251          | 807 Infinite Circle      |
| 252          | 32 Design Patterns Plaza |
| 253          | 9208 S. Java Ranch       |
| 254          | 4653 W. EJB Estate       |
| 255          | 8678 OOA&D Orchard       |
+--------------+--------------------------+
> SELECT address FROM pizza_deliveries WHERE order_num = 252;
+--------------------------+
| address                  |
+--------------------------+
| 32 Design Patterns Plaza |
+--------------------------+
1 row in set (0.04 sec)
```

Location, location, location

Now consider a realtor. He might want to have a separate column for the street number. He may want to query on a given street to see all the houses for sale by street number. For him, street number and street name are each atomic.

But for the realtor, separating street from street number lets him see all the houses for sale on a given street with an easy query.

File Edit Window Help IWantMyCommission

```
+---------------+-----------------------+---------------+---------+
| street_number | street_name           | property_type | price   |
+---------------+-----------------------+---------------+---------+
| 59            | N. Ajax Rapids        | condo         | 189000  |
| 849           | SQL Street            | apartment     | 109000  |
| 2348          | E. PMP Plaza          | house         | 355000  |
| 1978          | HTML Heights          | apartment     | 134000  |
| 24            | S. Servlets Springs   | house         | 355000  |
| 807           | Infinite Circle       | condo         | 143900  |
| 32            | Design Patterns Plaza | house         | 465000  |
| 9208          | S. Java Ranch         | house         | 699000  |
| 4653          | SQL Street            | apartment     | 115000  |
| 8678          | OOA&D Orchard         | house         | 355000  |
+---------------+-----------------------+---------------+---------+
> SELECT price, property_type FROM real_estate WHERE street_name = 'SQL Street';
+-----------+---------------+
| price | property_type |
+-----------+---------------+
| 109000.00 | apartment |
| 115000.00 | apartment |
+-----------+---------------+
2 rows in set (0.01 sec)
```

Atomic data and your tables

There are some questions you can ask to help you figure out what you need to put in your tables:

1. What is the one thing your table describes?

Does your table describe clowns, cows, doughnuts, people?

2. How will you use the table to get at the one thing?

Design your table to be easy to query!

3. Do your columns contain atomic data to make your queries short and to the point?

there are no Dumb Questions

Q: Aren't atoms tiny, though? Shouldn't I be breaking my data down into *really* tiny pieces?

A: No. Making your data atomic means breaking it down into the smallest pieces that you need to create an efficient table, not just the smallest possible pieces you can.

Don't break down your data any more than you have to. if you don't need extra columns, don't add them just for the sake of it.

Q: How does atomic data help me?

A: It helps you ensure that the data in your table is accurate. For example, if you have a column for street numbers, you can make sure that only numbers end up in that column.

Atomic data also lets you perform queries more efficiently because the queries are easier to write and take a shorter amount of time to run, which adds up when you have a massive amount of data stored.

Sharpen your pencil

Here are the official rules of atomic data. For each rule, sketch out **two** hypothetical tables that violate each rule.

RULE 1: A column with atomic data can't have several values of the same *type* of data in *that* column.

Greg's my_contacts column interests violates this rule.

RULE 2: A table with atomic data can't have multiple columns with the same *type* of data.

The easy_drinks table violates this rule.

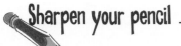

Sharpen your pencil Solution

Here are the official rules of atomic data. For each rule, sketch out **two** hypothetical tables that violate each rule.

RULE 1: A column with atomic data can't have several values of the same *type* of data in that column.

Of course, your answers will differ, but here is one example:

food_name	ingredients
bread	flour, milk, egg, yeast, oil
salad	lettuce, tomato, cucumber

Remember Greg's table? That has a column for hobbies that often contains multiple interests, making searching a nightmare!

It's the same here: imagine trying to find tomato amongst all those other ingredients.

RULE 2: A table with atomic data can't have multiple columns with the same *type* of data.

Too many student columns!

teacher	student1	student2	student3
Ms. Martini	Joe	Ron	Kelly
Mr. Howard	Sanjaya	Tim	Julie

Exercise

Now that you know the official rules and the three steps to making data atomic, take a look at each table from earlier in this book and explain why it is or isn't atomic.

Greg's table, page 47 ....

Donut rating table, page 78 ....

Clown table, page 121 ....

Drink table, page 59 ....

Fish info, page 160 ....

Reasons to be normal

When your data consultancy takes off and you need to hire more SQL database designers, wouldn't it be great if you didn't need to waste hours explaining how your tables work?

Well, making your tables NORMAL means they follow some standard rules your new designers will understand. And the good news is, our tables with atomic data are halfway there.

Making your data atomic is the first step in creating a NORMAL table.

Now that you know the official rules and the three steps to making data atomic, take a look at each table from earlier in this book and explain why it is or isn't atomic.

Greg's table, page 47 Not atomic. The "interest" and "seeking" columns violate rule 1.

Donut rating table, page 78 Atomic. Unlike the easy_drinks table, each column holds a different type of information. And, unlike the clown table "activities" column, each column has only one piece of information in it.

Clown table, page 121 Not atomic. The "activities" column has more than one activity in some records, and thus violates rule 1.

Drink table, page 59 Not atomic. There is more than one "ingredient" column, which violates rule 2.

Fish info, page 160 Atomic. Each column holds a different type of information. And each column has only one piece of information in it.

The benefits of normal tables

1. Normal tables won't have duplicate data, which will reduce the size of your database.

Avoiding duplicates will save your disk space.

2. With less data to search through, your queries will be faster.

My tables aren't that big. Why should I care about normalizing them?

Because, even when your tables are tiny, it adds up.

And tables grow. If you begin with a normalized table, you won't have to go back and change your table when your queries go too slowly.

Clowns aren't normal

Remember the clown table? Clown tracking has become a nationwide craze, and our old table isn't going to cut it because the `appearance` and `activities` columns contain *so* much data. For our purposes, this table is not atomic.

These two columns are really difficult to query because they contain so much data!

clown_info

name	last_seen	appearance	activities
Elsie	Cherry Hill Senior Center	F, red hair, green dress, huge feet	balloons, little car
Pickles	Jack Green's party	M, orange hair, blue suit, huge feet	mime
Snuggles	Ball-Mart	F, yellow shirt, baggy blue pants	horn, umbrella
Mr. Hobo	Eric Gray's Party	M, cigar, black hair, tiny hat	violin
Clarabelle	Belmont Senior Center	F, pink hair, huge flower, blue dress	yelling, dancing
Scooter	Oakland Hospital	M, blue hair, red suit, huge nose	balloons
Zippo	Millstone Mall	F, orange suit, baggy pants	singing
Babe	Earl's Autos	F, all pink and sparkly	balancing, little car
Bonzo	Dickson Park	M, in drag, polka dotted dress	singing, dancing
Sniffles	Tracy's	M, green and purple suit, pointy nose	climbing into tiny car

Sharpen your pencil

Let's make the clown table more atomic. Assuming you need to search on data in the `appearance` and `activities` columns, as well as `last_seen`, write down some better choices for columns.

Answers on page 195.

Halfway to 1NF

Remember, our table is only about halfway normal when it's got atomic data in it. When we're completely normal we'll be in the FIRST NORMAL FORM or 1NF.

To be 1NF, a table must follow these two rules:

We already know how to do this. →

Each row of data must contain atomic values.

To make our tables completely normal, we need to give each record a Primary Key. →

Each row of data must have a unique identifier, known as a <u>Primary Key</u>.

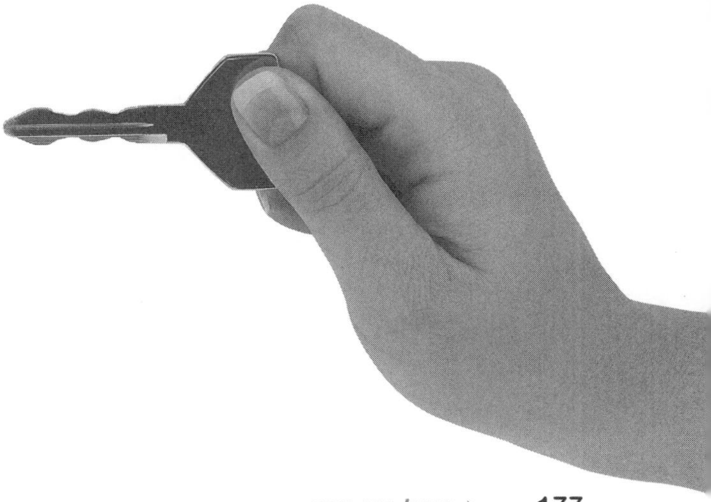

BRAIN POWER

What types of columns do you think would make good Primary Keys?

PRIMARY KEY rules

The column in your table that will be your primary key has to be designated as such when you create the table. In a few pages, we'll create a table and designate a primary key, but before that, let's take a closer look at what a primary key is.

A primary key is a column in your table that makes each record unique.

The primary key is used to uniquely identify each record

Which means that the data in the primary key column can't be repeated. Consider a table with the columns shown below. Do you think any of those would make good primary keys?

SSN	last_name	first_name	phone_number

Since Social Security Numbers are assigned uniquely to a particular person, maybe that could be a primary key.

These three columns can all contain duplicate values—for example, you will likely have a record for more than one person named John, or multiple people who live together and share a phone number, so they're probably not good choices for the primary key.

Watch it!

Take care using SSNs as the Primary Keys for your records.

With identity theft only increasing, people don't want to give out SSNs—and with good reason. They're too important to risk. Can you absolutely guarantee that your database is secure? If it's not, all those SSNs can be stolen, along with your customers' identities.

A primary key can't be NULL

If it's null, it can't be unique because other records can also be NULL.

The primary key must be given a value when the record is inserted

When you insert a record without a primary key, you run the risk of ending up with a NULL primary key and duplicate rows in your table, which violates First Normal Form.

The primary key must be compact

A primary key should contain only the information it needs to to be unique and nothing extra.

The primary key values can't be changed

If you could change the value of your key, you'd risk accidentally setting it to a value you already used. Remember, it has to remain unique.

BRAIN POWER

Given all these rules, can you think of a good primary key to use in a table?

Look back through the tables in the book. Do any of them have a column that contains truly unique values?

Wait, so if I can't use SSN as the primary key, but it still needs to be compact, not NULL, and unchangeable, what should I use?

The best primary key may be a *new* primary key.

When it comes to creating primary keys, your best bet may be to create a column that contains a unique number. Think of a table with people's info, but with an additional column containing a number. In the example below, let's call it `ID`.

If it weren't for the `ID` column, the records for John Brown would be identical. But in this case, they're actually two different people. The `ID` column makes these records unique. This table is in first normal form.

id	last_name	first_name	nick_name
1	Brown	John	John
2	Ellsworth	Kim	Kim
3	Brown	John	John
4	Petrillo	Maria	Maria
5	Franken	Esme	Em

A record for John Brown.

Also a record for John Brown, but the ID column shows that this is a unique record, so this is is a different John Brown from the first one.

Geek Bits

There's a big debate in the SQL world about using ***synthetic***, or made-up, primary keys (like the ID column above) versus using ***natural*** keys—data that is already in the table (like a VIN number on a car or SSN number). We won't take sides, but we will discuss primary keys in more detail in Chapter 7.

there are no Dumb Questions

Q: You said "first" normal form. Does that mean there's a second normal form? Or a third?

A: Yes, there are indeed second and third normal forms, each one adhering to increasingly rigid sets of rules. We'll cover second and third normal form in Chapter 7.

Q: So we've changed our tables to have atomic values. Are any of them in 1NF yet?

A: No. So far, not a single table we've created has a primary key, a unique value.

Q: The comments column in the doughnut table really doesn't seem atomic to me. I mean, there's no reasonable way to query that column easily.

A: You're absolutely correct. That field is not particularly atomic, but then our design of the table didn't require it to be. If we wanted to restrict the comments to a specific predetermined set of words, that field could be atomic. But then it wouldn't contain true, spontaneous comments.

Getting to NORMAL

It's time to step back and normalize our tables. We need to make our data atomic and add primary keys. Creating a primary key is normally something we do when we write our `CREATE TABLE` code.

BRAIN POWER

Do you remember how to add columns to an existing table?

Fixing Greg's table

From what you've seen so far, this is how you'd have to fix Greg's table:

Fixing Greg's table Step 1: SELECT all of your data and save it somehow.

Fixing Greg's table Step 2: Create a new normal table.

Fixing Greg's table Step 3: INSERT all that old data into the new table, changing each row to match the new table structure.

So now you can drop your old table.

Wait a second. I already have a table full of data. You can't seriously expect me to use the DROP TABLE command like I did in Chapter 1 and type in all that data again, just to create a primary key for each record...

So, we know that Greg's table isn't perfect.

It's not atomic and it has no primary key. But luckily for Greg, you ***don't*** have to live with the old table, and you **don't have to dump your data**.

We can add a primary key to Greg's table and make the columns more atomic using just one new command. But first, let's take a little trip to the past…

The CREATE TABLE we wrote

Greg needs a primary key, and after all the talk about atomic data, he realizes there are a few things he could do to make his columns more atomic. Before we look at how to fix the existing table, let's look at how we could have created the table in the first place!

Here's the table we created way back in Chapter 1.

```
CREATE TABLE my_contacts
(
    last_name VARCHAR(30),
    first_name VARCHAR(20),
    email VARCHAR(50),
    gender CHAR(1),
    birthday DATE,
    profession VARCHAR(50),
    location VARCHAR(50),
    status VARCHAR(20),
    interests VARCHAR(100),
    seeking VARCHAR(100)
);
```

No primary key here

Could these columns have been more atomic when we set up the table?

BRAIN POWER

But what if you don't have your old `CREATE TABLE` printed anywhere? Can you think of some way to get at the code?

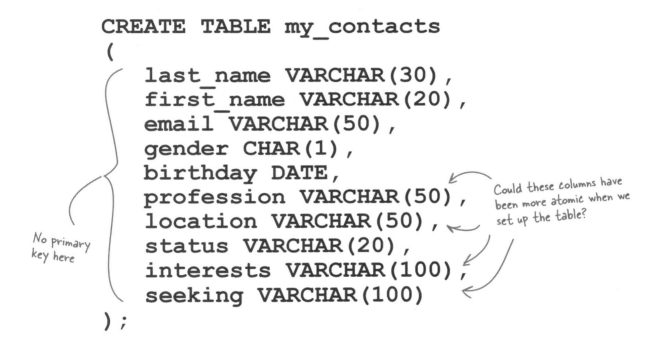

Show me the ~~money~~ table

What if you use the `DESCRIBE my_contacts` command to look at the code you used when you set up the table? You'll see something that looks a lot like this:

```
File  Edit  Window  Help  GregsListAgain
+------------+--------------+------+-----+---------+----------------+
| Column     | Type         | Null | Key | Default | Extra          |
+------------+--------------+------+-----+---------+----------------+
| last_name  | varchar(30)  | YES  |     | NULL    |                |
| first_name | varchar(20)  | YES  |     | NULL    |                |
| email      | varchar(50)  | YES  |     | NULL    |                |
| gender     | char(1)      | YES  |     | NULL    |                |
| birthday   | date         | YES  |     | NULL    |                |
| profession | varchar(50)  | YES  |     | NULL    |                |
| location   | varchar(50)  | YES  |     | NULL    |                |
| status     | varchar(20)  | YES  |     | NULL    |                |
| interests  | varchar(100) | YES  |     | NULL    |                |
| seeking    | varchar(100) | YES  |     | NULL    |                |
+------------+--------------+------+-----+---------+----------------+
```

But we really want to look at the **CREATE** code here, not the fields in the table, so we can figure out what we should have done at the very beginning without having to write the `CREATE` statement over again.

The statement `SHOW CREATE_TABLE` will return a `CREATE TABLE` statement that can exactly recreate our table, minus any data in it. This way, you can always see how the table you are looking at could be created. Try it:

```
SHOW CREATE TABLE my_contacts;
```

Time-saving command

Take a look at the code we used to create the table on page 183, and the code below that the SHOW CREATE TABLE my_contacts gives you. They aren't identical, but if you paste the code below into a CREATE TABLE command, the end result will be the same. You don't need to remove the backticks or data settings, but it's neater if you do.

The marks around the column names and the table name are called backticks. They show up when we run the SHOW CREATE TABLE command.

```
CREATE TABLE `my_contacts`
(
   `last_name` varchar(30) default NULL,
   `first_Name` varchar(20) default NULL,
   `email` varchar(50) default NULL,
   `gender` char(1) default NULL,
   `birthday` date default NULL,
   `profession` varchar(50) default NULL,
   `location` varchar(50) default NULL,
   `status` varchar(20) default NULL,
   `interests` varchar(100) default NULL,
   `seeking` varchar(100) default NULL,
) ENGINE=MyISAM DEFAULT CHARSET=latin1
```

Unless we tell the SQL software differently, it assumes all values are NULL by default.

It's a good idea to specify if a column can contain NULL or not when we create our table.

You don't need to worry about the last line of text after the closing parenthesis. It specifies how the data will be stored and what character set to use. The default settings are fine for now.

Unless you've deleted the original table, you'll have to give this one a new name.

Although you could make the code neater (by removing the last line and backticks), you can just copy and paste it to create a table.

The CREATE TABLE with a PRIMARY KEY

Here's the code our SHOW CREATE TABLE my_contacts gave us. We removed the backticks and last line. At the top of the column list we added a contact_id column that we're setting to NOT NULL, and at the bottom of the list, we're add a line PRIMARY KEY, which we set to use our new contact_id column as the primary key.

```
CREATE TABLE my_contacts
(
    contact_id INT NOT NULL,
    last_name varchar(30) default NULL,
    first_name varchar(20) default NULL,
    email varchar(50) default NULL,
    gender char(1) default NULL,
    birthday date default NULL,
    profession varchar(50) default NULL,
    location varchar(50) default NULL,
    status varchar(20) default NULL,
    interests varchar(100) default NULL,
    seeking varchar(100) default NULL,
    PRIMARY KEY (contact_id)
)
```

Remember, the primary key column has to be NOT NULL! If the primary key contains a value of NULL, or no value, you can't guarantee that it will uniquely identify each row of the table.

We've created a new column called contact_id that will hold an integer value that will be the primary key for our table. Each value in this column will be unique, and make our table atomic.

Here's where we specifying the primary key. Pretty simple syntax: we just say PRIMARY KEY and put in parentheses the name of the column we are using for it—in this case, our new contact_id column.

there are no Dumb Questions

Q: So you say that the PRIMARY KEY can't be NULL. What else keeps it from being duplicated?

A: Basically, you do. When you `INSERT` values into your table, you'll insert a value in the `contact_id` column that's new each time. For example, the first `INSERT` statement will set `contact_id` to `1`, the next `contact_id` will be `2`, etc.

Q: That's quite a pain to have to assign a new value to that PRIMARY KEY column each time I insert a new record. Isn't there an easier way?

A: There are two ways. One is using a column in your data that you know is unique as a primary key. We've mentioned that this is tricky (for example, the problem with using Social Security Numbers).

The easy way is to create an entirely new column just to hold a unique value, such as `contact_id` on the facing page. You can tell your SQL software to automatically fill in a number for you using keywords. Turn the page for details.

Q: Can I use SHOW for anything else besides the CREATE command?

A: You can use SHOW to display individual columns in your table:

```
SHOW COLUMNS FROM tablename;
```
This command will display all the columns in your table and their data type along with any other column-specific details.

```
SHOW CREATE DATABASE databasename;
```
Just like the SHOW CREATE table, you'll get the command that would exactly recreate your database.

```
SHOW INDEX FROM tablename;
```
This command will display any columns that are indexed and what type of index they have. So far, the only index we've looked at are primary keys, but this command will become more useful as you learn more.

And there's one more command that's VERY useful:

```
SHOW WARNINGS;
```
If you get a message on your console that your SQL command has caused warnings, type this to see the actual warnings.

There are quite a few more, but those are the ones that are related to things we've done so far.

Q: So what's up with that backtick character that shows up when I use a SHOW CREATE TABLE? Are you sure I don't need it?

A: It exists because sometimes your RDBMS might not be able to tell a column name is a column name. If you use the backticks around your column names, you can actually (although it's a very bad idea) use a reserved SQL keyword as a column name.

For example, suppose you wanted to name a column `select` for some bizarre reason. This column declaration wouldn't work:

```
select varchar(50)
```

But this declaration would work:

```
`select` varchar(50)
```

Q: What's wrong with using keywords as column names, then?

A: You're allowed to, but it's a bad idea. Imagine how confusing your queries would become, and the annoyance of typing those backticks when you can get away with not using them. Besides, `select` isn't a very good column name; it tells you nothing about what data is in it.

1, 2, 3... auto incrementally

Adding the keyword AUTO_INCREMENT to our contact_id column makes our SQL software automatically fill that column with a value that starts on row 1 with a value of 1 and goes up in increments of 1.

```
CREATE TABLE my_contacts
(
   contact_id INT NOT NULL AUTO_INCREMENT,
   last_name varchar(30) default NULL,
   first_name varchar(20) default NULL,
   email varchar(50) default NULL,
   gender char(1) default NULL,
   birthday date default NULL,
   profession varchar(50) default NULL,
   location varchar(50) default NULL,
   status varchar(20) default NULL,
   interests varchar(100) default NULL,
   seeking varchar(100) default NULL,
   PRIMARY KEY (contact_id)
)
```

That's it. Just add in the AUTO_INCREMENT keyword if you're using most flavors of SQL. (MS SQL users be warned, the keyword is INDEX, along with a starting value and increment value. Check your MS SQL reference for specific info.)

The keyword does pretty much what you'd expect it to: it starts at 1 and goes up by 1 each time you insert a new row.

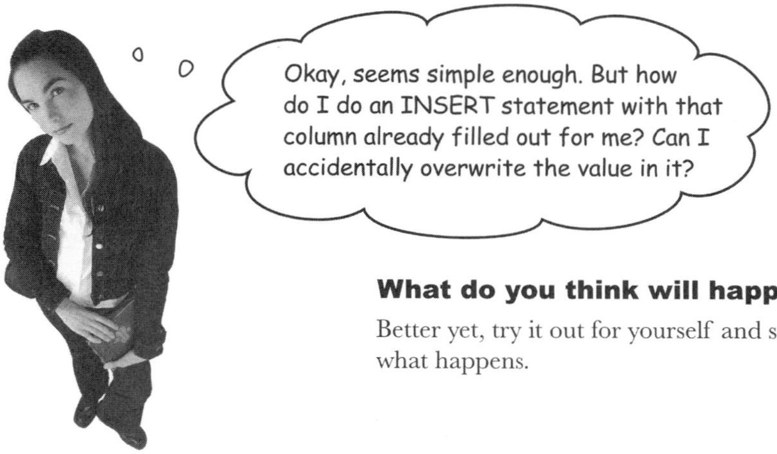
Okay, seems simple enough. But how do I do an INSERT statement with that column already filled out for me? Can I accidentally overwrite the value in it?

What do you think will happen?

Better yet, try it out for yourself and see what happens.

Exercise

1 Write a CREATE TABLE statement below to store first and last names of people. Your table should have a primary key column with AUTO_INCREMENT and two other atomic columns.

....

....

....

....

2 Open your SQL terminal or GUI interface and run your CREATE TABLE statement.

3 Try out each of the INSERT statements below. Circle the ones that work.

```
INSERT INTO your_table (id, first_name, last_name)
VALUES (NULL, 'Marcia', 'Brady');

INSERT INTO your_table (id, first_name, last_name)
VALUES (1, 'Jan', 'Brady');

INSERT INTO your_table
VALUES ('', 'Bobby', 'Brady');

INSERT INTO your_table (first_name, last_name)
VALUES ('Cindy', 'Brady');

INSERT INTO your_table (id, first_name, last_name)
VALUES (99, 'Peter', 'Brady');
```

4 Did all the Bradys make it? Sketch your table and its contents after trying the INSERT statements

your_table

id	first_name	last_name

Exercise Solution

1 Write a CREATE TABLE statement below. Your table should have a primary key column with AUTO_INCREMENT and two other atomic columns.

```
CREATE TABLE your_table
(
id INT NOT NULL AUTO_INCREMENT,
first_name VARCHAR(20),
last_name VARCHAR(30),
PRIMARY KEY (id)
);
```

2 Open your SQL terminal or GUI interface and run your CREATE TABLE statement.

3 Try out each of the INSERT statements below. Circle the ones that work.

```
INSERT INTO your_table (id, first_name, last_name)
VALUES (NULL, 'Marcia', 'Brady');

INSERT INTO your_table (id, first_name, last_name)
VALUES (1, 'Jan', 'Brady');

INSERT INTO your_table
VALUES ('', 'Bobby', 'Brady');

INSERT INTO your_table (first_name, last_name)
VALUES ('Cindy', 'Brady');

INSERT INTO your_table (id, first_name, last_name)
VALUES (99, 'Peter', 'Brady');
```

This last statement "works", but it overwrites the value in the AUTO_INCREMENT column.

4 Did all the Bradys make it? Sketch your table and its contents after trying the INSERT statements.

your_table

id	first_name	last_name
1	Marcia	Brady
2	Bobby	Brady
3	Cindy	Brady
99	Peter	Brady

Looks like we lost Jan because we tried to give her an index that was already assigned to Marcia. Marcia, Marcia, Marcia!

there are no Dumb Questions

Q: Why did the first query, the one with NULL for the `id` column, insert the row when `id` is NOT NULL?

A: Even though it seems like it shouldn't succeed, the AUTO_INCREMENT simply ignores the NULL. However, if it was not AUTO_INCREMENT, you would receive an error and it wouldn't insert the row. Give it a try.

Look, you're not reassuring me. Sure, I can paste in the code from SHOW CREATE TABLE, but I've still got the feeling that I'm going to have to drop my table and start over entering all those records again just to add the primary key column the second time around.

You won't have to start over; instead, you can use an ALTER statement.

A table with data in it doesn't have to be dumped, then dropped, then recreated. We can actually change an existing table. But to do that, we're going to borrow the `ALTER` statement and some of its keywords from Chapter 5.

Adding a PRIMARY KEY to an existing table

Here's the code to add an AUTO_INCREMENT primary
key to Greg's my_contacts table. (It's a long command,
so you'll need to turn your book.)

```
ALTER TABLE my_contacts
ADD COLUMN contact_id INT NOT NULL AUTO_INCREMENT FIRST,
ADD PRIMARY KEY (contact_id);
```

Here's our new SQL
command, ALTER.

ADD COLUMN does just that. It says
to add a column to the table and name
it contact_id.

Here's the code to add the
new column to the table.
Looks familiar, huh?!

You should recognize the line that
designates the primary key.

FIRST tells the software to
make the new column the first
one in the list. This is optional,
but it's good form to put your
primary key first.

BRAIN POWER

Do you think that this will add values to the new contact_id column for records
already in the table or only for newly inserted records? How can you check?

ALTER TABLE and add a PRIMARY KEY

Try the code yourself. Open your SQL terminal. `USE` the `gregs_list` database, and type in this command:

```
File Edit Window Help Alterations
> ALTER TABLE my_contacts
    -> ADD COLUMN contact_id INT NOT NULL AUTO_INCREMENT FIRST,
    -> ADD PRIMARY KEY (contact_id);

Query OK, 50 rows affected (0.04 sec)
Records: 50  Duplicates: 0  Warnings: 0
```

This tells us that it added the column to the 50 records we already have in our table. You won't have this many.

That's slick! I have a primary key, complete with values. Can ALTER TABLE help me add a phone number column?

To see what happened to your table, try a
SELECT * from my_contacts;

```
File Edit Window Help Alterations
+------------+-----------+------------+-------------------
| contact_id | last_name | first_name | email
+------------+-----------+------------+-------------------
|     1      | Anderson  | Jillian    | jill_anderson@yahoo.c
|     2      | Joffe     | Kevin      | kj@simuduck.com
|     3      | Newsome   | Amanda     | aman2luv@yahoo.com
|     4      | Garcia    | Ed         | ed99@mysoftware.com
|     5      | Roundtree | Jo-Ann     | jojo@yahoo.com
|     6      | Briggs    | Chris      | cbriggs@mymail.com
```

The contact_id column has been added first in the table before all the other columns.

Because we used AUTO_INCREMENT, the column was filled in as each record in the table was updated.

The next time we INSERT a new record, the contact_id column will be given a value one higher than the highest contact_id in the table. If the last record has a contact_id of 23, the next one will be 24.

Remember, this isn't the end of the table; Greg has a lot of contacts.

Will Greg get his phone number column? Turn to Chapter 5 to find out.

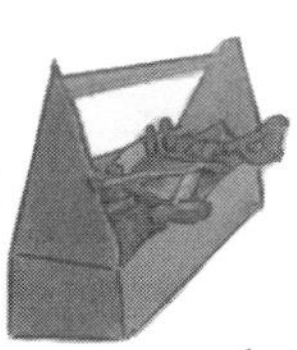

Your SQL Toolbox

You've got Chapter 4 under your belt. Look at all the new tools you've added to your toolbox now! For a complete list of tooltips in the book, see Appendix iii.

ATOMIC DATA

Data in your columns is atomic if it's been broken down into the smallest pieces that you need.

ATOMIC DATA RULE 1:

Atomic data can't have several bits of the same type of data in the same column.

ATOMIC DATA RULE 2:

Atomic data can't have multiple columns with the same type of data.

SHOW CREATE TABLE

Use this command to see the correct syntax for creating an existing table.

FIRST NORMAL FORM (1NF)

Each row of data must contain atomic values, and each row of data must have a unique identifier.

PRIMARY KEY

A column or set of columns that uniquely identifies a row of data in a table

AUTO_INCREMENT

When used in your column declaration, that column will automatically be given a unique integer value each time an INSERT command is performed.

Sharpen your pencil Solution

Let's make the clown table more atomic. Assuming you need to search on data in the `appearance` and `activities` columns, as well as `last_seen`, write down some better choices for columns.

There's no definite correct answer here.

The best you can do is to pull out things like gender, shirt color, pant color, hat type, musical instrument, transportation, balloons (yes or no for values), singing (yes or no for values), dancing (yes or no for values).

To make this table atomic, you've got to get those multiple activities into separate columns, and those multiple appearance features separated out.

Bonus points if you wanted to separate out the location column into address, city, and state!

5 ALTER

Rewriting the Past

If I had it to do over again, I would have gone for a bubble bath.

Ever wished you could correct the mistakes of your past?

Well, now is your chance. By using the **ALTER command**, you can apply all the lessons you've been learning to tables you designed days, months, even years ago. Even better, you can do it without affecting your data. By the time you're through here, you'll know what **normal** really means, and you'll be able to apply it to all your tables, past and present.

We need to make some changes

Greg wants to make a few more changes to his table, but he doesn't want to lose any data.

```
File Edit Window Help KeyedUp
+-------------+------------+-------------+-------------------
| contact_id  | last_name  | first_name  | email
+-------------+------------+-------------+-------------------
|     1       | Anderson   | Jillian     | jill_anderson@yahoo
|     2       | Joffe      | Kevin       | kj@simuduck.com
|     3       | Newsome    | Amanda      | aman2luv@yahoo.com
|     4       | Garcia     | Ed          | ed99@mysoftware.co
|     5       | Roundtree  | Jo-Ann      | jojo@yahoo.com
|     6       | Brigg      | Chri        | cbriggs
```

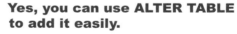

So, I *can* add that phone number column after all?

Yes, you can use ALTER TABLE to add it easily.

In fact, we think you should take a stab at it yourself since you've already met the `ALTER` command. Do the next exercise to get your code!

Sharpen your pencil

Take a close look at the ALTER TABLE command we used to add the primary key column in Chapter 4, and see if you can come up with your own command to add a phone column that can hold 10 digits. Note that you won't need to use all of the keywords in your new command.

```
ALTER TABLE my_contacts
ADD COLUMN contact_id INT NOT NULL AUTO_INCREMENT FIRST,
ADD PRIMARY KEY (contact_id);
```

Write your ALTER TABLE command here:

....

....

....

You can even tell the software where to put the phone column with the keyword AFTER. See if you can work out where to put the keyword to ADD the new column right after the first_name column.

Write your new ALTER TABLE command here:

....

....

....

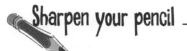

Sharpen your pencil Solution

Take a close look at the ALTER TABLE command we used to add the primary key column in Chapter 4, and see if you can come up with your own command to add that phone column. Note that you won't need to use all of the keywords in your new command.

```
ALTER TABLE my_contacts
ADD COLUMN contact_id INT NOT NULL AUTO_INCREMENT FIRST,
ADD PRIMARY KEY (contact_id);
```

The keywords we left out from the previous example are NOT NULL, AUTO_INCREMENT, and FIRST.

Write your ALTER TABLE command here:

```
ALTER TABLE my_contacts
ADD COLUMN phone VARCHAR(10);
```

The name of the table we're altering is still my_contacts.

We made an assumption that all our phone numbers will be 10 characters long. Greg didn't think about numbers for other countries.

Here's the bit that tells the ALTER command exactly how you want to change the table.

The name of the new column is phone.

You can even tell the software where to put the phone column with the keyword AFTER. See if you can work out where to put the keyword to ADD the new column right after the first_name column.

Write your new ALTER TABLE command here:

```
ALTER TABLE my_contacts
ADD COLUMN phone VARCHAR(10)
AFTER first_name;
```

The keyword AFTER followed by the name of the column you want the new column to be. This puts the phone column right after the first_name column.

AFTER is optional. If you don't use it, the column is added to the end of the table.

You've seen that you can use the keywords *FIRST* and *AFTER your_column*, but you can also use *BEFORE your_column* and *LAST*. And *SECOND*, and *THIRD,* and you get the idea.

Behind the Scenes

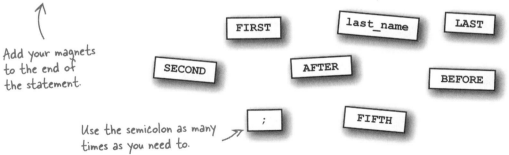

SQL Keywords Magnets

Use the magnets below to change the position of the phone column that's being added. Create as many different commands as you can, then sketch in the columns after you've run the command.

phone	contact_id	last_name	first_name	email

```
ALTER TABLE my_contacts
ADD COLUMN phone VARCHAR(10)
```

contact_id	last_name	first_name	email	phone

```
ALTER TABLE my_contacts
ADD COLUMN phone VARCHAR(10)
```

contact_id	phone	last_name	first_name	email

```
ALTER TABLE my_contacts
ADD COLUMN phone VARCHAR(10)
```

contact_id	last_name	phone	first_name	email

```
ALTER TABLE my_contacts
ADD COLUMN phone VARCHAR(10)
```

Add your magnets to the end of the statement.

Magnets: FIRST, last_name, LAST, SECOND, AFTER, BEFORE, ;, FIFTH

Use the semicolon as many times as you need to.

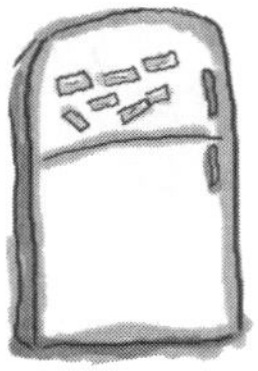

SQL Keywords Magnets SOLUTION

Use the magnets below to change the position of the phone column that's being added. Create as many different commands as you can, then sketch in the columns after you've run the command.

```
ALTER TABLE my_contacts
ADD COLUMN phone VARCHAR(10) FIRST ;
```

FIRST puts the phone column before all the other columns.

phone	contact_id	last_name	first_name	email

```
ALTER TABLE my_contacts
ADD COLUMN phone VARCHAR(10) LAST ;

ALTER TABLE my_contacts
ADD COLUMN phone VARCHAR(10) FIFTH ;

ALTER TABLE my_contacts
ADD COLUMN phone VARCHAR(10) ;
```

LAST puts the phone column after all the other columns, and so does FIFTH and not adding a position at all.

contact_id	last_name	first_name	email	phone

```
ALTER TABLE my_contacts
ADD COLUMN phone VARCHAR(10) SECOND ;

ALTER TABLE my_contacts
ADD COLUMN phone VARCHAR(10)
BEFORE last_name ;
```

SECOND puts the phone column second, and so does BEFORE (if you use it with the last_name column).

contact_id	phone	last_name	first_name	email

```
ALTER TABLE my_contacts
ADD COLUMN phone VARCHAR(10)
AFTER last_name ;
```

AFTER last_name puts the phone column third. If you'd had a THIRD magnet, that would have done the same thing.

contact_id	last_name	phone	first_name	email

Table altering

The ALTER command allows you to change almost everything in your table without having to reinsert your data. But be careful, if you change a column of one data type to a different one, you risk losing your data.

Dataville Alterations

OUR SERVICES FOR EXISTING TABLES:

CHANGE both the name and data type of an existing column *

MODIFY the data type or position of an existing column *

ADD a column to your table—you pick the data type

DROP a column from your table *

*** Possible loss of data may occur, no guarantees offered.**

ADDITIONAL SERVICES

Rearrange your columns
(only available when using ADD)

It's just a little alteration, it won't hurt a bit.

BRAIN POWER

Why might this table need altering?

projekts

number	descriptionofproj	contractoronjob
1	outside house painting	Murphy
2	kitchen remodel	Valdez
3	wood floor installation	Keller
4	roofing	Jackson

Extreme table makeover

Let's start our alterations with a table in need of a major makeover.

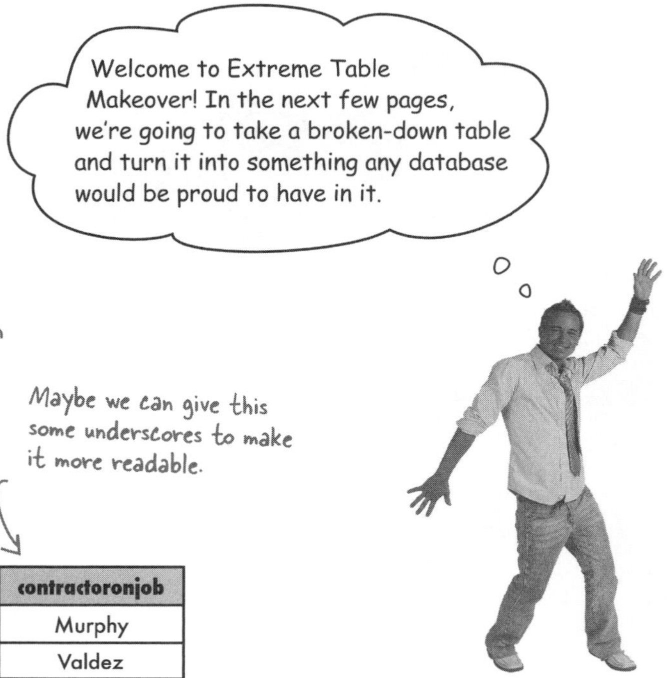

Welcome to Extreme Table Makeover! In the next few pages, we're going to take a broken-down table and turn it into something any database would be proud to have in it.

This doesn't tell us enough about what this table is supposed to contain.

This column name tells us nothing about what's in it.

Maybe we can give this some underscores to make it more readable.

projekts

number	descriptionofproj	contractoronjob
1	outside house painting	Murphy
2	kitchen remodel	Valdez
3	wood floor installation	Keller
4	roofing	Jackson

While the table and column names aren't great, the data in the table is valid, and we'd like to keep it.

Let's use DESCRIBE to see how this table is constructed. This shows us if a columns is the primary key and what type of data is being stored in each column.

```
File Edit Window Help BadTableDesign
--> DESCRIBE projekts;
+-------------------+-------------+------+-----+---------+-------+
| Field             | Type        | Null | Key | Default | Extra |
+-------------------+-------------+------+-----+---------+-------+
| number            | int(11)     | YES  |     | NULL    |       |
| descriptionofproj | varchar(50) | YES  |     | NULL    |       |
| contractoronjob   | varchar(10) | YES  |     | NULL    |       |
+-------------------+-------------+------+-----+---------+-------+
3 rows in set (0.01 sec)
```

Renaming the table

The table has some problems in its current state, but thanks to ALTER, we will make it suitable to contain a list of home improvement projects needed for a particularly run-down house. Our first step will be to use ALTER TABLE and give our table a meaningful name.

"projekts" is the old name of our table.

```
ALTER TABLE projekts
RENAME TO project_list;
```

It's practically English! We want to RENAME our table.

"project_list" is the new name we're giving our table.

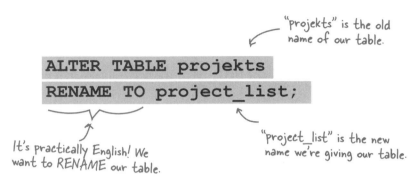

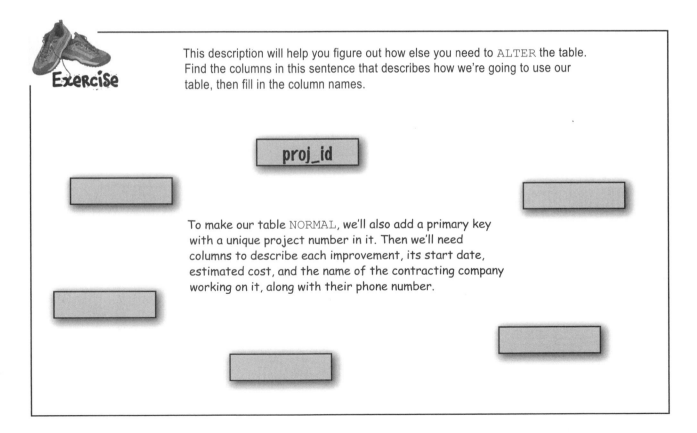

This description will help you figure out how else you need to ALTER the table. Find the columns in this sentence that describes how we're going to use our table, then fill in the column names.

proj_id

To make our table NORMAL, we'll also add a primary key with a unique project number in it. Then we'll need columns to describe each improvement, its start date, estimated cost, and the name of the contracting company working on it, along with their phone number.

Exercise Solution

This description will help you figure out how else you need to ALTER the table. Find the columns in this sentence that describes how we're going to use our table, then fill in the column names.

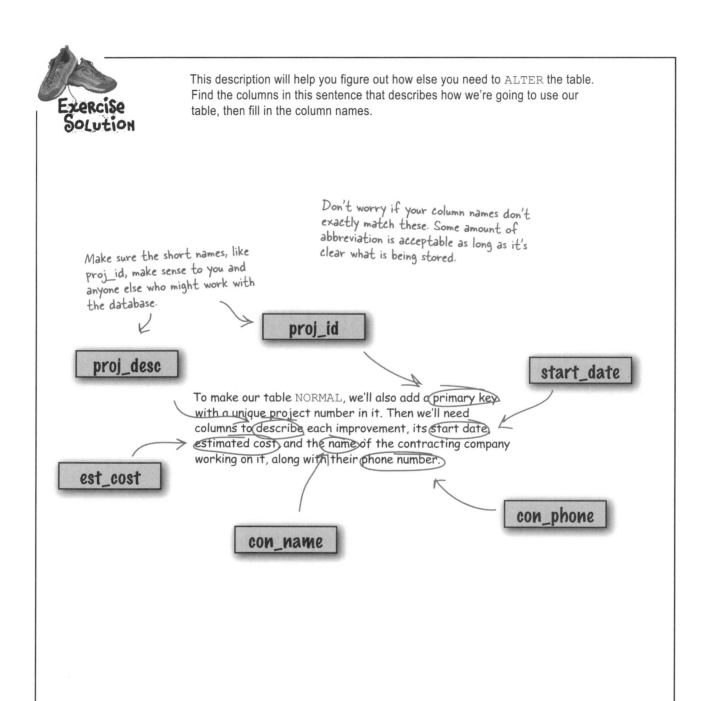

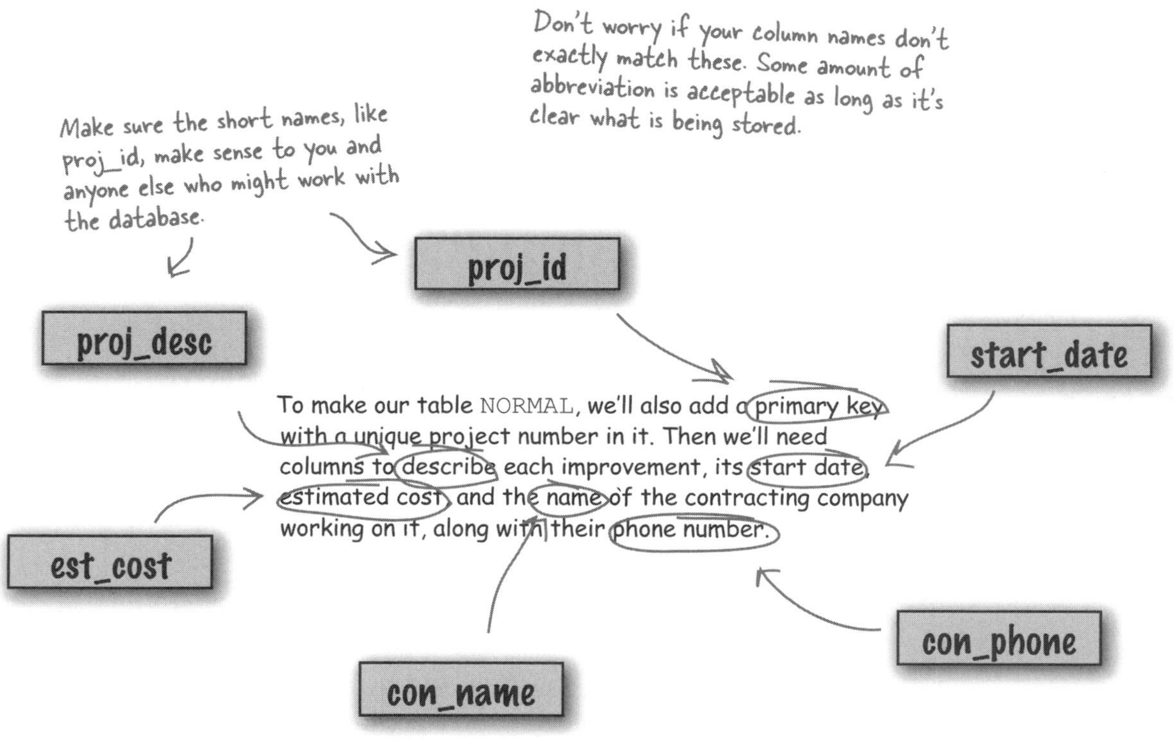
Don't worry if your column names don't exactly match these. Some amount of abbreviation is acceptable as long as it's clear what is being stored.
Make sure the short names, like proj_id, make sense to you and anyone else who might work with the database.
proj_id
proj_desc
start_date
To make our table NORMAL, we'll also add a primary key with a unique project number in it. Then we'll need columns to describe each improvement, its start date, estimated cost, and the name of the contracting company working on it, along with their phone number.
est_cost
con_phone
con_name

We need to make some plans

project_list

number	descriptionofproj	contractoronjob
1	outside house painting	Murphy
2	kitchen remodel	Valdez
3	wood floor installation	Keller
4	roofing	Jackson

It appears that data for three of our new columns is already in place. Instead of creating all new columns, we can RENAME our existing columns. By renaming these columns that contain valid data, we won't need to insert the data into new columns.

BRAIN POWER

Which existing column might be a good candidate for our primary key?

Retooling our columns

Now we have a plan to get us started,and we can `ALTER` the columns already in our table so they fit with three of our new column names:

- `number` is our primary key: **`proj_id`**
- `descriptionofproj` is a description of each improvement project: **`proj_desc`**
- `contractoronjob` is the name of the contracting company, or **`con_name`** for short

That just leaves us with the three columns called `est_cost`, `con_phone`, and `start_date` to add.

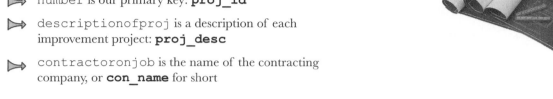

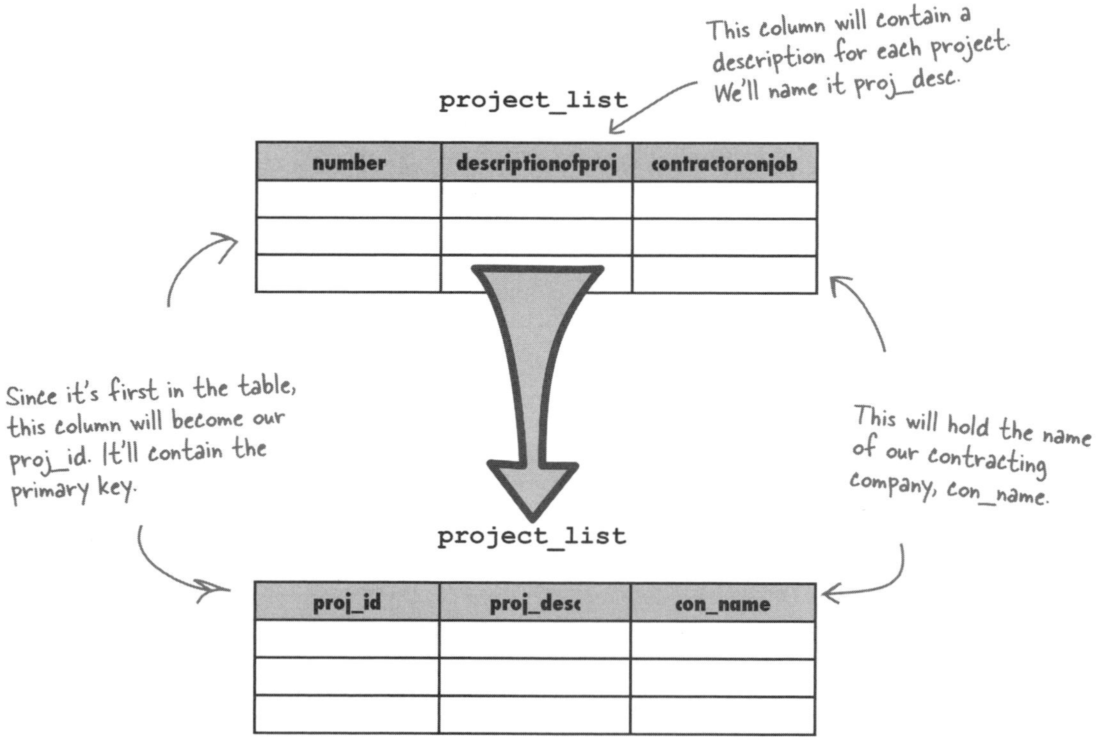

This column will contain a description for each project. We'll name it proj_desc.
project_list
number
descriptionofproj
contractoronjob
Since it's first in the table, this column will become our proj_id. It'll contain the primary key.
This will hold the name of our contracting company, con_name.
project_list
proj_id
proj_desc
con_name

Structural changes

We've decided to use existing columns for three of our needed columns. Beyond just changing the names, we should take a closer look at the data type that each of these columns stores.

Here's the description we looked at earlier.

```
File Edit Window Help BadTableDesign
--> DESCRIBE projekts;
+------------------+------------+------+-----+---------+-------+
| Field            | Type       | Null | Key | Default | Extra |
+------------------+------------+------+-----+---------+-------+
| number           | int(11)    | YES  |     | NULL    |       |
| descriptionofproj | varchar(50) | YES |     | NULL    |       |
| contractoronjob  | varchar(10) | YES  |     | NULL    |       |
+------------------+------------+------+-----+---------+-------+
3 rows in set (0.01 sec)
```

BRAIN BARBELL

Look at each of the columns' Type and decide if the current types are suitable for future data that we might be storing in this table.

ALTER and CHANGE

For our next step, we'll change the column `number` to have a new name, `proj_id`, and set it to `AUTO_INCREMENT`. Then we'll make it a primary key. It sounds complicated, but it really isn't. In fact, you can do it all in just one command:

This time we're using CHANGE COLUMN since we're changing both the name and the data type of the column formerly known as "number".

We're still using the same table, but remember, we gave it a new name.

"proj_id" is the new name we want our column to have...

... and we want it filled with auto incrementing integers and no NULL values.

```
ALTER TABLE project_list
CHANGE COLUMN number proj_id INT NOT NULL AUTO_INCREMENT,
ADD PRIMARY KEY ('proj_id');
```

Here's the part that tells our SQL software to use the newly named proj_id column as the primary key.

Sharpen your pencil

Sketch how the table will look after you run the command above.

Answers on page 233.

Change two columns with one SQL statement

We're going to change not one, but two columns in *just one statement*. We'll alter the names of the columns called `descriptionofproj` and `contractoronjob`, and at the same time we're also going to change their data types. All we have to do is include both `CHANGE COLUMN` lines in one `ALTER TABLE` statement and put a comma between them.

"descriptionofproj" is the name of the old column that we're changing in this command.

"proj_desc" is the column's new name.

We're increasing the number of characters so we can have longer descriptions.

```
ALTER TABLE project_list
CHANGE COLUMN descriptionofproj proj_desc VARCHAR(100),
CHANGE COLUMN contractoronjob con_name VARCHAR(30);
```

The other old column name, "contractoronjob", is also going to be changed...

... to con_name, and here's its new data type.

Watch it!

If you change the data type to something new, you may lose data.

If the data type you're changing to isn't compatible with the old data type, your command won't be carried out, and your SQL software will tell you that you have an error in your statement.

*But worse news is that if they **are** compatible types, your data might be **truncated**.*

For example: going from varchar(10) to char(1), your data will change from 'Bonzo' to just 'B'

The same thing applies to numeric types. You can change from one type to another, but your data will be converted to the new type, and you may lose part of your data!

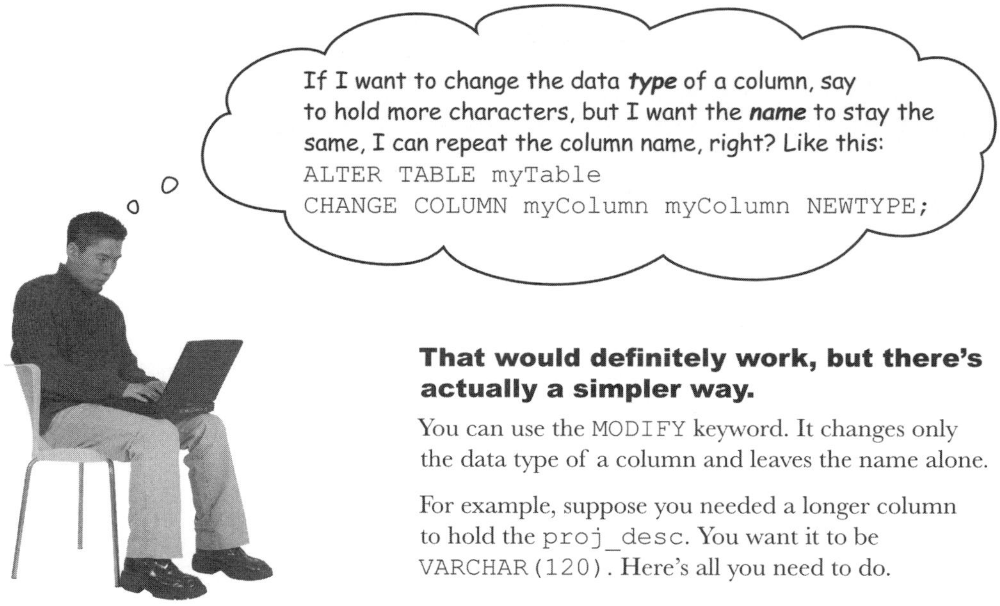
If I want to change the data *type* of a column, say to hold more characters, but I want the *name* to stay the same, I can repeat the column name, right? Like this:
ALTER TABLE myTable
CHANGE COLUMN myColumn myColumn NEWTYPE;

That would definitely work, but there's actually a simpler way.

You can use the MODIFY keyword. It changes only the data type of a column and leaves the name alone.

For example, suppose you needed a longer column to hold the proj_desc. You want it to be VARCHAR(120). Here's all you need to do.

```
ALTER TABLE project_list
MODIFY COLUMN proj_desc VARCHAR(120);
```

The name of the column we're modifying.

The new data type.

And of course you've made sure that the new data type won't cause you to truncate your old data!

there are no Dumb Questions

Q: What if I want ot change the order of my columns? Can I just do: ALTER TABLE MODIFY COLUMN proj_desc AFTER con_name;

A: You can't actually change the column order once the table already has been created. The best you can do is to add a new column into the position you want and drop the old one, but you'll lose all the data in the old column.

Q: But isn't it going to be a problem if the columns are stored in the wrong order?

A: No, because fortunately, in your SELECT queries, you can specify the order in which your columns will be displayed in the query results. It doesn't matter what order the data is stored in on your hard drive, since you can:

```
SELECT column3, column1 FROM your_table;
```

or:

```
SELECT column1, column3 FROM your_table;
```

or any other order you wish.

Exercise

Hey, I'm on the phone with my agent. You go ahead and add in those remaining columns, will you?

project_list

proj_id	proj_desc	con_name
1		
2		
3		

We still need to add in three more columns: a **phone number**, a **start date**, and an **estimated cost**.

Write a single ALTER TABLE statement below to do this, making sure to pay attention to those data types. Then complete the finished table below.

project_list

Exercise Solution

Hey, I'm on the phone with my agent. You go ahead and add in those remaining columns, will you?

project_list

proj_id	proj_desc	con_name
1		
2		
3		

We still need to add in three more columns: a **phone number**, a **start date**, and an **estimated cost**.

Write a single ALTER TABLE statement below to do this, making sure to pay attention to those data types. Then complete the finished table below.

```
ALTER TABLE project_table
ADD COLUMN con_phone VARCHAR(10),
ADD COLUMN start_date DATE,
ADD COLUMN est_cost DECIMAL(7,2);
```

A VARCHAR of 10 allows us to add the area code.

We're adding new columns, so we're using ADD.

Remember our DEC fields? We've set this so it's 7 digits long with two decimal places.

project_list

proj_id	proj_desc	con_name	con_phone	start_date	est_cost
1					
2					
3					

Quick! DROP that column

Stop everything!

We just found out that our project has been placed on hold. As a result, we can drop our `start_date` column. There's no point in having an unnecessary column lying about taking up space in the database.

It's good programming practice to have only the columns you need in your table. If you aren't using a column, drop it. With `ALTER`, you can easily add it back again, if you need it in the future.

The more columns you have, the harder your RDBMS has to work, and the more space your database takes up. While you might not notice it with a small table, when your tables grow, you'll see slower results, and your computer's processor will have to work that much harder.

Sharpen your pencil

Actually, you go ahead and write the SQL statement to drop the start_date column. We haven't shown you the syntax for it yet, but give it a try.

....

....

....

Sharpen your pencil Solution

Actually, you go ahead and write the SQL statement to drop the start_date column. We haven't shown you the syntax for it yet, but give it a try.

Here's our project_list.

```
ALTER TABLE project_table
DROP COLUMN start_date;
```

If you want to drop the start_date column, you can use the DROP command. That was easy!

The column to remove from the table

Watch it!

Once you've dropped a column, everything that was stored in it is removed too!

Use DROP COLUMN very cautiously. First you may want to do a SELECT from the column that you intend to drop to make absolutely certain that you want to drop it! You're better off having extra data in your table than missing a vital bit of data.

Exercise

Pimp My Table

It's time to turn your tired old hooptie table into a date magnet and take it to a level of table pimpification you never knew existed.

It's simple. Take this sorry little "before" table with used car data and `ALTER` it into that shiny, gorgeous "after" table. Part of the difficulty is to not disturb any of the data in the table, but to work around it. Are you up to the challenge?

Bonus points if you can do it all with a single `ALTER TABLE` statement.

Before

hooptie

color	year	make	mo	howmuch
silver	1998	Porsche	Boxter	17992.540
NULL	2000	Jaguar	XJ	15995
red	2002	Cadillac	Escalade	40215.9

After

car_table

car_id	VIN	make	model	color	year	price
1	RNKLK66N33G213481	Porsche	Boxter	silver	1998	17992.54
2	SAEDA44B175B04113	Jaguar	XJ	NULL	2000	15995.00
3	3GYEK63NT2G280668	Cadillac	Escalade	red	2002	40215.90

Exercise Solution

Pimp My Table

It's time to turn your tired old hooptie table into a date magnet and take it to a level of table pimpification you never knew existed.

It's simple. Take this sorry little "before" table with used car data and ALTER it into that shiny, gorgeous "after" table. Part of the difficulty is to not disturb any of the data in the table, but to work around it. Are you up to the challenge?

Bonus points if you can do it all with a single ALTER TABLE statement.

Before

hooptie

color	year	make	mo	howmuch
silver	1998	Porsche	Boxter	17992.540
NULL	2000	Jaguar	XJ	15995
red	2002	Cadillac	Escalade	40215.9

After

car_table

car_id	VIN	make	model	color	year	price
1	RNKLK66N33G213481	Porsche	Boxter	silver	1998	17992.54
2	SAEDA44B175B04113	Jaguar	XJ	NULL	2000	15995.00
3	3GYEK63NT2G280668	Cadillac	Escalade	red	2002	40215.90

You could have done a DESCRIBE first so you could see what the data types of each column were to be sure you weren't truncating any data.

```
ALTER TABLE hooptie
RENAME TO car_table,
ALTER TABLE car_table
ADD COLUMN car_id INT NOT NULL AUTO_INCREMENT FIRST,
ADD PRIMARY KEY (car_id),
ALTER TABLE car_table
ADD COLUMN VIN VARCHAR(16) SECOND,
CHANGE COLUMN mo model VARCHAR(20),
MODIFY COLUMN color AFTER model,
MODIFY COLUMN year SIXTH,
CHANGE COLUMN howmuch price DECIMAL(7,2);
```

You need to rename the column called "mo" to "model" before you move the color and year columns after it.

You have to give the renamed column "model" a data type.

You could also have put "year AFTER model" or "year BEFORE price."

there are no Dumb Questions

Q: Earlier you said that I couldn't reorder my columns with MODIFY. But my SQL software tool lets me reorder them. How is it doing that?

A: Your software is actually doing a bunch of commands behind the scenes. It is copying the values from the column you wish to move, saving them into a temporary table, dropping the column you wish to move, altering your table and creating a new column with the same name as the old one where you want it to be, copying all the values from the temporary table back into your new column, and deleting the temporary table.

It's usually better just to leave the position of your columns alone if they already have data in them and you aren't using software to do all those steps for you. You can SELECT your columns in any order you like.

Q: The only time it's easy to change the column order is when I'm adding in a new column?

A: Correct. The best choice is to think about the order as you design the table in the first place.

Q: What if I accidentally created a primary key, and then changed my mind and wanted to use a different column? Is there a way to remove the primary key designation without changing the data in it?

A: There is, and it's simple:

```
ALTER TABLE your_table DROP PRIMARY
KEY;
```

Q: What about AUTO_INCREMENT?

A: You can add it to a column that doesn't have it like this:

```
ALTER TABLE your_table CHANGE your_id
your_id INT(11) NOT NULL AUTO_INCREMENT;
```

And you can remove it like this:

```
ALTER TABLE your_table CHANGE your_id
your_id INT(11) NOT NULL;
```

It's important to keep in mind that you can only have one AUTO_INCREMENT field per table, it has to be an INTEGER data type and it can't contain NULL.

BULLET POINTS

- Use `CHANGE` when you want to change both the name and the data type of a column.
- Use `MODIFY` when you wish to change only the data type.
- `DROP COLUMN` does just that: it drops the named column from the table.
- Use `RENAME` to change the name of your table.
- You can change the order of your columns using `FIRST`, `LAST`, `BEFORE column_name`, `AFTER column_name`, `SECOND`, `THIRD`, `FOURTH`, etc.
- With some RDBMSs, you can only change the order of columns in a table when you add them to a table.

My table now has a primary key and a phone number column. But it's still not very atomic. Some of the queries I need to do are difficult—for example, querying by the state in the location field.

ALTER TABLE can help you improve your table design

By using `ALTER TABLE` together with `SELECT` and `UPDATE`, we can take awkward, non-atomic data columns and refine them into precise atomic columns. It's all about combining the SQL statements you've already learned in the right ways.

Let's take a look at the `CREATE TABLE` statement for Greg's `my_contacts` table.

```
CREATE TABLE my_contacts
(
    contact_id INT NOT NULL AUTO_INCREMENT
    last_name VARCHAR(30) default NULL,
    first_name VARCHAR(20) default NULL,
    email VARCHAR(50) default NULL,
    gender CHAR(1) default NULL,
    birthday DATE default NULL,
    profession VARCHAR(50) default NULL,
    location VARCHAR(50) default NULL,
    status VARCHAR(20) default NULL,
    interests VARCHAR(100) default NULL,
    seeking VARCHAR(100) default NULL,
    PRIMARY KEY (contact_id)
)
```

We added these two lines to create and designate our primary key.

These four columns aren't very atomic and could use some tweaking with ALTER TABLE.

A closer look at the non-atomic location column

Sometimes Greg just wants to know someone's state or city, so the `location` column is a good candidate to break apart into two columns. Let's see what the data in the column looks like:

A bit of the data from the location column of the my_contacts table.

Seattle, WA ← Two letter state abbreviation.
Natchez, MS ←
Las Vegas, NV
Palo Alto, CA
City name. → NYC, NY ← A comma.

This data is consistently formatted. First is the city name, followed by a comma, and then a two-letter state abbreviation. Because the data is consistent, we can separate the city from the state.

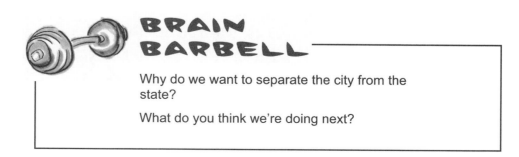

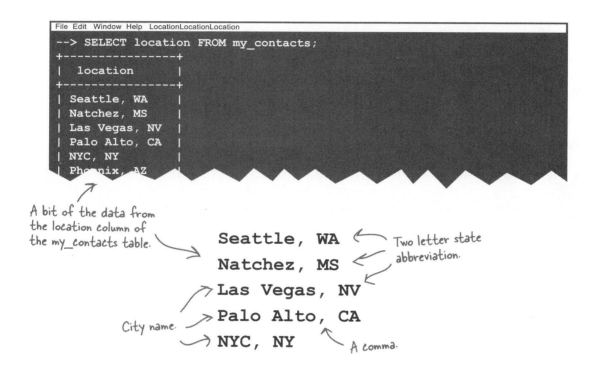

BRAIN BARBELL

Why do we want to separate the city from the state?

What do you think we're doing next?

Look for patterns

Every location column in the `my_contacts` table follows the same pattern: City Name, followed by a comma, and then the two-letter state abbreviation. The that fact it's consistent and follows a pattern will help us break it down so it's more atomic.

City Name, XX

These last two characters always contain the state abbreviation. If we had a state column in our table, this is the data we'd want in it.

This comma that's always in front of the state abbreviation may come in handy...

We can grab everything in front of the comma so we can put it in a column containing `city names`.

City Name ,

We need a function that allows us to grab everything before the comma...

And we can take the last two characters of our location column to put in a new column called `state`.

XX

... And we need a function that will grab. the last two characters.

Sharpen your pencil

Write an ALTER TABLE statement that adds city and state columns to my_contacts.

....

....

....

```
ALTER TABLE my_contacts
ADD COLUMN city VARCHAR(50),
ADD COLUMN state CHAR(2);
```

A few handy string functions

We've located two patterns. Now we need to grab the state abbreviation and add it to a new **state** column. We also need everything in front of the comma for a **city** column. After we create our new columns, here's how we can extract the values we need:

Text values and values stored in CHAR or VARCHAR columns are known as strings.

To SELECT the last two characters

Use RIGHT() and LEFT() to select a **specified number of characters** from a column.

```
SELECT RIGHT(location, 2) FROM my_contacts;
```

Start at the RIGHT side of the column. (You can use LEFT in exactly the same way.)

This is the column to use.

This is how many characters to select from the RIGHT side of the column.

String functions allow you to select part of a text column.

To SELECT everything in front of the comma

Use SUBSTRING_INDEX() to grab part of the column, or substring. This one will find everything **in front** of a **specific character or string**. So we can put our comma in quotes, and SUBSTRING_INDEX() will select everything in front of it.

```
SELECT SUBSTRING_INDEX(location, ',', 1) FROM my_contacts;
```

This grabs part of the column, or substring. It looks for the string in single quotes (in this case, it's a comma) and grabs everything in front of it.

Again, the column name.

Here's the comma the command is looking for.

This is the tricky part. It's "1" because it's looking for the first comma. If it were "2" it would keep going until it found a second comma and grab everything in front of that.

Try this at home

Exercise

SQL possesses a number of functions that let you manipulate string values in your tables. Strings are stored in text columns, typically `VARCHAR` or `CHAR` data types.

Here's a list of some of the more common and helpful string functions. Try each one for yourself by typing in the `SELECT` statements.

`SUBSTRING(your_string, start_position, length)` gives you part of `your_string`, starting at the letter in the `start_position`. `length` is how much of the string you get back.

```
SELECT SUBSTRING('San Antonio, TX', 5, 3);
```

`UPPER(your_string)` and **`LOWER(your_string)`** will change everything in the string to uppercase or lowercase, respectively.

```
SELECT UPPER('uSa');

SELECT LOWER('spaGHEtti');
```

`REVERSE(your_string)` does just that; it reverses the order of letters in your string.

```
SELECT REVERSE('spaGHEtti');
```

`LTRIM(your_string)` and **`RTRIM(your_string)`** returns your string with extra spaces removed from before (to the left of) or after (to the right of) a string.

```
SELECT LTRIM(' dogfood ');

SELECT RTRIM(' catfood ');
```

`LENGTH(your_string)` returns a count of how many characters are in your string.

```
SELECT LENGTH('San Antonio, TX ');
```

IMPORTANT: string functions do NOT change the data stored in your table; they simply return the altered strings as a result of your query.

WHAT'S MY PURPOSE?

We're trying to take the information in our location column and transfer it into two new columns, city and state.

Here are the steps we'll take to do that. Match each step to the SQL keyword or keywords that we need to accomplish that particular step.

SUBSTRING_INDEX()

SELECT

1. Take a look at the data in a particular column to find a pattern.

LEFT

ADD COLUMN

2. Add new empty columns into our table.

ADJUST

RIGHT

3. Grab part of the data from a text column.

ALTER TABLE

DELETE

4. Put the data we grabbed in step 2 into one of the empty columns.

UPDATE

INSERT

Answers on page 228.

We know how to use all the right pieces, but we still don't know how to put them together efficiently. Maybe we could try using those string functions with an UPDATE statement...

With what we know so far, we would have to do an UPDATE statement, one record at a time, with a SELECT to get the right data.

But with SQL, we can combine our statements. Turn the page to see how to put the values in our new columns.

WHAT'S MY PURPOSE?

We're trying to take the information in our location column and transfer it into two new columns, city and state.

Here are the steps we'll take to do that. Match each step to the SQL keyword or keywords that we need to accomplish that particular step.

SUBSTRING_INDEX()

SELECT

1. Take a look at the data in a particular column to find a pattern.

LEFT

ADD COLUMN

2. Add new empty columns into our table.

ADJUST

RIGHT

3. Grab part of the data from a text column.

ALTER TABLE

DELETE

4. Put the data we grabbed in step 2 into one of the empty columns.

UPDATE

INSERT

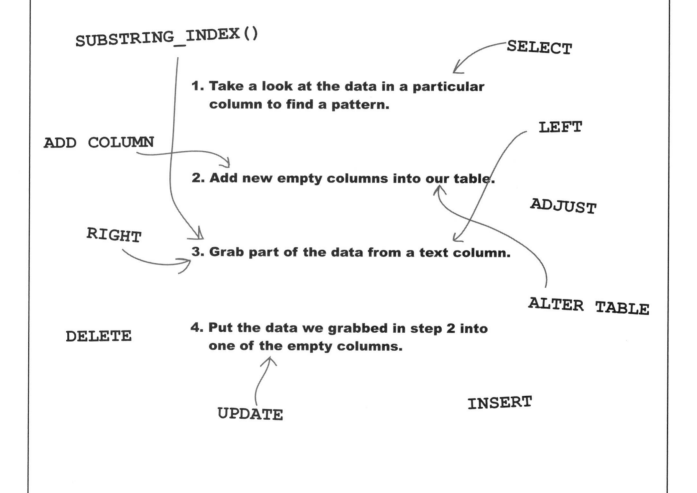

Use a current column to fill a new column

Remember our UPDATE syntax? We can use that to set every row in our table to contain the same new value. The statement below shows the syntax for **changing the value of every row in a column**. In place of newvalue, you can put a value or another column name.

```
UPDATE table_name
SET column_name = newvalue;
```

Each row in our table is set, one at a time, to this value.

To add data to our new city and state columns, we can use the string function RIGHT() inside that UPDATE statement. The string function grabs the last two characters from the old location column and puts them into the new state column.

```
UPDATE my_contacts
SET state = RIGHT(location, 2);
```

Here's the new column for our state data.

And here's the string function that grabs the last two characters from the location column.

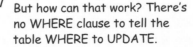

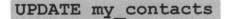

But how can that work? There's no WHERE clause to tell the table WHERE to UPDATE.

It will work without a WHERE clause. Turn the page to see how.

How our UPDATE and SET combo works

Your SQL software interprets the statement for each row in the table one at a time; then it goes back and starts over until all the state abbreviations are split out into their new `state` column.

my_contacts

contact_id	location	city	state
1	Chester, NJ		
2	Katy, TX		
3	San Mateo, CA		

Here's a simplified version of our table.

```
UPDATE my_contacts
SET state = RIGHT(location, 2);
```

And here's our SQL statement.

Let's see it in action on this example table. First time through, it takes the location for the first column and operates on it.

Then it starts to run through the whole table again a second time, finds the location in the second row, operates on it, and so on, until all the state records are split and it has no more records that match the statement.

You can use string functions in combination with SELECT, UPDATE, and DELETE.

First time through

```
UPDATE my_contacts
SET state = RIGHT('Chester,NJ',2)
```

Takes the first record's location column and operates on it

Second time through

```
UPDATE my_contacts
SET state = RIGHT('Katy, TX',2)
```

Now the second one

Third and final time through, because there are only three records

```
UPDATE my_contacts
SET state = RIGHT('San Mateo, CA',2)
```

And finally the third one

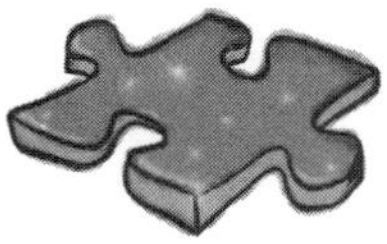

Altercross

How does a crossword help you learn SQL? Well, it makes you think about commands and keywords from this chapter in a different way.

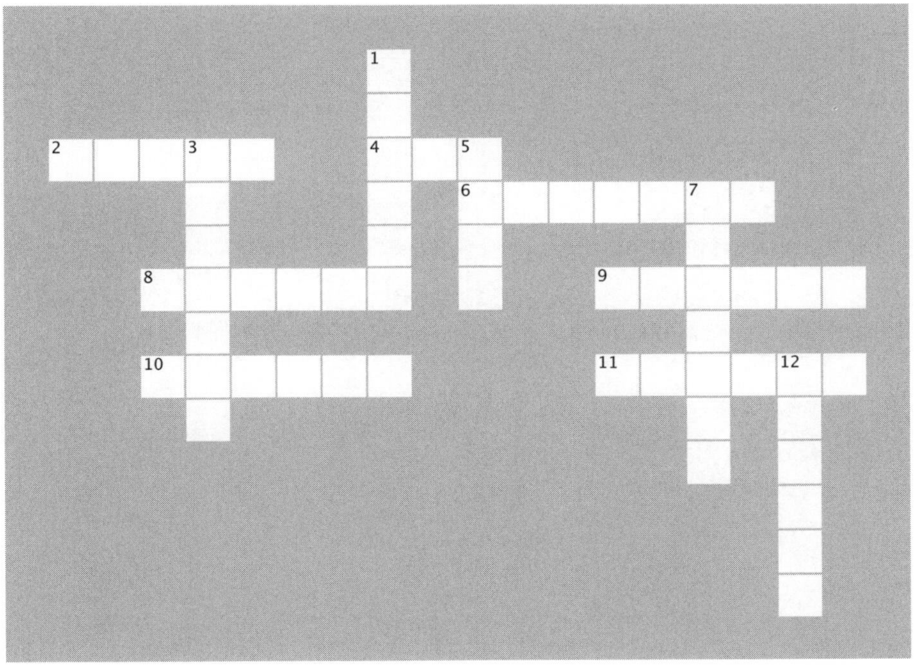

Across

2. _____(your_string) returns your string with extra spaces removed from before (to the left of) a string.
4. Our table can be given new columns with the ALTER statement and _____ COLUMN clause.
6. _____(your_string) does just that, it reverses the order of letters in your string.
8. ALTER TABLE projekts _____ TO project_list;
9. You can use _____ functions in combination with SELECT, UPDATE, and DELETE.
10. SUBSTRING(your_string, start_position, length) gives you part of your_string, starting at the letter in the start_position. _____ is how much of the string you get back.
11. Use _____ to change the name of your table.

Down

1. Use this keyword to alter the type of data stored in a column.
3. You can only have one AUTO_INCREMENT field per table, it has to be an _____ data type.
5. When you no longer need a column, use _____ COLUMN with ALTER.
7. Values stored in CHAR or VARCHAR columns are known as these.
12. Use this clause with ALTER when you only wish to change the data type.

CHAPTER 5

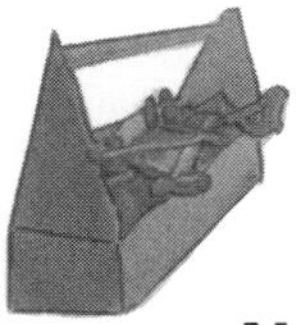

Your SQL Toolbox

Give yourself a hand. You've mastered Chapter 5, and now you've added ALTER to your toolbox. For a complete list of tooltips in the book, see Appendix iii.

ALTER TABLE

Lets you change the name of your table and its entire structure while retaining the data inside of it.

ALTER with CHANGE

Lets you change both the name and data type of an existing column.

ALTER with MODIFY

Lets you change just the data type of an existing column.

ALTER with ADD

Lets you add a column to your table in the order you choose.

ALTER with DROP

Lets you drop a column from your table.

String functions

Let you modify copies of the contents of string columns when they are returned from a query. The original values remain untouched.

Sharpen your pencil Solution

From page 210.

Sketch how the table will look after you run the command on page 210.

The old "number" has become proj_id, and that column contains the auto-incrementing primary key values.

project_list

proj_id	descriptionofproj	contractoronjob
1	outside house painting	Murphy
2	kitchen remodel	Valdez
3	wood floor installation	Keller
4	roofing	Jackson

Altercross Solution

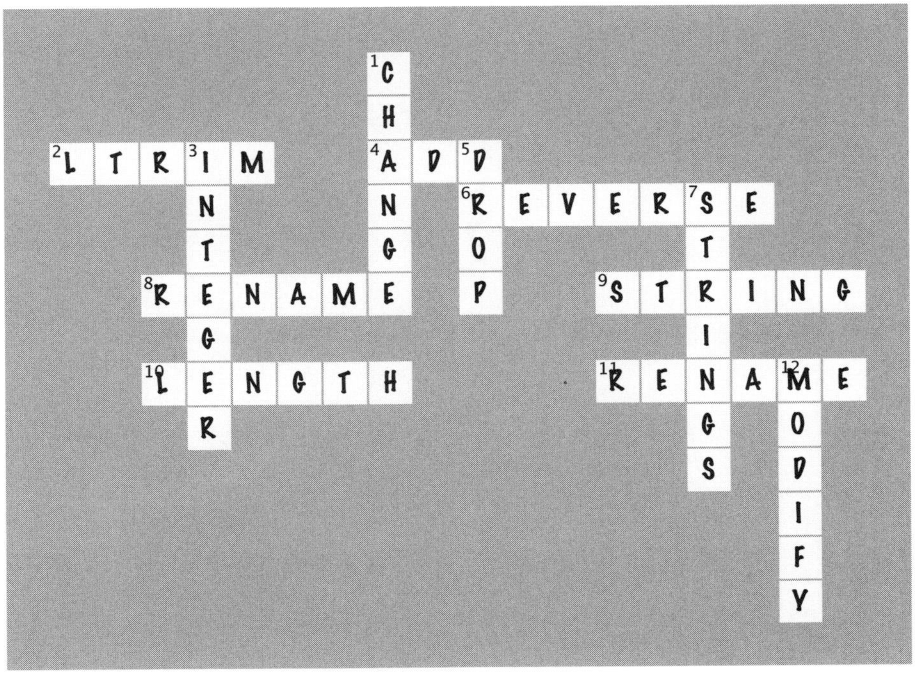

6 advanced SELECT

Seeing your data with new eyes

And then I was able to see just the enemy planes using a CASE statement! Kapow!

It's time to add a little finesse to your toolbox. You already know how to SELECT data and use WHERE clauses. But sometimes you need more **precision** than SELECT and WHERE provide. In this chapter, you'll learn about how to **order and group** your data, as well as how to **perform math operations** on your results.

Dataville Video is reorganizing

The owner of Dataville Video has a badly organized store. In his current system, movies can end up on different shelves depending on which employee is shelving them. He's ordered new shelves, and he thinks it's great time to finally label each of his movie categories.

To: Dataville Video Staff
From: The Boss
Subject: New shelves mean new categories!

Hi gang,

The new shelves are in, so I want you to organize our movies. We can use the following categories:

Action & Adventure
Drama
Comedy
Family
Horror
SciFi & Fantasy
Misc

I'll leave it to you to figure out how to make our current table work with these new categories.

Let's do lunch,

Your boss

In the current system, true and false values are used for types of movies. This makes figuring out how to categorize difficult. For example, if a movie has both T for comedy and T for scifi, where should it be shelved?

"T" and "F" are short for True and False.

This is when the store acquired a copy.

movie_table

movie_id	title	rating	drama	comedy	action	gore	scifi	for_kids	cartoon	purchased
1	Monsters, Inc.	G	F	T	F	F	F	T	T	3-6-2002
2	The Godfather	R	F	F	T	T	F	F	F	2-5-2001
3	Gone with the Wind	G	T	F	F	F	F	F	F	11-20-1999
4	American Pie	R	F	T	F	F	F	F	F	4-19-2003
5	Nightmare on Elm Street	R	F	F	T	T	F	F	F	4-19-2003
6	Casablanca	PG	T	F	F	F	F	F	F	2-5-2001

All these columns exist so that we can answer customer questions about the content of an individual movie.

Problems with our current table

Here's a rundown of the problems Dataville Video has with the current table.

When movies are returned, we don't know where they belong.

If we have T values for a number of the columns in the table, there's no clear way to know where that movie needs to be shelved. Movies should always be associated with a **single category**.

People aren't clear what the movie is about.

Our customers get confused when they spot a gory cover in the comedy section. Currently none of our T/F values take precedence over any others when movies are shelved.

Adding True and False data is time-consuming, and mistakes often happen.

Every time a new movie comes in, it has to be inserted with all those T/F columns. And the more of those that get entered, the more errors that crop up. Sometimes a column that should have been T is accidently entered as F, and vice versa. A category column would help us double-check our T/F columns, and eventually we might be able to get rid of those T/Fs altogether.

What we need here is a category column to speed up shelving, help customers figure out what type of movie it is they're renting, and limit errors in our data.

BRAIN POWER

How would you reorganize the current columns into new **categories**? Are there any films that might fit into more than one of the new categories?

Matching up existing data

You know how to ALTER your table to add in the new category column, but adding in the actual categories is a bit trickier. Luckily, the data that's already in the table can help us figure out the category for each movie, without us actually having to watch each one.

Let's rewrite the relationships in simple sentences:

If this column is 'T': **drama** we set the category column to 'drama'

If this column is 'T': **comedy** we set the category column to 'comedy'

If this column is 'T': **action** we set the category column to 'action'

If this column is 'T': **gore** we set the category column to 'horror'

If this column is 'T': **scifi** we set the category column to 'scifi'

If this column is 'T': **for_kids** we set the category column to 'family'

If this column is 'T': **cartoon** and this column is 'G': **rating** we set the category column to 'family'

If this column is 'T': **cartoon** and this column is **NOT** 'G': **rating** we set the category column to 'misc'

Not all cartoons are for kids. The rating column helps you determine if a film is in the family category or not, depending on whether it's true or false. If the rating is G, we can call it 'family'; if not, we'll call it 'misc'.

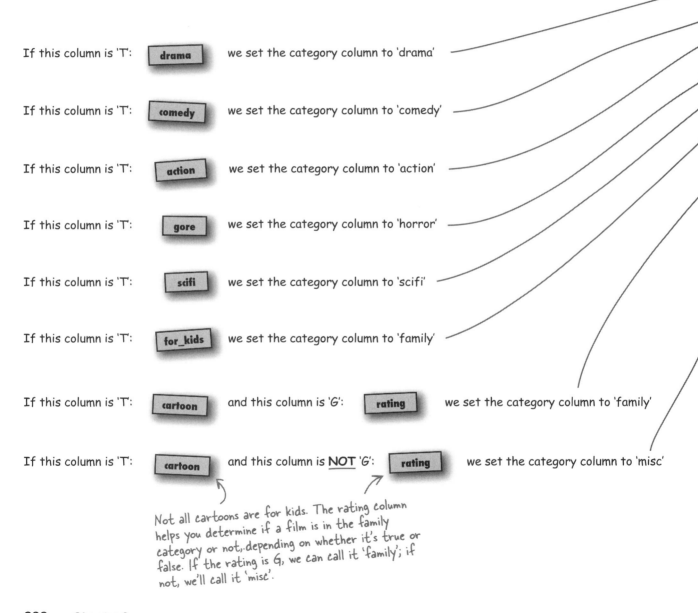

Populating the new column

Now we can translate those sentences into SQL UPDATE statements:

```
UPDATE movie_table SET category = 'drama' where drama = 'T';
UPDATE movie_table SET category = 'comedy' where comedy = 'T';
UPDATE movie_table SET category = 'action' where action = 'T';
UPDATE movie_table SET category = 'horror' where gore = 'T';
UPDATE movie_table SET category = 'scifi' where scifi = 'T';
UPDATE movie_table SET category = 'family' where for_kids = 'T';
UPDATE movie_table SET category = 'family' where cartoon = 'T' AND rating = 'G';
UPDATE movie_table SET category = 'misc' where cartoon = 'T' AND rating <> 'G';
```

Rating is not equal to 'G'.

Sharpen your pencil

Fill in the category value for these movies.

movie_table

title	rating	drama	comedy	action	gore	scifi	for_kids	cartoon	category
Big Adventure	G	F	F	F	F	F	T	F	
Greg: The Untold Story	PG	F	F	T	F	F	F	F	
Mad Clowns	R	F	F	F	T	F	F	F	
Paraskavedekatriaphobia	R	T	T	T	F	T	F	F	
Rat named Darcy, A	G	F	F	F	F	F	T	F	
End of the Line	R	T	F	F	T	T	F	T	
Shiny Things, The	PG	T	F	F	F	F	F	F	
Take it Back	R	F	T	F	F	F	F	F	
Shark Bait	G	F	F	F	F	F	T	F	
Angry Pirate	PG	F	T	F	F	F	F	T	
Potentially Habitable Planet	PG	F	T	F	F	T	F	F	

Does the order in which we evaluate each of the T/F columns matter? ....

Sharpen your pencil Solution

Fill in the category value for these movies.

movie_table

title	rating	drama	comedy	action	gore	scifi	for_kids	cartoon	category
Big Adventure	G	F	F	F	F	F	T	F	family
Greg: The Untold Story	PG	F	F	T	F	F	F	F	action
Mad Clowns	R	F	F	F	T	F	F	F	horror
Paraskavedekatriaphobia	R	T	T	T	F	T	F	F	?
Rat named Darcy, A	G	F	F	F	F	F	T	F	family
End of the Line	R	T	F	F	T	T	F	T	misc
Shiny Things, The	PG	T	F	F	F	F	F	F	drama
Take it Back	R	F	T	F	F	F	F	F	comedy
Shark Bait	G	F	F	F	F	F	T	F	?
Angry Pirate	PG	F	T	F	F	F	F	T	misc
Potentially Habitable Planet	PG	F	T	F	F	T	F	F	?

The question marks mean a column was changed by more than one UPDATE. This value will change depending on the order the UPDATEs were executed.

Does the order in which we evaluate each of the T/F columns matter? Yes, it does matter.

The order does matter

For example, if we go through the columns in order 'Paraskavedekatriaphobia' would end up being classified as scifi, even though it might be more of a comedy. We don't know if it should be considered comedy, action, drama, cartoon, or scifi. Since it's unclear where it belongs, it might best be placed in the misc category.

Order matters. Two UPDATE statements may change the same column's value.

That seems fine for a small table, but what if you had hundreds of columns? Is there some way we could combine all those UPDATE statements into one big one?

Well, you could write one big UPDATE statement, but there's a better way.

The CASE expression combines all the UPDATE statements by checking an existing column's value against a condition. If it meets the condition, the new column is filled with a specified value.

It even allows you to tell your RDBMS ***what to do if any records don't meet the conditions***

Here's its basic syntax:

```
UPDATE my_table
SET new_column =
CASE
  WHEN column1 = somevalue1
    THEN newvalue1
  WHEN column2 = somevalue2
    THEN newvalue2
  ELSE newvalue3
END;
```

The value in the column you specify here will be changed to the appropriate value below.

This begins the CASE expression.

WHEN this condition is met...

THEN set the value of new_column to this value.

WHEN a different condition is met...

THEN set the value of new_column to this different value.

The indenting doesn't do anything to the expression; it just makes it easier to track what's going on when you look at the code.

Anything that doesn't match either of the conditions gets this value instead.

This ends the CASE expression and the entire UPDATE statement (because it's followed by a semicolon).

UPDATE with a CASE expression

Let's see the CASE expression in action on our movie_table.

```
UPDATE movie_table
SET category =
CASE
  WHEN drama = 'T' THEN 'drama'
  WHEN comedy = 'T' THEN 'comedy'
  WHEN action = 'T' THEN 'action'
  WHEN gore = 'T' THEN 'horror'
  WHEN scifi = 'T' THEN 'scifi'
  WHEN for_kids = 'T' THEN 'family'
  WHEN cartoon = 'T' THEN 'family'
  ELSE 'misc'
END;
```

This is the same as saying UPDATE movie_table SET category = 'drama' WHERE drama = 'T'—but with a whole lot less typing!

Everything that doesn't match the conditions in the lines above is given a category value of 'misc'.

The values that were unknown when we used UPDATE on its own to populate the new column now have category values.

But notice how we also have new values for 'Angry Pirate' and 'End of the Line'.

movie_table

title	rating	drama	comedy	action	gore	scifi	for_kids	cartoon	category
Big Adventure	PG	F	F	F	F	F	F	T	family
Greg: The Untold Story	PG	F	F	T	F	F	F	F	action
Mad Clowns	R	F	F	F	T	F	F	F	horror
Paraskavedekatriaphobia	R	T	T	T	F	T	F	F	drama
Rat named Darcy, A	G	F	F	F	F	F	T	F	family
End of the Line	R	T	F	F	T	T	F	T	drama
Shiny Things, The	PG	T	F	F	F	F	F	F	drama
Take it Back	R	F	T	F	F	F	F	F	comedy
Shark Bait	G	F	F	F	F	F	T	F	family
Angry Pirate	PG	F	T	F	F	F	F	T	comedy
Potentially Habitable Planet	PG	F	T	F	F	T	F	F	comedy

As each movie title's T/F values are run through the CASE statement, the RDBMS is looking for the first 'T' to set the category for each film.

Here's what happens when 'Big Adventure' runs through the code:

```
UPDATE movie_table
SET category =
CASE
   WHEN drama = 'T' THEN 'drama'
   WHEN comedy = 'T' THEN 'comedy'
   WHEN action = 'T' THEN 'action'
   WHEN gore = 'T' THEN 'horror'
   WHEN scifi = 'T' THEN 'scifi'
   WHEN for_kids = 'T' THEN 'family'
   WHEN cartoon = 'T' THEN 'family'
   ELSE 'misc'
END;
```

FALSE: no category yet

FALSE: no category yet

FALSE: no category yet

FALSE: no category yet

FALSE: no category yet

FALSE: no category yet

TRUE: category set to 'family', and we skip to the END and exit the code.

Let's do one with multiple matches. Again, we're looking for the first 'T' value here to set the category.

Here's what happens when 'Paraskavedekatriaphobia' runs through the code:

```
UPDATE movie_table
SET category =
CASE
   WHEN drama = 'T' THEN 'drama'
   WHEN comedy = 'T' THEN 'comedy'
   WHEN action = 'T' THEN 'action'
   WHEN gore = 'T' THEN 'horror'
   WHEN scifi = 'T' THEN 'scifi'
   WHEN for_kids = 'T' THEN 'family'
   WHEN cartoon = 'T' THEN 'family'
   ELSE 'misc'
END;
```

TRUE: category set to drama; we skip to the END and exit the code. All our other T values are ignored.

Looks like we have a problem

We may have a problem. 'Great Adventure' is an R-rated cartoon. Somehow it ended up categorized as 'family'.

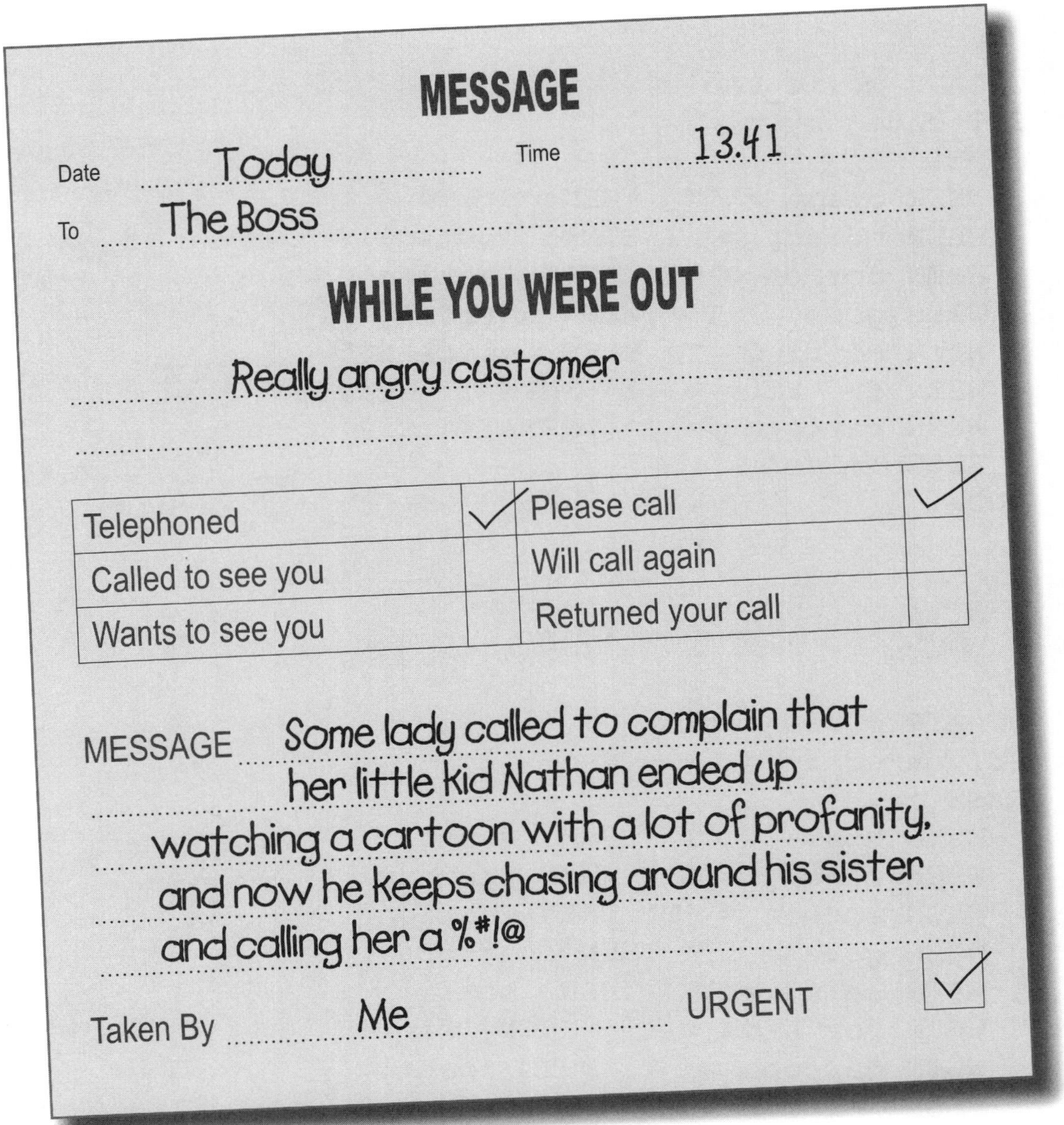

MESSAGE

Date: Today   Time: 13.41

To: The Boss

WHILE YOU WERE OUT

Really angry customer

Telephoned	✓	Please call	✓
Called to see you		Will call again	
Wants to see you		Returned your call	

MESSAGE: Some lady called to complain that her little kid Nathan ended up watching a cartoon with a lot of profanity, and now he keeps chasing around his sister and calling her a %*!@

Taken By: Me   URGENT ✓

Sharpen your pencil

Change the CASE expression so that cartoons get put in the 'misc' category, not 'family'.

....

....

....

....

....

....

....

....

....

....

....

....

BRAIN POWER

How might we use the R rating to keep this sort of thing from happening in the future?

Sharpen your pencil Solution

Change the CASE expression to test for the conditions that set a cartoon to 'misc' instead of 'family'.

```
UPDATE movie_table
SET category =
CASE
  WHEN drama = 'T' THEN 'drama'
  WHEN comedy = 'T' THEN 'comedy'
  WHEN action = 'T' THEN 'action'
  WHEN gore = 'T' THEN 'horror'
  WHEN scifi = 'T' THEN 'scifi'
  WHEN for_kids = 'T' THEN 'family'
  WHEN cartoon = 'T' AND rating = 'G' THEN 'family'
  ELSE 'misc'
END;
```

Your condition can have multiple parts: add an AND to your WHEN to test for whether the film is a cartoon AND it's rated 'G'. If it is, then it gets a category of 'family'.

there are no Dumb Questions

Q: Do I have to use the ELSE?

A: It's optional. You can simply leave that line out if you don't need it, but it's nice to have to update the value of your column when nothing else fits. It's better to have some sort of value than NULL, for example.

Q: What happens if I leave off the ELSE but none of the WHEN conditions match?

A: No values will be changed in the column you are updating.

Q: What if I want to only use the CASE expression on some columns but not others? For example, if I wanted to do a CASE where my category = 'misc'. Can I use a WHERE?

A: Yes, you can add a WHERE clause after the END keyword. The CASE will only apply to those columns that match the WHERE.

Q: Can I use a CASE expression with anything other than UPDATE statements?

A: Yes. You can use a CASE expression with SELECT, INSERT, DELETE, and, as you've seen, UPDATE.

CASE CONSTRUCTION

Your boss, always a bit wishy-washy, has decided to change things up a bit. Read his email and write a single SQL statement that will accomplish what he wants.

....
....
....
....
....
....
....
....
....

It turns out that the new categories are causing customers to have a tough time finding movies. Write a statement that gets rid of the new R-rated categories you just created.

....
....
....
....
....
....
....
....
....

Finally, delete all those T/F columns we don't need anymore.

....
....
....
....
....
....
....
....

To: Dataville Video Staff
From: The Boss
Subject: New sections mean new categories!

My happy video family,

I've decided to create some new sections. I'm thinking that R-rated movies should be shelved in a different section than G and PG. Let's just create 5 new categories:

horror-r
action-r
drama-r
comedy-r
scifi-r

And if there are any G-rated movies in the misc section, move 'em to Family.

Thanks. That'll be great,
Your boss

CASE CONSTRUCTION SOLUTION

Your boss, always a bit wishy-washy, has decided to change things up a bit. Read his email and write a single SQL statement that will accomplish what he wants.

```
UPDATE movietable
SET category =
CASE
  WHEN drama = 'T' AND rating = 'R' THEN 'drama-r'
  WHEN comedy = 'T' AND rating = 'R' THEN 'comedy-r'
  WHEN action = 'T' AND rating = 'R' THEN 'action-r'
  WHEN gore = 'T' AND rating = 'R' THEN 'horror-r'
  WHEN scifi = 'T' AND rating = 'R' THEN 'scifi-r'
  WHEN category = 'misc' AND rating = 'G' THEN 'family'
END;
```

> **To:**   Dataville Video Staff
> **From:**   The Boss
> **Subject:** New sections mean new categories!
>
> My happy video family,
>
> I've decided to create some new sections. I'm thinking that R-rated movies should be shelved in a different section than G and PG. Let's just create 5 new categories:
>
> horror-r
> action-r
> drama-r
> comedy-r
> scifi-r
>
> And if there are any G-rated movies in the misc section, move 'em to Family.
>
> Thanks. That'll be great,
> Your boss

It turns out that the new categories are causing customers to have a tough time finding movies. Write a statement that gets rid of the new R-rated categories you just created.

```
UPDATE movietable
SET category =
CASE
  WHEN category = 'drama-r' THEN 'drama'
  WHEN category = 'comedy-r' THEN 'comedy'
  WHEN category = 'action-r' THEN 'action'
  WHEN category = 'horror-r' THEN 'horror'
  WHEN category = 'scifi-r' THEN 'scifi'
END;
```

Finally, delete all those T/F columns we don't need anymore.

```
ALTER TABLE movietable
DROP COLUMN drama,
DROP COLUMN comedy,
DROP COLUMN action,
DROP COLUMN gore,
DROP COLUMN scifi,
DROP COLUMN for_kids,
DROP COLUMN cartoon;
```

Tables can get messy

When a movie arrives at the store, it gets added to our table and becomes the newest row in our table. There's no order to the movies in our movie table. And now that it's time to reshelve our movies, we have a bit of a problem. We know that each of the new shelves holds 20 movies, and every one of the more than 3,000 movies has to have a sticker on it indicating its category. ***We need to select the movies in each category, in alphabetical order within its category.***

We know how to query the database to find all of the movies in each category, but we need them listed alphabetically within their categories somehow.

movie_table

movie_id	title	rating	category	purchased
83	Big Adventure	G	family	3-6-2002
84	Greg: The Untold Story	PG	action	2-5-2001
85	Mad Clowns	R	horror	11-20-1999
86	Paraskavedekatriaphobia	R	action	4-19-2003
87	Rat named Darcy, A	G	family	4-19-2003
88	End of the Line	R	misc	2-5-2001
89	Shiny Things, The	PG	drama	3-6-2002
90	Take it Back	R	comedy	2-5-2001
91	Shark Bait	G	misc	11-20-1999
92	Angry Pirate	PG	misc	4-19-2003
93	Potentially Habitable Planet	PG	scifi	2-5-2001
9[illegible]	[illegible]	R	hor[illegible]	[illegible]

These are just a few of the more than 3,000 movies Dataville Video has in stock.

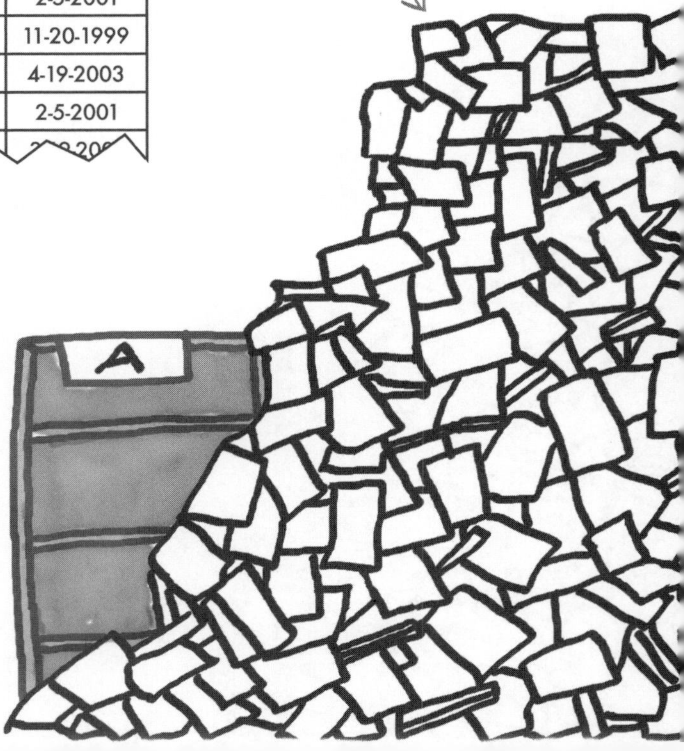

BRAIN BARBELL

How would you organize this data alphabetically using a SQL statement?

We need a way to organize the data we SELECT

Each one of the more than 3,000 movies has to have a sticker on it indicating its category. Then it has to be shelved in alphabetical order.

We need a master list of the movies in alphabetical order by title for each category. So far, we know how to SELECT. We can easily select movies by category, and we can even select movies by first letter of the title and by category.

But to organize our big list of movies means that we would need to write at least 182 SELECT statements: Here are a just a few of them:

```
SELECT title, category FROM movie_table WHERE title LIKE 'A%' AND category = 'family';
SELECT title, category FROM movie_table WHERE title LIKE 'B%' AND category = 'family';
SELECT title, category FROM movie_table WHERE title LIKE 'C%' AND category = 'family';
SELECT title, category FROM movie_table WHERE title LIKE 'D%' AND category = 'family';
SELECT title, category FROM movie_table WHERE title LIKE 'E%' AND category = 'family';
SELECT title, category FROM movie_table WHERE title LIKE 'F%' AND category = 'family';
SELECT title, category FROM movie_table WHERE title LIKE 'G%' AND category = 'family';
```

We need to know the title so we can dig in the pile to find it, and the category so we can sticker and shelve it.

This is the letter of the alphabet that the movie titles should begin with.

And this is the category we're looking for.

It's 182 queries because we have 7 categories and 26 letters of the alphabet. This number doesn't include movies that have a number at the beginning of their titles (like '101 Dalmatians' or '2001: A Space Odyssey').

BRAIN POWER

Where do you think titles that begin with a number or a non-letter character—like an exclamation point—will appear in the list?

Sharpen your pencil

We still have to manually alphabetize the titles within their category list using the letters that follow the initial 'A' to decide the order.

Take a closer look at some of the output from just one of our 182 (or more) queries. Try alphabetizing the list of movie titles by hand.

```
SELECT title, category FROM movie_table WHERE title LIKE 'A%' AND category = 'family';
```

A few of our query results

title	category
Airplanes and Helicopters	family
Are You Paying Attention?	family
Acting Up	family
Are You My Mother?	family
Andy Sighs	family
After the Clowns Leave	family
Art for Kids	family
Animal Adventure	family
Animal Crackerz	family
Another March of the Penguins	family
Anyone Can Grow Up	family
Aaargh!	family
Aardvarks Gone Wild	family
Alaska: Land of Salmon	family
Angels	family
Ann Eats Worms	family
Awesome Adventure	family
Annoying Adults	family
Alex Needs a Bath	family
Aaargh! 2	family

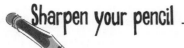

Sharpen your pencil Solution

We still have to manually alphabetize the titles within their category list using the letters that follow the initial 'A' to decide the order.

Take a closer look at some of the output from just one of our 182 (or more) queries. Try alphabetizing the list of movie titles by hand.

```
SELECT title, category FROM movie_table WHERE title LIKE 'A%' AND category = 'family';
```

title	category
Aaargh!	family
Aaargh! 2	family
Aardvarks Gone Wild	family
Acting Up	family
After the Clowns Leave	family
Airplanes and Helicopters	family
Alaska: Land of Salmon	family
Alex Needs a Bath	family
Andy Sighs	family
Angels	family
Animal Adventure	family
Animal Crackerz	family
Ann Eats Worms	family
Annoying Adults	family
Another March of the Penguins	family
Anyone Can Grow Up	family
Are You My Mother?	family
Are You Paying Attention?	family
Art for Kids	family
Awesome Adventure	family

How long did these 20 movies take you to order?

Can you imagine how long it would take to order 3,000 or more movies in this way?

The titles starting 'Are You...' come towards the end of the order since the letter following the initial 'A' is an 'r', but then we had to look at the seventh letter into the title before we could work out where each movie should be shelved.

Try a little ORDER BY

You say you need to order your query? Well, it just so happens that you can tell SQL to `SELECT` something and `ORDER` the data it returns `BY` another column from the table.

No surprises in this part. It's exactly the same as the SELECT query we just tried.

```
SELECT title, category
FROM movie_table
WHERE
title LIKE 'A%'
AND
category = 'family'
ORDER BY title;
```

Here's the new bit. Just like it sounds, it tells the program to return the data in alphabetical order by title.

Seriously. Are you telling me this is the only way we can alphabetize our results? There's NO WAY I'm doing that for every letter of the alphabet.

Sharpen your pencil

You're right. What can we take out of the query above to make it much more powerful?

....

....

....

....

STOP! Do this exercise before turning the page.

ORDER a single column

If our query uses `ORDER BY title`, we don't need to search for titles that start with a particular letter anymore because the query returns the data listed in alphabetical order by title.

All we need to do is take out the `title LIKE` part, and `ORDER BY title` will do the rest.

Sharpen your pencil Solution

What can we take out of the query above to make it much more powerful?

```
SELECT title, category
FROM movie_table
WHERE
title LIKE 'A%'
AND
category = 'family'
ORDER BY title;
```

(The lines `title LIKE 'A%'` and `AND` are crossed out.)

```
SELECT title, category
FROM movie_table
WHERE
category = 'family'
ORDER BY title;
```

This time we'll get the entire list of movies in the family category.

Even better, this list will include movies that begin with numbers in the title. They'll be first in the list.

This isn't the end of the results; we don't have room to show them all here. They continue all the way through Z titles.

ORDER BY allows you to alphabetically order any column.

Notice that the first few titles begin with a number.

title	category
1 Crazy Alien	family
10 Big Bugs	family
101 Alsatians	family
13th Birthday Magic	family
2 + 2 is 5	family
3001 Ways to Fall	family
5th Grade Girls are Evil	family
7 Year Twitch	family
8 Arms are Better than 2	family
Aaargh!	family
Aaargh! 2	family
Aardvarks Gone Wild	family
Acting Up	family
After the Clowns Leave	family
Airplanes and Helicopters	family
Alaska: Land of Salmon	family
Alex Needs a Bath	family
Andy Sighs	family
Angels	family
Animal Adventure	family
Animal Crackerz	family
Ann Eats Worms	family
Annoying Adults	family
Another March of the Penguins	family
Anyone Can Grow Up	family
Are You My Mother?	family
Are You Paying Attention	family
Art for Kids	family
Awesome Adventure	family

Exercise

Create a simple table with a single CHAR(1) column called 'test_chars'.

Insert the numbers, letters (both upper- and lowercase), and non-alphabet characters shown below in this column, each in a separate row. Insert a space and leave one row NULL.

Try your new ORDER BY query on the column and fill in the blanks in the *SQL's Rules of Order* book shown below.

0123ABCDabcd!@#$%^&*()-_
+=[]{};:'"\|`~,.<>/?

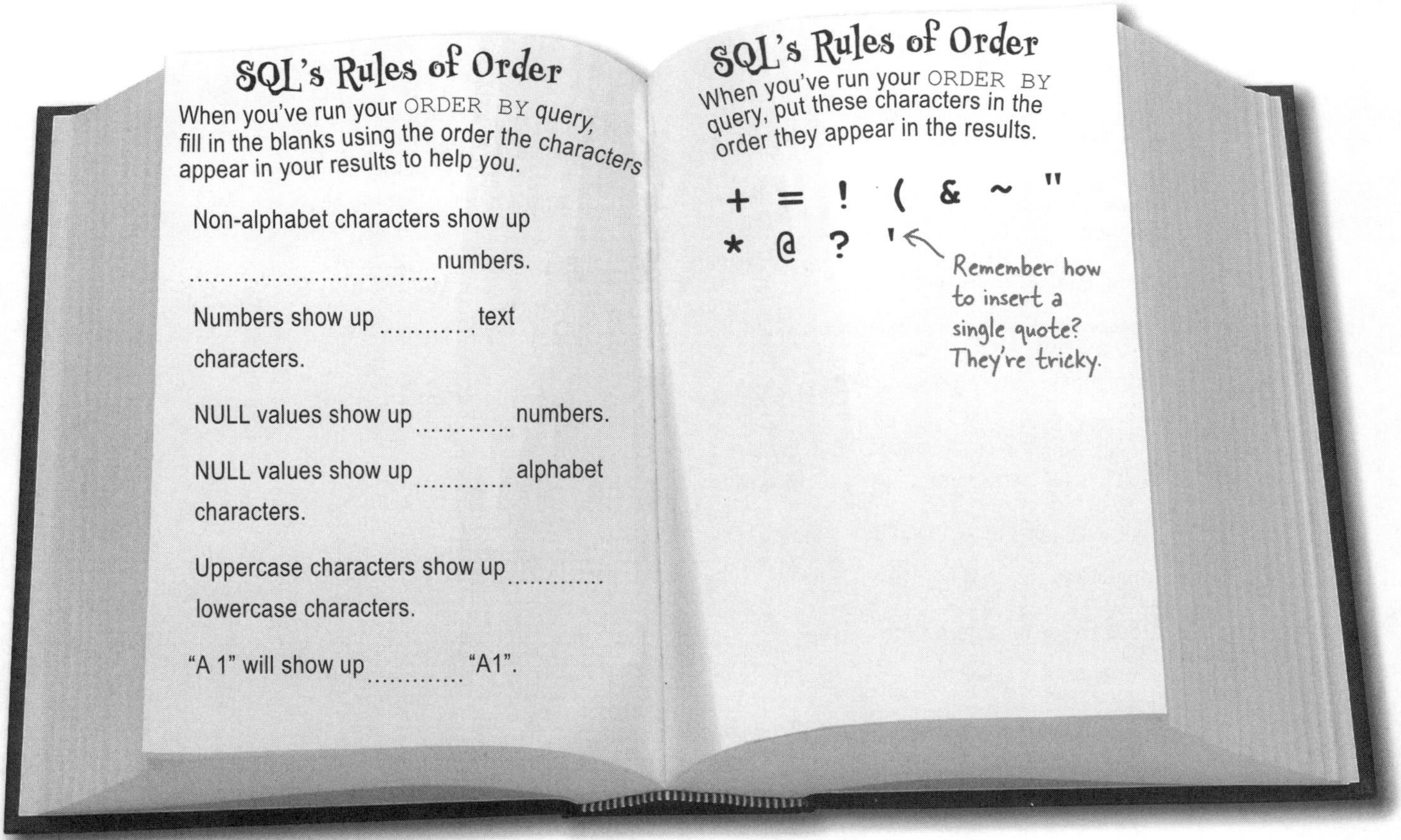
SQL's Rules of Order
When you've run your ORDER BY query, fill in the blanks using the order the characters appear in your results to help you.
Non-alphabet characters show up .... numbers.
Numbers show up .... text characters.
NULL values show up .... numbers.
NULL values show up .... alphabet characters.
Uppercase characters show up .... lowercase characters.
"A 1" will show up .... "A1".
SQL's Rules of Order
When you've run your ORDER BY query, put these characters in the order they appear in the results.
+ = ! (& ~ "
* @ ? '
Remember how to insert a single quote? They're tricky.

Exercise Solution

Create a simple table with a single CHAR(1) column called 'test_chars'.

Insert the numbers, letters (both upper- and lowercase), and non-alphabet characters shown below in this column, each in a separate row. Insert a space and leave one row NULL.

Try your new ORDER BY query on the column and fill in the blanks in the 'SQL's Rules of Order' book shown below.

```
 !"#$%&'()*+,-./0123:;<=>
?@ABCD[\]^_`abcd{|}~
```

The order that the characters may have shown up in your results. Note the space at the beginning. Your order may be a bit different depending on your RDBMS. The point here is to know that there IS an order, and what the order is for your RDBMS.

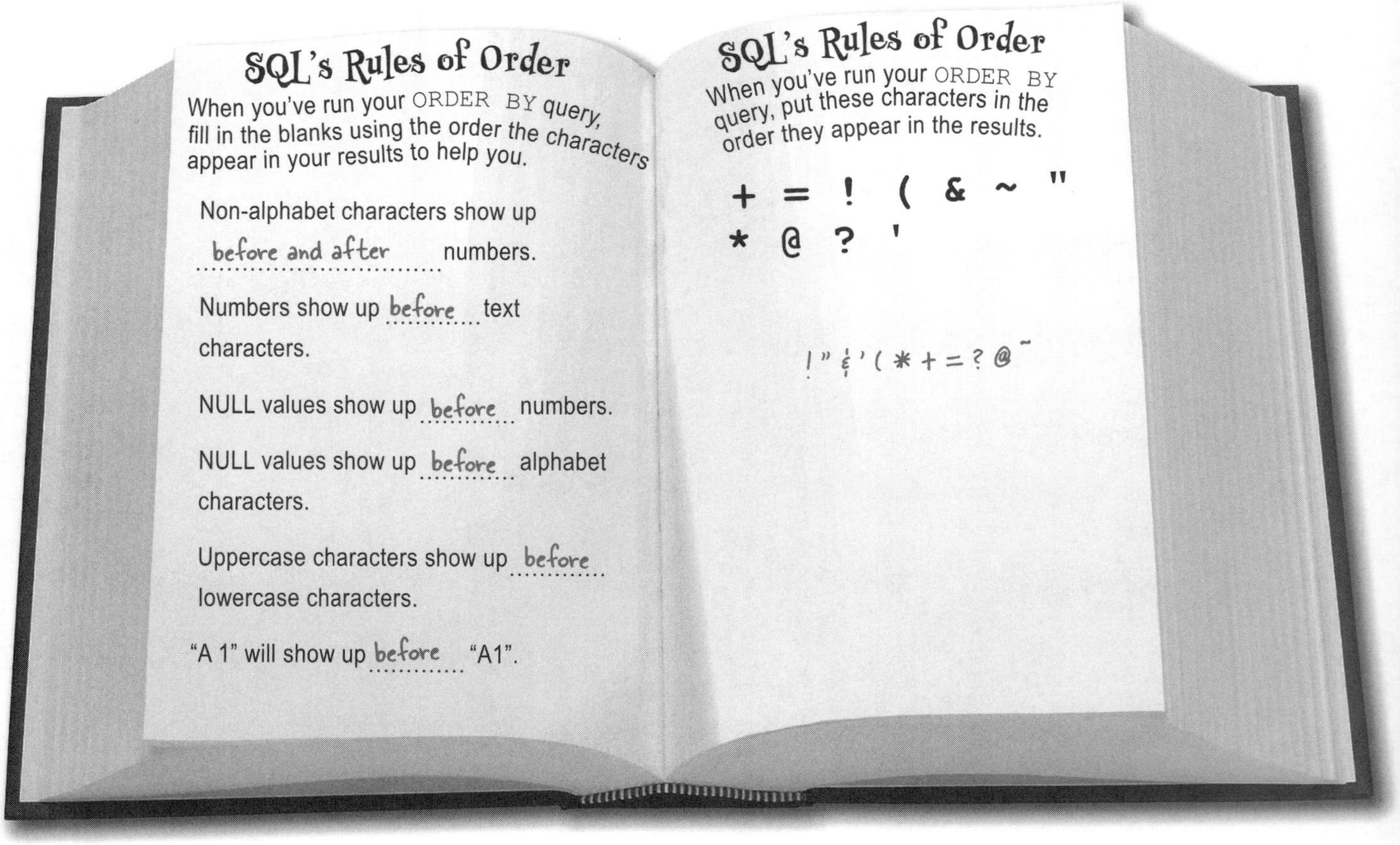
SQL's Rules of Order
When you've run your ORDER BY query, fill in the blanks using the order the characters appear in your results to help you.
Non-alphabet characters show up before and after numbers.
Numbers show up before text characters.
NULL values show up before numbers.
NULL values show up before alphabet characters.
Uppercase characters show up before lowercase characters.
"A 1" will show up before "A1".
SQL's Rules of Order
When you've run your ORDER BY query, put these characters in the order they appear in the results.
+ = ! (& ~ "
* @ ? '
! " & ' (* + = ? @ ~

ORDER with two columns

Seems like everything is under control. We can alphabetize our movies, and we can create alphabetical lists for each category.

Unfortunately, your boss has something else for you to do…

> **To:** Dataville Video Staff
> **From:** The Boss
> **Subject:** Out with the old (movies)
>
> Hey,
>
> I think we need to get rid of some of the movies we've had for the longest time. Can you come in this weekend and give me a list of movies in each category by order of purchase date?
>
> That would be great,
> Your boss

Fortunately, you can order multiple columns in the same statement.

We want to make sure the purchased date shows up in the results.

```
SELECT title, category, purchased
FROM movie_table
ORDER BY category, purchased;
```

This will be the first column ordered. We'll get a list of every movie in the store, ordered by category.

And this will be the second column ordered, AFTER the category column has been ordered.

BRAIN BARBELL

Will the oldest movies show up first or last in each category? And what do you think will happen if two movies are in the same category with the same purchase date? Which will show up first?

ORDER with multiple columns

You're not restricted to sorting by just two columns. You can sort by as many columns as you need to get at the data you want.

Take a look at this `ORDER BY` with three columns. Here's what's going on, and how the table gets sorted.

You can sort by as many columns as you need.

```
SELECT * FROM movie_table
ORDER BY category, purchased, title;
```

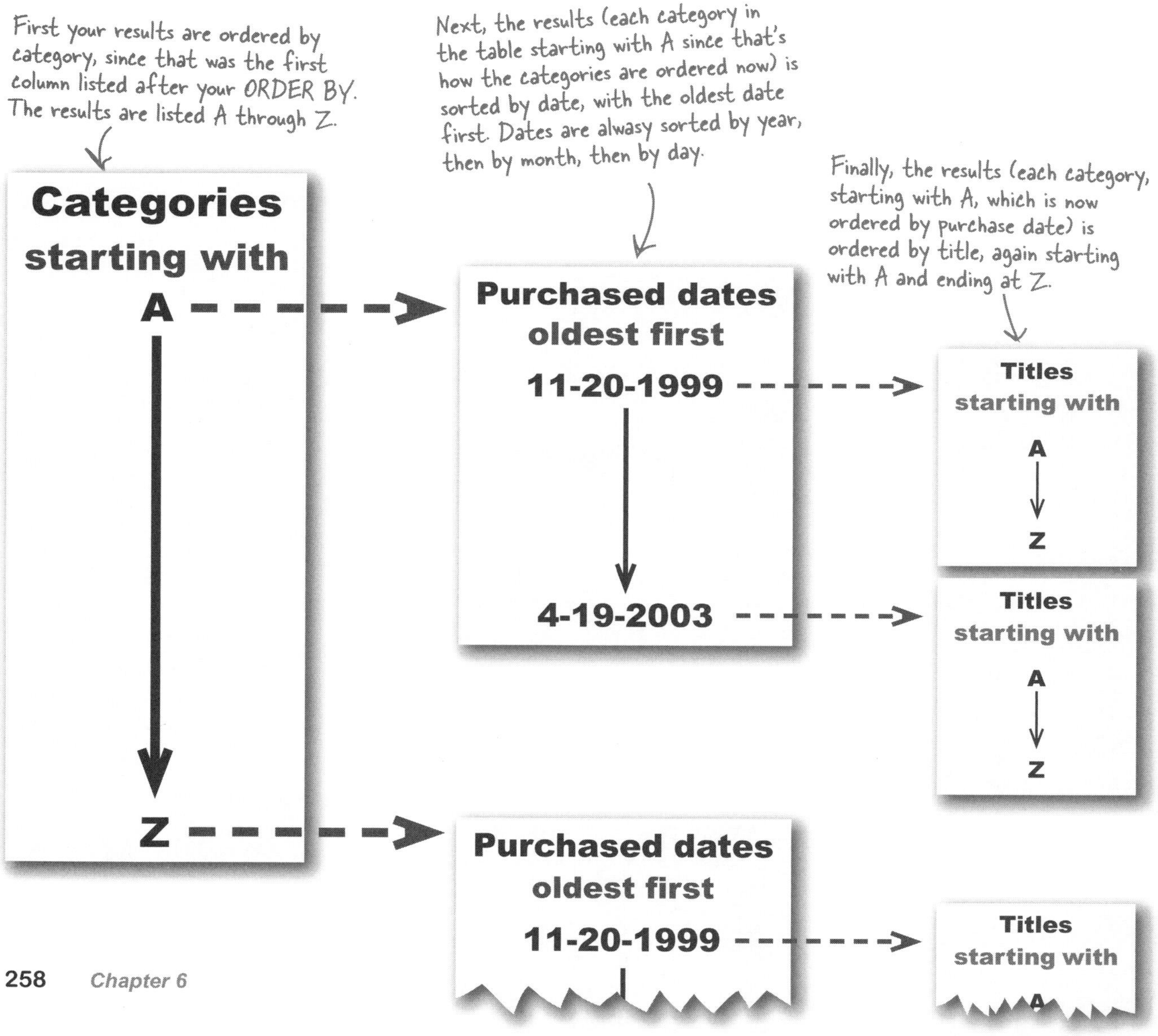
First your results are ordered by category, since that was the first column listed after your ORDER BY. The results are listed A through Z.
Next, the results (each category in the table starting with A since that's how the categories are ordered now) is sorted by date, with the oldest date first. Dates are alwasy sorted by year, then by month, then by day.
Finally, the results (each category, starting with A, which is now ordered by purchase date) is ordered by title, again starting with A and ending at Z.
Categories starting with
A
Z
Purchased dates oldest first
11-20-1999
4-19-2003
Purchased dates oldest first
11-20-1999
Titles starting with
A
Z
Titles starting with
A
Z
Titles starting with
A

An orderly movie_table

Let's see what this SELECT statement actually returns
when we run it on our original movie table.

Our original
movie_table

There's no real
order here;
movies just
show up in the
order in which
the records
were inserted
into the table.

movie_id	title	rating	category	purchased
83	Bobby's Adventure	G	family	3-6-2002
84	Greg: The Untold Story	PG	action	2-5-2001
85	Mad Clowns	R	horror	11-20-1999
86	Paraskavedekatriaphobia	R	action	4-19-2003
87	Rat named Darcy, A	G	family	4-19-2003
88	End of the Line	R	misc	2-5-2001
89	Shiny Things, The	PG	drama	3-6-2002
90	Take it Back	R	comedy	2-5-2001
91	Shark Bait	G	misc	11-20-1999
92	Angry Pirate	PG	misc	4-19-2003
93	Potentially Habitable Planet	PG	scifi	2-5-2001
9	C s G Wi	R	or	2 9 200

and the ordered results from our query:

Third column that
was ordered

First column that
was ordered

Second column that
was ordered

movie_id	title	rating	category	purchased
84	Greg: The Untold Story	PG	action	2-5-2001
86	Paraskavedekatriaphobia	R	action	4-19-2003
90	Take it Back	R	comedy	2-5-2001
89	Shiny Things, The	PG	drama	3-6-2002
83	Bobby's Adventure	G	family	3-6-2002
87	Rat named Darcy, A	G	family	4-19-2003
85	Mad Clowns	R	horror	11-20-1999
91	Shark Bait	G	misc	11-20-1999
88	End of the Line	R	misc	2-5-2001
93	Potentially Habitable Planet	PG	scifi	2-5-2001

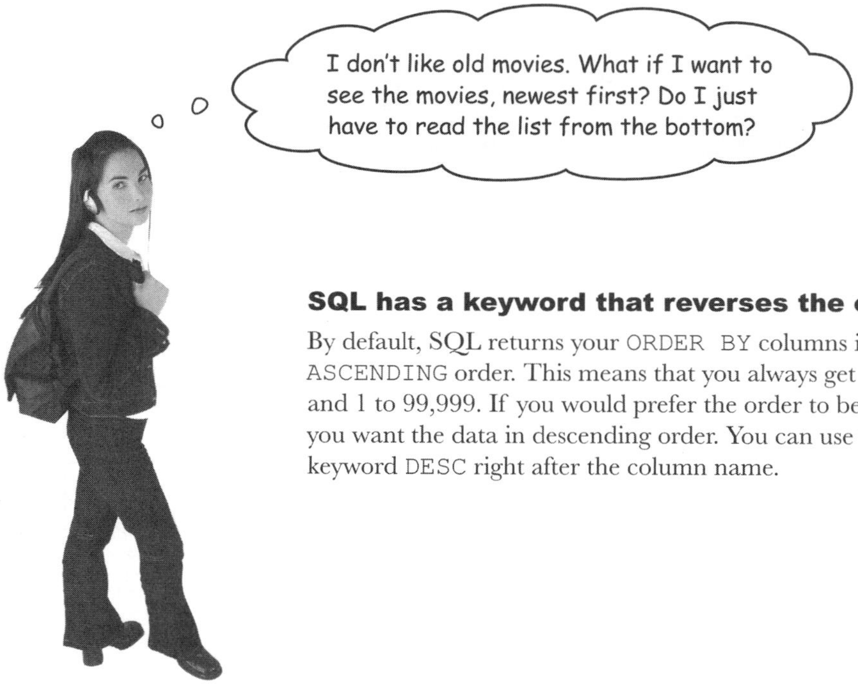
I don't like old movies. What if I want to see the movies, newest first? Do I just have to read the list from the bottom?

SQL has a keyword that reverses the order.

By default, SQL returns your `ORDER BY` columns in `ASCENDING` order. This means that you always get A to Z and 1 to 99,999. If you would prefer the order to be reversed, you want the data in descending order. You can use the keyword `DESC` right after the column name.

there are no Dumb Questions

Q: I thought that DESC was used to get the DESCRIPTION of a table. Are you sure this works to change the ORDER?

A: Yes. It's all about context. When you use it in front of a table name—for example, **`DESC movie_table;`**—you'll get a description of the table. In that case, it's short for **`DESCRIBE`**.

When you **use it in an `ORDER` clause**, it stands for **`DESCENDING`** and that's how it will order the results.

Q: Can I use the whole words DESCRIBE and DESCENDING in my query to avoid confusion?

A: You can use **`DESCRIBE`**, but `DESCENDING` won't work.

Use the keyword DESC after your column name in ORDER BY clauses to reverse the order of your results.

Reverse the ORDER with DESC

Picture your data on a staircase. When you **climb up** the stairs, you're **ascending**, and you reach A before B. When you come back **down** again, you **descend** and reach Z before A.

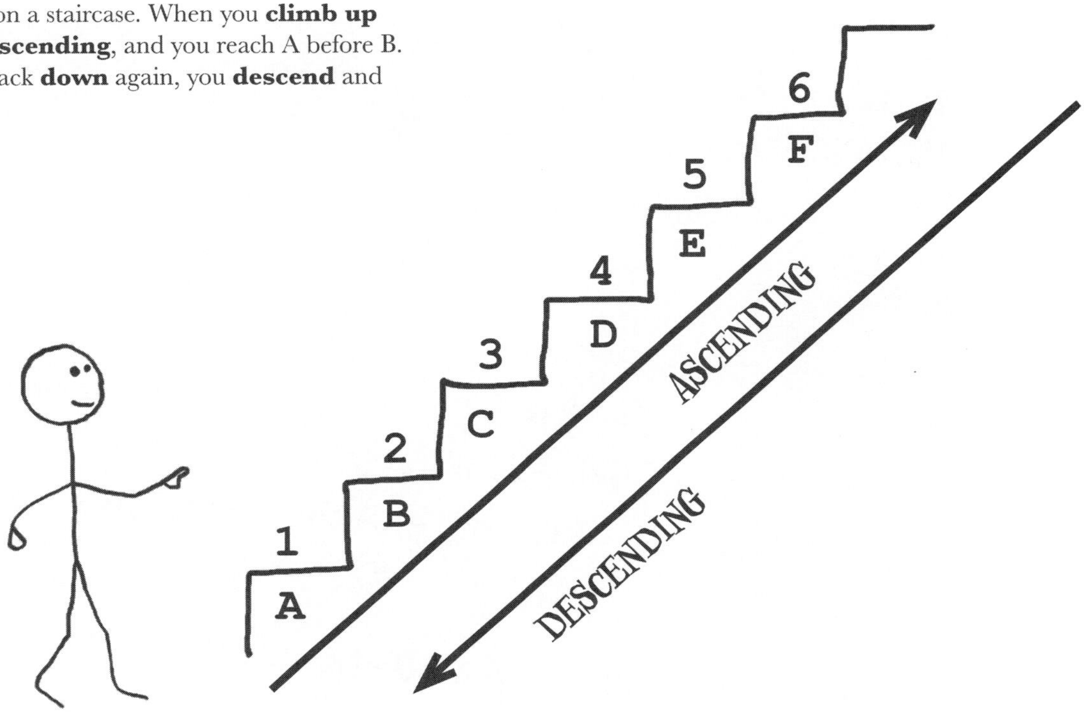

This query gives us a list of movies ordered by the purchase date, with the ***newest*** ones first. For each date, the movies purchased on that date are listed in alphabetical order.

```
SELECT title, purchased
FROM movie_table
ORDER BY title ASC, purchased DESC;
```

We can put ASC there, but it's not necessary. Just remember that ASC is the default order.

If we want to order our data from Z to A or from 9 to 1, we have to use the DESC keyword.

To: Dataville Video Staff
From: The Boss
Subject: Freebies all round!

Hey,

The store is looking great! You've got all those movies stacked in the right places, and, thanks to those fancy ORDER BY clauses in your SQL, everybody can find exactly what they're looking for.

To reward you for all of your hard work, I'm throwing a little pizza party at my house tonight. Show up at 6ish.

Don't forget to bring those reports!
Your boss

P.S. Don't wear anything too nice, I've got these bookshelves I've been itching to reorganize…

The Girl Sprout® cookie sales leader problem

The troop leader of the local Girl Sprout troop is trying to figure out which girl sold the most cookies. So far she's got a table of each girl's sales for each day.

I need to find the winner soon. No one likes an angry Girl Sprout.

Edwina, confused Girl Sprout troop leader

Girl Sprout who made the sale → first_name; Dollar amount earned → sales; Sales for this date → sale_date

cookie_sales

ID	first_name	sales	sale_date
1	Lindsay	32.02	3-6-2007
2	Paris	26.53	3-6-2007
3	Britney	11.25	3-6-2007
4	Nicole	18.96	3-6-2007
5	Lindsay	9.16	3-7-2007
6	Paris	1.52	3-7-2007
7	Britney	43.21	3-7-2007
8	Nicole	8.05	3-7-2007
9	Lindsay	17.62	3-8-2007
10	Paris	24.19	3-8-2007
11	Britney	3.40	3-8-2007
12	Nicole	15.21	3-8-2007
13	Lindsay	0	3-9-2007
14	Paris	31.99	3-9-2007
15	Britney	2.58	3-9-2007
16	Nicole	0	3-9-2007
17	Lindsay	2.34	3-10-2007
18	Paris	13.44	3-10-2007
19	Britney	8.78	3-10-2007
20	Nicole	26.82	3-10-2007
21	Lindsay	3.71	3-11-2007
22	Paris	.56	3-11-2007
23	Britney	34.19	3-11-2007
24	Nicole	7.77	3-11-2007
25	Lindsay	16.23	3-12-2007
26	Paris	0	3-12-2007
27	Britney	4.50	3-12-2007
28	Nicole	19.22	3-12-2007

Sharpen your pencil

The Girl Sprout with the largest total amount sold will win free horseback riding lessons. All of the Girl Sprouts want to win, so it's crucial that Edwina figure out the correct winner before things get ugly.

Use your new ORDER BY skills to write a query that will help Edwina find the name of the winner.

....

Sharpen your pencil Solution

The Girl Sprout with the largest total amount sold will win free horseback riding lessons. All of the Girl Sprouts want to win, so it's crucial that Edwina figure out the correct winner before things get ugly.

Use your new ORDER BY skills to write a query that will help Edwina find the name of the winner.

```
SELECT first_name, sales
FROM cookie_sales
ORDER BY first_name;
```

Here's our query...

...and here are the results.

first_name	sales
Nicole	19.22
Nicole	0.00
Nicole	8.05
Nicole	26.82
Nicole	7.77
Nicole	15.21
Nicole	18.96
Britney	3.40
Britney	2.58
Britney	4.50
Britney	11.25
Britney	8.78
Britney	43.21
Britney	34.19
Lindsay	17.62
Lindsay	9.16
Lindsay	0.00
Lindsay	32.02
Lindsay	2.34
Lindsay	3.71
Lindsay	16.23
Paris	26.53
Paris	0.00
Paris	0.56
Paris	1.52
Paris	13.44
Paris	24.19
Paris	31.99

96.03

107.91

81.08

98.23

The sales for each girl still had to be added together manually to find the winner..

SUM can add them for us

The stakes are high. We can't make a mistake and risk making our Girl Sprouts angry. Instead of adding these up ourselves, we can make SQL do the heavy lifting for us.

The SQL language has some special keywords, called *functions*. Functions are bits of code that perform an operation on a value or values. The first one we'll show you performs a mathematical operation on a column. We'll use the SUM function which works by ***totaling the values in a column*** designated by parentheses. Let's see it in action.

The SUM function totals the values in the sales column.

SUM is known as a function. This means that it performs an action on the column next to it that's in parentheses.

```
SELECT SUM(sales)
FROM cookie_sales
WHERE first_name = 'Nicole';
```

This restricts the query to only add up Nicole's sales. Otherwise it would be totaling the whole of the sales column.

```
File  Edit  Window  Help  TheWinnerIs
> SELECT SUM(sales) FROM cookie_sales
-> WHERE first_name = 'Nicole';
+------------+
| SUM(sales) |
+------------+
|      96.03 |
+------------+
1 row in set (0.00 sec)
```

Now we need the other three totals and we're done. But it would be easier if we could do it in one single query...

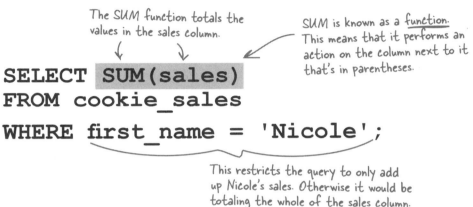

Try this at home

Try it yourself. Create a table like the cookie_sales table and insert some decimal values in it. Then work through the queries you'll find over the next few pages.

SUM all of them at once with GROUP BY

There is a way to SUM each of the girl's sales at the same time. We'll just add a GROUP BY to our SUM statement. This groups all of the first name values for each girl and totals the sales for this group.

```
SELECT  first_name, SUM(sales)
FROM cookie_sales
GROUP BY first_name
ORDER BY SUM(sales)DESC;
```

SUM all the sales column figures.

Group together all the first_name values.

We have to order by the same SUM that we selected with.

We want the values displayed high-to-low so we can see the winner more easily.

This statement totals all the sales values in each first name group.

first_name	sales
Nicole	19.22
Nicole	0.00
Nicole	8.05
Nicole	26.82
Nicole	7.77
Nicole	15.21
Nicole	18.96

first_name	sales
Paris	26.53
Paris	0.00
Paris	0.56
Paris	1.52
Paris	13.44
Paris	24.19
Paris	31.99

first_name	sales
Lindsay	17.62
Lindsay	9.16
Lindsay	0.00
Lindsay	32.02
Lindsay	2.34
Lindsay	3.71
Lindsay	16.23

first_name	sales
Britney	3.40
Britney	2.58
Britney	4.50
Britney	11.25
Britney	8.78
Britney	43.21
Britney	34.19

File Edit Window Help TheWinnerReallyIs

```
> SELECT first_name, SUM(sales)
-> FROM cookie_sales GROUP BY first_name
-> ORDER BY SUM(sales);
+------------+------------+
| first_name | sum(sales) |
+------------+------------+
| Britney    |     107.91 |
| Paris      |      98.23 |
| Nicole     |      96.03 |
| Lindsay    |      81.08 |
+------------+------------+
4 rows in set (0.00 sec)
```

And the winner is Britney!

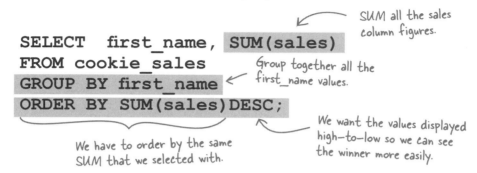

AVG with GROUP BY

The other girls were disappointed, so Edwina has decided to give another prize to the girl with the highest daily average. She uses the AVG function.

Each girl has seven days of sales. For each girl, the AVG function adds together her sales and then divides it by 7.

Again, we're grouping together all the first_name values...

... but this time we're averaging the value.

```
SELECT first_name, AVG(sales)
FROM cookie_sales
GROUP BY first_name;
```

AVG adds all of the values in a group and then divides by the total number of values to find the average value for that group.

first_name	sales
Nicole	19.22
Nicole	0.00
Nicole	8.05
Nicole	26.82
Nicole	7.77
Nicole	15.21
Nicole	18.96

first_name	sales
Paris	26.53
Paris	0.00
Paris	0.56
Paris	1.52
Paris	13.44
Paris	24.19
Paris	31.99

first_name	sales
Lindsay	17.62
Lindsay	9.16
Lindsay	0.00
Lindsay	32.02
Lindsay	2.34
Lindsay	3.71
Lindsay	16.23

first_name	sales
Britney	3.40
Britney	2.58
Britney	4.50
Britney	11.25
Britney	8.78
Britney	43.21
Britney	34.19

```
File Edit Window Help TheWinnerReallyIs
> SELECT  first_name, AVG(sales)
-> FROM cookie_sales GROUP BY first_name;
+------------+------------+
| first_name | AVG(sales) |
+------------+------------+
| Nicole     |  13.718571 |
| Britney    |  15.415714 |
| Lindsay    |  11.582857 |
| Paris      |  14.032857 |
+------------+------------+
4 rows in set (0.00 sec)
```

Oops, Britney did it again. We need to come up with some other way to find a second place winner.

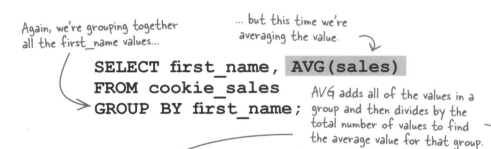

MIN and MAX

Not willing to leave anything out, Edwina takes a quick look at the `MIN` and `MAX` values from her table to see if any of the other girls had a larger sale value for a single day, or even if Britney had a worse day and got a lower value than any of the others…

We can use the function `MAX` to find the **largest value in a column**. `MIN` will give us the **smallest value in a column**.

```
SELECT first_name, MAX(sales)
FROM cookie_sales
GROUP BY first_name;
```

MAX returns the single largest sale value for each girl.

first_name	sales
Nicole	26.82
Britney	43.21
Lindsay	32.02
Paris	31.99

Surprise, Britney had the highest single day sales.

```
SELECT first_name, MIN(sales)
FROM cookie_sales
GROUP BY first_name;
```

MIN returns the single lowest sale value for each girl.

first_name	sales
Nicole	0.00
Britney	2.58
Lindsay	0.00
Paris	0.00

And while it looks like the other girls slacked off at least one day each, even on Britney's worst day she made money.

This is getting serious. Maybe I can give the prize to the girl who sold cookies on more days than any of the others.

COUNT the days

To figure out which girl sold cookies on more days than any other, Edwina tries to work out how many days the cookies were sold with the COUNT function. COUNT will return the ***number of rows in a column.***

```
SELECT COUNT(sale_date)
FROM cookie_sales;
```

COUNT returns the number of rows in the sale_date column. If the value is NULL, it isn't counted.

Sharpen your pencil

cookie_sales

ID	first_name	sales	sale_date
1	Lindsay	32.02	3-6-2007
2	Paris	26.53	3-6-2007
3	Britney	11.25	3-6-2007
4	Nicole	18.96	3-6-2007
5	Lindsay	9.16	3-7-2007
6	Paris	1.52	3-7-2007
7	Britney	43.21	3-7-2007
8	Nicole	8.05	3-7-2007
9	Lindsay	17.62	3-8-2007
10	Paris	24.19	3-8-2007
11	Britney	3.40	3-8-2007
12	Nicole	15.21	3-8-2007
13	Lindsay	0	3-9-2007
14	Paris	31.99	3-9-2007
15	Britney	2.58	3-9-2007
16	Nicole	0	3-9-2007
17	Lindsay	2.34	3-10-2007
18	Paris	13.44	3-10-2007
19	Britney	8.78	3-10-2007
20	Nicole	26.82	3-10-2007
21	Lindsay	3.71	3-11-2007
22	Paris	.56	3-11-2007
23	Britney	34.19	3-11-2007
24	Nicole	7.77	3-11-2007
25	Lindsay	16.23	3-12-2007
26	Paris	0	3-12-2007
27	Britney	4.50	3-12-2007
28	Nicole	19.22	3-12-2007

Here's the original table. What do you think will be returned by the query?

....

....

Does this number represent the actual number of days cookies were sold?

....

....

Write a query that will give us the number of days that each girl sold cookies.

....

....

....

Sharpen your pencil Solution

Here's the original table. What do you think will be returned by the query?

28 sales dates

Does this number represent the actual number of days cookies were sold?

No. This number simply represents the number of values in the table for sale_date.

Write a query that will give us the number of days that each girl sold cookies.

```
SELECT first_name, COUNT(sale_date)
FROM cookie_sales
GROUP BY first_name;
```

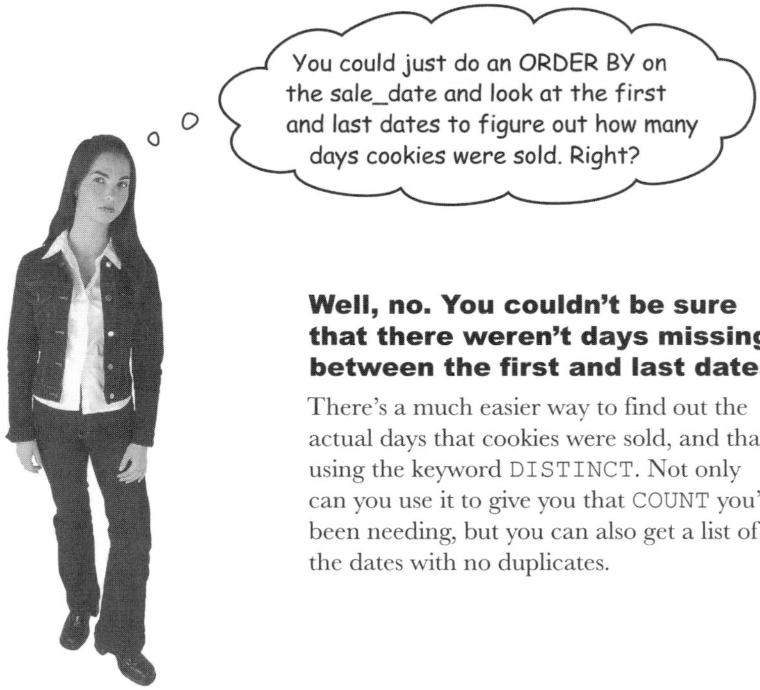
You could just do an ORDER BY on the sale_date and look at the first and last dates to figure out how many days cookies were sold. Right?

Well, no. You couldn't be sure that there weren't days missing between the first and last dates.

There's a much easier way to find out the actual days that cookies were sold, and that's using the keyword DISTINCT. Not only can you use it to give you that COUNT you've been needing, but you can also get a list of the dates with no duplicates.

SELECT DISTINCT values

First let's look at that keyword DISTINCT ***without*** the COUNT function.

Since DISTINCT is a keyword and not a function, you don't need parentheses around sale_date.

```
SELECT DISTINCT sale_date
FROM cookie_sales
ORDER BY sale_date;
```

Here's our ORDER BY so we can see the first and last sales dates.

```
File Edit Window Help NoDupes
> SELECT DISTINCT sale_date
FROM cookie_sales
 -> ORDER BY sale_date;
+------------+
| sale_date  |
+------------+
| 2007-03-06 |
| 2007-03-07 |
| 2007-03-08 |
| 2007-03-09 |
| 2007-03-10 |
| 2007-03-11 |
| 2007-03-12 |
+------------+
7 rows in set (0.00 sec)
```

Look at that, not a duplicate in the bunch!

Now let's try it ***with*** the COUNT function:

Notice that the DISTINCT goes inside the parentheses with sale_date.

```
SELECT COUNT(DISTINCT sale_date)
FROM cookie_sales;
```

We don't need an ORDER BY because COUNT will be returning a single number. Nothing to ORDER here.

BRAIN BARBELL

Try out this query, and then use it to figure out which girl sold cookies on the most days?

Answer: Britney

Who am I?

A bunch of SQL functions and keywords, in full costume, are playing a party game, "Who am I?" They'll give you a clue—you try to guess who they are based on what they say. Assume they always tell the truth about themselves. Fill in the blanks to the right to identify the attendees. Also, for each attendee, write down whether it's a function or keyword.

Tonight's attendees:

COUNT, DISTINCT, AVG, MIN, GROUP BY, SUM, MAX

	Name	function or keyword
The result you get from using me might not be worth much.	....	....
What I spit out is larger than anything I take in.	....	....
I'll give you one-of-a-kind results.	....	....
I'll tell you how many there were.	....	....
You need to use me if you want to get a sum.	....	....
I'm only interested in the big number.	....	....
How am I? Somewhere in the middle.	....	....

Answers on page 279.

there are no Dumb Questions

Q: Since you were looking for the highest values with AVG, MAX, and MIN, couldn't you have added an ORDER BY clause?

A: We could have, and it would have been a very good idea. We chose to leave it out so as to not clutter up the queries and make it easier for you to learn the new functions. Take a look back over those functions and visualize the ORDER BY there. See how it would change the results?

Q: That DISTINCT keyword seems pretty useful. Can I use it with any column I want?

A: You can. It's especially useful when you have multiple records with the same value in a single column, and you simply want to see the variety of the values, and not a long list of duplicate values.

Q: Doing the query for MIN() didn't really have anything to do with Edwina finding a winner, did it?

A: No, but it would have helped her find the girls who did the worst. Next year, she can keep an eye on them to motivate them more.

Q: Speaking of MIN, what happens if there's a NULL in the column?

A: Good question. No, NULL is never returned by any of these functions, because NULL is the absence of a value, not the same thing as zero.

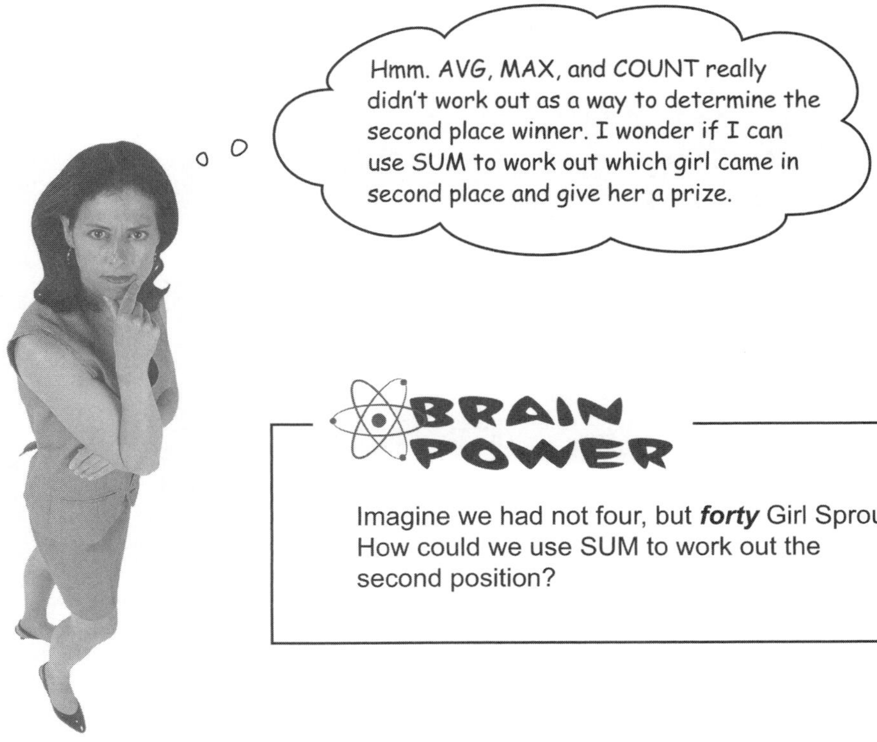
Hmm. AVG, MAX, and COUNT really didn't work out as a way to determine the second place winner. I wonder if I can use SUM to work out which girl came in second place and give her a prize.

BRAIN POWER

Imagine we had not four, but ***forty*** Girl Sprouts. How could we use SUM to work out the second position?

LIMIT the number of results

Now we're going to use SUM to determine second place. Let's look back at the original query and and results to help us figure out how to get that winner.

```
SELECT first_name, SUM(sales)
FROM cookie_sales
GROUP BY first_name
ORDER BY SUM(sales)DESC;
```

It's crucial that we use ORDER BY here; otherwise our results would be arbitrary.

first_name	sales
Britney	107.91
Paris	98.23
Nicole	96.03
Lindsay	81.08

We really only want the first two results.

Paris is our second-place winner! Nicole has stopped speaking to her.

Since we only have four results, it's easy to see who came in second place. But if we wanted to be even more precise, we could LIMIT the number of results just to the top two girls. That way we could see precisely the results we want. LIMIT allows us to specify exactly how many rows we want returned from our result set.

```
SELECT first_name, SUM(sales)
FROM cookie_sales
GROUP BY first_name
ORDER BY SUM(sales)DESC
LIMIT 2;
```

This is saying that you want to LIMIT your results to the first two.

It's a long query and gets you these two little results.

first_name	sales
Britney	107.91
Paris	98.23

While there are only four Girl Sprouts in the table and limiting it to two doesn't help a huge amount here, imagine that you were working with a much larger table. Suppose you had a list of the top 1,000 current songs playing at radio stations, but you wanted the top 100 in order of popularity. LIMIT would allow you to see only those and not the other 900 songs.

LIMIT to just second place

`LIMIT` even allows us to pinpoint the second place winner without having to see the first place winner. For this, we can use `LIMIT` with two parameters:

If you tried to guess what this would result in, you'd probably be wrong. When you have two parameters it means something completely different than with one.

```
LIMIT 0,4
```

This is the result to start with. SQL starts counting with 0.

This is how many results to return.

first_name	sales
Britney	107.91
Paris	98.23
Nicole	96.03
Lindsay	81.08

Britney is 0, Paris is 1, Nicole is 2, and Lindsay is 3

Remember our top 100 songs? Suppose we wanted to see songs 20 through 30. Adding an extra parameter to our `LIMIT` would really help us. We'd simply be able to order them by popularity and add `LIMIT 19, 10`. The `19` says to start with the 20th song since SQL counts starting with 0, and the `10` says to give us back 10 rows.

Sharpen your pencil

Write the query that will get us the second result ***and only the second result*** using the LIMIT clause with two parameters.

Sharpen your pencil Solution

Write the query that will get us the second result ***and only the second result*** using the LIMIT clause with two parameters.

```
SELECT first_name, SUM(sales)
FROM cookie_sales
GROUP BY first_name
ORDER BY SUM(sales) DESC
LIMIT 1,1;
```

Remember, SQL starts counting with 0. So 1 is actually 2.

My SQL statements are getting so long and complicated now, with all those new keywords. I like them, they're great, but isn't there a way I can simplify things?

Your queries are getting longer because your data is getting more complicated.

Let's take a closer look at your table, you may have outgrown it. Move along to Chapter 7...

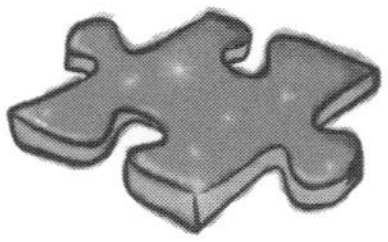

SELECTcross

It's time to give your right brain a break and put that left brain to work: all the words are SQL-related and from this chapter.

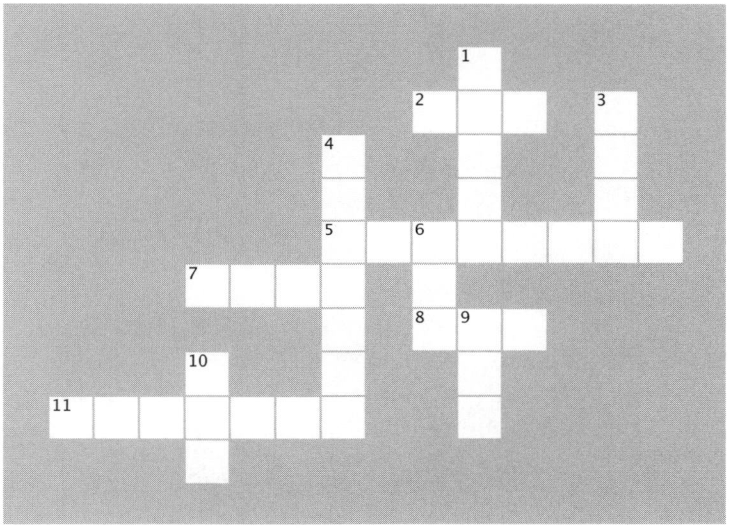

Across

2. You can find the smallest value in a column with this function.
5. This function returns each unique value only once, with no duplicates.
7. The _____ keyword in the CASE allows you to tell your RDBMS what to do if any records don't meet the conditions
8. You can find the largest value in a column with this function.
11. Use these two words to consolidate rows based on a common column.

Down

1. Lets you specify exactly how many rows to return, and which row to start with.
3. If you ORDER BY a column using this keyword, the value 9 in that column will come before 8.
4. Use these two words to alphabetically order your results based on a column you specify.
6. This function adds up a column of numeric values.
9. If you ORDER BY a column using this keyword, the value 8 in that column will come before 9.
10. Use this in a SELECT to return the number of results rather than the results themselves.

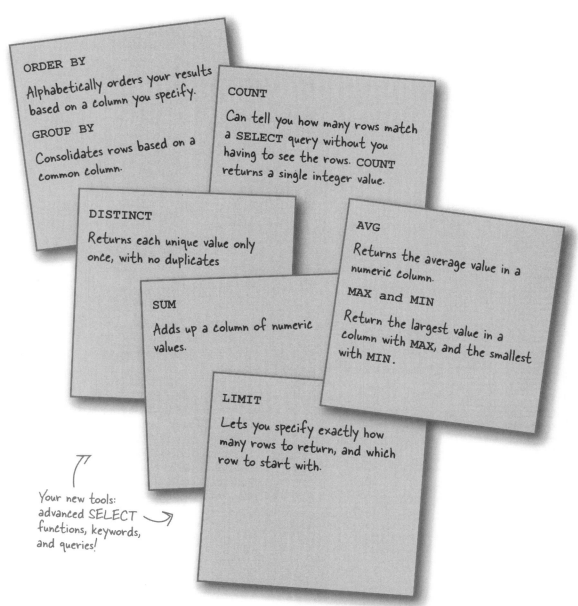

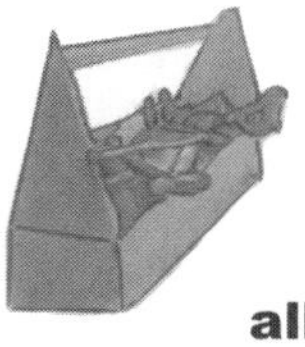

Your SQL Toolbox

You've got Chapter 6 under your belt, and you're really cruising now with all those advanced SELECT functions, keywords, and queries. For a complete list of tooltips in the book, see Appendix iii.

`ORDER BY`

Alphabetically orders your results based on a column you specify.

`GROUP BY`

Consolidates rows based on a common column.

`COUNT`

Can tell you how many rows match a `SELECT` query without you having to see the rows. `COUNT` returns a single integer value.

`DISTINCT`

Returns each unique value only once, with no duplicates

`AVG`

Returns the average value in a numeric column.

`MAX` and `MIN`

Return the largest value in a column with `MAX`, and the smallest with `MIN`.

`SUM`

Adds up a column of numeric values.

`LIMIT`

Lets you specify exactly how many rows to return, and which row to start with.

Your new tools: advanced SELECT functions, keywords, and queries!

Who am I?

from p. 272

A bunch of SQL functions and keywords, in full costume, are playing a party game, "Who am I?" They'll give you a clue—you try to guess who they are based on what they say. Assume they always tell the truth about themselves. Fill in the blanks to the right to identify the attendees. Also, for each attendee, write down whether it's a function or keyword.

Tonight's attendees:

COUNT, DISTINCT, AVG, MIN, GROUP BY, SUM, MAX

	Name	function or keyword
The result you get from using me might not be worth much.	MIN	function
What I spit out is larger than anything I take in.	SUM	function
I'll give you one-of-a-kind results.	DISTINCT	keyword
I'll tell you how many there were.	COUNT	function
You need to use me if you want to get a sum.	GROUP BY	keywords
I'm only interested in the big number.	MAX	function
How am I? Eh, so so.	AVG	function

SELECTcross Solution

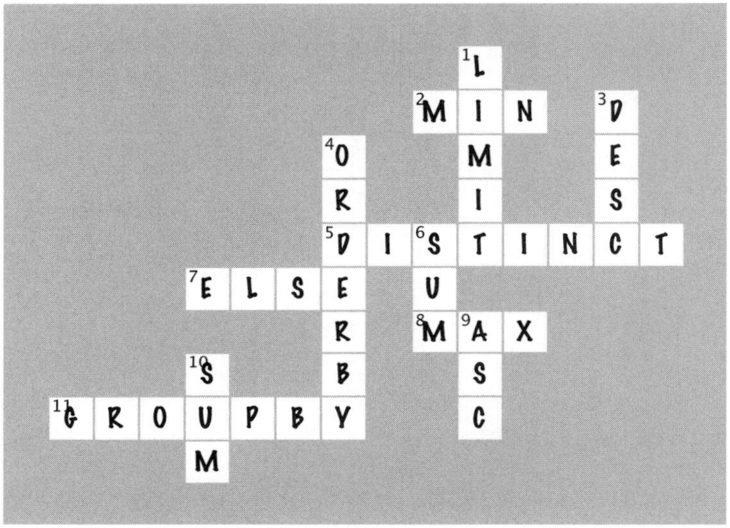

7 multi-table database design

Outgrowing your table

My little man is growing up.
Maybe he'll finally move out.

Sometimes your single table isn't big enough anymore.

Your data has become more complex, and that **one table** you've been using just **isn't cutting it**. Your single table is full of redundant data, wasting space and slowing down your queries. You've gone as far as you can go with a single table. It's a big world out there, and sometimes you need **more than one table** to contain your data, control it, and ultimately, be the master of your own database.

Finding Nigel a date

Greg's lonely friend Nigel has asked Greg to help him find a woman to date with similar interests. Greg begins by pulling up Nigel's record.

Here's Nigel:

```
contact_id: 341
last_name: Moore
first_name: Nigel
phone: 5552311111
email: nigelmoore@ranchersrule.com
gender: M
birthday: 1975-08-28
profession: Rancher
city: Austin
state: TX
status: single
interests: animals, horseback riding,
movies
seeking: single F
```

Nigel

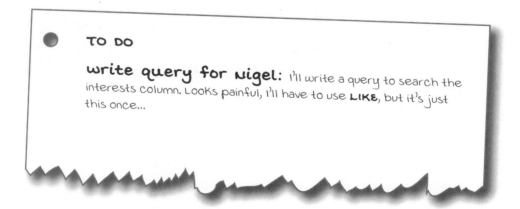

The `interests` column isn't atomic; it has more than one type of the same information in it. He's worried it won't be easy to query.

Greg adds Nigel's request to his TO DO list:

TO DO

write query for Nigel: I'll write a query to search the interests column. Looks painful, I'll have to use **LIKE**, but it's just this once...

Why change anything?

Greg's decided not to change the `interests` column at all. He's willing to write the difficult queries because he doesn't think he'll have to write them that often.

He uses the birthday `DATE` field to find matches that are no more than five years younger or five years older than Nigel.

Sharpen your pencil

Finish Greg's custom query to help Nigel find a compatible date who shares all of Nigel's interests. Annotate what each line of code does.

```
SELECT * FROM my_contacts
WHERE gender = 'F'
AND status = 'single'
AND state='TX'
AND seeking LIKE '%single M%'
AND birthday > '1970-08-28'
AND birthday < '1980-08-28'
AND interests LIKE ..............................
AND .....................................................................
AND .....................................................................
```

Sharpen your pencil Solution

Finish Greg's custom query to help Nigel find a compatible date who shares all of Nigel's interests.

Annotate what each line of code does.

```
SELECT * FROM my_contacts
WHERE gender = 'F'
AND status = 'single'
AND state='TX'
AND seeking LIKE '%single M%'
AND birthday > '1970-08-28'
AND birthday < '1980-08-28'
AND interests LIKE '%animals%'
AND interests LIKE '%horse%'
AND interests LIKE '%movies%';
```

Select everything from the my_contacts table that matches the following conditions.

Nigel wants to date a woman, so we're looking for a female...

...and we want her to be single.

...and at least live in the same state as Nigel.

She should be looking for a single guy.

He wants someone no more than 5 years older and no more than 5 years younger than he is.

These will pull out matches for Nigel's interests. We could have used OR here, but we really want to match all of his interests.

The query worked really well

Greg found the perfect match for Nigel:

```
contact_id: 1854
last_name: Fiore
first_name: Carla
phone: 5557894855
email: cfiore@fioreanimalclinic.com
gender: F
birthday: 1974-01-07
profession: Veterinarian
city: Round Rock
state: TX
status: single
interests: horseback riding, movies, animals,
mystery novels, hiking
seeking: single M
```

good age.

great profession.

even lives close by

matching interests!

Carla and Trigger

It worked too well

Nigel and Carla really hit it off. Now Greg's become a victim of his own success: *all* of his single friends want him to query the database. And Greg has a lot of single friends.

I can't keep writing these complicated queries every night.

Your table design should do the heavy lifting for you. Don't write convoluted queries to "get around" a badly designed table.

This is too time consuming. Greg adds a note to his TO DO list.

TO DO

~~**write query for Nigel:** I'll write a query to search the interests column. Looks painful, I'll have to use **LIKE**, but it's just this once...~~

in future, ignore the interests column for quicker and easier queries.

Ignoring the problem isn't the answer

Another friend, Regis, asks Greg to find him a date. He's looking for a girl who is no more than five years older and no less than five years younger than he is. He lives in Cambridge, MA and he has different interests than Nigel

Greg decides not to bother with the `interests` column to keep his queries short and simple.

Write a query for Regis without using the interests column.

```
contact_id: 873
last_name: Sullivan
first_name: Regis
phone: 5552311122
email: me@kathieleeisaflake.com
gender: M
birthday: 1955-03-20
profession: Comedian
city: Cambridge
state: MA
status: single
interests: animals, trading cards, geocaching
seeking: single F
```

Answers on page 342.

Too many bad matches

Greg gives Regis a long list of matches. After a few weeks, Regis calls Greg and tells him that his list is useless, and that not one of the women had anything in common with him.

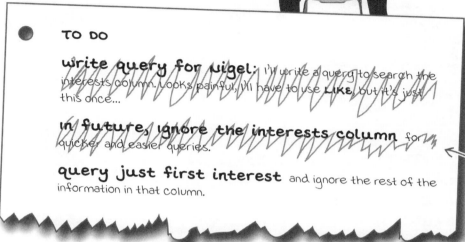

I can't ignore the interests column completely. There's ***got*** to be a better way...

TO DO

~~**write query for nigel:** I'll write a query to search the interests column. Looks painful, I'll have to use **LIKE**, but it's just this once...~~

~~**in future, ignore the interests column** for quicker and easier queries.~~

query just first interest and ignore the rest of the information in that column.

Interests ARE important. We shouldn't ignore them, there's some valuable information in there.

Use only the first interest

Greg now knows that he can't ignore all the interests. He's assuming that people gave him interests in order of importance and decides he'll query only the first one. His queries are still a little painful to write, but not as bad as when he included `LIKE` for all of the interests in the `interest` column.

Sharpen your pencil

Use the SUBSTRING_INDEX function to get only the first interest from the interests column.

Sharpen your pencil Solution

Use the SUBSTRING_INDEX function to get only the first interest from the interests column.

SUBSTRING_INDEX(interests, ',', 1)

This is "1" because it's looking for the first comma. If it were "2", it would keep going until it found a second comma and grab everything in front of that, which would be the first two interests.

This grabs everything in front of the comma in the interests column, or substring.

Here's the comma the command's looking for.

Then Greg writes a query to help Regis find a date using his SUBSTRING_INDEX and specifying that the first interest should match with 'animals'.

```
SELECT * FROM my_contacts
WHERE gender = 'F'
AND status = 'single'
AND state='MA'
AND seeking LIKE '%single M%'
AND birthday > '1950-08-28'
AND birthday < '1960-08-28'
AND SUBSTRING_INDEX(interests,',',1) = 'animals';
```

Only women who had 'animals' listed first in their interests will show up in the results.

A possible match

At last! Greg found a match for Regis:

```
contact_id: 459
last_name: Ferguson
first_name: Alexis
phone: 5550983476
email: alexangel@yahoo.com
gender: F
birthday: 1956-09-19
profession: Artist
city: Pflugerville
state: MA
status: single
interests: animals
seeking: single M
```

good age. (birthday)

lives near Regis (state)

matching interest (interests)

Mis-matched

Regis asked Alexis out on a date, and Greg waited anxiously to hear how it went. He began to imagine his `my_contacts` table as the start of a great social networking site.

The next day, Regis shows up at Greg's door, clearly upset.

Regis shouts, "She was definitely interested in animals. But you didn't tell me that one of her interests was taxidermy. Dead animals everywhere!"

TO DO

~~**write query for Nigel:** I'll write a query to search the interests column. Looks painful, I'll have to use **LIKE**, but it's just this once...~~

~~**in future, ignore the interests column** for quicker and easier queries.~~

~~**query just first interest** and ignore the rest of the information in that column.~~

create multiple columns to hold one interest in each because having all the interests in one column makes querying difficult.

Regis's perfect match was in the table, but was never discovered because her interests were in a different order.

Greg decides to redesign his table.

BRAIN POWER

What will Greg's next query look like after he adds in multiple interest columns?

Add more interest columns

Greg realizes that the single interest column makes query writing inexact. He has to use LIKE to try to match interests, sometimes ending up with bad matches.

Since he learned how to ALTER tables recently, as well as how to break apart text strings, he decides to create multiple interest columns and put one interest in each column. He thinks that four columns should be enough.

Sharpen your pencil

Use your ALTER and the SUBSTRING_INDEX function to end up with these columns. Write as many queries as it takes.

```
contact_id
last_name
first_name
phone
email
gender
birthday
profession
city
state
status
interest1
interest2
interest3
interest4
seeking
```

Answers on page 341.

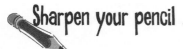

Starting over

Greg's been feeling bad about Regis's experience with Alexis, so he's going to try once more. He begins by pulling up Regis's record:

```
contact_id: 872
last_name: Sullivan
first_name: Regis
phone: 5554531122
email: regis@kathieleeisaflake.com
gender: M
birthday: 1955-03-20
profession: Comedian
city: Cambridge
state: MA
status: single
interest1: animals
interest2: trading cards
interest3: geocaching
interest4: NULL
seeking: single F
```

Four interests columns in our newly reformatted table

Then Greg writes a custom query to help Regis find a compatible date. He throws in everything he can think of to make a great match. He starts with the simpler columns—gender, status, state, seeking, and birthday—before querying all those interest columns.

Write his query here.

Exercise Solution

Then Greg writes a custom query to help Regis find a compatible date. He throws in everything he can think of to make a great match. He starts with the simpler columns, gender, status, state, seeking, and birthday before querying all those interest columns.

Write his query here.

```
SELECT * FROM my_contacts
WHERE gender = 'F'
AND status = 'single'
AND state='MA'
AND seeking LIKE '%single M%'
AND birthday > '1950-03-20'
AND birthday < '1960-03-20'
AND
(
interest1 = 'animals'
OR interest2 = 'animals'
OR interest3 = 'animals'
OR interest4 = 'animals'
)
AND
(
interest1 = 'trading cards'
OR interest2 = 'trading cards'
OR interest3 = 'trading cards'
OR interest4 = 'trading cards'
)
AND
(
interest1 = 'geocaching'
OR interest2 = 'geocaching'
OR interest3 = 'geocaching'
OR interest4 = 'geocaching'
);
```

Regis wants to date a single girl born between 1970 and 1980, who lives in Massachusetts and wants to date a single guy.

Greg has to look through each interest column to see if the values match Regis's interests since there could be a match in any of the four new columns.

Regis had a NULL value for interest4 so we only have to check for three interests, not four.

All is lost...

Adding the new columns did nothing to solve the basic problem; the table design does not make querying easy. Each version of the table violates the rules of atomic data.

TO DO

~~**write query for Nigel:** I'll write a query to search the interests column. Looks painful, I'll have to use LIKE, but it's just this once...~~

~~**in future, ignore the interests column** for quicker and easier queries.~~

~~**query just first interest** and ignore the rest of the information in that column.~~

~~**create multiple columns to hold one interest in each** because having all the interests in one column makes querying difficult.~~

?

This seemed like such a good a solution. But it made querying even more complicated.

...But wait

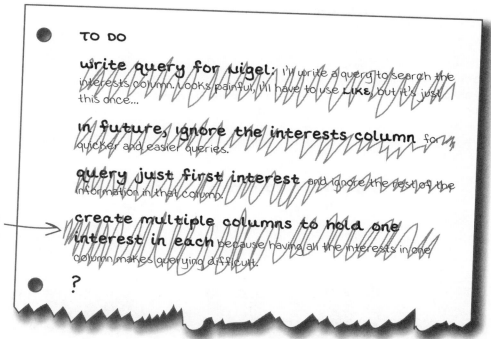

Could we create a table that just contained interests? Would that help?

BRAIN POWER

Would adding a new table help? How might we connect the data in a new table to our current table?

Think outside of the single table

We know that there's no good solution if we work within the current table. We tried many ways to fix the data, even altering the structure of the single table. Nothing worked.

We need to think outside of this table. What we really need are **more tables** that can ***work with*** the current one to allow us to **associate each person with more than one interest**. And this will allow us to keep the existing data intact.

We need to move the non-atomic columns in our table into new tables.

File Edit Window Help MessyTable

```
> DESCRIBE my_contacts;
+------------+-------------+------+-----+---------+----------------+
| Field      | Type        | Null | Key | Default | Extra          |
+------------+-------------+------+-----+---------+----------------+
| contact_id | int(11)     | NO   | PRI | NULL    | auto_increment |
| last_name  | varchar(30) | YES  |     | NULL    |                |
| first_name | varchar(20) | YES  |     | NULL    |                |
| phone      | varchar(10) | YES  |     | NULL    |                |
| email      | varchar(50) | YES  |     | NULL    |                |
| gender     | char(1)     | YES  |     | NULL    |                |
| birthday   | date        | YES  |     | NULL    |                |
| profession | varchar(50) | YES  |     | NULL    |                |
| city       | varchar(50) | YES  |     | NULL    |                |
| state      | varchar(2)  | YES  |     | NULL    |                |
| status     | varchar(20) | YES  |     | NULL    |                |
| interests  | varchar(100)| YES  |     | NULL    |                |
| seeking    | varchar(100)| YES  |     | NULL    |                |
+------------+-------------+------+-----+---------+----------------+
13 rows in set (0.01 sec) >
```

The multi-table clown tracking database

Remember our clown tracking table from chapter 3? The Dataville clown problem is still increasing, so we've altered the single table into a much more useful set of tables.

How the old clown_tracking table used to look.

clown_tracking

clown_info	name	last_seen	activities
Elsie	Cherry Hill Senior Center	F, red hair, green dress, huge feet	balloons, little car
Pickles	Jack Green's party	hair, blue suit, huge feet	mime
Snuggles	Ball-Mart	shirt, baggy blue pants	horn, umbrella
Mr. Hobo	Eric Gray's Party	hair, tiny hat	violin

info_activities

id 🔑
activity_id 🔑

activities

activity_id 🔑
activity

We'll explain the lines and arrows soon...

What used to be the main table has been whittled down to this.

clown_info

id 🔑
name
gender
description

info_location

id 🔑
location_id 🔑
when

location

location_id 🔑
location

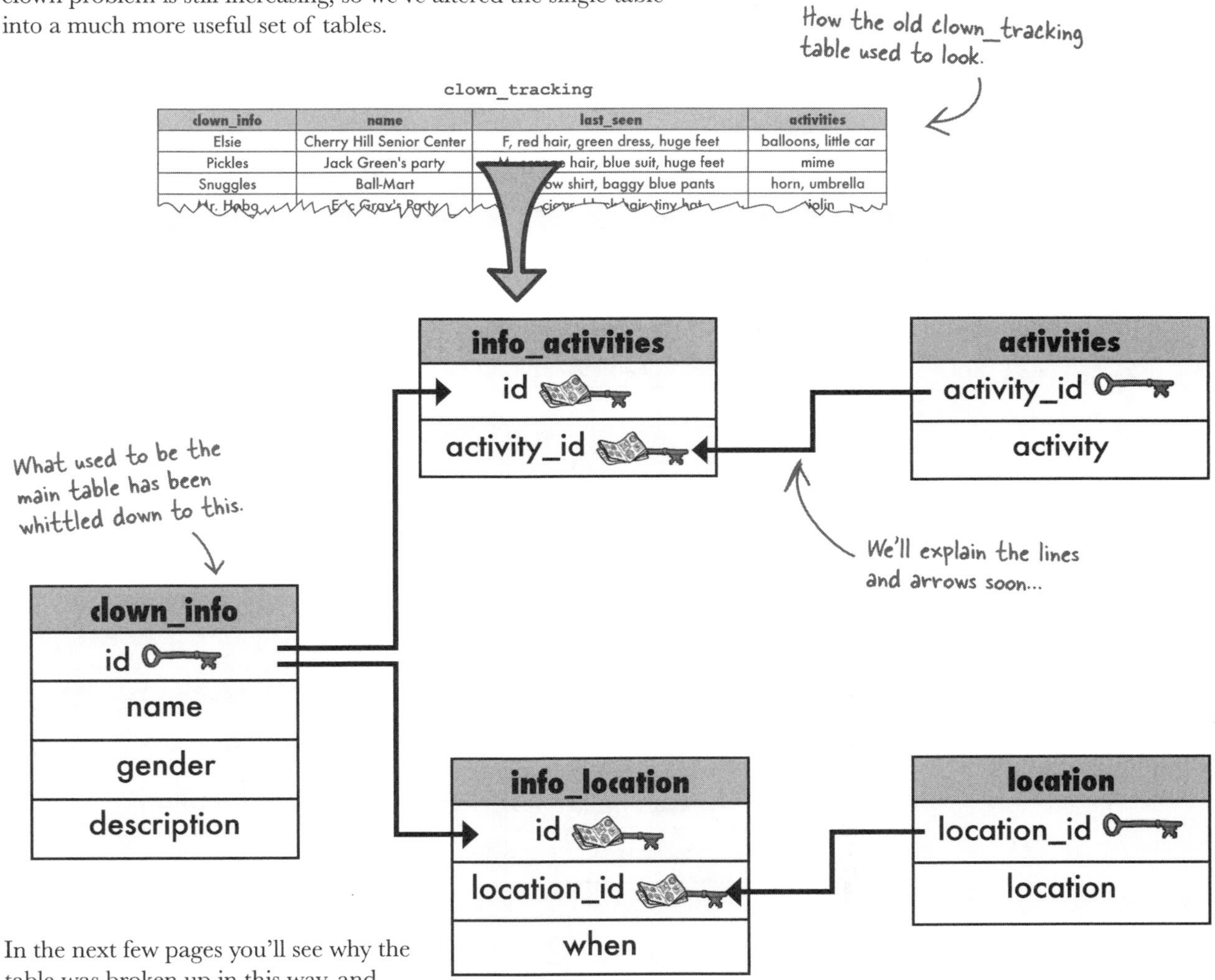

In the next few pages you'll see why the table was broken up in this way, and what the arrows and keys mean. When we've got through all that, we can apply the same rules to gregs_list.

BRAIN POWER

What do you think the lines with arrows mean? How about those key symbols?

The clown_tracking database schema

A representation of all the structures, such as tables and columns, in your database, along with how they connect, is known as a **schema**.

Creating a visual depiction of your database can help you see how things connect when you're writing your queries, but your schema can also be written in a text format.

The old table.

clown_tracking

clown_info	name	last_seen	activities
Elsie	Cherry Hill Senior Center	F, red hair, green dress, huge feet	balloons, little car
Pickles	Jack Green's party	[illegible] hair, blue suit, huge feet	mime
Snuggles	Ball-Mart	[illegible]ow shirt, baggy blue pants	horn, umbrella
Mr. Hobo	Eric Gray's Party	[illegible]	violin

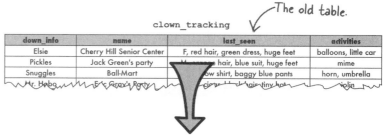

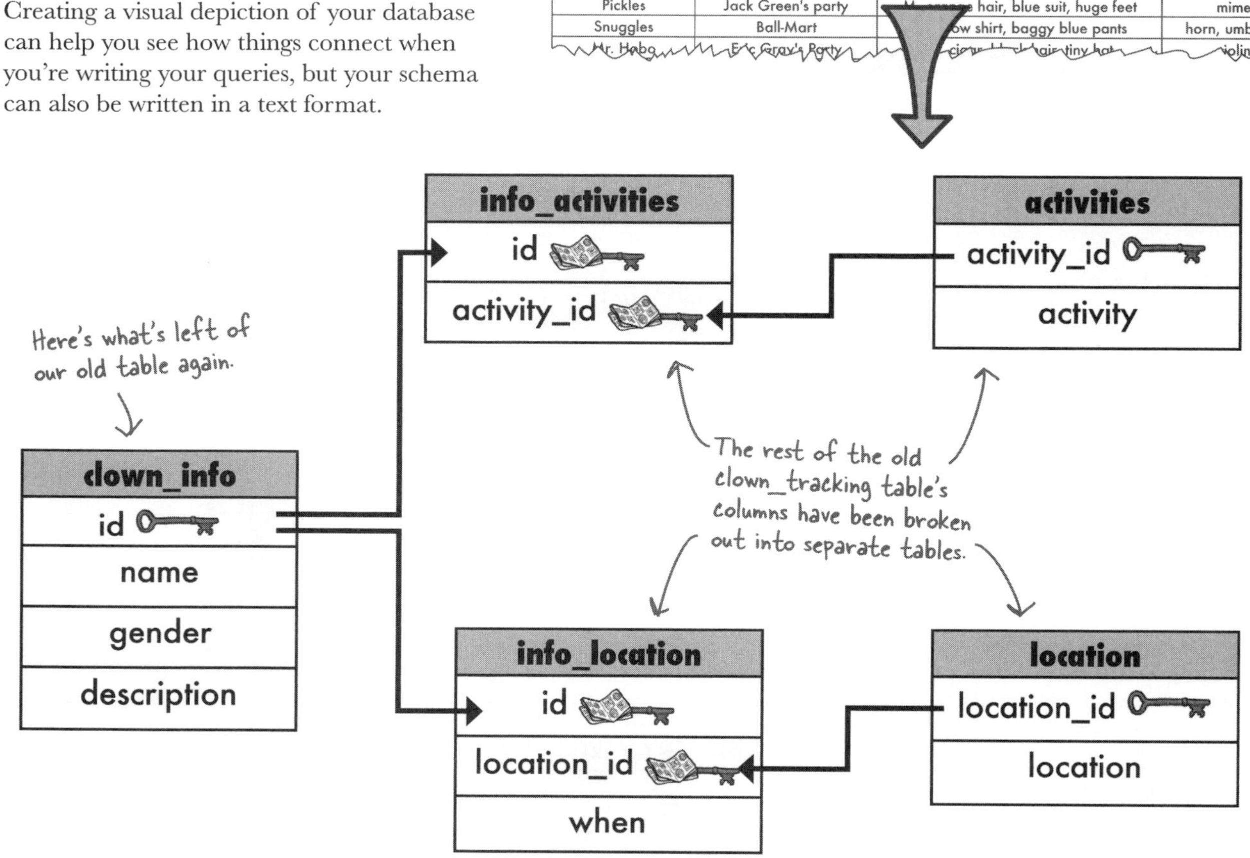

A description of the data (the columns and tables) in your database, along with any other related objects and the way they all connect is known as a SCHEMA

An easier way to diagram your tables

You've seen how the clown tracking table has been converted. Let's see how we can fix the `my_contacts` table in the same way.

Up to this point, every time we looked at a table, we either depicted it with the column names across the top and the data below, or we used a `DESCRIBE` statement in a terminal window. Those are both fine for single tables, but they're not very practical to use when we want to create a diagram of multiple tables.

Here's a shorthand technique for diagramming the current `my_contacts` table:

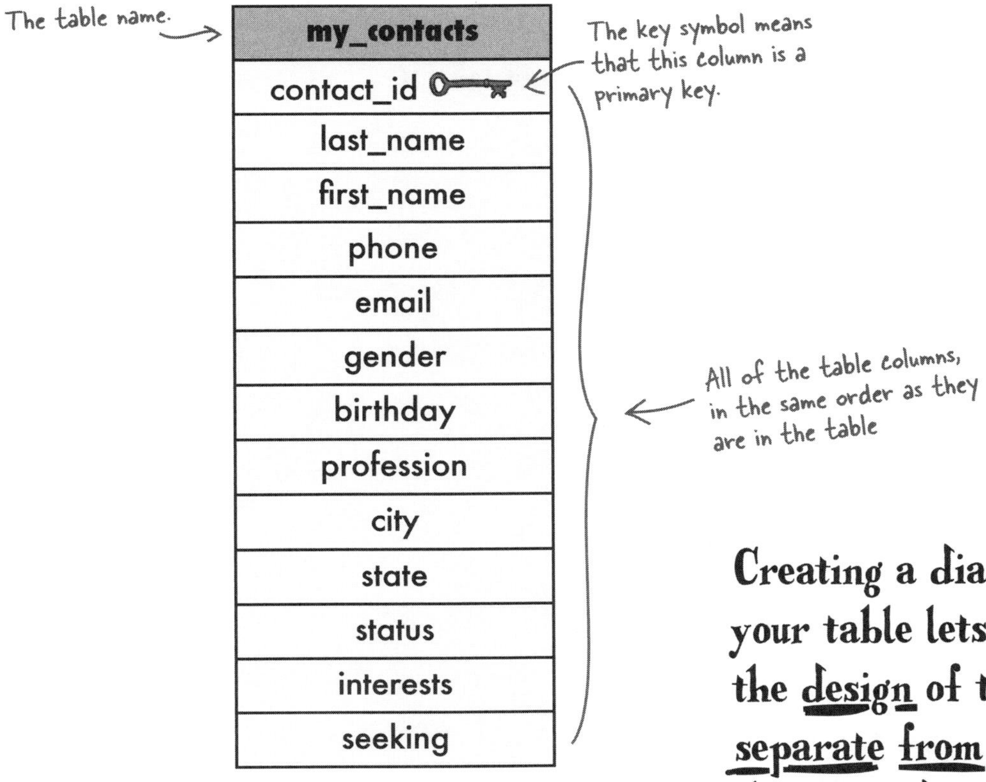

Creating a diagram of your table lets you keep the design of the table separate from the data that's inside of it.

How to go from one table to two

We know that the interests column is really difficult to query as it stands right now. It has multiple values in the same column. And even when we tried to create multiple columns for it, our queries were quite difficult to write.

Here's our current `my_contacts` table. Our interest column isn't atomic, and there's really only one good way to make it atomic: we need a new table that will hold all the interests.

We'll start by drawing some diagrams of what our tables could look like. We won't actually create our new table or touch any of the data until we figure out our new schema.

my_contacts
contact_id
last_name
first_name
phone
email
gender
birthday
profession
city
state
status
interests
seeking

Here's my_contacts. It's not atomic yet.

1 **Remove the interests column and put it in its own table.**

Here we've moved the interests colum into a new table.

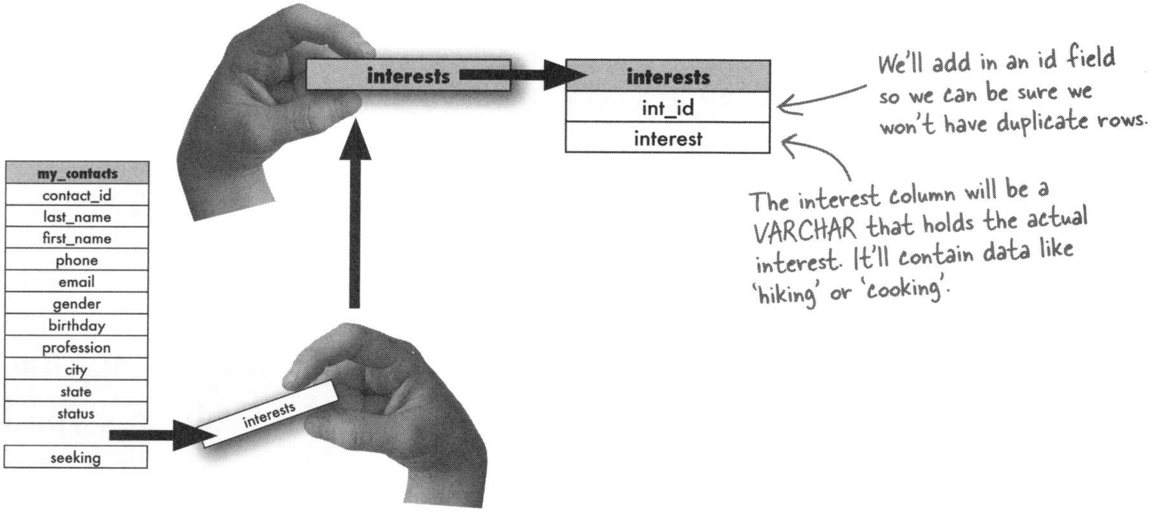
my_contacts
contact_id
last_name
first_name
phone
email
gender
birthday
profession
city
state
status
seeking
interests
interests
interests
int_id
interest
We'll add in an id field so we can be sure we won't have duplicate rows.
The interest column will be a VARCHAR that holds the actual interest. It'll contain data like 'hiking' or 'cooking'.

Our new interests table will hold all the interests from the `my_contacts` table, one interest per row.

2 **Add columns that will let us identify which interests belong to which person in the my_contacts table.**

We've moved our interests out of `my_contacts`, but we have no way of knowing which interests belong to which person. We need to use information from the `my_contacts` table and put it into the interests table to link these tables together.

One possible way is to add the `first_name` and `last_name` columns to the interests table.

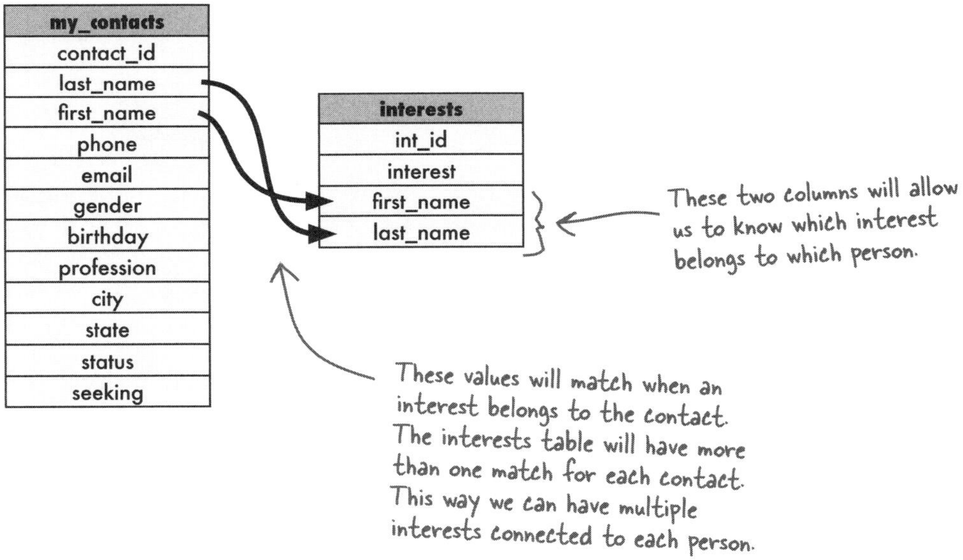
my_contacts
contact_id
last_name
first_name
phone
email
gender
birthday
profession
city
state
status
seeking
interests
int_id
interest
first_name
last_name
These two columns will allow us to know which interest belongs to which person.
These values will match when an interest belongs to the contact. The interests table will have more than one match for each contact. This way we can have multiple interests connected to each person.

BRAIN POWER

We have the right idea, but first_name and last_name aren't the best choice of columns to connect these tables.

Why is that?

Linking your tables in a diagram

Let's take a closer look at our idea for the `my_contacts` table.

Here's our initial sketch:

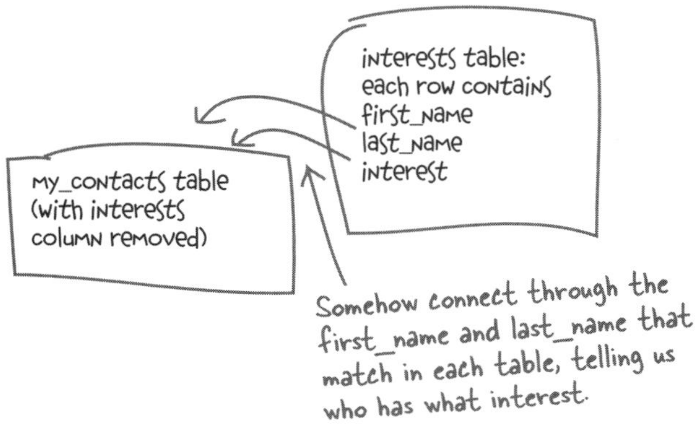
interests table:
each row contains
first_name
last_name
interest
my_contacts table
(with interests
column removed)
Somehow connect through the first_name and last_name that match in each table, telling us who has what interest.

And here's our new schema:

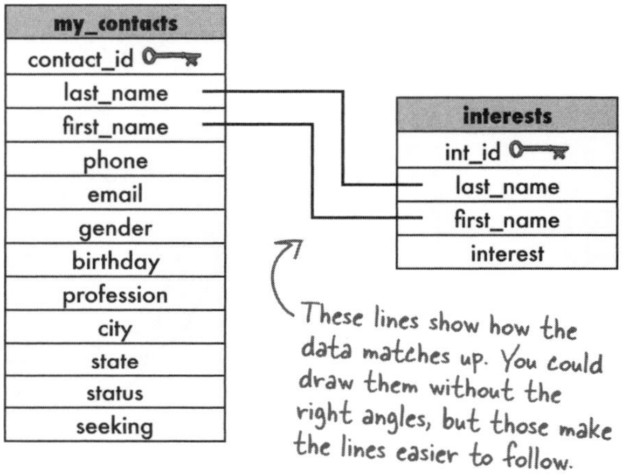
my_contacts
contact_id
last_name
first_name
phone
email
gender
birthday
profession
city
state
status
seeking
interests
int_id
last_name
first_name
interest
These lines show how the data matches up. You could draw them without the right angles, but those make the lines easier to follow.

Notice how the lines with right-angle bends between tables show the columns that match up in each table The schema allows us to tidy up our sketch in a way that any SQL developer will understand since it uses standard symbols.

And here is a series of `SELECT` statements that will let us use the data in both tables.

1

```
SELECT first_name, last_name
FROM my_contacts
WHERE (a bunch of conditions);
```

2

```
SELECT interest FROM interests
WHERE first_name = 'Somename'
AND last_name = 'Lastname';
```

Don't worry if this seems inefficient. It's just to show you how the data from one table can be used to pull out data from another. (We'll show you a better way soon.)

Sharpen your pencil

Use this space to sketch out more ideas for adding new tables to the gregs_list database to help us keep track of multiple interests.

Don't worry about making it as neat as our schema; we're at the ideas stage here. One idea is drawn for you already, but it has a flaw.

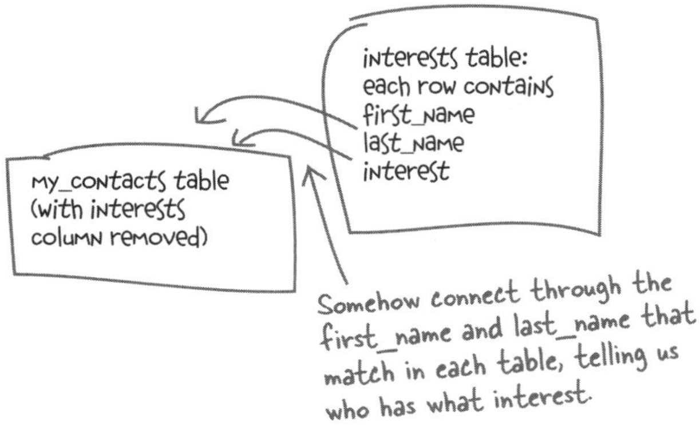
interests table:
each row contains
first_name
last_name
interest
my_contacts table
(with interests
column removed)
Somehow connect through the first_name and last_name that match in each table, telling us who has what interest.

Sharpen your pencil Solution

Use this space to sketch out more ideas for adding new tables to the gregs_list database to help us keep track of multiple interests.

Don't worry about making it as neat as our schema; we're at the ideas stage here. One idea is drawn for you already, but it has a flaw.

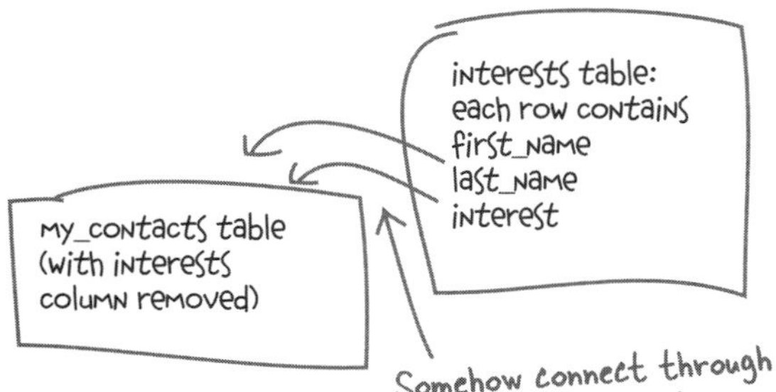

Somehow connect through the first_name and last_name that match in each table, telling us who has what interest.

Using the first name and last name to connect to the interests table isn't such a good idea, however. More than one person in my_contacts might share the same first and last name, so we could be connecting people to the wrong interests. We're better off using our primary key to make the connection.

Instead of using the first_name and last_name that might not truly be unique, we could use the contact_id to link our tables:

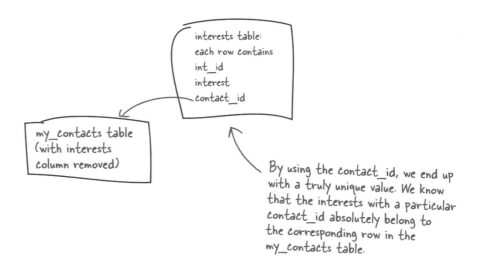

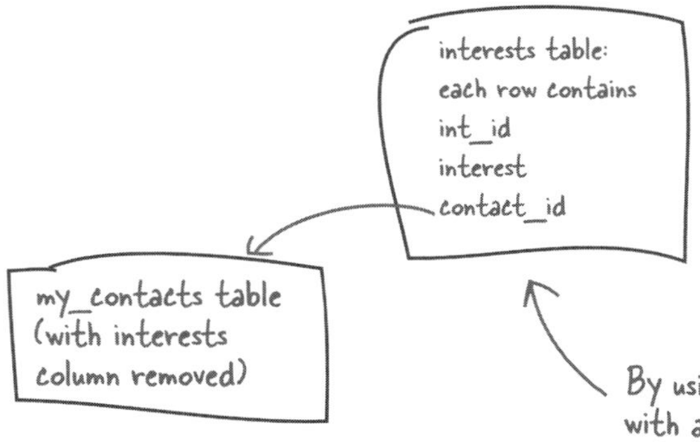

By using the contact_id, we end up with a truly unique value. We know that the interests with a particular contact_id absolutely belong to the corresponding row in the my_contacts table.

Connecting your tables

The problem with our first sketch of the connected tables is that we're trying to use `first_name` and `last_name` fields to somehow let us connect the two tables. But what if two people in the `my_contacts` table have the same `first_name` and `last_name`?

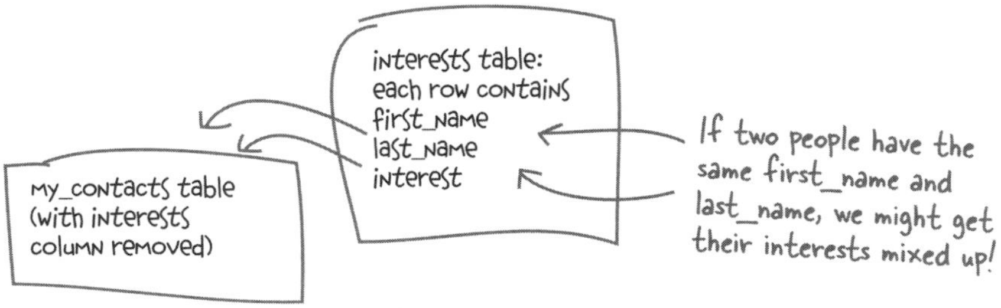
interests table:
each row contains
first_name
last_name
interest
my_contacts table
(with interests
column removed)
If two people have the same first_name and last_name, we might get their interests mixed up!

We need a **unique** column to connect these. Luckily, since we already started to normalize it, we have a truly unique column in `my_contacts`: the **primary key**.

We can use the value from the primary key in the `my_contacts` table as a column in the `interests` table. Better yet, we'll know which interests belong to which person in the `my_contacts` table through this column. It's called a **foreign key**.

The FOREIGN KEY is a column in a table that references the PRIMARY KEY of another table.

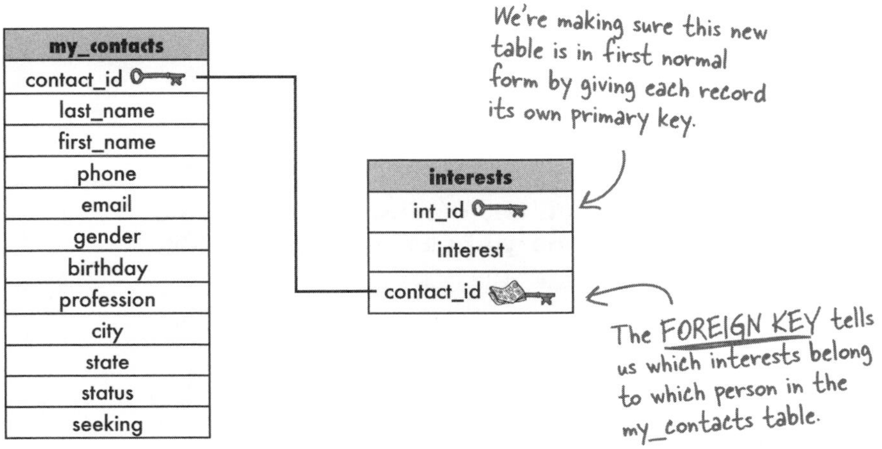
my_contacts
contact_id
last_name
first_name
phone
email
gender
birthday
profession
city
state
status
seeking
interests
int_id
interest
contact_id
We're making sure this new table is in first normal form by giving each record its own primary key.
The FOREIGN KEY tells us which interests belong to which person in the my_contacts table.

Foreign key facts

A foreign key can have a different name than the primary key it comes from.

The primary key used by a foreign key is also known as a *parent key.* The table where the primary key is from is known as a parent table.

The foreign key can be used to make sure that the rows in one table have corresponding rows in another table.

Foreign key values can be null, even though primary key values can't.

Foreign keys don't have to be unique—in fact, they often aren't.

I get that a foreign key lets me connect two tables. But what good is a NULL foreign key? Is there any way to make sure your foreign key is connected to a parent key?

A NULL foreign key means that there's no matching primary key in the parent table.

But we can make sure that a foreign key contains a meaningful value, one that exists in the parent table, by using a **constraint**.

Constraining your foreign key

Although you could simply create a table and put in a column to act as a foreign key, it's not really a foreign key unless you designate it as one when you `CREATE` or `ALTER` a table. The key is created inside of a structure called a **constraint**.

Think of a CONSTRAINT as a rule our table has to follow.

Creating a FOREIGN KEY as a constraint in your table gives you definite advantages.

You'll get errors if you violate the rules, which will stop you accidentally doing anything to break the table.

You will only be able to insert values into your foreign key that exist in the table the key came from, the parent table. This is called *referential integrity*.

Our original my_contacts table is now a parent table since part of its data has been moved to a new table, called a....

child table.

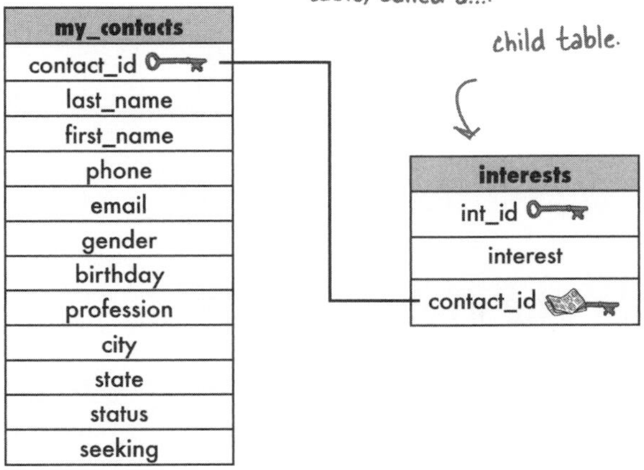
my_contacts
contact_id
last_name
first_name
phone
email
gender
birthday
profession
city
state
status
seeking
interests
int_id
interest
contact_id

Referential integrity means you can only put values in the child table's foreign key that already exist in the parent table.

You can use a foreign key to reference a unique value in the parent table.

It doesn't have to be the primary key of the parent table, but it must be unique.

Why bother with foreign keys?

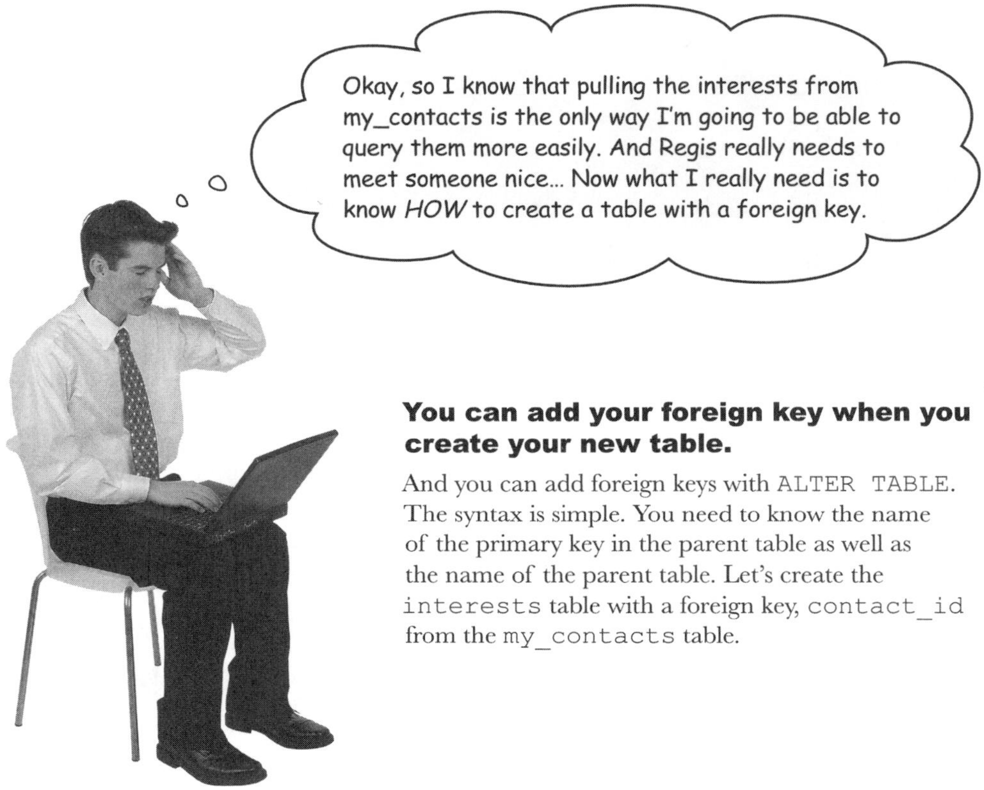
Okay, so I know that pulling the interests from my_contacts is the only way I'm going to be able to query them more easily. And Regis really needs to meet someone nice... Now what I really need is to know *HOW* to create a table with a foreign key.

You can add your foreign key when you create your new table.

And you can add foreign keys with `ALTER TABLE`. The syntax is simple. You need to know the name of the primary key in the parent table as well as the name of the parent table. Let's create the `interests` table with a foreign key, `contact_id` from the `my_contacts` table.

there are no Dumb Questions

Q: Once we get my interests pulled out from my_contacts, how will I query them?

A: We'll be getting to that in the next chapter. And you'll see that it really is easy to write queries that can pull our data from multiple tables. But for now we need to redesign my_contacts to make our queries simple and efficient.

CREATE a table with a FOREIGN KEY

Now that you know why you should create a foreign key with a
constraint, here's how you can actually do it. Note how we're
naming the CONSTRAINT so that we can tell which table the key
comes from.

Adding the PRIMARY KEY
command to the line where you set
it up is another (quicker) way to
designate your primary key.

We create the
foreign key
just like we
would any index
column: we set
it to INT and
NOT NULL.

```
CREATE TABLE interests (

int_id INT NOT NULL AUTO_INCREMENT PRIMARY KEY,

interest VARCHAR(50) NOT NULL,

contact_id INT NOT NULL,

CONSTRAINT my_contacts_contact_id_fk

FOREIGN KEY (contact_id)

REFERENCES my_contacts (contact_id);

)
```

We're naming this CONSTRAINT in a
way that tells us which table the key
comes from (my_contacts), what we've
named the key (contact_id), and that
it's a foreign key (fk).

If we change our minds
later, this name will be
what we use to undo it.
This line is optional, but
it's good form to use it.

This specifies where the
foreign key came from...

and what it's called in
the other table.

The column name in
parentheses is what
will become a foreign
key. You can name it
whatever you like.

Exercise

You try it. Open up your console window and type in the code above to create your
own interests table.

When you've created it, take a look at the structure of your new table. What new
information do you see that tells you your constraint is in there?

You try it. Open up your console window and type in the code above to create your own interests table.

When you've created it, take a look at the structure of your new table. What new information do you see that tells you your constraint is in there?

```
File Edit Window Help
> DESC interests;
+------------+-------------+------+-----+---------+----------------+
| Field      | Type        | Null | Key | Default | Extra          |
+------------+-------------+------+-----+---------+----------------+
| int_id     | int(11)     | NO   | PRI | NULL    | auto_increment |
| interest   | varchar(50) | NO   |     |         |                |
| contact_id | int(11)     | NO   | MUL |         |                |
+------------+-------------+------+-----+---------+----------------+
```

MUL means that multiple occurrences of the same value may be stored in this column. This is what allows us to keep track of multiple interests for each contact_id in my_contacts.

there are no Dumb Questions

Q: You go to all that trouble to create a foreign key constraint, but why? Couldn't you simply use the key from another table and call it a foreign key without adding the constraint?

A: You could, but by creating it as a constraint, you will only be able to insert values in it that exist in the parent table. It enforces the link between the two tables.

Q: "Enforces the link"? What does that mean?

A: The foreign key constraint ensures referential integrity (in other words, it makes sure that if you have a row in one table with a foreign key, it must correspond to a row in another through the foreign key). If you try to delete the row in a primary key table or to change a primary key value, you'll get an error if the primary key value is a foreign key constraint in another table.

Q: So that means I can never delete a row from my_contacts that has a primary key if it shows up in the interest table as a foreign key?

A: You can, you just have to remove the foreign key row first. After all, if you're removing the row from my_contacts, you don't need to know that person's interests anymore.

Q: But who cares if I have those rows left hanging around in the interests table?

A: It's slow. Those rows are called orphans, and they can really add up on you over time. All they do is slow down your queries by causing useless information to be searched.

Q: Okay, I'm convinced. Are there other constraints besides the foreign key?

A: You've already seen the primary key constraint. And using the keyword `UNIQUE` (when you create a column) is considered a constraint. There's also a type of constraint, not available in MySQL, called a `CHECK` constraint. It allows you to specify a condition that must be met on a column before you can insert a value into that column. You'll want to consult the documentation for your specific SQL RDBMS for more info on `CHECK`.

Relationships between tables

We know how to connect the tables through foreign keys now, but we still need to consider how the tables relate to each other. In the `my_contacts` table, our problem is that we need to associate **lots of people** with **lots of interests**.

This is one of three possible patterns you'll see again and again with your data: **one-to-one**, **one-to-many**, and **many-to-many**, and once you identify the pattern your data matches, coming up with the design of multiple tables—your **schema**—becomes simple.

Patterns of data: one-to-one

Let's look at the first pattern, **one-to-one**, and see how it applies. In this pattern a record in Table A can have at most ONE matching record in Table B.

So, say Table A contains your name, and Table B contains your salary details and Social Security Numbers, in order to ***isolate*** them from the rest of the table to keep them more secure.

Both tables will contain your ID number so you get the right paycheck. The `employee_id` in the parent table is a primary key, the `employee_id` in the child table is a foreign key.

In the schema, the connecting line is ***plain*** to show that we're linking **one** thing **to one** thing.

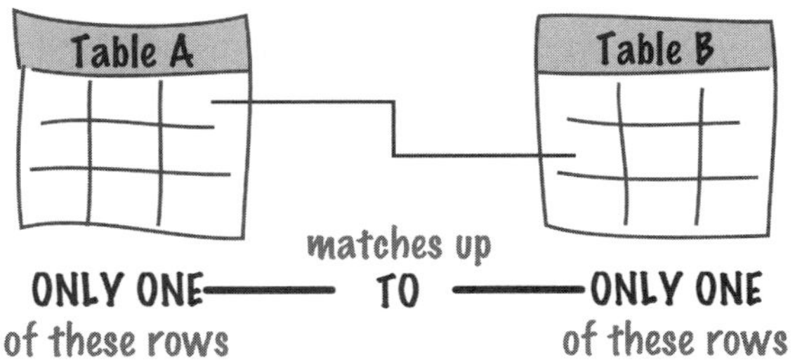

Each person in employees can only have one Social Security number, and each SSN maps to only one person. One person, one SSN, makes this a one-to-one relationship.

employees

employee_id	first_name	last_name
1	Beyonce	Knowles
2	Shawn	Carter
3	Shakira	Ripoll

salary

ssn	salary_level	employee_id
234567891	2	6
345678912	5	35
123456789	7	1

These tables also have a one-to-one relationship, since the primary key of the employee table, employee_id, is being used as the foreign key of the salary table.

Patterns of data: when to use one-to-one tables

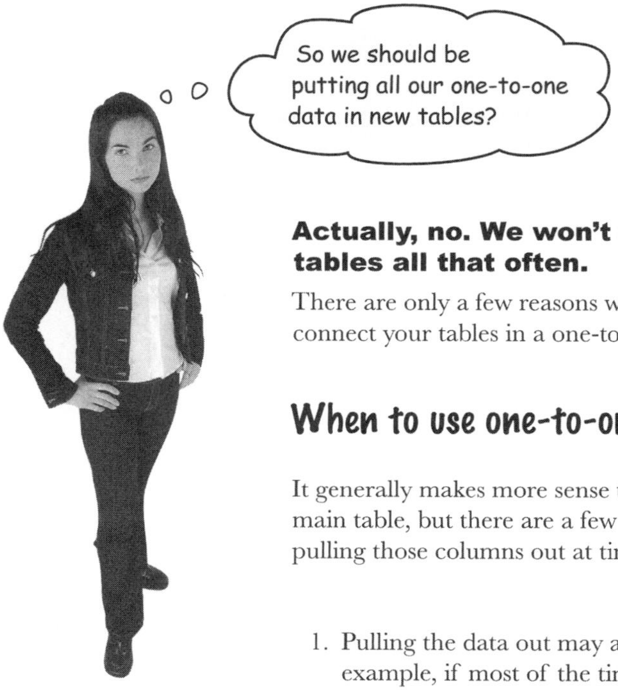
So we should be putting all our one-to-one data in new tables?

Actually, no. We won't use one-to-one tables all that often.

There are only a few reasons why you might connect your tables in a one-to-one relationship.

When to use one-to-one tables

It generally makes more sense to leave one-to-one data in your main table, but there are a few advantages you can get from pulling those columns out at times:

1. Pulling the data out may allow you to write faster queries. For example, if most of the time you need to query the SSN and not much else, you could query just the smaller table.
2. If you have a column containing values you don't yet know, you can isolate it and avoid `NULL` values in your main table.
3. You may wish to make some of your data less accessible. Isolating it can allow you to restrict access to it. For example, if you have a table of employees, you might want to keep their salary information out of the main table.
4. If you have a large piece of data, a BLOB type for example, you may want that large data in a separate table.

One-to-One: exactly one row of a parent table is related to one row of a child table.

Patterns of data: one-to-many

One-to-many means that a record in Table A can have **many** matching records in Table B, but a record in Table B can only match **one** record in Table A.

One-to-Many: a record in Table A can have MANY matching records in Table B, but a record in Table B can only match ONE record in Table A.

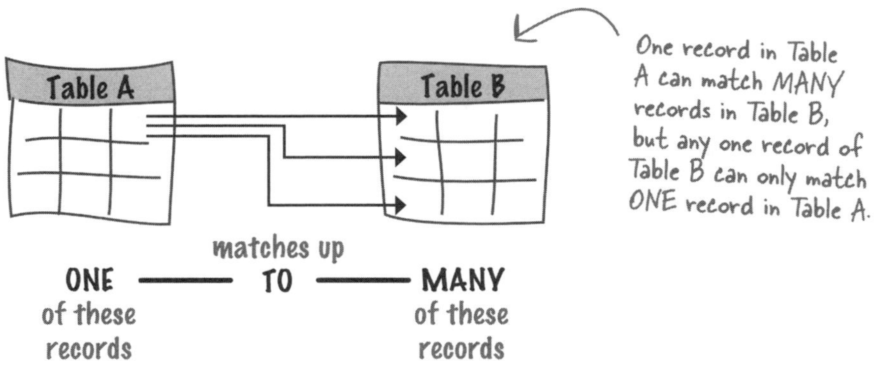
Table A
Table B
One record in Table A can match MANY records in Table B, but any one record of Table B can only match ONE record in Table A.
ONE of these records
matches up TO
MANY of these records

The prof_id column in my_contacts is a good example of a one-to-many relationship. Each person has only one prof_id, but more than one person in my_contacts may have the same prof_id.

In this example, we've moved the profession column to a new child table, and changed the profession column in the parent table to a foreign key, the prof_id column. Since it's a one-to-many relationship, we can use the prof_id in both tables to allow us to connect them.

The connecting line has a ***black arrow*** at the end to show that we're linking **one** thing **to many** things.

Each row in the professions table can have many matching rows in my_contacts, but each row in my_contacts has only one matching row in the professions table.

For example, the prof_id for Programmer may show up more than once in my_contacts, but each person in my_contacts will only have one prof_id.

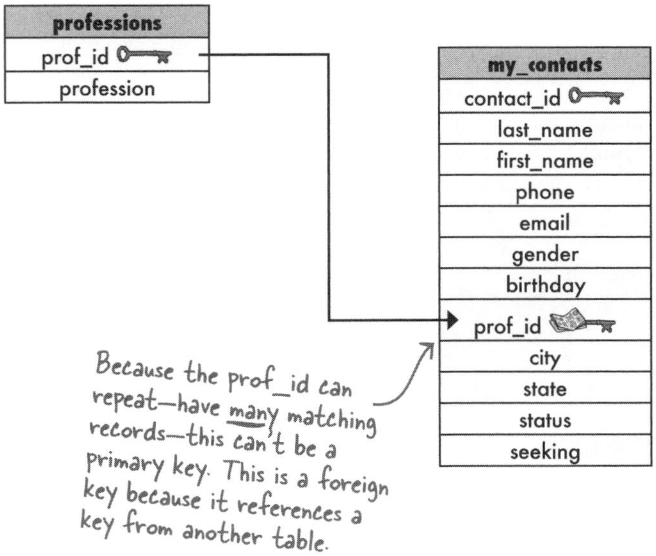
professions
prof_id
profession
my_contacts
contact_id
last_name
first_name
phone
email
gender
birthday
prof_id
city
state
status
seeking
Because the prof_id can repeat—have many matching records—this can't be a primary key. This is a foreign key because it references a key from another table.

Patterns of data: getting to many-to-many

Many woman own **many** pairs of shoes. If we created a table containing women and another table containing shoes to keep track of them all, we'd need to link many records to many records since more than one woman can own a particular make of shoe.

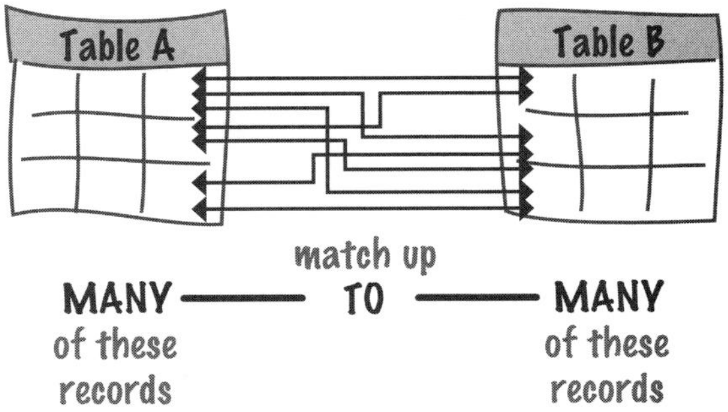

Suppose Carrie and Miranda buy both the Old Navy Flops and Prada boots, and Samantha and Miranda both have the Manolo Strappies, and Charlotte has one of each. Here's how the links between the `women` and `shoes` tables would look.

woman_id	woman
1	Carrie
2	Samantha
3	Charlotte
4	Miranda

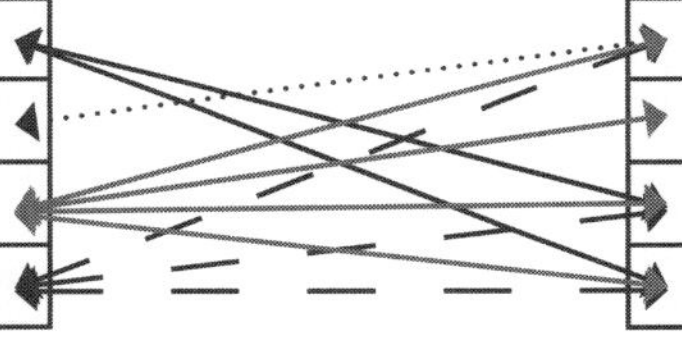

shoe_id	shoe_name
1	Manolo Strappies
2	Crocs Clogs
3	Old Navy Flops
4	Prada Boots

Imagine they loved the shoes so much, the women all bought a pair of the shoes they didn't already own. Here's how the links from women to each shoe name would look then.

The connecting lines have black arrows at both ends; we're linking many things to many things.

woman_id	woman
1	Carrie
2	Samantha
3	Charlotte
4	Miranda

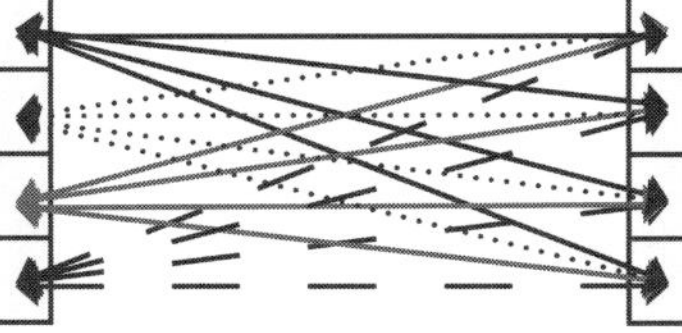

shoe_id	shoe_name
1	Manolo Strappies
2	Crocs Clogs
3	Old Navy Flops
4	Prada Boots

BRAIN POWER

How can we fix the tables without putting more than one value in a column (and winding up like Greg did with his interests column problems in his queries for Regis)?

Sharpen your pencil

Take a look at this first pair of tables. We tried to fix the problem by adding shoe_id to the table with women records as a foreign key.

woman_id	woman	shoe_id
1	Carrie	3
2	Samantha	1
3	Charlotte	1
4	Miranda	1
5	Carrie	4
6	Charlotte	2
7	Charlotte	3
8	Charlotte	4
9	Miranda	3
10	Miranda	4

shoe_id	shoe_name
1	Manolo Strappies
2	Crocs Clogs
3	Old Navy Flops
4	Prada boots

Now the two tables connect with the shoe_id column.

Sketch out the tables yourself, only this time put the woman_id in the shoe table as a foreign key.

When you've done that, draw in the links.

Sharpen your pencil Solution

Take a look at this first pair of tables. We tried to fix the problem by adding shoe_id to the table with women records as a foreign key.

woman_id	woman	shoe_id
1	Carrie	3
2	Samantha	1
3	Charlotte	1
4	Miranda	1
5	Carrie	4
6	Charlotte	2
7	Charlotte	3
8	Charlotte	4
9	Miranda	3
10	Miranda	4

shoe_id	shoe_name
1	Manolo Strappies
2	Crocs Clogs
3	Old Navy Flops
4	Prada boots

Now the two tables connect with the shoe_id column.

Notice the duplicates in the woman and shoe_name columns.

Sketch out the tables yourself, only this time put the woman_id in the shoe table as a foreign key.

When you've done that, draw in the links.

shoe_id	shoe_name	woman_id
1	Manolo Strappies	3
2	Crocs Clogs	2
3	Old Navy Flops	1
4	Prada boots	1
5	Crocs Clogs	3
6	Old Navy Flops	3
7	Prada boots	3
8	Manolo Strappies	4
9	Old Navy Flops	4
10	Prada boots	4

woman_id	woman
1	Carrie
2	Samantha
3	Charlotte
4	Miranda

Patterns of data: we need a junction table

As you just found, adding either primary key to the other table as a foreign key gives us duplicate data in our table. Notice how many times the women's names reappear. We should only see them once.

We need a table to step in between these two many-to-many tables and simplify the relationships to one-to-many. This table will hold all the `woman_id` values along with the `shoe_id` values. We need what is called a **junction table**, which will contain the primary key columns of the two tables we want to relate.

Linking these two tables directly to each other just won't cut it because we end up with duplicate data thanks to its many-to-many relationships.

woman_id	woman
1	Carrie
2	Samantha
3	Charlotte
4	Miranda

many-to-many

shoe_id	shoe_name
1	Manolo Strappies
2	Crocs Clogs
3	Old Navy Flops
4	Prada boots

Take the primary key from here...

... and the primary key from here...

... and put them both in a junction table.

one-to-many

woman_id	shoe_id
1	3
1	4
2	1
3	1
3	2
3	3
3	4
4	1
4	3
4	4

one-to-many

The junction table contains the primary keys of the two tables you want to relate.

Then you need to link the primary key columns of each of the two original tables, with the matching columns in the junction table.

Many-to-Many: a junction table holds a key from each table.

Patterns of data: many-to-many

Now you know the secret of the **many-to-many** relationship—it's usually made up of ***two one-to-many relationships***, with a ***junction table in between***. We need to associate **ONE** person in the `my_contacts` table with **MANY** interests in our new `interests` table. But each of the interests values could also map to more than one person, so this relationship fits into the **many-to-many** pattern.

The `interests` column can be converted into a many-to-many relationship using this schema. Every person can have more than one interest, and for every interest, there can be more than one person who shares it:

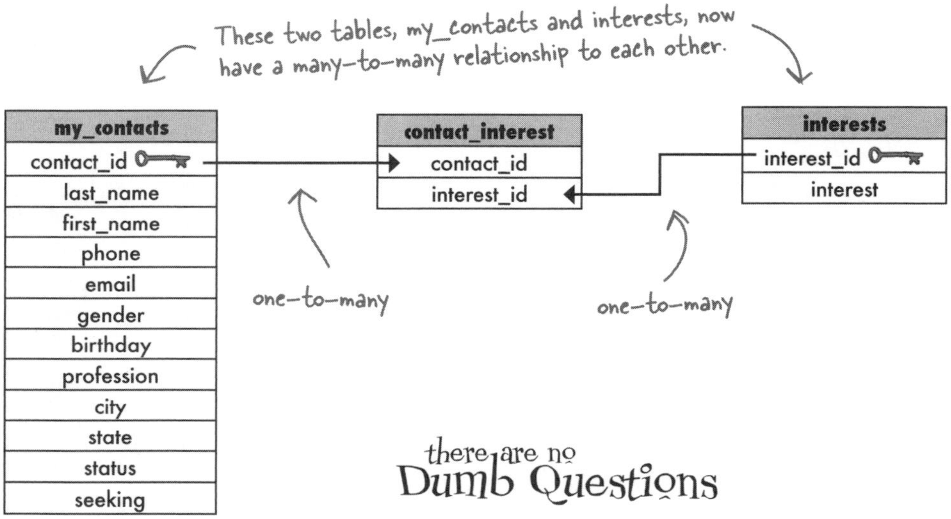

there are no Dumb Questions

Q: Do I have to create the middle table when I have many-to-many relationship?

A: Yes, you should. If you have a many-to-many relationship between two tables, you'll end up with repeating groups, violating first normal form. (A refresher on normalization is coming up in a few pages.)

There's no good reason to violate first normal form, and many good reasons not to. The biggest is that you'll have a very difficult time querying your tables with all the repeated data.

Q: What's the advantage to changing my table like this? I could just put all the interests in a table with contact_id and interest_name. I'd have repeats, but other than that, why not?

A: You'll definitely see an advantage when you start querying these multiple tables with joins in the next chapter. It can also help you, depending on how you'll use your data. You may have a table where you're more interested in that many-to-many connection than the data in either of the two other tables.

Q: What if I *still* don't mind repeats?

A: Joining tables helps preserve your data integrity. If you have to delete someone from `my_contacts`, you never touch the interests table, just the `contact_interest` table. Without the separate table, you could accidentally remove the wrong records. It's safer this way.

And when it comes to updating info, it's also nice. Suppose, you misspelled some obscure hobby name, like "spelunking." When you fix it, you only have to change one row in the interests table, and never touch the `contact_interest` or `my_contacts` tables.

NAME THAT RELATIONSHIP

In each of the partial tables below, decide if each of the ringed columns is best represented by a one-to-many or many-to-many relationship.

(Remember that if it's one-to-many or many-to-many, the column would be pulled from the table and linked with an ID field.)

COLUMN

RELATIONSHIP

doughnut_rating

(doughnut_type) 0—⚷

rating

....

clown_tracking

clown_id 0—⚷

(activities)

date

....

my_contacts

contact_id 0—⚷

(state)

(interests)

....

....

books

book_id 0—⚷

(authors)

(publisher)

....

....

fish_records

record_id 0—⚷

(fish_species)

(state)

....

....

NAME THAT RELATIONSHIP SOLUTION

In each of the partial tables below, decide if each of the ringed columns is best represented by a one-to-many or many-to-many relationship.

(Remember that if it's one-to-many or many-to-many, the column would be pulled from the table and linked with an ID field.)

COLUMN   RELATIONSHIP

doughnut_rating

doughnut_type O━

rating

............one-to-many............

clown_tracking

clown_id O━

activities

date

............many-to-many............

my_contacts

contact_id O━

state

interests

............one-to-many............

............many-to-many............

This one's tricky, but since a book can have more than one author, it's many-to-many.

books

book_id O━

authors

publisher

→ ....many-to-many............

............one-to-many............

fish_records

record_id O━

fish_species

state

............one-to-many............

............one-to-many............

Patterns of data: fixing

I know where you're going next. We're going to change the gregs_list database and my_contacts to a multi-table format. Right?

Almost. Now that you know about the patterns of data, we're nearly ready to redesign gregs_list.

We know that the interests column can be changed to a one-to-many relationship with another table. We also need to fix the seeking column in the same way. These changes will also put us into ***first normal form****.

But we can't just stop at first normal form. We need to normalize further. The more we normalize now, the easier it will be for you to get to your data with queries and, in the next chapter, joins. Before we create a new schema for `gregs_list`, let's take a detour to learn more levels of normalization.

my_contacts
contact_id (key)
last_name
first_name
phone
email
gender
birthday
profession
city
state
status
interests
seeking

* You may feel compelled to flip back a few chapters to refresh your memory of first normal form. No need, we talk about it on the next page.

Not in first normal form

We've talked about the First Normal Form. Let's take a look at it again, and then take our normalization even further, into Second and even Third Normal Forms.

But before we can go there, let's recap just what it is that puts a table into the 1NF.

First Normal Form, or 1NF:
Rule 1: Columns contain only atomic values
Rule 2: No repeating groups of data

The tables below are not in First Normal Form. Notice how the second table has had extra colors columns added, but the colors themselves still repeat one to a row in the new table:

Not in 1NF

toy_id	toy	colors
5	whiffleball	white, yellow, blue
6	frisbee	green, yellow
9	kite	red, blue, green
12	yoyo	white, yellow

To be atomic, the colors column should only contain one of those colors, not 2 and 3 per record.

Still not in 1NF

toy_id	toy	color1	color2	color3
5	whiffleball	white	yellow	blue
6	frisbee	green	yellow	
9	kite	red	blue	green
12	yoyo	white	yellow	

This table still isn't in 1NF because the columns themselves are holding the same category of data, all VARCHARs with the toy color.

Finally in 1NF

Take a look at what we've done here.

In 1NF

Primary key.

toy_id	toy
5	whiffleball
6	frisbee
9	kite
12	yoyo

Foreign key.

toy_id	color
5	white
5	yellow
5	blue
6	green
6	yellow
9	red
9	blue
9	green
12	white
12	yellow

Now we know that these tables are joined with the foreign key, we don't have to keep drawing lines everywhere.

None of the things are repeated inside a column. It's one color per row, and all of our rows are unique.

We can use both the toy_id and color value together to form a unique primary key.

If we add the `toy_id` to a separate table as the foreign key, that's fine because the values it holds don't have to be unique. If we add the color values to that table also, **all the rows are unique** because each color PLUS each `toy_id` together make up a ***unique combination.***

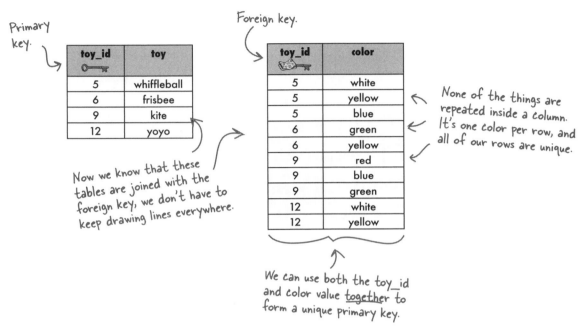

A multi-column primary key? But doesn't a primary key have to be just *one* column?

No. A key made of two or more columns is known as a composite key.

Let's take a look at how those work in some more tables.

Composite keys use multiple columns

So far we've talked about how the data in a table *relates to other tables* (one-to-one, one-to-many). What we haven't considered is **how the columns in a table *relate to each other***. Understanding that is the key to understanding second and third normal forms.

And once we understand those, we can create database schemas that will make querying multiple tables much easier.

You'll want well-designed tables when we get to joins in the next chapter!

So what exactly *is* a composite key?

A COMPOSITE KEY is a PRIMARY KEY composed of multiple columns, creating a unique key.

Consider this table of superheros. It has no unique key, but we can create a composite primary key from the `name` and `power` columns. While there are some duplicate names and powers, put them together, and the pair of them create a unique value.

We could create this table and designate these two fields to be a composite primary key. We're assuming that we'll never have exactly the same name and power so that this will be unique.

`super_heroes`

name	power	weakness
Super Trashman	Cleans quickly	bleach
The Broker	Makes money from nothing	NULL
Super Guy	Flies	birds
Wonder Waiter	Never forgets an order	insects
Dirtman	Creates dust storms	bleach
Super Guy	Super strength	the other Super Guy
Furious Woman	Gets really, really angry	NULL
The Toad	Tongue of justice	insects
Librarian	Can find anything	NULL
Goose Girl	Flies	NULL
Stick Man	Stands in for humans	games of Hangman

Stick Man, Stick Man,
Does whatever no human can
All you need is No. 2
To tell Stick Man what to do
Set your imagination free
Go draw
Your very own Stick Man!

Even superheros can be dependent

Our superheroes have been busy! Here's the updated `super_heroes` table. We're in 1NF, but there's another problem.

See how the `initials` column contains the initial letters of the name value in the `name` column? What would happen if a superhero changed their name?

Exactly. The initials column would change, too. The `initials` column is said to be **functionally dependent** on the `name` column.

When a column's data must change when another column's data is modified, the first column is functionally dependent on the second.

Here are our two identical names, with the power column added to create a truly unique composite primary key.

super_heroes

name	power	weakness	city	country	arch_enemy	initials
Super Trashman	Cleans quickly	bleach	Gotham	US	Verminator	ST
The Broker	Makes money from nothing	NULL	New York	US	Mister Taxman	TB
Super Guy	Flies	birds	Metropolis	US	Super Fella	SG
Wonder Waiter	Never forgets an order	insects	Paris	France	All You Can Eat Girl	WW
Dirtman	Creates dust storms	bleach	Tulsa	US	Hoover	D
Super Guy	Super strength	aluminum	Metropolis	US	Badman	SG
Furious Woman	Gets really, really angry	NULL	Rome	Italy	The Therapist	FW
The Toad	Tongue of justice	insects	London	England	Heron	T
Librarian	Can find anything	children	Springfield	US	Chaos Creep	L
Goose Girl	Flies	NULL	Minneapolis	US	The Quilter	GG
Stick Man	Stands in for humans	hang man	London	England	Eraserman	SM

Sharpen your pencil

Now you know that the initials column is dependent on the name column in the superhero table. Do you see any similar dependencies? Write them down here.

....

....

....

....

Sharpen your pencil Solution

Now you know that the initials column is dependent on the name column in the super_heroes table. Do you see any similar dependencies? Write them down here.

initials are dependent on name

weakness is dependent on name

arch_enemy is dependent on name

city is dependent on country

These don't mention which table the columns are from, which will matter when you add more tables. There's a shorthand way to indicate these dependencies and the tables they're from.

Shorthand notations

Notation Detour

A quick way to describe a functional dependency is to write this:

T.x ->; T.y ← The technical term for this is a shorthand notation.

Which can be read like this "in the relational table called T, column y is functionally dependent on column x." Basically, you read them from right to left to see what's functionally dependent on what.

Let's see that applied to our superheroes:

super_heroes.name ->; super_heroes.initials

"In the `super_heroes` relational table, the `initials` column is functionally dependent on the `name` column."

super_heroes.name ->; super_heroes.weakness

"In the `super_heroes` relational table, the `weakness` column is functionally dependent on the `name` column."

super_heroes.name ->; super_heroes.arch_enemy

"In the `super_heroes` relational table, the `arch_enemy` column is functionally dependent on the `name` column."

super_heroes.country ->; super_heroes.city

"In the `super_heroes` relational table, the `city` column is functionally dependent on the `country` column."

Superhero dependencies

So, if our superhero were to change his name, the initials column would change as well, making it **dependent** on the name column.

If our arch-enemy decides to move his lair to a new city, his location changes, but nothing else does. This makes the `arch_enemy_city` column in the table below completely **independent**.

A **dependent column** is one containing data that ***could change if another column changes***. **Non-dependent** columns ***stand alone***.

If Stick Man changed his name to The Sticky, the initials column will change, too.

Partial functional dependency

A **partial functional dependency** means that a non-key column is dependent on some, but not all, of the columns in a composite primary key.

In our superheroes table, the `initials` column is ***partially dependent*** on `name`, because if the superhero's name changes, the initials value will too, but if the power changes, and not the name, our superhero's initials will stay the same.

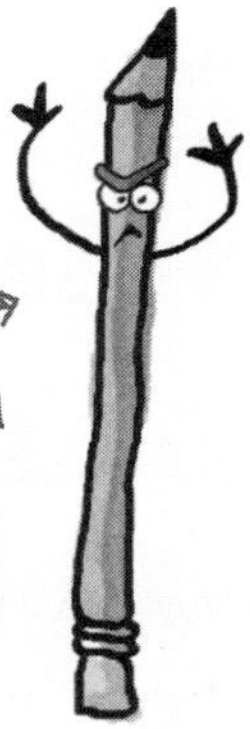

Meanwhile Eraserman has moved his pencil tin to a new desk in Borrowdale, but none of the other columns will be affected.

Intials depend on name, but not on power, so this table contains a partial functional dependency.

Name and power together make up the composite primary key.

super_heroes

name	power	weakness	city	initials	arch_enemy_id	arch_enemy_city
Super Trashman	Cleans quickly	bleach	Gotham	ST	4	Gotham
The Broker	Makes money from nothing	NULL	New York	TB	8	Newark
Super Guy	Flies	birds	Metropolis	SG	5	Metropolis
Wonder Waiter	Never forgets an order	insects	Paris	WW	1	Paris
Dirtman	Creates dust storms	bleach	Tulsa	D	2	Kansas City
Super Guy	Super strength	aluminum	Metropolis	SG	7	Gotham
Furious Woman	Gets really, really angry	NULL	Rome	FW	10	Rome
The Toad	Tongue of justice	insects	London	T	16	Bath
Librarian	Can find anything	children	Springfield	L	3	Louisville
Goose Girl	Flies	NULL	Minneapolis	GG	9	Minneapolis
The Sticky	Stands in for humans	hang man	London	S	33	Borrowdale

Transitive functional dependency

You also need to consider how each non-key column relates to the others. If an arch-enemy moves to a different city, it doesn't change his `arch_enemy_id`.

Verminator's arch_enemy_id hasn't changed, even though he's moved to Kansas City.

name ○╋☰	arch_enemy_id	arch_enemy_city
Super Trashman	4	Kansas City
The Broker	8	Newark
Super Guy	5	Metropolis
Wonder Waiter	1	Paris
Dirtman	2	Kansas City

If changing any of the non-key columns might cause any of the other columns to change, you have a transitive dependency.

Suppose a superhero changes his arch-enemy. The `arch_enemy_id` would change, and that ***could*** change the `arch_enemy_city`.

If changing any of the non-key columns might cause any of the other columns to change, you have a ***transitive dependency.***

If we update the arch_enemy_id that changes the value in the arch_enemy_city column.

name ○╋☰	arch_enemy_id	arch_enemy_city
Super Trashman	2	Kansas City
The Broker	8	Newark
Super Guy	5	Metropolis
Wonder Waiter	1	Paris
Dirtman	2	Kansas City

This is called a transitive functional dependency because the non-key arch_enemy_city column is related to arch_enemy_id, which is another of the non-key columns.

Transitive functional dependency: when any non-key column is related to any of the other non-key columns.

Take a look at this table listing book titles. pub_id identifies the publisher.
pub_city is the city where the book was published.

author ○✛☰	title ○✛☰	copyright	pub_id	pub_city
John Deere	Easy Being Green	1930	2	New York
Fred Mertz	I Hate Lucy	1968	5	Boston
Lassie	Help Timmy!	1950	3	San Francisco
Timmy	Lassie, Calm Down	1951	1	New York

Write down what will happen to the value in the copyright column if the title of the book in the
third row changes to: 'Help Timmy! I'm Stuck Down A Well'

If the title changes, the copyright value will, too. ← Copyright depends
on title, so its
value will change.

What will happen to the value in the copyright column if the author of the book in the third row
changes to 'Rin Tin Tin', but the title stays the same?

....

What would happen to 'Easy Being Green' if we changed its pub_id value to 1?

....

What would happen to the pub_id value of 'I Hate Lucy' if its publisher moved to Sebastopol?

....

What would happen to the pub_city value of 'I Hate Lucy' if we changed its pub_id value to 1.

....

Exercise Solution

Take a look at this table listing book titles. pub_id identifies the publisher. pub_city is the city where the book was published.

Write down what will happen to the value in the copyright column if the title of the book in the third row changes to: 'Help Timmy! I'm Stuck Down A Well'

If the title changes, the copyright value will, too. ← *Copyright depends on title, so its value will change.*

What will happen to the value in the copyright column if the author of the book in the third row changes to 'Rin Tin Tin', but the title stays the same?

If the author changes, and not the title, the copyright changes.

Author and title together make up the composite primary key.

Copyright depends on title. It also depends on author.

author	title	copyright	pub_id	pub_city
John Deere	Easy Being Green	1930	2	New York
Fred Mertz	I Hate Lucy	1968	5	Boston
Lassie	Help Timmy!	1950	3	San Francisco
Timmy	Lassie, Calm Down	1951	1	New York

What would happen to 'Easy Being Green' if we changed its pub_id value to 1?

The pub_city won't change. ← *The pub_city for pub_id 1 and pub_id 2 is New York, so the city won't change (even though pub_city is transitively dependent on pub_id).*

What would happen to the pub_id value of 'I Hate Lucy' if its publisher moved to Sebastopol?

pub_id is independent of the pub_city column, so the pub_id stays the same. → *The pub_id would stay the same.*

What would happen to the pub_city value of 'I Hate Lucy' if we changed its pub_id value to 1.

pub_city is transitively dependent on pub_id so the city value changes. → *The pub_city would become New York.*

Pub_city is dependent on the value in the pub_id column. Neither column is a key column, so this is a transitive functional dependency.

author	title	copyright	pub_id	pub_city
John Deere	Easy Being Green	1930	2	New York
Fred Mertz	I Hate Lucy	1968	5	Boston
Lassie	Help Timmy!	1950	3	San Francisco
Timmy	Lassie, Calm Down	1951	1	New York

there are no Dumb Questions

Q: Is there a simple way to avoid having a partial functional dependency?

A: Using an id field like we have in `my_contacts` allows you to completely avoid the issue. Since it's a new key that exists only to index that table, nothing is dependent on it.

Q: So, other than when I create junction tables, why would I ever want to create a composite key out of columns in my table? Why not just always create an id field?

A: It's certainly one way to go. But you'll find compelling arguments for both sides if you search the Web for "synthetic or natural key." You'll also find heated debates. We'll let you make up your own mind on the topic. In this book, we'll primarily stick with single, synthetic primary key fields to keep our syntax simpler so you learn the concepts and don't get bogged down with the implementation.

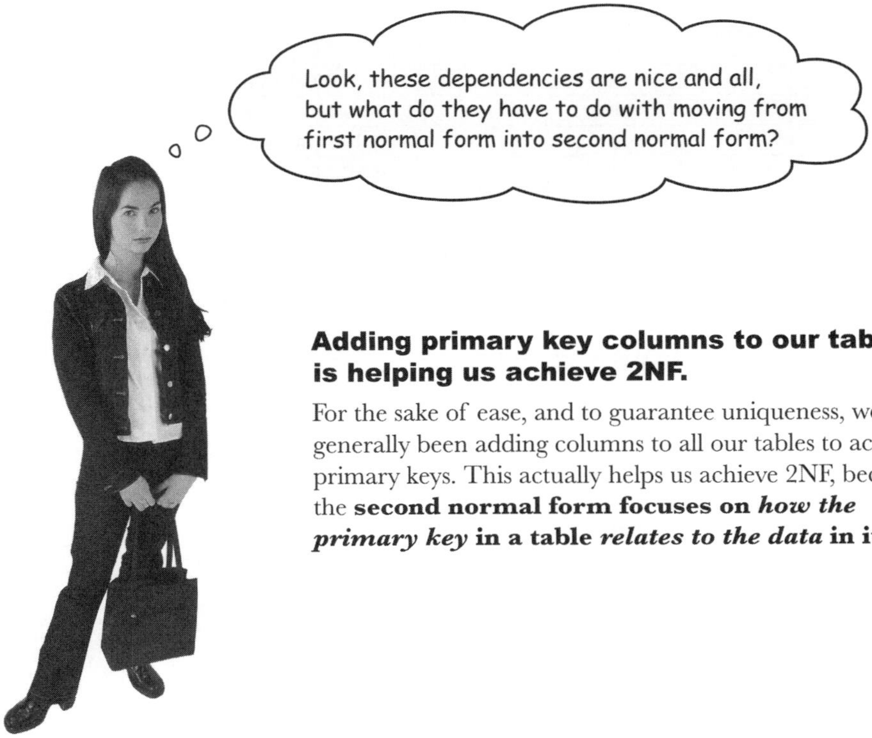
Look, these dependencies are nice and all, but what do they have to do with moving from first normal form into second normal form?

Adding primary key columns to our tables is helping us achieve 2NF.

For the sake of ease, and to guarantee uniqueness, we've generally been adding columns to all our tables to act as primary keys. This actually helps us achieve 2NF, because the **second normal form focuses on *how the primary key* in a table *relates to the data* in it**.

Second normal form

Let's consider two tables that exist to keep an inventory of toys to help us better understand how the second normal form focuses on the relationship between the table's primary key and the data in the table.

toy_id	toy
5	whiffleball
6	frisbee
9	kite
12	yoyo

Composite key.

toy_id	store_id	color	inventory	store_address
5	1	white	34	23 Maple
5	3	yellow	12	100 E. North St.
5	1	blue	5	23 Maple
6	2	green	10	1902 Amber Ln.
6	4	yellow	24	17 Engleside
9	1	red	50	23 Maple
9	2	blue	2	1902 Amber Ln
9	2	green	18	1902 Amber Ln
12	4	white	28	17 Engleside
12	4	yellow	11	17 Engleside

There are many repeats in this column. And it really doesn't have anything to do with the inventory; it has to do with the store.

We might want to rethink this column as well. It really belongs more in a toy table than in an inventory table. Our toy_id ought to identify both toy type AND toy color.

Inventory is dependent on both of the columns that make up the composite primary key, so it does not have a partial functional dependency.

Notice how the `store_address` is repeated when a toy is associated with that `store_id`. If we need to change the `store_address`, we have to change every row where it's referenced in this table. The more rows that are updated over time, the more possibility there is for errors to creep into our data.

If we pulled the `store_address` column into another table, we'd only have to make one change.

We might be 2NF already...

A table in 1NF is also 2NF if all the columns in the table are part of the primary key.

We could create a new table with a composite primary key with the `toy_id` and `store_id` columns. Then we'd have a table with all the toy information and a table with all the store information, with our new table connecting them.

Your 1NF table is also 2NF if all the columns in the table are part of the primary key

OR

It has a single column primary key

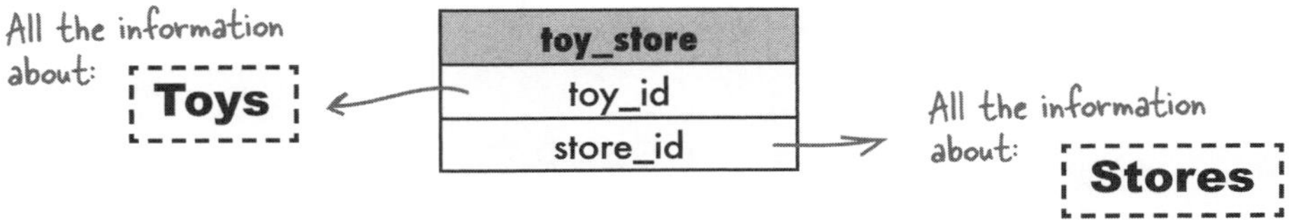

A table in 1NF is also 2NF if it has a single column primary key.

This is a great reason to assign an `AUTO_INCREMENT` id column.

Second Normal Form or 2NF:
Rule 1: Be in 1NF
Rule 2: Have no partial functional dependencies.

I don't think I have any partial functional dependencies in my_contacts, but I'm not sure...

That's why it's time to play...

BE the 2NF table with no partial functional dependencies

Your job is to play a table, and remove all the partial functional dependencies from yourself. Look at each table diagrammed below, and draw lines through the columns that are better moved to another table.

These two make up a unique composite primary key.

toy_inventory
toy_id
store_id

cookie_sales
amount
girl_id
date
girl_name
troop_leader
total_sales

singers
singer_id
last_name
first_name
agency
agency_state

movies
movie_id
title
genre
rented_by
due_date
rating

salary
employee_id
last_name
first_name
salary
manager
employee_email
hire_date

dog_breeds
breed
description
avg_weight
avg_height
club_id
club_state

Sharpen your pencil

Redesign these tables into three tables that are all 2NF.

One will contain info about the toy, one will have store info, and the third will contain the inventory and connect to the other two. Give all three meaningful names.

Finally, add in these additional columns to the appropriate tables:

toy_id	toy
5	whiffleball
6	frisbee
9	kite
12	yoyo

toy_id	store_id	color	inventory	store_address
5	1	white	34	23 Maple
5	3	yellow	12	100 E. North St.
5	1	blue	5	23 Maple
6	2	green	10	1902 Amber Ln.
6	4	yellow	24	17 Engleside
9	1	red	50	23 Maple
9	2	blue	2	1902 Amber Ln
9	2	green	18	1902 Amber Ln
12	4	white	28	17 Engleside
12	4	yellow	11	17 Engleside

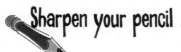

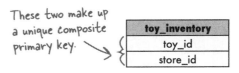

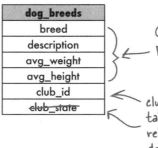

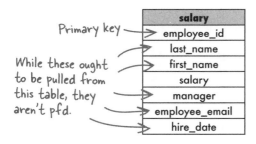

BE the 2NF table with no partial functional dependencies solution

Your job is to play a table, and remove all the partial functional dependencies from yourself. Look at each table diagrammed below, and draw lines through the columns that are better moved to another table.

These two make up a unique composite primary key.

toy_inventory
toy_id
store_id

Primary key.

singers
singer_id
last_name
first_name
agency
agency_state

While these ought to be an ID pulled from an agency table (because two agencies might have the same name), it's not a partial functional dependency.

cookie_sales
amount
girl_id
date
~~girl_name~~
~~troop_leader~~
~~total_sales~~

Once we've moved those columns out, the remaining columns can form a composite primary key.

Primary key

movies
movie_id
title
genre
rented_by
due_date
rating

These columns have transitive functional dependency only.

Primary key

salary
employee_id
last_name
first_name
salary
manager
employee_email
hire_date

While these ought to be pulled from this table, they aren't pfd.

dog_breeds
breed
description
avg_weight
avg_height
club_id
~~club_state~~

Composite primary key

club_id might belong in this table (if it's a one-to-one relationship), but club_state doesn't belong here. Even so, none of the columns are pfd.

Sharpen your pencil
Solution

Redesign these tables into three tables that are all 2NF.

One will contain info about the toy, one will have store info, and the third will contain the inventory and connect to the other two. Give all three meaningful names.

Finally, add in these additional columns to the appropriate tables:

toy_id	toy
5	whiffleball
6	frisbee
9	kite
12	yoyo

toy_id ○+☰	store_id ○+☰	color	inventory	store_address
5	1	white	34	23 Maple
5	3	yellow	12	100 E. North St.
5	1	blue	5	23 Maple
6	2	green	10	1902 Amber Ln.
6	4	yellow	24	17 Engleside
9	1	red	50	23 Maple
9	2	blue	2	1902 Amber Ln
9	2	green	18	1902 Amber Ln
12	4	white	28	17 Engleside
12	4	yellow	11	17 Engleside

The composite primary key is toy_id and store_id.

store_inventory

toy_id ○+☰	store_id ○+☰	inventory
5	1	34
5	3	12
5	1	5
6	2	10
6	4	24
9	1	50
9	2	2
9	2	18
12	4	28
12	4	11

toy_info

toy_id ○—☰	toy	color	cost	weight
1	whiffleball	white	1.95	0.3
2	whiffleball	yellow	2.20	0.4
3	whiffleball	blue	1.95	0.3
4	frisbee	green	3.50	0.5
5	frisbee	yellow	1.50	0.2
6	kite	red	5.75	1.2
7	kite	blue	5.75	1.2
8	kite	green	3.15	0.8
9	yoyo	white	4.25	0.4
10	yoyo	yellow	1.50	0.2

store_info

store_id ○—☰	address	phone	manager
1	23 Maple	555-6712	Joe
2	1902 Amber Ln.	555-3478	Susan
3	100 E. North St.	555-0987	Tara
4	17 Engleside	555-6554	Gordon

Third normal form (at last)

Because in this book we generally add artificial primary keys, getting our tables into second normal form is not normally a concern for us. Any table with an **artificial primary key** and no composite primary key is always 2NF.

We do have to make sure we're in 3NF, though.

If your table has an artificial primary key and no composite primary key, it's in 2NF

Third Normal Form or 3NF:
Rule 1: Be in 2NF
Rule 2: Have no transitive dependencies

Remember? A transitive functional dependency means that any non-key column is related to any of the other non-key columns.

If changing any of the non-key columns might cause any of the other columns to change, you have a transitive dependency.

Consider what would happen if we changed a value in any of these three columns: **`course_name`**, **`instructor`**, and **`instructor_phone`**.

We can ignore the primary key when considering 3NF.

courses
course_id
course_name
instructor
instructor_phone

- ⇨ If we change the `course_name`, neither `instructor` nor `instructor_phone` need to change.
- ⇨ If we change the `instructor_phone`, neither `instructor` nor `course_name` needs to change.
- ⇨ If we change the `instructor`, the `instructor_phone` will change. We've found our transitive dependency.

It should be pretty obvious at this point that instructor_phone doesn't belong in this table if we want it to be 3NF.

Exercise

So how does my_contacts stand up?

It does need a few changes. On the page below, start with the current my_contacts table and sketch out the new gregs_list schema. Show the relationships between foreign keys with lines, and the one-to-many relationships with arrows. Also indicate the primary keys or composite keys.

my_contacts
contact_id (key)
last_name
first_name
phone
email
gender
birthday
profession
city
state
status
interests
seeking

Hint: In our version on the next page, we have 8 tables. (We added in a column for zip code. Before that, we had 7.)

Exercise Solution

So how does my_contacts stand up?

It does need a few changes. On the page below, start with the current my_contacts table and sketch out the new gregs_list schema. Show the relationships between foreign keys with lines, and the one-to-many relationships with arrows. Also indicate the primary keys or composite keys.

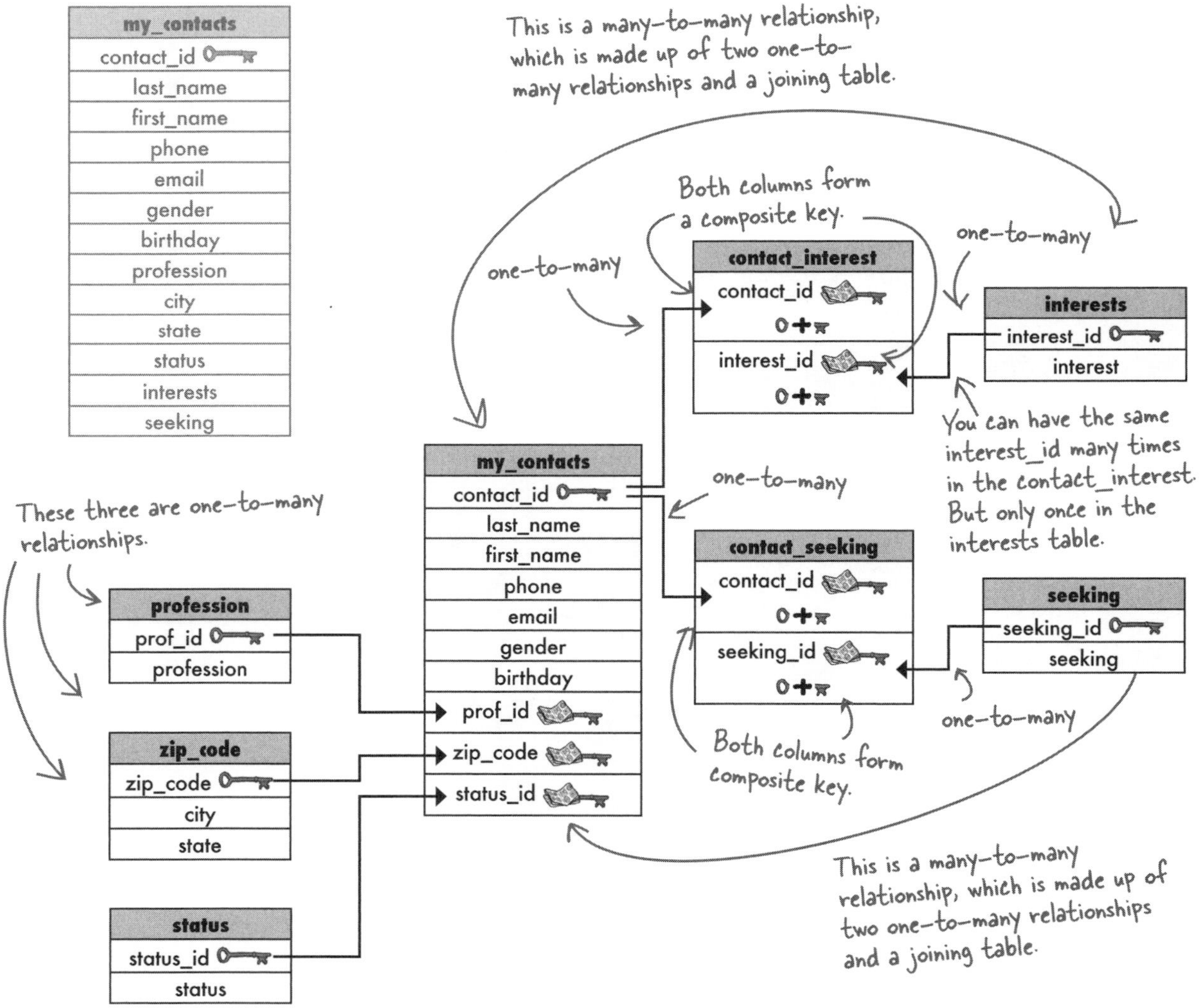

my_contacts
contact_id
last_name
first_name
phone
email
gender
birthday
profession
city
state
status
interests
seeking
This is a many-to-many relationship, which is made up of two one-to-many relationships and a joining table.
Both columns form a composite key.
one-to-many
one-to-many
contact_interest
contact_id
interest_id
interests
interest_id
interest
You can have the same interest_id many times in the contact_interest. But only once in the interests table.
These three are one-to-many relationships.
my_contacts
contact_id
last_name
first_name
phone
email
gender
birthday
prof_id
zip_code
status_id
one-to-many
contact_seeking
contact_id
seeking_id
seeking
seeking_id
seeking
one-to-many
Both columns form composite key.
profession
prof_id
profession
zip_code
zip_code
city
state
status
status_id
status
This is a many-to-many relationship, which is made up of two one-to-many relationships and a joining table.

And so, Regis (and gregs_list) lived happily ever after

Greg's able to find Regis's perfect match using his newly normalized database. Better yet, he's also able to easily find matches for more of his friends keeping the Greg's List dream alive.

The End

Not so fast! Now I have to query all these new tables and match them up by hand! How do I get at my data now with all those tables without writing a hundreds of queries?

That's where joins come in.

See you in the next chapter...

CHAPTER 7

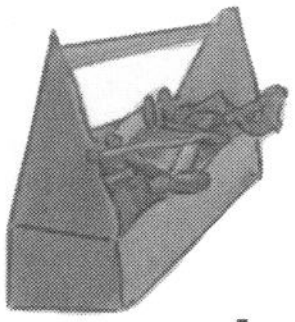

Your SQL Toolbox

Give yourself a hand, you're more than halfway through the book. Check out all the key SQL terms you learned in Chapter 7. For a complete list of tooltips in the book, see Appendix iii.

Schema

A description of the data in your database, along with any other related objects and the way they all connect.

One-to-One relationship

Exactly one row of a parent table is related to one row of a child table.

One-to-Many relationship

A row in one table can have many matching rows in a second table, but the second table may only have one matching row in the first.

Many-to-Many relationship

Two tables are connected by a junction table, allowing many rows in the first to match many rows in the second, and vice versa.

First normal form (1NF)

Columns contain only atomic values, and no repeating groups of data are permitted in a column.

Transitive functional dependency

This means any non-key column is related to any of the other non-key columns.

Second normal form (2NF)

Your table must be in 1NF and contain no partial functional dependencies to be in 2NF.

Third normal form (3NF)

Your table must be in 2NF and have no transitive dependencies.

Foreign key

Your table must be in 2NF and have no transitive dependencies.

Composite key

This is a primary key made up of multiple columns, which create a unique key value.

Sharpen your pencil
Solution

Use your ALTER and the SUBSTRING_INDEX function to end up with these columns. Write as many queries as it takes.

First of all you need to create the new columns:

```
ALTER TABLE my_contacts
ADD COLUMN interest1 VARCHAR(50),
ADD COLUMN interest2 VARCHAR(50),
ADD COLUMN interest3 VARCHAR(50),
ADD COLUMN interest4 VARCHAR(50);
```

Then you need to move the first interest to the new interest1 column.
You can do that with:

```
UPDATE my_contacts
SET interest1 = SUBSTRING_INDEX(interests, ',', 1);
```

Next we need to remove the first interest from the interests field since it's stored in interest1. We remove everything until right after the first comma with a string function:

TRIM removes the space left in front of the string after we removed everything in front of the comma.

RIGHT returns part of the interests column, starting from the righthand side.

```
UPDATE my_contacts SET interests = TRIM(RIGHT(interests,
(LENGTH(interests)-LENGTH(interest1) - 1)));
```

This scary-looking part computes how much of the interests column we need. It takes the total length of the interests column and subtracts the length of the part we moved to interest1. Then we subtract one more so we start after the comma.

And now we repeat those steps for the other interest columns:

```
UPDATE my_contacts SET interest2 = SUBSTRING_INDEX(interests, ',', 1);
UPDATE my_contacts SET interests = TRIM(RIGHT(interests, (LENGTH(interests)-
LENGTH(interest2) - 1)));
UPDATE my_contacts SET interest3 = SUBSTRING_INDEX(interests, ',', 1);
UPDATE my_contacts SET interests = TRIM(RIGHT(interests, (LENGTH(interests)-
LENGTH(interest3) - 1)));
```

For the last column, all we've got left in there is a single value:

```
UPDATE my_contacts SET interest4 = interests;
```

Now we can drop the interests column entirely. We also could have just renamed it interest4 and not needed the ADD COLUMN (assuming we just have four interests).

contact_id
last_name
first_name
phone
email
gender
birthday
profession
city
state
status
interest1
interest2
interest3
interest4
seeking

Exercise Solution

From page 286.

Write a query for Regis without using the interests column.

```
SELECT * FROM my_contacts
WHERE gender = 'F'
AND status = 'single
AND state='MA'
AND seeking LIKE '%single M%'
AND birthday > '1950-03-20'
AND birthday < '1960-03-20';
```

← This is essentially the same query as Greg used for Nigel,.except he's left off the interests.

8 joins and multi-table operations

Can't we all just get along?

Please go away, Jacques.
None of us is interested
in your "foreign key."

Welcome to a multi-table world. It's great to have **more than one table** in your database, but you'll need to learn some ***new tools and techniques*** to work with them. With multiple tables comes confusion, so you'll need **aliases** to keep your tables straight. And **joins** help you connect your tables, so that you can get at all the data you've spread out. Get ready, it's time to **take control of your database** again.

Still repeating ourselves, still repeating...

Greg noticed the same values for **status**, **profession**, **interests**, and **seeking** popping up again and again.

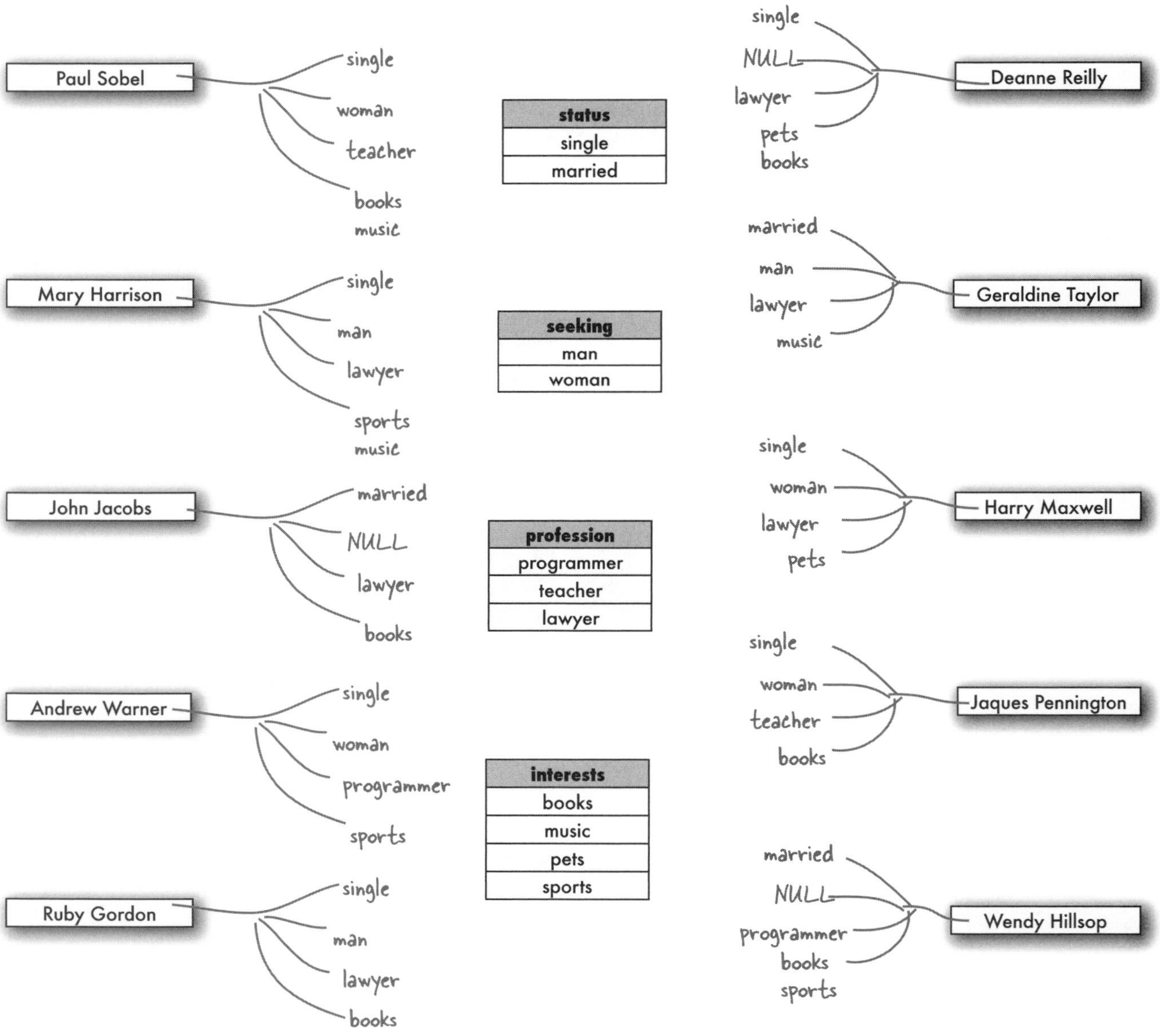

Prepopulate your tables

Having many duplicate values will make it easy to prepopulate the `status`, `profession`, `interests`, and `seeking` tables. Greg wants to load up those four tables with the values already in his old `my_contacts` table.

First he needs to query his table to find out what's already in there. But he doesn't want an enormous list of duplicate values.

Wouldn't it make sense to have a set list of values in some of the tables?

Sharpen your pencil

Write queries that can retrieve the status, profession, interests, and seeking values from the old my_contacts table, without producing any duplicates. You may want to refer back to the Girl Sprout cookie sales problem in Chapter 6.

Sharpen your pencil Solution

Write queries that can retrieve the status, profession, interests, and seeking values from the old my_contacts table, without producing any duplicates. You may want to refer back to the Girl Sprout cookie sales problem in Chapter 6.

```
SELECT status FROM my_contacts
GROUP BY status
ORDER BY status;
```

```
SELECT profession FROM my_contacts
GROUP BY profession
ORDER BY profession;
```

```
SELECT seeking FROM my_contacts
GROUP BY seeking
ORDER BY seeking;
```

Using GROUP BY combines the duplicates into one single value for each group.

Then using ORDER BY gives us the list alphabetically.

If you don't do them in this order, you get an error. ORDER BY always needs to be last.

~~SELECT interests~~
~~FROM my_contacts~~
~~GROUP BY interests~~
~~ORDER BY interest;~~

But that query doesn't work for the interests column. We've got multiple values in that one, remember?

We can't do a simple SELECT to get the interests column out.

Using that SELECT statement for the interests column isn't going to work when we have values in there like this:

interests
books, sports
music, pets, books
pets, books
sports, music

We got the "table ain't easy to normalize" blues

Like a dog that ain't got no bone, our un-normalized design has really hurt us. There's just no easy way to get those values out of the interests column in a way that we can see them one at a time.

We need to go from this

interests
first, second, third, fourth

Our column from the my_contacts table

to this

interests
first
second
third
fourth

A column in our new interests table.

BRAIN POWER

How can we get those multiple values into a single column in the interests table?

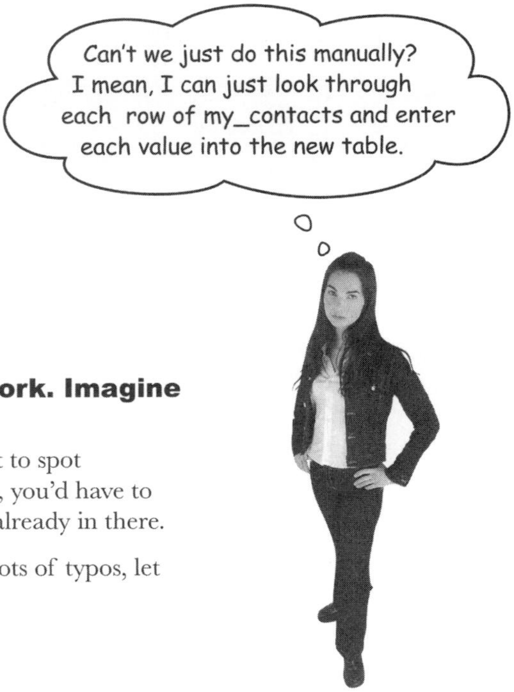
Can't we just do this manually? I mean, I can just look through each row of my_contacts and enter each value into the new table.

First, it's an enormous amount of work. Imagine thousands of rows.

And doing it by hand would make it very difficult to spot duplicates. When you have hundreds of interests, you'd have to look each time you enter a new one to see if it's already in there.

Instead of doing all that hard work, and risking lots of typos, let SQL do the tedious work for you.

The special interests (column)

One fairly straightforward way is to add four new columns to `my_contacts` where we can temporarily store the values as we separate them out. Then we can get rid of those columns when we finish.

Sharpen your pencil

You know how to ALTER tables at this point, so you need to ALTER my_contacts to have four new columns. Name them interest1, interest2, interest3, and interest4.

→ Answers on page 378.

Here's what the interests and new interest columns in my_contacts look like now that you've run `ALTER`.

interests	interest1	interest2	interest3	interest4
first, second, third, fourth				

We can easily copy the first interest and put it in the new `interest1` column with our `SUBSTRING_INDEX` function from Chapter 5:

```
UPDATE my_contacts
SET interest1 = SUBSTRING_INDEX(interests, ',', 1);
```

The name of our column — The character to look for, a comma — ...look for the first comma.

Run that, and this is what we get:

interests	interest1	interest2	interest3	interest4
first, second, third, fourth	first			

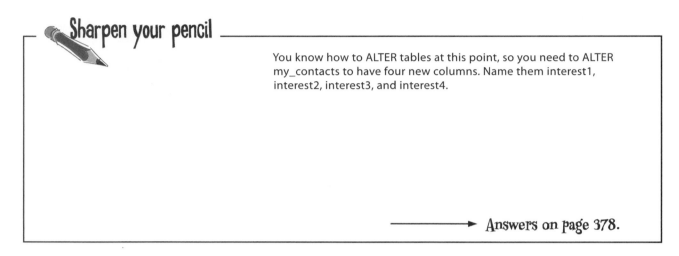

Keeping interested

Now for the tricky part: we're going to use another substring function to remove from the `interests` column the data we just moved into the `interest1` column. Then we can fill in the rest of the interest columns the same way.

interests	interest1	interest2	interest3	interest4
first, second, third, fourth	first			

We're going to remove the first interest, the comma that follows it, and the space that follows the comma from the interests column.

We'll use a `SUBSTR` function that will grab the string in the interests column and return part of it. We're telling it to return the same part we just put in interest1, plus two more characters (for the comma and space).

Translation: Change the value in the interests column to be whatever is in there now, without the part we put in interest1 and the comma and the space.

The length of the text in the interest1 field...

...plus 2 more characters: one for the comma, one for the space.

```
UPDATE my_contacts
SET interests = SUBSTR(interests, LENGTH(interest1)+2 );
```

SUBSTR returns part of the original string in this column. It takes the string and cuts off the first part that we specify in the parentheses, and returns the second.

Length returns a number that is the length of whatever string is in the parentheses that follow it.

In our example the length of the string 'first' is five characters.

Remember how some functions are different depending on which flavor of SQL you're using? Well, this one of those. Refer to a really useful reference—like SQL in a Nutshell from O'Reilly—for your particular brand of SQL.

So in our example, the number returned by LENGTH is 5+2, or 7, which is the number of characters that will be removed from the first of the string in the old interests column.

UPDATE all your interests

After we've run that UPDATE statement, our table looks like this. But we're not done yet. We've got to do the same thing for `interest2`, `interest3`, and `interest4` columns.

interests	interest1	interest2	interest3	interest4
second, third, fourth	first			

Sharpen your pencil

Fill in the blanks to complete Greg's update statement. We've given you a couple of notes to help you along.

Hint: Rhe interests column will change each time because the string value in the interests column is being shortened by the SUBSTR function.

```
UPDATE my_contacts SET
interest1 = SUBSTRING_INDEX(interests, ',', 1),
interests = SUBSTR(interests, LENGTH(interest1)+2),
interest2 = SUBSTRING_INDEX(.........................................),
interests = SUBSTR(.....................................................),
interest3 = SUBSTRING_INDEX(.........................................),
interests = SUBSTR(.....................................................),
interest4 = ....................................................................
```

After you've removed the first three interests from the interests column, all that is left is the fourth interest. What needs to be done here?

Fill in what's in each column after this big command.

interests	interest1	interest2	interest3	interest4
second, third, fourth	first			

Answers on page 378.

Getting all the interests

We've got all our interests separated at last. We can get to them with simple SELECT statements, but we can't get to them all at the same time. And we can't easily pull them all out in a single result set, since they're in four columns. When we try, we get:

```
File Edit Window Help TooManyColumns
> SELECT interest1, interest2, interest3, interest4 FROM my_contacts;

+-----------+-----------+-----------+-----------+
| interest1 | interest2 | interest3 | interest4 |
+-----------+-----------+-----------+-----------+
|  first    |  second   |  third    |  fourth   |
|  horses   |  pets     |           |           |
|  music    |  fishing  |  books    |  movies   |
|  painting |           |           |           |
|  horses   |  pets     |           |           |
|  music    |  sports   |  books    |  boating  |
|  travel   |  music    |           |           |
|  horses   |  pets     |           |           |
|  music    |  sports   |  books    |  knitting |
|  pets     |  writing  |  travel   |           |
|  dogs     |  hiking   |           |           |
|  movies   |  sports   |           |           |
+-----------+-----------+-----------+-----------+
```

But at least we can write four separate SELECT statements to get all the values out:

```
SELECT interest1 FROM my_contacts;     SELECT interest3 FROM my_contacts;

SELECT interest2 FROM my_contacts;     SELECT interest4 FROM my_contacts;
```

All we're really missing now is a way to take those SELECT statements and stuff the contents directly into our new tables. There's not just one way to do this; there are at least three!

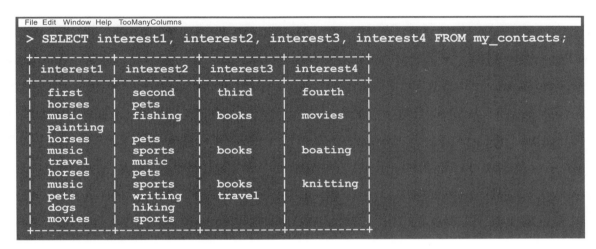

Try this at home

Consider the profession column SELECT statement you wrote on page 345:

```
SELECT profession FROM my_contacts GROUP BY profession
ORDER BY profession;
```

On the next page we're going to show you *THREE WAYS* to take advantage of these SELECT statements to get your new interests table pre-populated.

Play around with SELECT, INSERT, and CREATE to see what you come up with. And then look at the next page to see the three ways.

The point here is not to get this right, but to think about your possibilities.

Many paths to one place

While being able to do the same thing three (or more) different ways might seem fun to the crazy clowns, it can be confusing to the rest of us.

But it is useful. When you know three ways to do something, you can choose the way that best suits your needs. And as your data grows, you'll notice that some queries are performed more quickly by your RDBMS. When your tables become very large, you will want to optimize your queries, so knowing that you can perform the same task in different ways can help you do that.

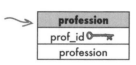

You know what's fun about SQL, kids?
There's usually more than one way to do the same thing!

On the next couple of pages are all three of the ways you can create and populate this table with distinct, alphabetically ordered values.

profession
prof_id (key)
profession

CREATE, SELECT and INSERT at (nearly) the same time

1. CREATE TABLE, then INSERT with SELECT

You know how to do this one! First you `CREATE` the `profession` table, then you populate the columns with the values from your `SELECT` on page 345.

```
CREATE TABLE profession
(
  id INT(11) NOT NULL AUTO_INCREMENT PRIMARY KEY,
  profession varchar(20)
);

INSERT INTO profession (profession)
  SELECT profession FROM my_contacts
  GROUP BY profession
  ORDER BY profession;
```

Create the profession table with a primary key column and a VARCHAR column to hold the professions.

Now fill up the profession column of the profession table with the values from your SELECT.

2. CREATE TABLE with SELECT, then ALTER to add primary key

Second way: CREATE the profession table using the data from a SELECT that grabs the values from the my_contacts table's profession column, then ALTER the table and ADD the primary key field.

```
CREATE TABLE profession AS
  SELECT profession FROM my_contacts
  GROUP BY profession
  ORDER BY profession;

ALTER TABLE profession
ADD COLUMN id INT NOT NULL AUTO_INCREMENT FIRST,
ADD PRIMARY KEY (id);
```

Create the profession table with one column, full of the values from the SELECT...

... then ALTER the table to add in the primary key field

CREATE, SELECT and INSERT at the same time

3. CREATE TABLE with primary key and with SELECT all in one

This is the one-step way: CREATE the profession table with a primary key column and a VARCHAR column to hold the profession values, and at the same time fill it with the values from the SELECT. SQL auto-increments, so your RDBMS knows the id column should be fed automatically, and that leaves only one column, which is where the data goes.

```
CREATE TABLE profession
(
  id INT(11) NOT NULL AUTO_INCREMENT PRIMARY KEY,
  profession varchar(20)
) AS
  SELECT profession FROM my_contacts
  GROUP BY profession
  ORDER BY profession;
```

Create the profession table with both a primary key and a profession column, and fill the profession column with the values from the SELECT.

I haven't seen AS before. It seems like it's being used to reference the results from one query to insert them into the new table.

Yes. The AS keyword does exactly what it sounds like it does.

It's all part of aliasing, which we're just coming to!

What's up with that AS?

AS populates a new table with the result of the SELECT. So when we used AS in the second and third examples, we were telling the software to take all the values that came out of the my_contacts table as a result of that SELECT and put it into a new profession table we just created.

If we hadn't specified that the new table have two columns with new names, AS would have created just one column, filled with the same name and data type as the column that's the result of the SELECT.

```
CREATE TABLE profession
(
  id INT(11) NOT NULL AUTO_INCREMENT PRIMARY KEY,
  profession varchar(20)
) AS
  SELECT profession FROM my_contacts
  GROUP BY profession
  ORDER BY profession;
```

We're creating a VARCHAR column in our new table and calling it profession.

If we hadn't given the new table two columns, AS would have created just one column and filled with the same name and data type as the column that is the result of the SELECT.

This little keyword is doing a big thing. It's funneling all the output of the SELECT into the new table.

These all refer to the profession column in my_contacts because they're all part of the SELECT.

Since we created the profession table with an auto_incrementing primary key, we only needed to add the values to the second column in that table, which we named profession.

I'm confused. "profession" shows up five times in that one query. The SQL software might know which profession is which, but how can *I* tell?

SQL let's you assign an alias for a column name so you won't get confused.

That's one of the reasons that SQL allows you to temporarily give your columns and tables new names, known as **aliases**.

Column aliases

Creating an alias couldn't be easier. We'll put it right after the initial use of the column name in our query with another AS to tell our software to refer to the `profession` column in `my_contacts` as some new name that makes it clearer to us what's going on.

We'll call the profession values that we're selecting from the `my_contacts` table **`mc_prof`** (`mc` is short for `my_contacts`).

```
CREATE TABLE profession
(
  id INT(11) NOT NULL AUTO_INCREMENT PRIMARY KEY,
  profession varchar(20)
) AS
  SELECT profession AS mc_prof FROM my_contacts
  GROUP BY mc_prof
  ORDER BY mc_prof;
```

Put your alias right after the first use of the original column name in the query to tell your software to refer to it as the alias from now on.

This query does exactly the same thing as the first one, but thanks to the alias, it's easier to understand.

There's one small difference between the two queries. All queries return the results in the form of tables. ***The alias changes the name of the column* in the results** but it ***doesn't change the original column name in any way***. An alias is **temporary**.

But since we overrode the results by specifying that our new table have two columns—the primary key and our profession column—our new table will still have a column called `profession`, not `mc_prof`.

profession
programmer
teacher
lawyer

The original query results with the original column name.

The results of the query using the alias. The column name is the same as the alias.

mc_prof
programmer
teacher
lawyer

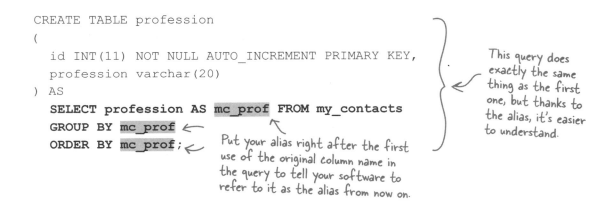

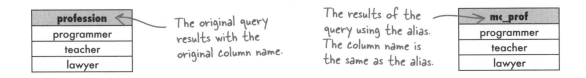

Table aliases, who needs 'em?

You do! We're about to dive head-first into the world of joins, where we are selecting data from more than one table. And without aliases, you're going to get tired of typing those table names again and again.

You create table aliases in the same way as you create column aliases. Put the table alias after the initial use of the table name in the query with another `AS` to tell your software to refer to the original `my_contacts` table as **mc** from now on.

Table aliases are also called correlation names

```
SELECT profession AS mcprof
FROM my_contacts AS mc
GROUP BY mc_prof
ORDER BY mc_prof;
```

Create your table alias exactly the same way as you create your column aliases.

Do I have to use "AS" each time I set up an alias?

No, there's a shorthand way to set up your aliases.

Just leave out the word AS. The query below does exactly the same thing as the one at the top of the page.

There's no difference in what these two queries do.

```
SELECT profession mc_prof
FROM my_contacts mc
GROUP BY mc_prof
ORDER BY mc_prof;
```

We've removed the AS. This works as long as the alias follows directly after the table or column name it is aliasing.

Everything you wanted to know about inner joins

If you've ever heard anyone talking about SQL, you've probably heard the word "join" tossed about. They're not as complicated as you might think they are. We're going to take you through them, show you how they work, and give you plenty of chances to figure out when you should use joins. And which one to use when.

But before we get to that, let's begin with the simplest type of join (that isn't a true join at all).

It has several different names. We'll call it a **Cartesian join** in this book, but it's also called a Cartesian product, cross product, cross join, and, strangely enough, "no join."

...and that's where
little result tables
really come from.

Suppose you have a table of children's names, and another table with the toys that those children have. It's up to you to figure out which toys you can buy each child.

toys

toy_id	toy
1	hula hoop
2	balsa glider
3	toy soldiers
4	harmonica
5	baseball cards

boys

boy_id	boy
1	Davey
2	Bobby
3	Beaver
4	Richie

Cartesian join

The query below gets us the Cartesian results when we query both tables at once for the toy column from toys and the boy column from boys.

```
SELECT t.toy, b.boy
FROM toys AS t
  CROSS JOIN
  boys AS b;
```

Remember our shorthand notations from last chapter? The name before the dot is the table, and the name after it is the name of a column in that table. Only this time around, we're using table aliases instead of the full table names.

We're using table aliases here, too.

This line says SELECT the column called 'boy' from the boy table and the column called 'toy' from the toy table. And the rest of the query joins those two columns in a new results table.

The Cartesian join takes each value in from the first table and pairs it up with each value from the second table.

The CROSS JOIN returns every row from one table crossed with every row from the second.

toys.toy

toy
hula hoop
balsa glider
toy soldiers
harmonica
baseball cards

boys.boy

boy
Davey
Bobby
Beaver
Richie

These lines show the results of the join. Each toy is matched up with each boy. There are no duplicates.

This join gets us 20 results. That's 5 toys * 4 boys to account for every possible combination.

Only because toys.toy had more results do these show up in groups. If we had 5 results for boy and 4 for toys, you'd see a boy's name grouped first. But remember, the order of results has no meaning with this query.

toy	boy
hula hoop	Davey
hula hoop	Bobby
hula hoop	Beaver
hula hoop	Richie
balsa glider	Davey
balsa glider	Bobby
balsa glider	Beaver
balsa glider	Richie
toy soldiers	Davey

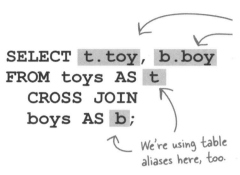

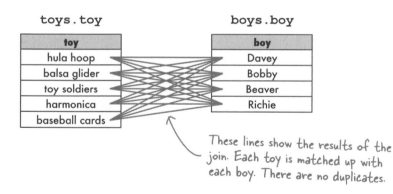

there are no Dumb Questions

Q: Why would I ever need this?

A: It's important to know about it, because when you're mucking around with joins, you might accidentally get Cartesian results. This will help you figure out how to fix your join. This really can happen sometimes. Also, sometimes cross joins are used to test the speed of your RDBMS and its configuration.The time they take is easier to detect and compare when you use a slow query.

Q: Say I'd used his query instead:

```
SELECT * FROM toys CROSS JOIN boys;
```

What happens if I use SELECT *

A: You should try it yourself. But you would still end up with 20 rows; they would just include all 4 columns.

Q: What if I cross join two very large tables?

A: You'd get an ***enormous*** number of results. It's best not to cross join large tables, you run the risk of hanging your machine because it has so much data to return!

Q: Is there another syntax for this query?

A: You bet there is. You can leave out the words CROSS JOIN and just use a comma there instead, like this:

```
SELECT toys.toy, boys.boy
FROM toys, boys;
```

Q: I've heard the terms "inner join" and "outer join" used before. Is this Cartesian join the same thing?

A: A Cartesian join is a type of inner join. An inner join is basically just a Cartesian join where some results rows are removed by a condition in the query. We're going to look at inner joins over the next few pages, so hold that thought!

An INNER JOIN is a CROSS JOIN with some result rows removed by a condition in the query.

BRAIN BARBELL

What do you think would be the result of this query?

```
SELECT b1.boy, b2.boy
FROM boys AS b1 CROSS JOIN boys AS b2;
```

Try it yourself.

Sharpen your pencil

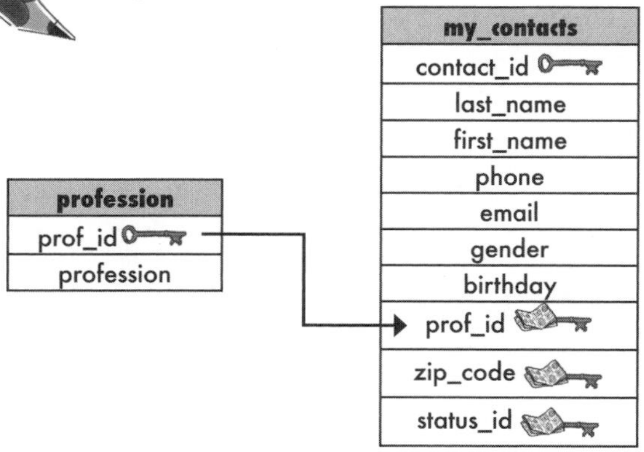

Here are two tables from the gregs_list database structure: profession, and my_contacts. Look at the query and write in the blanks what you think each line of the query is doing.

```
SELECT mc.last_name,                ..............................

mc.first_name,                      ..............................

p.profession                        ..............................

FROM my_contacts AS mc              ..............................

  INNER JOIN                        ..............................

  profession AS p                   ..............................

ON mc.contact_id = p.prof_id;       ..............................
                                    ..............................
```

Assume the data from the three stickies below is in the tables.
Draw what the resulting table might look like with results.

Joan Everett
Single
3-4-1978
Salt Lake City, UT
Artist
Female
jeverett@mightygumball.net
Sailing, hiking, cooking
555 555-9870

Tara Baldwin
married
1-9-1970
Boston, MA
Chef
female
tara@breakneckpizza.com
movies, reading, cooking
555 555-3432

Paul Singh
married
10-12-1980
New York City, NY
Professor
male
ps@tikibeanlounge.com
dogs, spelunking
555 555-8222

Sharpen your pencil Solution

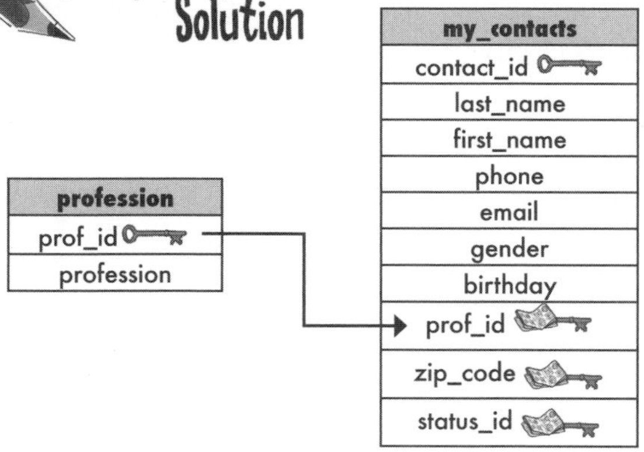

Here are two tables from the gregs_list database structure: profession, and my_contacts. Look at the query and write in the blanks what you think each line of the query is doing.

`SELECT mc.last_name,`	SELECT the last_name column in the my_contacts table (alias mc)
`mc.first_name,`	and the first_name column in the my_contacts table
`p.profession`	and the profession column in the profession table (alias p)
`FROM my_contacts AS mc`	FROM the my_contacts table (alias mc) and
`INNER JOIN`	use an INNER JOIN to join the SELECT results with
`profession AS p`	the profession table (alias p)
`ON mc.contact_id = p.prof_id;`	where the contact_id from my_contacts matches the id field in the profession table

Assume the data from the three stickies is in the tables.
Draw what the resulting table might look like with results.

last_name	first_name	profession
Everett	Joan	artist
Singh	Paul	professor
Baldwin	Tara	chef

Releasing your inner join

I get it! That's how I connect all my new tables to the new my_contacts. I don't have to write a bunch of SELECTs, I just join my tables with that INNER JOIN thingamabob and I'm done!

There's quite a bit more to learn.

You've just seen one small variation of one kind of join. And you've got a lot more to learn about it and the other joins before you can use them appropriately and effectively.

An `INNER JOIN` combines the records from two tables using comparison operators in a condition. Columns are returned only where the joined rows match the condition. Let's take a closer look at the syntax.

Whatever columns you need to see.

```
SELECT somecolumns
FROM table1
  INNER JOIN
  table2
ON somecondition;
```

We've left the aliases off to simplify matters.

The keyword WHERE will also work here.

This condition can use any of the comparison operators.

An INNER JOIN combines the records from two tables using comparison operators in a condition.

The inner join in action: the equijoin

Consider these tables. Each boy has only one toy. We have a one-to-one relationship, and `toy_id` is a foreign key.

boys

boy_id	boy	toy_id
1	Davey	3
2	Bobby	5
3	Beaver	2
4	Richie	1

toys

toy_id	toy
1	hula hoop
2	balsa glider
3	toy soldiers
4	harmonica
5	baseball cards

All we want to do is find out what toy each boy has. We can use our inner join with the = operator to match up the foreign key in boys to the primary key in toys and see what toy it maps to.

EQUIJOIN inner joins test for equality

```
SELECT boys.boy, toys.toy
FROM boys
  INNER JOIN
  toys
ON boys.toy_id = toys.toy_id;
```

boys

boy_id	boy	toy_id
1	Davey	3
2	Bobby	5
3	Beaver	2
4	Richie	1

toys

toy_id	toy
1	hula hoop
2	balsa glider
3	toy soldiers
4	harmonica
5	baseball cards

Our result table. We could have added an ORDER BY boys.boy if we'd wanted to.

boy	toy
Richie	hula hoop
Beaver	balsa glider
Davey	toy soldiers
Bobby	baseball cards

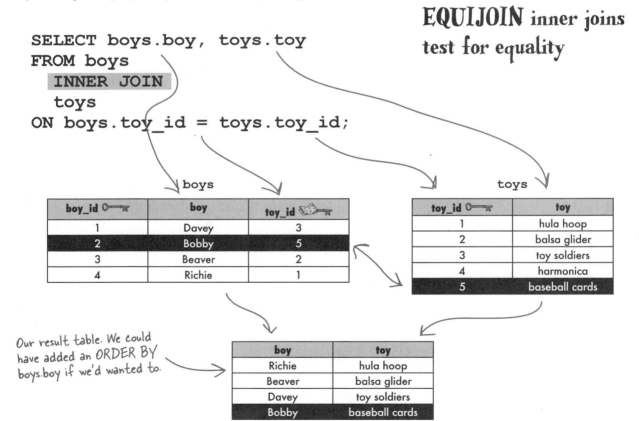

Sharpen your pencil

Write the equijoin queries for the gregs_list database below.

Query that returns the email addresses and professions of each person in my_contacts.

....

....

....

Query that returns the first name, last name, and status each person in my_contacts.

....

....

....

Query that returns the first name, last name, and state of each person in my_contacts.

....

....

....

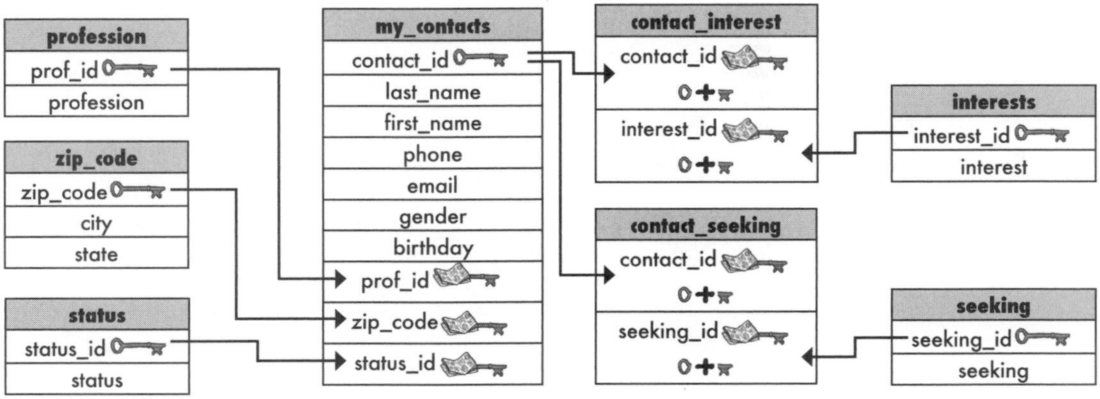

profession
prof_id
profession
zip_code
zip_code
city
state
status
status_id
status
my_contacts
contact_id
last_name
first_name
phone
email
gender
birthday
prof_id
zip_code
status_id
contact_interest
contact_id
interest_id
contact_seeking
contact_id
seeking_id
interests
interest_id
interest
seeking
seeking_id
seeking

Sharpen your pencil Solution

Write the equijoin queries for the gregs_list database below.

Query that returns the email addresses and professions of each person in my_contacts.

```
SELECT mc.email, p.profession FROM my_contacts mc
INNER JOIN profession p ON mc.prof_id = p.prof_id;
```

The foreign key prof_id connects to the prof_id in the profession table.

Query that returns the first name, last name, and status each person in my_contacts.

```
SELECT mc.first_name, mc.last_name, s.status FROM my_contacts mc
INNER JOIN status s ON mc.status_id = s.status_id;
```

The foreign key status_id connects to the status_id in the status table.

Query that returns the first name, last name, and state of each person in my_contacts.

```
SELECT mc.first_name, mc.last_name, z.state FROM my_contacts mc
INNER JOIN zip_code z ON mc.zip_code = z.zip_code;
```

This time we're using zip_code as the key that connects the two tables.

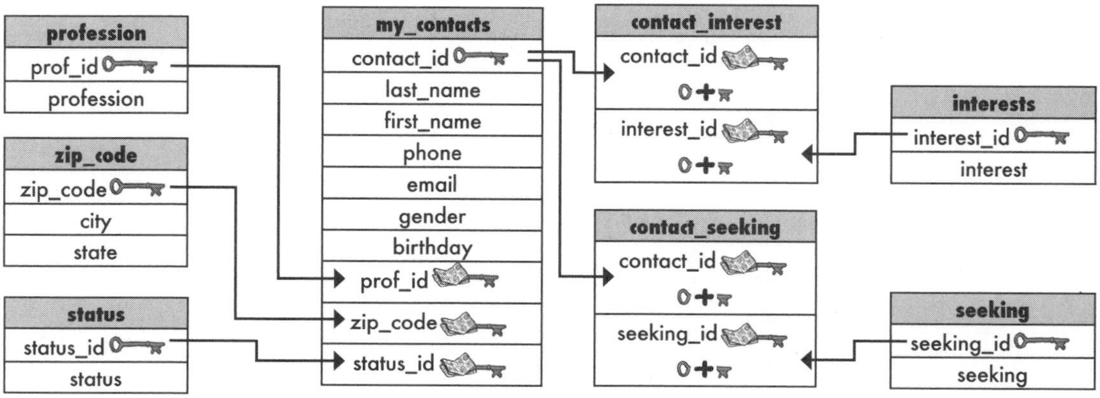

The inner join in action: the <u>non-equijoin</u>

The **non-equijoin** returns any rows that are not equal. Consider the same two tables, boys and toys. By using the non-equijoin, we can see exactly which toys each boy **doesn't** have (which could be useful around their birthdays).

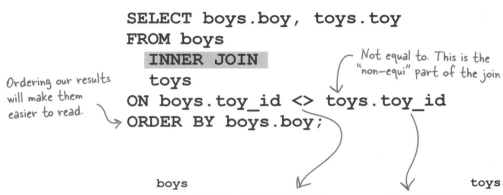

```
SELECT boys.boy, toys.toy
FROM boys
    INNER JOIN
    toys
ON boys.toy_id <> toys.toy_id
ORDER BY boys.boy;
```

Not equal to. This is the "non-equi" part of the join

Ordering our results will make them easier to read.

boys

boy_id ○━━	boy	toy_id 🔑
1	Davey	3
2	Bobby	5
3	Beaver	2
4	Richie	1

toys

toy_id ○━━	toy
1	hula hoop
2	balsa glider
3	toy soldiers
4	harmonica
5	baseball cards

boy	toy
Beaver	hula hoop
Beaver	toy soldiers
Beaver	harmonica
Beaver	baseball cards
Bobby	toy soldiers
Bobby	harmonica
Bobby	hula hoop
Bobby	balsa glider
Davey	hula hoop
Davey	balsa glider
Davey	harmonica
Davey	baseball cards
Richie	balsa glider
Richie	toy soldiers
Richie	harmonica
Richie	baseball cards

These are the four toys Beaver doesn't have yet.

NON-EQUIJOIN
inner joins test for inequality.

The last inner join: the natural join

There's only one kind of inner join left, and it's called a **natural join**. Natural joins only work if the **column you're joining by has the *same name in both tables***. Consider these two tables again.

Same column name

boys

boy_id	boy	toy_id
1	Davey	3
2	Bobby	5
3	Beaver	2
4	Richie	1

toys

toy_id	toy
1	hula hoop
2	balsa glider
3	toy soldiers
4	harmonica
5	baseball cards

Just as before, we want to know what toy each boy has. Our natural join will recognize the same column name in each table and return matching rows.

```
SELECT boys.boy, toys.toy
FROM boys
  NATURAL JOIN
  toys;
```

boys

boy_id	boy	toy_id
1	Davey	3
2	Bobby	5
3	Beaver	2
4	Richie	1

toys

toy_id	toy
1	hula hoop
2	balsa glider
3	toy soldiers
4	harmonica
5	baseball cards

We get the very same result set as we did with our first inner join, the equijoin.

boy	toy
Richie	hula hoop
Beaver	balsa glider
Davey	toy soldiers
Bobby	harmonica

NATURAL JOIN inner joins identify matching column names.

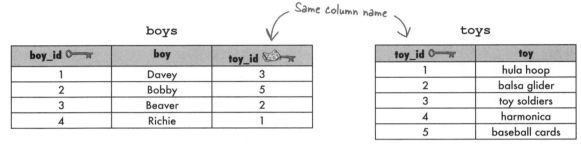

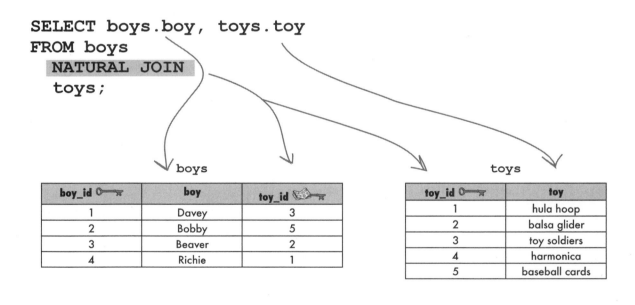

Sharpen your pencil

Write the queries for the gregs_list database below as natural joins or non-equijoins:

Query that returns the email addresses and professions of each person in my_contacts.

....

....

....

Query that returns the first name, last name, and any status that each person in my_contacts is not.

....

....

....

Query that returns the first name, last name, and state of each person in my_contacts.

....

....

....

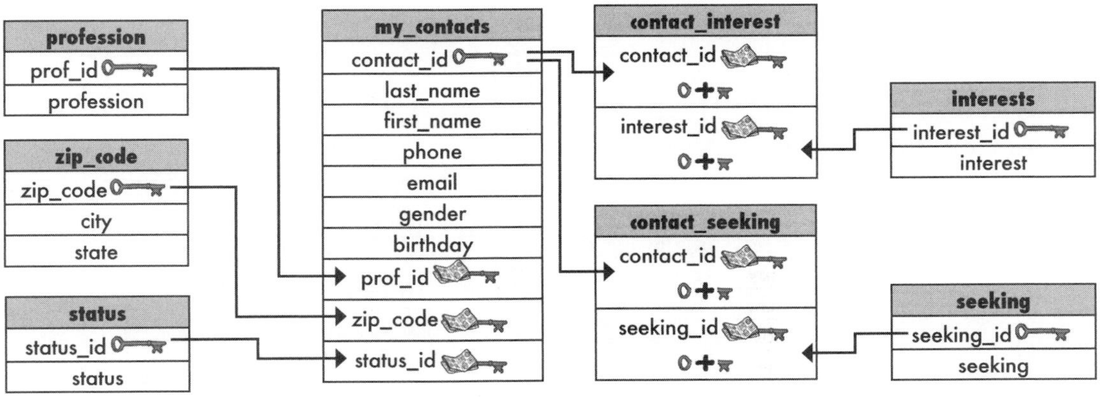

Sharpen your pencil Solution

Write the queries for the gregs_list database below as natural joins or non-equijoins:

Query that returns the email addresses and professions of each person in my_contacts.

```
SELECT mc.email, p.profession FROM my_contacts mc
INNER JOIN profession p;
```

Query that returns the first name, last name, and any status that each person in my_contacts is not.

```
SELECT mc.first_name, mc.last_name, s.status FROM my_contacts mc
INNER JOIN status s ON mc.status_id <> s.status_id;
```

You'll get back multiple rows for each person, with the statuses that they aren't linked to with the status_id.

Query that returns the first name, last name, and state of each person in my_contacts.

```
SELECT mc.first_name, mc.last_name, z.state FROM my_contacts mc
INNER JOIN zip_code z;
```

We don't need the ON part in the first and third queries because our foreign key and primary key names match up in each of these.

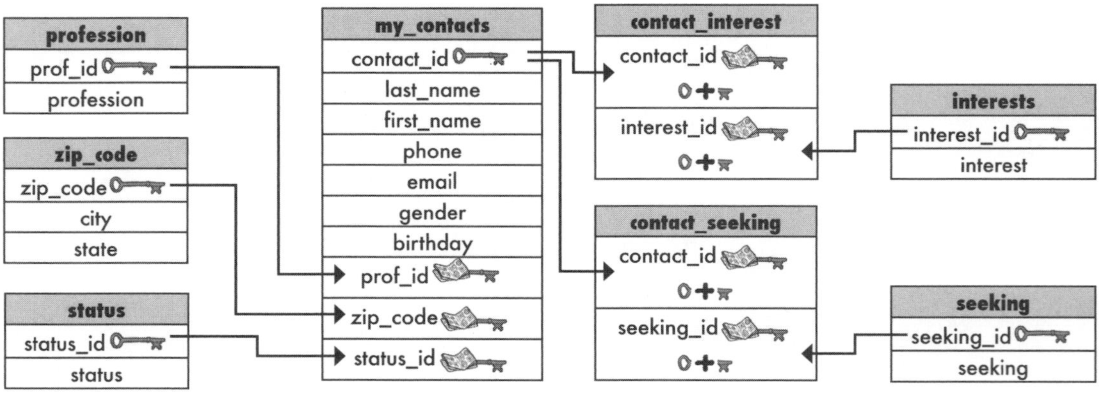

WHO DOES WHAT?

Match each join to the description of what it does. More than one join may match a description.

natural join	I return all rows where one column of a table does not match the other table's column.
equijoin	The order in which you join the tables matters to me.
cross join	I return all rows where one column of a table matches the other table's column, and I use the keyword ON.
outer join	I combine two tables that share a column name.
non-equijoin	I can return rows equal to the product of two tables' rows.
inner join	I return all possible rows and have no condition.
Cartesian join	I combine two tables with a condition.
cross product	

Who Does What?

Match each join to the description of what it does. More than one join may match a description.

- natural join
- equijoin
- cross join
- outer join
- non-equijoin
- inner join
- Cartesian join
- cross product

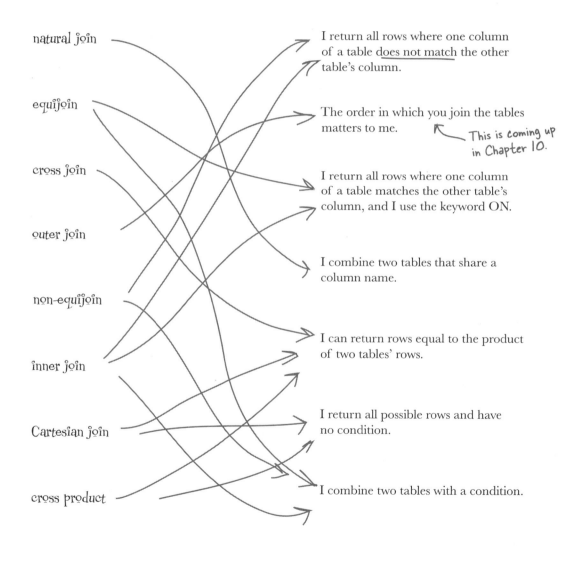

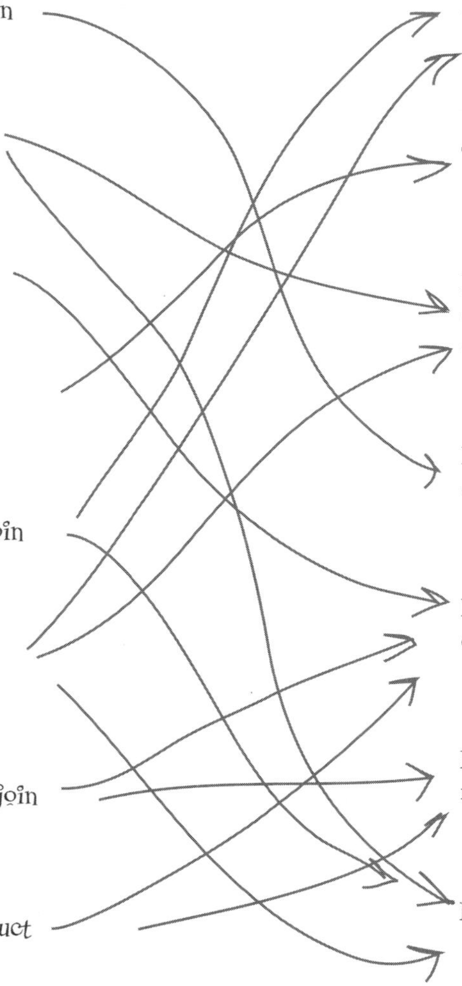

- I return all rows where one column of a table does not match the other table's column.
- The order in which you join the tables matters to me. ← This is coming up in Chapter 10.
- I return all rows where one column of a table matches the other table's column, and I use the keyword ON.
- I combine two tables that share a column name.
- I can return rows equal to the product of two tables' rows.
- I return all possible rows and have no condition.
- I combine two tables with a condition.

Use the diagram of the gregs_list database below to write SQL queries to get the information requested.

Write two queries, each with a different join, to get the matching records from my_contacts and contact_interest.

Write a query to return all possible combinations of rows from contact_seeking and seeking.

List the professions of people in the my_contacts table, but without any duplicates and in alphabetical order.

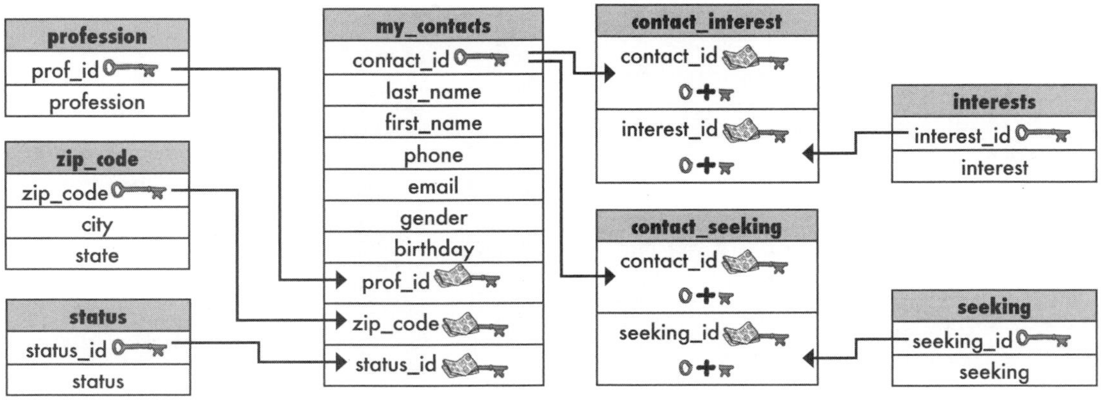

profession
prof_id
profession
zip_code
zip_code
city
state
status
status_id
status
my_contacts
contact_id
last_name
first_name
phone
email
gender
birthday
prof_id
zip_code
status_id
contact_interest
contact_id
interest_id
contact_seeking
contact_id
seeking_id
interests
interest_id
interest
seeking
seeking_id
seeking

Exercise Solution

Use the diagram of the gregs_list database below to write SQL queries to get the information requested.

Write two queries, each with a different join, to get the matching records from my_contacts and contact_interest.

```
SELECT mc.first_name, mc.last_name, ci.interest_id FROM my_contacts mc
INNER JOIN contact_interest ci ON mc.contact_id = ci.contact_id;

SELECT mc.first_name, mc.last_name, ci.interest_id FROM my_contacts mc
NATURAL JOIN contact_interest ci;
```

Write a query to return all possible combinations of rows from contact_seeking and seeking.

```
SELECT * FROM contact_seeking CROSS JOIN seeking;

SELECT * FROM contact_seeking, seeking;
```

There are two ways to do the same cross join.

List the professions of people in the my_contacts table, but without any duplicates and in alphabetical order.

```
SELECT p.profession FROM my_contacts mc
INNER JOIN profession p ON mc.prof_id = p.prof _ id GROUP BY profession ORDER BY profession;
```

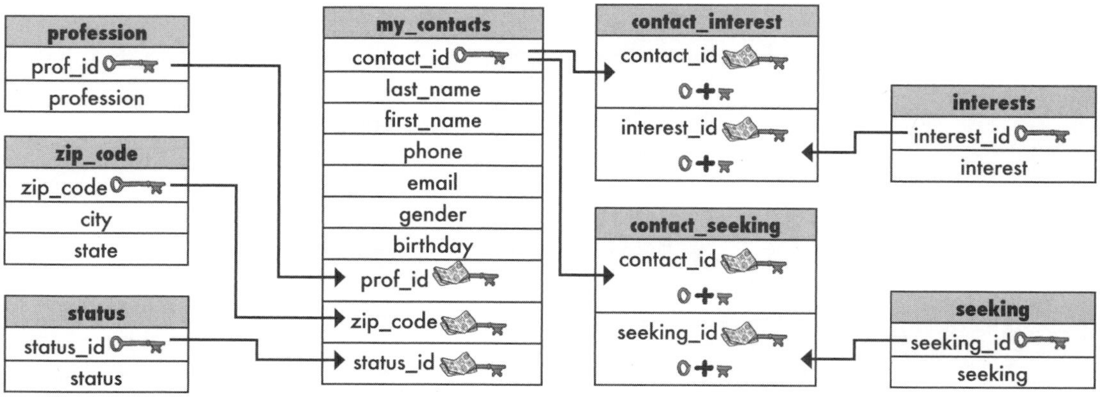

there are no Dumb Questions

Q: Can you join more than two tables?

A: You can, and we'll talk about that a little later. Right now we'll focus on getting the join concepts down.

Q: Aren't joins supposed to be more difficult than this?

A: Once you start getting into joins and aliases, SQL queries sound less English-like and more like a foreign language. Also using shortcuts (like replacing the keywords INNER JOIN with commas in queries, for example) could make things even more confusing. For that reason, this book favors more verbose SQL queries rather than less clear shortcuts.

Q: Does that mean there are other ways to write inner join queries?

A: There are, yes. But if you understand these, with the syntax we present, picking up syntax of the others will be easy. The concepts are much more important than you using `WHERE` or `ON` in a join.

Q: I noticed you used an ORDER BY in a join. Does that mean everything else is fair game too?

A: Yes. Feel free to use `GROUP BY`, `WHERE` clauses, and functions such as `SUM` and `AVG` anytime.

Joined-up queries?

Greg's really starting to appreciate joins. He's beginning to see that having multiple tables makes sense, and they aren't difficult to work with if they're well designed. He's even got some plans for expanding `gregs_list`.

But I still find myself typing one query, then using those results in a second query when it seems like I should be able to do it all in one... Wouldn't it be great if I could put a query inside another query? But that's just crazy talk.

A query inside another query? Is that possible?

Table and Column Aliases Exposed

This week's interview:
What are you hiding from?

HeadFirst: Welcome Table Alias and Column Alias. We're glad you could both be here. We're hoping you can clear up some confusion for us.

Table Alias: Certainly, great to be here. And you can call us **TA** and **CA** for short during this interview[laughs].

HeadFirst: Ha ha! That would certainly be appropriate. Okay, **CA**, let's begin with you. Why all the secrecy? Are you trying to hide something?

Column Alias: Absolutely not! If anything, I'm trying to make things more clear. I think I speak for both of us here, right TA?

TA: You are. In CA's case, it should already be clear what he's trying to do. He takes long or redundant column names and makes them easier to follow. More accessible. He also gives you result tables with useful column names. My story is a little different.

HeadFirst: I have to admit, I'm not as familiar with you, TA. I've seen how you operate, but I'm still not sure what it is you're doing. You don't show up at all in the results when we use you in a query.

TA: Yes, that's true. But I think you don't yet grasp my higher calling.

HeadFirst: Higher calling? Sounds intriguing. Go on.

TA: I exist to make joins easier to write.

CA: And you help me too in those same joins, TA.

HeadFirst: I'm not getting it. Can you show me an example?

TA: I can still show you the syntax. I think it will be pretty clear what it is I'm doing:

```
SELECT mc.last_name, mc.first_name, p.profession
FROM my_contacts AS mc
  INNER JOIN
  profession AS p
WHERE mc.contact_id = p.id;
```

HeadFirst: I see you! Everywhere I'd have to type `my_contacts`, I can just type `mc` instead. And `p` for `profession`. Much simpler. And really useful when I have to include two table names in a single query.

TA: Especially when the tables have similar names. Making your queries easier to understand not only helps you write them, but it helps you remember what they are doing when you come back to them later.

HeadFirst: Thanks very much, TA and CA. It's been.. uh... where'd they go?

Your SQL Toolbox

You've just completed Chapter 8 and can JOIN like a true SQL pro. Check out all the techniques you've learned. For a complete list of tooltips in the book, see Appendix iii.

INNER JOIN

Any join that combines the records from two tables using some condition.

NATURAL JOIN

An inner join that leaves off the "ON" clause. It only works if you are joining two tables that have the same column name.

EQUIJOIN and NON-EQUIJOIN

Both are inner joins. The EQUIJOIN returns rows that are equal, and the NON-EQUIJOIN returns any rows that are not equal.

CROSS JOIN

Returns every row from one table crossed with every row from the second table. Known by many other names including CARTESIAN JOIN and NO JOIN.

COMMA JOIN

The same thing as a CROSS JOIN, except a comma is used instead of the keywords CROSS JOIN.

Sharpen your pencil Solution

From page 348.

You know how to ALTER tables at this point, so you need to ALTER my_contacts to have four new columns. Name them interest1, interest2, interest3, and interest4.

```
ALTER TABLE my_contacts
ADD (interest1 VARCHAR(20), interest2 VARCHAR(20), interest3
VARCHAR(20), interest4 VARCHAR(20));
```

Sharpen your pencil Solution

From page 350.

Fill in the blanks to complete Greg's update statement. We've given you a couple of notes to help you along.

The difference between SUBSTRING_INDEX and SUBSTR is that SUBSTRING_INDEX is looking for a string *inside* the interests column—in this case, a comma—and returning everything in front of it. SUBSTR is shortening the length of the interest column—starting right after the first interest, a comma, and a space (the +2)—to the end of the string.

```
UPDATE my_contacts SET
interest1 = SUBSTRING_INDEX(interests, ',', 1),
interests = SUBSTR(interests, LENGTH(interest1)+2),
interest2 = SUBSTRING_INDEX(interests, ',', 1),
interests = SUBSTR(interests, LENGTH(interest2)+2),
interest3 = SUBSTRING_INDEX(interests, ',', 1),
interests = SUBSTR(interests, LENGTH(interest3)+2),
interest4 = interests;
```

After you've removed the first three interests from the interests column, all that is left is the fourth interest. This line is simply moving it to the new column. We could have simply renamed the interests column to interest4 at this point, instead.

The interests column is empty after we run the command.

interests	interest1	interest2	interest3	interest4
~~second, third, fourth~~	first	second	third	fourth

9 subqueries

Queries within queries

Will everyone else notice that I'm full of... (What's the right word? Exquisiteness? Resplendence? Pulchritude?)

Yes, Jack, I'd like a two-part question, please. Joins are great, but sometimes you need to ***ask your database more than one question***. Or ***take the result of one query and use it as the input to another query***. That's where **subqueries** come in. They'll help you **avoid duplicate data**, **make your queries more dynamic**, and even get you in to all those high-end concert afterparties. (Well, not really, but two out of three ain't bad!)

Greg gets into the job recruiting business

So far, the gregs_list database has literally been a labor of love. It's helped Greg find dates for his friends, but he's made no money from it.

It occurs to him that he could start a recruiting business where he matches his contacts up with possible jobs.

With the new recruiting functionality, I'm really going to make it big!
Greg's Recruiting Service

Greg knows he's going to need to add new tables for his contacts that are interested in the service. He decides to make them separate one-to-one tables rather than putting that information into my_contacts for two reasons.

First, not everyone in his my_contacts list is interested in the service. This way, he keeps NULL values out of my_contacts.

Second, he might hire people to help him with his business someday and the salary information might be considered sensitive. **He may only want to give access to those tables to certain people**.

Greg's list gets more tables

Greg's added new tables to his database to keep track of information on the **desired position** and **expected salary range**, as well as **current position** and **salary**. He also creates a simple table to hold the **job listing information**.

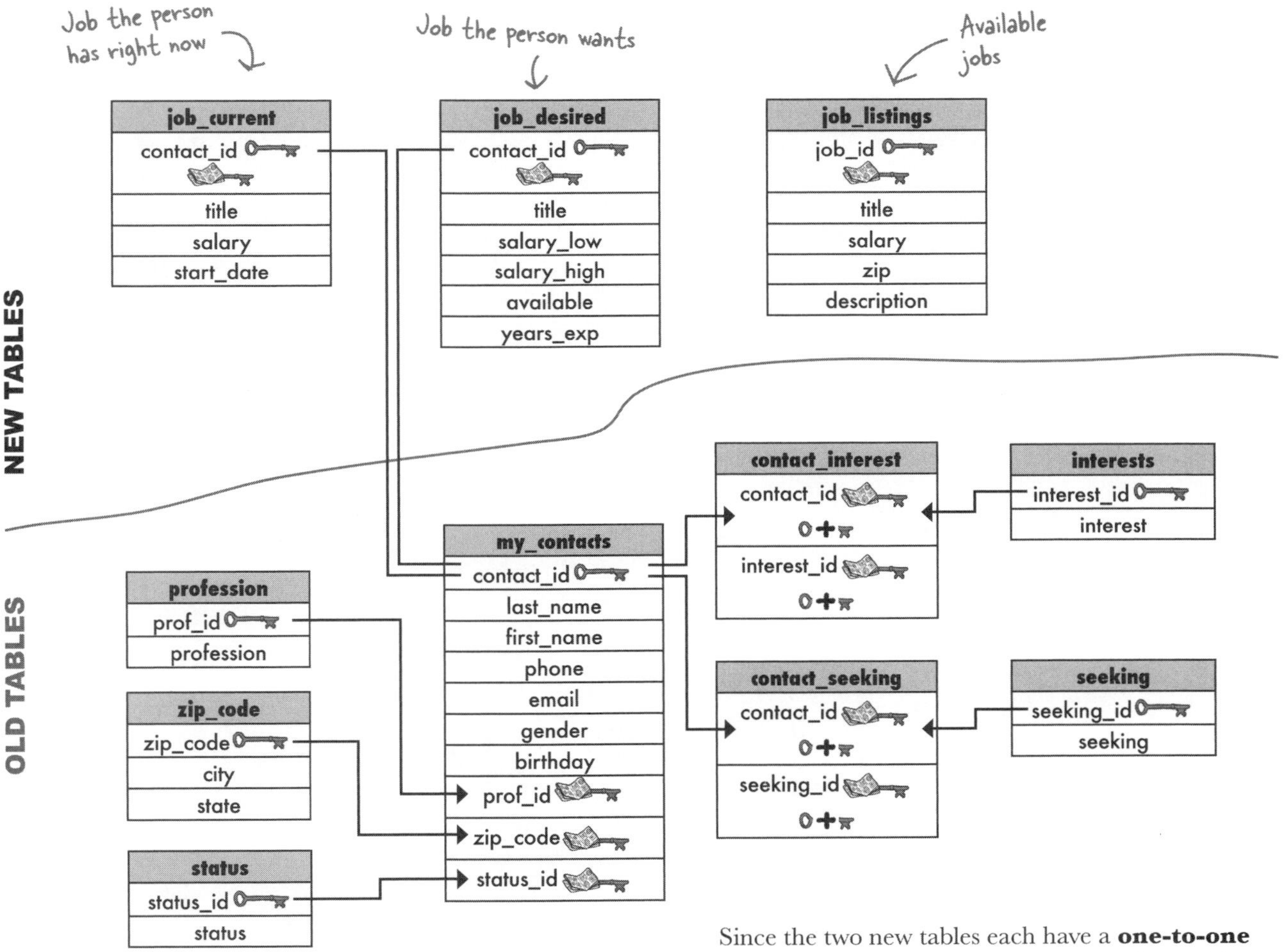

Since the two new tables each have a **one-to-one** relationship with `my_contacts`, he's been able to use **natural joins** so far with great success and ease.

Greg uses an inner join

Greg's got a hot job listing, and he's trying to match people in his database. He wants to find the best match for the job since he'll get a finder's fee if his candidate is hired.

Wanted: Web Developer

Looking for Web Developer with first rate HTML & CSS chops to work with our interaction and visual design teams. This is a tremendous opportunity for someone who's meticulous about web standards to shine with a highly-visible company. Work with an amazingly influential company operated by smart people who love what they do.

Salary: $95,000-$105,000

Experience: 5+ years

Once he finds the best few matches, he can call them up and screen them further. But first, he wants to pull out all the Web Developers with at least five years of experience and who don't require a salary higher than 105,000.

Sharpen your pencil

Write the query to get the qualified candidates from the database.

job_current
contact_id
title
salary
start_date

job_desired
contact_id
title
salary_low
salary_high
available
years_exp

job_listings
job_id
title
salary
zip
description

This is the lowest salary they'll accept for a new job. (→ salary_low)

This is the salary they're hoping for in a new job. (→ salary_high)

But he wants to try some other queries

Greg has more job openings than he can fill. He's going to look for people in his professions table to see if he can find any matches for his open job listings. Then he can do a natural join with `my_contacts` to get their contact info and see if they are interested.

First he selects all the titles from his job_current table.

```
SELECT title FROM job_listings
GROUP BY title ORDER BY title;
```

We use the GROUP BY so we only get one row for each job title. We also put them in alphabetical order.

The results

title
Cook
Hairdresser
Waiter
Web Designer
Web Developer

These are just a few of the titles in Greg's job_current table.

Sharpen your pencil Solution

Write the query to get the qualified candidates from the database.

```
SELECT mc.last_name, mc.first_name, mc.phone
FROM my_contacts AS mc
    NATURAL JOIN
    job_desired AS jd
WHERE jd.title = 'Web Developer'
AND jd.salary_low < 105000;
```

We only need to get the contact information since we know they're seeking Web Developer jobs.

Since both my_contacts and job_desired share contact_id as a primary key, we can simply use a natural join to connect them.

We're only interested in people who will consider the salary. We look at the salary_low figure to see if the salary offered is more than the least they'll accept.

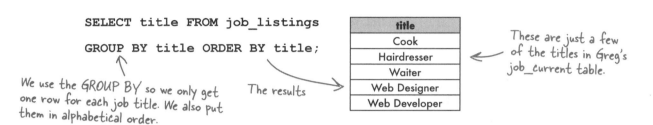

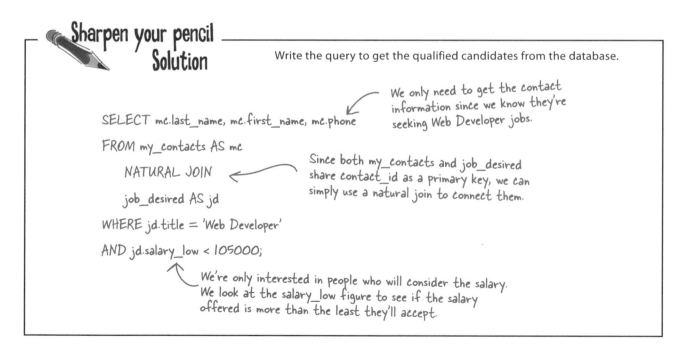

And now Greg uses the IN keyword to see if he has any matches for these job titles among his contacts.

```
SELECT mc.first_name, mc.last_name, mc.phone, jc.title
FROM job_current AS jc NATURAL JOIN my_contacts AS mc
WHERE
jc.title IN ('Cook', 'Hairdresser', 'Waiter', 'Web Designer', 'Web Developer');
```

Remember the IN keyword? It returns a row if jc.title is in the group of titles in parentheses.

Results from the first query

It works!

mc.first_name	mc.last_name	mc.phone	jc.title
Joe	Lonnigan	(555) 555-3214	Cook
Wendy	Hillerman	(555) 555-8976	Waiter
Sean	Miller	(555) 555-4443	Web Designer
Jared	Callaway	(555) 555-5674	Web Developer
Juan	Garza	(555) 555-0098	Web Developer

But he's still having to type in two separate queries...

BRAIN POWER

Try combining the two queries into a single query. Write that single query here.

Subqueries

To accomplish what those two queries do with just one query, we need to add a **subquery** into the query.

We'll call the *second* query we used to get the matches from the `professions` table the `OUTER` query because it will wrap up inside of itself the `INNER` query. Let's see how it works:

OUTER query

```
SELECT mc.first_name, mc.last_name, mc.phone, jc.title
FROM job_current AS jc NATURAL JOIN my_contacts AS mc
WHERE
jc.title IN ('Cook', 'Hairdresser', 'Waiter', 'Web Designer', 'Web Developer');
```

This part is the outer query.

This part can be removed and replaced with part of our first query, which will become the inner query.

All those professions in parentheses above came from the *first* query we did, the one to select all the titles from the `job_current` table. So—and this is the clever bit, so watch carefully—we can **replace that part of the outer query** with **part of our first query**. This will still produce all the results in parentheses above, but this query now gets encapsulated as the subquery:

A subquery is a query that is wrapped within another query. It's also called an INNER query.

INNER query

```
SELECT title FROM job_listings
GROUP BY title ORDER BY title;
```

This part of the first query will become the inner query, or subquery.

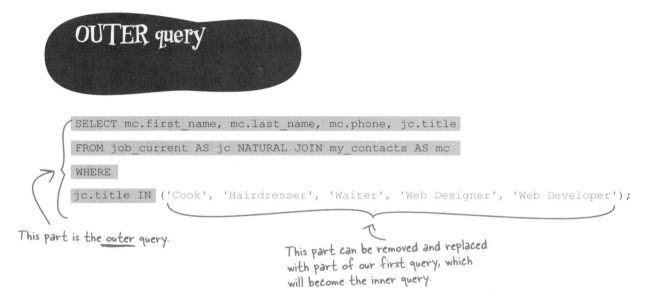

We combine the two into a query with a subquery

All we've done is combine the two queries into one. The first query is known as the **outer query.** The one inside is known as the **inner query**.

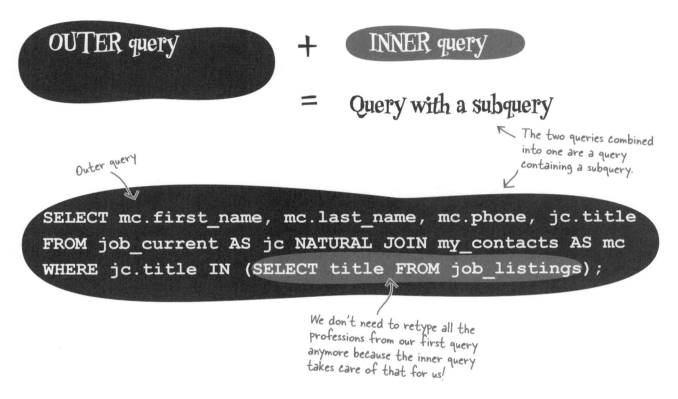

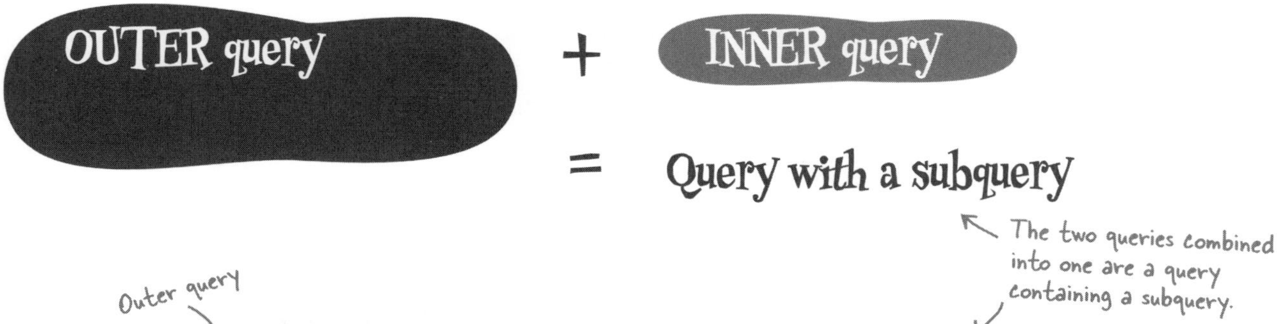
OUTER query
+
INNER query
=
Query with a subquery
The two queries combined into one are a query containing a subquery.
Outer query

```
SELECT mc.first_name, mc.last_name, mc.phone, jc.title
FROM job_current AS jc NATURAL JOIN my_contacts AS mc
WHERE jc.title IN (SELECT title FROM job_listings);
```

We don't need to retype all the professions from our first query anymore because the inner query takes care of that for us!

And these are the results we get when we run our query, precisely the same results as when we spelled out ***all*** the job titles in the `WHERE` clause, but with a lot less typing.

Same results as before, but with just one query!

mc.first_name	mc.last_name	mc.phone	jc.title
Joe	Lonnigan	(555) 555-3214	Cook
Wendy	Hillerman	(555) 555-8976	Waiter
Sean	Miller	(555) 555-4443	Web Designer
Jared	Callaway	(555) 555-5674	Web Developer
Juan	Garza	(555) 555-0098	Web Developer

Anatomy of a query within a query

As if one query wasn't enough: meet the subquery

A subquery is nothing more than a query inside another query.

The outside query is known as the **containing query,** or the **outer query**. The query on the inside is the **inner query**, or the **subquery**.

Outer query. Sometimes known as the containing query.

```
SELECT some_column, another_column
FROM table
WHERE column = (SELECT column FROM table);
```

Inner query, or subquery.

Outer query

```
SELECT some_column, another_column
FROM table
WHERE column = (SELECT column FROM table);
```

Inner query

Because it uses the = operator, this subquery will return a ***single value***, **one row from one column** (sometimes called a *cell*, but in SQL known as a *scalar value*), which is compared to the columns in the `WHERE` clause.

value

Our subquery returns a scalar value (one column, one row), which is then compared against the columns in the WHERE clause.

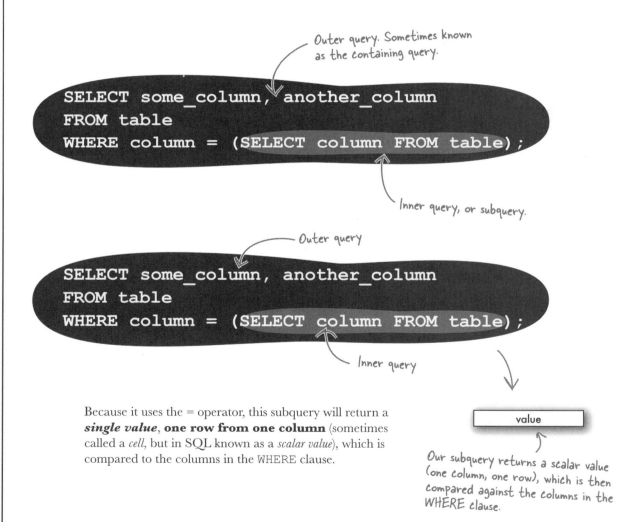

A subquery in action

Let's see a comparable query in action from the `my_contacts` table. First your RDBMS takes the scalar value from the `zip_code` table, then it compares that value to the columns in the `WHERE` clause.

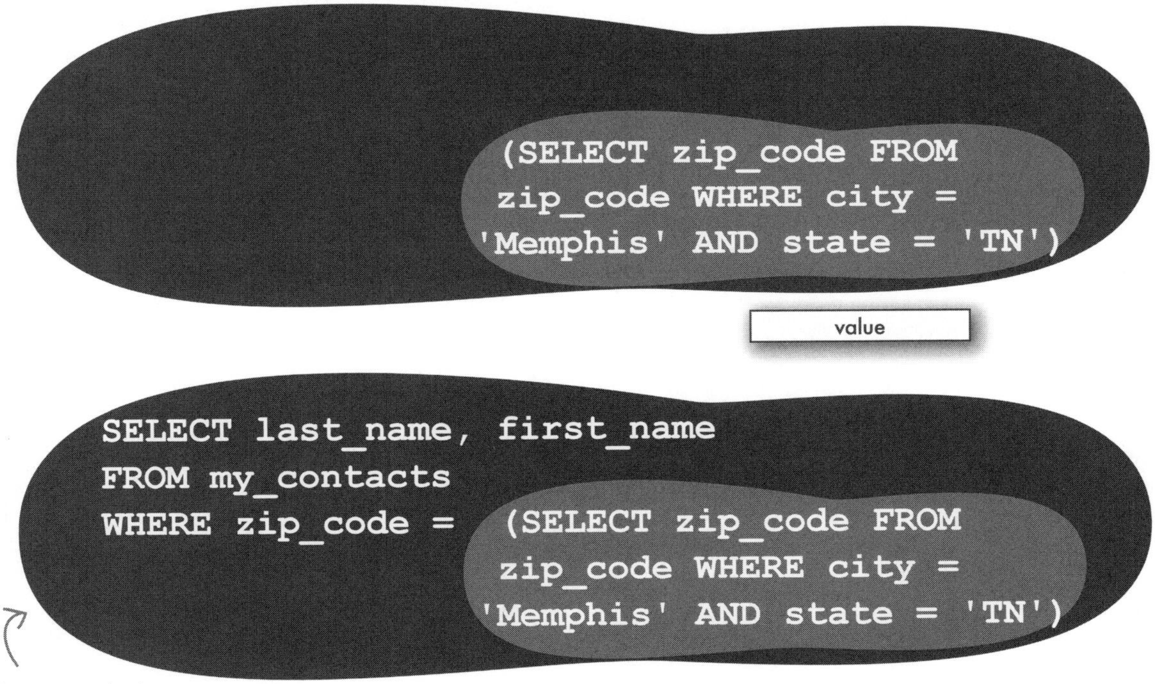
(SELECT zip_code FROM
zip_code WHERE city =
'Memphis' AND state = 'TN')
value
SELECT last_name, first_name
FROM my_contacts
WHERE zip_code =
(SELECT zip_code FROM
zip_code WHERE city =
'Memphis' AND state = 'TN')

This query selects the names of people in my_contacts in Memphis, Tennessee.

there are no Dumb Questions

Q: Why can't I just do this as a join?

A: You can. but some people find subqueries simpler to write than joins. It's nice to have the choice of syntax.

You can do the same query above this way:

```
SELECT last_name, first_name
FROM my_contacts mc
NATURAL JOIN zip_code zc
WHERE zc.city = 'Memphis'
AND zc.state = 'TN'
```

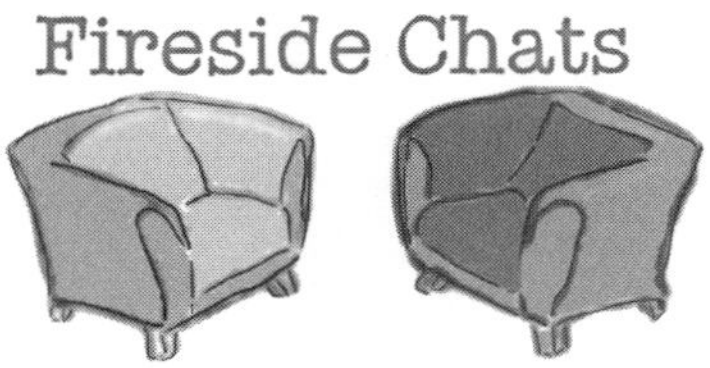

Tonight's talk: **Are you an INNER or an OUTER?**

Outer Query: I don't really need you, you know, Inner Query. I'd be just fine without you.

Inner Query: I could stand on my own as well. Do you think it's fun, giving you a specific, targeted result, only to have you take it and turn it into a bunch of matching rows? Quantity is not quality, you know.

Outer Query: Big whoop. You give me one little result. Users want data, and lots of it. I give them that. Why, I bet if you weren't there, they'd be even more pleased.

Inner Query: No, I give your results some kind of purpose. Without me, you'd be spouting all the data in the table.

Outer Query: Not if I added a WHERE clause.

Inner Query: That's just it, I AM your WHERE clause. And a very specific one I am, if I do say so myself. In fact, I don't really need you at all.

Outer Query: Oh yes, you do. What good is a single-row, single-column answer? It's not enough information.

Inner Query: So maybe we do work well together. I give your results direction.

Outer Query: Sure, but I stand alone.

Inner Query: As do I, most of the time.

Exercise

Subquery rules

There are some rules that all subqueries follow. Fill in the blanks using the words below (you might need some of them more than once).

SEMICOLON

SELECT

COLUMN LIST

END

PARENTHESES

DELETE

UPDATE

INSERT

SQL's Rules of Order

A subquery is always a single .... statement.

Subqueries are always inside ....

Subqueries do not get their own .... As always, one .... goes at the .... of the entire query.

SQL's Rules of Order

Subqueries can show up in four places in a query: .... clause, SELECT .... as one of the columns, ... clause, and in a .... clause.

Subqueries can be used with ....,................, ..., and, of course, ...

Exercise Solution

Subquery rules

Keep these rules in mind as you look at the subqueries in the rest of the chapter.

SQL's Rules of Order

A subquery is always a single **SELECT** statement.

Subqueries are always inside **PARENTHESES**.

Subqueries do not get their own **SEMICOLON**. As always, one **SEMICOLON** goes at the **END** of the entire query.

SQL's Rules of Order

Subqueries can show up in four places in a query: **SELECT** clause, SELECT **COLUMN LIST** as one of the columns, **FROM** clause, and in a **HAVING** clause.

Subqueries can be used with **INSERT**, **DELETE**, **UPDATE**, and, of course, **SELECT**.

there are no Dumb Questions

Q: So what is the inner query allowed to return? How about the outer query?

A: In most cases, the inner query can only return a single value—that is, one column with one row. The outer query can then take that value and use it to compare against all the values in a column.

Q: Why do you say "a single value" when the example on page 388 returns the entire column full of values?

A: Because the `IN` operator is looking at a set of values. If you use a comparison operator, like the = in the Anatomy, you can only have one value to compare to each value in your column.

Q: I'm still not clear on whether a subquery can return a single value or more than one value. What are the official rules?

A: In general, a subquery must return a single value. `IN` is the exception. Most of the time subqueries need to return a single value to work.

Q: So what happens if your subquery *does* return more than one value but isn't using a WHERE clause that contains a set of values?

A: Chaos! Mass destruction! Actually, you'll just get an error.

Yeah, these rules are cool or whatever, but what I want to know is how I can get rid of those long names in my result columns, like mc.last_name. Do you have a rule for that?

Actually, there are two things you can do that will help cut down on the clutter.

You can create alias names for your columns in your SELECT column list. The table you get back with your results is suddenly much clearer.

Here's the subquery we just created, but with short **column aliases**.

We'll give the my_contacts first_name column an alias of 'firstname' in our results.

... and the my_contacts last_name column will have an alias of 'lastname' in our results.

```
SELECT mc.first_name AS firstname, mc.last_name AS lastname,
mc.phone AS phone, jc.title AS jobtitle
FROM job_current AS jc NATURAL JOIN my_contacts AS mc
WHERE jobtitle IN (SELECT title FROM job_listings);
```

The my_contacts phone column will have an alias of 'phone' in our results... and so on. You get the picture!

Remember, the keyword AS is optional, so you can leave it out when creating your aliases.

Here are the results the query gives us.

Notice how using the column aliases makes the results much easier to understand.

And since aliases are temporary, we're not affecting any of the table or column names in either table.

firstname	lastname	phone	jobtitle
Joe	Lonnigan	(555) 555-3214	Cook
Wendy	Hillerman	(555) 555-8976	Waiter
Sean	Miller	(555) 555-4443	Web Designer
Jared	Callaway	(555) 555-5674	Web Developer
Juan	Garza	(555) 555-0098	Web Developer

A subquery construction walkthrough

The tricky part about subqueries isn't the structure; it's figuring out what part of the query needs to be the subquery. Or even if you need one at all.

Analyzing queries is very much like figuring out word problems. You identify words in the question that match things you know (like table and column names) and break things apart.

Let's go through an analysis of a question we want to ask our database and how to make a query out of it. First, the question:

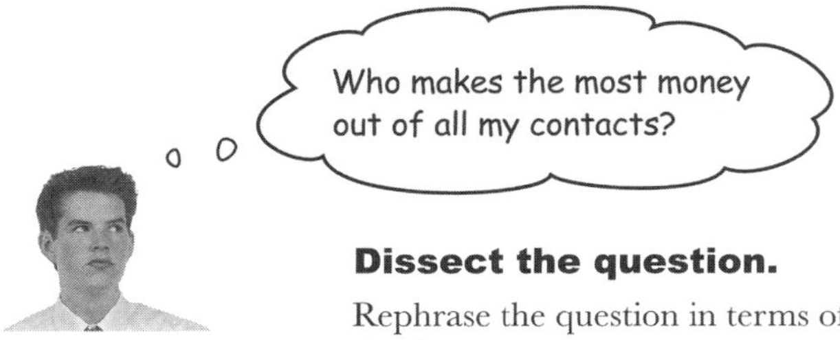
Who makes the most money out of all my contacts?

Dissect the question.

Rephrase the question in terms of the tables and columns in your database.

"Who" means you want a first and last name from `my_contacts`. "The most money" means you need a `MAX` value from your `job_current` table.

<u>Who</u> makes the <u>most money</u> out of all of my contacts?

first_name and last_name from my_contacts

MAX(salary) from the job_current table

Identify a query that answers part of the question.

Since we're creating a noncorrelated subquery, we can pick apart our question and build a query that answers part of it.

That `MAX(salary)` looks like a good candidate for our first query.

```
SELECT MAX(salary) FROM job_current;
```

Remember MAX? It returns the largest value from the column in parentheses.

Continue dissecting your query.

The first part of the query is also easy; we just need to select first and last names:

```
SELECT mc.first_name, mc.last_name
FROM my_contacts AS mc;
```

SELECT first and last names.

Finally, figure out how to link the two.

We not only need names of people in my_contacts, we need to know their salaries so we can compare them to our MAX(salary). We need a natural inner join to pull out the salary belonging to each person:

```
SELECT mc.first_name, mc.last_
name, jc.salary
FROM my_contacts AS mc
NATURAL JOIN job_current AS jc;
```

Use a NATURAL JOIN to pull out each person's salary.

And now add the WHERE clause to link the two

We create one big query that answers the question, "Who earns the most money?"

Here's the part we just did—it pulls out each person's salary.

```
SELECT mc.first_name, mc.last_name, jc.salary
FROM my_contacts AS mc NATURAL JOIN job_current AS jc
WHERE jc.salary =
(SELECT MAX(jc.salary) FROM job_current jc);
```

And here's the first part which is now our subquery to find the MAX salary value. The value from this is compared against the outer part of the query to get the results.

It's Mike? I should have known. He never picks up the check.

mc.first_name	mc.last_name	jc.salary
Mike	Scala	187000

It really seems like we could have done that without the subquery.

It's true, the subquery wasn't the only way to do it.

You could have done the same thing using a natural inner join and a `LIMIT` command. Like so many other things in SQL, there's more than one way to do it.

BRAIN POWER

Write another query to figure out who makes the most money out of all Greg's contacts.

I don't care if there are multiple ways of doing the same thing. I want to know the best way. Or at least some reason to choose one way over another.

Good point.

Why don't you check out the SQL Exposed interview on page 400?

A subquery as a SELECT column

A subquery can be used as one of the columns in a SELECT statement. Consider this query.

```
SELECT mc.first_name, mc.last_name,
(SELECT state
FROM zip_code
WHERE mc.zip_code = zip_code) AS state
FROM my_contacts mc;
```

We're setting up a column alias, 'state'.

We can dissect this query by first looking at the subquery. The subquery simply matches up the zip codes to the corresponding states in the `zip_code` table.

In simple terms, here's what this query is doing:

Go through all the rows in the my_contacts table. For each one, pull out the first name, last name, and state (where we find the state by taking the zip code and matching it up with the correct state in the zip code table).

If a subquery is used as a column expression in a SELECT statement, it can only return one value from one column.

Remember that the subquery may only return one single value, so each time it runs, a row is returned. Here's what some of the results of this query might look like:

mc.first_name	mc.last_name	state
Joe	Lonnigan	TX
Wendy	Hillerman	CA
Sean	Miller	NY
Jared	Callaway	NJ
Juan	Garza	CA

Another example: Subquery with a natural join

Greg's friend Andy has been bragging about what a great salary he gets. He didn't tell Greg how much, but Greg thinks he has that information in his table. He does a quick NATURAL JOIN to find it, using Andy's email address.

```
SELECT jc.salary

FROM my_contacts mc NATURAL JOIN job_current jc

WHERE email = 'andy@weatherorama.com';
```

This query will return Andy's salary, a single value.

This will be the inner query.

Greg notices that this query will only return a single result. Instead of running it and getting that value and plopping it into another query, he decides to turn it into a subquery.

He writes a single query that:

- gets Andy's salary and
- compares it to other salaries
- and returns the first and last names of people with their salaries
- who earn more than Andy.

This will use the > comparison operator.

Salaries greater than Andy's.

It's a long query, but it allows me to compare something I don't have to know to other things in my database.

Here's the outer query

```
SELECT mc.first_name, mc.last_name, jc.salary

FROM

my_contacts AS mc NATURAL JOIN job_current AS jc

WHERE

jc.salary > (ANDY'S SALARY QUERY WILL GO HERE)
```

A noncorrelated subquery

When we put the pieces together, here's the entire query. First the software processes the inner query once, then it uses that value to figure out the outer query result.

Get the first name, last name and salary.

The RDBMS processes this part first.

Only show the people who have greater salaries than Andy's.

These two queries are processed separately by the RDBMS.

```
SELECT mc.first_name, mc.last_name, jc.salary
FROM
my_contacts AS mc NATURAL JOIN job_current AS jc
WHERE
jc.salary > (SELECT jc.salary
FROM my_contacts mc NATURAL JOIN job_current jc
WHERE email = 'andy@weatherorama.com');
```

The subquery that gets Andy's salary for the outer query to compare against. This is processed second.

Here are a few of the results. We didn't use an ORDER BY, so they aren't in any order.

mc.first_name	mc.last_name	jc.salary
Gus	Logan	46500
Bruce	Hill	78000
Teresa	Semel	48000
Randy	Wright	49000
Julie	Moore	120000

If the subquery stands alone and doesn't reference anything from the outer query, it is a noncorrelated subquery.

(and if you can manage to fit "noncorrelated subquery" into a conversation, non-SQL users will be very impressed)

All of the subqueries you've seen so far are known as **noncorrelated subqueries**. The inner query gets processed first, then the result is used in the WHERE condition of the outer query. ***But the inner query in no way depends on values from the outer query; it can be run as a standalone query.***

Outer query gets processed second. Its results depend on the value from the inner query.

Inner query stands alone and gets processed first.

SQL Exposed

This week's interview: Choosing the best way to query when you have more than one choice

Head First SQL: Welcome, SQL. We appreciate the personal interview. We know things have been difficult.

SQL: Difficult? That's what you call it? I'd say things have been troubling, disturbing, and really hard to quantify while at the same time being very convoluted.

Head First SQL: Uh, right. That's kind of the point here. You're getting complaints that maybe you're too flexible. You give us too many choices when we ask you questions.

SQL: I admit that I'm flexible. That you can ask me the same question in a number of ways and I'll give you the same answers.

Head First SQL: Some people would say that you're wishy-washy.

SQL: I refuse to get defensive about this. I'm not the bad guy here.

Head First SQL: No, we know you aren't, it's just that you're so…imprecise.

SQL: HA! Me imprecise! I've had about enough of this. (standing)

Head First SQL: No, don't go. We just want a few answers. Sometimes you let us ask you the same thing in so many different ways.

SQL: And what's wrong with that?

Head First SQL: Nothing really, we just want to know WHAT we should be asking you. Does it matter, if you give us the same answer?

SQL: Of course it matters! Sometimes you ask me something, and it takes me a very long time to answer you. Sometimes, BANG, I'm done. The whole point is that you ask me the right way.

Head First SQL: So it's about how long you take to respond? That's how we pick how to ask you?

SQL: Well, duh. Of course it is. It's all about what you ask me. I'm just here to try to answer your questions, when they're accurate.

Head First SQL: Speed? That's the secret?

SQL: Look, I'll clue you in. The thing about databases is that they GROW. You want your questions to be as easy to answer as possible. Because if you ask me "Whodunnit" I need you to make me think about it as little as possible. Give me easy questions, and I'll give you quick answers.

Head First SQL: I get it. But how do we know what the easy questions are?

SQL: Well, for starters, cross joins are a huge waste of time. And correlated subqueries are on the slow side too.

Head First SQL: Anything else?

SQL: Well…

Head First SQL: Please, go ahead.

SQL: Experiment. Sometimes your best bet is to create test tables and try different queries. Then you can compare how long each one took. Oh, and joins are more efficient than subqueries.

Head First SQL: Thanks, SQL. Can't believe that's the big secret…

SQL: Yeah. Thanks for wasting my time.

Build-a-Subquery Workshop

Read through each of the scenarios below. Follow the instructions to write the two queries as requested, then combine them into a subquery.

1. Greg wants to see what the average salary is for a Web Developer in his `job_current` table. Then he wants to look at what people are actually making as compared to the average salary for that job. If he finds people earning less, he can use that to target them because they may be more interested in getting a new job.

   Write a query to get the average salary of a Web Developer from the `job_current` table.

   ....

   ....

   ....

2. Greg needs to get the first name, last name, and salary of all web developers in his `job_current` table.

   Write a query to get the first name, last name, and salary of all Web Developers in the `job_current` table.

   ....

   ....

   ....

3. Greg uses the average salary (and a little math) as a subquery to show each Web Developer and how much under or over the average salary they make.

   Combine the two queries. Use the subquery as part of the `SELECT` column list.

   ....

   ....

   ....

   ....

   ....

BUILD-A-SUBQUERY WORKSHOP SOLUTION

Read through each of the scenarios below. Follow the instructions to write the two queries as requested, then combine them into a subquery.

1. Greg wants to see what the average salary is for a Web Developer in his `job_current` table. Then he wants to look at what people are actually making as compared to the average salary for that job. If he finds people earning less, he can use that to target them because they may be more interested in getting a new job.

   Write a query to get the average salary of a Web Developer from the `job_current` table.

```
SELECT AVG(salary) FROM job_current WHERE title = 'Web Developer';
```

The AVG keyword is just what we need here.

2. Greg needs to get the first name, last name, and salary of all web developers in his `job_current` table.

   Write a query to get the first name, last name, and salary of all Web Developers in the `job_current` table.

```
SELECT mc.first_name, mc.last_name, jc.salary
FROM my_contacts mc NATURAL JOIN job_current jc
WHERE jc.title = 'Web Developer';
```

3. Greg uses the average salary (and a little math) as a subquery to show each Web Developer and how much under or over the average salary they make.

   Combine the two queries. Use the subquery as part of the `SELECT` column list.

Here's our subquery.

```
SELECT mc.first_name, mc.last_name, jc.salary,
jc.salary – (SELECT AVG(salary) FROM job_current WHERE title = 'Web Developer')
FROM my_contacts mc NATURAL JOIN job_current jc
WHERE jc.title = 'Web Developer';
```

A noncorrelated subquery with multiple values: IN, NOT IN

Consider that first query Greg tried all the way back on page 387. It helps him spot the people with job titles that ***match*** his listings. It takes the complete set of `titles` returned by the `SELECT` in the subquery and evaluates that against each row of the `job_current` table to find any possible matches.

```
SELECT mc.first_name, mc.last_name, mc.phone, jc.title
FROM job_current AS jc NATURAL JOIN my_contacts AS mc
WHERE jc.title IN (SELECT title FROM job_listings);
```

IN evaluates each row of jc.title values against the entire set returned by the subquery.

Using **NOT IN** would help Greg see job titles that ***don't match*** his listings. That takes the complete set of `titles` returned by the `SELECT` in the subquery and evaluates it against each row of the `job_current` table, returning any values that *are not a match* to those in the `job_current` table. Now Greg can focus on trying to find more job listings for those types of jobs.

```
SELECT mc.first_name, mc.last_name, mc.phone, jc.title
FROM job_current jc NATURAL JOIN my_contacts mc
WHERE jc.title NOT IN (SELECT title FROM job_listings);
```

NOT IN returns any current job titles that are not found in the job listings.

These types of queries are called **noncorrelated subqueries**, where IN or NOT IN tests the results of the subquery against the outer query to see if they match or not.

A noncorrelated subquery uses IN or NOT IN to test if the values returned in the subquery are members of a set (or not).

BRAIN POWER

Why not just type in the list of values instead of using a subquery?

Write queries with joins and noncorrelated subqueries when necessary to answer the questions below. Use the `gregs_list` database schema to help you.

Several of these need the aggregate functions you learned with the Girl Sprout cookie sales problem.

List titles for jobs that earn salaries equal to the highest salary in the job_listings table.

Answers on page 406.

List the first and last name of people with a salary greater than the average salary.

Answers on page 406.

Find all web designers who have the same zip code as any job_listings for web designers.

Answers on page 407.

List everyone who lives in the same zip code as the person with the highest current salary.

Answers on page 407.

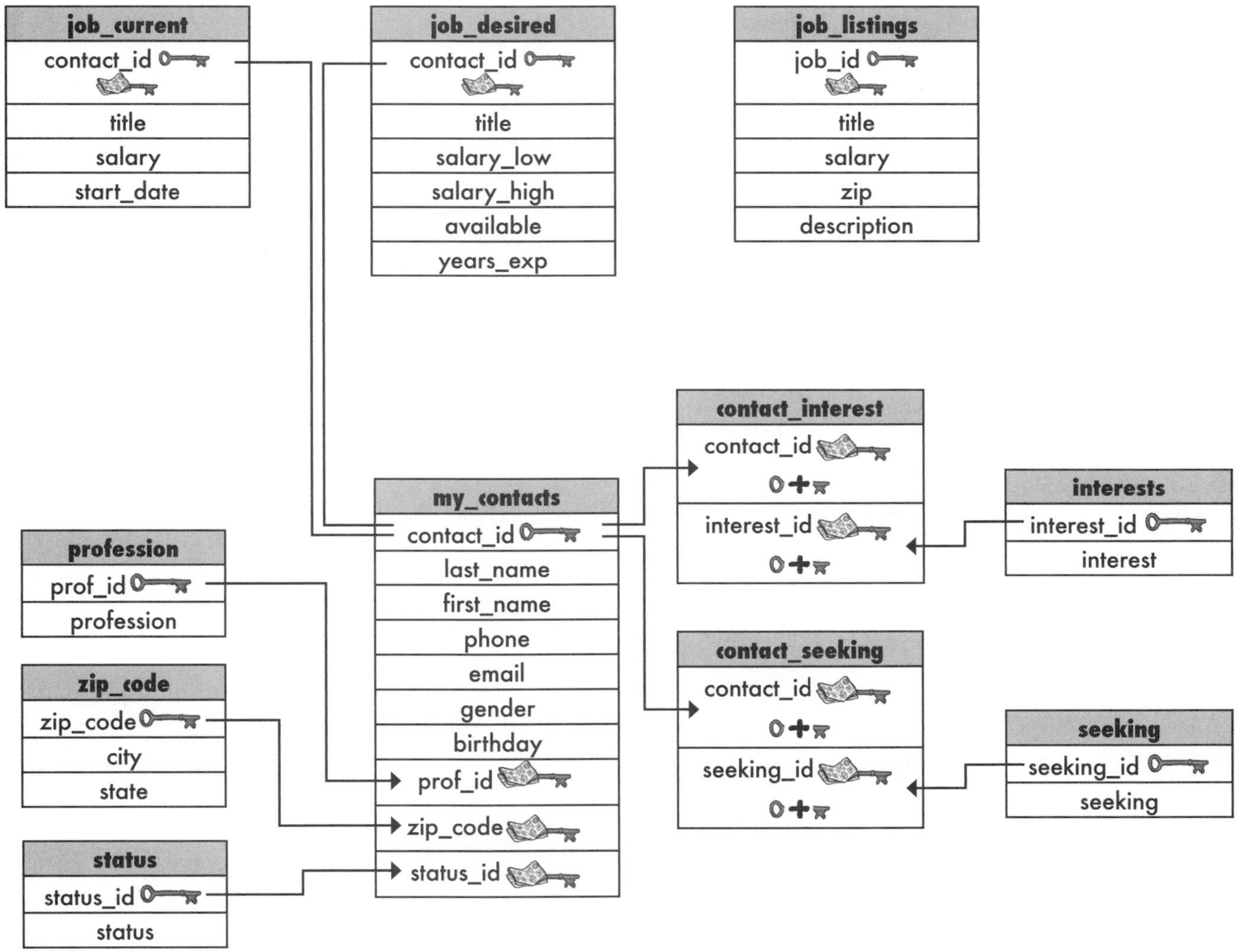
job_current
contact_id
title
salary
start_date
job_desired
contact_id
title
salary_low
salary_high
available
years_exp
job_listings
job_id
title
salary
zip
description
contact_interest
contact_id
interest_id
interests
interest_id
interest
my_contacts
contact_id
last_name
first_name
phone
email
gender
birthday
prof_id
zip_code
status_id
profession
prof_id
profession
zip_code
zip_code
city
state
status
status_id
status
contact_seeking
contact_id
seeking_id
seeking
seeking_id
seeking

Exercise Solution

Write queries with joins and noncorrelated subqueries when necessary to answer the questions below. Use the `gregs_list` database schema to help you.

List titles for jobs that earn salaries equal to the highest salary in the job_listings table.

The outer query matches against the MAX salary value.

The subquery returns a single value.

```
SELECT title FROM job_listings
WHERE salary = (SELECT MAX(salary)
FROM job_listings);
```

MAX returns the largest salary in the table.

List the first and last name of people with a salary greater than the average salary.

The outer query takes the result of the subquery and returns matches that are greater.

```
SELECT mc.first_name, mc.last_name
FROM my_contacts mc
NATURAL JOIN job_current jc
WHERE jc.salary > (SELECT AVG(salary) FROM job_current);
```

The natural join gives us the names of the people with salaries greater than the one returned by the inner query.

The subquery returns the average salary.

Find all web designers who have the same zip code as any job_listings for web designers.

We need to use a natural join to get useful info, like names and phone numbers, for the people we find.

```
SELECT mc.first_name, mc.last_name, mc.phone FROM my_contacts mc
NATURAL JOIN job_current jc WHERE jc.title = 'web designer' AND mc.zip_code
IN (SELECT zip FROM job_listings WHERE title = 'web designer');
```

Because there could be more than one zip code returned, we treat the results as a set and use "IN" to find the match.

The inner query returns all zip codes for web designer job listings.

List everyone who lives in the same zip code as the person with the highest current salary.

This is a trick question, because there could be more than one person with the highest salary. That means we'll need to use an IN. We also need to use two subqueries.

The outer query takes the zip codes and finds matches in the my_contacts table. Because the middle subquery could return more than one zip code, we use an IN.

The middle subquery finds zip codes of people who earn the maximum salary.

```
SELECT last_name, first_name FROM my_contacts
WHERE zip_code IN (SELECT mc.zip_code FROM my_contacts mc
NATURAL JOIN job_current jc
WHERE jc.salary = (SELECT MAX(salary) FROM job_current));
```

The innermost subquery gets the MAX salary from the job_current table. That will be a single value, so we can use =.

Correlated subqueries

If a noncorrelated subquery means the subquery stands alone, then I bet a correlated subquery is somehow dependent on the outer query.

Correct. In a noncorrelated subquery, the inner query, or subquery, gets interpreted by the RDBMS, followed by the outer query.

Which leaves us with a correlated subquery. A correlated subquery means that the inner query relies on the outer query before it can be resolved.

The query below counts the number of interests in the `interest` table for each person in `my_contacts`, then returns the first and last name of those people who have three interests.

```
SELECT mc.first_name, mc.last_name
FROM my_contacts AS mc
WHERE
3 = (
SELECT COUNT(*) FROM contact_interest
WHERE contact_id = mc.contact_id
);
```

The my_contacts alias is created in the outer query.

The subquery references the alias mc.

The outer query has to be executed before we know what the value of mc.contact_id is.

The subquery depends on the outer query. It needs the value for `contact_id` from the outer query before the inner query can be processed.

It uses the **same alias** or **correlation name** for `my_contacts`, `mc`, that was created in the outer query.

A (useful) correlated subquery with NOT EXISTS

A very common use for correlated subqueries is to find all the rows in the outer query for which no rows exist in a related table.

Suppose Greg needs more clients for his growing recruiting business, and wants to send out an email to everyone in my_contacts who **is not** currently in the **job_current** table. He can use a NOT EXISTS to target those people.

```
SELECT mc.first_name firstname, mc.last_name lastname, mc.email email

FROM my_contacts mc

WHERE  NOT EXISTS

(SELECT * FROM job_current jc

WHERE mc.contact_id = jc.contact_id );
```

NOT EXISTS finds the first and last names and email addresses of the people from the my_contacts table who are not currently listed in the job_current table.

WHAT'S MY PURPOSE?

Match each part of the query above to what it does.

mc.first_name firstname

WHERE NOT EXISTS

WHERE mc.contact_id = jc.contact_id

FROM my_contacts mc

mc.last_name lastname

SELECT * FROM job_current jc

mc.email email

Sets an alias for the mc.last_name field

If two contact_ids are true, a condition is met

Sets a field to "firstname" as an alias

Selects all fields for the table with alias "jc"

Sets a field to "email" as an alias

Specifies truth if something isn't found

Sets an alias for my_contacts

EXISTS and NOT EXISTS

Just like with `IN` and `NOT IN`, you can both use **EXISTS** and `NOT EXISTS` with your subqueries. The query below returns data from `my_contacts` where the `contact_ids` show up at least once in the `contact_interest` table.

```
SELECT mc.first_name firstname, mc.last_name lastname, mc.email email
FROM my_contacts mc
WHERE EXISTS
(SELECT * FROM contact_interest ci WHERE mc.contact_id = ci.contact_id );
```

EXISTS finds the first and last names and email addresses of the people from the my_contacts table whose contact_id shows up at least once in the contact_interest table.

WHAT'S MY PURPOSE?

Match each part of the query above to what it does.

`mc.first_name firstname`	Sets an alias for the mc.last_name field
`WHERE NOT EXISTS`	If two contact_ids are true, a condition is met
`WHERE mc.contact_id = jc.contact_id`	Sets a field to "firstname" as an alias
`FROM my_contacts mc`	Selects all fields for the table with alias "jc"
`mc.last_name lastname`	Sets a field to "email" as an alias
`SELECT * FROM job_current jc`	Specifies truth if something isn't found
`mc.email email`	Sets an alias for my_contacts

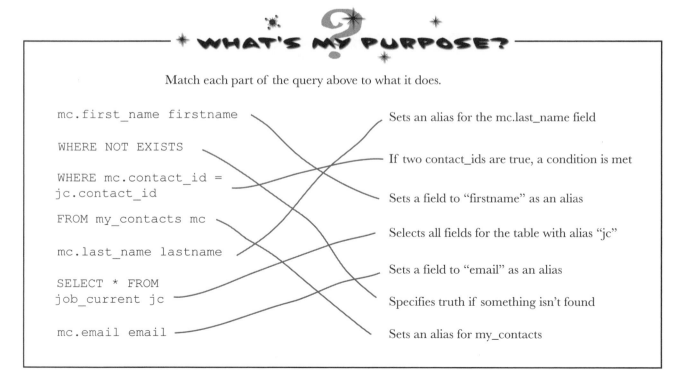

Sharpen your pencil

Write a query that returns the email of people who have at least one interest but don't exist in the job_current table.

Answers on page 416.

Greg's Recruiting Service is open for business

Greg is now comfortable getting to his data with subqueries. He even discovers he can use them in INSERT, UPDATE, and DELETE statements.

He rents a small office space for his new business, and decides to have a big kickoff party.

I wonder if I can find my own first employee in the job_desired table...

there are no Dumb Questions

Q: So can you put a subquery inside a subquery?

A: Definitely. There's a limit on how many nested subqueries you can use, but most RDBMS systems support far more than you'd ever easily be able to use.

Q: What's the best approach when trying to construct a subquery inside a subquery?

A: Your best bet is to write little queries for the various parts of the question. Then look at them and see how you need to combine them. If you're trying to find people who earn the same amount of money as the highest paid web designer, break it apart into:

Find the highest paid web designer
Find people who earn x amount of money

then put the first answer in place of the **x**.

Q: If I don't like using subqueries, is there a way I can use joins instead?

A: Most of the time, yes. You need to learn a few more joins first, though. Which leads us to...

On the way to the party

Greg spots this disturbing tabloid cover:

THE WEEKLY

INQUERYER

The SHOCKING TRUTH about Subqueries REVEALED!

JOINS IN HIDING

Neighbors say subqueries can't do "anything more" than joins, and "the truth needs to come out at last."

By Troy Armstrong
INQUERYER STAFF WRITER

DATAVILLE – What has only been speculation for many years has now been verified by Inqueryer sources. Joins and subqueries can be used to make exactly the same queries. Much to the confusion of local residents, anything you can do with a subquery, you can do with some type of join.

"It's terrible," sobbed schoolteacher Heidi Musgrove. "How can I tell the children that what they thought they knew about subqueries, all those hours spent learning how to use them, well, they could have just used joins. It's heartbreaking."

The fallout from this revelation can be expected to continue well into the next chapter, when outer joins are exposed to public scrutiny.

Local resident Heidi Musgrove was shocked to learn the truth about subqueries.

WAS IT ALL A WASTE OF TIME? ARE SUBQUERIES REALLY THE SAME AS JOINS? TURN TO THE NEXT CHAPTER TO FIND OUT.

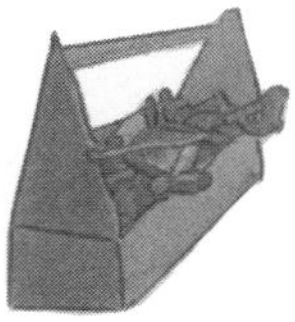

Your SQL Toolbox

You've completed Chapter 9 and mastered the art of the subquery. Take a look at all you've learned. For a complete list of tooltips in the book, see Appendix iii.

Outer query

A query which contains an inner query or subquery.

Inner query

A query inside another query. It's also known as a subquery.

Noncorrelated subquery

A subquery that stands alone and doesn't reference anything from the outer query.

Subquery

A query that is wrapped within another query. It's also known as an inner query.

Correlated Subquery

A subquery that relies on values returned from the outer query.

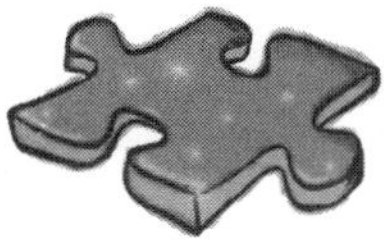

Subquerycross

You can tell your inner query from your outer query, but can you solve this crossword? All of the solution words are from this chapter.

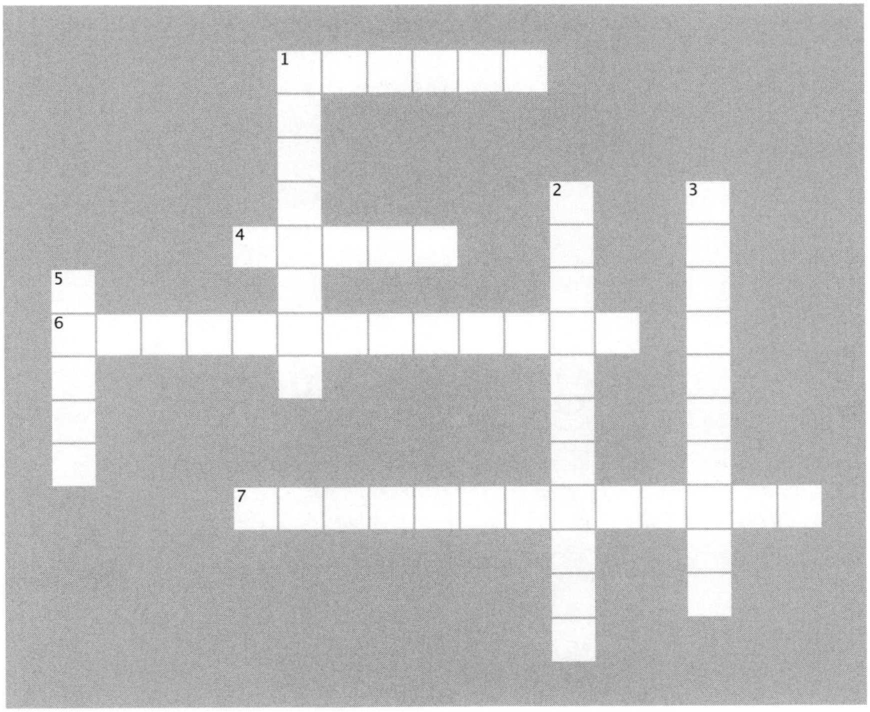

Across

1. A subquery is always a single _____ statement.
4. The _____ query contains the inner query, or subquery.
6. If the subquery stands alone and doesn't reference anything from the outer query, it is a _____ subquery.
7. In a _____ subquery, the inner query, or subquery, gets interpreted by the RDBMS, followed by the outer query.

Down

1. A query inside of another query is known as a _____.
2. Subqueries are always inside _____.
3. A _____ subquery means that the inner query relies on the outer query before it can be resolved.
5. The _____ query is called the subquery.

Sharpen your pencil
Solution

From page 411.

Write a query that returns the email of people who have at least one interest but don't exist in the job_current table.

SELECT me.email FROM my_contacts me WHERE

EXISTS

(SELECT * FROM contact_interest ci WHERE me.contact_ID = ci.contact_ID)

AND   *Just like any other two things that both need to be true, you can use an AND in your WHERE clause.*

NOT EXISTS

(SELECT * FROM job_current je

WHERE me.contact_id = je.contact_id);

Subquerycross Solution

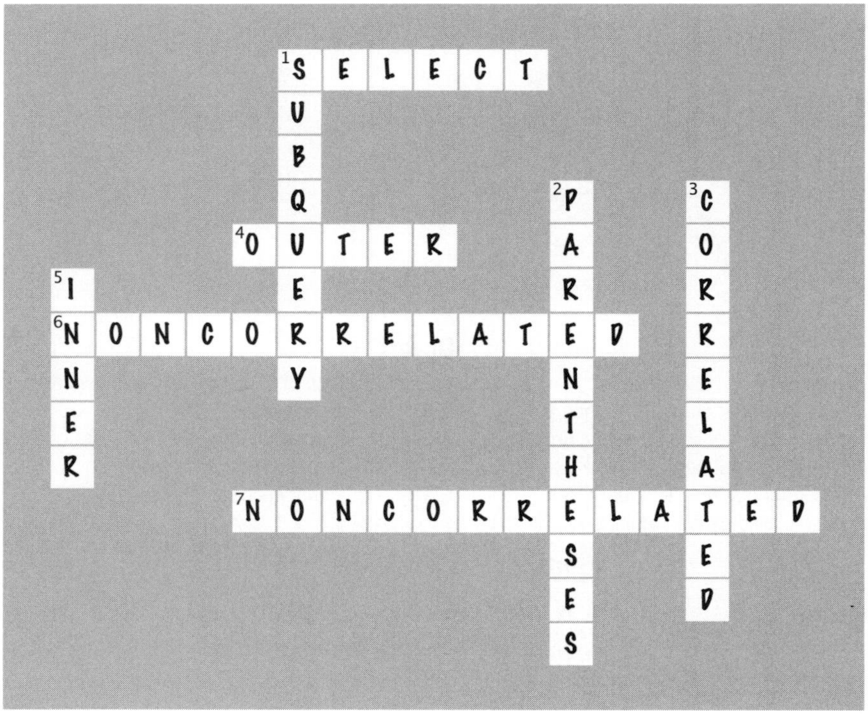

10 outer joins, self-joins, and unions

New maneuvers

And after the inner join, a left outer join for a figure eight. I'm gonna score big with the judges this time...

You only know half of the story about joins. You've seen cross joins that return every possible row, and inner joins that return rows from both tables where there is a match. But what you haven't seen are **outer joins** that give you back rows that *don't have matching counterparts in the other table*, **self-joins** which (strangely enough) *join a single table to itself*, and **unions** that *combine the results of queries*. Once you learn these tricks, you'll be able to get at all your data exactly the way you need to. (And we haven't forgotten about exposing the truth about subqueries, either!)

Cleaning up old data

I'd like to clean up my professions table. I think I might have some values in there that I'm not using anymore. How can I easily find professions that aren't connected to any of the records in the my_contacts table? I can't get an inner join to do that.

You can get that information with an outer join.

Let's take a look at what outer joins do, and then we'll show you how to find those professions you aren't using anymore.

An outer joins returns all rows from one of the tables, along with matching information from another table.

With an inner join, you're ***comparing rows from two tables***, but the **order of those two tables doesn't matter**.

Let's briefly review what the equijoin does. We get all the columns that match `toy_id` from both tables. It matches up the `toy_id` that exists in both tables:

```
SELECT g.girl, t.toy
FROM girls g
INNER JOIN toys t
ON g.toy_id = t.toy_id;
```

The equijoin compares rows from these two tables to get the result. It matches up the id values.

girls

girl_id	girl	toy_id
1	Jane	3
2	Sally	4
3	Cindy	1

toys

toy_id	toy
1	hula hoop
2	balsa glider
3	toy soldiers
4	harmonica
5	baseball cards
6	tinker toys
7	etch-a-sketch
8	slinky

Our results

girl	toy
Cindy	hula hoop
Jane	toy soldiers
Sally	harmonica

It's about left and right

By comparison, outer joins have more to do with the ***relationship between two tables*** than the joins you've seen so far.

A **LEFT** OUTER JOIN takes ***all the rows*** in the **left table** and **matches them to rows** in the **RIGHT** table. It's useful when the left table and the right table have a one-to-many relationship.

The left outer join matches EVERY ROW in the LEFT table with a row from the right table.

The big secret to understanding an outer join is to know which table is on the left and which is on the right.

In a **LEFT OUTER JOIN**, the table that comes after FROM and **BEFORE** the join is the **LEFT** table, and the table that comes **AFTER** the join is the **RIGHT table.**

The table that comes before whatever flavor of join you're using takes on the same flavor.

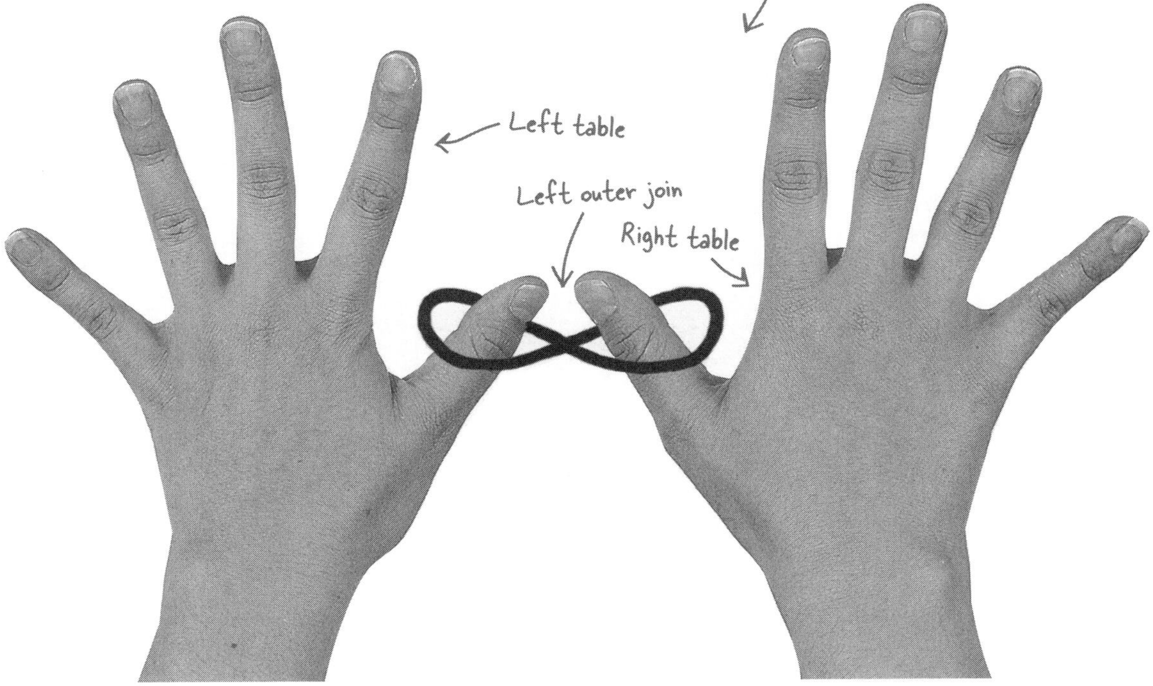

Here's a left outer join

We can use a left outer join to find out which girl has which toy.

Here's the syntax of a left outer join using the same tables as before. The `girls` table is first after `FROM`, so it's the `LEFT` table; then we have the `LEFT OUTER JOIN`; and finally, the `toys` table is the `RIGHT` table:

So, the LEFT OUTER JOIN takes all the rows in the left table (the girls table) and matches them to rows in the RIGHT table (the toys table).

```
SELECT g.girl, t.toy
FROM girls g
LEFT OUTER JOIN toys t
ON g.toy_id = t.toy_id;
```

It comes *before* the left outer join, so girls is the left table...

... and because it comes *after* the left outer join, toys is the right table.

It comes before the left outer join, so girls is the left table...

... and because it comes after the left outer join, toys is the right table.

girls

girl_id	girl	toy_id
1	Jane	3
2	Sally	4
3	Cindy	1

toys

toy_id	toy
1	hula hoop
2	balsa glider
3	toy soldiers
4	harmonica
5	baseball cards
6	tinker toys
7	etch-a-sketch
8	slinky

The results of the left outer join

Our results are the same as the inner join results.

Our results.

girl	toy
Cindy	hula hoop
Jane	toy soldiers
Sally	harmonica

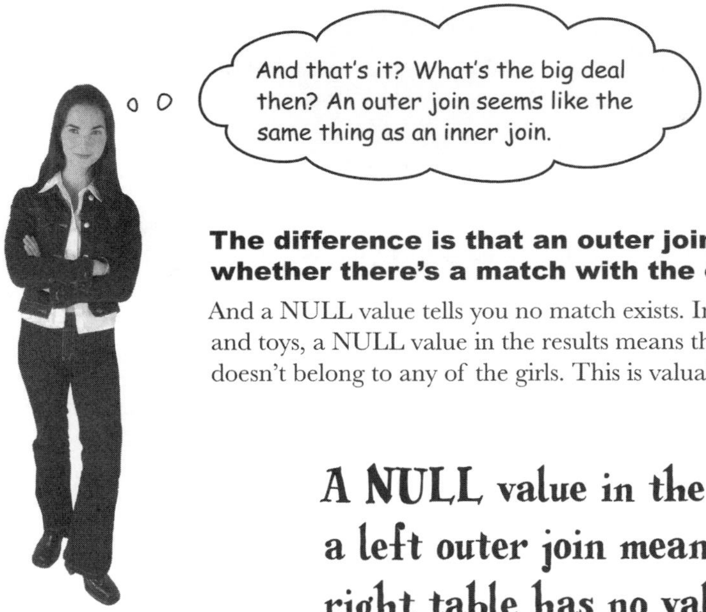
And that's it? What's the big deal then? An outer join seems like the same thing as an inner join.

The difference is that an outer join gives you a row whether there's a match with the other table or not.

And a NULL value tells you no match exists. In the case of our girls and toys, a NULL value in the results means that a particular toy doesn't belong to any of the girls. This is valuable information!

A NULL value in the results of a left outer join means that the right table has <u>no values</u> that correspond to the left table.

Sharpen your pencil

Sketch out what you think the result table of this query will be.

```
SELECT g.girl, t.toy
FROM toys t
LEFT OUTER JOIN girls g
ON g.toy_id = t.toy_id;
```

(Hint: There will be 8 rows in the results table.)

Sharpen your pencil Solution

Here's a query where we've swapped the order of our tables. Sketch what you think the results of this query will be.

```
SELECT g.girl, t.toy
FROM toys t        <- The left table.
LEFT OUTER JOIN girls g   <- The right table.
ON g.toy_id = t.toy_id;
```

This time around, every row in the toys table (the left table) is compared to the girls table (the right table).

The left table

toys

toy_id	toy
1	hula hoop
2	balsa glider
3	toy soldiers
4	harmonica
5	baseball cards
6	tinker toys
7	etch-a-sketch
8	slinky

The right table

girls

girl_id	girl	toy_id
1	Jane	3
2	Sally	4
3	Cindy	1

With the order of our tables changed, here's what we get:

girl	toy
Cindy	hula hoop
NULL	balsa glider
Jane	toy soldiers
Sally	harmonica
NULL	baseball cards
NULL	tinker toys
NULL	etch-a-sketch
NULL	slinky

If a match is found, it shows up as a result in our table. If no match is found, we still get a row in our table, but with NULL for the unmatched value.

The order the columns show up in the table is the order in which we SELECT them. This order has nothing to do with the LEFT join.

Below are two sets of results. For each result set, write a left outer join that could have created it, along with a girls table and toys table with data that matches the results.

The query

Result of a left outer join:

girl	toy
Jen	squirt gun
Cleo	crazy straw
Mandy	NULL

Left table

We did this one for you.

Right table

girls

girl_id	girl	toy_id
1	Jen	1
2	Cleo	2
3	Mandy	3

The query

Result of a left outer join:

This one's tricky.

girl	toy
Jen	squirt gun
Cleo	squirt gun
NULL	crazy straw
Sally	slinky
Martha	slinky

Left table

Right table

Below are two sets of results. For each result set, write a left outer join that could have created it, along with a girls table and toys table with data that matches the results.

The query

```
SELECT g.girl, t.toy
FROM girls g
LEFT OUTER JOIN toys t
ON g.toy_id = t.toy_id;
```

Result of a left outer join:

girl	toy
Jen	squirt gun
Cleo	crazy straw
Mandy	NULL

These are the toys that showed up in our results.

Left table

girls

girl_id	girl	toy_id
1	Jen	1
2	Cleo	2
3	Mandy	3

This can be any toy_id that doesn't actually exist in the toys table since the toy column ended up NULL in the results.

Right table

toys

toy_id	toy
1	squirt gun
2	crazy straw

The query

```
SELECT g.girl, t.toy
FROM toys t
LEFT OUTER JOIN girls g
ON g.toy_id = t.toy_id;
```

The repeated values mean that more than one girl has the same toy.

Result of a left outer join:

girl	toy
Jen	squirt gun
Cleo	squirt gun
NULL	crazy straw
Sally	slinky
Martha	slinky

And the NULL means that no girl has a crazy straw.

Left table

toys

toy_id	toy
1	squirt gun
2	crazy straw
3	slinky

Right table

girls

girl_id	girl	toy_id
1	Jen	1
2	Cleo	1
3	Sally	3
4	Martha	3

Outer joins and multiple matches

As you just noticed in the exercise, you'll get rows even when there are no matches in the other table, as well as multiple rows when there are multiple matches. Here's what the left outer join is actually doing:

```
SELECT g.girl, t.toy
FROM toys t
LEFT OUTER JOIN girls g
ON g.toy_id = t.toy_id;
```

toys

toy_id	toy
1	squirt gun
2	crazy straw
3	slinky

girls

girl_id	girl	toy_id
1	Jen	1
2	Cleo	1
3	Sally	3
4	Martha	3

The squirt gun `toys` row is compared to Jen's `girls` row: toys.toy_id = 1, girls.toy_id = 1
We have a match.
The squirt gun `toys` row is compared to Clea's `girls` row: toys.toy_id = 1, girls.toy_id = 1
We have a match.
The squirt gun `toys` row is compared to Sally's `girls` row: toys.toy_id = 1, girls.toy_id = 3
No match.
The squirt gun `toys` row is compared to Martha's `girls` row: toys.toy_id = 1, girls.toy_id = 3
No match.
The crazy straw `toys` row is compared to Jen's `girls` row: toys.toy_id = 2, girls.toy_id = 1
No match.
The crazy straw `toys` row is compared to Clea's `girls` row: toys.toy_id = 2, girls.toy_id = 1
No match.
The crazy straw `toys` row is compared to Sally's `girls` row: toys.toy_id = 2, girls.toy_id = 3
No match.
The crazy straw `toys` row is compared to Martha's `girls` row: toys.toy_id = 2, girls.toy_id = 3
No match.
End of table, row with NULL is created.
The slinky `toys` row is compared to Jen's `girls` row: toys.toy_id = 3, girls.toy_id = 1
No match.
The slinky `toys` row is compared to Clea's `girls` row: toys.toy_id = 3, girls.toy_id = 1
No match.
The slinky `toys` row is compared to Sally's `girls` row: toys.toy_id = 3, girls.toy_id = 3
We have a match.
The slinky `toys` row is compared to Martha's `girls` row: toys.toy_id = 3, girls.toy_id = 3
We have a match.

girl	toy
Jen	squirt gun
Cleo	squirt gun
NULL	crazy straw
Sally	slinky
Martha	slinky

The right outer join

The right outer join is exactly the same thing as the left outer join, except it compares the right table to the left one. The two queries below give you precisely the same results:

The <u>right outer join</u> evaluates the <u>right</u> table <u>against</u> the <u>left table</u>.

```
SELECT g.girl, t.toy
FROM toys t              ← The right table.
RIGHT OUTER JOIN girls g ←  The left table.
ON g.toy_id = t.toy_id;
```

```
SELECT g.girl, t.toy
FROM girls g         ←— The left table
LEFT OUTER JOIN toys t ←
ON g.toy_id = t.toy_id;
```

The right table

You already saw this query on page 420.

These two queries both make the girls table the left table.

The left table (in both queries)

The right table (in both queries)

girls

girl_id	girl	toy_id
1	Jane	3
2	Sally	4
3	Cindy	1

toys

toy_id	toy
1	hula hoop
2	balsa glider
3	toy soldiers
4	harmonica
5	baseball cards
6	tinker toys
7	etch-a-sketch
8	slinky

Our results →

girl	toy
Cindy	hula hoop
Jane	toy soldiers
Sally	harmonica

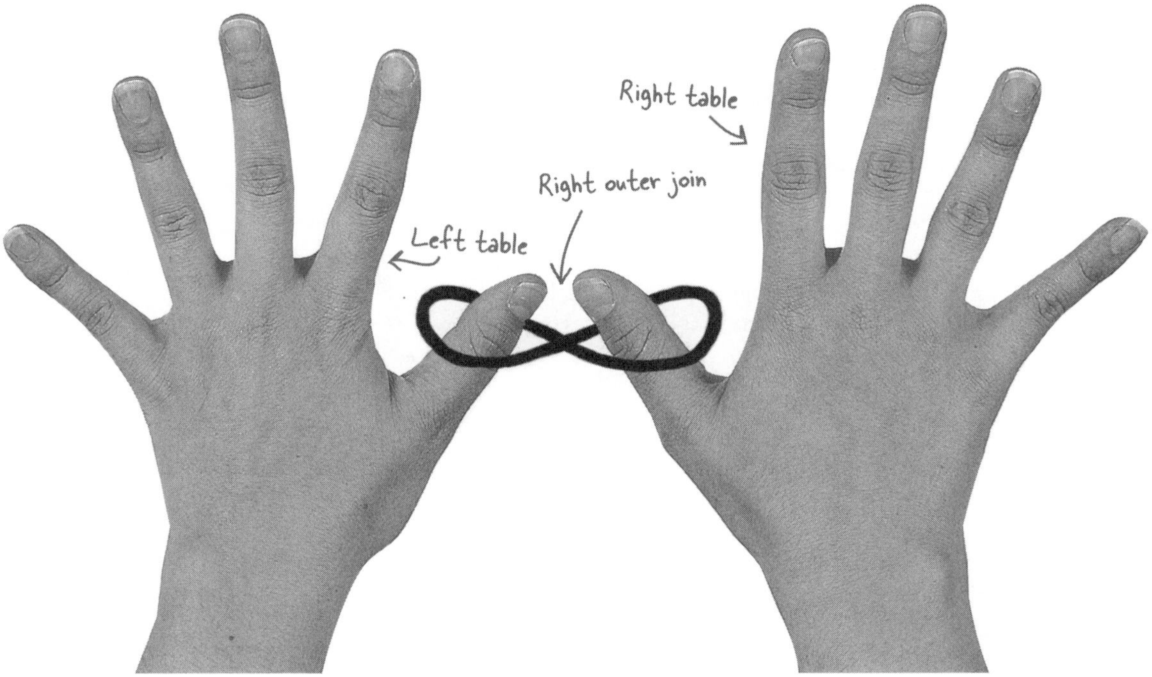

there are no Dumb Questions

Q: Is there any reason to use a left outer join instead of a right one?

A: Changing the word LEFT to RIGHT is easier than changing the order of the tables in the query. You only have to change one word, rather than swap the two table names and their aliases.

In general, though, it might actually be easier to always stick with one, say the left outer join, and change which table is left and which is right. That can be less confusing.

Q: So if there's a LEFT outer join, and a RIGHT outer join, is there a join that returns both the left and right results?

A: There is on some, but not all, RDBMS systems, and it's called the `FULL OUTER JOIN`. But it doesn't work with MySQL, SQL Server, or Access.

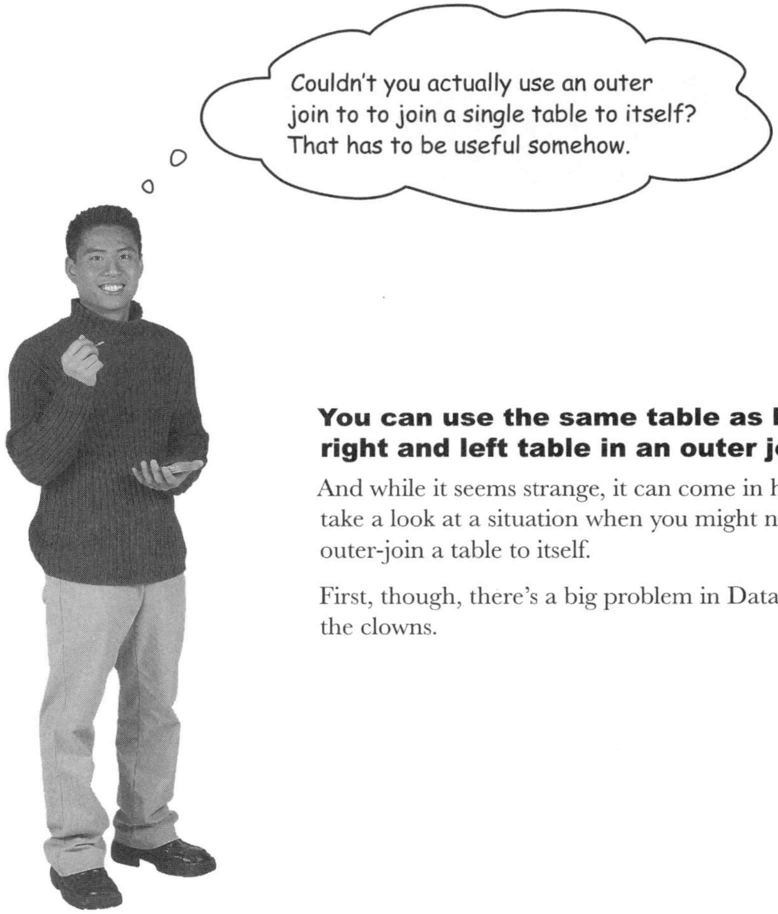
Couldn't you actually use an outer join to to join a single table to itself? That has to be useful somehow.

You can use the same table as both the right and left table in an outer join.

And while it seems strange, it can come in handy. Let's take a look at a situation when you might need to outer-join a table to itself.

First, though, there's a big problem in Dataville with the clowns.

While you were outer joining...

Back in Dataville, the clowns are organizing, and clown bosses are being put in charge. It's a frightening development, and we need to keep track of just who those bosses are, and which clowns report to which clown bosses.

Here's an example of the new clown hierarchy. Every clown has one boss, except for the head clown, Mister Sniffles.

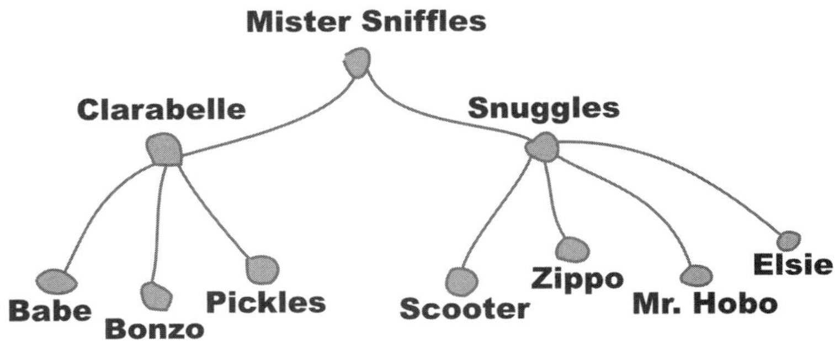

Let's take a look at our current schema and see how best to fit in this new information:

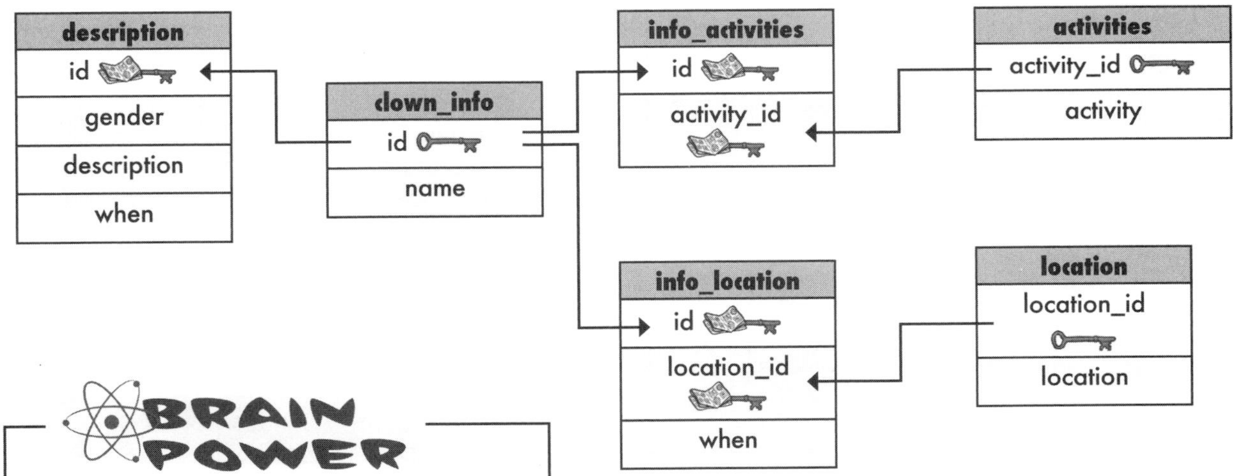

BRAIN POWER

How can you restructure your schema to store the information about boss clowns?

We could create a new table

We can create a table that lists each clown and the ID of his boss. Here's our hierarchy with the clown IDs of each clown.

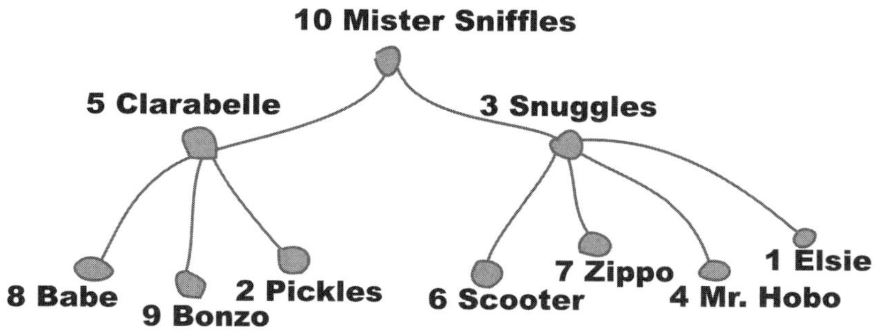

And here's a new table which lists each clown and the `id` of his boss from the `clown_info` table.

clown_boss

id	boss_id
1	3
2	5
3	10
4	3
5	10
6	3
7	3
8	5
9	5
10	10

We have a one-to-one relationship between the `clown_boss` table and the `clown_info` table.

Mister Sniffles has no boss, but he needs an id. We can give him his own id for boss_id and avoid a NULL in that column.

How the new table fits in

Let's take a look at our current schema and see how best to fit in this new table:

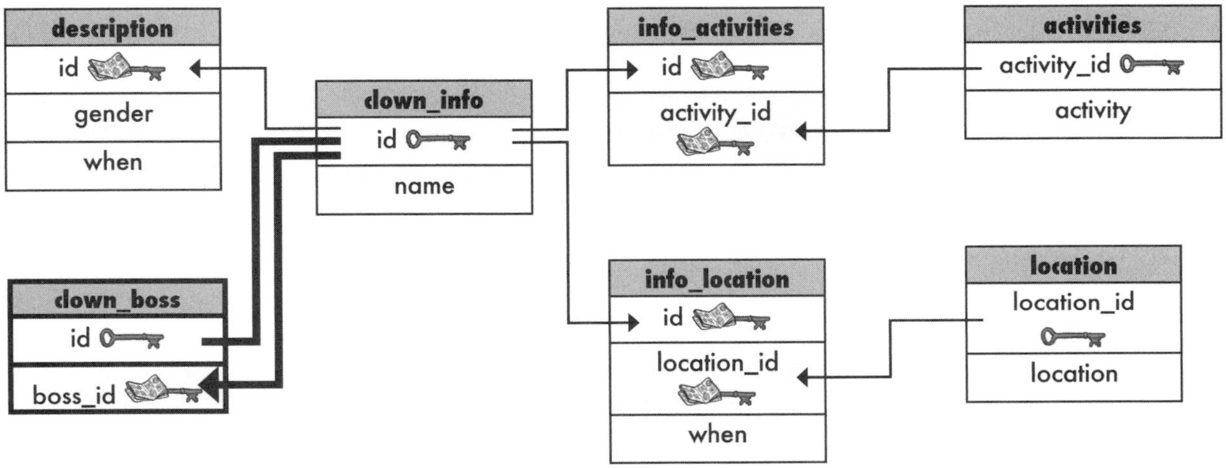

It's a little strange. We have a one-to-one relationship with `id`—our primary key—and a one-to-many relationship with `boss_id`. We have a primary key and a foreign key ***both from the clown_info table***.

It seems like you could use a one-to-one table, but since there's no private info there, can't we fit it into the main table somehow?

BRAIN POWER

Is there a way we can keep track of our clown bosses without creating a whole new table?

A self-referencing foreign key

What we need is a new column in our clown_info table that tells us who the boss of each clown is. The new column will contain the ID number of the clown's boss. We'll call it boss_id, just as we did in the clown_boss table.

In the clown_boss table, boss_id was a foreign key. When we add the column to clown_info, it's still a foreign key, even though it's in the clown_info table. This is known as a **self-referencing foreign key**. The self-referencing part means that it is a key that is referencing another field in the same table.

We assume Mister Sniffles is his own boss, so his boss_id is the same as his id. This means we can use a self-referencing foreign key as our boss_id.

A **self-referencing foreign key** is the ***primary key*** of a table ***used in that same table for another purpose***.

A SELF-REFERENCING foreign key is the primary key of a table used in that same table for another purpose.

This is the new boss_id column that we've simply added to the clown_info table. It holds a self-referencing foreign key.

clown_info

id	name	boss_id
1	Elsie	3
2	Pickles	5
3	Snuggles	10
4	Mr. Hobo	3
5	Clarabelle	10
6	Scooter	3
7	Zippo	3
8	Babe	5
9	Bonzo	5
10	Mister Sniffles	10

This references the id field in this same table to tell us which clown is the boss of Elsie.

Once again, Mister Sniffles' boss_id is his own id.

Join the same table to itself

Suppose we want to list each clown and who that clown's boss is. We can easily get a list of each clown's name and their boss's id with this SELECT:

```
SELECT name, boss_id FROM clown_info;
```

But what we really want is the clown's name and their boss's name:

name	boss
Elsie	Snuggles
Pickles	Clarabelle
Snuggles	Mister Sniffles
Mr. Hobo	Snuggles
Clarabelle	Mister Sniffles
Scooter	Snuggles
Zippo	Snuggles
Babe	Clarabelle
Bonzo	Clarabelle
Mister Sniffles	Mister Sniffles

Sharpen your pencil

Suppose you had identical tables, clown_info1 and clown_info2. Write a single join to get a table of results containing the name of each clown and the name of that clown's boss.

clown_info1

id	name	boss_id
1	Elsie	3
2	Pickles	5
3	Snuggles	10
4	Mr. Hobo	3
5	Clarabelle	10
6	Scooter	3
7	Zippo	3
8	Babe	5
9	Bonzo	5
10	Mister Sniffles	10

clown_info2

id	name	boss_id
1	Elsie	3
2	Pickles	5
3	Snuggles	10
4	Mr. Hobo	3
5	Clarabelle	10
6	Scooter	3
7	Zippo	3
8	Babe	5
9	Bonzo	5
10	Mister Sniffles	10

Sharpen your pencil Solution

Suppose you had identical tables, clown_info1 and clown_info2. Write a single join to get a table of results containing the name of each clown and the name of that clown's boss.

clown_info1

id	name	boss_id
1	Elsie	3
2	Pickles	5
3	Snuggles	10
4	Mr. Hobo	3
5	Clarabelle	10
6	Scooter	3
7	Zippo	3
8	Babe	5
9	Bonzo	5
10	Mister Sniffles	10

clown_info2

id	name	boss_id
1	Elsie	3
2	Pickles	5
3	Snuggles	10
4	Mr. Hobo	3
5	Clarabelle	10
6	Scooter	3
7	Zippo	3
8	Babe	5
9	Bonzo	5
10	Mister Sniffles	10

```
SELECT c1.name, c2.name AS boss
FROM clown_info1 c1
INNER JOIN clown_info2 c2
ON c1.boss_id = c2.id;
```

So that we don't get confused by two columns named 'name', we'll alias the second one as 'boss'.

Here's where we match up the boss_id from clown_info1 with the clown_info2 id.

We need a self-join

In the "Sharpen your pencil" you just did, you were given the same table twice. But in a normalized database, you would never have two copies of the same table. Instead, we can **use a self-join to *simulate* having two tables**.

Consider this query, which is almost identical to the solution of the "Sharpen," but has one obvious difference.

clown_info

id	name	boss_id
1	Elsie	3
2	Pickles	5
3	Snuggles	10
4	Mr. Hobo	3
5	Clarabelle	10
6	Scooter	3
7	Zippo	3
8	Babe	5
9	Bonzo	5
10	Mister Sniffles	10

```
SELECT c1.name, c2.name AS boss
FROM clown_info c1
INNER JOIN clown_info c2
ON c1.boss_id = c2.id;
```

We're using the clown_info table twice. It's aliased as c1 (where we'll get the boss_id) and c2 (where we'll get the name of the boss).

Instead of having two identical tables, we're using `clown_info` twice, first aliased at `c1`, then aliased as `c2`. Then we're doing an inner join to connect the `boss_id` (from `c1`) with the `name` of the boss (from `c2`).

This column comes from the INNER JOIN of boss_id in the first instance of the clown_info table (c1) and the name of that boss from the second instance of the clown_info table (c2).

name	boss
Elsie	Snuggles
Pickles	Clarabelle
Snuggles	Mister Sniffles
Mr. Hobo	Snuggles
Clarabelle	Mister Sniffles
Scooter	Snuggles
Zippo	Snuggles
Babe	Clarabelle
Bonzo	Clarabelle
Mister Sniffles	Mister Sniffles

The self-join allows you to query a single table as though there were two tables with exactly the same information in them.

Another way to get multi-table information

I'm trying to get a big list of all the job titles I use in gregs_list, but I can't figure out how to list all of the job titles in those three tables all at once.

These are the three tables Greg's talking about.

Job the person has right now ↘

Job the person wants ↓

Available jobs ↙

job_current
contact_id 🔑
title
salary
start_date

job_desired
contact_id 🔑
title
salary_low
salary_high
available
years_exp

job_listings
job_id 🔑
title
salary
zip
description

So far, he's created three separate SELECT statements:

```
SELECT title FROM job_current;
SELECT title FROM job_desired;
SELECT title FROM job_listings;
```

And they work, but he wants to combine the results in one single query and get a list of every title listed in those three tables.

You can use a UNION

There's another way of getting combined results from two or more tables, called a UNION.

A UNION combines the results of two or more queries into one table, based on what you specify in the column list of the SELECT. Think of the results of the UNION like they're the values from each SELECT that "overlap."

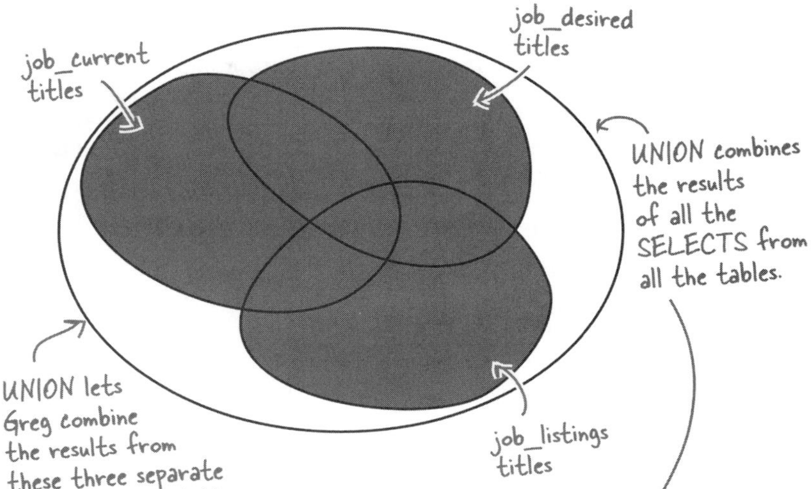
job_current titles
job_desired titles
UNION combines the results of all the SELECTS from all the tables.
job_listings titles

```
SELECT title FROM job_current
UNION
SELECT title FROM job_desired
UNION
SELECT title FROM job_listings;
```

UNION lets Greg combine the results from these three separate queries into one table of results.

These are a few of the hundreds of listings he gets in the combined results from all three tables.

title
Accountant
Lawyer
Programmer
Web Designer
Cat Herder
Chef
Psychologist
Barber
Teacher
Write

Greg notices that there aren't any duplicates in the results, but the titles aren't in order, so he tries the query again with an added ORDER BY in each SELECT statement.

```
SELECT title FROM job_current ORDER BY title
UNION
SELECT title FROM job_desired ORDER BY title
UNION
SELECT title FROM job_listings ORDER BY title;
```

Greg's added an ORDER BY to each statement so that the titles in the results table are listed alphabetically.

BRAIN POWER

What do you think happened when Greg ran this new query?

UNION is limited

Greg's query didn't work! Greg got an error, because his software didn't know how to interpret the ORDER BY multiple times.

UNION can only take **one ORDER BY at the *end* of the statement**. This is because UNION **concatenates and groups the results from the multiple SELECT statements.**

There are a few more things about unions you should know.

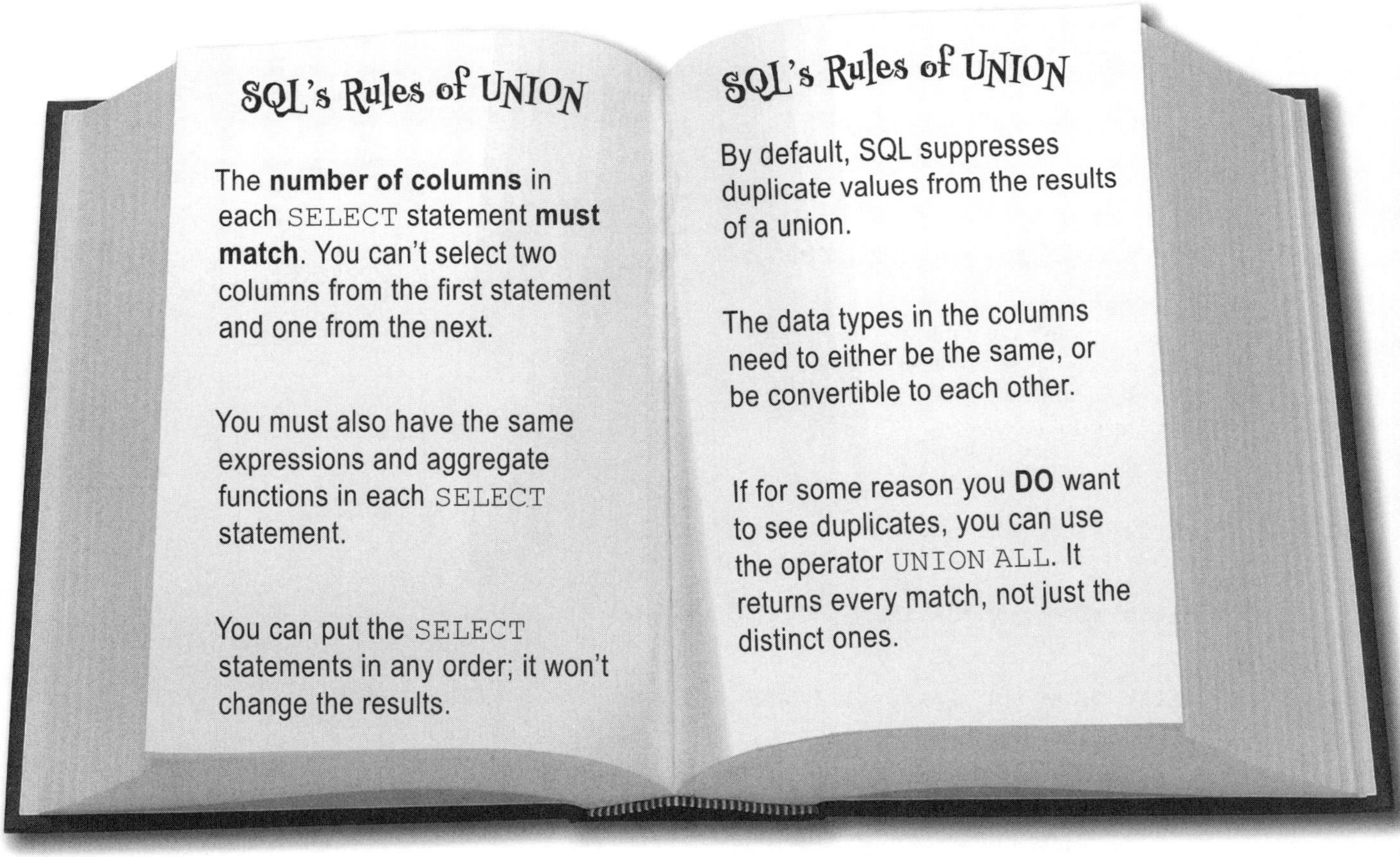
SQL's Rules of UNION
The **number of columns** in each SELECT statement **must match**. You can't select two columns from the first statement and one from the next.
You must also have the same expressions and aggregate functions in each SELECT statement.
You can put the SELECT statements in any order; it won't change the results.
SQL's Rules of UNION
By default, SQL suppresses duplicate values from the results of a union.
The data types in the columns need to either be the same, or be convertible to each other.
If for some reason you **DO** want to see duplicates, you can use the operator UNION ALL. It returns every match, not just the distinct ones.

UNION rules in action

The number of columns in the SELECT statements you're combining with UNION must match. You can't SELECT two columns from the first table and only one column from the next table.

You must use the same number of columns in each SELECT.

```
SELECT title FROM job_current
UNION
SELECT title FROM job_desired
UNION
SELECT title FROM job_listings
ORDER BY title;
```

If you want to order your results, use an ORDER BY after the last SELECT that you're combining. This orders the entire list of results.

title
Baker
Cat Herder
Cat Wrangler
Clown
Dog Trainer
Hairdresser
Jeweler
Lawyer
Mechanic
Neurosurgeon

Here's an example of the results we can expect to get back.

In this example, all three of the columns have the same data type, VARCHAR. As a result, the column returned by the query is also VARCHAR.

BRAIN POWER

What do you think would happen if the columns we unioned had different data types?

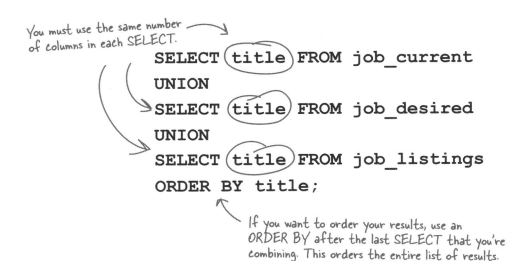

UNION ALL

UNION ALL works exactly the same way as UNION, except it returns all the values from the columns, rather than one instance of each value that is duplicated.

```
SELECT title FROM job_current
UNION ALL
SELECT title FROM job_desired
UNION ALL
SELECT title FROM job_listings
ORDER BY title;
```

This time we want to see all the values stored in the title columns from all three tables.

title
Baker
Baker
Cat Herder
Cat Wrangler
Clown
Clown
Clown
Dog Trainer
Dog Trainer
Hairdresser
Jeweler
Lawyer
Lawyer
Lawyer
Lawyer
Mechanic
Neurosurgeon

This time we get the same job listed more than once.

So far our UNIONs have used columns of the same data type. But you may want to create a UNION of columns with different data types.

When we say that the data types must be convertible to each other, we mean that the data types returned will be converted into compatible types if possible, and if they can't be, the query will fail.

Suppose you used a UNION on an INTEGER data type, and a VARCHAR type. Since the VARCHAR can't become an integer, the resulting rows would convert the INTEGER into a VARCHAR.

Create a table from your union

We can't easily see what the data type returned by our UNION is, unless we capture it somehow. We can use a CREATE TABLE AS to grab our UNION results and look at them more closely.

The CREATE TABLE AS statement takes the results of a SELECT query and makes a table out of them. In the example below, we are putting our title UNION into a new table named my_union.

The name of our new table

```
CREATE TABLE my_union AS
SELECT title FROM job_current UNION
SELECT title FROM job_desired
UNION SELECT title FROM job_listings;
```

This is the UNION you've already seen. You can create a table from any SELECT statement.

Sharpen your pencil

Create a UNION of the following: contact_id from job_current and salary from job_listings

....

....

Make a guess as to what the data type of the results will be, then write a CREATE TABLE AS statement with your UNION.

....

....

....

Do a DESC of your table and see if you were correct about the data type.

....

Answers on page 453.

INTERSECT and EXCEPT

Watch it! **These two operations DO NOT EXIST in MySQL.**

INTERSECT and EXCEPT are used in much the same way as UNION—to find parts of queries that overlap.

INTERSECT returns only those columns that are in the first query and also in the second query.

```
SELECT title FROM job_current
INTERSECT
SELECT title FROM job_desired;
```

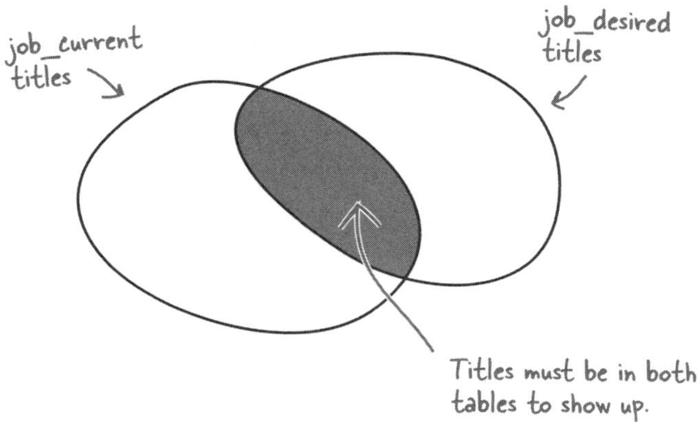
job_current titles
job_desired titles
Titles must be in both tables to show up.

EXCEPT returns only those columns that are in the first query, but **not** in the second query.

```
SELECT title FROM job_current
EXCEPT
SELECT title FROM job_desired;
```

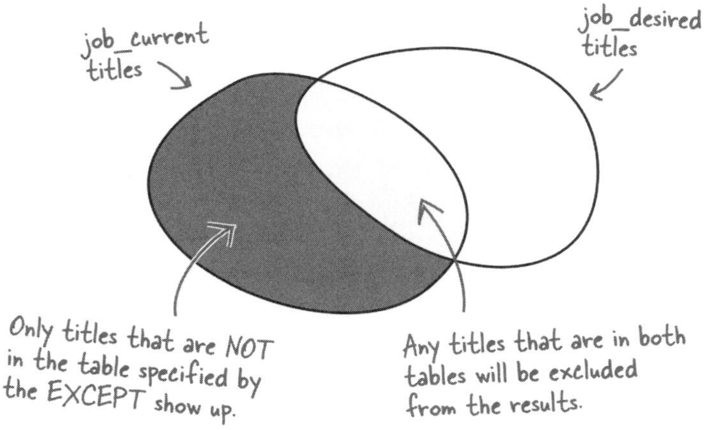
job_current titles
job_desired titles
Only titles that are NOT in the table specified by the EXCEPT show up.
Any titles that are in both tables will be excluded from the results.

We're done with joins, time to move on to

Wait a minute. You can't leave me in suspense. You said that joins and subqueries did the same thing. You need to prove it.

(Errr, yeah, what we meant to say was…)

Subqueries and joins compared

Practically anything you can do with subquery, you can do with a join. Let's step back a few pages to the beginning of Chapter 9.

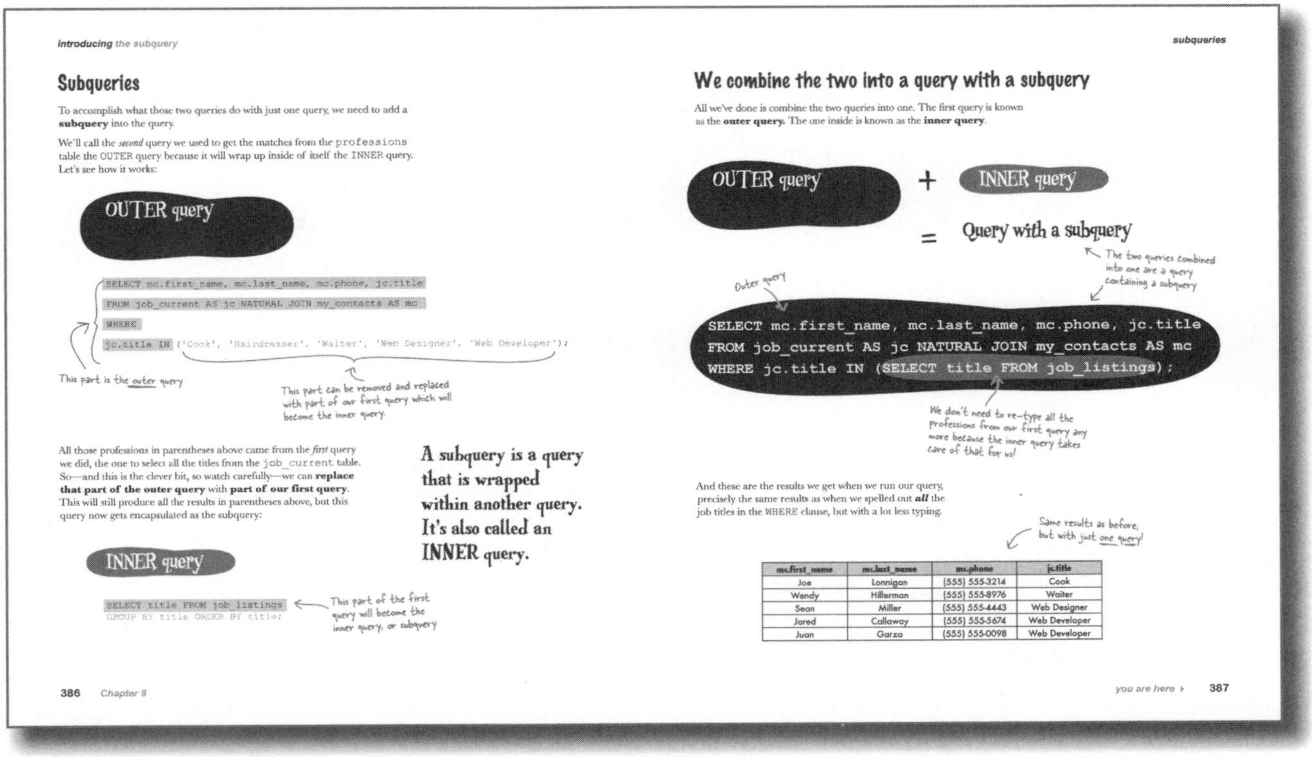

Subqueries

To accomplish what those two queries do with just one query, we need to add a **subquery** into the query.

We'll call the *second* query we used to get the matches from the `professions` table the `OUTER` query because it will wrap up inside of itself the `INNER` query. Let's see how it works:


```
SELECT mc.first_name, mc.last_name, mc.phone, jc.title
FROM job_current AS jc NATURAL JOIN my_contacts AS mc
WHERE
jc.title IN ('Cook', 'Hairdresser', 'Waiter', 'Web Designer', 'Web Developer');
```

This part is the outer query

This part can be removed and replaced with part of our first query which will become the inner query.

All those professions in parentheses above came from the *first* query we did, the one to select all the titles from the `job_current` table. So—and this is the clever bit, so watch carefully—we can **replace that part of the outer query** with **part of our first query**. This will still produce all the results in parentheses above, but this query now gets encapsulated as the subquery:

A subquery is a query that is wrapped within another query. It's also called an INNER query.


```
SELECT title FROM job_listings
GROUP BY title ORDER BY title;
```

This part of the first query will become the inner query, or subquery

We combine the two into a query with a subquery

All we've done is combine the two queries into one. The first query is known as the **outer query.** The one inside is known as the **inner query**.


```
SELECT mc.first_name, mc.last_name, mc.phone, jc.title
FROM job_current AS jc NATURAL JOIN my_contacts AS mc
WHERE jc.title IN (SELECT title FROM job_listings);
```

We don't need to re-type all the professions from our first query any more because the inner query takes care of that for us!

And these are the results we get when we run our query, precisely the same results as when we spelled out ***all*** the job titles in the `WHERE` clause, but with a lot less typing.

Same results as before, but with just one query!

mc.first_name	mc.last_name	mc.phone	jc.title
Joe	Lonnigan	(555) 555-3214	Cook
Wendy	Hillerman	(555) 555-8976	Waiter
Sean	Miller	(555) 555-4443	Web Designer
Jared	Callaway	(555) 555-5674	Web Developer
Juan	Garza	(555) 555-0098	Web Developer

Turning a subquery into a join

Back in Chapter 9, this was the first subquery we created:

Outer query

```
SELECT mc.first_name, mc.last_name, mc.phone, jc.title
FROM job_current AS jc NATURAL JOIN my_contacts AS mc
WHERE jc.title IN (SELECT title FROM job_listings);
```

Inner query

And these are the results we got when we ran our query:

mc.first_name	mc.last_name	mc.phone	jc.title
Joe	Lonnigan	(555) 555-3214	Cook
Wendy	Hillerman	(555) 555-8976	Waiter
Sean	Miller	(555) 555-4443	Web Designer
Jared	Callaway	(555) 555-5674	Web Developer
Juan	Garza	(555) 555-0098	Web Developer

Sharpen your pencil

Here's the WHERE clause with the subquery rewritten as an INNER JOIN:

```
SELECT mc.first_name, mc.last_name, mc.phone, jc.title
FROM job_current AS jc NATURAL JOIN my_contacts AS mc
INNER JOIN job_listings jl
ON jc.title = jl.title;
```

You can replace the WHERE containing the subquery with an INNER JOIN.

Explain why this INNER JOIN part of the query will get you the same results as the subquery.

....

....

....

Which one of these queries do you find easier to understand?

....

Answers on page 453.

If I've already got everything written using subqueries, should I go back and rewrite them as joins?

No, if you've got those subqueries doing what you need to do, you don't need to rewrite them.

But there are definitely reasons to choose one over the other at times...

Fireside Chats

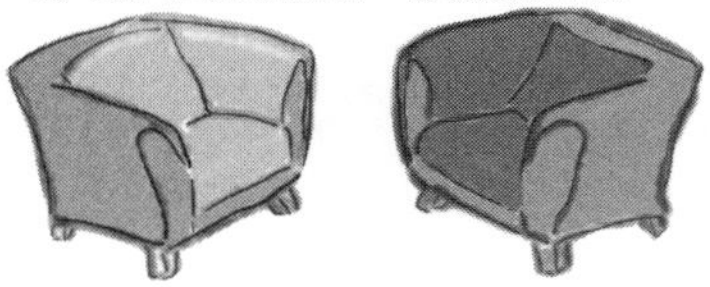

Tonight's talk: **Join versus Subquery, which is better**

Join: I'm clearly the best choice for most instances. I'm easier to understand, and I generally execute much more quickly than ol' Subquery over there.

Subquery: Excuse me? Who are you calling "old"? I wasn't even around until later in some RDBMSs. I was ADDED because so many programmers wanted to use me.

Join: I was doing just fine without you. I'm easier to understand than you are.

Subquery: Who are you trying to kid, with your INNER and OUTER claptrap? That stuff is confusing…

Join: Says you. What about that CORRELATED and NONCORRELATED malarkey?

Subquery: Okay, we've both got our own jargon; that's true. But with me, you can usually just figure out the inner part and then the outer part separately.

Continues on the next page.

Fireside Chats

Tonight's talk: **Join versus Subquery, which is better**

Join

Not always, Mr. CORRELATED Subquery. But okay, let's leave that for now. I'm the best choice when you need columns from multiple tables in your results. In fact, I'm the only choice when you need that.

That might be true, but it's not that hard to figure out what I'm doing. Why, you can even use aliases to avoid typing the table names again and again.

La dee da. Too good for aliases, are we? And you think you're so much simpler than me, but what about those correlated subqueries? Those are as convoluted as anything I can do.

Show off.

Subquery

Which is why you aren't so good with aggregate values. You can't use aggregates in a WHERE clause without a subquery. That makes up a bit for not returning multiple columns. You're so complicated.

Yeah, about those aliases, I think they make things even harder to follow. And for the record, I can use them too, you know. But when I use them, it's much more straightforward. Half the time I don't even bother with aliases.

Errr... true. But I know one thing that makes me much different than you. I can be used with UPDATE, INSERT, and DELETE.

Exercise

Take these queries with subqueries from Chapter 9 and see if you can write them without subqueries, or if you're just better off leaving subqueries in your query. Joins are allowed.

List titles for jobs that earn salaries equal to the highest salary in the job_listings table.

```
SELECT title FROM job_listings WHERE salary = (SELECT
MAX(salary) FROM job_listings);
```

Better off just using subqueries?

List the first and last name of people with a salary greater than the average salary.

```
SELECT mc.first_name, mc.last_name FROM my_contacts mc
NATURAL JOIN job_current jc WHERE jc.salary > (SELECT
AVG(salary) FROM job_current);
```

Better off just using subqueries?

Exercise Solution

Take these queries with subqueries from Chapter 9 and see if you can write them without subqueries, or if you're just better off leaving subqueries in your query. Joins are allowed.

List titles for jobs that earn salaries equal to the highest salary in the job_listings table.

```
SELECT title FROM job_listings WHERE salary = (SELECT
MAX(salary) FROM job_listings);
```

```
SELECT title FROM job_listings ORDER
BY salary DESC LIMIT 1;
```

This causes the query to only return a single result, the row with the largest salary.

Better off just using subqueries? No.

List the first and last name of people with a salary greater than the average salary.

```
SELECT mc.first_name, mc.last_name FROM my_contacts mc
NATURAL JOIN job_current jc WHERE jc.salary > (SELECT
AVG(salary) FROM job_current);
```

Uh oh, we can't use LIMIT and ORDER BY to get things that are average like we did up there.

Better off just using subqueries? Yes.

In the previous solution, we were able to use LIMIT to get the biggest salary out of an ordered salary list. Our greater-than-average salaries can't be ordered, so we can't use LIMIT to get them.

A self-join as a subquery

While you've seen how you can turn a subquery into a join, let's look at turning a self-join into a subquery.

Remember the clown `boss_id` we added to our `clown_info` table? Here's the self-join we used where we called one instance of the `clown_info` table `c1` and the second one `c2`.

Indicates which clown is the boss of which clown

clown_info

id	name	boss_id
1	Elsie	3
2	Pickles	5
3	Snuggles	10
4	Mr. Hobo	3
5	Clarabelle	10
6	Scooter	3
7	Zippo	3
8	Babe	5
9	Bonzo	5
10	Mister Sniffles	10

BEFORE

```
SELECT c1.name, c2.name AS boss
FROM clown_info c1
INNER JOIN clown_info c2
ON c1.boss_id = c2.id;
```

The first instance of clown_info (c1)

The second instance of clown_info (c2)

AFTER

When we turn the self-join into a subquery, the subquery is `CORRELATED` since it depends on the result of the outer query to get the correct `boss_id`, and it shows up in the `SELECT` column list.

Outer query.

The subquery is in the SELECT list.

```
SELECT c1.name,
(SELECT name FROM clown_info
WHERE c1.boss_id = id) AS boss
FROM clown_info c1;
```

The subquery depends on the result from the outer query to get the correct boss_id, so it's correlated.

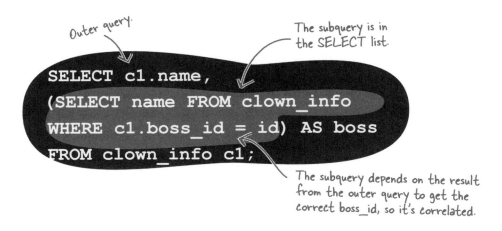

Greg's company is growing

Greg's been busy learning about joins and subqueries. He's hired some friends to help him with less complicated queries.

Too bad they don't know what they're doing. Greg's about to find out what happens when multiple people with shaky SQL skills work on the same database at the same time.

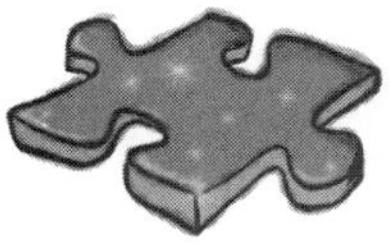

Joins&Unionscross

This has been a turbo-charged chapter, with lots to learn. Help it all sink in by doing this crossword. All answers come from the chapter.

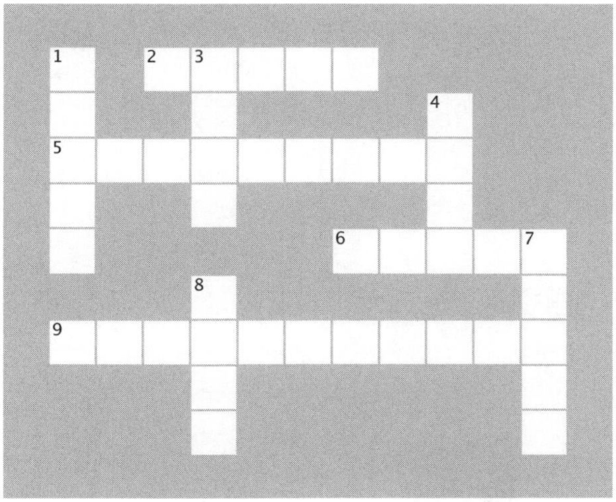

Across

2. This combines the results of two or more queries into one table, based on what you specify in the column list of the SELECT.
5. By default, SQL supresses _____ values from the results of a union.
6. An _____ join gives you a row whether there's a match with the other table or not.
9. A self-_____ foreign key is the primary key of a table used in that same table for another purpose.

Down

1. With an inner join, you're comparing rows from two tables, but the _____ of those two tables doesn't matter.
3. This in the results of a left outer join means that the right table has no values that correspond to the left table.
4. A _____ OUTER JOIN takes all the rows in the left table and matches them to rows in the RIGHT table.
7. The _____ outer join evaluates the right table against the left table.
8. We can use a _____-join to simulate having two tables.

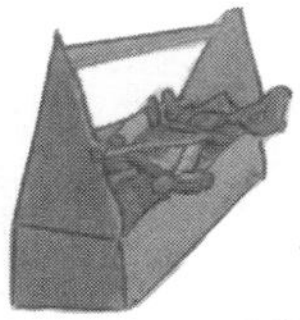

Your SQL Toolbox

You're really cruising now. You've covered outer joins, self-joins and unions, and you even know how to convert a join to a subquery and vice versa. For a complete list of tooltips in the book, see Appendix iii.

SELF-REFERENCING FOREIGN KEY

This is a foreign key in the same table it is a primary key of, used for another purpose.

LEFT OUTER JOIN

A LEFT OUTER JOIN takes all the rows in the left table and matches them to rows in the RIGHT table.

RIGHT OUTER JOIN

A RIGHT OUTER JOIN takes all the rows in the right table and matches them to rows in the LEFT table

SELF-JOIN

The SELF-JOIN allows you to query a single table as though there were two tables with exactly the same information in them.

UNION and UNION ALL

A UNION combines the results of two or more queries into one table, based on what you specify in the column list of the SELECT.

UNION hides the duplicate values, UNION ALL includes duplicate values.

CREATE TABLE AS

Use this command to create a table from the results of any SELECT statement.

INTERSECT

Use this keyword to return only values that are in the first query AND also in the second query

EXCEPT

Use this keyworld to return only values that are in the first query BUT NOT in the second query.

Sharpen your pencil Solution

From page 441.

Create a UNION of the following: contact_id from job_current and salary from job_listings

```
SELECT contact_id FROM job_current
UNION SELECT salary FROM job_listings;
```

Make a guess as to what the data type of the results will be, then write a CREATE TABLE AS statement with your UNION.

```
CREATE TABLE my_table SELECT
contact_id FROM job_current UNION
SELECT salary FROM job_listings;
```

Do a DESC of your table and see if you were correct about the data type.

DEC(12,2)

Sharpen your pencil Solution

From page 444.

Here's the WHERE clause with the subquery rewritten as an INNER JOIN:

```
SELECT mc.first_name, mc.last_name, mc.phone, jc.title
FROM job_current AS jc NATURAL JOIN my_contacts AS mc
INNER JOIN job_listings jl
ON jc.title = jl.title;
```

You can replace the WHERE containing the subquery with an INNER JOIN.

Explain why this INNER JOIN part of the query will get you the same results as the subquery.

The INNER JOIN only shows results when jc.title = jl.title, which is equivalent to the WHERE clause with the subquery:
WHERE jc.title IN (SELECT title FROM job_listings);

Which one of these queries do you find easier to understand?

There's no right answer here! But your answer shows that you're starting to think about what you might use in the future with your own data.

Joins&Unionscross Solution

1 O		2 U	3 N	I	O	N				
R			U					4 L		
5 D	U	P	L	I	C	A	T	E		
E			L					F		
R						6 O	U	T	E	7 R
			8 S							I
9 R	E	F	E	R	E	N	C	I	N	G
			L							H
			F							T

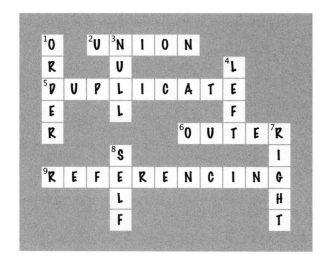

11 constraints, views, and transactions

Too many cooks spoil the database

See, this is where you went wrong. For "quantity" you entered "a whole bunch."

Your database has grown, and other people need to use it.

The problem is that some of them won't be as skilled at SQL as you are. You need ways to **keep them from entering the wrong data**, techniques for allowing them to **only see part of the data**, and ways to **stop them from stepping on each other when they try entering data at the same time**. In this chapter we begin protecting our data from the mistakes of others. Welcome to Defensive Databases, Part 1.

Greg's hired some help

Greg has hired two people to help him manage his growing business. Jim's going to handle entering new clients into the database, while Frank's in charge of matching people up to prospective jobs.

Greg has spent some time explaining his database to them and describing what each table does.

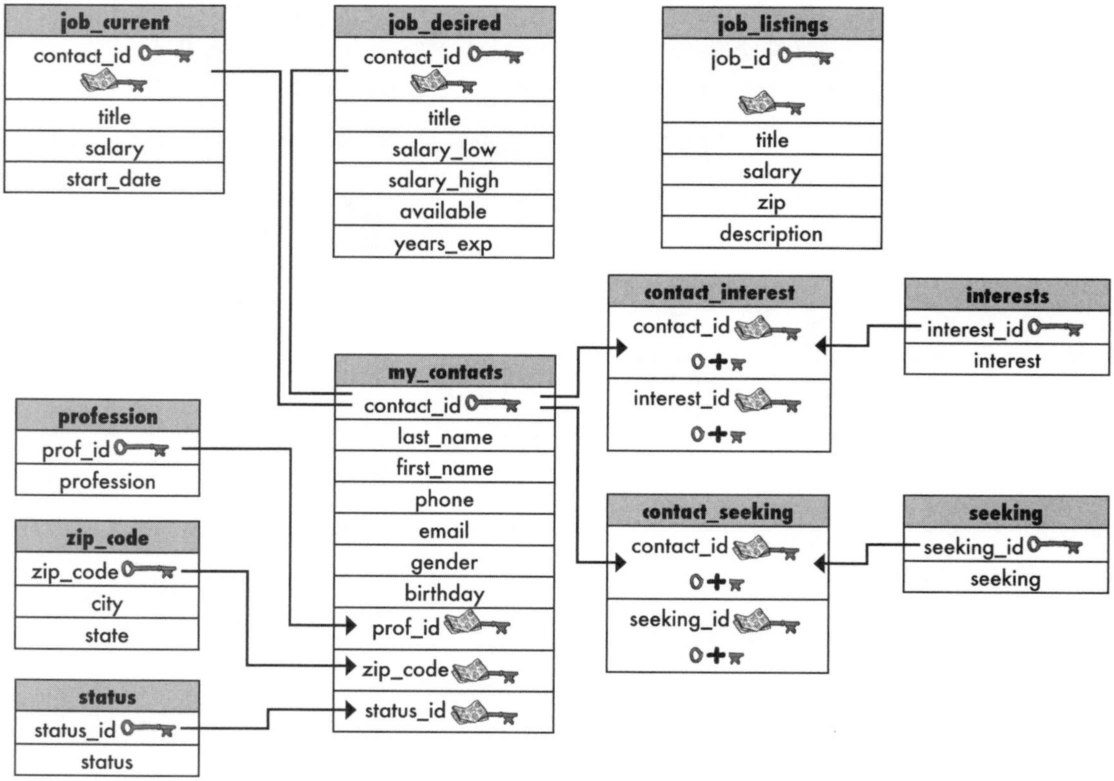

Jim's first day: Inserting a new client

Jim's sitting in his new cubicle and gets an IM from Greg:

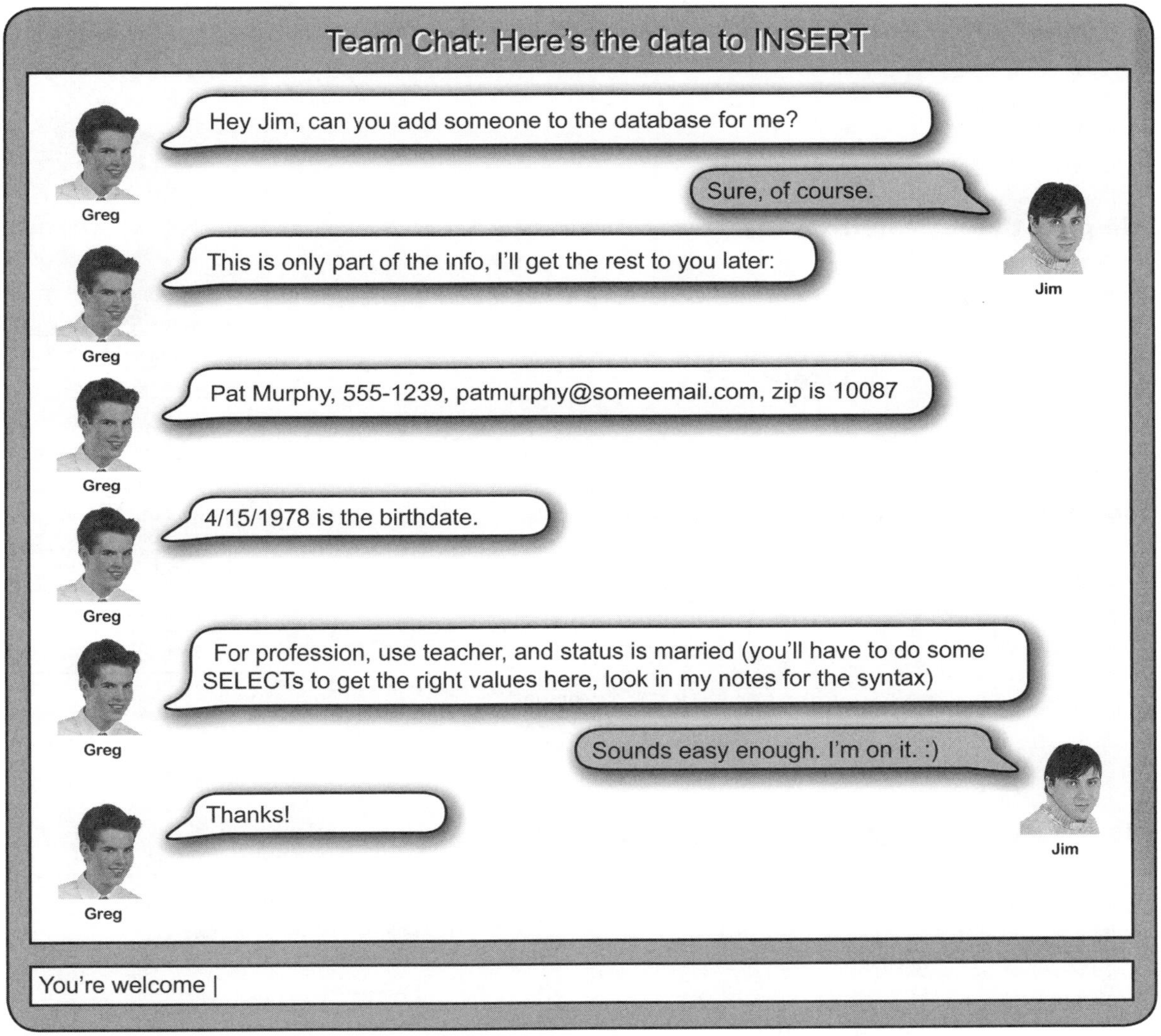

BRAIN POWER

Can you write the queries to insert this new person into the database?

Jim avoids a NULL

As he's entering the data, Jim realizes that he doesn't know if Pat is male or female. Greg isn't around, so he makes a command decision. He decides to enter 'X' for gender.

Here are his queries:

I've heard it's best to avoid NULLs, but I don't have a gender for this entry.

He gets the prof_id from the profession table

```
SELECT prof_id FROM profession WHERE profession = 'teacher';
```

prof_id
19

Here's the id that corresponds to 'teacher', so he can use that in his my_contacts query.

my_contacts
contact_id 0—🔑
last_name
first_name
phone
email
gender
birthday
prof_id 💰🔑
zip_code 💰🔑
status_id 💰🔑

He gets the status_id from the status table

```
SELECT status_id FROM profession WHERE status = 'single';
```

status_id
4

And here's the status_id that corresponds to 'married'.

He inserts these values and uses X for gender

When we have an AUTO_INCREMENT column, we don't need to put a value in. The two quotes tell the table to insert a value for us for the primary key column.

```
INSERT INTO my_contacts VALUES('', 'Murphy', 'Pat',
'5551239', 'patmurphy@someemail.com', 'X', 1978-04-15,
19, '10087', 3);
```

These are the IDs he found with the two queries up there. He could have done this with subqueries.

This is what Jim decides to enter for gender, rather than making a guess or entering NULL.

Flash forward three months

Greg's trying to figure out some demographic data. He wants to know how many of the people in `my_contacts` are male, how many are female, and how many total entries he has. He does three queries: first he gets a count of all the females and males, then he gets a total count.

```
SELECT COUNT(*) AS Females FROM my_contacts WHERE gender = 'F';
```

Females
5975

Greg discovers he's got 5,975 rows with 'F' for gender in his my_contacts table.

```
SELECT COUNT(*) AS Males FROM my_contacts WHERE gender = 'M';
```

Males
6982

And 6,982 'M' values in gender.

```
SELECT COUNT(*) AS Total FROM my_contacts;
```

Total
12970

He checks the total number of rows in his table with this query.

Greg notices that the numbers don't add up. He's got 13 rows that apparently don't show up under either the male or female query. He tries another query:

```
SELECT gender FROM my_contacts
WHERE gender <> 'M' AND gender <> 'F';
```

gender
X
X
X
X
X
X
X
X
X
X
X
X
X

When he looks for the missing records, he spots the 'X' gender values.

BRAIN POWER

How could Jim have avoided the X values altogether?

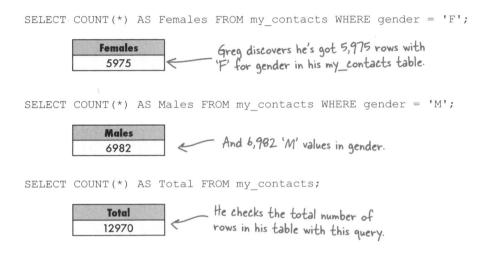

CHECK, please: Adding a CHECK CONSTRAINT

We've already seen a number of constraints on columns in earlier chapters. A **constraint** is a restriction on what you can insert into a column. Constraints are added when we create a table. Some of the constraints you've already seen include NOT NULL, PRIMARY KEY, FOREIGN KEY, and UNIQUE.

There's another sort of column constraint, called a **CHECK**. Here's an example of one. Suppose we have a piggy bank, and we want to keep track of the coins dropped in it. It only takes pennies, nickels, dimes, and quarters. We can use the letters P, N, D, and Q to stand for each type of coin. The table below uses a CHECK constraint to restrict the values that can be inserted into the coin column:

A CHECK constraint restricts what values you can insert into a column. It uses the same conditionals as a WHERE clause.

```
CREATE TABLE piggy_bank
(
  id INT AUTO_INCREMENT NOT NULL PRIMARY KEY,
  coin CHAR(1) CHECK (coin IN ('P','N','D','Q'))
)
```

This checks to see if the value for the coin column is one of these.

If the value you're trying to insert fails the CHECK condition, you get an error.

Watch it!

CHECK doesn't enforce data integrity in MySQL.

You can create your tables with CHECK constraints in MySQL, but it won't do anything for you. MySQL ignores them.

CHECKing the gender

If Greg could go back in time, he could have created `my_contacts` with a `CHECK` constraint on the gender column. Instead, he can fix it with an `ALTER TABLE`.

Why do I keep getting an error?

```
ALTER TABLE my_contacts
ADD CONSTRAINT CHECK gender IN ('M','F');
```

The next day, Jim finds himself unable to enter 'X' for gender. When he asks Greg about it, Greg explains the new constraint and tells Jim Since he can't go back in time, he makes Jim contact all the 'X' genders and figure out what they should be.

Sharpen your pencil

Write down what values you think are allowed in each of these columns.

```
CREATE TABLE mystery_table
(
  column1 INT(4) CHECK (column1 > 200),

  column2 CHAR(1) CHECK (column2 NOT IN ('x', 'y', 'z')),

  column3 VARCHAR(3) CHECK ('A' = SUBSTRING(column_3, 1, 1)),

  column4 VARCHAR(3) CHECK ('A' = SUBSTRING(column_4, 1, 1)
  AND '9' = SUBSTRING(column_4, 2, 1))
)
```

Column 1: ....

Column 2: ....

Column 3: ....

Column 4: ....

Sharpen your pencil Solution

Write down what values you think are allowed in each of these columns.

```
CREATE TABLE mystery_table
(
  column1 INT(4) CHECK (column1 > 200),

  column2 CHAR(1) CHECK (column2 NOT IN ('x', 'y', 'z')),

  column3 VARCHAR(3) CHECK ('A' = SUBSTRING(column_3, 1, 1)),

  column4 VARCHAR(3) CHECK ('A' = SUBSTRING(column_4, 1, 1)
  AND '9' = SUBSTRING(column_4, 2, 1))
)
```

You can combine conditions with AND and OR.

Column 1: Values inserted must be greater than 200

Column 2: Any characters other than x, y, or z can be inserted

Column 3: The first character of the string must be A

Column 4: The first character of the string must be A and the second must be 9

there are no Dumb Questions

Q: So I can use anything in my CHECK that I would in a WHERE clause?

A: Pretty much. You can use all the conditionals: AND, OR, IN, NOT, BETWEEN and others. You can even combine them, as you see in the example above. You can't use a subquery, though.

Q: So if I can't use these in MySQL, what can I use?

A: There's no easy answer for that. Some people use triggers, which are queries that will execute if a certain condition is met. But they just aren't as easy as `CHECK`, and are outside the scope of this book.

Q: What happens if you try to INSERT a value that doesn't satisfy the CHECK?

A: You'll get an error and nothing will be inserted.

Q: What good does that do?

A: It ensures that the data that gets entered into your table makes sense. You won't have end up with mystery values.

Frank's job gets tedious

Frank's been working on matching up people with jobs. He's noticing some patterns. He's got lots of job openings for web designers and not many applicants. He's got many technical writers seeking work, but not many positions open for them.

He performs the same queries every day to try to find matches for people and jobs.

I have to create the same queries over and over again every day. It's tedious.

BE Frank

Your job is to play Frank and write the queries that Frank writes every day. Write a query to find all the web designers from job_desired, along with their contact info. Write another query to find open positions for technical writers.

BE Frank SOLUTION

Your job is to play Frank and write the queries that Frank writes every day. Write a query to find all the web designers from job_desired, along with their contact info. Write another query to find open positions for technical writers.

```
SELECT mc.first_name, mc.last_name,
mc.phone, mc.email
FROM my_contacts mc
NATURAL JOIN job_desired jd
WHERE jd.title = 'Web Designer';
```

Greg typically capitalizes job titles in his database.

```
SELECT title, salary, description, zip
FROM job_listings
WHERE title = 'Technical Writer';
```

These aren't difficult queries, but in having to type them again and again, Frank is bound to make mistakes. He needs a way to save the queries and just see the output once a day without having to retype them.

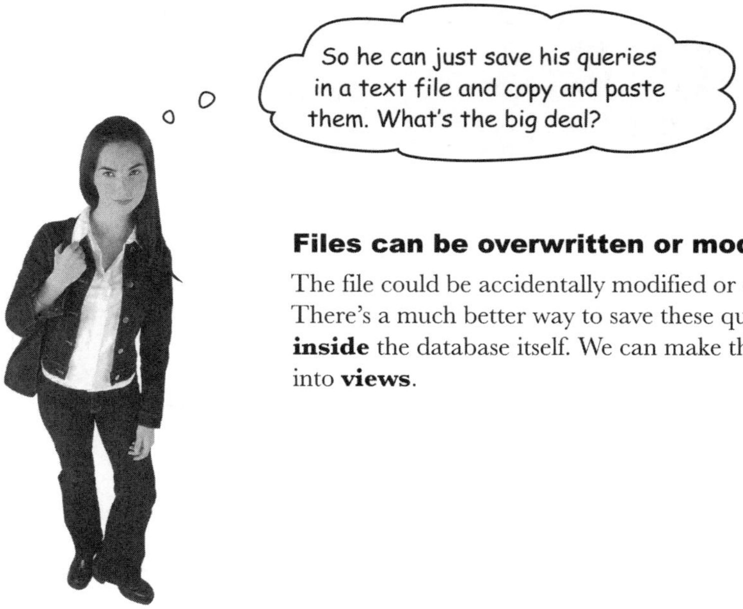
So he can just save his queries in a text file and copy and paste them. What's the big deal?

Files can be overwritten or modified.

The file could be accidentally modified or deleted. There's a much better way to save these queries **inside** the database itself. We can make them into **views**.

Creating a view

Creating a view is really simple. We add a CREATE VIEW statement to our query. Let's create two views from Frank's queries:

```
CREATE VIEW web_designers AS
SELECT mc.first_name, mc.last_name, mc.phone, mc.email
FROM my_contacts mc
NATURAL JOIN job_desired jd
WHERE jd.title = 'Web Designer';
```

This could also have been an INNER JOIN using:
ON mc.contact_id = jd.contact_id.

```
CREATE VIEW tech_writer_jobs AS
SELECT title salary, description, zip
FROM job_listings
WHERE title = 'Technical Writer';
```

Ah hah, easy! But how do I actually use the views I create?

BRAIN POWER

What do ***you*** think a SQL statement that uses a VIEW looks like?

Viewing your views

Consider the `web_designers` view we just created:

```
CREATE VIEW web_designers AS
SELECT mc.first_name, mc.last_name, mc.phone, mc.email
FROM my_contacts mc
NATURAL JOIN job_desired jd
WHERE jd.title = 'Web Designer';
```

Remember, we're allowed to leave out the AS keyword.

To see what's in it, we simply treat it as though it were a table. We can use a SELECT:

```
SELECT * FROM web_designers;
```

Here's the name of our view.

The output is:

first_name	last_name	phone	email
John	Martinez	5559872	jm@someemail.com
Samantha	Hoffman	5556948	sammy@someemail.com
Todd	Hertz	5557888	tod@someemail.com
Fred	McDougal	5557744	fm@someemail.com

And so on, until all the rows matching "Web Designer" are listed.

What your view is actually doing

When you actually use your view in a query, it's behaving as though it were a subquery. Here's what the SELECT we just used with our view is actually telling SQL to do:

```
SELECT * FROM web_designers;
```

This means, "Select everything from the subquery that returns the first name, last name, phone, and email of all the people from my_contacts who are looking for a job as a web designer."

```
SELECT * FROM
(SELECT mc.first_name, mc.last_name, mc.phone, mc.email
FROM my_contacts mc
NATURAL JOIN job_desired jd
WHERE jd.title = 'Web Designer') AS web_designers;
```

Here's what we used in our view.

We're giving our subquery an alias so that the query treats it as a table.

What's up with that AS web_designers part? Why do we need it?

The FROM clause expects a table.

And while our SELECT statement results in a virtual table, there's no way that SQL can grab onto it without that alias.

What a view is

A VIEW is basically a table that only exists when you use the view in a query. It's considered a **virtual table** because it acts like a table, and the same operations that can be performed on a table can be performed on a view.

But the virtual table doesn't stay in the database. It gets created when we use the view and then deleted. The named VIEW is the only thing that persists. This is good, because each time new rows are inserted into the database, when you use a view it will see the new information.

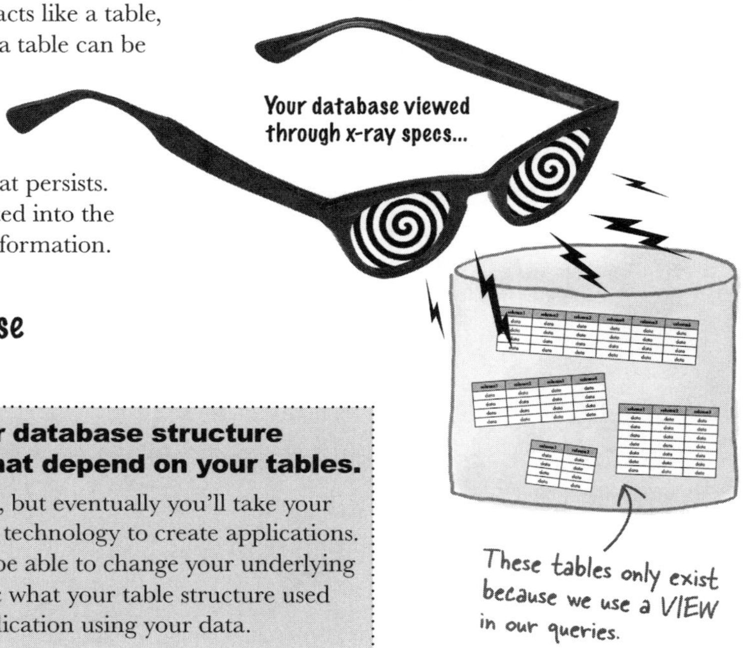

Your database viewed through x-ray specs...
These tables only exist because we use a VIEW in our queries.

Why views are good for your database

1 You can keep changes to your database structure from breaking applications that depend on your tables.

We haven't talked about it in this book, but eventually you'll take your SQL knowledge and use it with another technology to create applications. By creating views into your data, you will be able to change your underlying table structure but create views that mimic what your table structure used to be so you won't have to change the application using your data.

2 Views make your life easier by simplifying your complex query into a simple command.

You won't have to create complicated joins and subqueries repeatedly when you can create a view instead. Your view hides the complexity of the underlying query. And when you do tie your SQL into PHP or some other programming language, your view will be much easier to add to your code. You'll be using the simplified code of the view, not the big, complex query full of joins. Simplicity means there's less chance of typos, and your code will be that much easier to read.

3 You can create views that hide information that isn't needed by the user.

Consider the eventual addition of tables into gregs_list that contain credit card information. You can create a view to indicate someone has a card on file without revealing the details of that card. You can allow employees to see just the information they need, while keeping sensitive information hidden.

Okay, I've got a tough question for you. Could I create a view that would show me everyone in the job_current table who is also in the job_desired table, along with how much money they currently make, how much they want to make based on salary_low, and the difference between those two figures? In other words, the raise they'd want to change jobs? Oh, and give me their names, emails, and phone numbers.

Exercise

That's a tall order, but any query you can create as a SELECT you can turn into a view. Start by answering the questions below and then write Frank's query as a view called job_raises.

What are the tables that will need to be in this query?

....

What columns in which tables can be used to figure out the raise?

....

How can we use SQL to actually create a column named 'raise' in our results?

....

Write Frank's query:

....

....

....

....

....

....

Hint: Try writing it with two joins on three tables!

Exercise Solution

That's a tall order, but any query you can create as a SELECT you can turn into a view. Start by answering the questions below and then write Frank's query as a view called job_raises.

What are the tables that will need to be in this query?

job_current, job_desired, and my_contacts

What columns in which tables can be used to figure out the raise?

The salary column in job_current, and the salary_low column in job_desired

How can we use SQL to actually create a column named "raise" in our results?

Subtract current salary from salary_low and give it an alias

Write Frank's query:

Here, we create our new view named job_raises.

```
CREATE VIEW job_raises AS
SELECT mc.first_name, mc.last_name, mc.email, mc.phone, jc.contact_id, jc.salary, jd.salary_low,
jd.salary_low - jc.salary AS raise
FROM job_current jc
INNER JOIN job_desired jd
INNER JOIN my_contacts mc
WHERE jc.contact_id = jd.contact_id
AND jc.contact_id = mc.contact_id;
```

After we've created the view, the rest of the query uses two INNER JOINs to pull data from three tables. We also use a little math to create our new 'raise' column.

This subtracts the salary they want from the salary they get now and uses an alias to call the result 'raise'.

It's an enormous query, but now all Frank has to do is type

`SELECT * FROM job_raises;`

to see his information.

Answers on page 491.

Inserting, updating, and deleting with views

You can do more than just `SELECT` information from your tables with a view. In some instances, you can `UPDATE`, `INSERT`, and `DELETE` your data as well.

So I can create a view that will allow me to actually change what's in my tables?

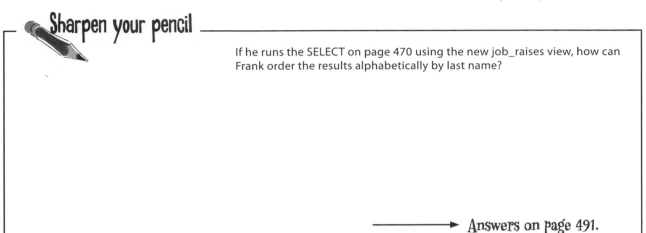

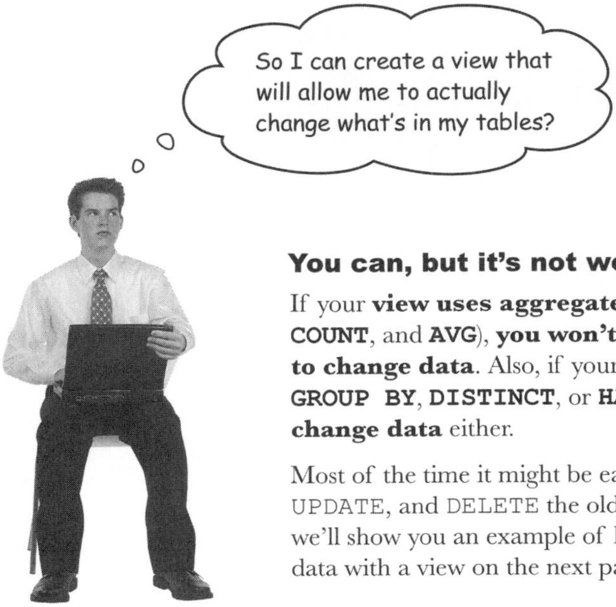

You can, but it's not worth the trouble.

If your **view uses aggregate values** (like **SUM**, **COUNT**, and **AVG**), **you won't be able to use it to change data**. Also, if your **view contains GROUP BY**, **DISTINCT**, or **HAVING**, it **won't change data** either.

Most of the time it might be easier to `INSERT`, `UPDATE`, and `DELETE` the old-fashioned way, but we'll show you an example of how to change your data with a view on the next page.

The secret is to pretend a view is a real table

Let's make a view from a new table called `piggy_bank`. This table contains coins we are collecting. There's an ID for each coin; a denomination column that indicates if it's a penny, nickel, dime, or quarter; and a year the coin was minted.

```
CREATE TABLE piggy_bank
(
  id INT AUTO_INCREMENT NOT NULL PRIMARY KEY,
  coin CHAR(1) NOT NULL,
  coin_year CHAR(4)
)
```

And here's the data currently in the `piggy_bank` table:

id	coin	coin_year
1	Q	1950
2	P	1972
3	N	2005
4	Q	1999
5	Q	1981
6	D	1940
7	Q	1980
8	P	2001
9	D	1926
10	P	1999

Let's write a view that only shows us rows containing quarters:

```
CREATE VIEW AS pb_quarters
SELECT * FROM piggy_bank
WHERE coin = 'Q';
```

BRAIN POWER

What will the table of results look like when we run this query?

```
SELECT * FROM pb_quarters;
```

Exercise

Try this at home. Create the piggy_bank table and the pb_quarters and pb_dimes views using the queries shown below.

```
INSERT INTO piggy_bank VALUES ('','Q', 1950), ('','P', 1972),('','N', 2005),
('','Q', 1999),('','Q', 1981),('','D', 1940),('','Q', 1980),('','P', 2001),('','D',
1926),('','P', 1999);

CREATE VIEW pb_quarters AS SELECT * FROM piggy_bank WHERE coin = 'Q';

CREATE VIEW pb_dimes AS SELECT * FROM piggy_bank WHERE coin = 'D' WITH CHECK OPTION;
```

↑ Try to figure out what this does as you work through the exercise.

Write what happens when you run each of these INSERT, DELETE, AND UPDATE queries. At the end of the exercise, sketch the final piggy_bank table.

```
INSERT INTO pb_quarters VALUES ('','Q', 1993);
```

```
INSERT INTO pb_quarters VALUES ('','D', 1942);
```

```
INSERT INTO pb_dimes VALUES ('','Q', 2005);
```

```
DELETE FROM pb_quarters WHERE coin = 'N' OR coin = 'P' OR coin = 'D';
```

```
UPDATE pb_quarters  SET coin = 'Q' WHERE coin = 'P';
```

Exercise Solution

Try this at home. Create the piggy_bank table and the pb_quarters and pb_dimes views using the queries shown below.

```
INSERT INTO piggy_bank VALUES ('','Q', 1950), ('','P', 1972),('','N', 2005),
('','Q', 1999),('','Q', 1981),('','D', 1940),('','Q', 1980),('','P', 2001),('','D',
1926),('','P', 1999);

CREATE VIEW pb_quarters AS SELECT * FROM piggy_bank WHERE coin = 'Q';

CREATE VIEW pb_dimes AS SELECT * FROM piggy_bank WHERE coin = 'D' WITH CHECK OPTION;
```

Try to figure out what this does as you work through the exercise.

Write what happens when you run each of these INSERT, DELETE, AND UPDATE queries. At the end of the exercise, sketch the final piggy_bank table.

```
INSERT INTO pb_quarters VALUES ('','Q', 1993);
```

This query will run appropriately.

```
INSERT INTO pb_quarters VALUES ('','D', 1942);
```

This inserts a new value into the table, even though you wouldn't think it could because of the WHERE clause.

```
INSERT INTO pb_dimes VALUES ('','Q', 2005);
```

This one gives you an error because of the CHECK OPTION clauses. That makes the data entered into a view be verified against the WHERE clause before being allowed to be added.

```
DELETE FROM pb_quarters WHERE coin = 'N' OR coin = 'P' OR coin = 'D';
```

This one does nothing at all to the table because it only looks at results with coin = 'Q'

```
UPDATE pb_quarters  SET coin = 'Q' WHERE coin = 'P';
```

This one does nothing at all to the table because no values of coin = 'P' are returned by the pb_quarters view.

The final table looks like this:

id	coin	coin_year
1	Q	1950
2	P	1972
3	N	2005
4	Q	1999
5	Q	1981
6	D	1940
7	Q	1980
8	P	2001
9	D	1926
10	P	1999
11	Q	1993
12	D	1942

View with CHECK OPTION

CHECK OPTION added to your view tells the RDBMS to check each statement you try to INSERT and DELETE to see if it's allowed according to the WHERE clause in your view. So, just how does CHECK OPTION affect your INSERT and UPDATE statements?

When you used CHECK OPTION in the previous exercise, your data was rejected in your INSERT if it didn't match the WHERE condition in the pb_dimes view. If you use an UPDATE you'll also get an error:

```
UPDATE pb_dimes SET coin = 'x';
```

The WHERE condition in pb_dimes has not been satisfied by 'x' so nothing is updated.

CHECK OPTION checks each query you try to INSERT or UPDATE to see if it's allowed according to the WHERE clause in your view.

Couldn't you use views with CHECK OPTION to create something kind of like a CHECK CONSTRAINT if you're using MySQL?

Yes, your views can precisely mirror what is in the table, but force INSERT statements to comply with WHERE clauses.

For example, with our gender problem earlier in this chapter we could create a view of the my_contacts table that Jim could use to update my_contacts. It could simply cause an error every time he tries to put X in the gender table.

In MySQL, you can imitate a CHECK CONSTRAINT using a CHECK OPTION

How could we create a view for my_contacts that would force Jim to enter either 'M' or 'F' for the gender field?

Your view may be updatable if...

In the piggy_bank table, both views we created were updatable views. An **updatable view** is a view that allows you to change the underlying tables. The important point here is that an updatable view includes all the NOT NULL columns from the tables it references. That way, when you INSERT using a view, you can be certain that you will have a value for every column you are required to have a value in.

Basically, this means that INSERT, UPDATE, and DELETE can all be used with the views we created. As long as the view returns any columns of the table that are not null, the view can enter the appropriate values into the table.

There are also non-updatable views. A **non-updatable view** is a view that doesn't include all the NOT NULL columns. Other than creating and dropping it, the only thing you can do with a non-updatable view is SELECT from it.

An updatable view includes all the NOT NULL columns from the tables it references.

Other than using a CHECK OPTION, I don't really see what the point of using a view and INSERT is.

It's true, you won't use views very often to INSERT, UPDATE, or DELETE.

While there are valid uses, such as forcing data integrity with MySQL, generally it's easier to simply use the table itself to INSERT, UPDATE, and DELETE. An INSERT into a view might come in handy if the view reveals only one column and the rest of the columns are assigned NULL or default values. In that case, then INSERT might make sense. You can also add a WHERE clause to your view that will restrict what you can INSERT, helping you imitate a CHECK constraint in MySQL.

To make things even more confusing, you can only update views that don't contain aggregate operators like SUM, COUNT, and AVG, and operators like BETWEEN, HAVING, IN, and NOT IN.

When you're finished with your view

When you no longer need one of your views, clean it up by using a DROP VIEW statement. It's as simple as:

```
DROP VIEW pb_dimes;
```

there are no Dumb Questions

Q: Is there a way to see what views you have created?

A: Views show up just like tables in your database. You can use the command SHOW TABLES to see all views and tables. And just like a table, you can DESC a view to see its structure.

Q: What happens if I drop a table that has a view?

A: It depends. Some RDBMSs will still allow you to use the view and will return no data. MySQL will not let you drop a view unless the table it was based on exists, even though you **can** drop a table that participates in a view. Other RDBMSs have different behaviors. It's a good idea to experiment with yours to see what happens. In general, it's best to drop the view before you drop a table it's based on.

Q: I see how useful CHECK constraints and views are for helping when more than one person is trying to do things to the database. But what happens if two people are trying to change the same column at the same time?

A: For that, we should talk about transactions. But first, Mrs. Humphries needs to get some cash.

CHECK constraints and views both help maintain control when you have multiple users.

When bad things happen to good databases

Mrs. Humphries wants to transfer 1,000 samoleons from her checking to her savings. She heads to the ATM...

She checks the balance of her checking and savings account.

1000 SAMOLEANS IN CHECKING

30 SAMOLEANS IN SAVINGS

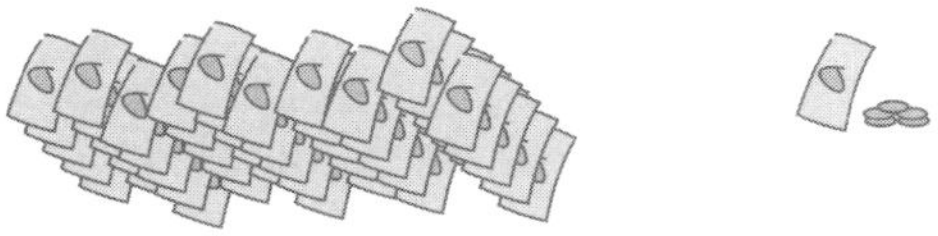

She selects.

TRANSFER 1000 SAMOLEONS FROM CHECKING TO SAVINGS

She pushes the button.

CHECKING → SAVINGS

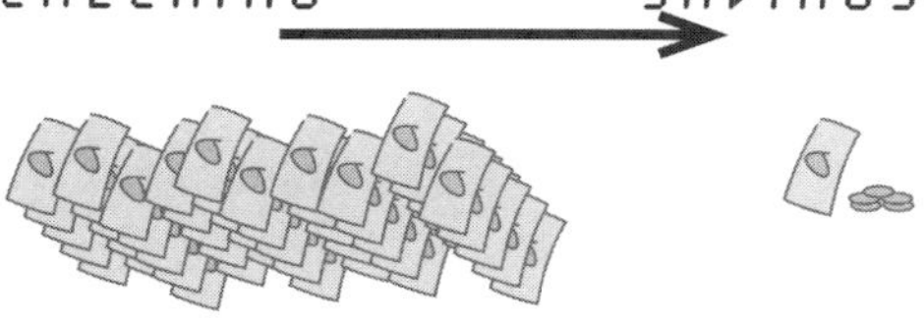

The ATM beeps then goes blank.

The power's gone out.

The power comes back on.

She checks her checking and savings balances.

0 SAMOLEANS IN CHECKING

30 SAMOLEANS IN SAVINGS

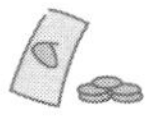

Where, oh where, did Mrs. Humphries' samoleons go?

What happened inside the ATM

ATM: LA LA LA LA LA.

ATM: HEY, IT'S MRS. ETHEL P. HUMPHRIES. HI MRS. ETHEL P. HUMPHRIES! (ACCOUNT_ID 38221)

Mrs. Humphries: Tell me how much money I have.

ATM: *Thinking* (SELECT BALANCE FROM CHECKING WHERE ACCOUNT_ID = 38221;
SELECT BALANCE FROM SAVINGS WHERE ACCOUNT_ID = 38221;)
SO THAT'S 1000 CHECKING, 30 SAVINGS

Mrs. Humphries: Transfer this 1000 samoleons from checking to savings.

ATM: THAT'S A TALL ORDER, MRS. HUMPHRIES, BUT HERE GOES:
(CHECKING_BAL > 1000, SO SHE HAS ENOUGH MONEY)
(REMOVE 1000 FROM CHECKING)
(INSERT BEEEP......

Here's where the power went out.

ATM:

ATM:

ATM: ZZZZZZZZZ

ATM: YAWN.

ATM: HEY, IT'S MRS. ETHEL P. HUMPHRIES. HI MRS. ETHEL P. HUMPHRIES! (ACCOUNT_ID 38221)

Mrs. Humphries: Tell me how much money I have.

ATM: *Thinking* (SELECT BALANCE FROM CHECKING WHERE ACCOUNT_ID = 38221;
SELECT BALANCE FROM SAVINGS WHERE ACCOUNT_ID = 38221;)
SO THAT'S 0 CHECKING, 30 SAVINGS

ATM: OWW! THAT'S MY SCREEN YOU'RE POUNDING ON.
BYE MRS. ETHEL P. HUMPHRIES!

BRAIN POWER

How could we have prevented the ATM from forgetting about the INSERT part of Mrs. Humphries' transaction?

Meanwhile, across town...

More trouble at the ATM

John and Mary share an account. On Friday, they ended up at two different ATM machines at the same time. They each try to withdraw 300 samoleons.

THE LEFT
BANK

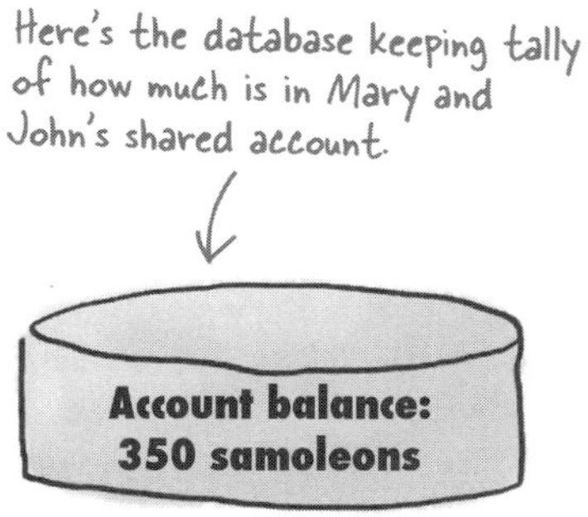
Here's the database keeping tally of how much is in Mary and John's shared account.
Account balance:
350 samoleons

1st National
Savings

ATM: OH, IT'S YOU AGAIN, JOHN. WHAT, YOU THINK I'M MADE OF MONEY?

John: What's my balance?

ATM: *Thinking* (SELECT CHECKING_BAL FROM ACCOUNTS;) 350 SAMOLEONS

John: Give me 300 samoleons

ATM: THAT'S ALL YOU THINK I'M GOOD FOR, TO GIVE ME MONEY. JUST USE ME AND THEN IGNORE ME.

(CHECKING_BAL > 300, HE HAS ENOUGH MONEY)

(REMOVE 300 FROM CHECKING)

(SUBTRACT 300 FROM CHECKING_BAL)

John takes the money and runs.

ATM: YOU NEVER CALL. YOU NEVER WRITE. BYE JOHN.

ATM: MARY, HIYA.

Mary: What's my balance?

ATM: *Thinking* (SELECT CHECKING_BAL FROM ACCOUNTS;) 350 SAMOLEONS

RING RING

Mary fiddles around in her purse looking for her cell phone.

Mary: Give me 300 samoleons.

ATM: YOU BETCHA

(CHECKING_BAL > 300, SHE HAS ENOUGH MONEY)

(REMOVE 300 FROM CHECKING)

(SUBTRACT 300 FROM CHECKING_BAL)

ATM: YOU'RE BADLY OVERDRAWN.

350 samoleons

350 samoleons

50 samoleons

This is where things went wrong.

-250 samoleons

Wouldn't it be dreamy if a series of SQL statements could be executed as a group, all at once, and if something goes wrong be rolled back as if they'd never been executed? But it's only a dream...

It's not a dream, it's a transaction

A **transaction** is a set of SQL statements that accomplish a single unit of work. In Mrs. Humphries' case, a transaction would consist of all the SQL statements needed to move the money from her checking account to her savings account:

These three actions make up a single unit of work. Here it's a transaction.

> **If the checking balance >= 1000**
>
> **Subtract 1000 from checking balance**
>
> **Add 1000 to savings balance**

John and Mary were each trying to perform *the same transaction* at the same time:

John and Mary were both trying to take out 300 samoleons at the same time.

> **If the checking balance >= 300**
>
> **Subtract 300 from checking balance**
>
> **Distribute 300 samoleons**

John's transaction at the Left Bank ATM

> **If the checking balance >= 300**
>
> **Subtract 300 from checking balance**
>
> **Distribute 300 samoleons**

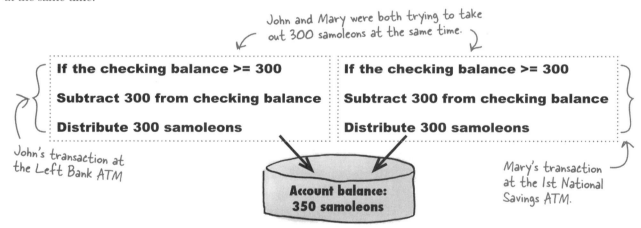

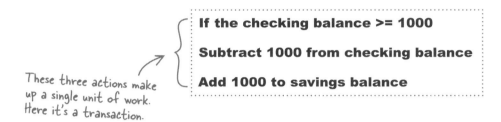

Mary's transaction at the 1st National Savings ATM.

Account balance: 350 samoleons

In the case of John and Mary, the 1st National Savings ATM shouldn't have been allowed to touch the account, even to query the balance, until the Left Bank ATM was finished with the transaction, thus unlocking it.

During a transaction, if <u>all</u> the steps can't be completed without interference, <u>none</u> of them should be completed.

The classic ACID test

To help you decide what steps in your SQL can be considered a transaction, remember the acronym **ACID**. There are four characteristics that have to be true before we can call a set of SQL statements a transaction:

ACID: ATOMICITY

All of the pieces of the transaction must be completed, or none of them will be completed. You can't execute part of a transaction. Mrs. Humphries' samoleons were blinked into non-existence by the power outage because only part of the transaction took place.

ACID: CONSISTENCY

A complete transaction leaves the database in a consistent state at the end of the transaction. At the end of both of the samoleon transactions, the money is in balance again. In the first case it's been transferred to savings; in the second it's been translated into cash. But no samoleons go missing.

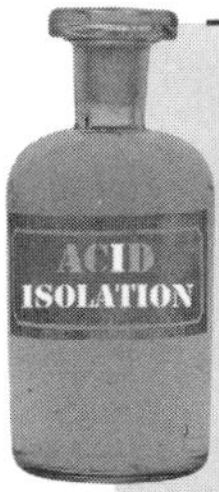

ACID: ISOLATION

Isolation means that every transaction has a consistent view of the database regardless of other transactions taking place at the same time. This is what went wrong with John and Mary: Mary's ATM could see the balance while John's ATM was completing the transaction. She shouldn't have been able to see the balance, or should have seen some sort of "transaction in progress" message.

ACID: DURABILITY

After the transaction, the database needs to save the data correctly and protect it from power outages or other threats. This is generally handled through records of transactions saved to a different location than the main database. If a record of Mrs. Humphries' transaction had been kept somewhere, then she might have gotten her 1,000 samoleons back.

SQL helps you manage your transactions

Let's consider a very simple bank database. Our database consists of a table of account holders, a checking account table, and a savings account table:

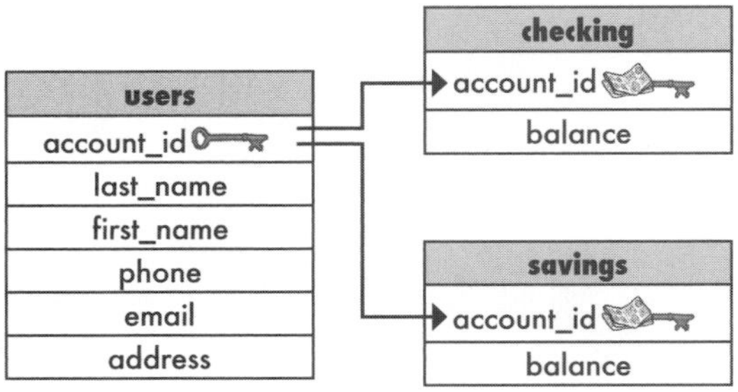

There are probably many more columns here, but you get the idea.

We've got three SQL transaction tools to help keep us safe:

`START TRANSACTION;`

This tracks what your SQL's doing.

Here's where your RDBMS starts to track your code.
Your code.

`START TRANSACTION` ***keeps track of all the SQL*** that follows until you enter either `COMMIT` or `ROLLBACK`.

`COMMIT;`

This commits all your code once you're happy with it.

If you've got all your statements in place and everything looks good, type **`COMMIT`** to ***make it permanent***.

`ROLLBACK;`

This takes you right back to before you started the transaction.

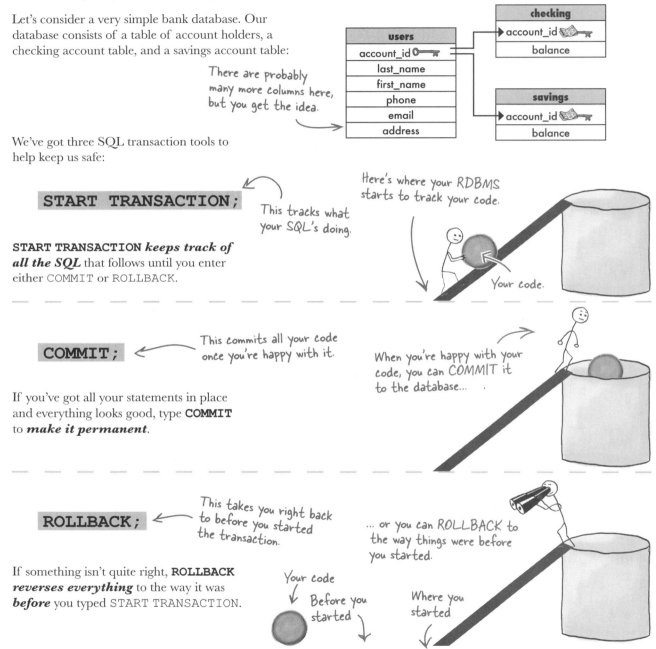

If something isn't quite right, **`ROLLBACK`** ***reverses everything*** to the way it was ***before*** you typed `START TRANSACTION`.

No changes will occur to the database until you COMMIT

What should have happened inside the ATM

ATM: LA LA LA LA LA.

ATM: HEY. IT'S MRS. ETHEL P. HUMPHRIES. HI MRS. ETHEL P. HUMPHRIES! (ACCOUNT_ID 38221)

Mrs. Humphries: Tell me how much money I have.

ATM: *Thinking* (SELECT BALANCE FROM CHECKING WHERE ACCOUNT_ID = 38221;
SELECT BALANCE FROM SAVINGS WHERE ACCOUNT_ID = 38221;)
SO THAT'S 1000 CHECKING, 30 SAVINGS

Mrs. Humphries: Transfer this 1,000 samoleons from checking to savings.

ATM: THAT'S A TALL ORDER, MRS. HUMPHRIES, BUT HERE GOES:
(START TRANSACTION;
SELECT BALANCE FROM CHECKING WHERE ACCOUNT_ID = 38221;)

ATM: SHE'S GOT 1000 IN CHECKING, SO I'LL KEEP GOING.

ATM: (UPDATE CHECKING SET BALANCE = BALANCE - 1000 WHERE ACCOUNT_ID = 38221;)

(INSERT BEEEP......

Here's where the power went out.

ATM ON EMERGENCY POWER: ROLLBACK;

ATM:

ATM:

ATM: ZZZZZZZZZ

ATM: YAWN.

ATM: HEY. IT'S MRS. ETHEL P. HUMPHRIES. HI MRS. ETHEL P. HUMPHRIES! (ACCOUNT_ID 38221)

Mrs. Humphries: Tell me how much money I have.

ATM: *Thinking* (SELECT BALANCE FROM CHECKING WHERE ACCOUNT_ID = 38221;
SELECT BALANCE FROM SAVINGS WHERE ACCOUNT_ID =38221;
)
SO THAT'S 1000 CHECKING, 30 SAVINGS

Thanks to ROLLBACK, the COMMIT statement was never entered, so nothing ever changed.

How to make transactions work with MySQL

Before you can use a transaction with MySQL, you need to use the correct **storage engine**. The storage engine is the behind-the-scenes structure that stores all your database data and structures. Some types allow transactions; some types do not.

Think back to Chapter 4 when you saw the

```
SHOW CREATE TABLE my_contacts;
```

This time we do care about the storage engine.

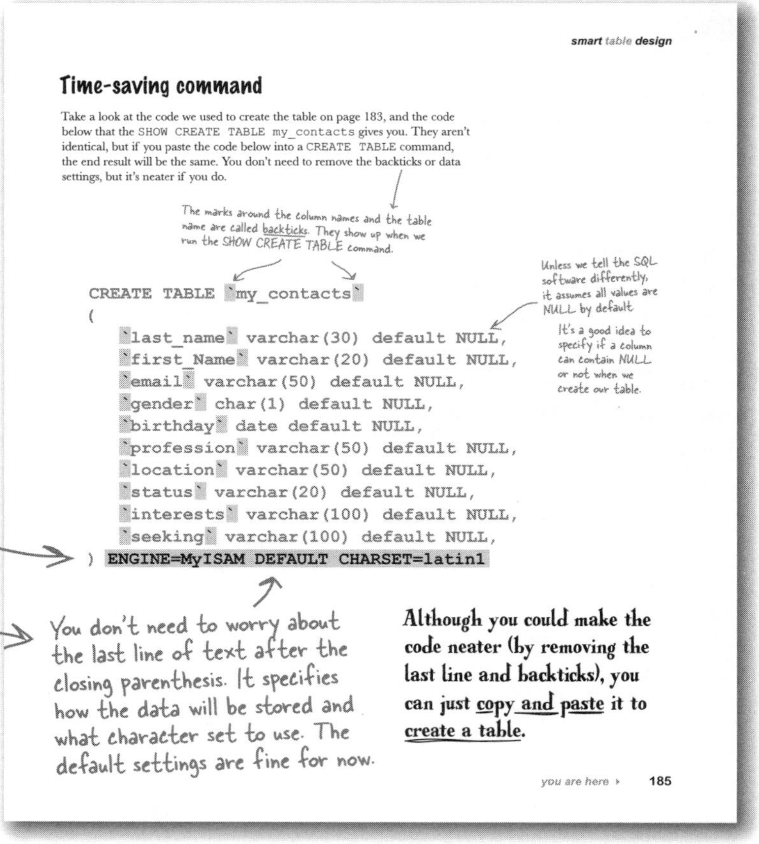
smart table design

Time-saving command

Take a look at the code we used to create the table on page 183, and the code below that the `SHOW CREATE TABLE my_contacts` gives you. They aren't identical, but if you paste the code below into a `CREATE TABLE` command, the end result will be the same. You don't need to remove the backticks or data settings, but it's neater if you do.

The marks around the column names and the table name are called backticks. They show up when we run the SHOW CREATE TABLE command.

```
CREATE TABLE `my_contacts`
(
  `last_name` varchar(30) default NULL,
  `first_Name` varchar(20) default NULL,
  `email` varchar(50) default NULL,
  `gender` char(1) default NULL,
  `birthday` date default NULL,
  `profession` varchar(50) default NULL,
  `location` varchar(50) default NULL,
  `status` varchar(20) default NULL,
  `interests` varchar(100) default NULL,
  `seeking` varchar(100) default NULL,
) ENGINE=MyISAM DEFAULT CHARSET=latin1
```

Unless we tell the SQL software differently, it assumes all values are NULL by default

It's a good idea to specify if a column can contain NULL or not when we create our table.

You don't need to worry about the last line of text after the closing parenthesis. It specifies how the data will be stored and what character set to use. The default settings are fine for now.

Although you could make the code neater (by removing the last line and backticks), you can just copy and paste it to create a table.

you are here ▸ 185

You need to make sure your storage engine is either BDB or InnoDB, the two choices that support transactions.

InnoDB and BDB are two possible ways that your RDBMS can store your data behind the scenes.

They're called storage engines, and using either of these types ensures that you can use transactions. Consult a reference for more differences between the storage engines MySQL offers.

For our purposes right now, it doesn't matter which you choose. To change your engine, use this syntax:

```
ALTER TABLE your_table TYPE = InnoDB;
```

Now try it yourself

Suppose we've upgraded all the pennies in our piggy bank to quarters.

Try the code below yourself on the piggy_bank table we created earlier in this chapter. First time around, we're going to use ROLLBACK because we decided not to go ahead with our changes:

```
START TRANSACTION;

SELECT * FROM piggy_bank;

UPDATE piggy_bank set coin = 'Q' where coin= 'P';

SELECT * FROM piggy_bank;  <-- Now you see the changes...

ROLLBACK;  <-- We changed our minds.

SELECT * FROM piggy_bank;  <-- ...and now you don't.
```

The second time we'll use COMMIT because we're okay with the changes:

```
START TRANSACTION;

SELECT * FROM piggy_bank;

UPDATE piggy_bank set coin = 'Q' where coin= 'P';

SELECT * FROM piggy_bank;  <-- Now you see the changes...

COMMIT;  <-- Make the changes stick.

SELECT * FROM piggy_bank;  <-- ...and now you still do.
```

Sharpen your pencil

Fill in the piggy_bank contents after these transactions. Here's how it looks now:

piggy_bank

id	coin	coin_year
1	Q	1950
2	P	1972
3	N	2005
4	Q	1999

```
START TRANSACTION;
UPDATE piggy_bank set coin = 'Q' where coin = 'P'
AND coin_year < 1970;
COMMIT;
```

id	coin	coin_year
1		
2		
3		
4		

```
START TRANSACTION;
UPDATE piggy_bank set coin = 'N' where coin = 'Q';
ROLLBACK;
```

id	coin	coin_year
1		
2		
3		
4		

```
START TRANSACTION;
UPDATE piggy_bank set coin = 'Q' where coin = 'N'
AND coin_year > 1950;
ROLLBACK;
```

id	coin	coin_year
1		
2		
3		
4		

```
START TRANSACTION;
UPDATE piggy_bank set coin = 'D' where coin = 'Q'
AND coin_year > 1980;
COMMIT;
```

id	coin	coin_year
1		
2		
3		
4		

```
START TRANSACTION;
UPDATE piggy_bank set coin = 'P' where coin = 'N'
AND coin_year > 1970;
COMMIT;
```

id	coin	coin_year
1		
2		
3		
4		

Answers on page 492.

there are no Dumb Questions

Q: Do you have to start with START TRANSACTION, or will COMMIT and ROLLBACK work without it?

A: You have to tell your RDBMS that you are starting a transaction with `START TRANSACTION`. It's keeping track of when the transaction started so it knows how far back to undo everything.

Q: Can I just use START TRANSACTION so that I can try out some queries?

A: You can and you should. It's a great way to practice queries that change the data in your tables without permanently changing the tables if you've done something wrong. Just be sure you `COMMIT` or `ROLLBACK` when you're finished.

Q: Why should I bother with the COMMIT or ROLLBACK?

A: Your RDBMS keeps a record of everything that has been done when you are inside a transaction. It's called a transaction log, and it keeps getting bigger and bigger the more you do. It's best to save using transactions for when you really need to be able to undo what you're doing to avoid wasting space and making your RDBMS have to work harder than necessary to keep track of what you've done.

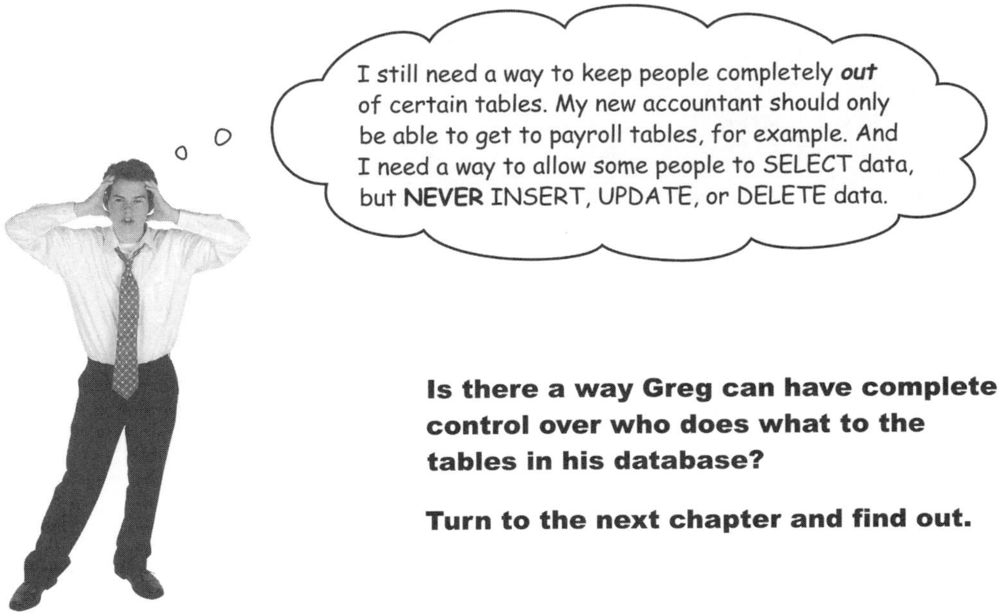
I still need a way to keep people completely *out* of certain tables. My new accountant should only be able to get to payroll tables, for example. And I need a way to allow some people to SELECT data, but **NEVER** INSERT, UPDATE, or DELETE data.

Is there a way Greg can have complete control over who does what to the tables in his database?

Turn to the next chapter and find out.

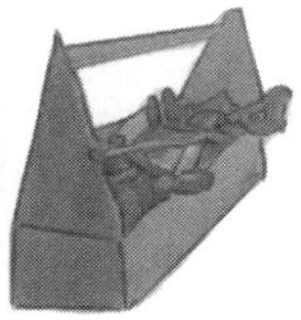

Your SQL Toolbox

You've got Chapter 11 under your belt, and almost filled your toolbox. You've seen how to VIEW your data and execute TRANSACTIONS. For a complete list of tooltips in the book, see Appendix iii.

TRANSACTIONS

This is a group of queries that must be executed together as a unit. If they can't all execute without interruption, then none of them can.

START TRANSACTION is

used to tell the RDBMS to begin a transaction. Nothing is permament until COMMIT is issued. The transaction will continue until it is committed or a ROLLBACK command is issued, which returns the database to the state it was prior to the START TRANSACTION.

VIEWS

Use a view to treat the results of a query as a table. Great for turning complex queries into simple ones.

UPDATABLE VIEWS

These are views that allow you to change the data in the underlying tables. These views must contain all NOT NULL rows of the base table or tables.

NON-UPDATABLE VIEWS

Views that can't be used to INSERT or UPDATE data in the base table.

CHECK CONSTRAINTS

Use these to only allow specific values to be inserted or updated in a table.

CHECK OPTION

Use this when creating an updatable view to force all inserts and updates to satisfy a WHERE clause in the view.

Sharpen your pencil Solution

From page 471.

If he runs the SELECT on page 470 using the new job_raises view, how can Frank order the results alphabetically by last name?

Add an ORDER BY last_name to either the view when it's created or the SELECT when it uses the view.

Sharpen your pencil Solution

From page 488.

Fill in the piggy_bank contents after these transactions. Here's how it looks now:

piggy_bank

id	coin	coin_year
1	Q	1950
2	P	1972
3	N	2005
4	Q	1999

```
START TRANSACTION;
UPDATE piggy_bank set coin = 'Q' where coin = 'P'
AND coin_year < 1970;
COMMIT;
```

No matches, so no change.

id	coin	coin_year
1	Q	1950
2	P	1972
3	N	2005
4	Q	1999

```
START TRANSACTION;
UPDATE piggy_bank set coin = 'N' where coin = 'Q';
ROLLBACK;
```

Rollback, no change.

id	coin	coin_year
1	Q	1950
2	P	1972
3	N	2005
4	Q	1999

```
START TRANSACTION;
UPDATE piggy_bank set coin = 'Q' where coin = 'N'
AND coin_year > 1950;
ROLLBACK;
```

Rollback, no change.

id	coin	coin_year
1	Q	1950
2	P	1972
3	N	2005
4	Q	1999

```
START TRANSACTION;
UPDATE piggy_bank set coin = 'D' where coin = 'Q'
AND coin_year > 1980;
COMMIT;
```

This row is affected.

id	coin	coin_year
1	Q	1950
2	P	1972
3	N	2005
4	D	1999

```
START TRANSACTION;
UPDATE piggy_bank set coin = 'P' where coin = 'N'
AND coin_year > 1970;
COMMIT;
```

This row is affected.

id	coin	coin_year
1	Q	1950
2	P	1972
3	P	2005
4	Q	1999

12 security

Protecting your assets

You've put an enormous amount of time and energy into creating your database. And you'd be devastated if anything happened to it. You've also had to give other people **access to your data**, and you're worried that they might insert or update something incorrectly, or even worse, **delete the wrong data**. You're about to learn how databases and the objects in them can be made more **secure**, and how you can have complete control over ***who can do what with your data.***

User problems

Clown tracking took off in such a big way that the Dataville City Council had to employ a whole team of people to track clowns and add the data to the `clown_tracking` database.

Unfortunately the team was infiltrated by a clown disguised in ordinary clothes who went by the codename of "George." He caused a number of problems in the database, including lost data, modified data, and nearly duplicate records that only exist because of his deliberate misspellings. Here are a few of the problems with the clown tracking database:

Snuggles, Snugles, and Snuggels all have rows in the clown_info table. We're pretty sure they are all the same clown because the gender and description columns are the same (except for misspellings).

With those multiple entries in the clown_info table, we've got a mess with our actual sightings. The info_location table uses the clown_info IDs for Snuggles, Snugles, and Snuggels.

The activities table is also full of misspellings. Snuggles is a juggeler, Snugles is a jugler, and Snuggels is a jugular.

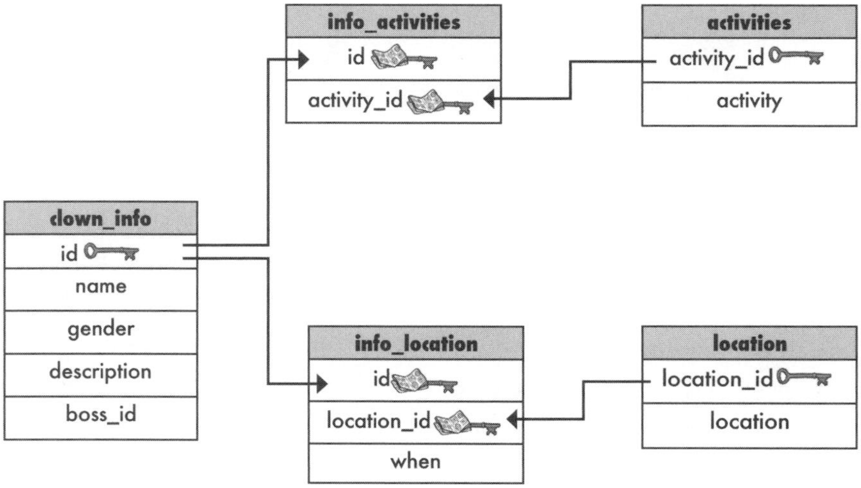

Avoiding errors in the clown tracking database

George quit before anyone noticed that he was sabotaging the data, and now we're left picking up the pieces. From now on, when we hire new people, we need to give them the ability to `SELECT` from the database so that they can identify clowns. But we want to keep them from `INSERTING` data. Or `UPDATING`. Or anything else until we've had time to do extensive background checks.

We'll also need to be careful; when we ask new employees to `DELETE` data to try to fix George's mistakes, they could end up deleting good data along with the bad.

It's time to protect the clown-tracking database before other clowns like George destroy it completely.

Sharpen your pencil

Protect the clown-tracking database from possible clown sabotage. On each side, write some queries that new employees should or should not be allowed to do. Include table names when possible.

New employees should be allowed to:

example: SELECT from activities

New employees should **not** be allowed to:

example: DROP TABLE on clown_info

Sharpen your pencil Solution

Protect the clown-tracking database from possible clown sabotage. On each side, write some queries that new employees should or should not be allowed to do. Include table names when possible.

New employees should be allowed to:

example: SELECT from activities

SELECT from clown_info, info_activities, activities, info_location, location

New employees should **not** be allowed to:

example: DROP TABLE on clown_info

DROP TABLE on clown_info, info_activities, activities, info_location, location

INSERT on clown_info, info_activities, activities, info_location, location

UPDATE on clown_info, info_activities, activities, info_location, location

ALTER on clown_info, info_activities, activities, info_location, location

DELETE on clown_info, info_activities, activities, info_location, location

There's good news, we *can* stop clowns like George from destroying our data!

SQL gives us the ability to control what our employees can and can't do to the clown-tracking database. Before we can, though, we need to give him, and everyone else who uses our database a **user account**.

Protect the root user account

Up to this point, we've only had one user in our database, and no password. Anyone with access to our terminal or graphical interface to our database has complete control over the database.

By default, the first user—the **root** user—has complete control over everything in the database. This is important, because the root user needs to be able to create user accounts for all other users. We don't want to limit what the root user can do, but we do want to give our root account a password. In MySQL, the command is simply:

```
SET PASSWORD FOR 'root'@'localhost' = PASSWORD('b4dcl0wnZ');
```

The username of our root user is simply 'root'.

'localhost' indicates that this is where the SQL software is installed and running.

This is the password we chose for our root user.

Other RDBMS techniques vary. Oracle uses:

```
alter user root identified by new-password;
```

If you're using a graphical interface to your database, you'll probably find a much easier dialog-driven way to change passwords. ***The important point is not so much* how *you do it, but that you definitely* should *do it.***

Consult RDBMS-specific documentation for information on protecting the root account.

there are no Dumb Questions

Q: I'm still not clear on what that "localhost" means. Can you explain in more detail?

A: `localhost` means that the computer you're using to run your queries is the same computer that your SQL RDBMS is installed on. `localhost` is the default value for this parameter, so including it is optional.

Q: But what I'm using an SQL client on a machine somewhere else.

A: This is known as remote access. You'll have to tell the query where the computer is. You can do that with an IP address or a hostname instead of localhost. For example, if your SQL software was installed on a machine called kumquats on the O'Reilly network, you might use something like `root@kumquats.oreilly.com`. But that's not a real SQL server, so of course it won't work.

Add a new user

Here's a question with an obvious answer for you:

How do you think SQL stores information about users?

In a table, of course! SQL keeps a database of data about itself. It includes user ids, usernames, passwords, and what each user is allowed to do to each database.

To create a new user, we can start with a username and a password. There's no actual SQL command to create a user, but most RDBMSs will use something like this:

Here's the user name for our newest employee, Elsie.

```
CREATE USER elsie
IDENTIFIED BY 'cl3v3rp4s5w0rd';
```

Here's her password

Watch it!

SQL does not specify how to manage users.

User creation varies from RDBMS to RDBMS. You need to check your documentation to find the correct way to create a user in your RDBMS.

Couldn't you have restricted Elsie from certain tables at the same time you created her account?

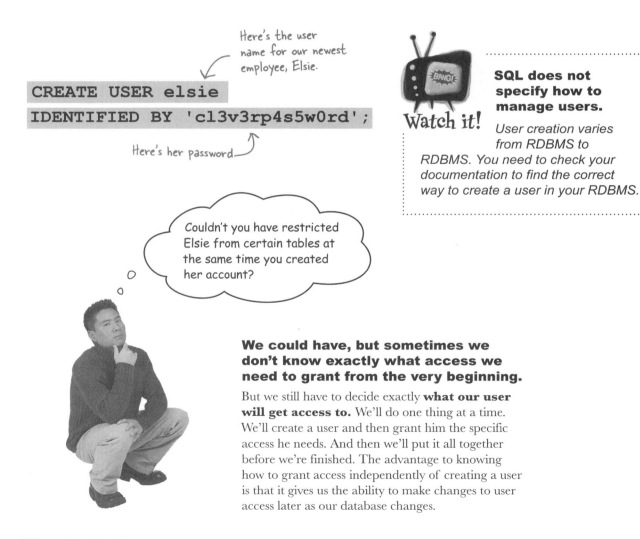

We could have, but sometimes we don't know exactly what access we need to grant from the very beginning.

But we still have to decide exactly **what our user will get access to.** We'll do one thing at a time. We'll create a user and then grant him the specific access he needs. And then we'll put it all together before we're finished. The advantage to knowing how to grant access independently of creating a user is that it gives us the ability to make changes to user access later as our database changes.

Decide exactly what the user needs

We've created Elsie's account. As it stands right now, she has no permission to do anything. We have to use a **GRANT** statement to ***give her permission*** to even `SELECT` from `clown_info`.

Unlike our root account, which has permission to run any SQL command on anything in the database, the new users we create have no permission. The `GRANT` statement can be used to give specific rights to users of our databases. Here's what the `GRANT` can allow us to do:

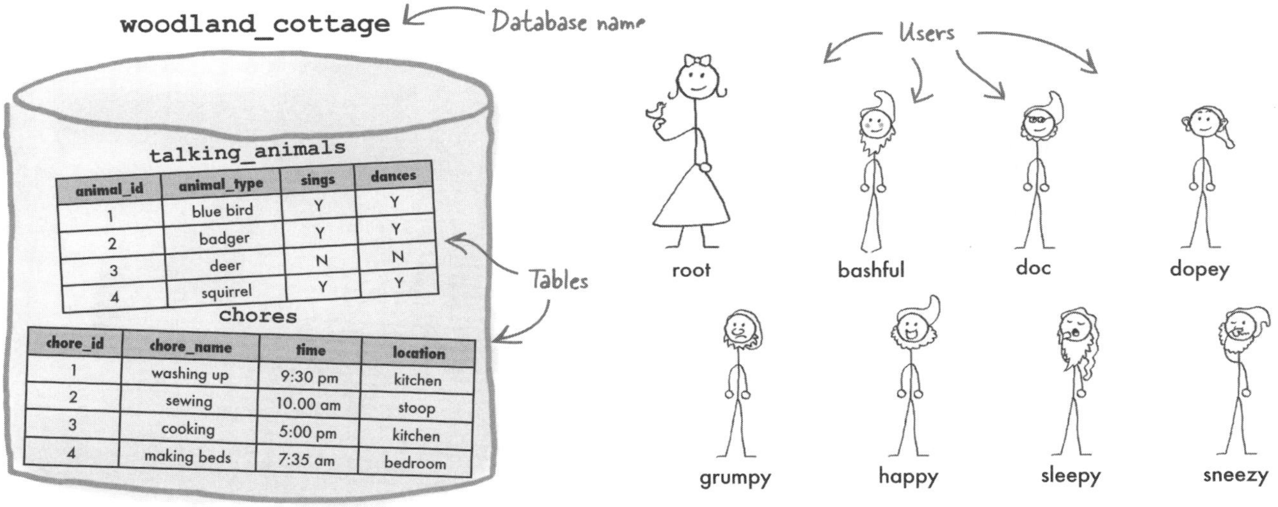

talking_animals

animal_id	animal_type	sings	dances
1	blue bird	Y	Y
2	badger	Y	Y
3	deer	N	N
4	squirrel	Y	Y

chores

chore_id	chore_name	time	location
1	washing up	9:30 pm	kitchen
2	sewing	10.00 am	stoop
3	cooking	5:00 pm	kitchen
4	making beds	7:35 am	bedroom

Only some users may modify particular tables.

Only the person in charge should be able to add new chores to the chores table. Only *root* can `INSERT`, `UPDATE`, and `DELETE` chores. However, *happy* is in charge of the `talking_animals` table and may `ALTER` the structure of it, as well as perform any other operations on it.

The data in a specific table may only be accessible to certain users.

Everyone except *grumpy* can `SELECT` from the `talking_animals` table. He doesn't like talking animals.

Even *within tables* there might need to be permissions: some users can see certain columns, but not others.

Everyone except *dopey* can see the instructions column in the chores table (it just confuses him).

You can control exactly what users can do to tables and columns with the GRANT statement.

A simple GRANT statement

We know that Elsie has no permission to do anything at this point. She can sign in to the SQL software using her username and password, but that's it. She needs to be able to SELECT from the clown_info table, so we can give her that **permission**. We need to GRANT permission TO Elsie. We'll use this statement:

User is granted permission to SELECT...

```
GRANT SELECT ON
clown_info
TO elsie;
```

...from the table we name here.

And the username we're granting the permission to is elsie.

Elsie also needs SELECT permission on the other clown-tracking tables so that she can use joins and subqueries in her SELECT statements. We need a separate GRANT statement for each table:

```
GRANT SELECT ON activities TO elsie;
GRANT SELECT ON location TO elsie;
GRANT SELECT ON info_activities TO elsie;
GRANT SELECT ON info_location TO elsie;
```

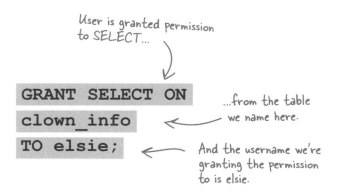

Now that we've got Elsie under control, try figuring out what these GRANT statements do to the woodland_cottage database you just saw on page 499.

The code	What does the code do?
1. `GRANT INSERT ON magic_animals TO doc;`	
2. `GRANT DELETE ON chores TO happy, sleepy;`	
3. `GRANT DELETE ON chores TO happy, sleepy WITH GRANT OPTION;`	
4. `GRANT SELECT(chore_name) ON chores TO dopey;` (Hint: It's a column name.)	
5. `GRANT SELECT, INSERT ON talking_animals TO sneezy;`	
6. `GRANT ALL ON talking_animals TO bashful;`	

Now try to write some of your own GRANT statements.

7.	Gives Doc permission to `SELECT` from chores.
8.	Gives Sleepy permission to `DELETE` from `talking_animals`, and it also gives Sleepy permission to `GRANT` the `DELETE` from `talking_animals` to anyone else.
9.	Gives ALL of the users all permissions on chores.
10.	This allows you to set the `SELECT` privilege for Doc all at once for every table in the `woodland_cottage` database.

Now that we've got Elsie under control, try figuring out what these GRANT statements do to the woodland_cottage database you just saw on page 499.

	The code	What does the code do?
1.	`GRANT INSERT ON magic_animals TO doc;`	Allows doc to INSERT into the magic_animals table.
2.	`GRANT DELETE ON chores TO happy, sleepy;`	Allows happy and sleepy to DELETE from the chores table.
3.	`GRANT DELETE ON chores TO happy, sleepy WITH GRANT OPTION;`	Allows happy and sleepy to DELETE from the chores table and give others the same permission.
4.	`GRANT SELECT(chore_name) ON chores TO dopey;`	Allows dopey to SELECT from just the chore_name column in the chores table.
5.	`GRANT SELECT, INSERT ON talking_animals TO sneezy;`	Allows sneezy to SELECT and INSERT into the talking_animals table.
6.	`GRANT ALL ON talking_animals TO bashful;`	Allows bashful to SELECT, UPDATE, INSERT and DELETE on the talking_animals table.

Now try to write some of your own GRANT statements.

7.	GRANT SELECT ON chores TO doc;	Gives Doc permission to `SELECT` from chores.
8.	GRANT DELETE ON talking_animals TO sleepy WITH GRANT OPTION;	Gives Sleepy permission to `DELETE` from `talking_animals`, and it also gives Sleepy permission to `GRANT` the `DELETE` from `talking_animals` to anyone else.
9.	GRANT ALL ON chores TO bashful, doc, dopey, grumpy, happy, sleepy, sneezy;	Gives ALL of the users all permissions on chores.
10.	GRANT SELECT ON woodland_cottage.* TO doc	This allows you to set the `SELECT` privilege for Doc all at once for every table in the `woodland_cottage` database.

GRANT variations

In the exercise you just did, you saw the major variations of the GRANT statement. Here they are:

1. **You can name multiple users in the same GRANT statement.**
   Each of the users named will get the same permission granted to them.

2. **WITH GRANT OPTION gives users permission to give other users the permission they were just given.**
   It sounds confusing, but it simply means that if the user was given a SELECT on chores, he can give any other user that same permission to do SELECTs on chores.

3. **A specific column, or columns, in a table can be used instead of the entire table.**
   The permission can be given to only SELECT from a single column. The only output the user will see will be from that column.

4. **You can specify more than one permission on a table.**
   Just list each permission you want to grant on a table using a comma after each.

5. **GRANT ALL gives users permission to SELECT, UPDATE, INSERT, and DELETE from the specified table.**
   It's simply a shorthand way of saying "give users permission to SELECT, UPDATE, INSERT, and DELETE from the specified table."

6. **You can specify every table in a database with database_name.***
   Much like you use the * wildcard in a SELECT statement, this specifies all the tables in a database.

REVOKE privileges

Suppose we decide to remove the SELECT privilege we gave to Elsie. To do that, we need the **REVOKE** statement.

Remember our simple GRANT statement? The REVOKE syntax is almost identical. Instead of the word "grant," it's "revoke," and instead of "to" we use "from."

We're removing the SELECT privilege.

```
REVOKE SELECT ON
clown_info
FROM elsie;
```

We revoke from a user instead of granting to.

You can also just revoke the WITH GRANT OPTION **but leave the privilege intact.** In this example, *happy* and *sleepy* can still DELETE things from the chores table, but they can't give anyone else that privilege any longer:

We're only removing the GRANT OPTION privilege.

```
REVOKE GRANT OPTION ON
DELETE ON chores
FROM happy, sleepy;
```

Users happy and sleepy can still DELETE, just not grant anyone else that privilege.

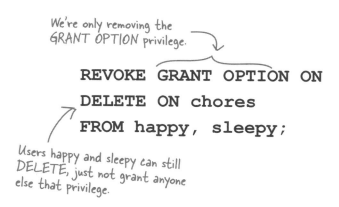

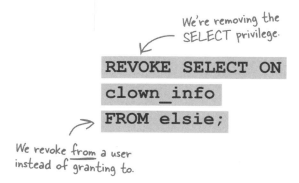

You do that, Jim, and I'll revoke all of your privileges for an entire month.

REVOKING a used GRANT OPTION

Consider this scenario. The root user gave *sleepy* DELETE privileges with GRANT OPTION on the chores table. Then *sleepy* gave *sneezy* DELETE privileges on chores, too.

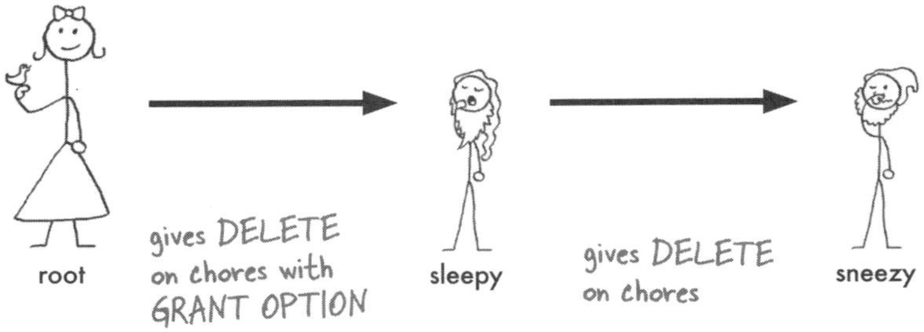
root
gives DELETE on chores with GRANT OPTION
sleepy
gives DELETE on chores
sneezy

Suppose the root user changes her mind and takes the privilege away from *sleepy*. It will also be revoked from *sneezy*, **even though she only revoked it from *sleepy***.

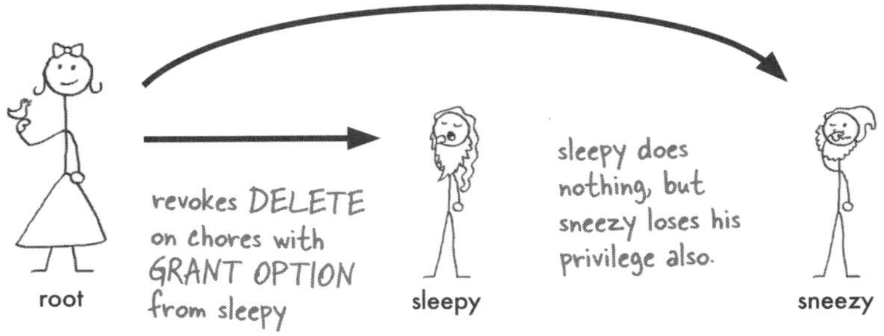
root
revokes DELETE on chores with GRANT OPTION from sleepy
sleepy
sleepy does nothing, but sneezy loses his privilege also.
sneezy

A side effect of the REVOKE statement was that *sneezy* also lost the privilege. There are two keywords you can use that will let you control what you want to happen when you're revoking.

BRAIN POWER

You're about to meet the keywords RESTRICT and CASCADE. What do you think each one does?

REVOKING with precision

There are two ways to revoke privileges and ensure that you're not affecting users other than the one you want to. You can use the keywords CASCADE and RESTRICT to target who keeps and who loses their privileges more precisely.

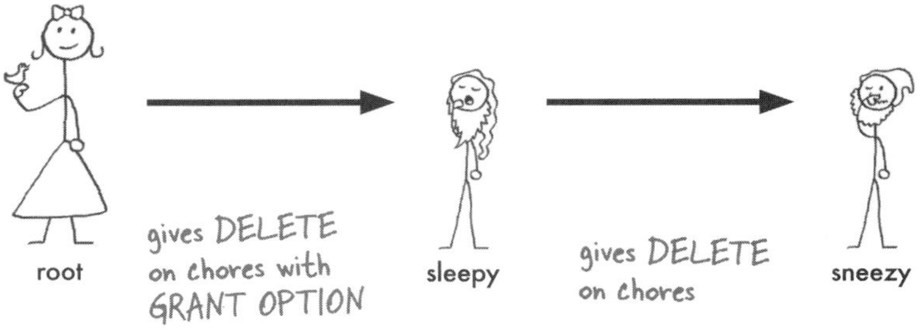
root
gives DELETE on chores with GRANT OPTION
sleepy
gives DELETE on chores
sneezy

The first, CASCADE, removes the privilege from the user you target (in this case, sleepy) as well as anyone else that that user gave permissions to.

```
REVOKE DELETE ON chores FROM sleepy CASCADE;
```

CASCADE means the revoke will affect anyone down the chain, as well as the original target.
root
revokes DELETE on chores with GRANT OPTION from sleepy.
sleepy
sleepy does nothing, but sneezy loses his privilege also.
sneezy

Using RESTRICT when you want to remove a privilege from a user will return an error if that user has granted privileges to anyone else.

```
REVOKE DELETE ON chores FROM sleepy RESTRICT;
```

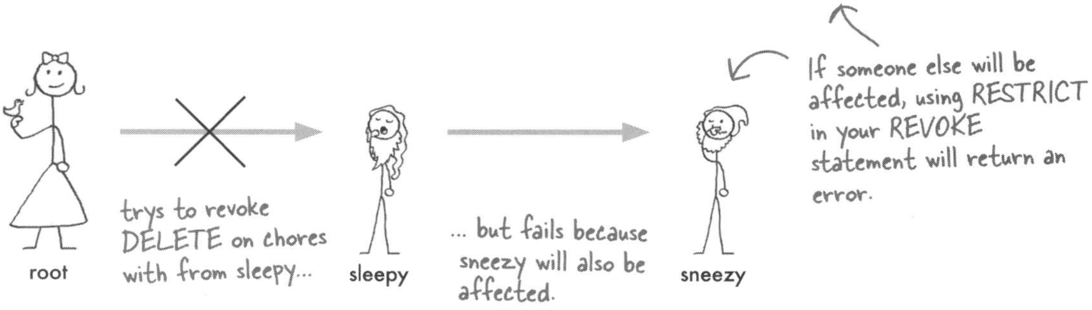
If someone else will be affected, using RESTRICT in your REVOKE statement will return an error.
root
trys to revoke DELETE on chores with from sleepy...
sleepy
... but fails because sneezy will also be affected.
sneezy

Both retain privileges, and *root* receives an error. She's stopped from making the change and gets an error because it will also have an effect on *sneezy*.

Sharpen your pencil

Someone keeps giving Elsie the wrong privileges. Write the appropriate REVOKE statements to return her to her safe SELECT-only status.

```
GRANT SELECT, INSERT, DELETE ON locations TO elsie;
```

....

```
GRANT ALL ON clown_info TO elsie;
```

....

```
GRANT SELECT, INSERT ON activities TO elsie;
```

....

```
GRANT DELETE, SELECT on info_location TO elsie
WITH GRANT OPTION;
```

....

```
GRANT INSERT(location), DELETE ON locations TO elsie;
```

....

Sharpen your pencil Solution

Someone keeps giving Elsie the wrong privileges. Write the appropriate REVOKE statements to return her to her safe SELECT-only status.

```
GRANT SELECT, INSERT, DELETE ON locations TO elsie;
```

REVOKE INSERT, UPDATE, DELETE ON locations FROM elsie;

```
GRANT ALL ON clown_info TO elsie;
```

REVOKE INSERT, UPDATE, DELETE ON clown_info FROM elsie;

We want to leave her with SELECT privileges, so we're not REVOKING everything.

```
GRANT SELECT, INSERT ON activities TO elsie;
```

REVOKE INSERT ON activities FROM elsie;

Another way you could have done these is to REVOKE everything and then GRANT what you need to.

```
GRANT DELETE, SELECT on info_location TO elsie
WITH GRANT OPTION;
```

REVOKE DELETE on info_location FROM elsie CASCADE;

```
GRANT INSERT(location), DELETE ON locations TO elsie;
```

REVOKE GRANT INSERT(location), DELETE ON locations FROM elsie;

Looks like we could also use a GRANT here to make sure she can still SELECT locations.

And we'd better make sure she hasn't given anyone else the same privileges she had.

there are no Dumb Questions

Q: I'm still thinking about GRANT statements that specify column names. What happens if you grant with INSERT on a single column of a table?

A: Good question. It's actually a pretty useless privilege to have. If you can only put a value into a single column, you can't insert an actual row into the table. The only way it can work is if the table only has the one column specified in the `GRANT`.

Q: Are there other GRANT statements that are just as useless?

A: Almost all privileges by column are pretty useless unless they are in conjunction with a SELECT in the `GRANT`.

Q: Suppose I want to add a user and let him SELECT from all of the tables in all of my databases. Is there an easy way to do that?

A: Like much in this chapter, it depends on your flavor of RDBMS. You can grant global privileges in MySQL like this:

```
GRANT SELECT ON *.*
TO elsie;
```

The first asterisk refers to all database, the second to all tables.

Q: So is CASCADE the default if you don't specify how you want to REVOKE?

A: Generally `CASCADE` is the default, but once again, check your RDBMS for specifics.

Q: What happens if I REVOKE something that the user didn't have to begin with?

A: You'll simply get an error telling you the GRANT didn't exist in the first place.

Q: What happens if two different people give the user *sneezy* the same privilege that *root* is revoking in the previous example?

A: That's when things start to get tricky. Some systems will not pay attention to where the `GRANT` came from when `CASCADE` is used, and some will ignore it. It's yet another case of checking the documentation on your particular software.

Q: Is there anything in addition to tables and columns that I can use GRANT and REVOKE with?

A: You can use them with views in exactly the same way you would a table, unless the view is non-updatable.In that case, you wouldn't be able to `INSERT` if you had permission to. And just like a table, you can grant access to specific columns in a view.

So if I want five different users to have the same permissions, I just add them all with commas at the end of the GRANT statements, right?

That will definitely work. And when you have a few users, that's definitely the way to go.

But as your organization grows, you'll start to have classes of users. You might have 10 people who are devoted to data entry, and only need to insert and select from certain tables. You might also have three power users who need to be able to do anything, and lots of users who just need to `SELECT`. You may even have software and web applications that connect to your database and need to query specific views in specific ways.

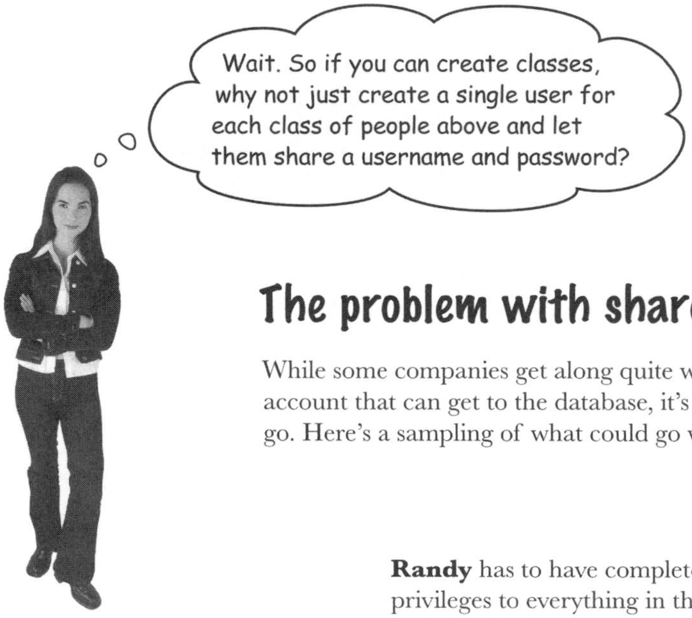
Wait. So if you can create classes, why not just create a single user for each class of people above and let them share a username and password?

The problem with shared accounts

While some companies get along quite well with a single user account that can get to the database, it's not the safest way to go. Here's a sampling of what could go wrong:

Randy has to have complete privileges to everything in the database to do his job. This makes the database vulnerable to other users who are not as knowledgeable about SQL and more prone to mistakes.

Simon changes the password and forgets to tell everyone else. No one can get into the database until he remembers to tell them.

Paula doesn't have a good grasp on how to write updates, and keeps messing up data. Nobody knows who is messing up the data, so no one can help her learn how to do it right.

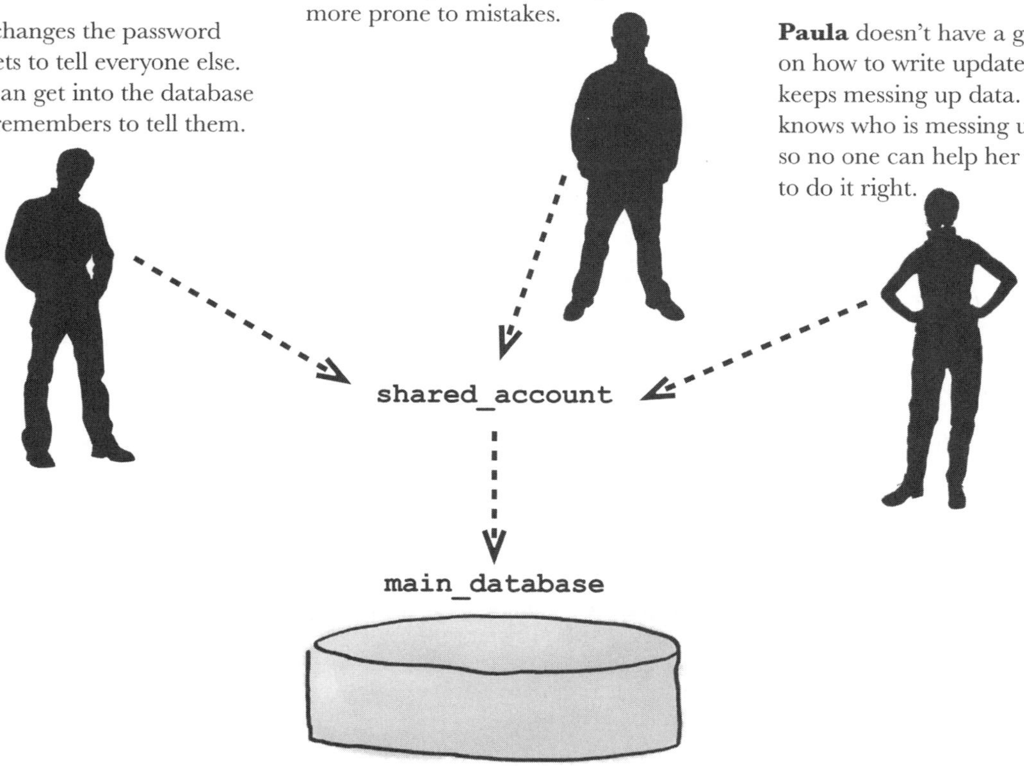
shared_account
main_database

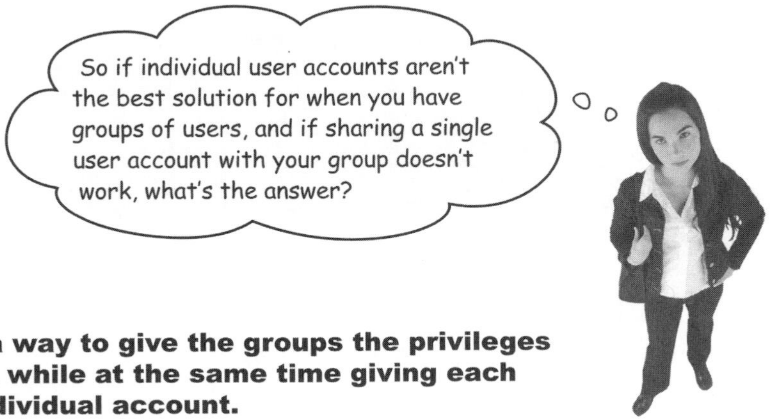

So if individual user accounts aren't the best solution for when you have groups of users, and if sharing a single user account with your group doesn't work, what's the answer?

You need a way to give the groups the privileges they need, while at the same time giving each user an individual account.

What you need are **roles**. A role is a way you can group together specific privileges, and apply those to everyone in a group. Your role becomes an object in your database that you can change as needed when your database changes, without having to explicitly change every single user's privileges to reflect the database changes.

And setting up a role is really simple:

```
CREATE ROLE data_entry;
```

The name of the role we're creating

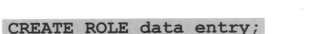

Watch it!

There are no roles in MySQL.

Roles are a feature that a future version of MySQL will probably have, but for now, you'll have to assign your privileges on a single user basis.

To add privileges to the role, you simply treat it as you would a username:

```
GRANT SELECT, INSERT ON some_table TO data_entry;
```

Instead of a user, we use the role name when we assign privileges.

We've created our role and given it privileges. Now we need to assign it to someone...

Using your role

Before creating our role, we could have given our data-entry users privileges directly using the GRANT statements, like so:

```
GRANT SELECT, INSERT
ON talking_animals
TO doc;
```

The old way.

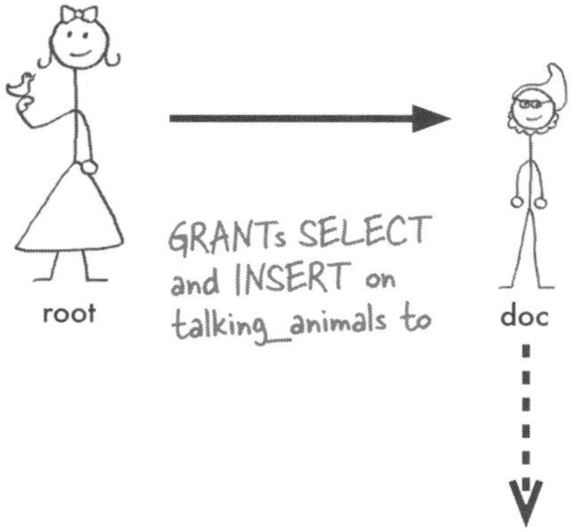

talking_animals

animal_id	animal_type	sings	dances
1	blue bird	Y	Y
2	badger	Y	Y
3	deer	N	N
4	squirrel	Y	Y

Now all we need to do is substitute the GRANT operation for our new role and apply it to *doc*. We don't need to mention the privileges or table because that's all stored in the data_entry role:

```
GRANT data_entry TO doc;
```

The role name takes the place of the table name and privileges.

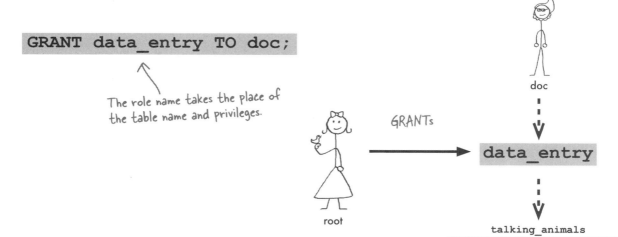

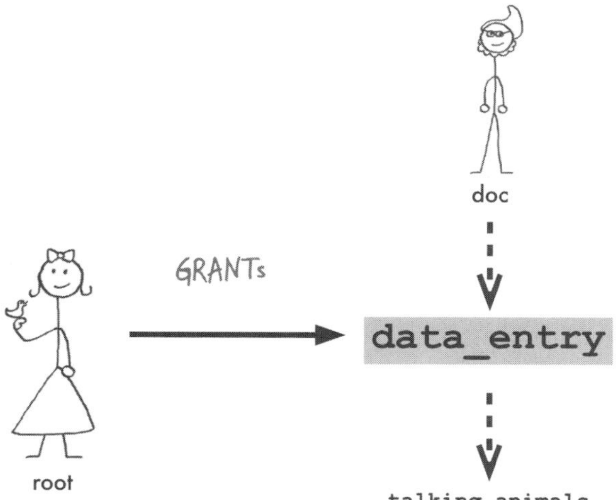

talking_animals

animal_id	animal_type	sings	dances
1	blue bird	Y	Y
2	badger	Y	Y
3	deer	N	N
4	squirrel	Y	Y

Role dropping

When you no longer need your role, there's no reason to keep it around. Use a DROP statement to get rid of it:

```
DROP ROLE data_entry;
```

there are no Dumb Questions

Q: What if I want to grant privileges for all the tables in a database? Do I have to type each one?

A: No, you can use this syntax:

```
GRANT SELECT, INSERT, DELETE
ON gregs_list.*
TO jim;
```

Just name the database and use the * to assign the privileges to all the tables in that database.

Q: If a role is assigned to a user, can you still drop it?

A: You can drop roles that are in use. Be very careful when dropping a role that you don't cut users off from the permissions that they need.

Q: That means that if a user has a role that is then dropped, he loses those permissions?

A: That's exactly right. It's as though you had explicitly granted him those permissions and then revoked them. Only instead of affecting a single user when you revoke FROM someone, you will have an effect on the permissions of all users assigned a role.

Q: Can a user have more than one role at a time?

A: Yes. Just make sure they don't have conflicting permissions, or you might cause yourself some problems. The denied permissions take precedence over the granted ones.

Sharpen your pencil

Revoking your role

Revoking a role works much like revoking a grant. See if you can write the statement to revoke data_entry from Doc ***without looking back in the chapter***.

Sharpen your pencil Solution

Revoking a role works much like revoking a grant. See if you can write the statement to revoke data_entry from Doc ***without looking back in the chapter***.

```
REVOKE data_entry FROM doc;
```

Using your role WITH ADMIN OPTION

Just like the `GRANT` statement has `WITH GRANT OPTION`, a role has the similar `WITH ADMIN OPTION`. This option allows anyone with that role to grant that role to anyone else. For example, if we use this statement:

```
GRANT data_entry TO doc WITH ADMIN OPTION;
```

WITH ADMIN OPTION allows user doc to grant the role of data_entry to anyone else.

doc now has admin privileges, and he can grant *happy* the `data_entry` role the same way it was granted to him:

```
GRANT data_entry TO happy;
```

When used with a role, the `REVOKE` command has the same keywords `CASCADE` and `RESTRICT`. Let's take a look at how they work:

REVOKE role with CASCADE

Used with `CASCADE`, the `REVOKE` affects everyone down the chain as well as the original target:

```
REVOKE data_entry FROM doc CASCADE;
```

Used with CASCADE, the revoke will affect anyone down the chain, as well as the original target.

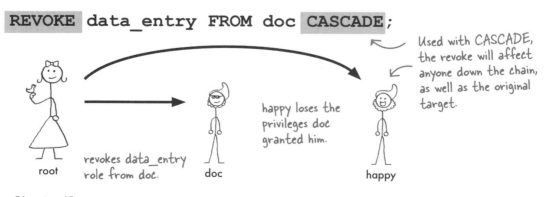

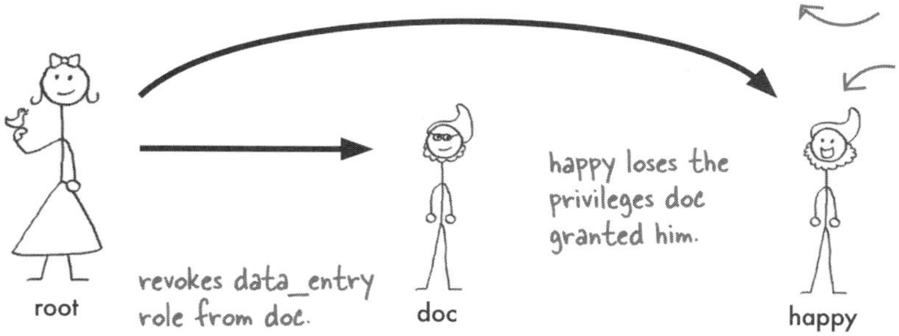
root
revokes data_entry role from doc.
doc
happy loses the privileges doc granted him.
happy

REVOKE role with RESTRICT

Using `RESTRICT` when you want to remove a privilege from a user will return an error if that user has granted privileges to anyone else.

```
REVOKE data_entry FROM doc RESTRICT;
```

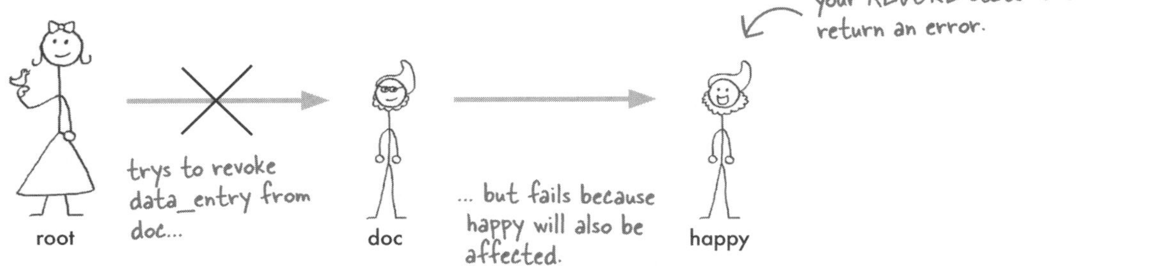
If someone else will be affected, using RESTRICT in your REVOKE statement will return an error.
root
trys to revoke data_entry from doc...
doc
... but fails because happy will also be affected.
happy

Both retain privileges, and *root* receives an error. She's stopped from making the change because it will also have an effect on user *happy*.

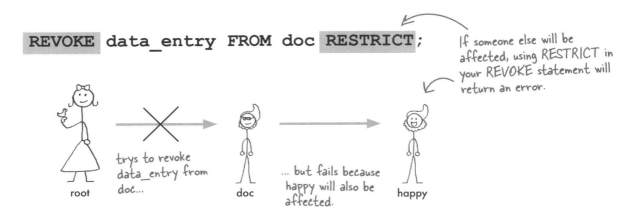

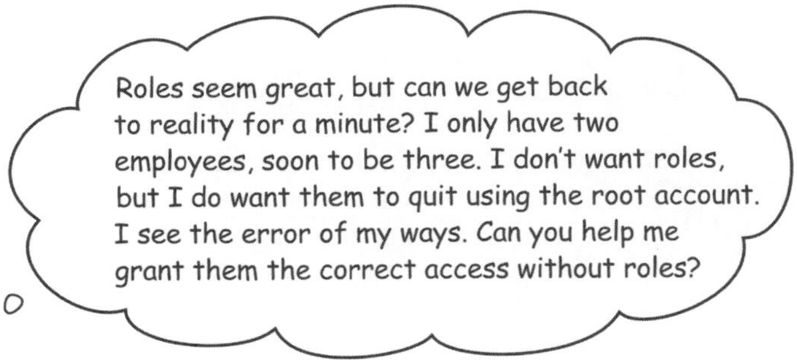
Roles seem great, but can we get back to reality for a minute? I only have two employees, soon to be three. I don't want roles, but I do want them to quit using the root account. I see the error of my ways. Can you help me grant them the correct access without roles?

Yes, it's time to get Greg's employees set up to use gregs_list more securely.

Greg will need to go through the steps in this chapter and protect the root account, figure out what his employees need, and give them the correct privileges.

Lucky you, you get to BE Greg...

BE Greg

Your job is to play Greg one last time and fix up the user side of his database so his employees can't accidentally mess things up.

Read the descriptions of the jobs for each user and come up with multiple GRANT statements that give them the data they need while not letting them access anything they shouldn't.

Frank: "I'm responsible for finding job matches for prospective job openings. I never enter anything in the database, although I do delete job listings when I find matches or the opening is filled. I sometimes need to look up contact info in `my_contacts` as well."

Jim: "I enter all the new data into the entire database. I've gotten really good at inserting, now that I can't accidentally enter an X for gender. I also update data. I'm learning to delete, but so far Greg tells me not to. Of course, what he doesn't know..."

Joe: "I was just hired by Greg to manage the matchmaking side of things. He wants to integrate his contact info into a web site. I'm more a web developer than an SQL guy, but I can do simple selects. I don't do inserts. Or Windows. Sorry, bad joke."

Take a look at the gregs_list database and give these guys some GRANTs before they damage some data.

Write the command to give the user currently known as "root" a password.

....

Write three commands to create user accounts for each of the three employees.

....

....

....

Write GRANT statements for each new employee to give him the correct permissions.

....

....

....

....

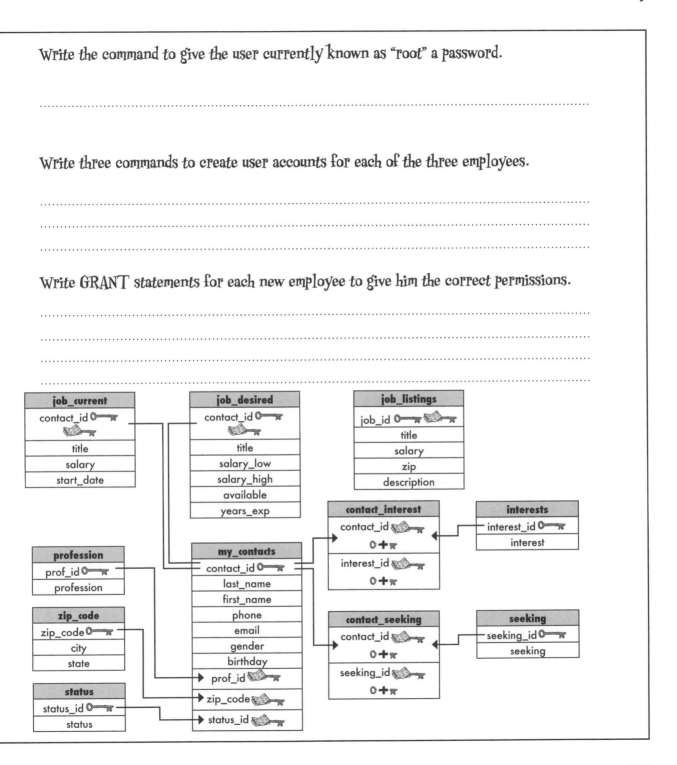

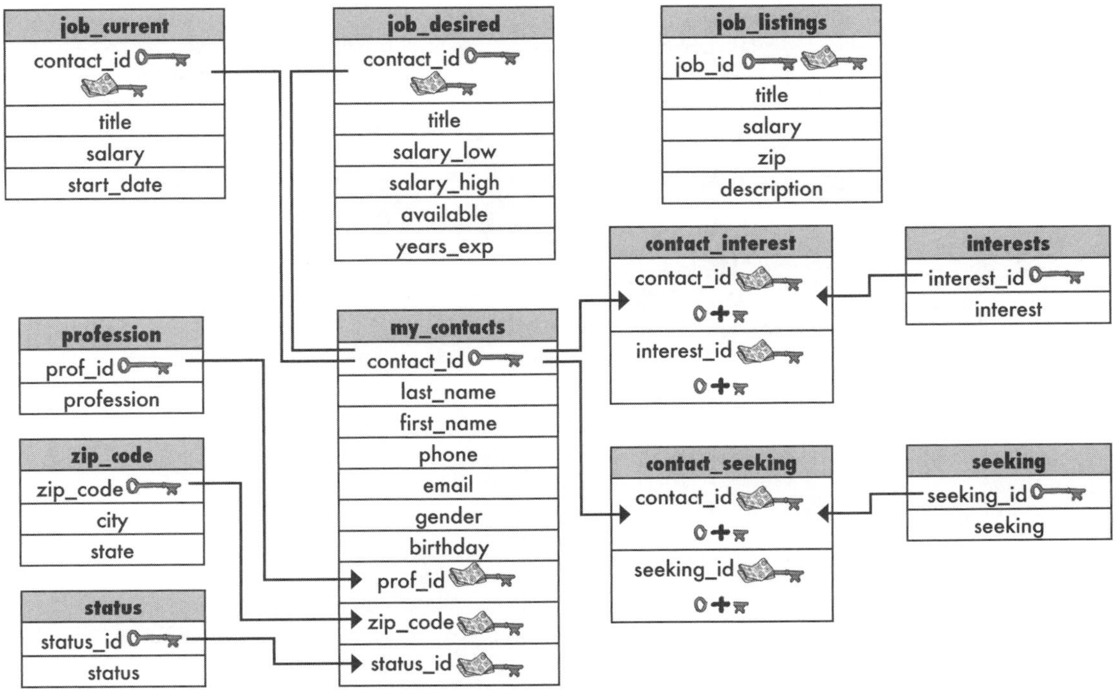

BE Greg SOLUTION

Your job is to play Greg one last time and fix up the user side of his database so his employees can't accidentally mess things up.

Read the descriptions of the jobs for each user and come up with multiple GRANT statements that give them the data they need while not letting them access anything they shouldn't.

Write the command to give the user currently known as "root" a password.

```
SET PASSWORD FOR root@localhost = PASSWORD('gr3GRulz');
```

Write three commands to create user accounts for each of the three employees.

```
CREATE USER frank IDENTIFIED BY 'jObM4teH';
CREATE USER jim IDENTIFIED BY 'NOmOr3Xs';
CREATE USER joe IDENTIFIED BY 's3LeCTdOOd';
```

Don't worry if your passwords are different. As long as you got the correct pieces of the commands in the right order, you're good to go!

Write GRANT statements for each new employee to give him the correct permissions.

```
GRANT DELETE ON job_listings TO frank;
GRANT SELECT ON my_contacts * TO frank;
```

Frank needs to be able to remove job listings and look up (select) from my_contacts.

```
GRANT SELECT, INSERT ON gregs_list * TO jim;
```

Jim needs access to the SELECT and INSERT from the whole of gregs_list. For now, we'll keep him away from DELETE.

```
GRANT SELECT ON my_contacts, profession, zip_code, status,
contact_interest, interests, contact_seeking, seeking TO joe;
```

Meanwhile Joe needs to be able to select from all the original tables, but not the tables that deal with jobs.

Combining CREATE USER and GRANT

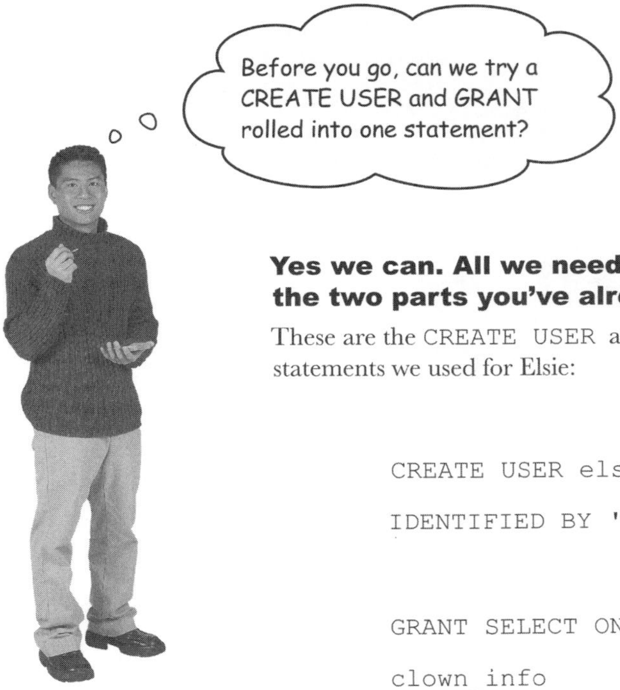
Before you go, can we try a CREATE USER and GRANT rolled into one statement?

Yes we can. All we need is to combine the two parts you've already seen.

These are the `CREATE USER` and `GRANT` statements we used for Elsie:

```
CREATE USER elsie
IDENTIFIED BY 'cl3v3rp4s5w0rd';

GRANT SELECT ON
clown_info
TO elsie;
```

We can combine them and leave out the `CREATE USER` part. Because the user *elsie* has to be created before she can have privileges granted to her, your RDBMS checks to see if she exists, and if not, it automatically creates her account.

```
GRANT SELECT ON
clown_info
TO elsie
IDENTIFIED BY 'cl3v3rp4s5w0rd';
```

Greg's List has gone global!

Thanks to all your help, Greg is now so comfortable with using SQL—and teaching Jim, Frank, and Joe how to use it—that he's expanded Greg's List to include to include local classified advertisements and forums as well.

And the best news of all? It's been such a success in Dataville that over 500 cities worldwide now have their own Greg's Lists, and Greg is front-page news!

Thanks guys, I couldn't have done it without you! Hey, I've got a franchise available in your city... Let's talk Greg's Lists!

THE WEEKLY

INQUERYER

The Rise and Rise of Greg's List

Franchises and Forums

Friends and relatives say fame hasn't changed Greg a bit.

By Troy Armstrong
INQUERYER STAFF WRITER

DATAVILLE – Local entrepreneur Greg has made it to the big time. His networking database grew from sticky notes, to a simple table, to a multi-table database that offers match-making, jobs, and much more.

If you'd like to join in the fun, visit:

www.gregs-list.net

to test your SQL skills. If you want to talk inner joins, transactions, and privileges with like-minded individuals, look no further than the SQL forum which can be found right here:

www.headfirstlabs.com

But most of all, you crazy SQL cats, have fun out there!

Has Greg's List reached your town yet? It's only a matter of time, say city data analysts

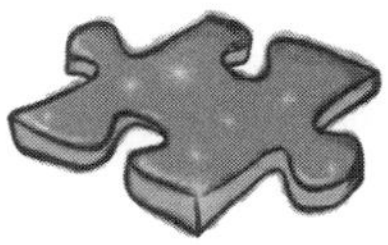

(the last) SQL Cross

Yes, it's a sad day, you're looking at the last crossword in the book. Take a deep breath, we've crammed this one full of keywords and commands to make it last longer. Enjoy!

Across

1. _____ _____ gives users permission to SELECT, UPDATE, INSERT, and DELETE from the specified table.

3. This function returns each unique value only once, with no duplicates.

6. _____tables won't have duplicate data, which will reduce the size of your database.

7. Granting a role WITH _____ OPTION allows a user ito grant the role to someone else.

11. _____PASSWORD FOR 'root'@'localhost' = PASSWORD('b4dcl0wnZ');

13. Values stored in CHAR or VARCHAR columns are known as these.

16. Using _____ when you want to remove a privilege from a user will return an error if that user has granted privileges to anyone else.

17. With an inner join, you're comparing rows from two tables, but the _____ of those two tables doesn't matter.

18. We can use a _____-join to simulate having two tables.

20. If changing any of the non-key columns might cause any of the other columns to change, you have a transitive _____.

23. If the subquery stands alone and doesn't reference anything from the outer query, it is a _____ subquery.

24. This means that your data has been broken down into the smallest pieces of data that can't or shouldn't be divided.

25. To help you decide what steps in your SQL can be considered a transaction, remember the acronym _____.

26. A _____ OUTER JOIN takes all the rows in the left table and matches them to rows in the RIGHT table.

27. A _____ subquery means that the inner query relies on the outer query before it can be resolved.

Down

1. You can control exactly what users can do to tables and columns with the _____ statement

2. A _____ functional dependency means that a non-key column is related to any of the other non-key columns.

4. You can only have one AUTO_ INCREMENT field per table, it has to be an _____ data type.

5. A _____ KEY is a PRIMARY KEY composed of multiple columns, creating a unique key.

8. You can find the largest value in a column with this function.

9. Assigning this is a way you can group together specific privileges, and apply those to everyone in a group.

10. Use these two words to alphabetically order your results based on a column you specify.

12. The non-equijoin returns any rows that are not _____.

13. Use this clause in your update statement to change a value.

14. A self-_____ foreign key is the primary key of a table used in that same table for another purpose.

15. During a _____, if all the steps can't be completed without interference, none of them should be completed.

19. A subquery is always a single _____ statement.

21. These joins only work if the column you're joining by has the same name in both tables.

22. A _____ constraint restricts what values you can insert into a column.

24. Our table can be given new columns with the ALTER statement and _____ COLUMN clause.

CHAPTER 12

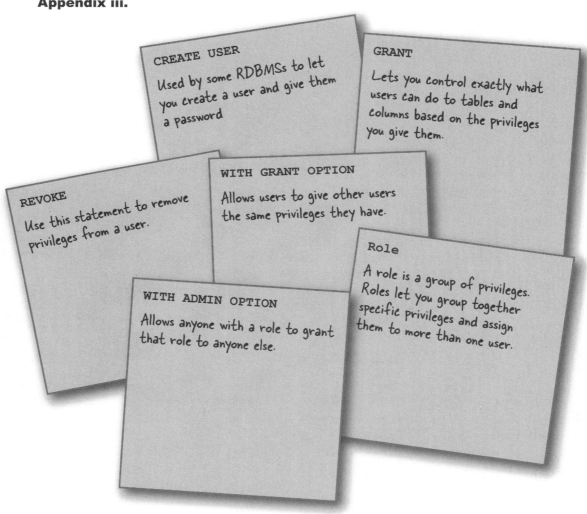

Your SQL Toolbox

Congratulations, you've completed Chapter 12! Take a minute and review the SQL security principles we just covered. For a complete list of tooltips in the book, see Appendix iii.

CREATE USER

Used by some RDBMSs to let you create a user and give them a password

GRANT

Lets you control exactly what users can do to tables and columns based on the privileges you give them.

REVOKE

Use this statement to remove privileges from a user.

WITH GRANT OPTION

Allows users to give other users the same privileges they have.

Role

A role is a group of privileges. Roles let you group together specific privileges and assign them to more than one user.

WITH ADMIN OPTION

Allows anyone with a role to grant that role to anyone else.

(the last) SQL Cross Solution

```
          ¹G R A N ²T A L L      ³D I S T ⁴I N C T
              R       R                   N
⁵C    ⁶N O R M A L    ⁷A D ⁸M I N         T
 O        N       ⁹R  N     A      ¹⁰O    E
 M      ¹¹S ¹²E T     O     S   ¹³S T R I N G S
 P      ¹⁴R  Q       L     I      E       E       ¹⁵T
 O       E   U    ¹⁶R E S T R I C T   ¹⁷O R D E R A
¹⁸S E L F F   A       I            R           N
 I       E   L    ¹⁹S  V            B           S
 T       R  ²⁰D E P E N ²¹N D E N ²²C Y         A
 E       E        L     A        H              T
      ²³N O N C O R R E L A T E D E  ²⁴A T O M I C
         C        C     U    ²⁵A C I D          T
         I     ²⁶L E F T R    K    D            I
         N              R                       O
         G    ²⁷C O R R E L A T E D             N
```

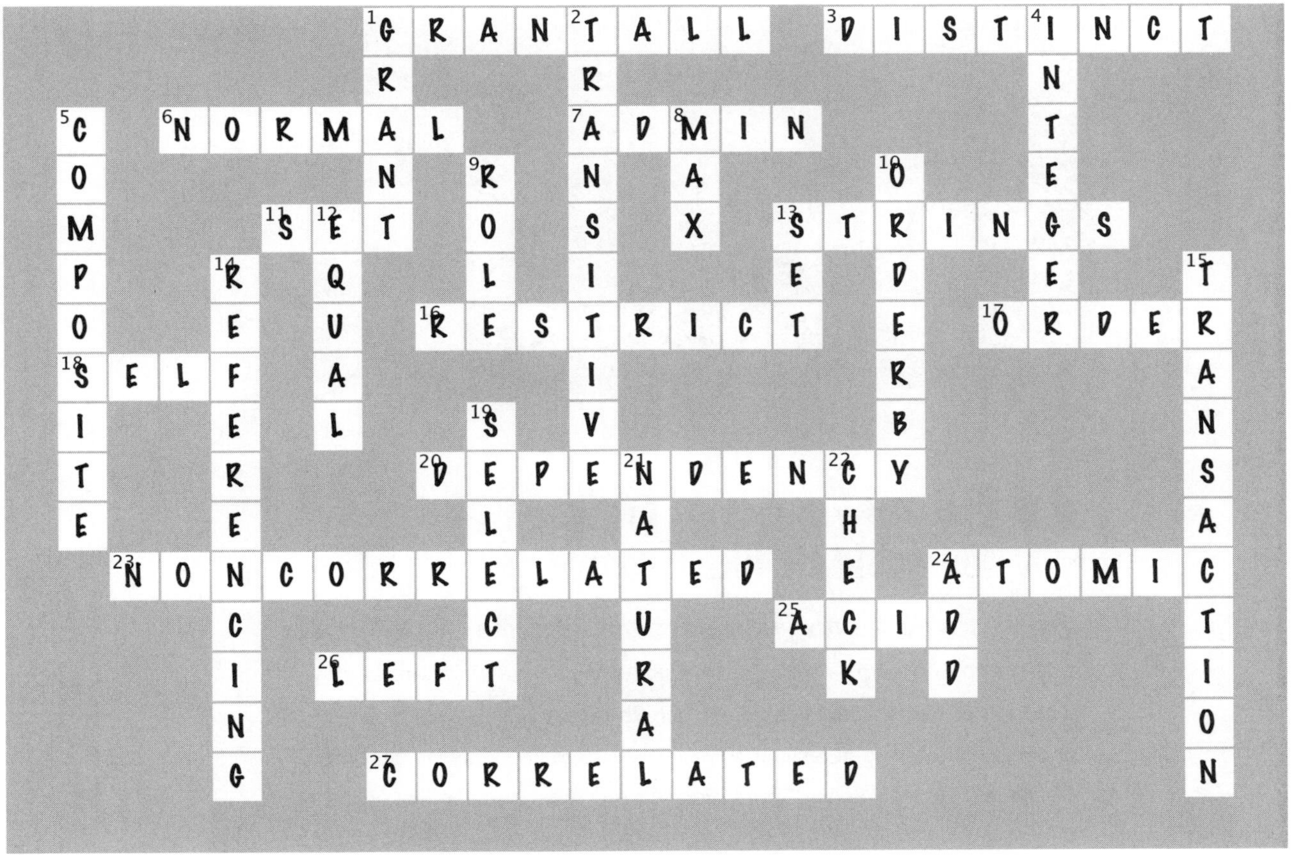

How about a Greg's List in your city?

Wow. A Super Bowl commercial for Greg's List. It's been a long journey, but look at me now!

Use SQL on your own projects, and you too could be like Greg!

We've loved having you here in Dataville. And we're sad to see you go, but there's nothing like *taking what you've learned* and **putting it to use in your own databases**—we're sure there are clowns that need tracking, or doughnuts that need testing, or [insert your name here]'s Lists that need creating wherever you are. There are still a few more gems for you in the back of the book, an index to read through, and then it's time to take all these new ideas and put them into practice. We're dying to hear how things go, so ***drop us a line*** at the Head First Labs web site, **www.headfirstlabs.com**, and let us know how SQL is paying off for **YOU**!

appendix i: leftovers

The Top Ten Topics (we didn't cover)

Even after all that, there's a bit more. There are just a few more things we think you need to know. We wouldn't feel right about ignoring them, even though they only need a brief mention. So before you put the book down, take a read through these **short but important SQL tidbits**. Besides, once you're done here, all that's left is another two appendixes... and the index... and maybe some ads... and then you're really done. We promise!

#1. Get a GUI for your RDBMS

While it's important to be able to code your SQL directly into a console, you know what you're doing now. You deserve an easier way to create your tables and see the contents of them.

Every RDBMS has some sort of graphical user interface associated with it. Here's a brief rundown of the GUI tools available for MySQL.

MySQL GUI tools

When you download MySQL, you can also download the MySQL GUI tools, and most importantly, MySQL Administrator. You can get the bundle directly from this page:

`http://dev.mysql.com/downloads/gui-tools/5.0.html`

It's available for Windows, Mac, and Linux. The MySQL Administrator allows you to easily view, create, and modify your databses and tables.

You'll also like the MySQL Query Browser. There, you can type your queries and see the results inside the software interface, rather than in a console window.

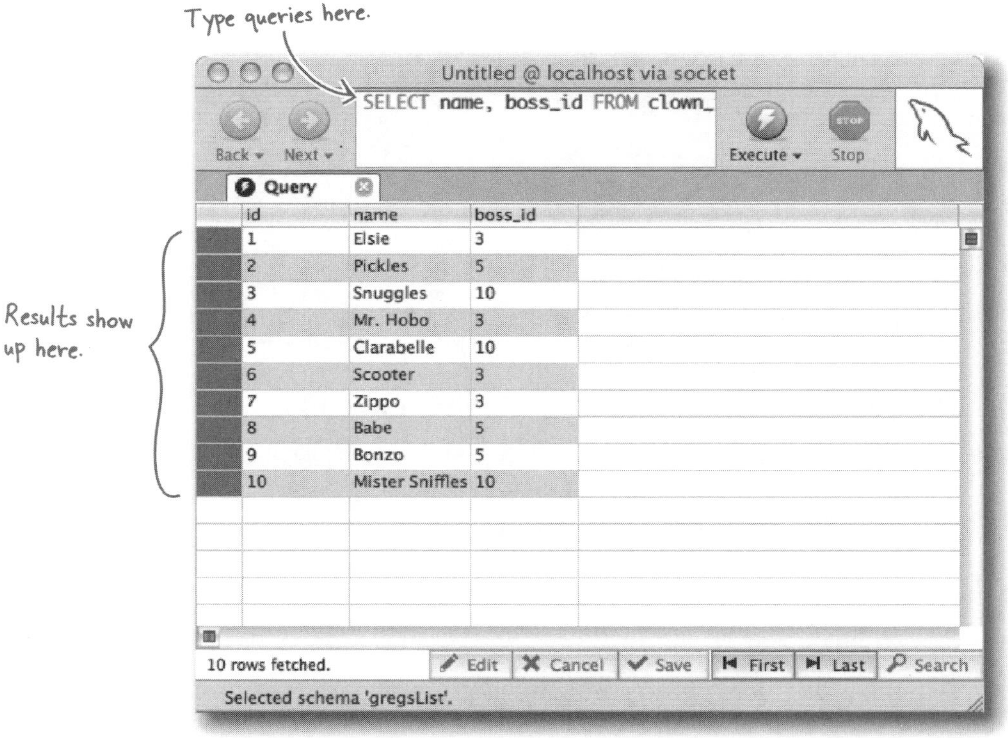

Other GUI tools

There are quite a few other options out there. We'll leave it to you to pick the one you like best from these. There are many more not mentioned here, which you can easily find by doing a web search.

For Mac, you might try CocoaMySQL:

`http://cocoamysql.sourceforge.net/`

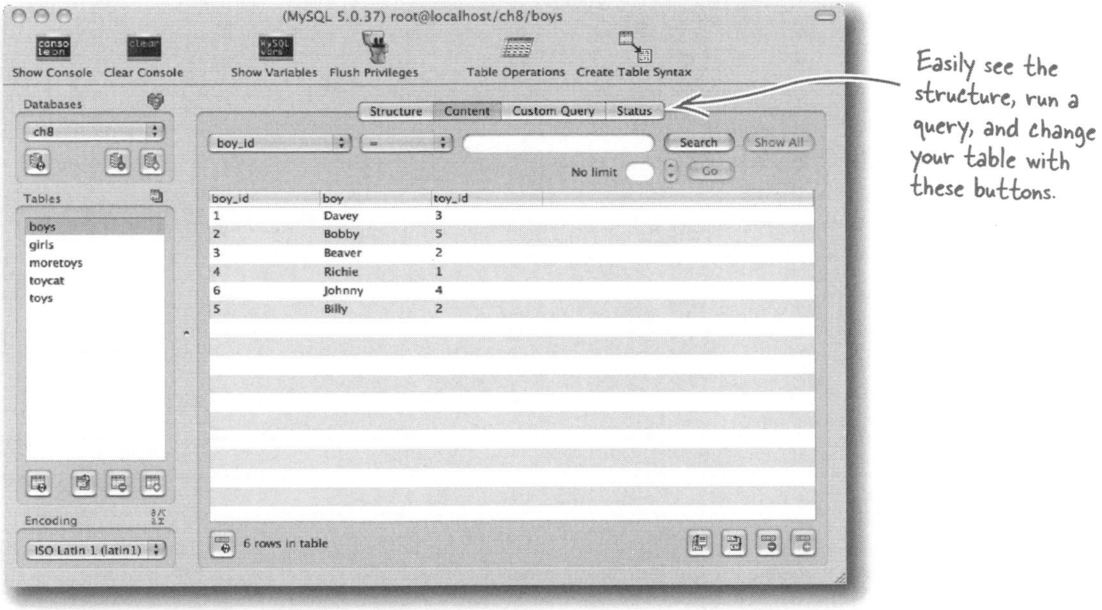

If you need a web-based solution, try phpMyAdmin. This works well if you are using a web hosting account with MySQL on a remote web server. It's not so good if you are using your local machine. More information can be found here:

`http://www.phpmyadmin.net/`

Here are a few more commonly used tools. Some are for PC only; your best bet is to visit the sites and read their latest release information to find out if they'll work for you:

Navicat offers a 30 day free trial here:

`http://www.navicat.com/`

SQLyog offers a free Community Edition here:

`http://www.webyog.com/en/`

#2. Reserved Words and Special Characters

The SQL language consists of quite a few reserved keywords. It's best to leave those words out of your database, table, and column names altogether. Even though you might like to name your new table "select", try to come up with something more descriptive, which doesn't use the word "select" at all. If you must use a reserved keyword, try to use it with other words and underscores so as not to confuse your RDBMS. For your convenience, on the righthand page is a list of those reserved words you'll want to avoid in your names:

To further complicate matters, SQL has a list of non-reserved words that may become reserved in future releases of SQL. We won't list those here, but you can find them in that RDBMS-specific reference book you should buy when you finish with this book.

Special Characters

Here's a list of most of the characters SQL uses and what they're used for. As with the reserved words, it's best to avoid using these in your names, with the exception of the underscore (_), which we encourage you to use in your names. In general, it's best to avoid anything except letters and underscores in your table names. And numbers aren't a great idea either, unless they are descriptive in some way.

*	Returns all the columns in a table from a SELECT statement.
()	Used to group expressions, specify the order in which to perform math operations, and to make function calls. Also used to contain subqueries.
;	Terminates your SQL statements.
,	Separates list items. Uses include the INSERT statement and the IN clause.
.	Used to reference names of tables and used in decimal numbers.
_	This is a wildcard that represents a single character in a LIKE clause.
%	Another LIKE clause wildcard, this one stands in for multiple characters.
!	The exclamation point stands for NOT. It's used with comparisons in the WHERE clause.
'	A pair of single quotes tells SQL that a string value is between them.
"	You can also use a pair of double quotes the same way, although it's better form to stick with single quotes.
\	This is used to allow you to put a single quote into a text column of your table.
+	In addition to using it for addition, you can also use the plus sign to join or concatenate two strings.

These are only wildcards when used with LIKE.

Here's a quick look at the mathematical operators:

+	Addition	+	Subtraction	*	*Between two values*, the asterisk acts as a multiplication symbol	+	Division

And the comparison operators:

>	Greater than	!>	Not greater than	>=	Greater than or equal to
<	Less than	!>	Not less than	>=	Less than or equal to
=	Equal to	<>	Not equal to	!=	Not equal to

&	|	^	~
Not covered in this book. Check your RDBMS's manual for info.			

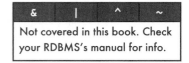

Reserved Words

It's a good idea to glance through these whenever you're giving something a single-word name to make sure you aren't using one of them.

A	ABSOLUTE ACTION ADD ADMIN AFTER AGGREGATE ALIAS ALL ALLOCATE ALTER AND ANY ARE ARRAY AS ASC ASSERTION AT AUTHORIZATION
B	BEFORE BEGIN BINARY BIT BLOB BOOLEAN BOTH BREADTH BY
C	CALL CASCADE CASCADED CASE CAST CATALOG CHAR CHARACTER CHECK CLASS CLOB CLOSE COLLATE COLLATION COLUMN COMMIT COMPLETION CONNECT CONNECTION CONSTRAINT CONSTRAINTS CONSTRUCTOR CONTINUE CORRESPONDING CREATE CROSS CUBE CURRENT CURRENT_DATE CURRENT_PATH CURRENT_ROLE CURRENT_TIME CURRENT_TIMESTAMP CURRENT_USER CURSOR CYCLE
D	DATA DATE DAY DEALLOCATE DEC DECIMAL DECLARE DEFAULT DEFERRABLE DEFERRED DELETE DEPTH DEREF DESC DESCRIBE DESCRIPTOR DESTROY DESTRUCTOR DETERMINISTIC DICTIONARY DIAGNOSTICS DISCONNECT DISTINCT DOMAIN DOUBLE DROP DYNAMIC
E	EACH ELSE END END_EXEC EQUALS ESCAPE EVERY EXCEPT EXCEPTION EXEC EXECUTE EXTERNAL
F	FALSE FETCH FIRST FLOAT FOR FOREIGN FOUND FROM FREE FULL FUNCTION
G	GENERAL GET GLOBAL GO GOTO GRANT GROUP GROUPING
H	HAVING HOST HOUR
I	IDENTITY IGNORE IMMEDIATE IN INDICATOR INITIALIZE INITIALLY INNER INOUT INPUT INSERT INT INTEGER INTERSECT INTERVAL INTO IS ISOLATION ITERATE
J	JOIN
K	KEY
L	LANGUAGE LARGE LAST LATERAL LEADING LEFT LESS LEVEL LIKE LIMIT LOCAL LOCALTIME LOCALTIMESTAMP LOCATOR
M	MAP MATCH MINUTE MODIFIES MODIFY MODULE MONTH
N	NAMES NATIONAL NATURAL NCHAR NCLOB NEW NEXT NO NONE NOT NULL NUMERIC
O	OBJECT OF OFF OLD ON ONLY OPEN OPERATION OPTION OR ORDER ORDINALITY OUT OUTER OUTPUT
P	PAD PARAMETER PARAMETERS PARTIAL PATH POSTFIX PRECISION PREFIX PREORDER PREPARE PRESERVE PRIMARY PRIOR PRIVILEGES PROCEDURE PUBLIC
Q	
R	READ READS REAL RECURSIVE REF REFERENCES REFERENCING RELATIVE RESTRICT RESULT RETURN RETURNS REVOKE RIGHT ROLE ROLLBACK ROLLUP ROUTINE ROW ROWS
S	SAVEPOINT SCHEMA SCROLL SCOPE SEARCH SECOND SECTION SELECT SEQUENCE SESSION SESSION_USER SET SETS SIZE SMALLINT SOME SPACE SPECIFIC SPECIFICTYPE SQL SQLEXCEPTION SQLSTATE SQLWARNING START STATE STATEMENT STATIC STRUCTURE SYSTEM_USER
T	TABLE TEMPORARY TERMINATE THAN THEN TIME TIMESTAMP TIMEZONE_HOUR TIMEZONE_MINUTE TO TRAILING TRANSACTION TRANSLATION TREAT TRIGGER TRUE
U	UNDER UNION UNIQUE UNKNOWN UNNEST UPDATE USAGE USER USING
V	VALUE VALUES VARCHAR VARIABLE VARYING VIEW
W	WHEN WHENEVER WHERE WITH WITHOUT WORK WRITE
X	
Y	YEAR
Z	ZONE

#3. ALL, ANY, and SOME

restaurant_ratings

name	rating
Pizza House	3
The Shack	7
Arthur's	9
Ribs 'n' More	5

There are three keywords that come in very handy with subqueries. These are ALL, ANY, and SOME. They work with comparison operators and sets of results. Before we get to those, let's take a quick peek back at the IN operator we talked about in Chapter 9:

```
SELECT name, rating FROM restaurant_ratings
WHERE rating IN
(SELECT rating FROM restaurant_ratings
WHERE rating > 3 AND rating < 9);
```

This subquery returns any ratings between 3 and 9—in this case, 7 and 5.

This query returns the name of any restaurant with the same rating as the result of our subquery in the set in parentheses. Our results will be: ***The Shack*** and ***Ribs 'n' More***.

Using ALL

Now consider this query:

```
SELECT name, rating FROM restaurant_ratings
WHERE rating > ALL
(SELECT rating FROM restaurant_ratings
WHERE rating > 3 AND rating < 9);
```

Greater than ALL finds any values larger than the biggest value in the set.

This time we're going to get any restaurants with a higher rating than all of the ratings in our set. Our result here will be ***Arthur's***.

Here's a query with <:

```
SELECT name, rating FROM restaurant_ratings
WHERE rating < ALL
(SELECT rating FROM restaurant_ratings WHERE
rating > 3 AND rating < 9);
```

Less than ALL finds any values smaller than the smallest value in the set.

We can also use >= and <= with ALL. This query will give us both ***Pizza Shack***, and ***Ribs 'n' More***. We get the ratings greater than our set, as well as any that equal the largest one in our set, which is 7:

```
SELECT name, rating FROM restaurant_ratings
WHERE rating >= ALL
(SELECT rating FROM restaurant_ratings
WHERE rating > 3 AND rating < 9);
```

Any values greater than our set, or equal to the highest result from our set will be matched.

Using ANY

ANY evaluates as true if ANY of the set matches the condition. Take the following example:

```
SELECT name, rating FROM restaurant_ratings
WHERE rating > ANY
(SELECT rating FROM restaurant_ratings WHERE
rating > 3 AND rating < 9);
```

We can read this as: select any rows where the rating is greater than any of (5, 7). Since ***The Shack*** has a rating of 7, which is greater than 5, it is returned. And ***Arthur's*** with a rating of 9 is also returned.

Greater than ANY finds any values larger than the smallest value in the set.

Less than ANY finds any values smaller than the largest value in the set.

Using SOME

SOME means the same thing as ANY in standard SQL syntax, and in MySQL. Check your flavor of RDBMS to confirm that it works that way for you.

#4. More on Data Types

You know the most common data types, but there are a few details that can help you fine-tune your columns even more. Let's take a closer look at some new types, and a closer look at some that you've already been using.

BOOLEAN

The boolean type allows you to store 'true', 'false', or it can be left NULL. It's great for any sort of true/false column. Behind the scenes, your RDBMS is storing a 1 for true values, and a 0 for false values. You can insert 1 or 'true', 0 or 'false'.

INT

We've used INT throughout the book. INT can hold **values in the range 0 to 4294967295**. That's if you only want to use positive values, and it's what is known as an ***unsigned integer***.

If you want to use negative and positive values in your integer, you need to make it a signed integer. A signed integer can hold values from –2147483648 to 2147483647. To tell your RDBMS that you want your INT signed, use this syntax when you create it:

```
INT(SIGNED)
```

Other INT types

You already know INT, but the two types SMALLINT and BIGINT fine-tune it a bit. They specify a maximum number that can be stored.

The ranges of values they can store vary according to your DBMS. MySQL ranges are:

	signed	unsigned
SMALLINT	-32768 to 32767	0 to 65535
BIGINT	-9223372036854775808 to 9223372036854775807	0 to 18446744073709551615

MySQL takes it a step farther and adds these types at well:

	signed	unsigned
TINYINT	-128 to 127	0 to 255
MEDIUMINT	-8388608 to 8388607	0 to 16777215

DATE and TIME types

Here's a rundown of the format in which MySQL stores your date and time data types:

`DATE`	`YYYY-MM-DD`
`DATETIME`	`YYYY-MM-DD HH:MM:SS`
`TIMESTAMP`	`YYYYMMDDHHMMSS`
`TIME`	`HH:MM:SS`

some_dates

a_date
2007-08-25 22:10:00
1925-01-01 02:05:00

When you `SELECT` a date or time type, you can modify what your RDBMS returns. Functions to do this vary by RDBMS. Here's an example of the MySQL function `DATE_FORMAT()`

Suppose you had the column, `a_date`:

Format strings must be quoted.

```
SELECT DATE_FORMAT(a_date, '%M %Y') FROM some_dates;
```

The `%M` and `%Y` tell the function how you want to format the dates. Here's what your results would look like:

a_date
August 2007
January 1925

We don't have room here to go into all the formatting options; there are a huge number of them. But with them, you can get exactly what you need from your date and time fields, without having to see what you don't need.

#5. Temporary tables

We've created lots of tables in this book. Each time we create a table, our RDBMS stores the structure of that table. When we insert data into it, that data is stored. The table and the data in it are saved. If you sign out of your SQL session in your terminal window or GUI software, that table and the data in it will still exist. The data stays around until you delete it; the table persists until you drop it.

SQL offers another type of table, known as a ***temporary table***. A temporary table exists from the time you create it until you drop it, or *until the user session ends*. By **session** we mean the time you are signed in to your account until you sign out or end your GUI program. You can also drop it explicitly with the `DROP` statement.

Reasons you might want a temporary table:

- You can use it to hold intermediate results—for example, performing some mathematical operation on a column, the results of which you will need to reuse during the session, but not the next session.
- You want to capture the contents of a table at a particular moment.
- Remember when we converted Greg's List from one table to many? You can create temporary tables to help you restructure your data, and know that they'll go away when you're finished with your session.
- If you eventually use SQL with a programming language, you can create temporary tables as you gather data, then store the final results in a persistent table.

Create a temporary table

The syntax to create a temporary table in MySQL is simple; you add the keyword `TEMPORARY`:

```
CREATE TEMPORARY TABLE my_temp_table
(
   some_id INT,
   some_data VARCHAR(50)
)
```

The word TEMPORARY is the only thing we need to add.

Watch it!

Temporary table-creation syntax varies greatly by RDBMS

Make sure to check your RDBMS's documentation for this feature.

A temporary table shortcut

You can create your temporary table from a query like this:

```
CREATE TEMPORARY TABLE my_temp_table AS
SELECT * FROM my_permanent_table;
```

Any query you like can go after the AS.

#6. Cast your data

Sometimes you have one type of data in a column, but you want it to be a different data type when it comes out. SQL has a function called CAST() that can take data of one type and convert it to another.

The syntax is:

```
CAST(your_column, TYPE)
```

TYPE can be one of these:

```
CHAR()
DATE
DATETIME
DECIMAL
SIGNED [INTEGER]
TIME
UNSIGNED [INTEGER]
```

Some situations where you might want to use CAST()

Convert a string with a date into a DATE type:

```
SELECT CAST('2005-01-01' AS DATE);
```

The string '2005-01-01' is formatted as a DATE.

Convert an integer to a decimal:

```
SELECT CAST(2 AS DECIMAL);
```

The integer 2 becomes the decimal 2.00.

Some other places you can use CAST() include the value list of an INSERT statement and inside the column list of a SELECT.

You can't use CAST() in these situations

* Decimal to integer

* TIME, DATE, DATETIME, CHAR to DECIMAL, or INTEGER.

But some other places you can use CAST() include the value list of an INSERT statement and inside the column list of a SELECT.

#7. Who are you? What time is it?

Sometimes you might have more than one user account on your RDBMS, each one with different permissions and roles. If you need to know which account you are currently using, this command will tell you:

```
SELECT CURRENT_USER;
```

This will also tell you what your host machine is. If your RDBMS is on the same computer as you are on, and you're using the root account, you'll see this:

```
root@localhost
```

You can get the current date and time with these commands:

```
File Edit Window Help
> SELECT CURRENT_DATE;
+--------------+
| CURRENT_DATE |
+--------------+
| 2007-07-26   |
+--------------+
1 row in set (0.00 sec)
```

```
File Edit Window Help
> SELECT CURRENT_TIME;
+--------------+
| CURRENT_TIME |
+--------------+
| 11:26:48     |
+--------------+
1 row in set (0.00 sec)
```

```
File Edit Window Help
SELECT CURRENT_USER;
+----------------+
| CURRENT_USER   |
+----------------+
| root@localhost |
+----------------+
1 row in set (0.00 sec)
```

#8. Useful numeric functions

Here's a rundown of functions that work with numeric data types.
Some you've seen already:

numeric function	what does it do?	
ABS(x)	Returns the absolute value of x	
	query	**result**
	SELECT ABS(-23);	23
ACOS(x)	Returns the arccosine of x	
	SELECT ACOS(0);	1.5707963267949
ASIN()	Returns the arcsine of x	
	SELECT ASIN(0.1);	0.10016742116156
ATAN(x,y)	Returns the arctangent of x and y	
	SELECT ATAN(-2,2);	-0.78539816339745
CEIL(x)	Returns the smallest integer that is greater than or equal to x. The return value will be a BIGINT.	
	SELECT CEIL(1.32);	2
COS(x)	Returns the cosine of x in radians	
	SELECT COS(1);	0.54030230586814
COT(x)	Returns the cotangent of x	
	SELECT COT(12);	-1.5726734063977
EXP(x)	Returns the value of e raised to the power of x	
	SELECT EXP(-2);	0.13533528323661
FLOOR(x)	Returns the largest integer that is less than or equal to x	
	SELECT FLOOR(1.32);	1
FORMAT(x,y)	Converts x to a formatted text string rounded to y decimal places	
	SELECT FORMAT(3452100.50,2);	3,452,100.50
LN(x)	Returns the natural logarithm of x	
	SELECT LN(2);	0.69314718055995
LOG(x) and LOG(x,y)	Returns the natural logarithm of x, or with two parameters returns the log of x for base y	
	SELECT LOG(2);	0.69314718055995
	SELECT LOG(2,65536);	16

Continues on the next page.

#8. Useful numeric functions (continued)

numeric function	what does it do?	
`MOD(x,y)`	Returns the remainder of x divided by y	
	query	**result**
	`SELECT MOD(249,10);`	9
`PI()`	Returns the value of pi	
	`SELECT PI();`	3.141593
`POWER(x,y)`	Returns the value of x raised to the power of y	
	`SELECT POW(3,2);`	9
`RADIANS(x)`	Returns x converted from degrees to radians	
	`SELECT RADIANS(45);`	0.78539816339745
`RAND()`	Returns a random floating-point value	
	`SELECT RAND();`	0.84655920681223
`ROUND(x)`	Returns the value of x rounded to the nearest integer	
	`SELECT ROUND(1.34);`	1
	`SELECT ROUND(-1.34);`	-1
`ROUND(x,y)`	Returns the value of x rounded to y decimal places	
	`SELECT ROUND(1.465, 1);`	1.5
	`SELECT ROUND(1.465, 0);`	1
	`SELECT ROUND(28.367, -1);`	30
`SIGN(x)`	Returns 1 when x is positive, 0 when x is 0, or -1 when x is negative	
	`SELECT SIGN(-23);`	-1
`SIN(x)`	Returns the sine of x	
	`SELECT SIN(PI());`	1.2246063538224e-16
`SQRT(x)`	Returns the square root of x	
	`SELECT SQRT(100);`	10
`TAN(x)`	Returns the tangent of x	
	`SELECT TAN(PI());`	-1.2246063538224e-16
`TRUNCATE(x,y)`	Returns the number x truncated to y decimal places	
	`SELECT TRUNCATE(8.923,1);`	8.9

#9. Indexing to speed things up

You know all about primary key and foreign key indexes. Those types of indexes are great for tying multiple tables together and enforcing data integrity. But you can also create indexes on columns to make your queries faster.

When a WHERE is done on an unindexed column, the RDBMS starts from the beginning of that column and works its way through, one row at a time. If your table is huge, and we mean 4 million rows huge, that can begin to take perceptible time.

When you create an index on a column, your RDBMS keeps additional information about the column that speeds that searching up tremendously. The additional information is kept in a behind-the-scenes table that is in a specific order the RDBMS can search through more quickly. The trade-off is that indexes take up space. So you have to consider creating some columns as indexes, the ones you'll search on frequently, and not indexing others.

Here's the ALTER table code to add an index to a column:

```
ALTER TABLE my_contacts
ADD INDEX (last_name);
```

There's a bit more theory behind indexing, but this is the basic idea.

#10. 2-minute PHP/MySQL

Before we leave, let's take a very quick look at how PHP and MySQL can interact together to help you get your data on the Web. This is only a tiny taste of what you can do, and you should certainly read more about this.

This example assumes you are somewhat familiar with PHP. And we know you're comfortable writing queries at this point. The code below connects to a database named `gregs_list` and selects all the first and last names of people in the `my_contacts` table. The PHP code takes all that data from the database and stores it in an array. The last part of the code prints all the first and last names on a web page:

```
<?php
$conn = mysql_connect("localhost","greg","gr3gzpAs");
if (!$conn)
  {
    die('Did not connect: ' . mysql_error());
  }

mysql_select_db("my_db", $conn);

$result = mysql_query("SELECT first_name, last_name FROM my_contacts");

while($row = mysql_fetch_array($result))
  {
    echo $row['first_name'] . " " . $row['last_name'];
    echo "<br />";
  }

mysql_close($conn);
?>
```

We'll save this file as `gregsnames.php` on a web server.

A closer look at each line

```
<?php
```

This first line tells the web server that PHP code follows.

```
$conn = mysql_connect("localhost","greg","gr3gzpAs");
```

To connect to `gregs_list`, we have to tell the web server where our RDBMS is located, what our username is, and what our password is. We create a connection string with this information, and we name it `$conn`. The PHP function `mysql_connect()` takes that info and reaches out to our RDBMS to see if it can communicate with it.

```
if (!$conn)
  {
    die('Did not connect: ' . mysql_error());
  }
```

If it didn't succeed, PHP will send us a message telling us why it couldn't connect to the RDBMS, and the PHP will stop being processed.

```
mysql_select_db("my_db", $conn);
```

Okay, so our connection to the RDBMS works. We now have to tell the PHP which database we're interested in. We want to `USE` our favorite database, `gregs_list`.

```
$result = mysql_query("SELECT first_name, last_name FROM my_contacts");
```

We've got our database selected, and we're connected, but we have no query. We write one and use the `mysql_query()` function to send it to the RDBMS. All the rows returned get stored in an array named `$result`.

```
while($row = mysql_fetch_array($result))
  {
```

Now we use PHP to get all those rows out of `$result` and on to the web page. This is done by a while loop, which goes through, one row at a time, until it reaches the end of the data.

```
    echo $row['first_name'] . " " . $row['last_name'];
    echo "<br />";
  }
```

These two PHP `echo` statements write the first and last name of each row to the web page. An HTML `<br>` tag is inserted between each line.

```
        lose($conn);
```

When we finish writing all the names, we close the connection to the RDBMS. It's just like logging out of your terminal.

```
?>
```

Finally, we end the PHP script.

appendix ii: MySQL installation

Try it out for yourself

All your new SQL skills won't do you much good without a place to apply them. This appendix contains instructions for installing your very own MySQL RDBMS for you to work with.

Get started, fast!

Because it's no fun to have a book on SQL without being able to try it out for yourself, here's a brief introduction to installing MySQL on Windows and Mac OS X.

NOTE: This section covers Windows 2000, XP, or Windows Server 2003, or other 32-bit Windows operating system. For Mac, it applies to Mac OS X 10.3.x or newer.

We'll take you through the downloading and installing of MySQL. The official name for the free version of the MySQL RDBMS server these days is **MySQL Community Server**.

Instructions and Troubleshooting

The following is a list of steps for installing MySQL on Windows and Mac OS X. This is *not* meant to replace the excellent instructions found on the MySQL web site, and **we strongly encourage you to go there and read them!** For much more detailed directions, as well as a troubleshooting guide, go here:

Get version 5.0 or newer.

http://dev.mysql.com/doc/refman/5.0/en/windows-installation.html

You'll also like the MySQL Query Browser we talked about on pages 526–527. There, you can type your queries and see the results inside the software interface, rather than in a console window.

Steps to Install MySQL on Windows

1 Go to:

`http://dev.mysql.com/downloads/mysql/5.0.html`

and click on the MySQL Community Server download button.

You may have to scroll down a little.

Get version 5.0 or newer.

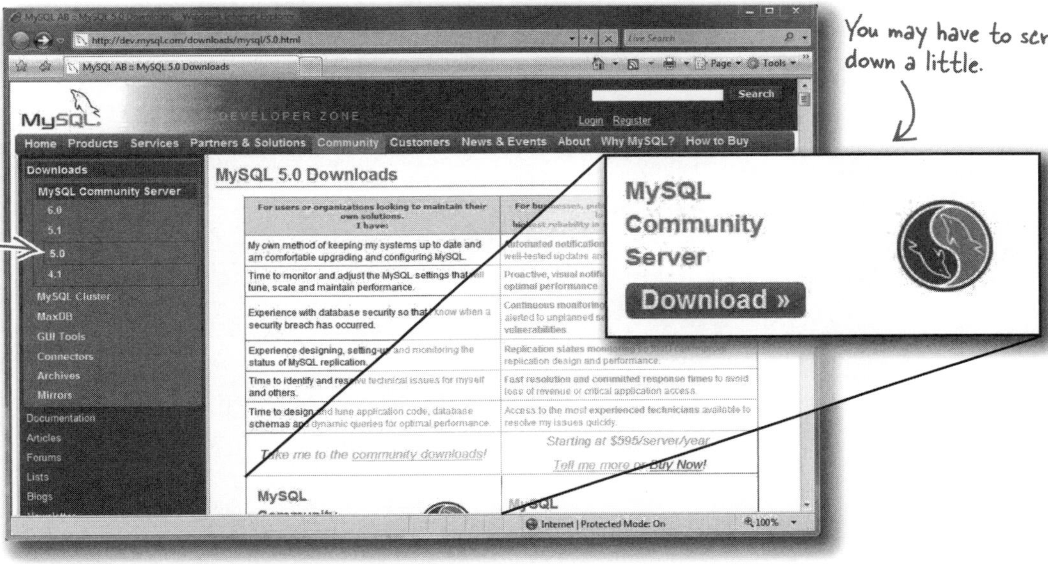

2 Choose **Windows** from the list.

The top one!

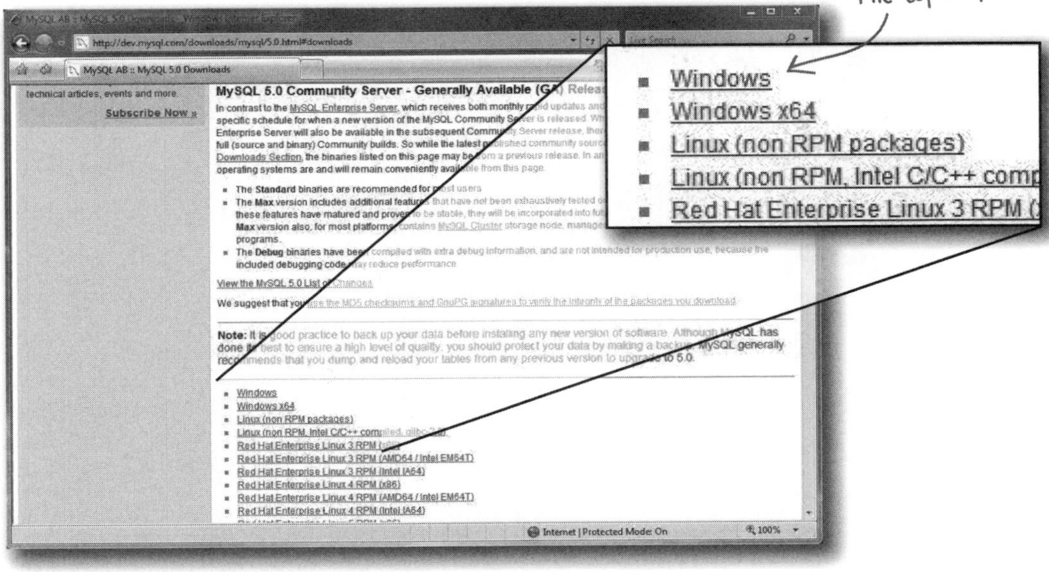

Download your installer

3 Under **Windows downloads**, we recommend that you choose the `Windows ZIP/Setup.EXE` option because it includes an installer that greatly simplifies the installation. Click on **Pick a Mirror**.

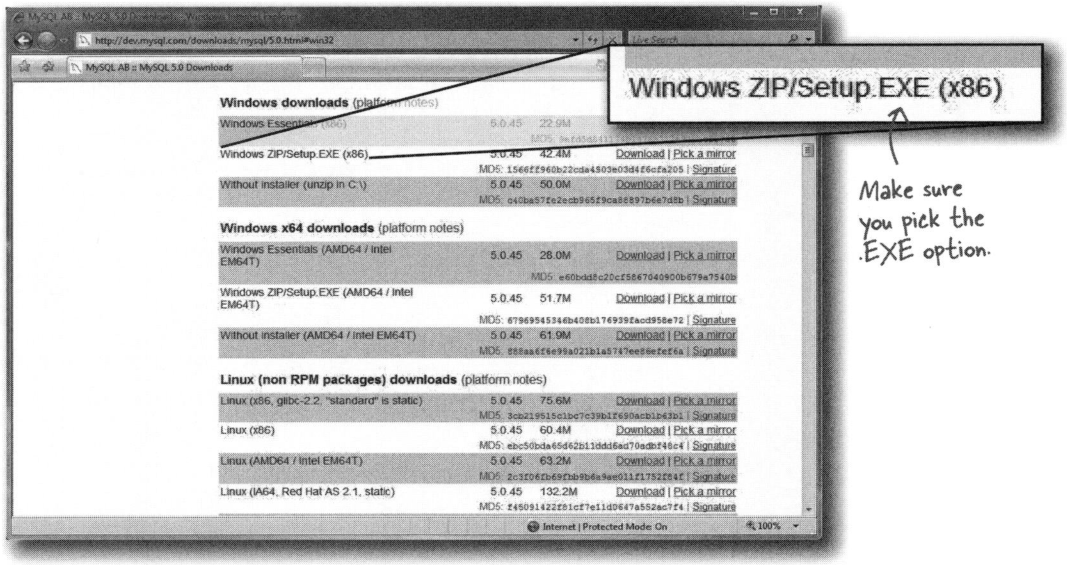

4 You'll see a list of locations that have a copy you can download; choose the one closest to you.

5 When the file has finished downloading, double-click to launch it. At this point, you will be walked through the installation with the **Setup Wizard**. Click the ***Next*** button.

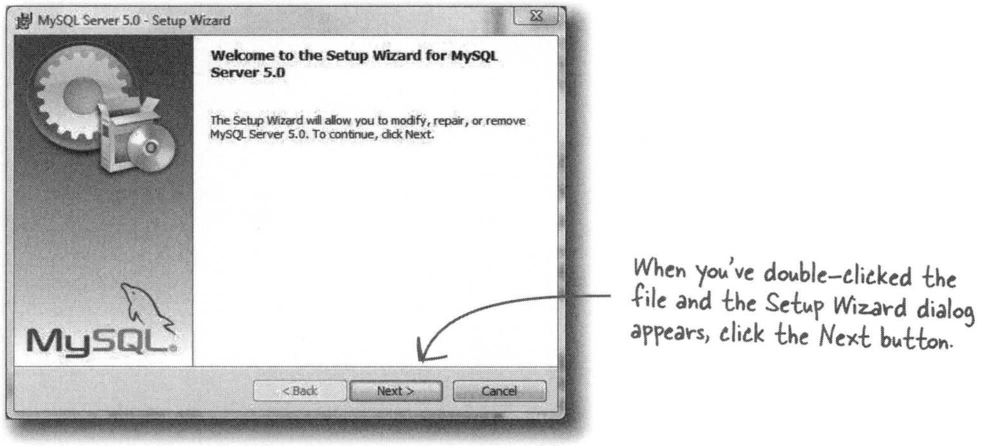

Pick a destination folder

6 You'll be asked to choose Typical, Complete, or Custom. For our purposes in this book, choose **Typical**.

You can change the location on your computer where MySQL will be installed, but we recommend that you stay with the default location:

```
C:\Program Files\MySQL\MySQL Server 5.0
```

Click the ***Next*** button.

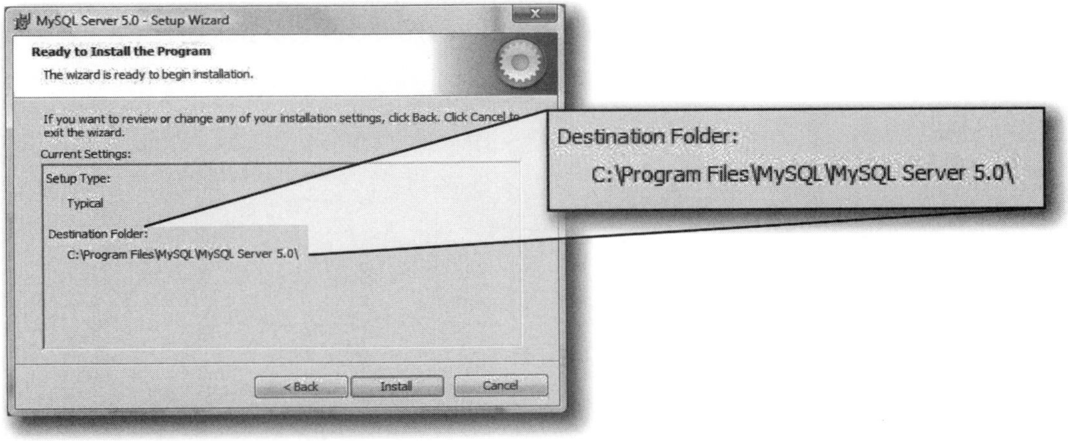

Click "Install" and you're done!

7 You'll see the "Ready to Install" dialog with the Destination Folder listed. If you're happy with the destination directory, click Install. Otherwise, go ***Back***, ***Change*** the directory, and return here.

Click ***Install***.

Steps to Install MySQL on Mac OS X

If you are running Mac OS X Server, a version of MySQL should already be installed.

Before you begin, check to see if you already have a version installed. Go to **`Applications/Server/MySQL Manager`** to access it.

1. Go to:

   `http://dev.mysql.com/downloads/mysql/5.0.html`

   and click on the MySQL Community Server download button.

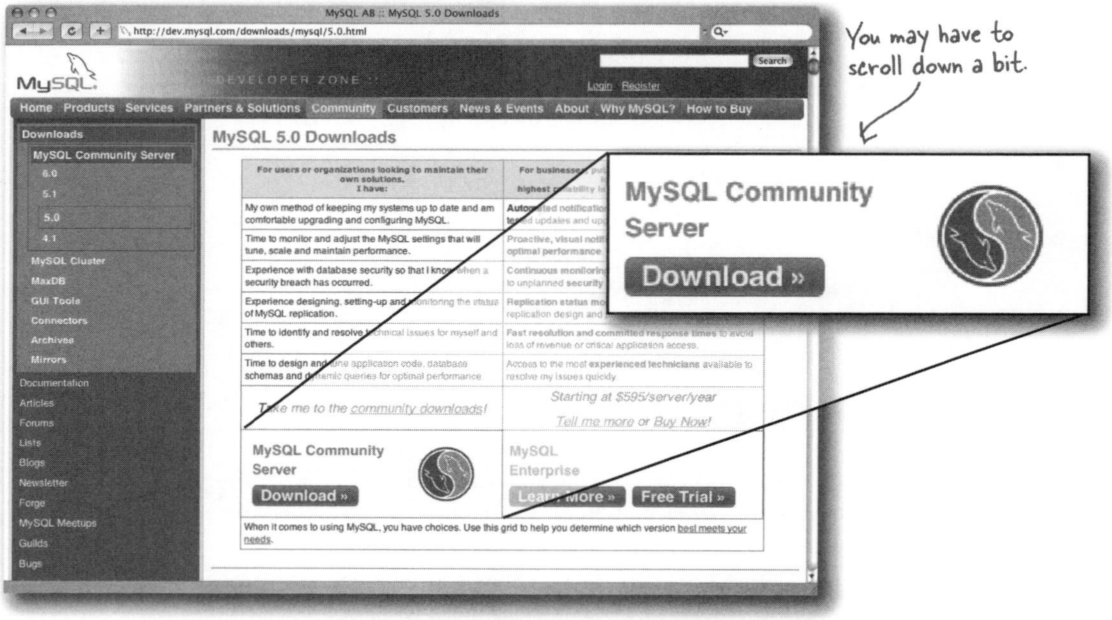

2. Choose **Mac OS X (package format)** from the list.

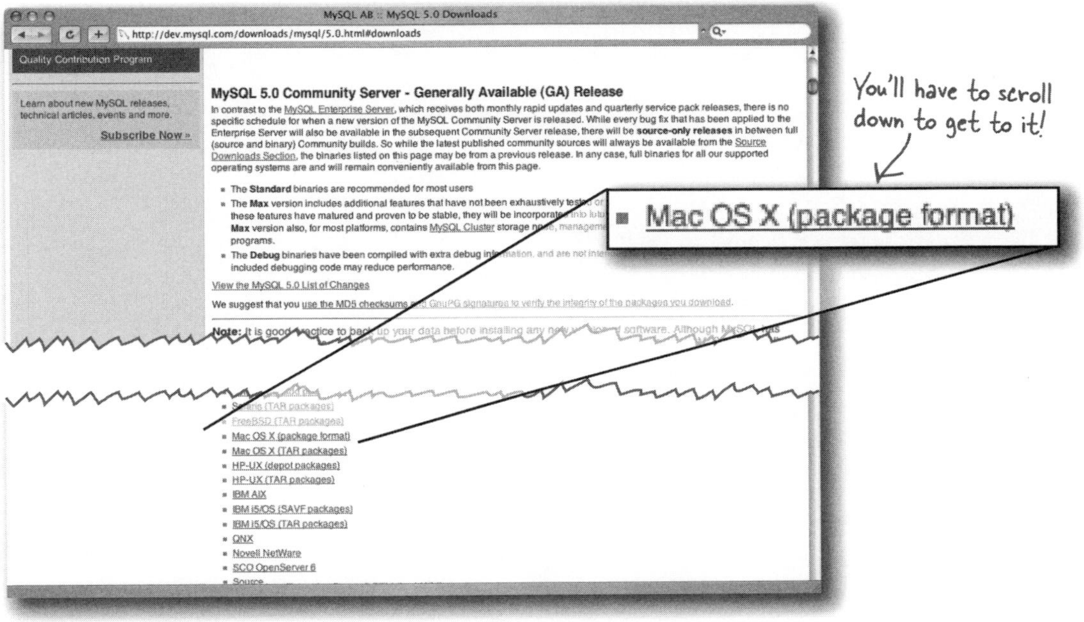

3. Choose the appropriate package for your Mac OS X version. Click on **Pick a Mirror**.

4. You'll see a list of locations that have a copy you can download; choose the one closest to you.

5. When the file has finished downloading, double-click to launch it. When you've installed MySQL, go look at the online documentation for how to access your install using the query browser we talked about on pages 526–527.

But if you're in a hurry, here's a quick way in using the Terminal.

You can now open a Terminal window on your Mac and type:

```
shell> cd /usr/local/mysql
shell> sudo ./bin/mysqld_safe
```

(Enter your password, if necessary)

(Press Control-Z)

```
shell> bg
```

(Press **`Control-D`** or enter **`exit`** to exit the shell)

appendix iii: tools roundup

All your new SQL tools

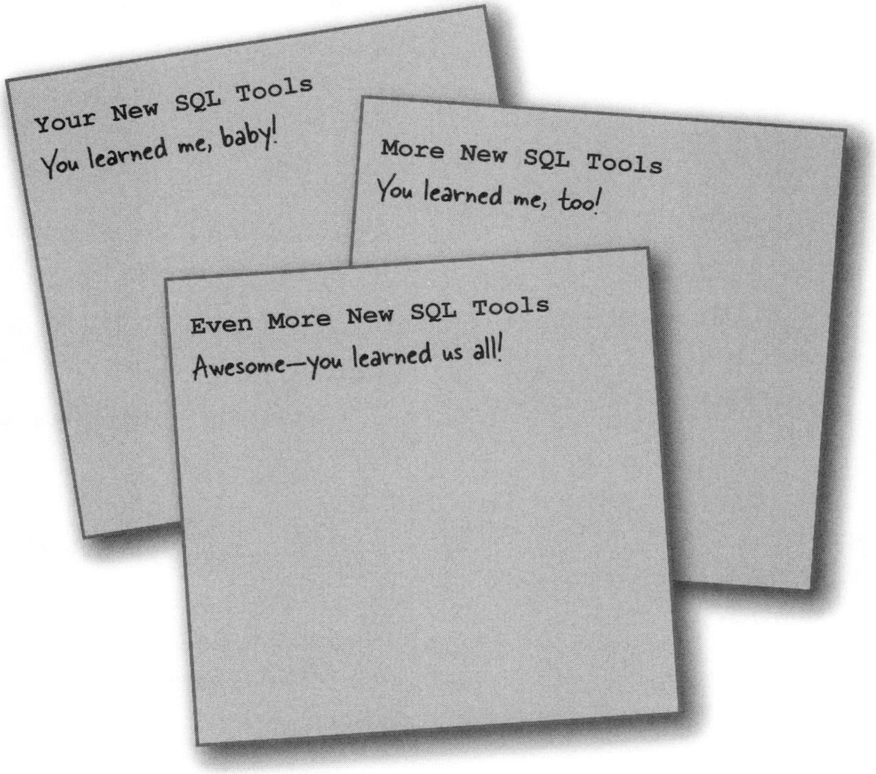

Your New SQL Tools
You learned me, baby!
More New SQL Tools
You learned me, too!
Even More New SQL Tools
Awesome—you learned us all!

Here are all your SQL tools in one place for the first time, for one night only (kidding)! This is a roundup of all the SQL tools we've covered. Take a moment to *survey the list and feel* ***great*****—you learned them all**!

Symbols

= <> < > <= >=

You've got a whole bunch of equality and inequality operators at your disposal.

Chapter 2

A

ALTER with CHANGE

Lets you change both the name and data type of an existing column.

Chapter 5

ALTER with MODIFY

Lets you change just the data type of an existing column.

Chapter 5

ALTER with ADD

Lets you add a column to your table in the order you choose.

Chapter 5

ALTER with DROP

Lets you drop a column from your table.

Chapter 5

ALTER TABLE

Lets you change the name of your table and its entire structure while retaining the data inside of it.

Chapter 5

AND and OR

With AND and OR, you can combine your conditional statements in your WHERE clauses for more precision.

Chapter 2

ATOMIC DATA

Data in your columns is atomic if it's been broken down into the smallest pieces that you need.

Chapter 4

ATOMIC DATA RULE 1

Atomic data can't have several bits of the same type of data in the same column.

Chapter 4

ATOMIC DATA RULE 2

Atomic data can't have multiple columns with the same type of data.

Chapter 4

AUTO_INCREMENT

When used in your column declaration, that column will automatically be given a unique integer value each time an INSERT command is performed.

Chapter 4

AVG

Returns the average value in a numeric column.

Chapter 6

B

BETWEEN

Lets you select ranges of values.

Chapter 2

C

CHECK CONSTRAINTS

Use these to only allow specific values to be inserted or updated in a table.

Chapter 11

CHECK OPTION

Use this when creating an updatable view to force all inserts and updates to satisfy a WHERE clause in the view.

Chapter 11

COMMA JOIN

The same thing as a CROSS JOIN, except a comma is used instead of the keywords CROSS JOIN.

Chapter 8

Composite key

This is a primary key made up of multiple columns which create a unique key value.

Chapter 7

COUNT

Can tell you how many rows match a SELECT query without you having to see the rows. COUNT returns a single integer value.

Chapter 6

CREATE TABLE

Starts setting up your table, but you'll also need to know your COLUMN NAMES and DATA TYPES. You should have worked these out by analyzing the kind of data you'll be putting in your table.

Chapter 1

CREATE TABLE AS

Use this command to create a table from the results of any SELECT statement.

Chapter 10

CREATE USER

Statement used by some RDBMSs that lets you create a user and give him a password.

Chapter 12

CROSS JOIN

Returns every row from one table crossed with every row from the second table. Known by many other names including Cartesian Join and No Join.

Chapter 8

D

DELETE

This is your tool for deleting rows of data from your table. Use it with a WHERE clause to precisely pinpoint the rows you want to remove.

Chapter 3

DISTINCT

Returns each unique value only once, with no duplicates.

Chapter 6

DROP TABLE

Lets you delete a table if you make a mistake, but you'll need to do this before you start using INSERT statements which let you add the values for each column.

Chapter 1

E

EQUIJOIN and NON-EQUIJOIN

Both are inner joins. The equijoin returns rows that are equal, and the non-equijoin returns any rows that are not equal.

Chapter 8

Escape with ' and \

Escape out apostrophes in your text data with an extra apostrophe or backslash in front of it.

Chapter 2

EXCEPT

Use this keyword to return only values that are in the first query BUT NOT in the second query.

Chapter 10

F

FIRST NORMAL FORM (1NF)

Each row of data must contain atomic values, and each row of data must have a unique identifier.

Chapter 4

Foreign Key

A column in a table that references the primary key of another table.

Chapter 7

G

GRANT

This statement lets you control exactly what users can do to tables and columns based on the privileges you give them.

Chapter 12

GROUP BY

Consolidates rows based on a common column.

Chapter 6

I

INNER JOIN

Any join that combines the records from two tables using some condition.

Chapter 8

Inner query

A query inside another query. Also known as a subquery.

Chapter 9

INTERSECT

Use this keyword to return only values that are in the first query AND also in the second query.

Chapter 10

IS NULL

Use this to create a condition to test for that pesky NULL value.

Chapter 2

L

LEFT OUTER JOIN

A LEFT OUTER JOIN takes all the rows in the left table and matches them to rows in the RIGHT table.

Chapter 10

LIKE with % and _

Use LIKE with the wildcards to search through parts of text strings.

Chapter 2

LIMIT

Lets you specify exactly how many rows to return, and which row to start with.

Chapter 6

M

Many-to-Many

Two tables are connected by a junction table, allowing many rows in the first to match may rows in the second, and vice versa.

Chapter 7

MAX and MIN

Return the largest value in a column with MAX, and the smallest with MIN.

Chapter 6

N

NATURAL JOIN

An inner join that leaves off the "ON" clause. It only works if you are joining two tables that have the same column name.

Chapter 8

Noncorrelated Subquery

A subquery which stands alone and doesn't reference anything from the outer query.

Chapter 9

NON-UPDATABLE VIEWS

Views that can't be used to INSERT or UPDATE data in the base table.

Chapter 11

NOT

NOT lets you negate your results and get the opposite values.

Chapter 2

NULL and NOT NULL

You'll also need to have an idea which columns should not accept NULL values to help you sort and search your data. You'll need to set the columns to NOT NULL when you create your table.

Chapter 1

O

One-to-Many

A row in one table can have many matching rows in a second table, but the second table may only have one matching row in the first.

Chapter 7

One-to-One

Exactly one row of a parent table is related to one row of a child table.

Chapter 7

ORDER BY

Alphabetically orders your results based on a column you specify.

Chapter 6

Outer Query

A query which contains an inner query or subquery.

Chapter 9

P

PRIMARY KEY

A column or set of columns that uniquely identifies a row of data in a table.

Chapter 4

RIGHT OUTER JOIN

A RIGHT OUTER JOIN takes all the rows in the right table and matches them to rows in LEFT table.

Chapter 10

S

Schema

A description of the data in your database along with any other related objects and the way they all connect.

Chapter 7

Second Normal Form (2NF)

Your table must be in 1NF and contain no partial functional dependencies to be in 2NF.

Chapter 7

SELECT *

Use this to select all the columns in a table.

Chapter 2

SELF-JOIN

The self-join allows you to query a single table as though there were two tables with exactly the same information in them.

Chapter 10

SELF-REFERENCING FOREIGN KEY

This is a foreign key in the same table it is a primary key of, used for another purpose.

Chapter 10

SET

This keyword belongs in an UPDATE statement and is used to change the value of an existing column.

Chapter3

SHOW CREATE TABLE

Use this command to see the correct syntax for creating an existing table.

Chapter 4

String functions

Lets you modify copies of the contents of string columns when they are returned from a query. The original values remain untouched.

Chapter 5

Subquery

A query that is wrapped within another query. It's also known as an inner query.

Chapter 9

SUM

Adds up a column of numeric values.

Chapter 6

T

Third Normal Form (3NF)

Your table must be in 2NF and have no transitive dependencies.

Chapter 7

Transitive functional dependency

When any non-key column is related to any of the other non-key columns.

Chapter 7

U

UNION and UNION ALL

UNION combines the results of two or more queries into one table, based on what you specify in the column list of the SELECT. UNION hides the duplicate values, UNION ALL includes duplicate values.

Chapter 10

UPDATABLE VIEWS

These are views that allow you to change the data in the underlying tables. These views must contain all NOT NULL rows of the base table or tables.

Chapter 11

UPDATE

This statement updates an existing column or columns with a new value. It also uses a WHERE clause.

Chapter 3

USE DATABASE

Gets you inside the database to set up all your tables.

Chapter 1

V

VIEWS

Use a view to treat the results of a query as a table. Great for turning complex queries into simple ones.

Chapter 11

W

WITH GRANT OPTION

Allows users to give other users the same privileges they have.

Chapter 12

Index

Numbers

Symbols

A

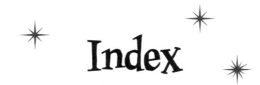

D

S

U

V

W

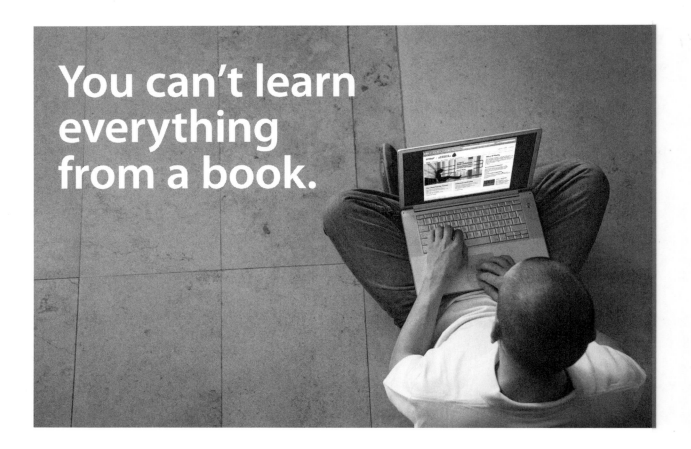

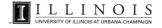

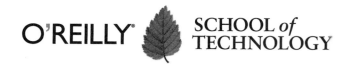